China in Revolution: The First Phase 1900–1913

China in Revolution: The First Phase

1900-1913

Edited and with an introduction by

Mary Clabaugh Wright

New Haven and London: Yale University Press

Library of Congress catalog card number: 68–27770
ISBN: 0–300–01460–0 (paper)

Designed by John O. C. McCrillis,
set in Baskerville type,
and printed in the United States of America by
The Murray Printing Company,
Westford, Massachusetts.

14 13 12 11 10 9 8 7 6 5

Preface

The fiftieth anniversary of the Chinese Revolution of 1911 was the occasion for a flood of publication. Collections of documents, reminiscences, and interpretations poured forth, and the flow is continuing. Historians of modern China scattered around the world sampled the new evidence rather casually at first, and then, with growing excitement, found that the picture of China in the early twentieth century which we all lectured on and included in textbooks was almost completely wrong. Few independent scholars had consciously accepted either the Kuomintang or the Communist stereotype of the period, but the dullness that seemed to invest the period from 1900 to 1913 made us happy to give it only summary attention.

In the Kuomintang stereotype, a Sun Yat-sen larger than life had been the leader of a powerful Revolutionary Alliance that had led a revolutionary upsurge motivated primarily by anti-Manchu feelings—one that would have solved China's problems but for the treachery of Yuan Shih-k'ai. The Kuomintang made so much of the Revolution of 1911 that the Communists for a time ignored it; a 1949 middle-school reader on the history of the Chinese Revolution did not even mention the events of 1911. When the Revolution of 1911 was discussed in more comprehensive Chinese Communist books, the interpretations varied according to the time of writing. In 1929, the 1911 revolutionaries were charged with basing themselves on the support of the upper bourgeoisie, intellectuals, artisans, and peasants. They failed because they did not win the support of the working class and the petty bourgeoisie, and because they did not recognize the danger of foreign imperialism. By 1938 the treatment of the early revolutionary movement was less absurd, but far from satisfactory. The movement failed, it was charged, because it had not really worked for a mass mobilization of the peasantry or mounted a real attack on the traditional social system. As of 1953, the official stereotype embalmed in a handbook on the meaning of various national holidays stated that 1911 marked China's bourgeois-democratic revolution, which had failed because Sun Yat-sen had spent his time abroad seeking the support of the imperialist powers and because no suitable leader had emerged at home.

As the new evidence poured in from every side after 1961, it became clear that we had been discounting, out of ignorance and a resistance to dogmatic encapsulations, one of history's truly exciting subjects. Individual scholars—some in leading university centers, some isolated by thousands of miles from anyone with related interests—began corresponding and exchanging data and preliminary ideas. In recognition of this burgeoning but scattered interest, the Joint Committee on Contemporary China of the American Council of Learned Societies and the Social Science Research Council provided the funds for a research conference of twenty-two scholars held at Wentworth-by-the-Sea, Portsmouth, New Hampshire, in August 1965.

Substantial research papers were circulated in advance so that our almost round-the-clock sessions could be devoted to discussion and debate. At the outset we did not expect our conference to produce a publishable volume. The field was new and not one tenth explored; most of the participants were young and, it was thought, perhaps not yet ready to publish; and seven countries, with different scholarly climates, were represented. Yet by the end of the week we had concluded that, although we were far from ready to collaborate in a synthesis of this first phase of the Chinese Revolution and that to attempt to do so prematurely would do great damage, we had, rather to our surprise, the makings of a book.

The selection of papers to be included in this volume was determined by caucus and consensus. Several stimulating papers were bright sparks cast from the grinding wheels of dissertation research. Some authors felt that their particular essays might better appear in other forms of publication. Still others had topics that might best be treated by development into independent monographs. All these papers have been or soon will be published in other forms; I mention them here because their authors joined fully in the conference and, through their comments and criticisms, are silent coauthors of this book.

We agreed that each of us who was to contribute an essay would use much of his time for a further year or more of research and reflection along the lines suggested in our conference discussions. Although we remained in regular correspondence, circulating drafts through many revisions, our locations and other commitments precluded a fast operation. Yet during this interval, we wanted our first results to be of use to others. We therefore placed thirty sets of the conference papers in the most generally accessible libraries in all countries where there is scholarly interest in modern Chinese history. According to all reports, these have proved of great value to students attempting independent work and to the coming generation of young scholars. We have received nearly two hundred additional requests for permission to photocopy the papers, and to these we have gladly agreed. Yet I should emphasize that the present volume represents three years of further work and, once published, completely supersedes the draft papers.

Several points about the organization of this volume should be noted here. Chinese political organizations are referred to by English translations which have been made uniform and which appear in a table in an appendix. A composite list of abbreviated forms of reference to frequently cited works follows the table of contents. We have followed the modified Wade-Giles system of Chinese romanization, with very few exceptions for names widely known in other forms, for example, Sun Yat-sen; for a few words where the system is clearly faulty, we have included alternate readings.

We have a major intellectual debt to four outstanding senior scholars who found time to participate in the conference as critics and to offer continuing counsel, and to one who, though not present at the conference, has cheerfully volunteered hundreds of hours of help on the development of conference papers into the chapters of a book. They are: John King Fairbank, Francis Lee Higginson Professor of History at Harvard University; Albert Feuerwerker, Professor of History at the University of Michigan; Marius Jansen, Professor of History at Princeton University; G. William Skinner, Professor of Anthropology at Stanford University; and Arthur Frederick Wright, Charles Seymour Professor of History at Yale University.

We wish here to acknowledge our appreciation for the generous support of the Joint Committee on Contemporary China not only of the 1965 conference but of much of the later editorial work, and also for substantial supplementary support from Yale University, notably a grant from the university's Concilium on International and Area Studies. We have other debts to many people: to the late Mrs. Hope M. Wright for her translation of

Mme. Bergère's chapter; to Mrs. Wen-yen Wu, who wrote the characters for the glossary; to Mrs. Ethel Himberg and Miss Jennifer Josephy, who struggled through several stages of amended typescript; to Mrs. Judith Maclay, Mrs. Mary Shuford, and Miss Joan Wallstein for their skilled editing; and to Mrs. Gail M. Mau for her expert index of an unusually difficult text.

We also owe a great debt to many of our colleagues who have taken time to solve a variety of problems. Among them are Professor K. C. Liu of the University of California at Davis; Mr. Weiying Wan, Curator of the East Asian Collections at the Yale University Library; and Dr. Eugene Wu, director of the Chinese-Japanese Library of Harvard University. We should also like to thank four of the conference participants for efforts beyond the norm in the common interest: Mr. P'eng-yüan Chang of Academia Sinica, who checked a number of technical points for others; Professor Akira Iriye of the University of Rochester, who volunteered at the conference as an interpreter; Dr. John Schrecker of Princeton University, who handled many of the practical arrangements; and Professor Jonathan Spence of Yale University, who performed superbly as rapporteur.

MARY CLABAUGH WRIGHT

YALE UNIVERSITY
June 1968

Contents

Part IV The Limitations of Revolutionary Leadership

Abbreviations

CCF	France, Ministère des Affaires Etrangères, Correspondance Consulaire Francaise: French consular correspondence deposited in the archives of the Quai d'Orsay, Paris; still in process of classification, and not yet listed under reference numbers; the reports consulted come under the section entitled: CHINE, Politique intérieure, Révolution de Chine.
CHS ts'ung-k'an	Wu Hsiang-hsiang, ed., *Chung-kuo hsien-tai shih ts'ung-k'an* (Selected Writings on Modern Chinese History), continuing series (6 vols. Taipei, 1960–64).
CHS ts'ung-shu	Wu Hsiang-hsiang, ed., *Chung-kuo hsien-tai shih-liao ts'ung-shu* (Library of Chinese Contemporary Historical Materials), 1st series (16 vols. Taipei, 1962).
Feng, *Chung-hua*	Feng Tzu-yu, *Chung-hua min-kuo k'ai-kuo ch'ien ko-ming shih* (Revolutionary History Prior to the Founding of the Republic of China) (The editions referred to by the various authors are specified in the notes).
Feng, *I-shih*	Feng Tzu-yu, *Ko-ming i-shih* (Fragments of Revolutionary History) (The editions referred to by the various authors are specified in the notes).
FO	Great Britain, Foreign Office, Archives, Public Record Office, London.
HHKM	Chung-kuo shih-hsüeh hui (Chinese Historical Association), ed., *Hsin-hai ko-ming* (The Revolution of 1911), Ch'ai Te-keng et al., comp. (8 vols. Shanghai, 1957).

HHKMHIL Chung-kuo jen-min cheng-chih hsieh-shang hui-i ch'üan-kuo wei-yüan hui wen-shih tzu-liao yen-chiu wei-yüan-hui (Committee on Written Historical Materials of the National Committee of the Chinese People's Political Consultative Conference), ed., *Hsin-hai ko-ming hui-i-lu* (Memoirs of the Revolution of 1911) (Peking, 1961– , *1*–).

HMTP Liang Ch'i-ch'ao, ed., *Hsin-min ts'ung-pao* (The New People's Miscellany) (Yokohama, 1902–07, 96 issues).

HT Hsüan-t'ung.

JAS *Journal of Asian Studies, 1*, 1, 1941–).

KFCC Chinese Kuomintang Archives, ed., *Kuo-fu ch'üan-chi* (Complete Works of Sun Yat-sen) (6 vols., rev. ed. Taipei, 1957).

KFNP Chinese Kuomintang, Committee for the Compilation of Historical Material on Party History, eds., *Kuo-fu nien-p'u ch'u-kao* (Draft Chronological Biography of Sun Yat-sen), Lo Chia-lun, chief ed. (2 vols. Taipei, 1958).

KFP Liang Ch'i-ch'ao, ed., *Kuo-feng-pao* (National Trends) (Shanghai, 1910–11, 52 issues).

KH Kuang-hsü.

KKWH Chung-hua min-kuo k'ai-kuo wu-shih-nien wen-hsien pien-tsuan wei-yüan-hui (Committee on the Compilation of Documents on the Fiftieth Anniversary of the Founding of the Republic of China), ed., *Chung-hua min-kuo k'ai-kuo wu-shih-nien wen-hsien* (Documents on the Fiftieth Anniversary of the Founding of the Republic of China) (Taipei, 1963– , *1*–).

KMWH	Chinese Kuomintang, Central Executive Committee, Committee for the Compilation of Materials on Party History, comp., Lo Chia-lun, chief ed., *Ko-ming wen-hsien* (Documents of the Revolution), *1–* (Taipei, 1953–).
Liang . . . nien-p'u	Ting Wen-chiang, comp., *Liang Jen-kung hsien-sheng nien-p'u ch'ang-pien, ch'u-kao* (A Chronological Biography of Liang Ch'i-ch'ao, unabridged first draft) (38 chüan in 3 vols. Taipei, 1958).
Morrison Papers	George Ernest Morrison Papers, Uncatalogued Manuscripts, Mitchell Library, Sydney, Australia.
NCH	*North China Herald* (Shanghai, weekly edition of *North China Daily News*).
PP	Great Britain, Foreign Office, *Parliamentary Papers* (Blue Books), *Correspondence Respecting the Affairs of China.*
SCMP	*South China Morning Post* (Hong Kong).
SLHC	Chang Nan and Wang Jen-chih, eds., *Hsin-hai ko-ming ch'ien shih-nien chien shih-lun hsüan-chi* (Selection of Topical Articles from the Decade before the 1911 Revolution) (The editions referred to by the various authors are specified in the notes).
TFTC	*Tung-fang tsa-chih* (Eastern Miscellany) (Shanghai, 1904–48, monthly).
TR	Chinese Imperial Maritime Customs, *Returns of Trade and Trade Reports* (Shanghai).
USDS	U.S. Department of State, *Records Relating to Internal Affairs of China, 1910–29,* microfilm, 893.00/351/2-10700, National Archives, Washington, D.C.

Introduction: The Rising Tide of Change

Mary Clabaugh Wright

Rarely in history has a single year marked as dramatic a watershed as did 1900 in China. The weakness laid bare by the Allied pillage of Peking in the wake of the Boxer Rebellion finally forced on China a polar choice: national extinction or wholesale transformation not only of a state but of a civilization. Almost overnight Chinese—imperial government, reformers, and revolutionaries—accepted the challenge. Easily three quarters of the foreign nonofficial observers—journalists, missionaries, businessmen, doctors, teachers—were dumbfounded at the change. Letters flowed home assuring friends and colleagues who had left China only a few years earlier that they simply would not recognize the country today. A few called the changes superficial, but the great majority supported their impression of a vastly altered ambience with specific observations and experiences.

The general assessment of Chinese society offered in his earlier writings by the observant missionary Arthur Henderson Smith had been mordant and pessimistic. In 1907, his *China and America Today* presented a very different and highly optimistic estimate. Another veteran, Calvin Mateer, who had been highly critical of earlier Sinophiles like Anson Burlingame, wrote to a friend in 1905: "The state of things today presents a great contrast with what it was when I arrived here forty-one and a half years ago. Then everything was dead and stagnant; now all is life and motion . . . [with] promise of great things in the near future."[1] W. A. P. Martin, reviewing the changes up to 1906, concluded: "China is the theatre of the greatest movement now taking place on the face of the globe."[2] Similar assessments, based on factual reports, could be multiplied a hundredfold and still be restricted to people like G. E. Morrison, the London *Times* correspondent who had lived

1. Quoted in Daniel W. Fisher, *Calvin Wilson Mateer; Forty-five Years a Missionary in Shantung China* (Philadelphia, 1911), pp. 311–12.
2. W. A. P. Martin, *The Awakening of China* (New York, 1907), Preface.

in China for some years, or Sir Robert Hart and Griffith John, who had been active in China for half a century.

The observers included not only missionaries and journalists, but hardheaded representatives of Great Britain, the chief imperial power. Admiral of the Fleet Sir Edward Seymour, who had had experience on the China Station, wrote: "The present revolution in China is the most startling change of a government since the great French cataclysm."[3] The outgoing governor of Hong Kong warned the Colonial Office that the new governor

> will require an entirely revised estimate of Chinese character from that which has been hitherto accepted. . . . [if he] is able to contrast the new with the old, he will be able to recognize the significance of the remarkable reversal of what have hitherto been considered as essential characteristics of the Chinese and to attach to them the importance they deserve . . .[4]

The general European journals were filled with articles of similar import; one of the most prophetic reads in part:

> While the man who would read as he runs is curious to know whether the rising was caused by the nationalization of certain railways or by the local dearth of food, the philosopher discerns tokens of the elements of volcanic eruption and confidently looks for seismic manifestations 10,000 miles away. The real issues raised by the Chinese Revolution will appear clear-cut and formidable before the present generation has vanished. . . . Whatever else it may create or destroy, it will cut deep into the life of all civilized nations. . . .[5]

Many of the West's radicals looked at China seriously for the first time. Lenin, writing in *Pravda* of November 8, 1912 and May 31, 1913 shared the enthusiasm of missionaries, naval officers, colonial governors, and businessmen when he wrote almost lyrically that a quarter of the earth's population was moving forward, that hundreds of millions of men were awakening to life, to light, and to freedom.[6]

3. Seymour, "Chinese Changes," *Cornhill Magazine* (Dec. 1911), pp. 721–31.

4. Lugard to Colonial Office (hereafter CO), CO 1899/11/12 in CO 129 (Hongkong), 381.

5. E. J. Dillon, "The Most Momentous Event for 1000 Years," *Contemporary Review* (Dec. 1911), pp. 874, 880. Dillon, an amateur orientalist who wrote a dozen books on current world affairs, was the John Gunther of his time.

6. Quoted in K. A. Wittfogel, *Der Erwachende China* (Vienna, 1926).

The observations of this multitude of witnesses, even assuming some degree of wishful thinking, are persuasive. The general picture of the state of China emerges slowly and unevenly in the midst of detailed discussions of specific questions, but with due allowance for different conditions in different parts of a vast country, the general import year by year is unmistakable: This is not the China we have known; "New China" has arrived and is gathering momentum.

Chinese sources confirm the impression of a new era, indeed of a new world. The flow of edicts and memorials continued, but even these had a different tone and texture. Meanwhile affairs of state were beginning to be reported fully in the *Tung-fang tsa-chih* (Eastern Miscellany) and in the host of other magazines, newspapers, and pamphlets that mushroomed in the coastal cities and found their way across the country. The headlines, the cartoons, the feature stories, the letters to the editor belong to our own era. They are not reminiscent of the end of any earlier dynasty, or even of the 1890s.

As a traveler who has emerged from the study of the nineteenth century in China to survey the broad outlines of the early twentieth I cannot escape the conclusion that 1900 was the major turning point of modern Chinese history.[7] Here is the evidence.

Nationalism: The Moving Force

The paramount issue that concerned New China—China in the first phase of revolution—was nationalism, a nationalism directed toward action and change in three different, though related spheres. First it called for action not only to halt but to roll back the tide of imperialism. New China meant to reclaim everything imperial China had ever lost to foreign powers, and in some cases to advance beyond the claims of the Ch'ing Empire at its height.

7. My impressions of the views of foreign nonofficial observers are based in part on my examination of 547 items of this period in the library on China collected by George E. Morrison, now deposited in the Tōyō Bunko, Tokyo, supplemented by the resources of the Yale University Library, where interest in China was strong immediately after 1900. My summaries of the international aspects of the revolution and of the views of official observers are derived from reading the China files of the British Foreign Office Archives, 1900–13, and portions of the War Office, Colonial Office, and Admiralty Archives. My references to Chinese accounts are drawn from several years' reading in a wide sampling of the primary documentation available.

Since an introduction cannot be a series of monographs, I have given footnotes only for direct quotations, or occasionally to illustrate the type of materials on which summary statements are based.

Although this was of course an "antiforeign" sentiment, it should be sharply distinguished from the primitive xenophobia to which the reformers and revolutionaries of the time attributed the antiforeign uprisings of the nineteenth century, which culminated in the Boxer Rebellion of 1900.

Nationalism demanded secondly the organization of a modern, centralized nation-state, capable both of forcing back the imperialists and of forwarding the country's new aspirations in political, social, economic, and cultural life. And thirdly, nationalism meant to overthrow the Manchu dynasty. This anti-Manchuism seems to me to have been less important at the time, and far less important retrospectively, than the anti-imperialist and centralizing thrusts of the new nationalism.

Resistance to Imperialism

The watchword of New China was "recovery of sovereign rights." This is not the place to discuss the issue of when and how Chinese came to accept the idea of a world made up of many sovereign states, thus renouncing the idea of the universal domain of the Son of Heaven. By the late nineteenth century, the newly coined terms "national sovereignty" and "sovereign rights"—ideas learned from the West to use in argument with the West—begin to appear here and there in state papers. After 1900, the phrases seem to appear on nearly every page one reads.

The sharp reaction against imperialism after 1900, the cry to "buy back China," is easy enough to understand in its historic context. Beginning with the Opium War (1839–42), China had succumbed to a series of foreign attacks each of which was concluded with an "unequal treaty" which required China to pay an indemnity and to concede privileges, rights, and territory to the victorious foreigner. The Sino-Japanese War of 1894–95 revealed a China too weak to refuse anybody anything. In the ensuing "scramble for concessions" the powers shifted from checking one another to outgrabbing one another. The scramble increased to uncontrolled pillage after the Allied Expedition of 1900, when the carpetbaggers of the earth rushed to China to buy up the mining rights of whole provinces for a song.

The effect on China was the opposite of what had been casually expected. Internal Chinese policy differences as to whether one should concede to Japan or to Russia in the north in order to ward off a greater threat from the other, to France or to Britain along the long and ill-defined southern frontier, were buried under a wave of determination to strengthen the country and reclaim *all* that had been lost.

A new province of China proper was carved out of those portions of Tibet lying closest to Szechwan Province. Chinese claims on their takeover were substantiated by Western firsthand reports, for example: "The Chinese talk of the submission of these tribesmen very often in a rather ridiculous fashion, but this time it really has been a submission to the Chinese Government."[8] Chinese troops moved by degrees to occupy the rest of Tibet, including Lhasa. This expedition was clearly intended not as an isolated thrust but as a reorganization of Tibet under Chinese sovereignty, all the way to the Indian frontier. Chinese garrisoned and governed the towns, altered many of the customary administrative procedures, and stripped a number of princes of their authority. According to both Chinese and British accounts they met with little resistance. The tea planters of Assam screamed to the home government in vain, for the Foreign Office recognized the weakness of its right to interfere in Tibet. Britain had the right to preserve law and order only in areas adjacent to India that were beyond effective Chinese control. China was now in the process of establishing that control.

As of January 31, 1910 the British government seemed prepared to accept the Chinese claim to Tibet as sovereign and not suzerain territory, and the Foreign Office noted that it had "no ground for objecting to the abolition of Tibetan autonomy."[9] A few days later the Dalai Lama fled to Darjeeling. On April 18, the Chinese Ministry of Foreign Affairs made a formal statement of its claims to Tibet in terms of the sovereign rights of China, which by now had become the stock phrase of any Chinese discussing any issue with any foreigner.[10]

From this point, Chinese control in Tibet was rapidly extended, and "Chinese officials became still more enterprising on other portions of the frontier."[11] Along the whole northern frontier of India, the Chinese and British were asserting claims to territory that had

8. Muir, Batang, to Wilkinson, Chengtu (Jan. 29, 1910), FO 371/1612, no. 12233. An official Chinese map of the new province, tentatively named only Kuan-wai, is attached to FO 371/853, no. 13351.

9. Minute on FO 371/853, no. 13351.

10. Note the comment of Max Müller on FO 371/854, no. 16007.

11. Review memorandum on Tibet, prepared for distribution to the Cabinet, FO 371/1609, no. 10240.

never really belonged to either. There was therefore little basis for negotiating a border; instead both sides were racing to extend *de facto* administration to serve as the basis for legal claims.

China considered Bhutan as tributary, but the relationship was so loose that the British could ignore it until the thrust of China's new forward policy began to be felt. When it was, early in 1910, Britain maneuvered quickly to get Bhutan to declare fealty to India in foreign relations to provide a legal basis for intervention against China if necessary. Within a few months China did reassert her historic claim to Bhutan, backing her case with a list of precedents extending from the Yung-cheng to the Kuang-hsü reigns. Those few months of early 1910 were precious indeed, for the British presented them as outweighing Chinese centuries. The India Office was straining more than history when it dismissed the Chinese claims as having "succumbed to the logic of events and the lapse of time." A year later, at the end of 1911, the Chinese amban at Lhasa was still addressing peremptory letters to the Maharaja of Bhutan—letters which could now be left unanswered as the Chinese central authority crumbled.[12]

The race for the allegiance of Nepal was similar. As late as 1908 a Nepalese mission in Chinese official dress had proceeded to Peking, an event to which China pointed as confirmation of Nepal's tributary status. Although the British again outmaneuvered the Chinese, it was a close contest whose outcome might well have been different if the Chinese central government had remained stable. As for Sikkim, Chinese troops were poised on the frontier of a state whose ruler was still conventionally portrayed in the dress of a Chinese official.

A different race for the same goal was in progress along the Burma frontier, where the Chinese had a distinct logistical advantage: their lines from secure bases to the outposts they claimed in the disputed territory were shorter and better than those of the British. Chinese miners were moving far beyond the "frontier" in search of gold. Chinese officials were busily appointing village headmen to Chinese official ranks, collecting taxes, and establishing Chinese schools deep in Shan territory. The British could no longer relax with their earlier vague claims; they had to decide what portions of Burma were vital to their interests and to occupy them before the Chinese got there. The contest was still close as

12. FO 371/1337, passim; FO 371/859, nos. 6193, ff.; FO 371/1330, no. 652.

late as 1913. After several collisions between the Burma military police and parties of Chinese, the Foreign Office noted: "We were evidently only just in time to prevent the country being taken over by the Chinese."[13]

The Indochinese border was as sensitive as those further West; the Chinese went so far as to design a railway whose route would be economically pointless but which would cripple French-held Kwangchow-wan and curtail further French activity in the area. The recovery of Macao was included in the anti-imperialist drive, particularly after the overthrow of the Portuguese monarchy in 1910, but demands for the return of Hong Kong and Weihaiwei were curiously muted for the moment. Here the effort seems to have been to contain rather than to expel for a variety of tactical reasons, a policy perhaps comparable to the successful containment of Germany's effort to expand the Shantung base she had acquired only a decade earlier.[14]

China's frontiers to the north posed similar general problems. There had been considerable anti-Russian feeling in China at the time of the Russian occupation of Manchuria in 1902–03 and this was intensified after 1905 when, having been set back in Manchuria by Japan's victory, Russia turned her attention to Mongolia. Mongolia posed essentially the same issues as Tibet. China's claim to suzerainty, but not sovereignty, had been recognized, and China had been forced to agree to special rights for Russia. Now with Russia weakened and Chinese anti-imperialist sentiment at fever pitch, Peking's policy changed to one of asserting her full sovereignty over her dependency. Local officials along the whole border, from Manchuria to Turkestan, were enjoined to combat Russian influence. The flow of Chinese colonists into Outer Mongolia was encouraged, a Chinese type administration was set up under an able, modern-minded official, and Chinese garrison troops were sent out.

In the Manchurian homeland, Chinese emigration was speeded, the old special Manchu offices were abolished, and the whole area was divided into three provinces, to be governed like any other. The ultimate intention was to redeem the Chinese Eastern Railway and to block Japan's expansion along the projected line of the South Manchurian Railway.

13. Minute on FO 371/1603, no. 32502.

14. I am indebted to John Schrecker for information on the containment of Germany in Shantung.

I have not attempted in these paragraphs to trace the subtleties of multilateral diplomatic maneuvering or of local conditions in each area around the vast periphery of China. My purpose has been to underscore the territorial aspect of the intense anti-imperialist nationalism of the period, and the degree of success achieved. Much remains to be examined area by area, but the sources leave no doubt as to the general picture. There is no evidence of a Manchu-Chinese, central-provincial, or gentry-peasantry cleavage on this point. What the Chinese sources record was duly recognized by a startled outside world.

One may well ask what is anti-imperialist or revolutionary about the attempts of the Chinese government to join in great power diplomacy on an equal footing. The answer lies in history, geography, and the connection with the other changes taking place in China at this time. For centuries Chinese frontier policy had been based on maintaining a screen of buffer states, autonomous in minor local matters but never in matters that might affect China. When foreign powers began infiltrating these buffer areas, Chinese interpreted this as a further step in aggression that would lead to partition. Hence counterattack did not appear as Chinese imperialism against the Mongols or Tibetans, but as resistance to Russian or British imperial expansion at the expense of China. That the British and French might move from Burma and Indochina into Yunnan seemed quite likely; that the Chinese might move out from Yunnan to conquer the world was patent nonsense. In this historic-geographic context, in a country smarting under 65 years of defeat, the massive nationalism that supported the policies outlined above proved potently revolutionary.

By massive nationalism I mean an intense, widespread fear that China would be partitioned and the Chinese disappear as a people. Since foreign policy has become the issue of mass demonstrations and protests in Western countries only in recent times, and then often been attributed to the work of a handful of agitators, the Westerner may easily regard the issues summarized above as of no interest to Chinese as a whole, and the Chinese government's statements as characteristic of the oratory of leaders without followers. This was clearly not the case with avowed revolutionaries. Underground revolutionary pamphlets like *Ko-ming hsien-feng* (Vanguard of the Revolution) compared China's fate to that of Poland and India. So did the revolutionary newspapers like *Min-li-pao*.

The real question is: What response did the issues of frontier policy receive from the general public? A primary-school song from Wusih in Kiangsu exhorted the government to stand firm on the frontiers so that the sleeping lion, finally awakened, might come roaring onto the battlefield.[15] Similar songs were sung in schools throughout China. According to the correspondent of *Le Temps,* they showed "better than anyone could explain, the changes which are operating in the soul of the Chinese, whose ideal not long ago was limited to success in personal affairs and whose spirit of solidarity, though very strong, did not go beyond the guild or town."[16] In the long comfortable foreign bastion of Shanghai, at highly charged meetings led by students and singers, hysterical women demanded arms to fight. It was reported that both audiences and leaders left these meetings in a state of indescribable delirium compounded of heroism and fury.[17] Theatricals showing French *colons* beating their Annamite coolies and British officers striking Indian troops on parade were shown repeatedly in South China. The press of Yunnan and Kweichow spread reports that in the forthcoming partition of China, these provinces would go to France. The popular reaction was sharp: We would rather die than submit to the fate of Annam.[18] Szechwan was plastered with posters to the effect that only armed force would prevent Szechwan from sharing the fate of India.[19] In the disputed area of Burma the British had to alter their strategy; they could not rely on Chinese muleteers to "take any share in assisting us to seize what is regarded by China as a portion of Chinese soil."[20]

These issues were discussed not only in the local but in the national press, and in the new assemblies. Nor were the hot spots limited to South China. For example, Japanese announcements of plans for the reconstruction of the Mukden-Antung Railway line, a part of the broader South Manchurian Railway plan, produced sharp reactions as far as Canton. On the issue of Mongolia, pro-

15. Quoted in Fernand Farjenel, "La Transformation politique de la Chine," *Revue politique et parlementaire* (Dec. 10, 1908), p. 534.

16. Jean Rodes, *La Chine nouvelle* (Paris, 1910), pp. 249–52.

17. Jean Rodes, *Scènes de la vie révolutionnaire en Chine, 1911–1914* (Paris, 1917), pp. 72–76.

18. FO 371/873, no. 35724; FO 371/864, no. 23052; Albert Maybon, *La Politique chinoise: Études sur les doctrines des partis en Chine* (Paris, 1908), Pt. 3, pp. 151–52; Jean Rodes, *Le Céleste Empire avant la révolution,* commissioned by the Geographical Society and the Colonial Ministry (Paris, 1914), pp. 23–26.

19. Texts in FO 371/1615, no. 8861.

20. FO 371/1615, no. 8861.

vincial governors and assemblies from Manchuria to Kwangtung called for war against Russia.[21]

The anti-American boycott of 1905 over the Exclusion Act and the anti-Japanese boycott over the *Tatsu Maru* case in 1908 were two of the most conspicuous indications that a new Chinese public had been aroused to a new nationalism which, although it evoked overtones of the tributary system, was in the main a new, anti-imperialist drive. The anti-American boycott, which began early in 1905 at Shanghai, soon shifted its center to Canton. Although it was officially ended late that year, meetings and demonstrations continued into 1907. Numerous incidents accompanying the boycott show that Chinese merchants and workers were prepared to make substantial material sacrifices in order to achieve the broad objectives of the new nationalism. Morrison of *The Times* reported: "The Chinese have awakened to a consciousness of nationality. Outrages on Cantonese who have emigrated to the Pacific coast are no longer resented only by the people of Kwantung. They make *all* China indignant."[22] When a young student returned from Japan heard that the American consul had been quoted as saying that a Chinese was incapable of acting except in self-interest, he poisoned himself on the doorstep of the consulate. His martyrdom set off demonstrations in all the major cities of China.[23]

Early in 1908 the *Tatsu Maru* was seized carrying contraband, and the Japanese flag was hauled down. Japan, in the time-honored manner, demanded and received an apology and compensation, and the Chinese officials concerned were punished. The Chinese nationalist reaction was intense: merchants burned their stocks of Japanese goods and workers refused to unload Japanese ships. The news was spread through the vernacular press, and protest demonstrations swept the country. New songs were composed and physical education suddenly became very popular. Although the economic effects were not serious in this case, it was one more incident that fed growing nationalism. It also demonstrates that although this nationalism was revolutionary, the revolutionaries were not the leading force in its formation; the

21. Press clippings enclosed in FO 371/1338, no. 51899; report to the Admiralty of the Senior Naval Officer at Canton, FO 371/1615, no. 8861.

22. G. E. Morrison, quoted in F. A. McKenzie, "Four Hundred Million Chinamen Awaken" (an interview with Morrison), *The London Magazine,* 25, no. 150 (Feb. 1911), 702.

23. Maybon, Pt. 3, pp. 196–201.

contraband cargo had been arms believed intended for the revolutionaries. The popular outcry ignored this; it was directed against the violation of the sovereign rights of any Chinese government.

Chinese bitterness over loss of sovereign rights within China was as intense as the resentment over foreign encroachment on the frontiers. By successive treaties and agreements, foreigners had gained the right to administer an increasing number of the settlements and concessions in which their businesses and residences were located. They were subject to their own laws as administered by their own courts rather than to Chinese law. The Maritime Customs Service was managed by foreigners. By treaty, the tariff on imports and exports was limited to 5 percent ad valorem, and had become in fact considerably less. China was still powerless to prohibit the import of Indian opium. Foreigners exercised their treaty right to patrol inland waterways against piracy and to land forces where foreign interests seemed jeopardized.

Foreign interests had greatly expanded after 1895. Syndicates raced to lend money secured on railways to be built or mines to be developed. The railways and mines were the security for the loans, which added to the already strangling burden of debt that China had accumulated in a succession of indemnities for the wars she had lost. In Sun Yat-sen's famous phrase, China's position was worse than that of a colony. She was at the mercy of the powers, yet there was no one paternalistic colonial power to whom she could turn for mercy.

It is well known that cancellation of special foreign rights was later a battle cry of the Nationalists, and that in the years after 1949 the Communists simply denounced what remained of foreign special privilege and expropriated foreign property they regarded as stolen from the Chinese people. What is not generally recognized is that these were deep-seated grievances that would have been forcibly righted by any Chinese government strong enough to do so, and that the imperial government, with full popular support, started a movement to recover full sovereignty at the beginning of the twentieth century.

Extraterritoriality, according to which the foreigner resident in China was subject to the jurisdiction of foreigners rather than of local Chinese officials, had not aroused particular Chinese fears when it was incorporated into the Sino-American Treaty of Wanghia in 1844. By 1900, however, this and related privileges had produced safe, comfortable, and prosperous enclaves that were visible symbols of foreign power. No Chinese, however close his connections with the foreigners, failed to resent this; and no revolutionary, however convenient it might be to have a place to hide from the Chinese police, failed to denounce the flag that in protecting him denied Chinese sovereignty on Chinese soil. On this the revolutionaries and reformers were agreed—and so was the imperial government.

The steps taken seem mild enough today, for the Chinese government probed gently, awaiting the time when its modernized armed forces would be strong enough to make a foreign power hesitate to start a land war in Asia over issues which, though of intense importance to the China traders, were trivial in the worldwide concerns of the imperial powers. In 1912, for example, there was a collision between the Chinese police and the foreign police of the Municipal Council at Shanghai over who should patrol roads outside but adjacent to the International Settlement. The Municipal Council claimed the right based on long usage; the Chinese protested as a means of testing the legality of certain supplementary land regulations. The British minister characterized the incident thus: "The spirit of latent hostility under the old regime has become one of active aggression."[24]

Take another small case: in 1905 a widow of good Cantonese family was arrested in Shanghai by the foreign police on a kidnapping charge. The Chinese judges of the Mixed Court opposed imprisonment, but without effect. Protests against the prison sentence included street rioting, petitions from both merchants and gentry, and a protest by the taotai. The widespread protest was caused by resentment of the limited authority of Chinese judges in the Mixed Courts and, more basically, of the fact that Chinese had no voice in the government of the International Settlement.[25]

The public reaction to the death of a Chinese in the foreign settlement of Kiukiang in 1909, allegedly caused by the British Superintendent of Police, was another sign of the changing temper. In earlier years the accidental killing of a Chinese by a foreigner, even if proven, would have caused no stir. In 1909 there was public excitement, and when after a long trial the Superintendent of Police was exonerated, there was a boycott of British goods.

24. FO 371/1347, no. 2350; see also no. 43730.
25. Maybon, Pt. 3, pp. 211–14; Martin, pp. 255–56.

Beneath a multiplicity of incidents of this type lay one underlying cause. The Chinese were finding foreign jurisdiction on Chinese soil intolerable. Since the original justification had been the objectionable character of the Chinese criminal code and judicial proceedings, a commission proceeded to plan the reorganization of both. In the meantime, China made a clever move by establishing in 1906 new judicial establishments, the Shen-pan-t'ing. By 1910, these existed in areas as remote as Kweilin and Wuchow in Kwangsi. The foreigners saw no problem at first, since in cases involving foreigners, the appropriate consul would be present. As cases came to trial, however, they found that their consuls were expected to be silent observers present at the pleasure of the Chinese magistrate. This was a long way from the effective consular supervision of trials they thought the treaties guaranteed.[26]

Of more importance were the steps quietly taken to make the Imperial Maritime Customs Service a normal arm of the Chinese government through the establishment in 1906 of a Customs Bureau (Shui-wu chü) to which the elaborate system established by treaty and manned by foreigners would be subordinate.[27] In his way, Sir Robert Hart, Inspector General of the Customs, had served China well for half a century, as a kind of special agent of the throne upon whom he had originally been forced but whom he never failed to recognize as his employer. But however much Hart himself, old and ill, might deny it, the time had passed when even a "good" institution manned by foreigners according to treaty terms was acceptable to a China in the midst of a radical nationalist revolution. The British Foreign Office's reaction was to stand firm and refuse to discuss even revision of the 1902 tariff schedule to bring it up to an effective 5 percent, not because they were totally unreasonable but because to be adamant on the taxation of foreign trade was "the only effective stick, with which we can beat China" to force her to observe her treaty obligations with respect to opium and Tibet.[28]

And so it was with a dozen lesser "sovereign rights." The Chinese press announced that the Cantonese were ready to attack British gunboats if they continued to patrol China's inland waterways as protection against piracy. The Chinese government

26. FO 371/1628, no. 4762.
27. FO 371/682, nos. 14689 and 15267.
28. FO 371/1349, no. 41411.

insisted that the principle of reciprocity required that they be allowed to establish Chinese consulates abroad. An edict of April 10, 1911 foreshadowed a move to take control of the postal system and put it under China's new Ministry of Communications. This was alarming to the legations in Peking, which often confused a current practice with a treaty right. As the British Foreign Office noted, although the system might be less efficient in Chinese hands, "we have no other grounds, and certainly no treaty rights to oppose the change."[29]

One of the most emotion-laden areas in which the Chinese were determined to recover their sovereign rights concerned Britain's treaty right to import Indian opium into China. The British Government, long uneasy about forcing China to import opium, had taken refuge in the argument that China herself produced most of the opium she consumed and that therefore to deny this treaty-guaranteed trade to British merchants would serve no purpose. They had however agreed that if China should *prove* that she had completely eradicated the production of opium in China, Britain would reciprocate. By edict of September 20, 1906, a ten-year campaign to remove the poppy from China was begun, and its results were astonishing. The anti-opium campaign may have been the largest and most vigorous effort in world history to stamp out an established social evil. Since the stakes of the opium traders were large and their lobby efficient, the evidence had to be supplied not by Chinese reports but by hard-nosed British inspectors. Not every remote valley in China could be visited in season, but the general trend of the voluminous reports suggests that by 1911 80 percent of the land where the opium poppy had been grown had been converted to food crops and that whatever opium smoking continued was done in private.

The anti-opium campaign was an extraordinarily dangerous one. Opium was the most profitable crop in many of the poorest areas. Addiction was common at every level of society, and corrupt officials had long since found a way to tap the profits of this lucrative trade.

The campaign, reinforced by a Draconian further edict of January 1911, almost succeeded. With a little less British legalism it might have truly succeeded. The Foreign Secretary, Sir Edward Grey, looking over the wealth of reports, expressed real admiration

29. FO 371/1343, no. 8057; FO 371/1090, no. 16901; see also nos. 18989, 19455, 23899.

for the Chinese performance. Yet, when the governor of Anhwei ordered the burning of British opium stocks at Anking on the ground that the province was now free of opium, the consul general at Shanghai sailed up in a gunboat to protest. When the governor of Kiangsi took similar action on similar grounds, the British again cried "treaty violation." British opium was also confiscated at Hangchow and other cities. In each case, the British dodged the issue on the ground that all opium must disappear from all China before a particular opium-free area could demand the suspension of imports. In the temper of the times, Chinese protest mounted, and the vernacular press was filled with denunciations and threats of a reverse Opium War.[30]

The targets of the anti-imperialist drive also included most of the Western investment in China; in the mood of the period the extent of these investments seemed to presage the turning over of most of China's natural resources to foreign enterprises protected by the hated treaties.

The Chinese government had always kept a close watch on unauthorized mining, even by its own subjects. However, at the lowest ebb of China's strength, there had been a rush by foreigners to buy up rights to China's fabled mineral wealth. With the rise in anti-imperialist mood, there was a drive to recover these rights. For example, in the bleak year of 1898, the Peking Syndicate had secured extensive rights to mine in Honan Province. By 1909, opposition in the province was so strong that test-holes were being destroyed and operations could not proceed. Officials and gentry at the provincial capital, especially the leaders of the Provincial Assembly, argued that the benefits promised to China had not been forthcoming and that therefore the old agreement was void; in this they had the full support of the Chinese Ministry of Foreign Affairs. Endless meetings were held, at which the British minister was instructed to assist the Syndicate but with the private notation of the Foreign Office that "his chance of vindicating the rights acquired by the Syndicate appears . . . rather small in the

30. The documentation is enormous. For key policy statements and Chinese press clippings, see FO 371/1330, 1331, 1333; FO 228/1849. The facts of the matter were that Sassoon alone had on hand some 32,000 chests of opium, valued at £12,000,000. They were badly overstocked with opium they could not sell in the face of Chinese opposition, yet they had to keep buying in India to prevent a fall in price which would have been ruinous to their existing holdings. The foreign banks in China had advanced loans amounting to several million pounds, and many failures were feared if these could not be repaid.

present temper of the Chinese."[31] The central government offered to buy back the rights, the usual procedure in this period of fear of foreign reprisal, but the question was at what price and with what funds. When the Chinese had bought back German gold mining rights in Shantung, alleged to be worth £4,000,000, for £50,000, the British Foreign Office remarked: "It is consoling to find that we are not the only victims of the China for the Chinese policy."[32]

Illustrations could be drawn from every part of the country. When the joint Anglo-French Yunnan Syndicate plans were announced in 1910, there were meetings of protest, a press campaign, and the threat of riot if the mines opened. The population was reported as menacing.[33] In Shensi in 1911 the rumor that the new governor had pledged the oil wells of the provinces as security for a foreign loan led to an uproar in the provincial assembly and the press.[34]

The drive to recover China's railways—most of which had been built by or were heavily mortgaged to imperialist interests—is in some ways the most dramatic aspect of the Rights Recovery Movement, because it precipitated the nationwide uprising of 1911 that was the climax of the first stage of the Chinese Revolution. Railways in China generally operated at a good profit, including a few of those owned and operated by Chinese. But for the necessary capital, foreign loans were almost the only recourse. The Chinese government had been bankrupted by three quarters of a century of wars, indemnities, rebellions, and natural disasters; in comparison, extravagance and peculation in high places seems to have been quantitatively trivial. As Mme. Bergère explains in chapter 5, the high yield on safe investments like land limited the flow of Chinese private capital into the tiny and risky modern sector of the economy.

The Chinese government had first fought the very idea of railways, appealing to everything from disturbance of graves to the prospect of unemployment of carters and boatmen. Chinese officials had also argued that foreigners had established commercial bases wherever there were navigable rivers along which gun-

31. FO 371/857, nos. 11707, 13190; no. 2421ff.; no. 2594ff.; no. 846ff.

32. FO 371/860, no. 1972.

33. FO 371/873, no. 35723; Rodes, *Céleste Empire*, pp. 23–26.

34. E. R. Beckman, *The Massacre at Sianfu* (Chicago, 1913), p. 55; John C. Keyte, *The Passing of the Dragon; the Story of the Shensi Revolution and Relief Expedition* (London and New York, 1913), p. 17.

boats could be brought up to support them. Might they not use a railway network as they had used the rivers?

In New China, after 1900, opposition to railways had dissolved, but Chinese railways were to be owned by and operated for Chinese, not foreigners. This is not the place to analyze the central-vs.-local and public-vs.-private conflicts on the Chinese side, still less the efforts of the various international banking groups to secure exclusive rights to float the loans. In perspective, the important point is that by 1909, as the British recognized, all railway plans had suffered a setback from the point of view of the foreign investor.[35] There was now evidence that Chinese were capable of operating railway lines effectively; the question was how to find the capital. The foreign powers were appalled when in 1909 the Chinese government invited applications for railway loans from Chinese financiers.[36]

This step, along with wildcat borrowing from Chinese and foreign sources, was correctly interpreted by the Foreign Office: "It is undoubtedly true that the Chinese government and people are showing increasing signs of resentment at what they consider the harsh and unreasonable conditions imposed by the foreign financial interests in China . . . against the tightening grip of foreign financiers on the nation's purse strings."[37]

The correspondent of *Le Temps* reported that the protest in August 1907 against the British and Chinese Corporation's contract for the Shanghai-Ningpo line included leaders of the gentry and merchants, 6,000 weeping coolies, and 2,000 beggars—not to mention actors and priests. Members of the gentry proposed to go to Peking and commit suicide in front of the British legation, as did one of the most prominent businessmen of Shanghai, who declared, "To die for one's country is glorious." The same man wrote the British minister, saying that unless the minister arranged a cancellation of the loan within a month he would be labeled "an enemy of the Chinese people," who would retaliate with a boycott of British goods. The "people" of both provinces concerned declared that they would rather be shot by imperial troops than submit to the new foreign loan. An engineer and a student at the Railway Technical School reportedly starved themselves to death at Hangchow. A professor at Ningpo was reported to have

35. FO 371/861, no. 5829.
36. FO 371/851, no. 4324.
37. FO 371/871, no. 37193.

died of sadness. Weeping crowds viewed the bodies and threatened an uprising and refusal to pay the land tax.[38] Thirty million taels were reportedly pledged toward redemption of the line. The accuracy of the precise details is less important than the fact that they filled the national press, and that the area directly concerned was plastered with posters.

During the first decade of the twentieth century, every possible method of redeeming China's railways was attempted. In Canton, with the support of merchant organizations, a merchant raised more capital than had been believed possible. Subscriptions poured in from the provinces of Kwangtung, Kwangsi, Hupeh, and Hunan, the city of Shanghai, and the Overseas Chinese in Cochin China and Singapore. Coolies and blind musicians were reported to have joined merchants and gentry in their eagerness to finance a Canton-Hankow line free of foreign and central government control.[39] The two were now becoming identified as targets, in spite of the government's own efforts to free itself, because it had too often been forced to pledge railways as security for the loans without which it could not have survived for long.

A similar but more explosive situation was developing in Szechwan, as is well known. Yet the capital was inadequate, and after a short time investment dwindled as the enormity of the problem became clear.

Whatever one may think of widespread stories of little girls who saved for months to send a dollar "to help buy back China," protests and suggestions came from all quarters, reaching a peak in 1909–11. When electric lights were introduced into Hunan in 1911, the province was placarded with statements that this was the way to fight foreign petroleum.[40] The leading reform-minded officials were urged to form an organization to put pressure on all officials to donate 30 percent of their salaries; a youth group suggested collecting two dollars from every man, woman, and child in China; student organizations hoped that a sweeping drive for small contributions might prove infectious. Provincial assemblies demanded publication of the full facts as a basis for concerted action. The imperial princes were reported to have taken the lead in contributing sums up to $50,000.[41]

38. Rodes, *Chine nouvelle,* pp. 191–93, 254–57.
39. *NCH* (March 16, 1906); Maybon, Pt. 3, pp. 207–11.
40. Rodes, *Céleste Empire,* pp. 128–29.
41. *Notes on Money Matters with Special Reference to China,* reprinted from the *National Review* (Shanghai, 1910).

Out of all this turmoil a National Debt Redemption Association was formed. It did not accomplish its purpose, but in its formation and activities it revealed the depth and passion of the nationalism behind the drive to recover national independence by paying off national debts, a passion that reached a new pitch in 1911, when the new catchword "blood and iron" was everywhere in the news. Persistent rumors of the impending partition of China led to an increased number of mass meetings, in the schools and in public, as did the increasingly wide distribution of revolutionary pamphlets with titles like "Disaster! Help!" (*Shou-k'u chiu-nan*). News of a patriotic character from the remotest part of China was broadcast everywhere. All over, projects were put forward for "saving the nation," including the proposal, given more and more prominence, to establish a people's army for defense against the imperial powers.

China might still be weak, but popular feeling was so aroused that the British consul in Chungking warned that if any power intervened, "the resentment of the people will be so great that I doubt if any one person will leave this port alive."[42]

Nationalism vs. Provincialism

Nationalism, in this first phase of the revolution, meant more than anti-imperialism. It meant also the triumph of nationalism over provincialism.

In response to several years of widespread press agitation and massive petitions, the imperial government in 1908 authorized the election of provincial assemblies in every province of China except Sinkiang, where the literacy rate in Chinese was minimal. These provincial assemblies in turn elected the National Assembly. Nearly 90 percent of the men elected had received degrees under the now defunct Examination System, but approximately half were holders of lower degrees, the lower gentry who, even in more stable periods, were far more varied in background and occupation than the upper gentry. These gentry assemblymen did not function as the solid phalanx of the old elite, determined to preserve the status quo. On the contrary, they reflected their fluid status in a new China and their passionate concern with national as distinct from local issues.

Mr. Chang and Mr. Fincher both treat these questions in de-

42. Brown, Chungking (Oct. 31, 1911), FO 371/1098, no. 51644; Amoy Consular Intelligence Report for quarter ending June 1911, FO 228/1801; Hankow Consular Intelligence Report for quarter ending March 1911, FO 228/1801.

tail in this volume and conclude that the provincial assemblies and various province-centered activities of the period not only were of more significance than we have hitherto thought but were steps toward, rather than away from, the creation of a new national society and polity. As Mr. Fincher puts it, "Through the cultivation of abstract loyalties such as allegiance to large territorial units, and to a people conceived as voting citizens, Chinese provincialism facilitated the rise of nationalism."

Historians of China have overlooked the unprecedented character of the elections of 1909 and 1912, the rapid expansion of the electorate from 1 to 25 percent of the adult male population, and the manner in which, in the process of discussion, yesterday's most advanced proposal was today assumed as established practice. We have also overlooked the speed with which the assemblymen acquired parliamentary skills, and the fact that by January 1911 they had forced upon the imperial government what almost amounted to a parliament.

This form of nationalism may not have evoked such strong passions as did the fear of imperialism, but the issues debated in the assemblies were not academic; there were suicides and self-mutilations to underscore the demands for a national constitutional government.

The assemblies were not the only instruments through which local interest became a propelling force of the new nationalism. This was an era of societies for the prohibition of opium, for the abolition of footbinding, for equal rights for women, and so on, and the meetings of these societies gave local leaders platforms on which to develop their forensic skills and organizations through which they could and did cooperate with like-minded groups elsewhere. The mushrooming of publications and the extension of rail and postal services added to the channels through which local interests and loyalties were increasingly seen in a national context.

In his discussion of the new armies, Mr. Hatano similarly notes that the new provincial institutions were transitional to nationalism, and not vice versa. Mme. Bergère points out that if it was to develop, China's new bourgeoisie needed a national market and reforms that only an effective national government could institute. For example, the Provincial Assembly of Kwangtung, often considered the most self-centered province of China, declared that the abolition of the hated likin tax would be "useless unless coordinated with measures taken by a central government for the restoration of external customs duties and for the establishment of a civil and commercial code." She concludes that "the import-export trade replaced Confucian doctrines as the school in which the bourgeoisie learned the principles of national unity."

Discussion of many local issues inevitably led to national issues concerned with resistance to imperialism; for example, when a local branch of the Self-Government Association of Kwangtung objected to the visit of a British river patrol, it was led inexorably to challenge the validity of the whole treaty structure. Similarly the frustrations of a local chamber of commerce trying to expand trade through zones with different currencies led directly to a demand for national monetary reform. The point is so obvious, and the evidence so overwhelming, that it is curious that we have for so long considered the provincial constitutionalists to be of little importance except as being nationally divisive.

Opposition to Manchu Rule

In the Kuomintang orthodoxy that has influenced so much writing on this period, revolutionary nationalism has had a third, and to the Kuomintang, major meaning—Chinese ethnic opposition to alien Manchu rule as reactionary in domestic policy and cowardly in foreign affairs. Viewed dispassionately, the evidence suggests that this anti-Manchu strain of nationalism was probably the least important and certainly the least revolutionary of the three. Although the constitutional reformers made increasingly sharp demands on the court, they would generally have agreed with their leading spokesman Liang Ch'i-ch'ao that the Chinese monarchy was by this time no more alien to its people than was the British monarchy.

It should be remembered that the Manchus were not a single ruling group with a single policy. The Sino-Manchu amalgam that had been developing since the eighteenth century had reached its full maturity in the mid-nineteenth century, when domestic rebellion threatened the entire upper class and foreign aggression threatened the entire country. Reforms of the old regime in the early twentieth century—characteristic of this as of other great revolutions—were reforms in which divisions on policy did not match ethnic divisions. Among the imperial princes there were reformers and antireformers, as there were throughout the bureaucracy. Indeed, as Mr. Chang shows, the Manchu Bannermen were among the groups to which the provincial assembly leaders appealed for support, along with such groups as the Associations of Education and of Commerce and the Overseas Chinese.

When in July 1905 the revolutionary Wu Yüeh threw a bomb at a party of high officials about to go abroad to study reform in various fields, he was not attacking the Manchus, for there were Chinese in the mission. Of the two who then withdrew from the group in fright, one was Manchu, one Chinese. As I see it, Wu was unconsciously attacking reform for ambivalent reasons: he doubted the efficacy, the "sincerity" of reform from the top and at the same time he feared that it might be effective enough to dissipate revolutionary pressures.

As the Sino-Manchu elite included both reformers and reactionaries, so also it included both fiery anti-imperialists and compromisers. Here again it seems impossible to draw an ethnic policy line. There seems little foundation for the charges by revolutionaries that the Manchus as *Manchus* were wrecking the country by opposition to modernization and by pusillanimity in the face of imperialism. The proper target for such charges was the whole of the traditional Chinese state and society, and the charge could legitimately be made only by the extreme radical wing of the revolutionaries. Revolutionary pamphlets like "T'ien-t'ao" (Heaven's Punishment) attacked leading Chinese statesmen from Tseng Kuofan to Yuan Shih-k'ai. This obviously was an attack on the imperial system rather than on the Manchus as such. As the historian Ku Chieh-kang later recalled: "A race revolution was only an insignificant part of our program. We would not consider our revolutionary tasks accomplished until we had abolished government, had discarded the family system, and had made currency unnecessary." The gentry, of whom Ku himself was a member, was the real barrier. "I could not rest until this class was eliminated."[43]

This "Great Leap" strain, prominent in the whole history of the Chinese Revolution, was based on the belief that China could by an act of will skip the stages of history that the reformers were so fond of discussing, On such an assumption, it was a foregone conclusion that the monarchy and much else would be promptly dispatched; but the ethnic issue was irrelevant.

Simple anti-Manchu xenophobia certainly existed, but it was most prominent in limited geographic areas and in those wings

43. Ku Chieh-kang, *The Autobiography of a Chinese Historian,* trans. and annotated by Arthur W. Hummel (Leyden, 1931), p. 28.

of the revolutionary movement least concerned with revolution as social upheaval. In Kwangtung and in the Overseas Chinese communities the slogan "Overthrow the Manchus, restore the Chinese" aroused real feeling. Whenever the revolutionaries attempted to work with the secret societies, the old slogan could be used.

The intensity of anti-Manchu sentiment differed by time as well as by place. The deaths in 1908, both of the Empress Dowager Tz'u-hsi who had held the imperial apparatus together for nearly half a century, and of the Kuang-hsü Emperor, a pathetic and popular figure who had been under palace arrest since 1898, produced a crisis in leadership since the new Emperor was a child. The last three years of the dynasty were marked by court rivalries between the factions of the inept Prince Regent and the new Empress Dowager. The regent did not block the reform program—on the contrary it was accelerated—but he allowed the imperial princes to play an increasing role in government and assembled more and more Manchus around him in high place. On this score, he broke nearly every rule of Manchu self-restraint established by his ancestors in their consolidation of power in the mid-seventeenth century. The Manchu throne thus became an easier target for Chinese nationalism. Veiled protest often took the form of crossroad shrines to the memory of the late Kuang-hsü Emperor, where irate local gentry could insist that unpopular officials dismount in humility. It was a curious mixture.

Thus in some circumstances anti-Manchu sentiment could feed the new nationalism by arousing racist sentiments and by providing symbolic acts of liberation such as the cutting off of the queue. The revolutionaries' later treatment of the Manchus, however, supports the hypothesis that the depth of this sentiment in the country as a whole has been grossly exaggerated. In some instances, massacre may not be too strong a word to use, although the firsthand accounts vary widely. More often, it proved impossible to distinguish Manchu from Chinese, and the Manchus disappeared into the population at large. The ruling house was accorded extraordinarily favorable treatment, but aside from a few high Chinese officials who honored the Confucian code of loyalty to their sovereign and the later Japanese conquerors, who misread modern Chinese history, the world forgot the Ch'ing dynasty.

The Imperial Reforms

Nationalism propelled the imperial government into a series of reforms that proved to be one of the main revolutionary forces of the period both indirectly and directly; indirectly because of the fundamental changes they instituted in nearly every sphere of Chinese life, and directly because they precipitated political revolution. Most of the imperial government and bureaucracy shared the anti-imperialist nationalism and the centralizing nationalism that were agitating the country as a whole. It hoped to combat the anti-Manchu element in the new nationalism by demonstrating that it could provide the ideas, plans, and leadership for a united national effort. I have already discussed those which, like the campaign against opium, were directly related to foreign relations. I turn now to those that were more generally related to the modernization of the country's institutions.

In an era where one new idea led to another with the force and speed of converging rapids, there was a drive to change almost everything except land tenure. The most important reforms, viewed retrospectively, were the creation of an educational system new in both form and substance in a country with the world's oldest continuously educated upper class; the modernization of the army in the country that had invented gunpowder; and the introduction of the electoral process and organs of local self-government in a country where an elite of merit had impressive claims to moral and political preeminence.

The first steps were taken immediately after the government resumed power following the Allied occupation of Peking in 1900. The dispatch in 1905 of a mission to study constitutional government abroad marked the first acceleration of reform. Then came a retrenchment in consequence of the bombing of the mission by a revolutionary, immediately followed by a further acceleration, a more severe retrenchment in the wake of the assassination of the governor of Anhwei in 1907, and then from 1908 until the abdication, a leaping reform thrust. The point here is not that court politics and other complex factors affected the trends of the weeks, but that the trend of the years is unmistakably clear.

The abolition of the Examination System in 1905 and the simultaneous creation of a Ministry of Education altered with one stroke the basis of gentry power and of the recruitment of the bureacracy, points which I shall discuss below. It also removed much of the premium on Chinese classical learning and cleared the way for the new educational system, the first steps toward which had already been taken. A careful study concluded: "Never has a country accomplished more in so short a time after the establishment of a new system of education."[44]

The new schools began opening immediately in 1901–02. A few random examples illustrate the staggering proportions of what followed. In Kansu, where deforestation and the great mid-century rebellions had wreaked havoc, there were by 1910 seven modern high schools with adequate libraries, plus a number of technical schools. Foreign languages were being taught by the Berlitz system in Lanchow.[45] In Sian, in addition to new schools there were two well-equipped "colleges" with 800 politically attuned, idealistic students who spent their spare time spreading the slogan of "China for the Chinese." In Yunnanfu (Kunming) there were nine primary schools, one middle school, one high school, one normal school, and, in addition, technical schools and girls' schools. The educational plan for Kwangtung and Kwangsi was nearing complete realization except for some lag in the elementary school program. There were of course greater numbers of new schools in the long-established centers of learning, but it is the activity in areas that had been beyond the cultural pale—or disadvantaged at least—that is the most impressive. Education was perhaps the single most talked of subject in the country, not only in the new journal *Chiao-yü shih-chieh* (Educational World) but in the whole range of new publications.

The new schools' limitations were clearly apparent. There was a shortage of trained teachers and texts; and the fervor of demonstrations with what seemed facile slogans caused European observers to doubt the academic solidity of the new institutions. The more one reads, however, the more one is impressed with how much was in fact accomplished.

There was certainly some local misappropriation of educational funds, and in some cases sharp resistance by the peasantry to an innovation for which they payed extra taxes but which seemed for gentry benefit. Schoolboys, proud of their new uniforms, seemed arrogant. But on the basis of the available firsthand ac-

44. Harry Edwin King, *The Educational System of China as Recently Reconstructed,* U.S. Bureau of Education Bulletin no. 15 (Washington, D.C., 1911), p. 103.

45. G. E. Morrison from Lanchow, Feb. 24, 1910, in the *Times* (London, April 9, 1910).

counts, I have the impression that in the majority of towns and villages the new schools were welcomed. The propagandists of the new learning were skilled orators and they were addressing audiences who were accustomed to the idea that education opened the path to advancement; when they were told that the new education opened paths to an advancement that would save China, there was often a powerful response.

The campaigns to raise private funds for education met with surprising success. High officials, wealthy merchants, and prominent gentry seemed to respond to such appeals willingly. Tuan-fang established a girls' school in a part of his official residence. People of modest means also contributed, and patriotic suicides left notes asking that contributions in their memory be made to education. The total sums raised were hopelessly inadequate, as in the case of the campaign to buy back the railways, but the general public concern with modern education for a widening sector of society was manifest.

Change in the subjects studied was accompanied by change in the language itself. For several years a national commission under the direction of the distinguished scholar-entrepreneur Chang Chien worked on the problem of establishing a national language (*kuo-yü*) and simplifying the characters in which it was written. Language specialists from all provinces worked for a time in Peking and then returned home to set up national language centers. Formal proposals for establishing the basis of nationwide action were completed in June 1911.[46] Meanwhile, new phrases had been coined for new ideas; foreigners who had known the pre-1900 Chinese language well had to study the newspapers to add to their vocabularies the Chinese expressions for ideal, purpose in life, society, reform, the public good, taking the initiative, volunteering one's services, sweeping away obstructions, and so on.

In the long run—if there had been a long run—China might have followed the Japanese pattern; she seemed at the time to be lagging by no more than twenty years and to be capable of making up time. In the short run, the new schools funneled into an already strained society hundreds of thousands of young people, touched in one way or another by the new schools and new ideas, confident of their own mission to create a new world, and exerting an influence out of all proportion to their numbers.

46. Wen-tzu kai-ko ch'u-pan she, *Ch'ing-mo wen-tzu kai-ko wen-chi* (Documents on Language Reform at the End of the Ch'ing Period) (Peking, 1958), pp. 143–44.

The imperial government's military reforms were, like its educational reforms, double-edged, as the chapters by Mr. Hatano and Mr. Young demonstrate. The modern armies made possible the Chinese Empire's resistance to foreign encroachment on her frontiers, but this very role, coupled with their modern training, made them highly receptive to ideas of revolution in the name of nationalism.

Chinese military prowess came as a revelation to observers with a knowledge of the defeats of China's demoralized and underequipped armies during the nineteenth century. Behind the mounting of the Tibetan expedition and the firmness on all frontiers stood the new programs of recruitment, training, supply, and indoctrination. There is abundant outside professional evidence on the scope of the military reforms and the speed with which results were obtained.

A German officer who watched the maneuvers of the Yunnan forces in 1909 and again in January 1911 commented that although there were some tactical errors as a result of the youth and inexperience of the officers, remarkable progress had been made in only two years.[47] As of 1910, the British Foreign Office review of military intelligence reported that it was no longer feasible to exert local pressure on China through gunboats. "The Chinese forces have improved enormously in the last year or two" and might well retaliate by seizing the legations. The War Office concurred: "The new model Chinese army has been made to prevent foreign powers exerting pressure except at the cost of a war." When the revolution broke out in Wuhan it was noted that "the very business-like conduct of this army has been a revelation to those here." The supply system was good; "Professional pride is noticeable in each branch." The men were cheerful and quick to joke, "but there is a decided air of independence which is admitted by all to be quite 'New China.' "[48]

The third major group of imperial reforms included general reorganization of the entire administrative apparatus of the Empire, of which the most important feature for the present study was the authorization of elected assemblies at the provincial and national levels and of other organs of local self-government. Although the assemblies were intended to be consultative at the outset, their leaders quickly seized the reins. Petitions for an early

47. Enclosure in FO 228/1809.

48. FO 371/867, nos. 10962 and 11571.

convening of a true parliament and the inauguration of constitutional government seemed to flood the country in 1910. The number of signatures on the petitions reportedly increased from 200,000 in January to 25,000,000 in October of that year. The imperial government responded by moving the date forward to 1913. Mr. Chang and Mr. Fincher describe and analyze these changes in detail.

The government's purpose was to increase the efficiency of administration and to maintain centralized government in a rapidly changing country by providing new channels for the upward flow of information and opinion and the downward flow of power. But like the military and educational reforms, these structural reforms undermined the state even as they served it. The assemblies provided national forums for sharp debate, the substantive issues of which were potentially revolutionary. The assemblies in turn were influenced by the rapid spread of local self-government associations, which conducted campaigns on all current issues, freely discussed the decisions of high officials, and brought pressure to bear through public meetings and demonstrations.

The fourth series of major reforms were those intended to encourage industry, a dramatic reversal of an imperial policy that had been taken for granted for two millennia. Even in the late nineteenth century, resistance to industrialization was overpowering. Against this background, the imperial edict of 1903 ordering the establishment of a Ministry of Commerce underscored the fundamental character of the changes that had occurred. The edict declared:

> Commerce and the encouragement of industries have ever been from ancient times to the present matters of real importance to governments, but according to an old tradition we have looked upon matters of industries and commerce as matters of the last importance. That the policy of the Government and the labor of the people result in daily increasing poverty can have no other reason than this.[49]

The barriers to industrialization were formidable, but this move is no more to be discounted than the other imperial reforms. Chang Chien's example was observed and his was a powerful voice. As far away as Lanchow, Tso Tsung-t'ang's woolen mill, long closed,

49. *Peking Gazette* (April 22, 1903).

was reopened and expanded and new industries were begun. These are discussed by Mme. Bergère.

The position of the Chinese merchant had already begun to rise. His new social status was now confirmed, and in their new citywide chambers of commerce merchants now began to formulate their interests as a new class, as a nascent bourgeoisie. Since this was the group most visibly affected by the special privileges of foreign businessmen, nationalism had a strong appeal. And so once again the reforms of the imperial government aided in the creation of voices that would soon demand more than the imperial system was able to offer.

Commissions were also laying the groundwork for a dizzying series of other reforms: of currency, of criminal law, of commercial law, of transportation and communication. In time the tricky subject of land reform might have been broached, for of all Chinese dynasties the Ch'ing had been the most insistent on a freeholding peasantry as the basis of a stable society.

A monarch with imagination could have made a good case that the imperial reforms were offering all that the constitutional reformers and moderate republicans were demanding and that the small clusters of socialists and anarchists were talking to nobody but themselves. As Mr. Gasster points out in chapter 1, a revolution is not necessarily the only or most effective way to achieve revolutionary aims. But the Prince Regent was a feeble, frightened man, and the press was full of complaints at the high cost of the reforms and reports of popular resistance and riots. Mr. Ichiko has emphasized peasant resistance, but there is ample evidence of gentry resistance as well, a fact that affects his major thesis: that the so-called revolutionary movement was primarily a series of end-of-dynasty maneuvers by the gentry to expand their power. I interpret the resistance to the imperial reforms differently. The reforms were expensive, the government bankrupt. The cost had to be paid by raising funds locally and the new taxes were resented. A great many fundamental changes were introduced very rapidly, and change is always suspect in wide sections of any society. Many urged the government to proceed more slowly, but it seemed obsessed with the idea—an idea that characterized revolutionary thinking as well—that China could and must move forward with giant strides.

The reforms thus added to the growing revolutionary pressures in society in two ways: by the new forces they set in motion and by the resistance they generated—resistance not to their goals but to the only means the imperial government had to achieve them.

A New Society in the Making

China after 1900 was in many ways a new world, the result in part of the same forces that led to the imperial reforms and in part of the changes introduced by those reforms. From the heart of China, G. E. Morrison reported: "No one who has seen the change which is taking place in the country served by the [Peking-Hankow] railroad can long remain pessimistic as to the future of China."[50] And he found similar changes in Sinkiang in the far northwest: population and revenues were increasing, a modernizing spirit was felt everywhere, the vigorous campaign against opium was making progress, able officials were on the job, and corruption was less easy.[51]

Rapidly improving communications made it possible for groups in widely separated parts of the country to act simultaneously, as the boycotts and other popular protests showed. Railways and telegraph lines were rapidly being extended. The postal service expanded along with and beyond the lines of the railways. To attempt to give precise figures would be futile because of the different records kept by the three services. For our purposes it is sufficient to say that in 1910 Chinese were sending and receiving at least twenty-five times as many letters, newspapers, and magazines as they had in 1901. A veteran China journalist of ten years' experience concluded:

> For the first time in history the Chinese have discovered a common ground of union which has appealed to men of all classes and trades, of all religions, and all sections of the community. Unconsciously the Chinese have welded themselves into a nation.[52]

There was a different look to the cities. From Peking to Chengtu, streets were being cleaned, paved, and lighted. They were well policed and crime seemed no threat. New buildings were under construction. Beggars and prostitutes were becoming a rare sight except in the foreign-dominated ports. It was reported that they had been rounded up for vocational training in special insti-

50. From Sianfu, Jan. 31, 1910, in the *Times* (London, March 3, 1910).
51. From Urumchi, May 5, 1910, in the *Times* (London, June 13, 1910).
52. Douglas Story, *Tomorrow in the East* (London, 1907), pp. 170–73.

tutes,[53] not by order of the central government but through the cooperation of municipal officials and the various new citizens' organizations, in a burst of civic pride. Customs too were changing. Everywhere there were local societies to stamp out footbinding, gambling, opium smoking—anything that was regarded as one of the evils of Old China.

Newspapers were a prime force in expressing and in turn reinforcing this emergent public opinion. Their numbers and their distribution expanded rapidly. Travelers found an ample supply of newspapers at all the stopping places of the riverboat service on the Yangtze and reported that Chinese provincial readers were better informed about world affairs than the readers of the European provincial press. Others reported that while in 1895 the people only knew that China had been beaten, by 1908 any schoolboy could give a fairly accurate account of the Russo-Japanese War. The press was sufficiently informative for a village teacher who had never left home to discuss, with an interested local audience, the coming constitution, educational policy, and changes in the appointments of high officials.

The press affected politics directly as well as indirectly. In one case, for example, the governor-general at Nanking wrote letters to the papers explaining policies for which he had been attacked. The press also provided an alternative hearing for the victim of an alleged miscarriage of justice. Formerly he could petition the governor, of course, but he had no way of commanding the governor's attention. Now he could write a letter to a newspaper which the governor would read and, in most cases, investigate.

The magazines of the time, even those that were purely commercial ventures, concentrated on educating the literate public to China's needs; the contents of these magazines, like those of the newspapers, were then spread by word of mouth beyond their immediate office. In literature the realistic novel, often serialized, was predominant. Bitterness over the Allied occupation of Peking in 1900, nationalism, and satires on officials were recurrent themes. Even the archconservative Lin Shu elected to translate *Uncle Tom's Cabin*. The theater followed fiction's example: the old heroic legends and bawdy comedies were giving way to a patriotic repertory. Apparently this was what the audiences wanted, since

53. Roger Sprague, *From Western China to the Golden Gate* (Berkeley, 1911), pp. 107–13. The author had taught English in the new Chinese schools and knew the Chinese language.

the playwright-director had to count on paid admissions to cover expenses.

In this new world, old classes were changing and new classes emerging. But several of those most important to the developing revolutionary movement were dynamic new groups that it would be difficult to call social classes. Therefore I shall not base this brief discussion on an account of how the old four-class (scholar [gentry], peasant, artisan, merchant) society had broken down, but rather begin with the new groups and classes that were being formed and proceed to the old classes that were being transformed.

Youth

Students, and youth generally, were in many ways the most important group to gain prominence in China in the first phase of the revolution. There had been many upheavals in China's long history, but only after 1900 did young people, mainly from the new schools, take the lead. It is a Western truism that the younger generation is seldom satisfied with the world left them by their elders. This has obscured the significance of the fact that in a country where, more than anywhere else, youth had bowed to the authority of age both in times of peace and in times of crisis, youth—precisely because of its lack of trammeling experience and of habitual acceptance of the world as it is—suddenly became the most vibrant force in the nation. The Chinese youth movement, of which we have not yet seen the end, began in this period rather than in 1919. The May Fourth Movement was its second stage, not its origin.

Intelligence, courage, and indifference to death for their cause gave the new youth an influence out of all proportion to their numbers. One of them, as a schoolteacher, could start the awakening of a whole county. One of them, in a military training school or army unit, could give shape to the passionate but often formless ideas that were abroad everywhere. At the same time, the social position they had inherited and the respect with which they were listened to in a country accustomed to respecting the educated gave them something of the aura of the old elite even as they called for its destruction.

As is well known, the most politically active youth studied in Japan, where many of the reformist and revolutionary organizations and journals were based. In addition, some who were from southwest China picked up their new ideas in British Burma or French Indochina, where the contrast between the English and

French books they read and the behavior of British and French colonials toward natives seemed to them to underscore the significance of Western European liberal and radical ideas. Those who studied in America or Europe were on the whole younger, and they were widely scattered in countries where Chinese politics were of little interest. They tended to study technical subjects and on the whole had little interest in or influence on the revolutionary movement at this time.

Thus not every student who returned took to the platform or the barricades. As one student who had studied in Japan remarked, Chinese students returning from abroad often dumped their consciences into the Yellow Sea as Europeans coming out East dumped theirs into the Red Sea.[54] Mrs. Rankin's chapter vividly illustrates the process by which young anarchists of gentry background, imbued with ideas of revolutionary romanticism and heroic self-sacrifice, tried to foment revolution in the countryside.

Women

Girls and young women played a prominent role in the revolutionary youth movement. Many of the activists attended the new girls' schools established by the imperial reforms or the private schools that wealthy high officials had done so much to encourage. In Canton, where girls of good family had lived entirely within the family courtyard until a few years before, girl students joined in the patriotic demonstrations over the *Tatsu Maru* case in 1908. Thousands were reported to have marched out of their academies to hold meetings, wearing mourning white and rings engraved "National Humiliation." On April 6 they joined other women of Canton in forming a National Humiliation Society. Their fainting at emotionally supercharged meetings was interpreted as showing the depths of their despair for the country, as the first step toward suicide, the final protest. There is no doubt that such news, dramatized in the press but based on fact, contributed to the revolutionary élan of the era.

In even more conservative Foochow, girls formed a Patriotic Society to which they contributed their jewelry, and when the revolution broke out, they, like the girl students of Canton, struggled for the right to fight. At their meetings they were described as looking tiny and dainty, weary but determined. In Shanghai,

54. Interview in *Min-li-pao,* quoted in Rodes, *Céleste Empire,* pp. 186–95.

where old customs yielded sooner, there was in 1910 a wave of militant, defiant, nationalist demonstrations by well-disciplined schoolgirls and their teachers.

China's new feminism took many forms. When the revolution broke out in Wuchang, it was the boatwomen of the Canton area who went to the revolutionary front, probably the first nurses ever assigned to Chinese troops in combat. At the other extreme, one of the new journals said to be read by court ladies, *Pei-ching nü-pao* (Peking Woman), ran a series of articles on the equality of all human beings. In some areas, women won the right to participate in the new provincial organs of self-government. The militant woman schoolteacher quickly emerged as a new "type." Mrs. Rankin describes the career of the best known of these, Ch'iu Chin, whose execution in 1907 on well-founded charges of revolutionary conspiracy set off a national wave of protest. Sophia Chang, who adopted the personal name of the Russian revolutionary heroine Sophia Perovskaya, was a leader in the Revolutionary Alliance. She organized the women of Shanghai and raised funds through performances of plays dealing with three great revolutions: the American,[55] the French, and, as the final culmination, the Chinese. She too was a schoolmistress, and there were many like her throughout the country.

The new sense of freedom reached beyond politics. Women were increasingly seen in public, and footbinding was starting to die out. Newspapers reported the suicides of women whose mothers-in-law forbade them to unbind their feet or take courses at the new schools. When in 1909 a young woman in a village in remote Kansu killed herself because her husband's parents opposed her plans to unbind her feet and to enter school, her farewell letter was widely circulated in the press. "Indeed, there should be no sympathy for me, but the mere thought of the destruction of my ideals and my young children, who will without doubt be compelled to live in the old way, makes my heart almost break."[56]

The shift in the position and aspirations of women was as swift and dramatic as the shift in the role of youth as a whole. Chinese women had traditionally been less confined than women

55. The magnitude and radicalism of the American Revolution were curiously overestimated in China at this time. Washington was the one Western name known everywhere. I have found one case where it was taken to mean the president of any republic.

56. Text in Paul S. Reinsch, "The New Education in China" *The Atlantic Monthly* (April 1909), p. 520.

in many countries—they had ranged all the way from the dominating wives of henpecked peasant husbands to the talented daughters privately tutored on the insistence of doting fathers. But they had been subject not only to legal disabilities but to social pressures and a code of behavior that kept them—whether sheltered or shackled—at home.

The change in the position of women, like that of youth, was lasting and irreversible, as the later history of China has shown. In this sense, it was one of the hallmarks of a major social revolution.

The New Military Men

The military had played a prominent role in most periods of Chinese history, and the predominant role more than once, but the officers and men of the new armies constituted a genuinely new group. The imperial government wanted officers and soldiers of a new stamp, and they succeeded in getting more than they had perhaps intended. According to the well-informed correspondent of the London *Times,* "The Chinese soldier of today is a different man from his fellow of even ten years ago."[57] The correspondent of *Le Temps*—in spite of many things that struck him as quaint, such as drilling before Confucian shrines—agreed on the importance of this new military element and of the new prestige of a military career. "It is thus that a people prepares itself for the use of force."[58] An Anglo-Indian journalist concluded after a tour of training facilities and arsenals that they "are turning out officers as different from the past as the modern Mauser rifles and cartridges which the factories are producing by the hundred thousand and the million, are different from the ancient blunderbusses with which the Chinese of yesterday were armed."[59]

The professional accomplishments of the military reform program are well attested, as I have indicated above in discussing the imperial reforms. Morale was good because of vastly improved organization and because the men believed that they could become heroes in the national drive to repel the foreigner and to restore China to greatness.

Once the revolution broke out, however, there are scores of witnesses to the vastly superior morale both of the imperial units who went over to the republican side and of the raw, hastily recruited

57. G. E. Morrison, quoted in McKenzie, pp. 702–03.

58. Rodes, *Chine nouvelle,* p. 248.

59. Everard Cotes, *Signs and Portents in the Far East* (London, 1907), pp. 22–23.

new revolutionary units. There were loyal imperial forces who did not collapse, but they seemed to have lost their former sense of purpose and to be fighting from habit rather than from conviction; they certainly lacked the passionate élan of their revolutionary adversaries.

The most unimpeachable testimony to the fact that the revolutionary troops believed in what they were fighting for comes from foreign professionals trained to ignore the oratory and watch the artillery, for example, the Senior British Naval Officer in Hankow: "Above all, the Revolutionary principles seem to have worked up their troops almost into an enthusiastic condition for their cause."[60] This sense of purpose was reflected not only in fighting spirit but in the revolutionaries' humane treatment of the civilian population. The imperial forces were trained to battle discipline, but except in battle, their discipline was much poorer than that of the heterogeneous, untrained revolutionary troops.[61]

There is considerable evidence to suggest that the new armies—first the imperial forces and later the revolutionary forces—were more than agents of modernization in the upper strata of Chinese society. They may have been the agency through which part of the peasantry too was involved in the Chinese Revolution from the outset. Mr. Dutt's chapter notes that in the Wuchang Uprising, it was the enlisted men and officers of the lowest rank who took the lead in revolt and forced their superiors to follow. Mr. Hatano's chapter on the new armies as a whole concludes that they, rather than the revolutionary groups, were the organizations that channeled peasant discontent into uprisings that toppled the dynasty. I shall return later to the controversial question of how deeply into Chinese society the revolution reached.

The Overseas Chinese

The first phase of the Chinese Revolution marked the emergence into the national public life of a fourth new group—the Overseas Chinese. For generations, despite legal prohibitions, Chinese, especially from the overcrowded southeastern provinces, had been emigrating to Southeast Asia and more recently to the Americas

60. Commander H. Lynes to Admiral Sir Alfred Winslow (Dec. 3, 1911), Section 4 of Admiralty M–6990/12, attached to FO 371/15, no. 2185. Commander Lynes gave full evidence for this statement, with which he said all those who had watched the fighting in its later stages would agree, and concluded "that the day may not be long distant when the word patriotism will have a meaning in China."

61. Conclusion to Lt. Col. Willoughly's Annual Report for 1911, FO 371/1347, no. 30250.

and Africa. A few became wealthy, and a large number became reasonably prosperous by moving in to supply whatever skills or services were lacking and in demand. The majority were shipped out in the notorious coolie trade to meet the demand for labor in Africa, Borneo, or building American railways. Those who lived made their way up. But assimilation to the areas in which they settled did not begin until much later. All their loyalties were focused on their native places in China, but the most they could hope for was to send money home and eventually to be buried there.

With the turn of the century, all factions of New China sought their support. The imperial government made more vigorous efforts to control the coolie trade and to establish Chinese consulates to look after the welfare of its overseas subjects. Many returned home and found careers in the new enterprises. The reformers and the revolutionaries who traveled abroad contended for the support of the Chinese communities wherever they went. Sun Yat-sen's Society to Restore China's Prosperity and several ephemeral early revolutionary groups were essentially Overseas Chinese organizations.

Not all Overseas Chinese were revolutionaries; the reformers had their following and the Overseas communities would have sent their representatives to the Imperial Parliament scheduled to convene in 1913. But in a broader sense, all the Overseas Chinese—offered a place in Chinese public life for the first time, adding a new and different element to the new public and the new public opinion—were, like the new youth, the new woman, and the new military, a revolutionary social force.

Others have emphasized more than I do here the role of the Overseas Chinese. If one focuses on Sun Yat-sen and the Revolutionary Alliance, the picture of the revolution is different. In that case, the ability of the Overseas communities to supply funds, the influence of their newspapers, and the competition for their support are central factors. If on the other hand one starts with the general history of this revolutionary decade, the Revolutionary Alliance is not at the center of the stage, nor are the Overseas Chinese.

The Working Class

The fifth of the new groups to enter Chinese public life and politics was the small working class. Here I mean not the traditional artisans, although apparently they often took part in nationalist demonstrations, but the workers employed in such modern industries as textiles, railways, and mining. Despite their small numbers, there were large concentrations of them at critical times and places. In October of 1911, for example, there were 6,000 railway workers from North China in the Yangtze River port of Ichang.[62]

In this early period, as Jean Chesneaux has shown, the strikes were invariably political rather than economic. The workers shared the general anti-imperialist mood of the times and, for example, refused to unload Japanese ships following the *Tatsu Maru* incident. The number of strikes rose sharply whenever political tension was heightened; the period just prior to the outbreak of the Revolution of 1911 was one of the peaks.[63]

These new industrial workers were recruited not from the artisanate but directly from the poorer peasantry, and they maintained close ties with their villages. They were important in this period because they could put teeth into protests initiated by others and because, with their periodic visits home, they constituted one of the channels through which the new ideas were beginning to affect the so-called vast immovable mass of the Chinese peasantry.

The five new groups on the political scene—youth, women, the modern military, the Overseas Chinese, and industrial labor—make a strange company, but they have in common several important features. All had been subject to more than average deprivation in traditional Chinese society; all were in situations where they were more aware than most of what foreign pressure had cost China; all were in positions where action seemed possible; all had a less than average stake in the preservation of existing institutions. This of course does not mean that they constituted a solid revolutionary phalanx. Obviously as the first phase of the revolution subsided many students decided to get on with their careers, many women to look after their households, many Overseas Chinese to make fortunes, and many workers to save a little money to buy land to reenter the landowning peasantry. What it does mean is that there were substantial groups, volatile because of their newness, with sharp discontents, each capable of a distinct and major contribution to the creation of a New China. The educated and aroused young could analyze China's plight and fire off ideas—

62. FO 371/1098, no. 52197.

63. Jean Chesneaux, *The Chinese Labor Movement, 1919–1927* (Stanford, Calif., 1968). (Original French edition 1962.)

some sparks, some rockets. The soldiers could offer their training and their arms. The Overseas Chinese—the poor as well as the rich—could provide money and entrepreneurial and technical skills. The workers could back up their ideas with strikes that really hurt.

This was an impressive revolutionary striking force—many revolutions have succeeded with less—but none of its components was central to existing Chinese society. The Chinese "establishment" was vast and deeply rooted. I therefore turn now to change, and resistance to change, among existing classes: the gentry, merchants, and peasants.

The Gentry

For centuries the Chinese gentry had gained access to public office through the Examination System. Their status carried with it a host of tangible and intangible benefits: a virtual monopoly of the higher culture, leisure, great respect and deference, certain legal immunities, and opportunities to accumulate land. They were the social class with the highest stake in the old order. The question here is whether this class was undergoing significant change after 1900, and if so in what ways.

There are enough studies to show that the gentry of the nineteenth century and earlier were very different from what was called the gentry in community studies of the 1930s and 1940s. The slim evidence that we have suggests that this transformation of the gentry began and progressed surprisingly far in the decade after 1900. The abolition of the Examination System in 1905 destroyed the primary basis of their status. They were quick to see this and to adjust to it by preparing their children for the newly opening careers in business and the professions, and for posts in a quite different kind of government. Land rents were important—they remained so until 1949—but it was a rare gentry family that could live on land rents alone; holdings even of substantial gentry families were quickly broken up through the equal division of property among all sons and the provision of substantial dowries for daughters. This process was not new; what was new was the availability of new occupations and sources of income.

There can have been scarcely a gentry family that did not include a radical student, an officer in the new armies, or an investor in modern enterprises. The gentry do not seem to have been isolated from the main currents of the time. They read newspapers and wrote letters to the editor. They were the leaders of the local self-government associations and dominated the provincial assemblies, as Mr. Chang's chapter demonstrates in detail. The records show that these organizations concentrated on the great national issues of the day: resistance to Western encroachment, domestic social reforms, constitutional government. Mr. Fincher offers considerable evidence to show that these new provincial and local institutions were transitional steps toward a new nationalism. Mr. Chang argues that the gentry were in fact the active constitutionalists—the men who organized petitions and protests and made speeches, as distinct from the theorists of constitutional monarchy.

Mr. Ichiko presents a directly opposing hypothesis: that as the central power failed, the gentry, freed of legal obligations and customary restraints, seized the opportunity to maximize their local power, in a typical end-of-dynasty fashion. In so doing, he argues, they prevented any social change and were successful in maintaining the status quo until 1949. I find Mr. Ichiko's statement eloquent, but the evidence now available does not seem to me to support it. I have no doubt that many gentry families compromised on all sides to stay out of trouble. But men like Chang Ping-lin, at this time a far more radical revolutionary than Sun Yat-sen, were members of the gentry and maintained their gentry connections. New entrepreneurs like Chang Chien, a member of the exalted upper reaches of the gentry, were leaders in the assemblies and in the constitutional movement.

Admittedly this is an impression, based on limited information and a negative logic that says that the gentry cannot have been unaffected by the great changes taking place in their whole world. Mr. Ichiko's answer is that no great changes were in fact taking place. On this the evidence is stronger. I have summarized some of it; the other contributors present particular facets of change in detail.

The Bourgeoisie

Merchants in imperial China had suffered from both legal disabilities and lack of social standing. Some had been enormously wealthy, but their position was always precarious. Confiscatory taxes in the form of forced contributions to the state were not uncommon, and merchant property was always in jeopardy. In these circumstances, merchants had to curry favor with officials, and they nearly always attempted to escape upward into the scholar-gentry class by educating their sons for the official examinations. All these factors prevented the emergence of a strong, self-conscious, independent merchant class.

The opening of the treaty ports provided new opportunities for merchants, and their numbers greatly expanded. By the beginning of the twentieth century it was beginning to be recognized that they had an essential role to play in the development of the Chinese economy by Chinese rather than foreigners. As the foundations of gentry status were undermined, many members of the gentry saw the advantages of modern enterprise. A new class, a bourgeoisie, was thus recruited from both the merchants and the gentry of traditional society. Merchants took their place, long denied, in the councils of the local elite and a new compound term, gentry-merchant (*shen-shang*), came into general use. Industry and commerce were specifically encouraged by an imperial edict of 1903, as noted above.

Some merchants in the older handicraft centers remained aloof from the new currents and continued to work, and sometimes to live, with their artisans in the old way and in relatively small units. So did merchants at the street stall or peddler level. All these seem to have taken part in the nationalist demonstrations, but apparently they were not part of the flow either into the nascent bourgeoisie or into the nascent industrial labor force. The continued existence of these master-apprentice units, located in areas where wealthy Chinese and foreigners were concentrated and producing articles for their use, perhaps contributed to the persistent myth of an unchanging China.

The origins, development, and political role of the new bourgeoisie are analyzed in Mme. Bergère's chapter. She demonstrates the fallacy of the popular Communist distinction between a national bourgeoisie, playing its historic role in the evolution of society toward socialism, and a compradore bourgeoisie, running dogs of the imperial powers. She shows that the *whole* Chinese bourgeoisie was nationalistic in its opposition to foreign special privilege and in its demand for a strong central government capable of providing the conditions in which a national market could develop, of issuing a uniform national currency, and of enforcing a modern commercial code. But the national bourgeoisie was no more able than the compradores to develop independently, since foreign interests, supported by the advanced economies of their home countries and protected by treaty from Chinese law and from all but nominal taxation, dominated the entire modern sector of the Chinese economy.

Nonetheless, when it came the revolution was distinctly not a bourgeois revolution; the bourgeoisie's role was important but always auxiliary. They were, along with the gentry, leaders in the constitutional movement and in the formation of a new public opinion. When fighting broke out, they sometimes gave the revolutionaries active support without thought of property loss—local variations were enormous on this point—but generally they attempted to work out an orderly transfer of power; for long periods their chambers of commerce were often the only stable source of authority.

There is a strange discrepancy between the interests and role of the bourgeoisie and its ideology. Its members talked vaguely but passionately of liberty, equality, and fraternity; of nationalism, democracy, and mass welfare. These ideas were neither coherently thought out nor expressive of their class interests, for theirs was in no way the position of the French bourgeoisie in the eighteenth century. Yet the very fact that these words, however poorly understood, were so constantly used, may have been one of the most important contributions of the bourgeoisie to the revolutionary movement.

In this first stage of the revolution, the bourgeoisie—even the Cantonese bourgeoisie—did not show the regional particularism and resistance that characterized its attitude in the second phase of the revolution in the 1920s. Had Yuan Shih-k'ai's political neutralization of the bourgeoisie in 1913 proved permanently effective? Had businessmen come to understand the implications of what they had been saying and been frightened? Or did the Chinese Revolution pass them by as it sped in two generations from a traditional society that gave the bourgeoisie little scope to a socialist society that gave them none?

The Peasantry

To what degree did the revolutionary changes of the early twentieth century affect the peasantry? Were the peasants, as some have claimed, largely ignorant of what was going on in the upper layers of society, a passive mass that was indifferent unless one or another of the contesting parties pressed them too hard in the demand for grain and manpower? Or were they ready to provide a mass base for revolution if the revolutionary leaders had only understood how to reach them?

Here I think we must recognize the illogical but real distinction between the "people of China" and the peasantry who constituted 80 percent of that people. It is clear that the British minister was greatly in error when he reported that the revolution was based on "the usual platitudes about the struggle for freedom . . . in which not more than five percent of the population of China take the slightest interest." The Foreign Office found this "remarkable" in view of the information coming in, but noted that even so, 5 percent of the population of China was 20,000,000 people.[64]

It is abundantly clear that considerably more than 5 percent of the population was involved in the massive boycotts and demonstrations to which I have referred above. The people of China were certainly affected by and contributing to these changes, if by people one means the visible 20 percent. One need only recall, as noted above, that the proportion of the electorate expanded from 1 percent of the adult male population in 1909 to 25 percent in 1912; or that the signatures to the petitions demanding a speedier convening of a parliament expanded from a reported 200,000 signatures in June 1910 to a reported 25 million in October of that year. In my opinion, on the evidence now available, these changes were also reaching into the peasantry.

The fallacy of an inert peasantry that characterized so many contemporary accounts and continues, in my view, to distort research, was well expressed by a careful observer who was, surprisingly, General Frey of the French colonial army. In his opinion, there was ample evidence of the nationalism of the Chinese peasant: that he was concerned with the fate of the country as a whole at the hands of foreigners and with the problems of remote areas within China. Frey attributed widespread European belief in the self-centeredness of a self-sufficient peasantry to the fact that many of the writers had little knowledge of the Chinese countryside and were prone to generalize on the basis of their acquaintance with what he called the mercenary uprooted Chinese of the coastal cities. He pointed out that peasants must work without interruption or starve.[65] The fact that they continued to work in the fields did not prove that their interests were limited to those fields.

64. FO 371/15, no. 952. The Foreign Office cover minute was marked for the attention of the cabinet.

65. General H. Frey, *L'Armée chinoise* (Paris, 1904), pp. 85–95.

General Frey presumably reached this conclusion from close observation of Chinese soldiers, who were of course peasants.

A veteran English journalist reported that the societies protesting the American Exclusion Act of 1905 served as links through which reform groups "now reach and direct social forces which have hitherto lain beyond their control."[66] One should remember that the people being excluded from the United States were mainly peasants, certainly the poor. Another long-time resident and close observer summarizing the various changes—the press, foreign trade, new schools, the postal service, the activities of the provincial assemblies—concluded: ". . . all had combined, without perhaps changing the people, gradually to accustom them to the idea of change. It is a process that has gone deeper and had more considerable consequences than is generally supposed."[67]

Since the issue is still speculative, let us turn the question around. The new armies were recruiting and indoctrinating peasant troops who displayed high morale. The industrial labor force, removed from the peasantry only seasonally, was calling patriotic strikes. Newspapers were widely disseminated and they emphasized national and international issues; these were read aloud in villages by old literati trying to catch up with the times as well as by students from the new schools. Storytellers and traveling theater troupes played up the themes of New China to peasant audiences. How reasonable is it to suppose that Chinese peasants, illiterate but cultivated and excellent conversationalists, let all this pass them by, and talked only of crops and marriages in the hours of teahouse talk on market days?

One qualified observer found them poorly informed on politics, but highly responsive to revolutionary slogans:

> They possess the moral qualities that go to the making of a great nation . . . They would be a great power in the hands of anyone who could coordinate their scattered units and induce them to follow his lead.[68]

66. Story, *Tomorrow in the East*, p. 173.

67. Percy H. Kent, *The Passing of the Manchus* (London, 1912), pp. 63–64. The author was legal adviser to the (Chinese) supervisor of industries in Chihli Province.

68. Fernand Farjenel, *Through the Chinese Revolution*, trans. Margaret Vivian (London, 1915), p. 142. The author, who taught courses on China at the Collège Libre des Sciences Sociales, traveled in China immediately before and during the revolution.

Revolutionary Organizations and Ideologies

In the foregoing discussion, the reader may have wondered where the revolutionaries are. I have talked about the revolutionary implications of nearly everything that was happening in the New China of the early twentieth century, but societies have changed rapidly in circumstances where the word revolution should be used only in quotation marks. For a real revolution, must there not be at the center of action organized bodies of men who, by a combination of ideas and violence, overthrow the existing authority and succeed to power?

The answer for the Chinese Revolution as a whole is yes; for the early phase, a tentative no. Revolutionary organizations did of course exist in the first phase of the revolution and they created a revolutionary tradition honored today, though in different ways, by all Chinese. But though not for lack of courage, they created a tradition rather than a revolution. All circumstances save one—a decisive factor to which I shall shortly turn—were propitious, but the revolutionary organizations of the time were frail instruments indeed for the Herculean task at hand.

Sun Yat-sen's first party, the Society to Restore China's Prosperity, was founded in Honolulu in 1894 and never at its height attracted more than 500 members, nearly all poor, nearly all illiterate, nearly all from a few districts near Canton. Few had even the advantage—if it were one—of active secret society membership, although most, including Sun himself, had loose ties with either the Triad Society or its counterpart in the Overseas Chinese communities, the Hung Society. One would not expect any such group to be able to capitalize on the main revolutionary currents of Chinese society as a whole, and such proved to be the case.

This was not the only early party; there were others, discussed in various chapters of this book, some that were more intellectual, some that were less remote from the mainstream of Chinese national life. These organizations usually had their main base in Japan, where Chinese students could be trained as revolutionaries to be sent home to circulate clandestine publications or to encourage underground railways for wanted men.

Since a series of uprisings had failed, these small but important groups decided in 1905 that their members should join a united group called the Revolutionary Alliance. After this merger, of the early parties only the Restoration Society continued to maintain a separate identity.

The Revolutionary Alliance[69] was China's first modern political party. It found ways to plant sympathizers in nearly all the new schools, including the military schools, to add to the effectiveness of the major demonstrations, and generally to exert an influence quite out of proportion to its numbers. It should be remembered that even as an alliance of all revolutionary parties, it began with a membership of less than 400 and that, at the time of the Wuchang Uprising in October 1911, it still numbered less than 10,000. Its strong point was supposed to be its ability to appeal to students and to the educated, disaffected elite, yet less than one third of its members were educated.

The claims later made that the history of the Revolutionary Alliance is the history of the revolution are manifestly unfounded. The party did not compensate for its numerical weakness either by a tight organization or by a well-articulated program. Agitation and leadership in the Wuhan area, as Mr. Dutt's chapter shows, was the work of the Literary Institute and of the Progressive Association, whose links to the Revolutionary Alliance were nebulous. The Literary Institute had a membership of 3,000 in Wuchang alone. It is more than symbolic that Sun Yat-sen, leader of the Revolutionary Alliance, was in Denver, Colorado when he heard about the outbreak of the revolution.

The only organizations seemingly in a position to lead a popular revolution of disaffected elements from the lower strata were the secret societies. These societies had had a long history and had provided, in earlier times, some of the motive power in small uprisings and major rebellions. Their organizations offered a network of mutual assistance functions over vast areas of China, extending into overseas communities, to peasants, laborers, small merchants, boatmen, and the like. No less an authority than Chu Te has stated that the cellular structure of the Chinese Communist Party derives from the secret societies rather than from an imported model.[70] During the anti-Japanese war, Mao Tse-tung recalled the participation of the Elder Brother Society in the Revolution of 1911.[71]

69. The most informative account is the late Shelley Cheng's "The T'ung-meng-hui: Its Organization, Leadership, and Finances, 1905–1912" (unpublished Ph.D. dissertation, Department of History, University of Washington, 1962).

70. Jean Chesneaux, *Les Sociétés secrètes en Chine* (*19e et 20e siècles*) (Paris and the Hague, 1965), 204.

71. Address of July 15, 1936, *China Quarterly*, no. 27 (1966), p. 12.

Yet there emerged no "united front" between the secret societies and the revolutionary parties; as Mr. Schiffrin's chapter shows, Sun tried to use the societies in the Waichow uprising of 1900 and failed. The organization of the societies into local units, often called lodges, without strong central control, may have been one of the factors which prevented their use in mobilizing a national revolutionary force. Further, many of the societies had elaborate rituals dating back many generations and quite unrelated to the realities of a revolutionary situation.

An important question is whether the societies were anything more than "primitive rebels" in Hobsbawm's definition.[72] Indeed, at times, they were less: they were blackmailers, strong-armed gangs, and racketeers who connived with officials to exploit the public. Were they capable of grasping the national issues and making common cause with the predominantly upper-class leadership of the various New China groups—many of whom had been brought up to fear these clandestine organizations? Or did they have the potential for developing a peasant revolution, as some of the evidence from Shensi and Szechwan suggests?

The role of the secret societies is one of the least understood problems in the early Chinese revolutionary movement. Until we have solid understanding of it, we lack an essential key to relating this period backward to the cycles of Chinese rebellions and forward into the later phases of the revolution.

The dominant theme in the ideology of the revolutionary activists was nationalism, but it was nationalism that included a number of strains, as I have indicated: the reassertion of Chinese power along the frontiers, anti-imperialism, China for the Chinese, modernization, and anti-Manchuism. These nationalisms were interwoven with a host of more or less ephemeral movements, each of which had its own slogans, and they developed in a rapidly changing climate of opinion. It is not surprising that the revolutionaries developed no coherent ideology, if by ideology we mean a more or

72. ". . . when the jaws of the dynamic modern world seize the static communities in order to destroy and transform them . . . social banditry, though a protest, is a modest and unrevolutionary protest. It protests not against the fact that the bandits are poor and oppressed, but against the fact that they are sometimes excessively poor and oppressed. Bandit heroes are not expected to make a world of equality. They can only right wrongs and prove that sometimes oppression can be turned upside down." E. J. Hobsbawm, *Primitive Rebels: Studies in Archaic Forms of Social Movements in the 19th and 20th Centuries* (New York, 1965), p. 24.

less systematic body of ideas meant to guide action, to marshal public opinion, and to define the kind of future that a country should have. There had been no time for the slow germination of ideas and their translation into programs that had preceded the Revolution of 1789. And the problems facing the Chinese revolutionaries were greater, for they had to contemplate not a mere change in social system, but a change that would telescope time and bridge the gulf between two civilizations.

It is scarcely to be wondered at that Sun Yat-sen failed to rise to this formidable challenge. As Mr. Schiffrin shows, Sun was remarkably vague and self-contradictory. He combined a smattering of Western knowledge with a superficial understanding of traditional Chinese thought and a penchant for grandiose programmatics. In this first decade of the twentieth century even the relative coherence of his later ideology was not yet visible. He emphasized anti-Manchuism and avoided the anti-imperialist issue for sound tactical reasons, but a tactic is not an ideology.

Outside Sun's circle were intellectuals of many persuasions. Chang Ping-lin, who is customarily thought of as a classical scholar and as the most traditional of the literati nationalists, appears in Mr. Bernal's chapter as a young radical who maintained that all Chinese institutions had tended toward socialism and who later moved left to anarchism. There we also find Chu Chih-hsin who, in anticipation of Mao, argued that the peasantry should participate actively in social revolution. Other examples in this volume demonstrate that the strain of extreme radicalism in modern Chinese thought has deeper roots than has been supposed and that the first decade of the twentieth century was the seedbed for many of the ideas that much later emerged to dumbfound the world, including the Communist world.

Radical ideas in this period were not confined to intellectual cliques or to particular geographical enclaves. Mrs. Rankin's chapter, for example, traces the process by which anarchism filtered into one province, and this account would find parallels in other regions. But the ideas of the early radicals remained ideas. They were not at this time translatable, by political leaders or influential writers, into one or more ideologies of political action.

THE REVOLUTION: EXPLOSION AND COLLAPSE

The period I have been describing appears to me characteristically prerevolutionary. Intense foreign pressure had produced a sharp anti-imperialist reaction. Desperate internal problems were felt to require a new and strong hand at the helm. All society was in a state of flux: new social groups had moved to the center of the political stage and the traditional classes were in the process of transformation. A strain of extremism was evident in the cascade of new ideas that was reaching an ever-widening, more demanding public. The imperial government had embarked on a series of reforms which, far from stabilizing the situation, contributed to the general ferment.

Violence had been spreading; the uprising at Wuchang that marked the beginning of the Revolution of 1911 was the ninth in a series of revolutionary attempts to seize power. Lesser riots against specific grievances were increasing. The cost of living was rising. According to the press, early in 1911 the price of flour had risen 30 percent in five years and the price of rice in Shanghai, which was reported to have doubled during the past decade, was rising at a rate of about 2 percent per day.

Floods in Central China in the autumn of 1910 climaxed years of bad harvests. Whole cities became lakes, whole towns were wiped out, and not only in Central China. In January 1911 the Central China Famine Relief Committee, in a desperate appeal, stated that between one and three million people were in immediate danger of starvation. On September 12, 1911 the Yangtze stood at its highest recorded mark and the dykes could not hold. And still the rains came; in the most productive areas the entire 1911 crop was lost. Some observers said that it was the worst disaster since the great famine of 1877. The *North China Herald* predicted the greatest suffering in the history of the Empire for the autumn and winter of 1911.

Disaster has been so frequent in China that the word must be used with caution; nonetheless the accounts, with grisly photographs of the bodies of the drowned caught by the piers of the new bridges, seem to portray suffering extraordinary even for China.[73]

Meanwhile the central government was proceeding with its reforms. Imperial reformers had inherited an historic bias in favor of state control of the critical sectors of the economy, and their studies of other late modernizing countries reinforced their conviction that national railway networks were best developed and operated by governments. Unfortunately, the government did not start with

73. Central China Famine Relief Committee (CCFRC), *Famine Scenes in China, 1910–1911* (Shanghai, 1911). *Report of the Secretary of the CCFRC* (April 2, 1912). CCFRC, *Reports and Accounts, 1910–11* (Shanghai, 1912). FO 228/1804, 1809, and 1836. *NCH,* passim for the period in question.

a clear field. A number of lines had been begun by local gentry and officials, and when capital ran short, eager foreign lenders were waiting.

In this chaos, the reforming central government chose the not unreasonable course of attempting to buy up, refinance, and rationalize all these lines into a national system. The reformers and revolutionaries, if faced with the responsibilities of power, might well have done the same thing. But here, as in a number of other instances, reform destroyed the reforming government; it could not control the forces to whose acceleration its own policies had contributed. The specific incident that precipitated the Revolution of 1911 was the central government's decision to buy up a line in Szechwan in which the local gentry had invested heavily. In the opinion of Western financial specialists at the time the price offered was fair, but many investors stood to lose because of ineptness in the line's management and of the Shanghai stock-market crisis of 1910, in which a goodly portion of the railway's capital had been lost. On May 9, 1911 the nationalization of all trunk lines was announced and shortly afterward the infamous—to Chinese patriots—Hukuang foreign loan agreement was signed.

The Szechwan uprising, led by the moderate constitutionalists of the Railway Protection League, sparked widespread disturbances that often had no connection with the railway issue and were generally believed to have been led by the secret societies. By late summer the Szechwan authorities were calling for outside troops. A substantial number were transferred from Wuchang, leaving the Wuhan area's forces well under normal strength.

Mr. Dutt's chapter discusses in detail the outbreak of the revolution at Wuchang. By the end of 1911, Hunan, virtually all of Hupeh, Chekiang, Fukien, Kwangtung, Kwangsi, Yunnan, Kweichow, and at least half of Anhwei and Kiangsu were under revolutionary control of one kind or another. Most of east China north of the Yangtze was still under imperial control but there were fierce battles in these provinces too.

The speed with which an imperial government still superficially stable in the autumn of 1911 was succeeded by a conservative republican government under the leadership of a former imperial official in the spring of 1912 has led many to believe that this was a fake revolution, that no real change occurred. It should therefore be noted that the fighting, though short, was intense. In the imperial counterattack on Hankow beginning October 28, 1911, massive "coolie" resistance could have lasted indefinitely in the labyrinth of narrow streets in the immense city despite the superior firepower of the reinforced imperial troops.

Feeling was so intense that wounded revolutionary soldiers who were lucky enough to reach a hospital reportedly jumped out of bed to strangle wounded imperial soldiers. The imperial forces solved the problem by burning the city to the ground. After a furious blaze lasting more than a week, only a few foundations remained among ashes several yards deep, where occasional curious crystals of melted porcelain caught the eye. Not one person, not one sampan was to be seen. We have ample accounts of journalists, and photographs from some areas, to demonstrate the fact that the fury at Hankow was by no means unique.

Yet as of 1913, the revolution seemed to many to have accomplished nothing worthy of the name and therefore to be unworthy of the name. The rubber-stamp parliament was disbanded, the revolutionary party declared illegal, and one of its most determined leaders, Sung Chiao-jen, assassinated. The so-called "Second Revolution" of 1913 attracted no more than passing notice and was quickly suppressed.[74]

Yet some of the revolutionary changes were uninterrupted. Anti-imperialist nationalism continued unabated. As the British Foreign Office noted, ". . . the Republic will be as aggressive and as regardless of Treaty rights as the Empire if it is given the opportunity." "It seems determined to continue a forward policy in Tibet when it cannot maintain order in its capital . . ."; ". . . and it once indicated that it would need foreign help in maintaining order in the International Settlement at Shanghai for a brief period only."[75] The new schools and the new ideas continued, youth and women remained active, and so on. Even at the height of the reaction around 1915, China was a vastly different country from what it had been fifteen years earlier.

Yet even granting all this, the spirit of New China had been dissipated and it is obvious that the revolutionary movement had suffered a serious—some thought mortal—injury in 1912. Mr. Young's chapter makes it impossible for any serious scholar to con-

74. Earlier the British Foreign Office had watched the Chinese Revolution with some care. When the reports on the revolution of 1913 came in, they were filed, still half-sealed, with the notation: "This is purely an account of the insurrection in the provinces." FO 371/1620, no. 52154.

75. FO 371/1329, no. 53850; FO 371/1619, no. 18459; FO 371/15, no. 838.

tinue to attribute this setback to the chicanery of Yuan Shih-k'ai. What then does account for it?

THE LIMITATIONS OF REVOLUTIONARY LEADERSHIP

The most immediate and obvious cause of the failure of 1912 was the limited vision of the revolutionary leaders and their inability to organize effectively. They tended at the same time to be nearsighted and farsighted; when they looked out to their distant goals, as they frequently did, they could not bring Utopia into focus and resorted to rhetoric; when they looked at China's immediate problems, which they seldom did, they had to stand back to see them at all.

Sun Yat-sen was clearly not the leader needed. Against the background of the heroic mold in which he has usually been cast, Sun emerges as a pallid figure. He appealed to some audiences and was an excellent fund raiser, but he had little idea of what a transfer of power would mean; he was equally vague on the subject of China's relation to the West. He was not alone among Chinese revolutionaries in admiring many of the achievements of Western civilization, but he was nearly alone in inviting a degree of Western tutelage of China that would have amounted, in fact, to enlightened colonialism. Except for his humble origins, he in many ways resembled the Westernized compradore so vividly described in Mme. Bergère's chapter.

He had other deficiencies as a revolutionary leader: to the intellectuals his writings did not begin to probe the issues, and despite his origins and early secret society connections, he seems to have made little effort to recruit a mass following for his movement or to tackle agrarian problems in his programs. He was also a poor organizer. Sun's personality and role remain puzzling, for if he was not an effective leader denied fulfillment of his role by the treachery of Yuan Shih-k'ai, he was not merely an anomaly either. I believe Mr. Schiffrin's chapter is the most thoughtful, carefully researched effort in any language to date, to portray fairly a man who remains to this day a hero to nearly all Chinese everywhere.

Li Yüan-hung's lack of qualifications are worth no more than a line. He refused to assume leadership until he was asked by his subordinates whether he wanted to go down in history as a Washington or a Napoleon, or to be executed on the spot.

The problem did not lie with the top leadership alone. In locality after locality, there were followers without active leaders. A perceptive British consul who constantly moved among local revolutionary forces asking questions, reported: "The one strikingly weak spot is that such a unanimous revolutionary spirit should lack capable leaders and proper organization."[76] Mrs. Rankin concludes in her case study that Ch'iu Chin and Hsü Hsi-lin were "exactly opposite to the Leninist type of revolutionary. Their efforts ended in personal testimonies of faith in revolution with no thought of preserving the party organization." The revolutionaries themselves were aware of the problem of leadership. Chang Ping-lin thought that revolution would pose fewer problems than constitutional reform because, as he saw it, the revolutionaries, though lacking in leadership, did have popular support, while the reformers had neither leadership nor wide support.

Mr. Young remarks that the "revolution was bigger than Yüan." I would say that it was, in all its phases, bigger than all its leaders. The issue between Mr. Ichiko and some of his colleagues derives mainly from the fact that he takes the men who succeeded to provincial power as leaders of the revolution, and from this concludes that what they led was not a revolution. I would turn the proposition around: The revolution generally failed to produce adequate leadership at any level and therefore power went by default to conservative local notables who certainly were not revolutionaries. Their success proved not that there had been no revolution but that it had been a revolution without real leadership.

But why was no adequate leadership forthcoming? In the general history of protest movements in the modern world, we are more familiar with potentially outstanding leaders who fail to attract a mass following than with a leaderless revolutionary surge. There is truth, but only partial truth, in the answer given by one close observer:

> Much rubbing has removed all excrescences of character that might develop into unusual powers. There is simply no room for initiative. The experimenter has always desired privacy and leisure of which there is none in Chinese villages.[77]

It is obvious that to survive the communal and interdependent life of a crowded Chinese family in a crowded Chinese village was possible only through the observation of an elaborate code of social

76. FO 371/1313, no. 7145.

77. Henry Graybill, *The Educational Reform in China* (Hongkong, 1911), p. 24. Graybill was acting president of Canton Christian College.

norms. The premium was on conformity, not bold independence, the latter being virtually impossible in any case. In the past China had produced the necessary leadership, but that leadership, recruited young and thoroughly indoctrinated in tradition, had clear points of reference.

It may well be that the development of bold, imaginative leadership able to envision a new order of society—difficult enough in any civilization—was peculiarly difficult in China. In my opinion, however, the fundamental reason for the failure of adequate leadership to emerge was the lack of time. Leadership does not mature rapidly even in small countries, or in countries that face crises of limited scope. China was huge, the sources of the revolutionary movement complex, and the problems were almost unlimited in scope. The body of revolutionary tradition and doctrine was thin, and there was no time.

There was no time because all Chinese believed, not without reason, that prolonged disorder would bring foreign intervention and partition of the country. As Mr. Young puts it, the leadership was *handed* to Yuan Shih-k'ai "as the one man who could achieve the dynasty's abdication and at the same time retain national unity and keep the powers at bay."

The Foreign Omnipresence

The foreign powers congratulated themselves on having preserved an admirable neutrality during the revolution; this neutrality was based in the last analysis on an indifference to the outcome so long as they were assured, as they were, that neither side would dare take any step that might directly or indirectly jeopardize foreign interests. Since by 1911 there were foreign interests in every corner of China, the revolution had to be kept within tidy bounds. On the available military evidence, the revolutionaries did not compromise and stop short because they feared the superior power of the enemy. On the contrary, they were winning battles and gathering recruits. But as the revolution gathered momentum, increasing violence could be expected. If mass uprisings of the type begun by secret societies in Szechwan, Shensi, and elsewhere were allowed to run their course, foreign intervention was certain. The substratum of Chinese society shared the anti-imperialist sentiments of the upper quarter, but they were not likely to be timid if treaty rights and other things of which they knew little got in their way. The upper classes, including revolutionary youth, were not prepared to pay the price, which they believed to be partition of the country. And so they accepted the compromise that stopped the revolution short and brought Yuan Shih-k'ai to power. The determining factor was the foreign omnipresence.

Let me give a few illustrations of this "omnipresence." In 1911, a French specialist estimated that China would need 1,617,000,000 francs to buy back her railways. If all went well this could be accomplished by 1954.[78] The total British claim under the Boxer indemnity amounted to nearly 7,600,000 pounds sterling. By the end of 1910, the amount of *principal* repaid had been less than 150,000 pounds, the rest of the payments having gone to interest.[79] China's total foreign debt at this time amounted to between 800 million and 1000 million taels. While some of this had undoubtedly been misspent or privately pocketed, China had reached a stage where most of the funds she had to raise merely serviced earlier debts resulting from earlier wars, loans, and indemnities.

There was a default in indemnity payments in October 1911, and the economic stranglehold grew tighter during the course of the revolution. The British Foreign Office noted: "The financial situation in China appears to be gradually drifting towards bankruptcy and foreign financial control, which would probably mean further uprisings and possible foreign intervention."[80] In conference with representatives of the Hongkong and Shanghai Banking Corporation, it was agreed that foreigners might have to control vital parts of the Chinese government in order to secure their loans. These men did not think of themselves as plotting the takeover of China. On the contrary, "Our aim should be to consider with how little control we can safely be content."[81] This language illustrates what I mean by the foreign omnipresence; the foreign interests were there, everywhere, taken for granted. They wanted no more control than was necessary to secure those interests; but that degree of control was more than any sovereign state could concede.

Anyone who is in doubt should read the minutes of the meetings between the Six Groups (the bankers of Britain, France, Belgium, Germany, Russia, and the United States) and the Republican Min-

78. Edouard de Laboulaye, *Les Chemins de fer de la Chine* (Paris, 1911), pp. 328–37.

79. FO 371/1093, no. 41063.

80. FO 371/1317, no. 18469.

81. FO 371/1316, no. 13578.

ister of Finance in December 1912. It was clear that China would be required to accept a short-term, high-interest loan, with no knowledge of the selling price of the issue; that the loan would be guaranteed by sweeping mortgages on whatever China had left unmortgaged; and that most of what China thus added to her foreign debt would never leave the West; it would go directly to payment of arrears on earlier indemnities and services on previous loans. Meanwhile there was strong pressure for a new indemnity to cover damage to foreign property during the revolution.[82] Western terms were growing stiffer, because as Sir John Jordan noted, "China no longer has any tangible security to offer . . ."[83]

Loans did not represent the only pressure on China. There were now branches and native agents of the foreign firms everywhere, looking for quite illegal treaty protection throughout the interior. The revolution broke out at Wuchang, and the Chinese section of Hankow, across the river, was shortly burned, as I have noted above. But the fighting had to be conducted in such a way that no warehouse of any foreign firm was hit. Revolutionary and imperial forces alike accepted this condition; they knew what foreign intervention would mean. In the strategically critical fighting in the area between Shanghai and Nanking, the revolutionary forces *walked* beside the Shanghai-Nanking railway line. The British consul noted: "It is I think most extraordinary that the revolutionaries acquiesced . . . when their forces were toiling along the ill-kept paths in full view of passing trains of which it was at any time in their power to take possession."[84]

Everywhere the revolutionaries and even the constitutionalists turned they faced a foreign interest and accepted it. When in 1910 the Provincial Assembly at Nanking impeached the conservative Shanghai taotai Ts'ai Nai-huang, four of the six charges concerned action he had taken on consular insistence that the treaties were involved. In West China, where the fighting was most severe, the young educated revolutionary leaders were almost obsessed with the fear that the secret societies would get out of hand and that a foreigner would be hurt. This was not love of the foreigner, in spite of the fact that the educated youth greatly admired some of the achievements of Western civilization—of which the secret societies knew nothing—but a fear of massive foreign retaliation.

82. FO 371/1590, nos. 1493, 2763.
83. Jordan to Grey (Jan. 6, 1913), FO 371/1590, no. 861.
84. FO 371/1097, no. 50208.

This foreign omnipresence in China that simply by existing prevented the revolution from developing and running its course is quite different from the foreign intervention *after* the French Revolution of 1789 and after the Russian Revolution of 1917. In these last two cases, outside intervention pressed successful revolutions toward extremism. This phenomenon did not occur until much later in the Chinese Revolution when during the Korean War General Douglas MacArthur ordered the drive to the Yalu River. The foreign omnipresence in this early phase compelled moderation and compromise to a degree that temporarily blocked the revolutionary process and thereby denied it the time to develop leadership.

The price China paid for premature stability was high. The Chinese government's 5 percent Reorganization Gold Loan of 1913 amounting to £25,000,000 was oversubscribed without any advertising or other expense. The Five-Power Agreement (the United States had withdrawn) broke down as everybody tried to lend China more money, for the interest on cash advances was an immediate 7 percent.[85]

China would now promise anything for cash, and the lenders did not worry about the security or whether the loan would be used for a productive purpose that would make repayment possible. There were always ways to make China pay. A sad footnote was the British Foreign Office's refusal to support a loan for the reconstruction of the city of Hankow, guaranteed on the general revenue of the city, and strongly urged by city, provincial, and national authorities. The purpose was admirable, the security inadequate.[86] The idea that a gesture of aid toward rebuilding Hankow might serve the long-term interests of the Western powers occurred to no one.

Among foreigners, the old stiff attitude that had been yielding in the course of the first decade of the century returned reinforced. One sharp example: the Peking Syndicate's mining rights in Honan, which a few years earlier the British minister had declared unenforceable in the altered temper of New China, were now in 1913 declared to be British rights that China must respect. If she did not, the British legation recommended sending in British troops in the old manner.[87]

85. FO 371/1594, nos. 22122–22706, 23339.
86. FO 371/1617, no. 24465.
87. FO 371/1626, no. 21603.

It did not seem to matter how great the Chinese interest, how trivial the British interest in a given case; every treaty right was once again supreme. A provincial governor could not forbid the export of beans in time of famine. It was not necessary for the foreigner even to consider whether the governor's action had been in fact necessary. All that need be said was that under an agreement of 1902, China had no right to interfere in the bean trade.[88]

Retrospect and Prospect

The Dynastic Cycle

I have already explained why I do not think the first decade of the twentieth century can be usefully considered in the context of the dynastic cycle, even though of course the Ch'ing dynasty did fall. It would be unnecessary to return to this point except for the fact that the idea of a basically unchanging China proceeding through cycles continues to crop up. Henry L. Stimson, writing in 1929 when he thought there were signs of the *beginning* of a permanent change, still reflected:

> Nevertheless, one cannot but bear in mind that the Chinese are probably the most peculiar people in the world; that a recorded history of over four thousand years seems to indicate that their changes and progress are marked by curious inhibitions, that again and again they have been subject to great new emeuts and convulsions which have seemed to presage radical development and progress, yet which after a century or more of turmoil have subsided and led them down to where they were before.[89]

Even today, there is confusion between the view that the People's Republic of China is the product of Chinese history and cannot be understood outside that history, and the view that the People's Republic is another dynasty. As I read the evidence, the former is demonstrably true, the latter palpably absurd.

The last imperial state transformed itself through reforms into something new, and the other new forces in every sphere of life were so different from the dissident movements that characterized the end of other dynasties as to make comparison meaningless. Nor do I believe that the Chinese Revolution of the twentieth century

88. FO 371/1626, no. 21603.

89. Henry L. Stimson letter of Sept. 14, 1929, Stimson Manuscripts, Yale University Library.

is in any important way comparable to earlier rebellions of Chinese history, including those that swept China in the mid-nineteenth century.

In fact, are we sure that the dynastic cycle continued to operate after the consolidation of the imperial power at the height of the Ming dynasty? One wonders whether Li Tzu-ch'eng in 1644 could have played the role of Chu Yüan-chang in 1368, even without the defection of Wu San-kuei. Perhaps the Manchus as outsiders could seize the throne of the Son of Heaven for the last time because they had already formed a state outside the wall and could move in laterally at the top. Considerations of this type are of interest but they do not illumine, and are not illuminated by, investigations of either the constitutionalist or the revolutionary leadership of the early twentieth century.

Comparison with Other Revolutions

At first glance, the events of the early twentieth century in China can readily be sorted into the standard categories that are generally used in histories of Western revolutions: the old régime speeding its own destruction by reform; the alienation of the intellectuals; the spread of new ideas; the subversion of the armed forces; the propulsion into prominence of new pressure groups with new demands; some deeply felt long-standing grievance capable of unifying disparate groups and imparting to them a heroic élan; and then some incident that appears as a concrete and passion-laden illustration that the old order has become intolerable. Violence spreads, and at the end, old institutions have been eliminated and new ones created. But at this point, and it is a crucial point, the Chinese Revolution no longer "fits," because the old elite does not disappear, to be replaced by a new one. There was no class or group, articulate and well-formed, ready to replace the old elite. And so power devolved on an unstable amalgam of a gentry that had lost the old basis of its elite status, the frail skeleton of a bourgeois class, and miscellaneous military adventurers.

The comparison seems to conceal as much as it reveals. This is one of the reasons that have led Mr. Schiffrin and Mme. Bergère to suggest that comparisons with more recent nationalist revolutions in underdeveloped countries might be more apt. However, if one presses these comparisons, one finds that they are not very enlightening. The characteristics in common with the Chinese Revolution of 1911 are sharp nationalism, the weakness or absence of a bourgeoisie, inadequate leadership, and a rather hastily assembled ideology. The great differences are that China has been a powerful unified empire for two millennia, accustomed to dealing with other peoples as subordinates; that it had a long, highly developed, and continuous bureaucratic tradition and a rich and sophisticated body of ideas relating to political economy. The list of differences could of course be extended.

Seeds of the Future

The Chinese revolutionary movement, from the very beginning and on all fronts, was enormously ambitious and proudly unrealistic, by ordinary standards, about what could be accomplished overnight by a mighty effort of the human will. Once Chinese decided that they had to enter the world of the modern great powers, they decided that they could and would leapfrog over the stages of the development of other countries. If this is true—and I shall give illustrative evidence shortly—then the extreme voluntarism that has characterized Chinese Communist theory and been epitomized in action by the Great Leap Forward must be seen in a new historical perspective.

As early as 1896 Sir Robert Hart, one of China's most experienced advisers, wrote of the Chinese plan to create her own modern, independent postal service that the Chinese demands for

> haste generally—for running before we can crawl—make me feel like a man who is shut in a coach with a driver on the box who wants to start his untrained team down a declivity to the left instead of toiling up the hill that is in front.[90]

The astonishing pace—the wide ambition of the imperial reforms—struck all observers: ". . . in our times seed are germinating in this immense empire the harvest from which will some day stagger humanity," and the course will probably be by "big, brutal leaps."[91] Varying observers translated this tremendous Chinese drive into their own idiom, but they all saw it. An American businessman wrote: "We cannot help but admire their energy and get-up in trying to do what would seem impossible to almost any

90. Quoted in H. B. Morse, *The International Relations of the Chinese Empire* (London, 1918), *3*, 68.

91. Henri Borel, *The New China* (London, 1912), p. 134. The author, a Chinese interpreter in the government of the Netherlands East Indies, wrote for the Amsterdam press during his study and travel in China.

other nation . . . China, the old slow country, has suddenly as if by magic, changed to the new fast China . . . When we come to think of the great changes that have taken place in the last ten years, it looks as if they could accomplish almost anything."[92]

Opium was to be abolished *now*. The country was to be remade by reform *now*. As a sympathetic English journal published in China put it:

> All these require money and a great deal of it. We have expressed our admiration of Chinese patriotism. If the event should prove that China is able to unearth hoards sufficient to finance all these undertakings satisfactorily, then our admiration of the wisdom of her course may grow with that of its audacity.[93]

The constitutionalists, gradualists by definition, were also moving ahead at an accelerating rate. The members of the provincial assemblies seemed from the beginning to be conducting business as if they had had many years of experience instead of only a few days.[94] Money poured in for reform and revolutionary groups. It was not uncommon for a member of an organization whose salary might be $25 per month, to live on one quarter and to contribute the other three quarters to the cause. Westerners in far corners of the world could hardly believe it, but their Chinese houseboys were sending most of their salaries to patriotic organizations. Of all this, the experienced Alfred Hippisley who had designed the Open Door notes wrote, "A country whose people act thus may accomplish much."[95]

Life, like money, was laid on the line. A careful observer wrote concerning the frequency of patriotic suicide: "A nation in which a spirit of ruthless self-sacrifice is still so common may bring forth things that will astonish the world."[96] Whether observers were hostile to this strange quality of reckless ambition or whether they understood that they were somehow witnessing a great moment in human history, they reported the same mood.

92. Robert Dollar, *Private Diary of Robert Dollar on his Recent Visits to China* (San Francisco, 1912), pp. 91–113, 202–03.

93. *The National Review, Notes on Money Matters . . .*, pp. 111–13.

94. G. E. Morrison in the *Times* (London, March 8, 1910).

95. A. E. Hippisley, "The Awakening of China," *The National Review* (March 1906), p. 54.

96. Reinsch, "The New Education . . .", pp. 519–20.

> The clue to the Republic is that it was an imaginative inspiration . . . A people's government required the coining of a new word; and out of the same mint there poured a flood of strange and inspiring ideas. . . . The people reacted to the new regime with a vitality which the Republicans themselves never controlled and only imperfectly understood.[97]

The gradualism of Liang Ch'i-ch'ao, brilliantly argued though it was, fell on deaf ears. In the radical wing, Marxism is a counsel of gradualism; it is not surprising that the anarchist strain triumphed. When a French-educated revolutionary was asked by the correspondent of *Le Temps* in December 1911 whether he did not fear that a republic would lead to a reaction as tyrannical as the Empire had been, he replied: "Oh, we won't imitate the French; we'll establish a republic once and for all."[98]

In this context, Sun Yat-sen's vast, impracticable plans take on a new significance. He proposed a great bridge across the Yangtze at Wuhan "as a lasting memorial to the Revolution."[99] It remained for Mao Tse-tung to build it, as a prelude to the Great Leap Forward.

The later course of the Chinese Revolution cannot be fully explained by its origins, but the more I reflect on this first phase, the more clearly it seems to me that there has been one single revolution, the salient features of which were rooted in this early twentieth century experience: the persistent prominence of educated youth, the unusually prominent role of women, the insistence on strong leadership and revolutionary discipline (for the initial absence of these had been tragic), suspicion of all foreign powers, and finally a kind of "great leap" psychology, a disinterest in classic Marxism and other theories that assume a slow and to us rational development of society, and a conviction that by superhuman effort of an indoctrinated elite, China could bypass the usual stages and achieve its own kind of good society through sheer application of human energy and willpower.

The second phase of the Chinese Revolution, 1919–27, continued the major themes of the first with mounting intensity. It began with the May Fourth Movement of 1919, touched off by the news from Paris that the Allies had turned defeated Germany's

97. G. L. Harding, *Present Day China* (New York, 1916), pp. 24–25.

98. Rodes, *Vie révolutionnaire,* pp. 46–49.

99. Speech by Sun at Wuhan in early April 1912, FO 228/1841.

concessions in Shantung over to Japan rather than back to China. It ended with the nominal reunification of the country in 1926–28 by the united Kuomintang-Communist forces of the Northern Expedition. On the eve of victory, the conservative wing of the Kuomintang gained control, and once again the revolution was prematurely halted.

There were marked gains in the recovery of sovereign rights, largely the work of the Kuomintang, and further mobilization of the peasantry and labor, largely the work of the Communists. There was also an important new element: the example of the Russian Revolution of 1917 and the work of Comintern advisers in China solved the problem of tight pyramidal organization for both the Chinese parties. This new element has received so much attention that it is essential to remember that the revolution of the 1920s was an acceleration of forces clearly discernible in China fifteen years earlier.

No historian of China would deny that the transfer of power in 1949 and the wholesale reordering of Chinese society marked the sharpest forward thrust of the Chinese revolutionary movement until perhaps the recent Cultural Revolution. The point is that the roots not only of the post-1919 phases but of the post-1949 phases of the Chinese Revolution lie in the first decade of the twentieth century.

PART I

Political and Ideological Movements

1. Reform and Revolution in China's Political Modernization

Michael Gasster

> "Truth is stranger than Fiction, but it is because Fiction is obliged to stick to the possibilities, Truth isn't."
>
> —MARK TWAIN

In this revolutionary age of ours, it is not always apparent that revolutionary situations need not necessarily lead to revolutions. A revolutionary situation develops from a growing lack of confidence in the existing order and a number of related phenomena that add up to the loss of a people's "sense of community." When this occurs, however, it may be possible to stave off revolution if the governing group takes adequate steps to restructure the community.[1] If, however, there is "intransigent resistance" by the "status quo elite" to correcting the multiple "dysfunctions" in a given social system, revolution will occur.[2]

There can be little argument about the existence of a revolutionary situation in China before 1911; it had been developing for decades. But discussion of the steps that were taken to alleviate the situation may shed some new light on twentieth-century Chinese history.[3]

A substantial number of people were losing confidence in the existing order in China during the nineteenth century, and many of them favored radical solutions. By the early 1900s, a growing number were coming to the conclusion that the Ch'ing court's attempts at reform would not bring about satisfactory changes. They felt that the ruling elite was so dedicated to preserving the status

1. The preceding is inspired largely by R. R. Palmer, *The Age of the Democratic Revolution, I,* "The Challenge" (Princeton, 1959), 21.

2. Chalmers Johnson, *Revolution and the Social System,* Hoover Institution Studies, 3 (Stanford, 1964), 6–7.

3. I shall deal with these issues more fully in a book scheduled for publication by the University of Washington Press in 1969.

quo that genuine reformers could no longer remain loyal subjects of the Manchu dynasty; to be a genuine reformer one had to be a revolutionary. Between about 1902 and 1905, this sentiment burgeoned so powerfully that a languid revolutionary movement which had been sputtering along for a decade was suddenly rejuvenated and converted into a widespread, organized, articulate, and serious contender for political power. The founding of the Revolutionary Alliance in 1905 reflected a growing belief that the steps taken by the Manchus to relieve the dysfunction in Chinese society were hopelessly inadequate and that a new and very different effort was needed.

A considerable body of recent scholarship supports the revolutionaries' evaluation of China's situation.[4] Much less attention has been paid to those who wanted similarly profound changes but who came to feel that cooperating with the Manchus offered greater possibilities than overthrowing them, and that a constitutional monarchy might be more suitable for China than a republic. I think it worthwhile to try to ascertain the grounds for this belief and compare it with the revolutionaries' views. The similarities and differences between such revolutionaries as Sun Yat-sen and Wang Ching-wei on the one hand, and reformers like Liang Ch'i-ch'ao on the other, raise a number of questions about the relationship between revolution and modernization in modern China.

Liang Ch'i-ch'ao, in the five years after the 1898 debacle, was as much a revolutionary as Sun. The Manchus had put a price on his head after the Hundred Days' Reform, he had helped provide funds for T'ang Ts'ai-ch'ang's uprising in 1900, and even the Society to Protect the Emperor was an implicit challenge to the Empress Dowager.[5] Liang is also known to have been interested in formal cooperation with Sun Yat-sen.

Liang was not simply a revolutionary in spirit and action from 1898 to 1903, but in a sense he may even be considered to have done more to sire the Revolution during that period than Sun.

4. One of the most recent works of this kind is Y. C. Wang, *Chinese Intellectuals and the West, 1840–1937* (Chapel Hill, 1966). See especially pp. 226 and 299, where Professor Wang asserts that the Manchus were "impotent" and that Chinese institutions "had acquired a rigidity that prevented modification."

5. Chang P'eng-yüan points out that Liang rarely used the phrase "protect the Emperor" (*pao-Huang*) alone; he spoke of "Emperor-protection in name, revolution in fact." Chang, *Liang Ch'i-ch'ao yu Ch'ing-chi ko-ming* (Liang Ch'i-ch'ao and the Revolutionary Movement in the Late Ch'ing Period) (Taipei, 1964), p. 182.

Liang was surely the most prolific writer of the time, and the influence of such essays as the "Hsin-min shuo" (A People Made New) probably exceeded that of any other author. In these writings Liang at times ridiculed gradualism and demanded that "we must shatter at a blow the despotic and confused governmental system of some thousands of years; we must sweep away the corrupt and sycophantic learning of these thousands of years."[6]

Joseph R. Levenson points out that in this period Liang's references to the classics "seem parenthetical, not central"; in a discussion of a certain economic problem, for example, a quotation from the *Ta-hsüeh* (The Great Learning) was "no more than rhetorical baggage."[7] The prophet Confucius became merely one among many Chinese and Western heroes.[8] In 1901 Liang rejected attempts others had made to portray the abdications of Yao and Shun as examples of ancient Chinese democracy; even if they really did abdicate, he noted skeptically, "that still is entirely different from modern democracy." Furthermore, he said, democracy is a "universal principle. Where universal principles are concerned, one must not consider as a matter of any importance whether or not the ancients previously applied it."[9]

As Levenson notes, it had now become less important that the Chinese be culturally orthodox than that what they did be useful to the nation.[10] The preservation of the nation was at stake, and in this contest "the means of survival are the ultimate national values; if adherence to tradition is incompatible with the adoption of these means, tradition will go."[11] Although he believes that they approached it by significantly different routes, Levenson affirms that Liang and the revolutionaries reached the same conclusion about tradition.[12]

Up to 1903 at least, and in fact for some time thereafter, Liang shared other views with the revolutionaries. For example, he placed great stress on the importance of making China strong;[13] he attributed Europe's progress to its tradition of popular repre-

6. Liang Ch'i-ch'ao, "Hsin-min shuo" (A People Made New), quoted in *Sources of the Chinese Tradition,* ed. W. T. deBary et al. (New York, 1960), p. 759.

7. Joseph R. Levenson, *Liang Ch'i-ch'ao and the Mind of Modern China* (Cambridge, Mass., 1953), pp. 88–89.

8. Ibid., p. 121.

9. Quoted in ibid., p. 92.

10. Ibid., p. 110.

11. Ibid., p. 119.

12. Ibid., p. 167.

13. Ibid., p. 117.

sentation;[14] he criticized his countrymen for having a slave mentality and lacking enterprise and initiative;[15] and on occasion he became so exasperated with China's backwardness that he uncharacteristically praised revolution and permitted himself an anti-Manchu outburst.[16] Chang P'eng-yüan points out that for the pre-1903 period this position was not as atypical of Liang as Levenson suggests; in those years his anti-Manchuism was similar to that of the revolutionaries.[17]

In 1903–04, however, Liang underwent an intellectual crisis. For about eight months during 1903 he traveled in Canada and the United States, where he was consumed by a growing sense of emptiness. For reasons that remain obscure he lost confidence in what he had been doing. As China's plight worsened and there seemed to be no time to waste, Liang was stricken with uncertainty about how to help save his country.[18] By 1905, a number of factors had combined to propel him along a new path. At odds with the revolutionaries for personal and intellectual reasons, under pressure from his teacher K'ang Yu-wei, and increasingly fearful that in the chaos of revolution China might be partitioned by the foreign powers, Liang abandoned his advocacy of revolution and took up the cause of peaceful reform.[19]

The major influence upon Liang Ch'i-ch'ao during his period of indecision seems to have been exerted by Huang Tsun-hsien.[20] Friends since 1896,[21] Liang and Huang exchanged numerous letters between 1902 and Huang's death in 1905. Huang's ideas of moderate reform were based on the conviction that destructive violence should be avoided and a kind of partnership between ruler and ruled be worked out instead; as the people's understanding of freedom grew they would be guided toward democracy while maintaining respect for monarchy. Huang's belief that conditions in China in 1904 were not suitable for the establishment of a republic struck a responsive chord in Liang and prompted him to support peaceful reform leading toward constitutional monarchy under the Manchus.[22]

14. Ibid., p. 138.
15. Ibid., p. 140.
16. Ibid., pp. 156–59.
17. Chang P'eng-yüan, pp. 171–72; see Levenson, *Liang*, p. 159.
18. Chang P'eng-yüan, pp. 177–82.
19. Ibid., pp. 167–72, 208.
20. Poet and reformer, 1848–1905.
21. Ssu-yü Teng and John K. Fairbank, *China's Response to the West* (Cambridge, Mass., 1954), p. 149.
22. Chang P'eng-yüan, pp. 174–75; also, *Liang . . . nien-p'u* (Taipei, 1964), 2, 195–97.

Several specific features of Huang's thinking suited Liang's temperament particularly well. Among these were Huang's observation that patriotic spirit and universal education had been important factors in Japan's success and were similarly important for China, and his suggestion to pursue revolution without calling it one.[23]

Huang's views reflected his considerable experience abroad. From 1877 to 1882 he served in the Chinese legation in Japan; from 1882 to 1885 he was consul-general in San Francisco; in 1890–91 he served in London; and from 1891 to 1894 he served in Singapore. His writings about Japan and the United States indicate that he was observant, critical, and devoted to reform.[24] In particular, Huang's stay in the United States had underlined for him the vast gulf between East and West and convinced him that China was not ready for a republic.[25] It is therefore striking that Liang's change of heart came during and after a visit to the United States. It was then that he began to criticize republicanism and to argue, for example, that the difference between the American and French revolutions was that the American colonists' greater experience with a parliamentary system and self-government facilitated a successful republican revolution; China, he maintained, was more like France than the United States in this respect, and therefore a republican revolution in China would bring results more like those in France.[26] It does not seem too speculative to suggest that he may have been particularly sensitive to the way in which Robespierre's dream of a "Republic of Virtue" yielded to the Reign of Terror, the short-lived Directory, and the coups of 1797 and 1799, for in his subsequent debates with the Revolutionary Alliance, Liang's chief argument was that revolution would ultimately produce only chaos and a takeover by a military strong-man.[27] The point is that although it was not in the United States that Liang first became acquainted with the French Revolution, he did see a modern Western society for the first time. If it is merely a

23. Ibid., pp. 196, 202. See also Chang P'eng-yüan, p. 182.

24. See Arthur W. Hummel, ed., *Eminent Chinese of the Ch'ing Period* (Washington, D.C., 1943–44), *1*, 350–51; also, Teng and Fairbank, p. 149.

25. *Liang . . . nien-p'u*, *2*, 195–96.

26. Chang P'eng-yüan, pp. 164, 173–74. It is very interesting to read Liang in light of the differences between America and France noted by R. R. Palmer, p. 189.

27. See Liang's explicit reference to the French Revolution and the dangers of republican revolution in his article, "Cheng-chih-hsüeh ta-chia Po-lun-chih-li chih hsüeh-shuo" (The Thought of the Great Political Theorist Bluntschli), Liang, *Yin-ping-shih wen-chi* (Shanghai, 1932), *13*, 83–86. I am grateful to Dr. Philip C. Huang for calling this item to my attention.

coincidence that his thinking changed so radically at precisely this time,[28] it is surely a most startling one. A more interesting and at least equally plausible interpretation is that Liang's first contact with a modern Western society revealed to him just how far behind China was.[29] This would have made him all the more responsive to Huang Tsun-hsien's influence and, combined with the other forces we have noted, could have been decisive in persuading him to abandon revolution in favor of peaceful reform and constitutional monarchy.

After 1903 the clash between Liang and the revolutionaries crystallized. It is at this point that the differences between the reformists and the revolutionaries became of major significance, for an important shift in the character of the revolutionary movement also occurred after 1903. Until then, revolutionary propaganda had concentrated overwhelmingly on China's weakness vis-à-vis the foreign powers. Beginning in about 1903 a more strident attack upon the Manchus began to find expression. A pamphlet by Tsou Jung,[30] one of the most famous writings of the time, was one of the first and most systematic indictments of the Ch'ing as a racist regime. In addition to blaming the Manchus for weakening China until she was at the mercy of foreign powers, Tsou accused the Ch'ing of showing bias against the Chinese and favoritism to Manchus in such things as job appointments and taxes, establishing a brutal rule by military force, and more.[31]

The opening lines are typical of the new rancor and emotionalism that permeated and heightened the revolutionary spirit:

> To sweep away thousands of years of despotism, to throw off thousands of years of slavery, to wipe out the five million barbarian Manchus, to wash away the shame of two hundred and sixty years of cruelty and oppression, to make the China mainland clean once again, [let] every descendant of Huang Ti [become a] George Washington; return to life from the

28. Chang P'eng-yüan believes that Liang's writings before and after 1903 are so different on the question of revolution that they seem almost to represent two different men. Chang, p. 163.

29. Philip C. Huang, "A Confucian Liberal: Liang Ch'i-ch'ao in Action and Thought" (unpublished doctoral dissertation, University of Washington, 1966), pp. 125–27.

30. Tsou Jung, "Ko-ming chün" (The Revolutionary Army), *HHKM, 1*. See pp. 331–64 for the full text, an introduction by Chang Ping-lin that appeared originally in the *Su-pao* (June 10, 1903), and a brief biographical note on Tsou.

31. Tsou Jung, pp. 335–49.

> eighteen layers of hell and arise to heaven . . . the most revered and exalted, the one and only, the supreme and unparalleled goal that we call the Revolution![32]

By broadening the attack upon the Manchus in this fashion, Tsou Jung blazed a trail that Revolutionary Alliance writers were to extend much further after 1905. A deep split had riven the new intelligentsia; its two segments now turned their backs on each other and their faces toward two increasingly different visions of a strong and modern China.

By 1905, then, the issue had taken shape. For several years a debate raged, chiefly between Liang Ch'i-ch'ao, writing in his *Hsin-min ts'ung-pao* (New People's Miscellany), and Wang Ching-wei supported by several other *Min-pao* (People's Report) writers.[33] Neither side possessed a unified or entirely consistent point of view, but each shared some common ground that linked its factions in the struggle against the other.[34]

The Revolutionary Alliance indicted the Manchus on three general counts. First, they had conquered China by brute force, and once in power they had carried out discriminatory policies and a host of other oppressive measures that relegated the Chinese people to an inferior position in society. Second, they were foreign barbarians, an inferior race. Third, they were attempting to deceive the Chinese by promising a "pseudo-constitution."

It would be tedious to recount in full the crimes with which the revolutionaries charged the Manchus. But production of the anti-Manchu vitriol that was splashed across the pages of *Min-pao* and other revolutionary publications was a major Revolutionary Alliance activity. It commands some of our attention because it spilled

32. Ibid., p. 333.

33. An interesting treatment of the debate is Chang Nan and Wang Jen-chih, "Hsin-hai ko-ming ch'ien tzu-ch'an chieh-chi ko-ming-p'ai ho kai-liang-p'ai ti tou-cheng" (Struggle between the Bourgeois Revolutionists and the Reformists before the Revolution of 1911), *Li-shih yen-chiu* (Historical Research) (1962), *6,* 32–46. An older treatment that provides a convenient summary of the debate is Kao Liang-tso, "K'ai-kuo ch'ien ko-ming yü chün-hsien chih lun-chan" (The Debate on Revolution and Constitutional Monarchy before the Founding of the Republic), *Chien-kuo yüeh-k'an* (The Nation-Building Monthly), *7:* 3–6 (1932); and *8:* 5–6 (1933). (Pagination of each article in this publication began with p. 1; the 6 articles total 85 pages.) Ch'i Ping-feng's new book, *Ch'ing-mo ko-ming yu chün-hsien ti lun-cheng* (Controversy between the Revolutionaries and the Constitutional Monarchists in the Late Ch'ing Period) (Taipei, 1966) reached the United States too late for discussion here.

34. Chang Nan and Wang Jen-chih, pp. 35–38, 42–46, refer to some of the points of agreement and disagreement on each side.

over into the more temperate ideas of the revolutionaries, and because it consumed much energy that could have been devoted to other purposes. However creditable their effort to discuss more positive and far-reaching goals, the revolutionaries were, as Wang Ching-wei and others pointed out, primarily concerned with the immediate and pressing problems of acquiring the power to move toward those goals.[35] Thus they were activists and agitators first, and theorists second. To acquire power they had to arouse anti-Manchu sentiment and discredit constitutional monarchy. This meant opposing constitutional monarchy in principle, but it also meant proving that the Manchus were incapable of instituting a genuine constitutional government.

The keynote of the revolutionaries' argument was the difference between the races:

> The Manchu government is evil because it is the evil race which usurped our government, and their evils are not confined to a few political measures but are rooted in the nature of the race (*chung-hsing*) and can neither be eliminated nor reformed. Therefore, even if there are a few ostensible reforms, the evils will remain just the same. The adoption of Western constitutional institutions and law will not change the situation ... [contrary to the view of Liang Ch'i-ch'ao].[36]

Similar sentiments were voiced by Ch'en T'ien-hua: "The present government is not a Chinese government but that of a foreign tribe. Since our interests are thus mutually opposed, our aims cannot but be different."[37] The evidence cited by the polemicists was usually confined to instances of Manchu mistreatment of the Chinese and concessions to the foreign powers. But some aspects of the racial arguments deserve more attention.

Wang Ching-wei argued that nations should be organized by people who possessed a common history and culture. He based his discussion upon his definition of a nation as a "continuing human group [possessing] common characteristics": consanguinity, a common spoken and written language, the same territorial abode, common customs, a common religion, and "common spiritual and

35. For example, see Wang Ching-wei, "Min-tsu ti kuo-min" (Citizens of a Nation), part 2, *Min-pao, 2,* 17.

36. Hu Han-min, "The Six Principles of the People's Report," deBary et al., pp. 763–64. See *Min-pao, 3,* 8, for the Chinese text, "Min-pao chih liu ta chu-i."

37. Ch'en T'ien-hua, "Lun Chung-kuo i kai-ch'uang min-chu cheng-t'i" (China Should Change to a Democratic Form of Government), *Min-pao, 1,* 49.

physical [characteristics]." Wang emphasized that the ties binding such a group had to have existed continuously over a long period of time, so that in its history there had developed a common identity that made the nation "indestructible."[38]

One issue dividing Liang Ch'i-ch'ao and the revolutionaries now emerges clearly. For Liang employed exactly the same definition of "nation," but he then proceeded to argue that Chinese and Manchus could not clearly be distinguished, on the grounds that they had long since been assimilated; in any case, even if the Manchus were racially different, they were too small a fraction of China's population to be of any consequence as a racial group.[39]

Of all the ideas advocated by the Revolutionary Alliance, anti-Manchuism was the supreme propaganda weapon. It offered a simple explanation for every ill with which China was afflicted, and it provided a convenient scapegoat. It also enabled the revolutionaries to attack the Manchus' proposed constitutional government in an effective, if only because easily understandable, way. In addition to attacking it as a "pseudo-constitution" that did not alter the fundamentally autocratic nature of the government, they also argued that as barbarian conquerors, the Manchus were incapable of carrying out political reforms. Especially in the period before the constitution was proclaimed, this was an extremely important argument.

In September 1906, shortly after the return of the constitutional mission they had sent abroad a year earlier, the Manchus announced that a constitution and a series of administrative reforms were being prepared. The new system was soon proclaimed, and within a year there were a flurry of reforms which, even if more nominal than real, caused the revolutionaries much anxiety.

Convinced that the Manchus were only disguising and not relinquishing their control, the Revolutionary Alliance writers could not be sure that the Chinese at home and abroad shared this view. It also appeared likely that the foreign powers, especially Japan, would now consider the revolutionaries even less deserving of support than before.[40] Subsequent Ch'ing measures only height-

38. Wang Ching-wei, "Min-tsu ti kuo-min," part 1, pp. 1–2.

39. Levenson, *Liang*, pp. 160–61. Tseng Yu-hao, *Modern Chinese Legal and Political Philosophy* (Shanghai, 1930), pp. 122–23, suggests that these criteria of "nation" came from Bluntschli's conception of "volk."

40. Marius B. Jansen has pointed out that Japan preferred a weak but friendly constitutional monarchy in China and even helped the Ch'ing government to plan its constitution. Jansen, *The Japanese and Sun Yat-sen* (Cambridge, Mass., 1954), p. 130.

ened the revolutionaries' concern. These included the establishment of a Bureau for the Compilation of a Constitution, the dispatch of another overseas mission, the announcement of regulations for the establishment of provincial and district assemblies and the election of their members, and, finally, in September 1908, the publication of the outline of the constitution, the parliament, and the election laws. These were to be brought into final shape within nine years.

The revolutionaries attacked each measure as it was announced. But until the constitution itself was actually produced, it was an elusive target. They found much to criticize, for example, in the government's declared intention to imitate the Japanese system, for they knew how the Japanese constitution served the purposes of the oligarchy and how, during a similar period of preparation in Japan, political opposition and discussion were stifled. However, residing in Japan, frequently in trouble with the Japanese authorities, and anxious to obtain Japanese support for their movement, the revolutionaries were unable to use their knowledge to attack the Manchus' proposals.[41] Moreover, even if the Manchus themselves did not make extravagant claims for their constitution, there was always the eloquent Liang Ch'i-ch'ao to contend with. Thus the Ch'ing reforms of 1905–08 and Liang's support of them created a political environment that greatly intensified the revolutionaries' sense of urgency.

The Revolutionary Alliance therefore mounted an offensive against the "pseudo-constitution" that began with the first issue of *Min-pao* and was maintained to the last. Again it was Wang Ching-wei who carried most of the journalistic burden. A constitution, he argued, represented the Manchus' last desperate hope for retaining political power; every other prop supporting their government had either been destroyed or seriously weakened.[42] Analyzing the recommendations made by the first constitutional mission and approved by the court, he showed how they were aimed at limiting regional power and returning authority to the central government. This, he contended, was not really a question of political relationships, but a racial matter. "Therefore the problem can be summarized in one brief statement: The reason the Manchu govern-

41. As I have noted above, Hu Han-min wrote of the Ch'ing adoption of Western, not Japanese, institutions.

42. Wang Ching-wei, "Min-tsu ti kuo-min," part 1, p. 24.

ment is planning centralization is that it is the inevitable result of a minority race controlling a majority race."[43]

The Revolutionary Alliance's anti-Manchuism, more than anything else, united the diverse elements in the revolutionary movement. Furthermore, the issue inflamed China's political and intellectual atmosphere with an emotion-charged racism that contrasted sharply with the genuinely humanitarian elements in the revolutionary program and, one may speculate, interfered with rational discussion of more substantive issues. Anti-Manchuism may even have been a convenient way of avoiding a full-scale frontal assault on traditional Chinese government,[44] but it left unanswered the questions of what was wrong with that government and what was to be done about it.

Whether China should have a constitutional monarchy or a republic was not debated solely as a racial issue. In spite of their limited exposure to Western ideas and their natural preoccupation with the immediate political struggle in which they were engaged, both Liang Ch'i-ch'ao and Wang Ching-wei stated a number of significant problems connected with democratic government. For example, they discussed how to guarantee the responsibility of elected officials to the electorate, how to ensure that the popular will would be adequately expressed and implemented, how to avoid majority tyranny, the role of the monarch in a constitutional monarchy, the nature and locus of sovereignty in a representative system, Rousseau's concept of the general will, the role of law, separation of powers, and the power to tax.

For present purposes, only a few features of these discussions require our attention. First, they were based upon a very narrow range of Western political thought. Liang drew his ideas chiefly from Johann Kaspar Bluntschli (1808–81), Max von Seydel (1846–1901), and Conrad Bornhak (1861–1944); Wang leaned heavily upon Paul Laband (1838–1918) and Georg Jellinek (1851–1911). Thus Wang's defense of republicanism was based on the ideas of devout monarchists who sought to justify the authority of an imperial government by making it a *Rechtsstaat,* a state whose activi-

43. Wang Ching-wei, "Man-chou li-hsien yü kuo-min ko-ming" (The Manchu Constitution and the National Revolution), *Min-pao, 8,* 35.

44. K'ang Yu-wei, for example, had pointed out that if China's government was bad, it was also the government of Han, T'ang, and Sung, not a peculiarly Manchu government. Quoted in Kao Liang-tso, in *Chien-kuo yüeh-k'an, 3* (1932), 4.

ties are under legal limitations.[45] His ingenuity in adapting these ideas in his debates with Liang is impressive,[46] but his failure to call upon republican theorists is equally striking. The problem was essentially that Wang and the other revolutionaries had had too little time to learn very much about republican government. They had at hand a limited body of information taken from societies whose differences from China they had not had the opportunity to analyze. What republicanism really was and especially how it could solve China's political problems were questions that the revolutionaries hardly considered. Wang Ching-wei, who wrote far more on the subject than any other revolutionary, concentrated on trying to show merely that the principles of political science neither made a monarchy mandatory nor ruled out the possibility of popular self-government, and that a republic was a theoretically viable system.

A second feature of the Wang-Liang debate is that they agreed on the desirability for China of representative government. A typical statement of the republican position was made by Wang to the effect that a representative system is the basic principle of true democratic government, because elected representatives "represent the people in the exercise of their rights."[47] The revolutionaries' demand for democracy and republicanism was voiced by other writers as well.[48]

Liang Ch'i-ch'ao did not lose all sympathy for democratic revolution even though he played a leading role in the constitutional monarchist movement.[49] An eminent authority maintains that Liang was a "moderate democrat";[50] compared with the revolutionaries, Liang's political ideas were closer to traditional English liberalism, and among writers of the late Ch'ing and early re-

45. See Rupert Emerson, *State and Sovereignty in Modern Germany* (New Haven, 1928), pp. 74–76, for a discussion of these thinkers' respect for monarchy and the weakness of the idea of popular sovereignty in Germany at this time. Also, Frank O. Miller, *Minobe Tatsukichi* (Berkeley, 1965), pp. 60–67.

46. For example, see Wang Ching-wei, "Po *Hsin-min ts'ung-pao* tsui-chin chih fei ko-ming lun" (In Refutation of the *Hsin-min ts'ung-pao's* Most Recent Anti-Revolutionary Essay), *Min-pao, 4,* 8–11, 20, 22–23, and "Tsai po *Hsin-min ts'ung-pao* chih cheng-chih ko-ming lun" (Further Refutation of the *Hsin-min ts'ung-pao's* Essay on Political Revolution), *Min-pao, 6,* 84, 88–90.

47. Ibid., p. 95.

48. See, for example, Sun Yat-sen, "Chung-kuo ying chien-she kung-ho-kuo" (China Ought to Establish a Republic), *KFCC* (Taipei, 1957), *3,* 1–6; also, Ch'en T'ien-hua, pp. 41–50.

49. Hsiao Kung-ch'üan, Preface to Chang P'eng-yüan, *Liang Ch'i-ch'ao,* p. 1.

50. Hsiao Kung-ch'üan, *Chung-kuo cheng-chih ssu-hsiang shih* (History of Chinese Political Thought) (6 vols. Taipei, 1954), *6,* 753.

publican period "he was the one most deeply imbued with the 'democratic attitude.' "[51] The differences between Liang and the revolutionaries were real enough, but they cannot be explained by labeling Liang a "traditionalist," "reactionary," or even "conservative" in contrast with "modernizing" or "progressive" Revolutionary Alliance writers. According to Chang P'eng-yüan Liang was consistently dedicated to transferring sovereignty from the Ch'ing court to the whole people.[52] Although he preferred a constitutional monarchy to a republic, it is clear even in Liang's plea for "enlightened autocracy" that he was objecting not to democracy but to revolution.[53]

It is probably safe to say that Liang regarded violent revolution with more distaste than the republicans did but that, as we have seen, he did not shrink from it altogether. The reformers, by no means satisfied with what they regarded as a protracted and limping program for introducing constitutional government, nevertheless believed that the Ch'ing government's willingness to establish a constitution opened the door to a peaceful and legal struggle. By a combination of requesting, proposing, remonstrating, and urging they felt it would be possible to accelerate and broaden the Manchus' reforms, thereby avoiding violent revolution and achieving genuine representative government.[54]

The revolutionaries insisted that the Manchus would never allow more than a facade of popular government to be created and that destruction of the Manchu dynasty was therefore the essential prerequisite to effective change. In any case, a constitutional monarchy would not do, even as an interim step; as Sun Yat-sen put it, "the future of China is like building a railroad. Thus if we were now building a railroad would we use the first locomotive ever invented or today's improved and most efficient model?"[55]

51. Hsiao, Preface to Chang P'eng-yüan, *Liang Ch'i-ch'ao,* p. 2. See also Chang, p. 174, on Liang's admiration for the British system.

52. Chang P'eng-yüan, *Liang Ch'i-ch'ao,* pp. 195–97.

53. See Liang's "K'ai-ming chuan-chih lun" (On Enlightened Autocracy), *HMTP,* particularly no. 75, pp. 14–48 and no. 77, pp. 1–10.

54. Chang Nan and Wang Jen-chih, pp. 33–34, 36–38; Chang P'eng-yüan, *Liang Ch'i-ch'ao,* pp. 182–86, 208. On Liang's effort to win over and collaborate with certain Manchu princes, see Ernest P. Young, "The Reformer as a Conspirator: Liang Ch'i-ch'ao and the 1911 Revolution," in A. Feuerwerker, R. Murphey, and M. C. Wright, eds., *Approaches to Modern Chinese History* (Berkeley and Los Angeles, 1967), pp. 244–51.

55. Sun Yat-sen, "Chung-kuo ying chien-she kung-ho kuo" (China Ought to Establish a Republic), p. 4.

The questions of whether the Ch'ing should be considered foreign rulers, whether there had been racial subjugation, and whether military force should be used to overthrow the central government were indeed the ones that were argued most heatedly.[56] But the question that loomed largest in the background and the one to which all others pointed was how China could establish a government that would be not only democratic but strong and efficient as well.

Liang argued that for republican government to be successful, the people had to have reached a certain level of education and to have experience participating in political affairs. Parliament, after all, was the most important organ of such a government; were the Chinese people ready to manage complex affairs ranging from impeachment and law making to evaluating budgets? Would politically immature people fulfill their duty to vote? Would they not be subject to bribes, pressures, and selfish interests?[57] Moreover, there were numerous practical problems to deal with: defining for voting purposes the requirements for Chinese citizenship, delimiting voting districts, taking a census, appointing officials and police to supervise elections, devising civil and criminal codes, and so forth. In sum, constitutional government could not be established overnight and without careful planning and preparatory work.[58]

The revolutionaries answered that speed was of the essence, that Liang's was the gloomy pessimism of the timid, that he underestimated the Chinese people and failed to see the many elements in China's past that fitted her for democracy, and that China could learn from the examples of the West and Japan. It is a striking feature of the revolutionaries' interest in the experience of other countries that, except in regard to Japan, they spoke less of copying or imitating than they did of learning from others' mistakes and avoiding them. In the case of Japan, the revolutionaries particularly stressed that their goals for China had successfully been accomplished elsewhere. Ch'en T'ien-hua and Sun Yat-sen spoke for the vast majority of the revolutionaries when they placed the greatest stress upon China becoming a world power. They pointed to Japan not as an example of republicanism, obviously, but

56. Chang Nan and Wang Jen-chih, p. 41.

57. Liang Ch'i-ch'ao, "K'ai-ming chuan-chih lun," *HMTP*, No. 77, pp. 1–6.

58. Ibid., pp. 6–9.

as proof that a weak and threatened country could quickly become a powerful and independent one.[59] Ironically, it was the Manchus for whom Japan was a model to be consciously imitated.

The first conclusion I wish to draw from this very brief sketch of the reformist-revolutionary controversy is that the fundamental similarity between the reformers and the revolutionaries was their dedication to bringing about far-reaching changes in China's political organization. They shared the view that it should be a democratic system and each advocated popular sovereignty. Both wanted as efficient a government as possible, at least partly in order to permit China to improve her international standing. In general, by their own standards of modern government, reformers and revolutionaries were advocates of political modernization.

The issues between the two groups concerned the form of modern government China should have and the method by which modern government should be introduced. Their differences stemmed partly from reasoned choices they made between the merits of constitutional monarchy and those of republicanism, but the more profound source of their differences flowed from their estimates of the Manchus' performance and potential, their willingness to cooperate with the Manchus, and their assessment of how extensively and how quickly change could be effected in China. A discussion of the concept of modernization will assist us in examining these differences.

Modernization is a concept that had prominent critics at least as long ago as 1932, when R. H. Tawney referred to it in passing as a "common, though ambiguous, expression."[60] In recent years it has been employed in so many different ways and has acquired such a host of meanings that a prominent political scientist has recommended suspending use of the terms "modern" and "modernity."[61] Others have proposed less drastic remedies in order to dis-

59. See, for example, Sun Yat-sen, "Chung-kuo ying chien-she kung-ho kuo," pp. 2–3, and Sun, "Po Pao-huang pao" (In Refutation of the Emperor Protection Newspaper), *KFCC, 6,* 229–30; also, Ch'en T'ien-hua, pp. 42–44. Ch'en's central concern with making China strong emerges clearly in Ernest P. Young, "Ch'en T'ien-hua (1875–1905): A Chinese Nationalist," Harvard University, East Asian Research Center, *Papers on China, 13* (Cambridge, Mass., 1959), 113–62.

60. R. H. Tawney, *Land and Labour in China* (London, 1932), p. 16.

61. Joseph LaPalombara, "Bureaucracy and Political Development: Notes, Queries, and Dilemmas," in LaPalombara, ed., *Bureaucracy and Political Development* (Princeton, 1963), p. 35.

tinguish it from related concepts, such as "development," with which it has come to be identified.[62]

When one analyzes the concept of modernization he finds himself sooner or later trying to define the modern condition and the processes by which a society approaches it. These questions are very much like the ones Chinese intellectuals had been asking, explicitly or implicitly, since the latter part of the nineteenth century: What are the essential features of Western societies? Are they the same as the distinguishing characteristics of modern civilization? Which of these characteristics are most important? How does a non-Western society acquire them? Does it mean abandoning all of one's own tradition and becoming Western? If not, which elements must be given up and which can or should be saved? What sequence is to be followed? What kind of government is most modern? And so on and on.

In addition to the more obvious and measurable indices such as industrialization (usually measured in terms such as GNP or per capita production), urbanization, and literacy,[63] a number of more elusive and often more subtle features of modern societies have been identified. Among them are such attitudes as the belief in change and the possibility of expanding knowledge by rational means.[64] These have been summarized as the attitude of "creative rationality"[65] or the view that life consists of alternatives, preferences, and choices, from which it follows that modern man will possess a rationalist and positivist spirit and have opinions, debate, and discuss.[66] Modern society is therefore "participant," and

62. See Samuel P. Huntington, "Political Development and Political Decay," *World Politics, 17*:3 (1965). Note especially pp. 386–93. For another example see Lucian W. Pye, "Introduction: Political Culture and Political Development," in Pye and Sidney Verba, eds., *Political Culture and Political Development* (Princeton, 1965), pp. 11–13.

63. See J. W. Hall, "Changing Conceptions of the Modernization of Japan," in M. B. Jansen, ed., *Changing Japanese Attitudes Toward Modernization* (Princeton, 1965). P. 19 has a typical list.

64. Cyril E. Black, "Political Modernization in Russia and China," in Kurt London, ed., *Unity and Contradiction* (New York, 1962), pp. 3–4. See also Black's more general "Change as a Condition of Modern Life," in Myron Weiner, ed., *Modernization: The Dynamics of Growth* (New York, 1966), pp. 17–27. His most recent formulation, *The Dynamics of Modernization* (New York, 1966), reached me too late for discussion here.

65. James O'Connell, "The Concept of Modernization," *South Atlantic Quarterly, 64*:4 (1965), 549–64.

66. David E. Apter, *The Politics of Modernization* (Chicago, 1965), p. 10, and Daniel Lerner, *The Passing of Traditional Society* (Glencoe, Ill., 1958), pp. 45–49.

a society's system of communications becomes another index and agent of change.[67]

This list of elements comprising the modern condition could be lengthened a great deal. But valuable as they are, they fall short; for studies of modernization have shown, more clearly than anything else, that there is no such thing as *the* modern condition. There is only an unlimited number of approximations to it, many societies at varying stages of many differing processes of modernization. Some modern elements are present to some degree in almost all societies. All societies are either traditional or transitional and most are in the latter category. Most societies, Western as well as non-Western, are dualistic, in the sense that they are *mixtures* of the modern and the traditional, not *either* modern *or* traditional. They are "systems in which cultural change is taking place," and they are distinguished from each other in terms of the type of relationship between the "modern" and the "traditional" components that exists in each.[68] The problem is therefore to analyze this relationship in each society rather than to grapple with empirically unverifiable ideal "modern" types or models.

From this point of view, modernization is best understood as a process *leading toward* a condition of modernity but never quite reaching it; indeed, there is no final condition of modernity but only a continuing process of adjustment among many modernizing and traditional forces. Societies reflect different degrees of modernization; no society has made a clean break with its past.[69] On the contrary, it is sometimes essential for a society to preserve or at least adapt certain traditional elements, even nonrational ones that might conflict with the needs of modernization.[70] The ques-

67. Ibid., pp. 50 ff.

68. Gabriel A. Almond, "A Functional Approach to Comparative Politics," in Almond and James S. Coleman, eds., *The Politics of the Developing Areas* (Princeton, 1960), pp. 17–25. This early formulation has been developed in different ways by a number of scholars. One important approach to the study of transitional societies is that of Fred W. Riggs; among his many writings see "The Prevalence of Clects," *American Behavioral Scientist, 5* (June 1962), 15–18; "The Theory of Developing Politics," *World Politics 16:*1 (1963), 147–71; "Bureaucrats and Political Development: A Paradoxical View" in LaPalombara, ed., pp. 120–67; and *Administration in Developing Countries: The Theory of Prismatic Society* (Boston, 1964). Marion J. Levy's new book, cited in n. 78, effects a number of breakthroughs, among them a fruitful distinction between relatively modernized and relatively nonmodernized societies.

69. See Apter, p. xi.

70. Sidney Verba, "Comparative Political Culture," in Pye and Verba, p. 516.

tion of whether to eliminate or adapt traditional institutions during modernization may become irrelevant owing to their staying power; usually there is no alternative to adaptation.[71] Choice may be exercised only within the framework of adaptation, the only choice being how and in what sequence to adapt. Since some features of the traditional society must survive during modernization to ensure stability, those features may even be strengthened.[72] The modernization process is certain to be disruptive, but modernizers who attempt to adjust the modern and the traditional might minimize the disruption.[73]

Of relevance to our study is the hypothesis that all societies are transitional or dualistic; all represent a unique blend of the traditional and the modern, and not all traditional features of society need be destroyed during the modernization process. The most successful modernization processes are those that most harmoniously fuse traditional and modern elements. Japan is one of the best illustrations of this, and for us the most relevant one, since so many Chinese were influenced by the Japanese.

"The distinctive quality of Japanese modernization was the extraordinary degree to which the past could be adapted to the needs and purposes of the present."[74] Recent studies have elaborated this theme with remarkable frequency. One scholar stresses dualism, the coexistence of traditional and modern factors in a "symbiotic rather than antagonistic" relationship, and concludes that in view of her long preparation for modernization, Japan's was not an example of rapid political development.[75] Another has made a study of Nishimura Shigeki in which Japan's moderniza-

71. See LaPalombara, pp. 12–13.

72. On the question of strengthening institutions see Huntington, pp. 393 ff.; cf. Stephen N. Hay, "Western and Indigenous Elements in Modern Indian Thought: The Case of Rammohun Roy," in Jansen, ed., p. 312.

73. The disruption or "dysfunction" involved is why the term "modernization" is preferable to development, which has a greater connotation of growth or an unfolding of latent possibilities in some gradual and uniform way. One of Huntington's most interesting points is that modernization can interfere with development, that is, that too much social mobilization can interfere with the institutionalization of political organizations and procedures. Note also the inference drawn by LaPalombara from Merle Fainsod's work "that a bureaucracy can instill and implement economic modernity without its absorbing any of the changes it seeks to disseminate." (Huntington, pp. 393 ff.; LaPalombara, pp. 11–12.)

74. Robert A. Scalapino, "Ideology and Modernization—The Japanese Case," in David E. Apter, ed., *Ideology and Discontent* (Glencoe, Ill., 1964), p. 97.

75. Robert E. Ward, "Japan: The Continuity of Modernization," in Pye and Verba, especially pp. 32–33 and 77–82.

tion is characterized as a "curious blending of tradition with Westernization." Nishimura tried to work out a modernized system that would unify and stabilize Japan in a period of rapid change; the system he developed shows how Japan's Westernized exterior was "braced" by the use of tradition. Modernizers who were more anxious than Nishimura to Westernize emphasized such things as natural rights, popular sovereignty, and equality of classes and sexes, "but their ideas outran their times. Similarly, Nishimura's more progressive suggestions attracted little attention, but when he applied tradition to current problems, some of his ideas were eventually picked up and utilized."[76] Slogans like "Civilization and Enlightenment," which were popular in Japan during the Western fever or "intoxication" of the 1870s and 1880s, tended to overshadow "Enrich the Nation, Strengthen its Arms." The latter slogan, however, was closer to representing "the true character of Meiji Japan." It "meant modernization in the selective way in which it was actually carried out in the Meiji period." This selective method was to change only those elements in Japanese culture that interfered with creating a centralized state based on military and industrial strength. This was the aim, and it did not matter whether the means came from East or West, or from liberal or authoritarian traditions.[77]

China's tradition was of course very different, and such scholars as Marion J. Levy have convincingly demonstrated the significance of those differences in explaining the great contrast between the modernization processes in the two countries.[78] But is it not possible that there nevertheless may have been elements in Chinese tradition, particularly in the political and intellectual spheres, that were not incompatible with and might have been selectively built upon to further modernization? It seems reasonable that those very differences and incompatibilities inevitably would make China's

76. Donald H. Shively, "Nishimura Shigeki: A Confucian View of Modernization," in Jansen, ed., pp. 240–41.

77. Ibid., pp. 196–98. See also Robert E. Ward, "Political Modernization and Political Culture in Japan," *World Politics, 15*:4 (1963), 578–81, and J. W. Hall, pp. 37–38.

78. See Marion J. Levy, *The Family Revolution in Modern China* (Cambridge, 1949), especially pp. 164–65, 171, 218–23, 297–98, 350–65; also, Levy's "Contrasting Factors in the Modernization of China and Japan," *Economic Development and Cultural Change, 2*:3 (1953), especially pp. 163–70, 174–75, 178–95; also, "Some Aspects of 'Individualism' and the Problem of Modernization in China and Japan," *Economic Development and Cultural Change, 10*:3 (1963), 225–40. Levy's most recent and comprehensive formulation is *Modernization and the Structure of Societies* (2 vols. Princeton, 1966).

process of modernization slower and more in keeping with her own cultural peculiarities than Japanese and Western modernization. Indeed, if my conception of modernization has any merit it suggests that "incompatibilities" have to be analyzed in very specific terms. Certain features of a tradition may be utterly incompatible with modernization, but others inevitably will be more adaptable. There can be no incompatibility between an entire tradition and modernization unless the latter is conceived of as a very narrowly defined phenomenon, analogous, for example, to the experience of Western Europe and the United States. It is possible that a tendency toward a narrow definition of modernity has prevented scholars from recognizing modernizing trends that follow different patterns. The process in China may well be such a case.

It is unlikely that China could have accomplished as much as Japan did, even under a constitution modeled on the Meiji document. It is even more unlikely that China could have been modernized the same way Japan was. The many differences between Chinese and Japanese tradition cannot be written off, nor can the fact that the Manchu dynasty was in an advanced state of decay by the end of the nineteenth century. But perhaps we underestimate the steps toward modernization that were taken in China under the Manchus from 1860 to 1911 because we cannot help comparing the pace of change in China with that of Japan and the West, and perhaps we also exaggerate how rapidly Japan (and even the West) changed. Just as modern societies develop unevenly, traditional societies decay unevenly. Granting the decay of Manchu China and the many elements in late Ch'ing society that may have been "incompatible" with modernization, may there not also have been elements in the political system that could have been adapted to modernization? The characteristics of a politically modern state include, for example, the presence of rational and secular techniques of decision-making and government involvement in the regulation of economic and social life. Were there in late Ch'ing China at least remnants of such characteristics out of which a modern state could have developed under a constitutional monarchy? In brief, was there at least a chance that Confucian China could have transformed itself?

These questions help to clarify the issues that divided the reformers and the revolutionaries. Positive answers to them seem to reflect the assumptions of such men as Liang Ch'i-ch'ao; negative ones suggest the reasoning of Revolutionary Alliance members. There are grounds for believing that the reformers' position had at least as sound an underpinning as that of the revolutionaries.

It has been shown, for example, that despite the limited success of China's attempt to develop a new approach to foreign relations in the 1860s, "a real change in outlook did occur" on the part of Chinese officials. The hypothesis that "the Tsungli-yamen was tentatively introducing a radically new view of China's foreign relations" is, I think, correct, and it suggests that the Confucian view of the world could be revised and adapted to modern conditions when it was clear to Chinese leaders that there were immediate and concrete political advantages to be gained.[79]

China's value system has frequently been cited as a major impediment to modernization, especially insofar as Chinese values were expressed in "particularistic" tendencies which affected social, economic, and political institutions.[80] To the extent that this value system was Confucian, some observations by Hellmut Wilhelm are relevant. He discerns the growth of "ideas within a developed Chu Hsi system which might have become germinating points of modernization."[81] He by no means minimizes the obstacles to such a possibility, but he does think it worth writing about those "thinkers whose ideas pointed in new directions." And I cannot help agreeing that "it is tempting to speculate what might have happened if thoughts like these could have been given another generation's time to mature."[82] In more concrete terms, one wonders why the values that failed to produce the entrepreneurial spirit in China[83] did not also stifle that spirit among Overseas Chinese, and why the family system operated in the same contradictory way.[84] Did Chinese values have to be shifted to promote modernization?

79. See Mary C. Wright, *The Last Stand of Chinese Conservatism* (Stanford, 1957), pp. 279–95, for the discussion on which this paragraph is based.

80. For example, Robert N. Bellah, *Tokugawa Religion* (Glencoe, Ill., 1957), pp. 188 ff.; cf. Marion Levy, cited in n. 78.

81. Hellmut Wilhelm, "Chinese Confucianism on the Eve of the Great Encounter," in Jansen, ed., p. 303.

82. Ibid., p. 310.

83. See Albert Feuerwerker, *China's Early Industrialization* (Cambridge, Mass., 1958), pp. 32–33.

84. See Frank H. H. King, *Money and Monetary Policy in China, 1845–95* (Cambridge, Mass., 1965), p. 232; Chi-ming Hou, *Foreign Investment and Economic Development in China, 1840–1937* (Cambridge, Mass., 1965), p. 161; Myron Weiner, pp. 6 and 10.

If so, which ones? Were they being revised significantly before 1911? Could environmental changes precede and encourage changes in values?

We are far from being able to answer such questions, but recent research suggests how we might at least approach them. Chi-ming Hou argues that tradition and the Manchu government have been blamed too much for China's slow modernization, that there were other important factors, and that tradition could have in some ways promoted modernization in China. He points out that traditional technology satisfied much of Chinese demand and that therefore we must reconsider the sense in which Ch'ing economic development was a "failure." Furthermore, in view of the tenacity of the traditional sector of the economy, some form of "economic dualism [i.e. a compromise between modern and traditional technology] may not really be undesirable . . . Technological progress should include creative adaptation of the traditional methods . . . "[85] And that is what seems to have happened. The modern sector of the Chinese economy grew steadily from 1840 to 1937, and while the West played a significant role in this growth, Chinese capital and entrepreneurship also made very important contributions. This was true even under the Manchus, whose investment in the economy amounted to a sizable portion of central government revenue.[86] Thus the traditional sector existed quite well alongside the modern sector of the Chinese economy.[87]

While economic change before 1895 was confined largely to the treaty ports and was limited even there, the industry that was developed provided at least a basis for further expansion.[88] This assumes greater significance if it is true that "before the Sino-Japanese War the disparity between the degree of modern economic development in these two countries was not yet flagrant."[89] When and how did the disparity become flagrant?

One factor that does not always receive the stress it deserves is the different positions of the two countries in relation to the foreign powers. Perhaps there existed in Japan the right combination

85. Chi-ming Hou, "Economic Dualism: The Case of China, 1840–1937," *Journal of Economic History, 23*:3 (1963), 296–97; "Some Reflections on the Economic History of Modern China (1840–1949)," *Journal of Economic History, 23*:4 (1963), 599–605. See also Professor Hou's book (cited in n. 84), pp. 165–88.

86. Chi-ming Hou, *Foreign Investment,* pp. 131–32.

87. Ibid., p. 178.

88. King, p. 19.

89. Feuerwerker, p. 53.

of ingredients—enough of a threat to stimulate but not enough real interference to slow modernization. If there was no great disparity between Chinese and Japanese economic modernization before 1895, it is highly significant that Japan freed herself of the unequal treaties at almost exactly the time when the disparity began to become significant.

One final evidence of change in prerepublican China seems particularly relevant at this point. In the most exhaustive study of the Ch'ing bureaucracy yet undertaken, Esther Morrison has found that a process of modernization began in the middle of the nineteenth century and accelerated until the fall of the dynasty. During this process a modern sector developed and expanded alongside a contrasting traditional sector. Although the Ch'ing bureaucratic system

> had badly disintegrated during the late nineteenth century yet the structure remained intact awaiting modernization. Coexisting beside the traditional bureaucracy was a small sphere of modern activities supported by a bureaucratic dynamics, which had drawn upon the flexibilities in the traditional system, and yet was in no aspect entirely identical with the essential features [of the traditional system].[90]

Professor Morrison by no means exaggerates the limited extent of modernization, nor does she overlook the remaining obstacles.[91] But she marshals impressive evidence for her contention that a modern sector of bureaucratic government grew steadily from 1850 to 1901,[92] until in the last decade of Ch'ing rule, "political acculturation" (i.e. the use of foreign models) was made national policy: an "all-out reform program," now "on an empire-wide scale," was accompanied "by major institutional changes."[93]

Among the many important aspects of Ch'ing bureaucratic modernization noted by Professor Morrison, one that particularly interests me is that the Manchus, while deliberately choosing the Japanese model, also took into account differences between China and Japan as well as between China and the West.[94] This seems

90. Esther Morrison, "The Modernization of the Confucian Bureaucracy" (unpublished Ph.D. dissertation, Department of History and Far Eastern Languages, Radcliffe College, 1959), p. 14.

91. See, for example, ibid., pp. 455–56, 625 ff., 745, 944–47, 968, 988, 1009–10, 1201–02.

92. Ibid., pp. 367–82.

93. Ibid., pp. 684–88 ff.

94. Ibid., pp. 695–98, 969, 1016.

important because the lesson to be learned from a comparison of Japan's modernization with China's may not be simply that a certain kind of tradition facilitates the process; it may be more that modernization will inevitably grow out of tradition no matter what kind of traditional culture it is.

By studying in the context of modernization the controversy between the reformers and the revolutionaries, we gain the following perspectives:

1. Modern societies grow out of their own traditions. Therefore the pace and pattern of each society's modernization, at least in its early stages, will vary as much as traditions vary. Modernization is never likely to be smooth or even, but it will be less disjointed to the extent that it is geared to tradition. This is all the more so in a country like China, where the very strength of tradition dictates that modernizers compromise with it.

2. The decline of the Manchus, while undeniable, did not reduce the Ch'ing to impotence, nor did the Manchu rulers become intransigent opponents of reform. In fact, given the massiveness of the problems they faced, their reforms were far from insignificant.

3. It is highly problematical whether the eventual failure of reform can be attributed to the rigidity or sterility of Chinese tradition or its incompatibility with modernization.

4. None of this could have been apparent to Chinese intellectuals in the beginning of the twentieth century, but these three points reflect the assumptions of the reformers more than they do those of the revolutionaries. Moreover, to the extent that they have any validity, these points suggest that as a program for modernization the revolutionaries' proposals were premature and, for the time, excessively radical.

My purpose is not to argue that the reformers' program, if adopted, would necessarily have provided a smoother or more successful path to modernization. Although the rapid failure of the Republic tempts one to suggest that Liang's program could hardly have been less successful, this takes us too far into speculation.[95] I am chiefly concerned with how the revolutionaries arrived at their position, what the nature of their dissatisfaction was, and what the factors were that led them to appraise the Manchus' performance and potential so differently from modernizers like

95. It might not be impossible to support the hypothesis that the Republic slowed China's modernization. It might be instructive to compare the last decade of the Ch'ing with the first decade or two of the Republic.

Liang: What led them to believe that China could move farther and faster as a republic than she had and could under Manchu leadership and how did that decision affect China's modernization?

To the Chinese revolutionaries, the facts that dominated the political environment in which they had spent their entire lives were that China had no effective central government and was continually subject to defeats, humiliations, and the threat of dismemberment at the hands of foreign powers. They also lived with the memory of China's greatness, which further dramatized her present plight. It was logical to blame the Manchu government. The revolutionaries began to define their differences from the Manchus and, consequently, to define what it meant to be Chinese. This conscious attempt at self-analysis and self-definition, combined with the effort to arouse their countrymen to an awareness of their identity and the desire to achieve for China a position in the world comparable to that of other nation-states, ushered in modern Chinese nationalism. Establishment of an effective central government and elimination of foreign privileges in China became the overriding goals of Chinese revolutionary-modernizers. The increasing urgency with which they pursued their political goals illustrates the accelerating pace of intellectual modernization in China, and their repeated failures widened the gap between intellectual and political change, between their ideas and the possibility of implementing those ideas. The result was another aspect of what I have referred to elsewhere as China's disjointed modernization.[96]

From the very beginning of China's modernization, the process was uneven, and China surely was not unique in this. Ideas may not change quite as rapidly as they often appear to, but new ideas tend to make their weight felt more quickly and more profoundly than do new institutions; at least new ideas seem to be more easily adopted than are new institutions.[97] In nineteenth-century China,

96. "Some Recent Books on the Rise of Chinese Communism," *Slavic Review, 23*:2 (1964), 340–41.

97. I am oversimplifying matters in this paragraph, but the essential point, the uneven character of modernization, is undeniable. A provocative analysis of one aspect of this complex question may be found in the article by G. William Skinner. Note especially part 2, pp. 216–27, where a distinction is drawn between false and true modernization and differences are noted between different parts of China. G. William Skinner, "Marketing and Social Structure in Rural China," *JAS, 24*:1 (1964), 3–43; *24*:2 (1965), 195–228; *24*:3 (1965), 363–99. (To appear shortly as a book, Stanford University Press.)

reform ideas pulled steadily ahead of institutional change until during the Hundred Days' Reform the link between them snapped. The Manchus repaired it by reining in reformist ideas, reducing the pace from K'ang Yu-wei's canter to a comfortable trot more like the self-strengtheners. In 1905 the Manchus accelerated again, but by this time a new set of ideas, those of revolution, had forged ahead. It is my thesis that from the time revolutionary doctrine began to be formulated, a broadening gulf was created between thought and the possibilities for action that led to some of the major frustrations plaguing Chinese intellectuals in the twentieth century. These frustrations were due to institutional change that lagged ever farther behind the intellectuals' galloping ideals. They produced among Chinese intellectuals what Schumpeter has termed "the kind of radicalism whose intensity is in inverse proportion to its practical possibilities, the radicalism of impotence."[98]

It is this, I submit, that constitutes the fundamental difference between the ideas of the reformist Liang Ch'i-ch'ao and those of the Revolutionary Alliance intellectuals. The issue is crucial because the split in China's intelligentsia before 1911 seems to have anticipated the split after 1919.[99] The revolutionary spirit that increasingly claimed the lead in Chinese thought and politics after May Fourth and culminated in the establishment of a Communist regime had its origins in the last years of the nineteenth century and crystallized after 1905.

Reformers like Liang Ch'i-ch'ao were reconciled to, if not counting on, a greater degree of coexistence between the modern and the traditional than were the revolutionaries. The latter, of course, were by no means unanimously opposed to such coexistence. In their ranks were men like Chang Ping-lin who were traditionalists at heart, and even many of the more modern-minded also retained strong attachments to tradition. The most relevant example is Sun Yat-sen's five-power constitution, which he outlined for the first time in 1906. Thus both the reformers and the revolutionaries maintained quite conscious ties to traditional ideas and practices. That the difference is one of degree rather than of kind makes it no less significant. At least as significant as Sun's enunciation of the five-power constitution is his complaint (in 1921) that Revolu-

98. Joseph A. Schumpeter, *Capitalism, Socialism, and Democracy* (New York, 1950), p. 328.

99. For the post-1919 split see Chow Tse-tsung, *The May Fourth Movement* (Cambridge, Mass., 1960), pp. 215 ff.

tionary Alliance members had paid no attention to it; they preferred a three-power constitution resembling that of the United States.[100]

Before 1900, reformers remained anchored in tradition. With Liang Ch'i-ch'ao, reformism ventured toward sweeping and rapid change but then retreated to a program which, if it was irrational at all, was irrational in a way that resembled the self-strengthening movement more than the New Culture and Communist movements. The Revolutionary Alliance marks the beginning of a new kind of radicalism, one more similar to what Robert Lifton describes as the "irrational urge to reform" of the Communists.[101]

The new nationalism that appeared in the revolutionaries' writings may have been needed if China was to modernize. But it is worth noting, first, that in these respects their nationalism was scarcely different from Liang Ch'i-ch'ao's. Liang's definition of a nation differed from Wang Ching-wei's only in that Liang believed it included the Manchus and Wang did not. Second, even if the racist anti-Manchuism was a mere propaganda device to foment revolution, the sheer volume of it must have been important. If it did not completely swallow up other elements in the new nationalism, anti-Manchuism surely left enough teeth-marks in them that they were not easily recognizable as independent elements. Anti-Manchuism and republicanism, I suggest, were at best peripheral or tangential to the long-range goals of modernization and at worst irrelevant to or inconsistent with them. To create a unified, modern, wealthy, powerful, and democratic state it did not really matter whether China was ruled exclusively by the Han Chinese. Nor was it essential that China be a republic rather than a constitutional monarchy.

My point is not that Confucian China could have been saved or that the revolutionaries were wrong or foolish. Much of their criticism of the Manchus was well founded and perceptive. But we have seen that Chinese modernization was more rapid and substantial from 1850 to 1911 than the revolutionaries estimated; and events of the decade or two after 1911 suggest that their hopes of hastening the process were too high. Sun Yat-sen spent far more time in the West than did Liang Ch'i-ch'ao, but the gap between China

100. See Sun's lecture on the five-power constitution, translated in Leonard Shihlien Hsu, *Sun Yat-sen, His Political and Social Ideals* (Los Angeles, 1933), p. 91.

101. Robert J. Lifton, *Thought Reform and the Psychology of Totalism* (New York, 1963), p. 413.

and the West did not impress him as it had Liang. Liang was more impressed by what he felt China could *not yet* have, Sun by what he wanted China *to* have. Thus, Sun's government–locomotive analogy is an early form of a "great leap" outlook. The development of this outlook is not easily explained, but I believe that to a considerable degree it resulted from the revolutionaries' reactions to their experiences abroad, especially in Japan.

Liang Ch'i-ch'ao was also impressed by Japan's progress, but this apparently inclined him to support the Manchus, who were trying to learn from Japan's example. Furthermore, he had little taste for violent change, and his temperament was such that a trip to the United States which would exhilarate Sun Yat-sen only chastened Liang. (One can hardly imagine Sun visiting J. P. Morgan and, like Liang, leaving immediately for want of something to say.[102]) Perhaps most important of all, Liang assimilated such experiences into a very different personal history. The crucial differences are, first, that Liang's association with K'ang Yu-wei, his involvement in the 1898 reform, and his narrow escape after its failure, exposed him to a side of politics that the revolutionaries had never seen. However limited this exposure was, it afforded more of an insight into the complexities of effecting social and political change than any of the revolutionaries had. It was at least a brief view from the seat of power, and it may have provided a different perspective; later Chinese revolutionaries, such as the Communists, have also discovered that new perspectives are gained from exposure to the inside of government. Second, Liang, however much he was at times inclined to be revolutionary, was basically more disposed to seek a cultural synthesis;[103] he could never quite shake off a belief in gradual change that maintained some ties to tradition. Liang's view of modernization, revolution, and republicanism had an evolutionary component that bears a close resemblance to Yen Fu's.[104]

The revolutionaries, in contrast, conceived of social and political change as allowing for shortcuts to the highest level. If what Japan had done was good, others had done still better; China could draw confidence from Japan's experience but her model should be the most "advanced" form of government. For largely unexamined

102. See Levenson, *Liang*, p. 70, for Liang's meeting with Morgan.

103. See Philip C. Huang, n. 29 above, for a more detailed discussion of this point.

104. See Benjamin Schwartz, *In Search of Wealth and Power* (Cambridge, Mass., 1964), pp. 143–47.

reasons, this was assumed to be a republic. This radicalism finally produced an impatient urge for more drastic changes than China could assimilate. Their inability to accomplish the changes they desired led the revolutionaries to conclude that stronger efforts rather than milder ones were required. Later advocates of great leaps forward were heirs to this radicalism.

Both the reformers and the revolutionaries were patriots and nationalists, but the one identified the Manchus with Chinese nationalism and the other directed its nationalism chiefly against the Manchus. Both groups were concerned about foreign domination, but they disagreed as to whether a revolution would facilitate or eliminate it; the reformers feared foreign intervention while the revolutionaries counted on foreign sympathy and help. Both groups favored democracy and constitutional government, but one decided to preserve the monarchy and work toward a system like Britain's while the other demanded a more radical departure from tradition.[105] Both wanted extensive changes but one believed violence could be avoided, and the other did not. The foundation of these divergent views is the assessment of the Manchus' performance and potential, which derived in part from what the Manchus had actually done, but also from the expectations and desires of the two groups. Both groups developed their ideas under enormous political pressures in an atmosphere of intensifying emotions that at times approached hysteria. As the gap between Liang's ideas and the possibility of implementing them began to seem too wide, he shortened his vision and modified his ideas. When the same gap yawned before the Revolutionary Alliance, their movement began to turn into a "revolution of rising frustrations."[106] Before 1911 this did not become a "secularized millenarianism" equivalent to that of the Jacobins,[107] but the extremism and utopianism that germinated in the Revolutionary Alliance blossomed amidst the failures of the Republic into something closely akin to

105. Note Fred W. Riggs' comment: "The Japanese example—and indeed, the British case itself—suggests the possibility of evolving a modern democratic polity within the chrysalis of a fossilized monarchy." Riggs, "Bureaucrats and Political Development: A Paradoxical View," p. 160. Cf. Robert E. Ward's analysis of how the Meiji constitution began a process of democratization and modernization in Japan. Ward, "Political Modernization and Political Culture in Japan," pp. 588–96.

106. The term is Daniel Lerner's. See his "Toward a Communication Theory of Modernization," in Lucian W. Pye, ed., *Communications and Political Development* (Princeton, 1963), p. 330.

107. See Lewis A. Coser, *Men of Ideas* (New York, 1965), pp. 150–52.

Jacobin radicalism. Revolutionary Alliance radicalism prepared the ground for the deeper radicalism that followed: seeking more than the level of modernization sought by Liang but less than the Westernization advocated in the New Culture Movement, Revolutionary Alliance intellectuals may eventually go down in history as the earliest evidence for the hypothesis that "rapid modernization . . . produces not political development, but political decay."[108]

108. Huntington, p. 386.

2. The Triumph of Anarchism over Marxism, 1906-1907

Martin Bernal

Socialism in China and Japan Before 1906

From 1895 until 1919 China was almost completely dependent on Japan for its knowledge of the West. With the notable exception of Yen Fu, nearly all of the Chinese purveyors of Western culture were men whose only foreign language was Japanese.[1] Even Sun Yat-sen relied on Japanese sources more than he cared to admit.[2] Therefore in any history of Chinese revolutionary ideas of this period it is necessary to pay considerable attention to their Japanese counterparts.

Japanese socialism antedated the Chinese type by several years. It originated from two very different sources, the Christian and the liberal. However, in the early years the Christians clearly dominated the movement.[3] The chief reason why so many Christians became Socialists or sympathetic toward socialism, was that their Christianity was often a symptom of a more general revolt against the values and methods of Meiji Japan. By becoming

1. See the chart in Chang Ching-lu, *Chung-kuo chin-tai ch'u-pan shih-liao* (Historical Materials on Modern Chinese Publishing) (2 vols. Shanghai, 1953–54), 2, 100–01, showing that 60 percent of the translations into Chinese from 1902 to 1904 were of Japanese works, and Sanetō's note that "an extremely large number" of the European works were retranslated into Chinese from their Japanese translations. Sanetō Keishū, *Chūgokujin Nihon ryūgaku-shi* (A History of Chinese Students in Japan) (Tokyo, 1960), p. 283.

2. For example, concerning his exaggeration of the influence of his stay in London on the formation of his concept of mass welfare (*min-sheng chu-i*), see Hatano Yoshihiro, "Shoki ni okeru Son Bun no 'heikei chigen' ni tsuite" (Concerning Sun Yat-sen's Policy of Equal Land Rights in the Early Period), *Shakai keizai shigaku, 21:* 5,6 (1955), 479–502.

3. The most influential Christian Socialists at this time were Abe Isō, Katayama Sen, Kinoshita Naoe, and Nishikawa Kōjirō.

Christians the future Socialists had already alienated themselves from their background—they were nearly all Samurai—and from Japanese society. Thus in many ways the adoption of socialism was only one step more on their path of revolt.[4] All of the Japanese Christian Socialists appear to have been educated by low-church American missionaries, many of whom were concerned about the "social problem"—the problem of increasing poverty under capitalism—which appeared to contemporaries to be particularly severe in the United States during the last decades of the nineteenth century.[5] It was through their contact with American Christian reformers in either Japan or the United States, where many of them had studied, that the future Japanese Christian Socialists first came to be influenced by socialism.[6] They were introduced to four or five key books on socialism by American writers, who while not Socialists themselves were very sympathetic toward it. The most influential of these books were popular digests of socialism, treating the fundamentals of socialist belief but devoting more space to describing the actual Socialist politicians and parties.[7] The authors of these books consciously set out to be objective about the controversial topic of socialism, and to a large extent they succeeded. However, as they had a distinct bias toward socialism, they tended to emphasize what they considered to be its more favorable aspects: its altruistic and idealistic nature and the writers' opinion that many socialist leaders were less materialistic than they themselves supposed. The writers also played down the violence and class conflict in socialism, stating that these were the preserves of the anarchists. Generally their writings implied that a socialist world was inevitable but that it would come about through parliamentary means, and great portions of the books were devoted to demonstrating the steady increase of the Social Democratic parties

4. Cyril H. Powles, "Abe Isoo and the Role of Christians in the Founding of the Japanese Socialist Movement (1895–1905)," Harvard University, East Asian Research Center, *Papers on Japan, 1* (Cambridge, Mass., 1961), 89–130.

5. See for example the lectures on socialism given by the Reverend D. M. Learned at Dōshisha University, *Papers on Japan, 1*, 100.

6. Abe, Katayama, and Kawakami Kiyoshi all studied in the U.S.

7. The books were Richard Ely, *Socialism and Social Reform* (New York, 1894), and *French and German Socialism in Modern Times* (London, 1886); W. D. P. Bliss, *A Handbook of Socialism* (London, 1895); and *The Quintessence of Socialism,* the English translation of the Austrian economist A. Schläffle's detached but not unsympathetic study of socialism, *Die Quintessenz des Socialismus* (1st ed. Gotha, 1875; translated from the 8th ed. London, 1889). The only key book that was not a general survey was Edward Bellamy's novel, *Looking Backwards, 2000–1887* (Boston, 1888).

in both size and votes. These books and the ideas they expressed formed the basis of Japanese socialism, and through the Japanese they exerted a considerable influence on the Chinese variety.

The liberal strand of Japanese socialism was dominated by the brilliant journalist Kōtoku Shūsui. Kōtoku was steeped in the Japanese liberal tradition, and was deeply influenced by the struggle for a constitution and political rights in the 1880s. Thus he always had the deep concern with liberty which was later to lead him to anarchism. Kōtoku was converted to socialism by the same American books but his predilections, unlike those of the Christians, did not tally neatly with the Western authors. Although he was equally concerned with the immorality of existing society, as a materialist he did not shrink from violence and was therefore much more in accord with the Social Democrats themselves than with their religious apologists.

In the late 1890s Christian Socialists started labor agitation and trade unions, while Kōtoku and his colleagues began writing articles in support of Western socialism which gained widespread publicity.[8] At the same time Socialists and socialist sympathizers formed a series of study groups to discuss socialism in general and its possible application to Japan. In 1901 members of these groups decided to link up with the new trade unions and form the Social Democratic Party (Shakai minshutō) in the approved German manner. In retrospect the Meiji period seems to have been one of relative freedom, but the formation of a Socialist Party was too much for the government and it was banned on the day of its foundation.[9]

Despite references to it by Yen Fu and K'ang Yu-wei, it can safely be said that the introduction of Western socialism to China only began after 1902.[10] In that year Liang Ch'i-ch'ao and his

8. For a description of the early labor movement see H. Kublin, *Asian Revolutionary, the Life of Sen Katayama* (Princeton, 1964), pp. 105–28; and Kōsaka Masaaki, "Shisō genron," in *Meiji bunka shi* (Tokyo, 1955), *4*, trans. D. Abosch, *Japanese Thought in the Meiji Era,* in *Japanese Culture in the Meiji Era, 9* (Tokyo, 1958), 323–24.

9. Powles, p. 109; Kublin, *Sen Katayama*, pp. 146–49.

10. Yen Fu referred to the chün-fu tang (equalizing wealth parties) in *Yüan ch'iang*. See Benjamin Schwartz, *In Search of Wealth and Power* (Cambridge, Mass., 1964), p. 63. K'ang Yu-wei mentioned Mr. Fu (Fourier) and his communism (*kung-ch'an chih fa*) and another theory, the theory of joint equal ownership (*ho-ch'ün chün-ch'an chih shuo*). See K'ang, *Ta Tung Shu: The One World Philosophy of K'ang Yu-wei,* trans. L. G. Thompson (London, 1958), p. 211, and *Ta-t'ung shu,* edi-

reformist supporters founded a publishing house, the Kuang-chih shu-chü (Extension of Knowledge Book Company) in Shanghai, and a magazine, *Hsin-min ts'ung-pao* (New People's Miscellany), in Yokohama. In 1903 the Kuang-chih shu-chü brought out three books on socialism and in the same year two others were brought out by different publishers in Shanghai. All these books were translations of Japanese surveys of socialism which were themselves modeled after the American works mentioned above.[11] The books repeatedly emphasized the moderation and devotion to parliamentary means of the European Socialist parties and stressed the very real connection between the socialism and the political democracy of the Social Democrats. The books shared the belief expressed in the American works that nearly all the violence in the socialist movement was attributable to the Anarchists and Nihilists.

1903 was a boom year for the translation of books from Japanese into Chinese.[12] In the years that followed, the number of books published on all Western subjects fell drastically and until 1911 no further books on socialism appeared. However, articles on socialism continued to appear and increase in number after 1903. Many of these appeared in *Hsin-min ts'ung-pao* describing European

---

tion unspecified, p. 105, quoted by Jung Meng-yüan, "Hsin-hai ko-ming ch'ien Chung-kuo shu-k'an shang tui Ma-k'o-ssu chu-i ti chieh-shao," (The Introduction of Marxism in Chinese Publications Before the Revolution of 1911) *Hsin chien-she* (1953), no. 3, p. 7. As early as 1901 Liang Ch'i-ch'ao referred to K'ang's grand harmony (*ta-t'ung*) as socialism (*she-hui chu-i*) or communism (*kung-ch'an chih lun*). See *Yin-ping-shih wen-chi* (Taipei, 1960), *3*, ch. 6, 73.

11. The books were: (1) Fukui Junzō, *Kinsei shakaishugi* (Modern Socialism) (Tokyo, 1899), translated into Chinese by Chao Pi-chen under the title *Chin-shih she-hui chu-i*. For descriptions of this work see Li Chu, "Lun she-hui chu-i tsai Chung-kuo ti ch'uan-po" (On the Propagation of Socialism in China), *Li-shih yen-chiu* (1954), *3*, 3, and Jung Meng-yüan, p. 8. (2) Nishikawa Kōjirō, *Shakaitō* (The Socialist Party) (Tokyo, 1901), translated by Chou Pai-kao under the title *She-hui-tang*. There is a copy of the work in the library of the University of California at Berkeley. (3) Murai Chishi, *Shakai shugi* (Socialism) (Tokyo, 1899), translated by Lo Ta-wei under the title *She-hui chu-i*. Another translation of this work was brought out by the Wen-ming ch'u-pan-she in the same year; see Chang Ching-lu, *1*, 174. This publishing house was connected with the *I-shu hui-pien* (Collected Translations). T'an Pi-an (in "O-kuo min-tsui chu-i tui T'ung-meng-hui ti ying-hsiang" [The Influence of Russian Populism on the Revolutionary Alliance] *Li-shih yen-chiu* [1959], *1*, 36) says that the book was translated by Chang Chi, but this is unlikely. (4) Shimada Saburō, *Shakai shugi gaihyō* (General Critique of Socialism) (Tokyo, 1901) was brought out in translation as *She-hui chu-i kai-p'ing* by still another publishing house. There is a copy of this also at the University of California at Berkeley.

12. Sanetō, p. 544, chart.

socialism or its relation to China. From them one can gain a general understanding of the attitudes toward socialism held by Liang and his supporters during the years from 1902 to 1905. Liang clearly sympathized with the European Socialists; he was distressed by the Western "social problem" and believed that a socialist solution was not only just but almost unavoidable.[13] Liang was somewhat inconsistent on the question of whether the "social problem" would necessarily cause a violent social revolution; at times he stated that social revolutions were inevitable all over the Western world; at others he thought that they could be avoided in countries like Germany where there was not only a strong Socialist party but a government which itself practiced state socialism.[14] Viewed in this way socialism appeared to be not a force for revolution but a method of avoiding it through reform. This view was reinforced by the Japanese picture of socialism as a moderate nonviolent movement.

To Liang socialism, with its emphasis on social harmony and its devotion to the common good, seemed in many ways more sympathetic and less revolutionary than liberalism and social Darwinism, with their creeds of individual struggle and competition. Liang believed that socialism, as the equivalent to the traditional Chinese concepts of grand harmony (*ta-t'ung*) and the well-field system of land tenure (*ching-t'ien*), was suitable to the Chinese temperament and applicable to China.[15] Thus socialism appealed to the political reformers in many ways.

This did not mean that Liang thought the application of socialism in China was an urgent matter. In his eyes China's lack of industry meant that she had no class system and that the "social problem" had not yet arisen there. Therefore no immediate solution to it was necessary. For Liang, the political problem of reforming the government and the economic problem of building up industry were far more pressing, because China would need to solve them before she could effectively resist foreign domination. Liang's program was for political reform and the creation of industry to be followed by state socialist measures such as insurance for the workers and railway nationalization. Apart from their intrinsic

13. "Wai-tzu shu-ju wen-t'i" (The Problem of the Introduction of Foreign Capital), *HMTP, 3:* issues 4, 5,6, 8 (Sept.-Nov. 1904).

14. Ibid., p. 98.

15. See "Chung-kuo chih she-hui chu-i" (China's Socialism), *HMTP,* joint numbers 46–48 (Feb. 14, 1904), 302–03.

justice he believed that these measures would be advantageous because they would prevent the "social problem" from arising and thus check the danger of a social revolution. Liang's program did not go beyond state socialism but he was sympathetic to other socialists. Like them he believed that the final stage of world history would be one of "perfect socialism" or grand harmony. He only disagreed that it could be practiced immediately. He maintained that it would take centuries for it to be possible in Europe and even longer in China.[16]

While Chinese were absorbing the ideas of the Japanese Christian Socialists, changes were taking place within the Japanese socialist movement itself. After the suppression of the ephemeral Social Democratic Party, its members continued their old activities, agitation, lecturing, and above all journalism. Their main aim was to propagate socialism, but they also joined in agitation on the political problems of the day, adult suffrage, and the Russo-Japanese War. From 1903 to 1905 the Japanese Socialists united in opposing the war. Despite constant harassment from the police and very little response from the public, they published antimilitarist books and articles, carried on correspondence with Russian radicals, and gave hundreds of lectures and speeches against the war.[17]

In the midst of this activity, many Socialists, particularly those in the liberal or "political" wing of the movement, found time to enlarge their knowledge of Western socialism. More translations of Western works appeared, and men like Kōtoku began to understand and accept such Marxist concepts as economic determinism and the idea of class conflict as the mainspring of history.[18]

When the war ended in September 1905, the challenge which had united the movement was removed. Almost immediately there was a split between its political and Christian wings, each founding its own journal.[19] However, early in 1906 the new Saionji government came to power and passed a bill allowing limited freedom of association. The political faction of the Socialists immediately took advantage of the situation: they came to a compromise with

16. "Wai-tzu-shu-ju wen-t'i," *HMTP, 8* (1904), 13.

17. Kublin, "The Japanese Socialists and the Russo-Japanese War," *Journal of Modern History*, 22 (1950), 322–40.

18. Kublin, *Sen Katayama*, p. 154, and Kosaka, pp. 342–54.

19. The Christian journal was called *Shinkigen* (New Era) and the more political one *Hikari* (*The Light*).

some of the Christians, and together they formed a new party which they called the Japanese Socialist Party.[20]

Sun Yat-sen first became aware of the Western "social problem" during his stay in England in 1896–97.[21] There for the first time he realized that even in a powerful country with political freedom the people were not prosperous or contented. His impressions of the West led him to the conclusion that the radicals who said that a social revolution was inevitable were correct, but he thought this was only true in the advanced West, and that in underdeveloped China it was still possible to prevent the injustice of the class system and the catastrophe of a violent social revolution. If China could have a bloodless social revolution at the same time as her political revolution she could avoid the mistakes of the West and become a modern industrial nation without creating a "social problem."[22] Thus the main aim of Sun's social policies at this stage was not the reform of existing Chinese society, but the prevention of future disaster.

Sun found what he thought was the way to achieve this aim in a group of theories which were widely prevalent at the turn of the century, especially in English-speaking countries. These theories belonged to two related schools of thought known as "single tax" and "land nationalization."[23] From 1897 onward Sun accepted ideas from both these schools. At first he seems to have favored land nationalization, but during the years from 1902 to 1905 he

20. Kublin refers to this as the Nihon shakaitō; however the members themselves used the more nationalistic form Nippon. See the English column of *Hikari, 1:* 11 (April 20, 1906). I have used the reprint of *Hikari* in the series *Meiji shakaishugi shiryō shū,* ed. Ōkochi Kazuo and others (8 vols. Tokyo, 1960–62, 1st printing), p. 83.

21. The purpose of Sun's exaggeration of the length of time he spent in England would seem to be that he wished to stress the amount of knowledge that he received from the West and to minimize the amount gained from his stays in Japan.

22. It is unlikely that Sun fully developed this last theory before 1905. The concept of simultaneous "political" and "social" (capitalist and socialist) revolutions probably came from the example of the 1905 Revolution in Russia, which was seen by many in these terms. See for example Lenin, "Lecture on the 1905 Revolution," *Selected Works* (12 vols. London, 1936), *3,* 3. I can find no evidence that Sun expounded this theory before February 1905.

23. See G. D. H. Cole, *A History of Socialist Thought* (London, 1954), *2,* 370–74 and 383–84. Harold Schiffrin, "Sun Yat-sen's Early Land Policy," *JAS, 16* (1957), 557–61, and Wang Te-chao, "T'ung-meng-hui shih-ch'i Sun Chung-shan hsien-sheng ko-ming ssu-hsiang ti fen-hsi yen-chiu" (An Analytical Study of Sun Yat-sen's Revolutionary Thought During the Revolutionary Alliance Period), *CHS ts'ung-k'an, 1,* 261–66.

became increasingly attracted to the theory of single tax: all rent on site value should go to the state, and other forms of taxation should be abolished. Throughout his life Sun acknowledged his debt to Henry George, the most famous Single Taxer, but evidence from Sun's statements at the time shows that even after 1902 he greatly modified Henry George's ideas or derived his own from other thinkers.[24]

After its introduction in 1902 Sun's policy of Equal Land Rights (*p'ing-chün ti-ch'üan*) became one of the four planks of the platform of the Society to Restore China's Prosperity.[25] The term "mass welfare" (*min-sheng chu-i*) first appeared in the Introduction to *Min-pao* (People's Report) in November 1905, and both of these concepts were promoted by Sun in the Revolutionary Alliance.

Usually Sun preferred talking in generalities, but in a speech in December 1906, he gave some indication of the specific policies he had in mind. These, though similar to those of Henry George, were closer to those of John Stuart Mill and some other economists. Sun urged that all land prices be fixed immediately after the political revolution, and that landowners pay to the government any increase in the value of their property brought about by the advance of civilization—the growth of towns and the extension of railways. He maintained that with a rapidly developing economy this sum alone would provide sufficient revenue for the state and all other taxes could be abolished.[26]

Sun published no further details of his proposals for another five years, and the picture of his social policies was even more blurred by the slightly different proposals put forward by other party spokesmen in their articles. Most of these articles were written by men with ideas of their own, some of which will be dealt with later. However an article written by Hu Han-min in May 1906 probably reflects Sun's views; Hu was an intimate friend of Sun, and at the early stage of their acquaintance Hu's concepts of the principles of mass welfare and socialism were derived entirely from Sun.[27] In

24. Schiffrin, p. 560; Wang, p. 165.

25. The standard date given for the introduction of the policy is the summer of 1903, at the foundation of the School for Revolutionary Soldiers (Ko-ming chün-shih hsüeh-hsiao). See Feng, *I-shih* (5 vols. Chungking, 1945), *3*, 205–06. I see no reason to doubt Jung Meng-yüan's statement that it was first used at the foundation of the branch of the Society to Restore China's Prosperity in Vietnam in 1902; Jung, p. 10.

26. Section on mass welfare (*min-sheng chu-i*) in Sun's speech in *Min-pao, 10,* 89–95.

27. "Hu Han-min tzu-chuan" (Autobiography of Hu Han-min), *KMWH, 3,* 386. Hu clearly stated that before he met Sun he knew nothing about socialism.

his article Hu proposed land nationalization (*t'u-ti kuo-yu*), a system under which the government would rent land for money to people prepared to cultivate it.[28] This proposal, as the opponents of the Revolutionary Alliance quickly pointed out, appeared to contradict Sun's plan, which was merely to tax the increase of land values.[29] The two proposals were later reconciled and made to fit into one scheme by Chu Chih-hsin.[30] But it seems unlikely that Sun had any such master plan; probably the two were simply different points on the range of opinions held by him at the time.

Hu Han-min's article also described the position of mass welfare within socialism. He said that the Revolutionary Alliance's policy was land nationalization, which was in turn part of collectivism (*chi-ch'üan chu-i*), that is, social democracy as opposed to anarcho-communism (*kung-ch'an chu-i*).[31]

Sun's sympathy with Western socialism, unlike that of Liang Ch'i-ch'ao, did not extend to state socialism. He firmly believed in the connection between democracy and socialism. The socialism of the Prussian monarchy was to him only a trick to deceive the workers and to delay though it could not prevent social revolution.[32] Although Sun wanted to minimize violence in China, as a revolutionary himself he could not share Liang's absolute horror of social revolution. For Sun there was no incompatibility between the high moral sense of the Western Socialists and their work for revolution. Sun had no hesitation in identifying the Revolutionary Alliance with the world socialist movement. He simply looked upon mass welfare as the form of socialism suitable for China. During 1905 and 1906 the unity of the two was so obvious to Sun that he and the other party spokesmen used the two words *min-sheng chu-i* (mass welfare) and *she-hui chu-i* (socialism) interchangeably.[33] *Min-sheng* was a traditional term denoting the government's responsibility to maintain standards of living,

28. "*Min-pao* chih liu ta chu-i" (The Six Great Principles of *Min-pao*), *Min-pao, 3,* 12–14.

29. Liang Ch'i-ch'ao, "She-hui ko-ming kuo wei chin-jih Chung-kuo so pi-yao hu?" (Is a Social Revolution Really Necessary in China Today?), *HMTP,* no. 86; reprinted in *SLHC* (2 vols. with two sections each, Peking, 1962–1963), *2,* section 1, 346–47.

30. Chu Chih-hsin, "T'u-ti kuo-yu yü ts'ai-cheng" (Land Nationalization and Finance), part 2, *Min-pao, 16,* 34–35.

31. Hu Han-min, "*Min-pao* chih liu ta chu-i," p. 11.

32. Hu specifically attacked the use of social policies by constitutional countries that have not yet forgotten autocracy. "*Min-pao* chih liu ta chu-i," p. 13.

33. Robert Scalapino and Harold Schiffrin, "Early Socialist Currents in the Chinese Revolutionary Movement," *JAS, 18* (1959), 334.

but euphony seems to have been the chief reason why Sun created the new term *min-sheng chu-i*. It was simply that it fitted more easily with nationalism (*min-tsu chu-i*) and democracy (*min-ch'üan chu-i*).

JAPANESE SOCIALISM FROM FEBRUARY TO JUNE 1906

For the members of the newly founded Japanese Socialist Party, the spring and early summer of 1906 was a period of optimism. As well as instituting such state socialist policies as railway nationalization, the new Saionji government appeared to be susceptible to popular pressure and for the first time it seemed possible for a Social Democratic party of the approved Western pattern to function in Japan. The first article of the new party's constitution clearly illustrated its nonrevolutionary nature—"Our party advocates socialism within the limits of the law."[34] To the party leaders Sakai Toshihiko, Nishikawa Kōjirō, and Katayama Sen, the most important immediate task was the campaign for adult suffrage as prerequisite to social democracy, and a considerable amount of the party's energy went into this cause.[35] Party members also worked for the alleviation of immediate economic difficulties. They agitated on behalf of the vast number of unemployed thrown out of work by the postwar depression; their most striking action was a mass demonstration organized in March against a proposed rise in tram fares which succeeded in keeping them down. On the whole, however, the party did not show much activity during the first year of its existence.[36]

Nevertheless, the Socialist leaders were not idle. In 1906 a large number of translations were made from Western languages, and Japanese knowledge of socialism increased proportionately.[37] Many of the translations appeared in *Shakai-shugi kenkyū* (*The Study of Socialism*), a new theoretical magazine which was founded in March.[38] The magazine was modeled on the English *Social Democrat* and the following list of articles in its first issue shows

34. *Hikari*, reprint cited above (n. 20), p. 64.

35. *Hikari*, reprint, pp. 7, 23, 42, 49, 57, 203, 226, 233, 241, 249.

36. Kublin, *Sen Katayama*, p. 193.

37. See the bibliography of books on socialism by Shimoide Hayakichi in *Meiji bunka zenshū, 21* (Tokyo, 1928), 603–22, and Shioda Shōbei and Watanabe Yoshimichi, *Nihon shakaishugi bunken kaisetsu* (Explanation of Japanese Books on Socialism) (Tokyo, 1958).

38. This magazine has also been reprinted in the series Ōkochi Kazuo, ed., *Meiji shakaishugi shiryō shū*.

that its political leanings were much the same: "The Communist Manifesto," "Life of Marx" by Liebknecht, "Life of Engels" by Kautsky, and "A Short History of International Socialist Congress" (sic).[39] On the other hand later issues contained articles on Kropotkin and anarcho-communism, and it is clear that these reflected an interest in the subject probably caused by the Russian Revolution of 1905. However the editor, Sakai Toshihiko, balanced articles sympathetic to Kropotkin with "objective" descriptions of anarchism by authors in favor of social democracy who regarded anarchism as impracticable and dangerous.[40] The first issue of *The Study of Socialism* also published a list of books on socialism available in Japanese, and this too showed the great strength of Social Democratic influence: over twenty-five books sympathetic to social democracy and social reform, but only two concerned with anarchism and nihilism.[41]

Russian populism was not considered worthy of serious theoretical study, and although *Hikari* (*The Light*) published fairly frequent reports of events in Russia, including the spectacular activities of the neopopulist Social Revolutionaries in the continuing revolution in Russia, even these reports had a Western Social Democratic slant.[42] A considerable number of articles ostensibly about the Russian situation were in fact concerned with Western demonstrations of sympathy for the revolutionaries.[43] The journal also gave a good deal of space to analyses of the situation by such Marxist leaders as Kautsky.[44]

In April 1906 *Hikari* published in its English column a description of the situation of Japanese socialism:

> There are three schools so to speak of Japanese Socialism. The first is the Nippon Shakwito [sic] Japanese Socialist party to which we belong. The second is a school of Christian Socialism . . . They are also Social-Democrats. Only they strive

39. The first was a slightly abridged version of the translation by Kōtoku and Ōsugi Sakae, which had been banned by the Katsura government in 1904. See the introduction by Shioda Shōbei to the journal *Shakai-shugi kenkyū* (March 1906), p. vii. The other articles were translated by Shizuno Matao, Sakai Toshihiko, and Ōsugi respectively.

40. See *Shakai-shugi kenkyū,* reprint, no. 2, where the writings of Kropotkin are followed by those of W. D. P. Bliss.

41. *Shakai-shugi kenkyū,* reprint, no. 1, pp. 85–87.

42. See for example *Hikari,* reprint, p. 47.

43. Ibid., pp. 39 and 55.

44. Ibid., p. 60.

> to develop the spiritual side of Socialism. The third is the Kokka Shakwaito State Socialist party. Mr. Yamaji is its leader. He is also a scientific socialist.[45]

There was no mention of any anarchist or populist faction. Thus in June 1906 the Japanese socialist movement appeared to be overwhelmingly dominated by Marxist "scientific socialism" and social democracy. However all was not still beneath the surface and many Japanese radicals were already being stirred by the Russian Revolution and the possibilities it seemed to offer of reaching socialism without going through the slow processes thought necessary by Marx and Lassalle.

The Socialism of the Min-pao Group

Chinese intellectuals appear to have shown a deeper interest in social democracy and Marxism during the eight months from November 1905 to June 1906 than at any time until the 1920s. Over ten articles directly or indirectly concerned with Western socialism appeared in the five issues of *Min-pao* (People's Report) during these months. Of these Hu Han-min's article mentioned above and the translation of a short passage from Henry George were commissioned by Sun Yat-sen or at least reflected his point of view.[46]

It is also clear that Sun's advocacy of mass welfare as a type of socialism suitable to China was a very important factor behind the revolutionaries' interest in socialism in general. There were however other factors involved. Two of the *Min-pao* articles were by Miyazaki Tamizō. One of these was the program of his Society for the Restoration of Land Rights (Tochi fukken dōshikai), whose policy was land nationalization: land should be available to anyone who wanted it, so that the industrial workers would not be completely dependent on the employers.[47] The other was a survey of the different currents of socialism from the same point of view.[48] It is probable that Miyazaki and his younger brother Torazō had an even greater effect on the Chinese students through

45. Ibid., p. 83.

46. Feng, *I-shih, 3,* 216.

47. Miyazaki Tamizō, "T'u-ti fu-ch'üan t'ung-chih hui chu-i shu," *Min-pao,* reprint, 2, correspondence section (*Lai-kao*), 2–5.

48. Miyazaki using the pen name Junkō, "Ou-Mei she-hui ko-ming yün-tung chih chung-lei chi p'ing-lun" (Forms and Criticisms of the Western Social-Revolutionary Movement), *Min-pao, 4,* 123–33.

personal contact. On New Year's Day 1906, Sung Chiao-jen wrote in his diary:

> Fine; got up early, ate and drank with Chang Chi, Ho Hsiao-liu, and T'ien Tzu-ch'in [T'ien T'ung]. At ten we all went to Miyazaki Tōten's [Miyazaki Torazō] house to wish him happy new year. Saw Tōten's elder brother Miyazaki Tamizō, the Japanese socialist. We talked for a long time and left at one.[49]

This is only one of many similar entries.[50] However the Miyazakis were not in the mainstream of Japanese socialism and there is no reason to suppose that at that time the Chinese students had any direct contact with it.[51] This does not mean that the Japanese socialist movement and its interest in social democracy had no influence on Revolutionary Alliance leaders.

In May 1906 *Hikari* welcomed the founding of "Minpo" (*Min-pao*).[52] It is probable that this belated recognition was due to Sung Chiao-jen, who noted in his diary on the 15th of April: "Wrote a letter to the *Heiminsha,* the organ of the Japanese Socialist Party, asking whether they had *Heimin shimbun* or *Chokugen* and whether they would like to exchange them for *Min-pao.*"[53] Sung's request illustrates both his interest in the Japanese Socialists and his lack of contact with them: *Heimin shimbun* had been closed for seventeen months and *Chokugen* had been prohibited the previous October. However we know from Sung's diary that he read articles on socialism in both socialist and bourgeois journals. In April 1906 he read the first issue of *Shakai-shugi kenkyū* (*The Study of Socialism*) and made a translation of one of its articles, "Bankoku shakaitō taikai ryakushi" (Brief History of the Socialist International), which was published in the fifth issue of *Min-pao.*[54] The article was a history of the Second International from 1877 to the Sixth Congress at Amsterdam in 1904, giving lists of the different delegations present and summaries of the resolutions passed. Although the compiler, Ōsugi Sakae, later became an An-

49. Sung Chiao-jen, *Wo-chih li-shih* (My Diary), reprinted in *CHS ts'ung-k'an,* 1st collection (Taipei, 1962), p. 89.

50. Ibid., pp. 95 and 129.

51. For the socialists' view of Miyazaki Tamizō as an eccentric see *Shakai-shugi kenkyū,* 2, 151.

52. *Hikari,* reprint, p. 91.

53. Sung Chiao-jen, p. 141.

54. Ibid., p. 138.

archist, the article was written from an impeccably social democratic standpoint.

Another Chinese interested in socialism at this period was Feng Tzu-yu. In December 1905 Feng published an article in *Chung-kuo jih-pao* (China Daily News) entitled "She-hui chu-i yü Chung-kuo cheng-chih chih ch'ien-t'u" (Socialism and China's Future Political Path). Months later, in the spring of 1906 he changed the word socialism (*she-hui chu-i*) to mass welfare (*min-sheng chu-i*) and the piece was reprinted in the fourth issue of *Min-pao*.[55] Fundamentally the article was an attempted synthesis by Feng of his picture of Western socialism with his understanding of Sun's economic program. Feng followed Sun closely on many points, such as the timing of the social revolution to coincide with the political one and his emphasis on the land question.[56] However, in his analysis of Western socialism he was closer to Liang Ch'i-ch'ao than to Sun, admiring the state socialism of Germany and Japan even more than their Social Democratic parties.[57] On the other hand, Feng's views on the application of socialism in China were more radical than those expressed by Sun at that time. He proposed that "postal services, land, electricity, railways, banks, steamship lines, tobacco, sugar, and all rights affecting the public interest should be nationalized."[58]

Sun himself did not mention the public ownership of any industry until after 1911. However it would probably be safe to believe Hu Han-min when he said in 1907 that Sun's conception of mass welfare involved the nationalization of all "natural monopolies"—a term that conventionally covered many but not all of the items mentioned above.[59] Feng was also more radical than Sun in his land policy. He followed Henry George in saying that all rent from land should go to the state, and not merely the increase in rent as proposed by Sun.[60]

Chu Chih-hsin was another writer who tried to reconcile his concept of orthodox Western socialism to Sun's social policies. In the first five issues of *Min-pao* he wrote five articles, some concerned

55. Scalapino and Schiffrin (pp. 326–29) give an excellent summary of this article.

56. Feng, "Min-sheng chu-i yü Chung-kuo cheng-chih chih ch'ien-t'u" (Mass Welfare and China's Future Political Path), *Min-pao, 4,* 109, 110.

57. Ibid., pp. 98, 109.

58. Ibid., p. 109.

59. Hu Han-min, "Kao fei-nan min-sheng chu-i che" (To the Traducers of Mass Welfare), *Min-pao, 12,* 100.

60. Feng, "Min-sheng chu-i," p. 110.

simply with Western social democracy and others with its application to China.[61] In the first category there were detailed and sympathetic biographies of Marx and Lassalle, and an intelligent assessment of the prospects of the British Labor Party after its successes in the election of 1906. In these pieces Chu showed that he was closer to the Japanese Socialists than to Sun in his analysis of the European situation, believing that violent social revolution was not inevitable in the West and that socialism would triumph there through parliamentary means. This did not make him disagree with Sun's advocacy of simultaneous political and social revolutions in China. Indeed, Chu's most brilliant and original article was written to justify this policy.[62] He also agreed with Sun's belief that in China the social revolution would be more a preventative than a cure.[63] However, although Chu paid lip service to the importance of land nationalization, his chief interest was in the public ownership of industry.[64]

Chu was in fact as near as a Chinese could ever be to being an orthodox Socialist of the Second International. As such he was very much opposed to anarcho-communism and other forms of "unscientific socialism."

> Formerly there were people who rejected socialism, but what they rejected was not modern socialism but pure communism. When people say that this cannot be practiced today I cannot contradict them. Now since Marx all the theories have been changed and are gradually being put into effect, and few scholars can absolutely denounce what is generally known as "scientific socialism" [English in the original], only our opponents do not know this. What our group pro-

61. The articles were: "Te-i-chih she-hui ko-ming-chia hsiao-chuan" (Short Biographies of German Social Revolutionaries), hereafter cited as "Hsiao-chuan," part 1, Marx, *Min-pao, 2,* 1–18, part 2, Lassalle, *Min-pao, 3,* 1–19; "Ying-kuo hsin tsung-hsüan-chü lao-tung-che chih chin-pu" (The Progress of the Workers in the Recent British General Election), *Min-pao, 3,* sect. 6–10; "Ts'ung she-hui chu-i lun t'ieh-tao kuo-yu chi Chung-kuo t'ieh-tao chih kuan-pan ssu-pan" (Discussion from a Socialist Point of View of Railway Nationalization and Official and Private Management of China's Railways), *Min-pao, 4,* 45–56; "She-hui ko-ming yü cheng-chih ko-ming ping-hsing" (That the Social and Political Revolutions Be Carried Out Together), *Min-pao, 5,* 43–66.

62. Scalapino and Schiffrin have summarized this article on pp. 329–33 of their article.

63. Chu Chih-hsin, "Ko-ming ping-hsing," p. 49.

64. Ibid., p. 63.

pose is state socialism, a principle not at all difficult to practice.[65]

If Chu thought himself a "scientific socialist," what did he mean by the term? His articles show that he had a moderately good grasp of Marxist theory. He understood and accepted such Marxist concepts as surplus value, economic determinism, class analysis, and the role of class conflict in history. It is even more interesting to note the points he understood but could not accept, either because the Japanese Socialists had objected to them or through his own independent judgment. Chu agreed that the proletariat would lead the social revolution, but he felt obliged to use his own term *hsi-min* for proletarian, because the term commoner, *p'ing-min,* included many of the rich and the word laborer, *lao-tung-che,* excluded the peasants; "therefore one cannot say it is suitable [for China]."[66] Chu also disagreed with Marx's view that "all capital is plunder." While he admitted that the modern Western capitalists accumulated their fortunes by exploiting the workers—according to the law of surplus value—he believed that it was possible for small businessmen to accumulate capital through their own efforts.[67]

Thus Chu believed that the peasants should take part in the social revolution, and implied that the petty bourgeoisie need not be its enemy, an interesting anticipation of Leninism and Maoism. Through their vagueness and inconsistency, the articles on the social policies of the Revolutionary Alliance by Sun and Hu Han-min must have caused considerable confusion. The articles by Miyazaki, Feng, Chu, and others can only have increased the bewilderment of anyone trying to discover the precise meaning of the party's social policies. On the other hand these articles greatly increased the Chinese students' knowledge of Western socialism. They also show the pervading influence of Marxist social democracy in Revolutionary Alliance circles at the time.

Japanese Knowledge of Anarchism and Nihilism Before June 1906

Information on Russian narodism (populism) and nihilist terrorism became available in Japan within months of its reaching

65. Ibid., p. 45.
66. Ibid., p. 53.
67. Chu Chih-hsin, "Hsiao-chuan," part 1, pp. 14–15.

the West. In 1882 and 1883, years of great terrorist activity in Russia, several books on the Nihilists were published in Japan. These books, all of which appear to have been based on works available in English and French, included translations of such vivid and sympathetic accounts of the revolutionaries as Stepniak's *Underground Russia.*[68] It would be difficult to say how much immediate impact these books had on Japan. The early 1880s, the era of the Popular Rights Movement, were years of violent political struggle, and some contemporary commentators saw the influence of Russian Nihilists in the activities of radical supporters of the Liberal Party.[69] Kōtoku Shūsui maintained that Russian nihilism was influential in the foundation in 1882 of the Eastern Socialist Party.[70] This small and ephemeral party was more radical than the Liberal Party but like the Russian terrorists of the time its radicalism was more political than economic. As the Anarchist Kōtoku approvingly pointed out, the Eastern Socialist Party had a clearly antiauthoritarian bent; it was to have no leaders and no headquarters. Kōtoku believed that it was the "unscientific" pioneer of Japanese socialism, taking very much the same stand as Fourier and Weitling in the French and German movements.[71]

The late 1880s and the 1890s were years of relative social calm in both Russia and Japan. No books on Russian nihilism appear to have been published in Japan between 1884 and 1902. As we have seen, the Japanese Socialist movement, which grew up at the same time as the Russian Social Democratic Party in the late 1890s, was very hostile to anarchism and terrorism. There is no reason to doubt the sincerity of the Declaration of the Japanese Social Democratic Party in 1901 when it stated: "It is only the Nihilist and the Anarchist who brandish a sword and throw bombs. Since our Social-Democratic Party resolutely opposes the use of force, we

68. This was published under the title *Kyōmutō jitsu denkiki shu shu* (Tokyo, 1883), trans. Miyazaki Muryū. The other books were *Rokoku kyōmutō ji ji* (Facts About the Russian Nihilists) (Tokyo, 1882), trans. Nishikawa Michitetsu. There was also a report of Vera Zasulich's assassination of General Trepov: *Rokoku kibun retsujo no gigaku* (Tokyo, 1882), trans. Somayama Sakutarō, and *Kyōmutō taiji kidan* (Tokyo, 1882), trans. Kawajima Todanosuke from P. Vernier's *La Chasse aux Nihilistes.* See Shimoide Hayakichi and Watanabe Yoshimichi and Shioda Shōbei.

S. Stepniak was the pen name of Serghei Kravchinsky.

69. See quotation in R. A. Scalapino, *Democracy and the Party Movement in Pre-War Japan* (Berkeley, 1953), p. 77.

70. Kōtoku Shūsui and Ishikawa Kyokusan, *Nippon shakaishugi shi* (History of Japanese Socialism) (Tokyo, 1908), reprinted in *Meiji bunka zenshū, 21,* 339.

71. Ibid., p. 338.

will never imitate the foolishness of the Nihilist and Anarchist Parties."[72]

From 1902 to 1904, however, a number of books were published on anarchism, a word that was beginning to replace nihilism and terrorism as the term for revolutionary assassination. The indiscriminate use of these three words by popular writers in every country later had a great effect on Japanese and Chinese radicals who, impressed by nihilist or populist terrorism, turned toward anarchism, which they assumed to be very much the same. The most influential of the new books was *Kinsei museifu shugi* (Modern Anarchism) by Kemuyama Sentarō, a teacher at Waseda University and a journalist specializing in Russian affairs.[73] Most of the book was not about anarchism but was a general history of the Russian revolutionary movement. It described the Decembrists, the Russian Hegelians, the Nihilists, the movement "to the people," and the assassinations of "Narodnia Volia" (The Will of the People). Russian revolutionary history and, by implication, world revolutionary history were divided up into three periods—revolutionary literature; propaganda and agitation; assassination and terror—a scheme that was later to have great influence on the Chinese revolutionaries. The book also contained details of the organization of assassination groups, factories for making explosives, and secret presses. However, influential though this book was, it was offset by the dozens that appeared on social democracy. Until the end of 1904 the Japanese Socialists were almost exclusively interested in German rather than Russian socialism.

In 1904 the Russo-Japanese War focused Japanese attention on Russia. Katayama Sen's handshake with Plekhanov at the meeting of the Second International in Amsterdam and an exchange of letters between *Heimin shimbun* and the Russian journal *Iskra* brought the Japanese Socialists into direct contact with the Russian Social Democrats, linking them in opposition to the militarism of their governments. Despite the cordiality of the correspondence there was an interesting and significant difference

72. Nobutaka Ike, "Kōtoku: Advocate of Direct Action," *JAS, 3* (1944), 227.

73. Among the other books were: *Museifutō no ichiya* (Night of the Anarchists) (Tokyo, 1903) translated by Hara Hoichian from a short story by Sir Arthur Conan Doyle which I have been unable to trace; *Kyōmutō* (The Nihilists) (Tokyo, 1904), a novel by Tsukahara Shibukakizono; and *Kyōmutō no kidan* (Strange Tales of the Nihilists) (Tokyo, 1904) by Matsui Matsuba.

between *Heimin shimbun* and *Iskra,* which was then under Menshevik control.[74] Kōtoku and Sakai Toshihiko wrote:

> We are neither Nihilists nor Terrorists but Social Democrats and are always fighting for peace. We object absolutely to using military force in our fighting. We have to fight by peaceful means; by reason and speech. It may be very difficult for you to fight with speech and produce revolution by peaceful means in Russia, where there is no constitution, and consequently you may be tempted to overthrow the government by force. But those who are fighting for humanity must remember that the end does not justify the means.[75]

The condescension in this letter may have come from a feeling held even by antimilitarist Japanese, that Japan's victories in Manchuria had proved that the country was more civilized and advanced than Russia. It is hardly surprising that the editors of *Iskra* rejected both the tone and the content of this part of the letter:

> Force against force, violence against violence! And in saying this we speak as neither Nihilists nor Terrorists. . . . Against Terrorism as an improper method of action we have never since the establishment of the Russian Social-Democratic Party ceased to fight. But regrettable as it may be, the ruling classes have never submitted to the forces of reason, and we have not the slightest ground for believing that they ever will.

However they did not want "this question of secondary importance" to obscure "the feeling of solidarity which the Japanese comrades have expressed in their message."[76]

The immediate Japanese comment on the Russian reply appeared to overlook the general challenge to their policy of moderation and gradualism. It treated *Iskra's* position simply as an unfor-

74. Cole, *A History of Socialist Thought, 3,* part 2, 935, and Kublin, *Sen Katayama,* p. 239, are mistaken when they say that Lenin may have written the reply. March 1904 is the earliest month in which it could have been written, by which time Plekhanov had brought back Martov and the other Mensheviks and Lenin had resigned from the editorial board. See I. Deutscher, *The Prophet Armed: Trotsky, 1879–1921* (London, 1954), p. 86, and T. Dan, *The Origins of Bolshevism* (London, 1964), p. 248. It is possible however that it was written by Trotsky.

75. *Heimin shimbun* (Proletarian News) (March 20, 1904), p. 1, English column reprinted in *Meiji shakaishugi shiryō shū,* 2nd series, *3,* 155.

76. *Heimin shimbun* (July 31, 1904), *4,* 1. English Column, *4,* 307.

tunate result of the peculiar Russian situation. "On reading this we deeply love and respect the spirit of the Russian Socialist Party. However, regarding our advice concerning the use of violence, we see that they still say that it is a situation where they cannot avoid force. We profoundly hate the Russian situation."[77] There seems to have been no further discussion in *Heimin shimbun* of this aspect of the correspondence. Like socialists in many other countries they continued to imagine that the Russian Social Democrats were relatively orthodox members of the International. This belief was reinforced by the resolution on violence passed by the First Congress of the Russian Social Democratic Labor Party in 1898, which Kōtoku quoted in *Heimin shimbun's* successor, *Chokugen.*[78] The resolution stated that the time was not yet ripe for organized violence. Thus the Japanese Socialists were able to accept the convenient conceptual dichotomy between social democratic moderation and anarchist and nihilist violence.[79]

Chinese Interest in Anarchism and Nihilism Before 1906

1903 seems to have been the year in which the word anarchism (*wu-cheng-fu chu-i*) was first used in China. At least one article was published describing the feats of the Western Anarchist assassins in favorable terms.[80] Also in that year a pamphlet appeared which its translator Chang Chi (Chang P'u-ch'üan) entitled *Wu-cheng-fu chu-i* (Anarchism).[81] The pamphlet, a description of

77. *Heimin shimbun* (July 24, 1904), *4*, 303.

78. *Chokugen* (Speak Out!) (February 19, 1905), pp. 1, 17.

79. Tanaka Sogorō, *Kōtoku Shūsui, ichi kakumeika no shisō to shōgai* (Kōtoku Shūsui, the Thought and Career of a Revolutionary) (Tokyo, 1955), p. 261, points out that Kōtoku and the other Japanese socialists did not see the importance of the Bolsheviks in the Revolution of 1905 and overestimated the role of the Social Revolutionaries. Although the pendulum has swung rather far in the opposite direction since 1917, Tanaka's point is valid not only for Japan but for the whole contemporary world, where the sensational activities of the S.R.'s were much more fully reported than the more solid work of the Bolsheviks and Mensheviks.

80. Su Man-shu under the pen name Tzu-ku, "Nü-chieh Kuo-erh-man" (The Heroine [Emma] Goldman), *Kuo-min jih-jih pao* (October 7/8, 1903). This revolutionary journal has been reissued in the series *Chung-kuo shih-hsüeh ts'ung-shu,* ed. Wu Hsiang-hsiang, *19* (Taipei, 1965), 330–31, 340–41. Parts of the article are quoted by Henry McAleavy, *Su Man-shu (1884–1918): A Sino-Japanese Genius* (London, 1960), p. 7.

81. This pamphlet is generally supposed to have been a translation of Enrico Malatesta's *Anarchia,* a pamphlet first published in August 1896. See Chang Ching-lu, n. 1, p. 174. Chang Ching-lu's evidence for this attribution seems to be: (1) that advertisements for a pamphlet by Chang Chi called *Wu-cheng-fu chu-i* (Anarchism) opened with a quotation from Malatesta. See *Chung-kuo pai-hua pao* (Chinese Vernacular

Western European anarchism, was part of the wave of translations that appeared during this year.[82] Many of the full-length books on socialism published at this time included passages on anarchism. But as they were written from a Social Democratic or Christian Socialist point of view they were extremely hostile, and the few pieces in favor of anarchism were greatly outnumbered by those written against it.

However, this lack of sympathy was restricted to Western anarchism. In the three years from 1902 to 1904 there was considerable interest in and support of Russian nihilism (*hsü-wu chu-i*). Numerous works touched on the subject and three books were specifically written about it. The most influential of these was a translation by Chin I (Chin Sung-ts'en) of Kemuyama Sentarō's *Kinsei museifu shugi* (Modern Anarchism), which appeared in 1904 as *Wu-cheng-fu chu-i* (Anarchism) but was better known under its later title of *Tzu-yu hsüeh* (Freedom's Blood).[83] Nearly all of these works in Chinese deplored the Russian autocracy and expressed sympathy with the terrorism of the Nihilists. However, there was no such general support for Nihilist goals if only because the writers were very confused as to whether the Nihilists were Communists and Anarchists or simply political revolutionaries. Liang Ch'i-ch'ao, for instance, who at that time thought that they advocated communist egalitarianism (*kung-ch'an chün-fu chu-i*), wrote, "The methods of nihilism receive my respect, but I cannot support their

---

Paper), no. 1 (December 1903), advertisement section, p. 2; and (2) that Chang Chi did at some stage translate Malatesta's pamphlet. However a summary of Chang Chi's pamphlet in an advertisement in *Min-pao, 10* (December 1906) lists contents totally different from those of Malatesta's original. Furthermore Chang Chi says in his memoirs that he translated Kōtoku's Japanese version of Malatesta in 1907; see "Hui-i-lu" (Memoirs) in *Chang P'u-ch'üan hsien-sheng ch'üan-chi* (Complete Works of Chang Chi) (2 vols. Taipei, 1951–52), *1*, 236. This seems likely, as Chang's only foreign language was Japanese, and Kōtoku's translation, the first in Japanese, only came out in 1907 or 1908. Thus it would appear that Chang translated a Japanese survey of anarchism in 1903 and Malatesta's pamphlet in 1907. Chang Ping-lin's introduction, written in January 1908, was for the second pamphlet, *Min-pao, 20,* p. 129.

82. See chart, Sanetō, p. 544.

83. The other works were: Tu-li chih ko-jen (pen name "Independent Individual") trans., *O-lo-ssu ta feng-ch'ao* (Great Tide in Russia) (1902), which may be a chapter of T. Kirkup's *History of Socialism* (1st ed. London, 1892). See Chang Ching-lu, p. 179, and *Hsü-wu-tang* (The Nihilists), which was written or translated by Ch'en Leng-hsüeh in 1904. Three important articles on the subject were: Liang Ch'i-ch'ao, "Lun O-lo-ssu hsü-wu tang" (Discussion on the Russian Nihilists), *HMTP, 40* and *41* (1903); Yüan Sun, "Lu-hsi-ya hsü-wu tang" (The Russian Nihilists), in *Chiang-su* and "Hsü-wu tang," in *Su-pao,* both reprinted in *SLHC, 1,* part 1, 369–76, part 2, 565–71 and 696–98, respectively.

principles."[84] Most of the other writers seemed to agree with Liang and likewise supported the political aims of the Nihilists while opposing or neglecting to mention their social or economic goals.

Liang had no qualms about the use of revolutionary terror in Russia: "Thus the latest methods of the Nihilists are the most suitable methods; for the Russian government there are no alternatives."[85] In 1903 and 1904 he believed that these methods could be modified to fit China. The revolutionaries went even further. According to them the situation in China was even worse than in Russia.

> In Russia the sovereign and the people are both of the same Slav race, but simply because the people cannot bear the poison of autocracy, they are willing to sacrifice millions of lives to buy freedom. . . . But when I look at our country I cannot control my feelings. For not only has it the same autocracy as Russia but for 200 years we have been trampled upon by foreign barbarians.[86]

Thus the anti-Manchu revolutionaries were unlike the Japanese radicals in that their concern with the methods and political aims of the Nihilists was not merely academic. In 1903 they began to investigate ways of imitating the Russians. The key figure in this movement of imitation was Yang Tu-sheng (Yang Yü-lin) (1872–1911).[87] In November 1902, as a student in Japan, he, together with Ch'en T'ien-hua and other Hunanese students, edited a magazine entitled *Yu-hsüeh i-pien* (Translations from Students Abroad) advocating revolution.[88] In May 1903 Yang was in-

84. Liang Ch'i-ch'ao, "Lun O-lo-ssu hsü-wu tang" (On the Russian Nihilists), reprinted in *SLHC, 1,* part 1, 375.

85. Ibid., p. 374.

86. Yüan Sun, p. 567.

87. Yang, who later changed his personal name to Shou-jen, was born of an official family in Changsha. He became a provincial degree holder (*chü-jen*) in 1897, but did not take up an official appointment. He was involved in the educational activities of Liang Ch'i-ch'ao and other reformists at Changsha, and was apparently in danger after the collapse of the reform movement in 1898. However the next year he felt secure enough to take up a teaching post in Kiangsu. In 1902 he went to Japan where, supported by a friend, he entered the Kōbungakuin and then Waseda University; see three biographies collected by Ts'ao Ya-po, reprinted in *HHKM, 4,* 316–24.

Shih Chien-ju's use of explosives in his attempt to assassinate Te-shou in 1900 strongly suggests that he was influenced by anarchism, nihilism, or both. However I can find no evidence to show that this was in any way conscious.

88. Chün-tu Hsüeh, *Huang Hsing and the Chinese Revolution* (Stanford, 1961), p. 91.

volved in the formation of the Volunteer Corps to Oppose Russia, a military training group organized by Chinese students in Japan to fight the Russians who were encroaching on Manchuria.[89] The corps was immediately prohibited by the Japanese government. The following week Yang and some friends formed an ephemeral Chinese Revolutionary Party (Chung-kuo ko-ming-tang), of which he was elected leader.[90] This party merged almost immediately with the Society for the Education of a Militant People which was founded in Tokyo on May 11.[91]

This organization was a continuation on a smaller scale of the Volunteer Corps to Oppose Russia. Its overt purpose was to oppose the Russian advance in Manchuria, while secretly it planned for a revolution. Its revolutionary activities were divided into three sections: propaganda, uprisings, and assassination. In June Huang Hsing, its leading figure, left Japan for Shanghai and Hunan to organize an uprising. Yang stayed in Japan studying chemical techniques with a Mr. Liang in Yokohama and seems to have become quite proficient at making explosives, although in an unfortunate accident he lost the sight of one eye.[92]

In the autumn of 1903 Yang appears to have gone to China and possibly was present at the foundation of the Society for China's Revival in Changsha that December.[93] In any case he knew enough about the ideas behind the organization to write, some time in 1903, the movement's apologia, a pamphlet entitled *Hsin Hu-nan* (The New Hunan). From this and articles written by Yang in *Yu-hsüeh i-pien* (Translations from Students Abroad) it is possible to see the extent to which he and presumably the other Chinese students were influenced by the Russian revolutionary tradition.

In *Hsin Hu-nan* Yang, whose chief motive was nationalism, went to great lengths to show that countries could become powerful only after violent revolution and that for this a "spirit of destruction" was necessary. It was the absence of this spirit that blocked China's

89. Feng, *I-shih, 1*, 104–07.

90. Ts'ao Ya-po, p. 319. The only other known members were Su P'eng and Chou Lai-su.

91. Kuo T'ing-i, *Chin-tai Chung-kuo shih-shih jih-chih* (A Daily Chronology of Modern Chinese History) (2 vols., Taipei, 1963), 2, 1179. This society should not be confused with its namesake, which was founded in Shanghai in response to the student action in Japan. Nor should it be confused with the Chün-shih hsüeh-hsiao (military school) founded by Sun Yat-sen and some Japanese officers the same summer; see Feng, *I-shih, 1*, 109–12, 132–34.

92. Ts'ao Ya-po, p. 319.

93. Kuo T'ing-i, 2, 1193, says Yang was present, but I have found no corroborative evidence.

advance into the modern world. He maintained that to gain it China should imitate Russia. "Of all the countries in the world today the spirit of destruction is strongest in the Russian Anarchist Party."[94] Then, drawing presumably from Kemuyama's book, Yang outlined the pattern of the Russian revolution: "Thus Russian nihilism rose from a period of revolutionary literature to a period of propaganda and agitation, and from propaganda and agitation to a period of assassination and terror."[95]

Yang firmly believed that the Chinese equivalent of the Russian term for youth was what he called "middle classes" (*chung-teng she-hui*) and that it should lead the revolutionary movement. Addressing a student audience he wrote: "Your position in Hunan is to be the saviors of the lower classes and the supplanters of the upper classes, supporting the lower classes and correcting the upper ones."[96] Elsewhere he stated: "The Chinese people's revolution must have the lower classes as its basis, and the middle classes as its field of action. Thus the lower classes are the core of the revolution and the middle classes its vanguard."[97] As in Russia "agitation had begun with students joining with groups of convicts, then with peasants, and finally with soldiers," Yang believed that the "middle classes" should join the secret societies (*mi-mi she-hui*), the labor organizations (*lao-tung she-hui*), and then the soldiers' societies (*chün-jen she-hui*).

Yang followed Kemuyama in using the words anarchist and nihilist indiscriminately to describe the Russian revolutionaries. He did not, however, support anarchism;[98] as a fervent nationalist he believed that the state was absolutely necessary. Neither was he a socialist; "What are the theories that we want to promote? They are simply the principles of establishing a national state and individual rights."[99]

The activities of the Society for China's Revival in 1904 are beyond the scope of this paper, but its use of the Ming-te School in

94. *Hsin Hu-nan,* reprinted in *SLHC, 1,* part 2, 612–49.

95. Ibid., p. 641. Yang's terms for these periods *ko-ming wen-hsüeh, yu-shuo shan-tung* and *an-sha k'ung-p'u,* and much of his terminology are the same as that used by Kemuyama Sentarō, *Kinsei museifushugi* (Modern Anarchism) (Tokyo, 1902), reprinted Tokyo, 1965, in the series *Meiji bunken shiryō soshō, 5;* see *Min-pao, 11* and *17.* Kemuyama taught at Waseda, where Yang was a student.

96. Ibid., p. 615.

97. Yang Tu-sheng, "Min-tsu chu-i chih chiao-yü" (Education for Nationalism), *Yu-hsüeh i-pien, 10,* reprinted in *SLHC, 1,* part 1, 408, 409.

98. T'an Pi-an, "O-kuo min-tsui chu-i tui T'ung-meng-hui ti ying-hsiang," *Li-shih yen-chiu* (1959), *1,* 35–44.

99. *Hsin Hu-nan,* p. 631.

Changsha for propaganda, its alliance of students and secret societies, and its plan to blow up the chief officials of the Ch'ing regime in Hunan show both the extent to which it was influenced by nihilism and the relevance of the Russian experience to the Chinese situation. However there was an important point on which the society and *Hsin Hu-nan* (The New Hunan) diverged from the Russian terrorist tradition, though not from populist theory. This was the policy of the revolutionaries not to strike at the Empress Dowager or the central government, but first of all to overthrow the regime locally. In their view Hunan would then become "a Switzerland or Belgium" and an inspiration to the rest of China, which would rise up and join with it to form a free nation united from the bottom up.

This divergence seems to have been too great for Yang, who became determined to strike the regime at its center. While continuing to act as an agent for the Society for China's Revival he went north, first to Tientsin and then to Peking.[100] Together with Chang Chi and a few friends he organized an assassination group which made plans to blow up both the Forbidden City and the Summer Palace. However, seeing no chance of success, the conspirators were forced to abandon the attempt.[101]

During 1904 a group of students at the Paoting Higher School established relations with the student revolutionary movement at Shanghai and formed a branch of the Society for the Education of a Militant People. Yang, who spent this year traveling between Shanghai and Peking, visited Paoting several times and often talked with the group, upon which he appears to have had considerable influence. Yang and the group agreed that there was a place for both uprisings and assassinations, and Yang, who retained his special interest in the latter, found a kindred spirit in a member of the group called Wu Yüeh (Meng-hsia) (1878–1905).[102] Yang and

100. Su P'eng, "Chi Chün-kuo-min chiao-yü-hui" (Note on the Society for the Education of a Militant People), reprinted in *KKWH, 10, Ko-ming chih ch'ang-tao yü fa-chan* Hsing-Chung-hui, pp. 100–01.

101. Ts'ao Ya-po, p. 319.

102. Wu was born at Tungcheng in Anhwei; his father was an official who left his position to become a merchant. After repeatedly failing official examinations and wandering through the country, Wu finally entered the Paoting senior school through the recommendation of a family friend. In 1902 or 1903 he became a revolutionary but later in 1903, influenced by the *Ch'ing-i-pao,* he became a reformist. By 1904 more revolutionary literature had led him back to the fold, leaving him with a bitter hatred for the reformists who had "tricked" him. Wu Yüeh, "Tzu-yü" (Personal Introduction), *T'ien t'ao* (Heaven's Punishment), supplement to *Min-pao* (April 1907), p. 1.

Wu discussed various techniques of assassination and gave a practical demonstration of the effectiveness of explosives.[103] In the spring and summer of 1905 Wu and a small band made plans to blow up T'ieh-liang, the chief of staff who became Minister of War in March 1905. But the task appeared too difficult and the attempt was abandoned. Then, prompted by Yang, who stayed in Peking to advise them, Wu and his group planned to attack the five ministers who were about to leave for Europe to investigate possible models for a Chinese constitution. Various difficulties checked the conspirators, but on September 24 Wu Yüeh, growing desperate, made the attempt on his own and threw a bomb at the ministers just before their departure. The explosion killed Wu and badly frightened the ministers, two of whom withdrew from the mission. Yang managed to avoid suspicion and escaped from Peking, going to Tokyo where he joined the newly formed Revolutionary Alliance.

Wu Yüeh clearly saw his attempt as an act of "propaganda by deed."[104] He wrote extensively explaining his political beliefs hoping that because of his action his writings would have a considerable impact, which they did when they were fully published in 1907.[105] These writings show that the Russian revolutionary tradition had a very great influence on him. We know that Wu had read *Hsin Hu-nan* and *Tzu-yu hsüeh,* and from them and his talk with Yang he had adopted the concept of a period of assassination.[106] However by the time that he was writing, the summer of 1905, it seemed that this period was coming to an end in Russia. He wrote:

> at present there is nothing in the world that attracts so much awe and attention as the fame of the Nihilist Party. In what period is the Russian Nihilist Party today? Or in what period was it formerly? If I dared be arbitrary I should say that the last half of the nineteenth century was the Nihilists' period of assassination and the first half of the twentieth century is their period of revolution. Without the former how could you obtain today's results? Where are we Han people? Where are

103. Ts'ao Ya-po, p. 320.

104. "Wu Yüeh i-shu" (Wu Yüeh's Posthumous Writings), *T'ien t'ao,* p. 7.

105. A letter by Wu Yüeh attacking the plans for a constitution was printed in *Min-pao, 3* (April 1906). Much longer writings were published in *T'ien t'ao* (April 1907).

106. Wu, "Tzu-yü," p. 1.

> we comrades? We comrades are in the period of assassination, and future years will bring the Han people's period of revolution.[107]

Like Yang, Wu was entirely absorbed in the methods of the Russian revolutionaries and their applicability to China. His aims were purely political; at no point did he show the slightest interest in the basic ideas of anarchism or socialism. However the publication of his writings in April 1907 not only caused a revival of interest in assassination but also played a considerable part in the awakening of interest in anarchism among Chinese revolutionaries.

Kōtoku Shūsui and the Japanese Conversion to Anarchism, February 1905–February 1907

The first signs of Kōtoku's conversion to anarchism appeared in February 1905, the month in which he began a five-month prison sentence for the publication of a special anniversary edition of *Heimin shimbun* which had included a translation of the *Communist Manifesto*. In that month he published two articles in *Çhokugen,* the successor to *Heimin shimbun,* on Russian revolutionaries, a subject that had become very topical since the beginning of the revolution on the 9th of January.[108] The articles concentrated on the Social Revolutionary Party, the heir to the nihilist tradition of the 1880s, toward both of which Kōtoku was very sympathetic. These articles contained the first criticisms by a Japanese Socialist of a Social Democratic party: "The moderation of the Social Democratic Party being unsatisfactory, a revolutionary socialist party was organized and . . . the majority of the youth were attracted to it."[109] He qualified his attacks by saying, "I am sure that the Social Democratic Party has had great achievements in strikes and demonstrations."[110] Furthermore, he made it clear that he believed that revolutionary violence was justifiable only in unconstitutional

107. "Wu Yüeh i-shu," pp. 7–8. Wu was not consistent in his theory that assassination was simply a prelude to revolution. At another point he suggested that assassination by itself could overthrow the Manchu regime. "Wu Yüeh i-shu," p. 10.

108. The articles were: "Rokoku kakumei no sobo" (Grandmother of the Russian Revolution: A Biography of K. Breshko-Breshkovskaya), *Chokugen* (February 12, 1905), p. 3, *Meiji shakai shugi shiryō shū, 1,* 11, and "Rokoku kakumei ga ata uru kyōkun" (The Lesson of the Russian Revolution), *Chokugen* (February 19, 1905), *1,* 17.

109. "Rokoku kakumei no sobo," p. 11.

110. Ibid.

Russia and not in Japan. Nevertheless he had made his first step away from parliamentary social democracy.

The clearest way of regarding Kōtoku's change of ideas is as a liberation from the straitjacket of Marxist social democracy. Lacking the Christian background of many Japanese Socialists, Kōtoku had no horror of violence. Indeed, as a Samurai brought up in the strife of the Popular Rights Movement he seems to have been predisposed toward it and hence had no particular attachment to moderate parliamentary methods. Kōtoku's choice of the name Shūsui—the title of the seventeenth chapter of the *Chuang Tzu*—and constant Taoist allusions in his poetry, very rare during that period, suggest that he was always interested in rural social integration.[111] He was born and brought up in Tosa, a *han* with a strong radical agrarian tradition. Furthermore he was the pupil and biographer of Nakae Chōmin, "the Japanese Rousseau." Thus throughout his socialist career Kōtoku chafed against the Marxist emphasis on the urban proletariat and the belief that socialism could come only after the full development of capitalism. Kōtoku always preferred the populist view of a revolution of the "majority of the people" led by "youth" *before* the triumph of capitalism.

Given those proclivities it is surprising not that Kōtoku became an Anarchist, but that he ever called himself a Social Democrat. The fundamental reason for this was that before 1905 Kōtoku and the other Japanese Socialists believed that no rational man could deny Marxist socialism. With his economic and historical analysis, Marx and Marx alone had raised socialism from a beautiful inspiration to a science. In their eyes the pre-Marxist Socialists were admirable but unpractical. In May 1904 Kōtoku wrote: "Most of Fourier's schemes failed not because his basic reasoning was bad, but because his practical plans were unscientific and unnatural."[112]

In addition to believing that Marxism was the only "scientific socialism," the early Kōtoku also thought that Kautsky was the only true interpreter of Marx. Thus despite his basic prejudices, Kotoku felt obliged to admit that the Western Social Democratic parties represented the wave of the future and that anarchism was only a moribund relic from the primitive past. In August 1904 *Heimin shimbun* reported: "As in other countries, there has

111. Shioda Shōbei, ed., *Kōtoku Shūsui no nikki to shokan* (The Diaries and Correspondence of Kōtoku Shūsui) (Tokyo, 1954), p. 54. See also the poems he wrote in prison, p. 189.

112. *Heimin shimbun*, 3 (May 8, 1904), 215.

been a decline in the Anarchist Party since the appearance of the [Russian] Social Democratic Party."[113]

Apparently there were three major reasons why by February 1905 Kōtoku had begun to reconsider his position. First was the closure of *Heimin shimbun* and his sentence to a term of imprisonment. These events increased his skepticism about Japanese constitutional government, and doubts arose in his mind about the possibility of progress by moderate parliamentary means.[114]

Second, and most important of all, was the massacre of workers on Bloody Sunday, January 9, 1905, and the wave of strikes and demonstrations that opened the revolution in Russia. These events, which were fully reported in *Chokugen* and the rest of the Japanese press, clearly had a considerable impact on Kōtoku. He believed that the Russian Revolution had worldwide significance and would serve as a model particularly in East Asia:

> Russia at the beginning of the twentieth century is like France at the beginning of the nineteenth. As revolutionaries in Western countries looked to a signal from France, now all the lost countries of the East look for a sign from the Russian Revolution . . . Look at China; look at Korea.[115]

Not only did the new manifestations of revolutionary spirit inspire him but they also cast a glow in retrospect on the past activities of Russian revolutionaries. "Going to the people" and terrorism, which had previously seemed pathetic attempts of "unscientific" and hopeless idealists, could now be seen as the planting and hoeing necessary for the harvest of revolution.

The third factor in Kōtoku's conversion was his relationship with Albert Johnson, an elderly Californian Anarchist with whom he began a correspondence in the autumn of 1904. Johnson immediately set about converting Kōtoku to his own ideas, sending him anarchist books and pictures of Anarchists and Social Revolutionaries. Like many others, Johnson was mistakenly convinced that the theories of anarchism and the activities of the Social Revolutionaries were two sides of the same coin. This combination, which Kōtoku accepted, gave to the Social Revolutionaries the

113. Ibid., 2 (August 14, 1904), 327.

114. See his letter to Albert Johnson, December 30, 1904, reprinted in Hyppolyte Havel, "Kotoku's Correspondence with Albert Johnson," *Mother Earth, 6:* 6–7, 9 (1911), 181.

115. Kōtoku quoted by Tanaka Sogorō in *Kōtoku Shūsui,* p. 261.

"scientific" theory of Kropotkin's anarcho-communism, and to anarchism an almost irresistible revolutionary glamour.

Kōtoku spent his five months in prison in reading and in intense thought, and his progress toward anarchism continued. In August 1905 he wrote: "Indeed, I had gone [to Sugamo Prison] as a Marxian Socialist, and returned a radical Anarchist."[116] While in prison Kōtoku decided to crystallize his new ideas by going to America after his release, and in November he set off for San Francisco.[117] He stayed there for seven months, seeing a great deal of Johnson, and studying all the radical ideas of the Bay Area. The only significant addition to the ideas that he had formed in Japan was the concept of "direct action" which came from the Industrial Workers of the World, which had been founded in June 1905 and had its main strength in the Pacific states. Its leaders rejected the craft unionism of the American Federation of Labor and the electoral tactics of the American Socialist Party. They wanted to overthrow the economic power of the capitalists and their state by direct action—demonstrations and strikes backed by violence and refusal to pay taxes or be conscripted. They maintained that when the working class had become sufficiently class conscious and militant by these means, it would be able to start and maintain a general strike that would bring about the collapse of capitalist society. After this the government would be replaced by trade unions and eventually the world would be federated under "one big union."[118] These ideas, similar but unconnected to those of the contemporary French syndicalists, had a great effect on Kōtoku. They provided a policy more immediately applicable to Japan than the assassinations and peasant risings of the Russian Social Revolutionaries. Thus Kōtoku saw himself as a "scientific" anarcho-communist identified with Social Revolutionary tactics in Russia and "the lost countries of Asia" and advocating immediate "direct action" for Japan and the West.

Kōtoku first began to expound his changed views while he was still in San Francisco in letters to *Hikari,* the new socialist journal.[119] But they made no impact until his return to Japan on June 22, 1906. Six days later he gave a lecture on "Trends in the World Revolutionary Movement" which caused a sensation: "Kō-

116. Kōtoku to Johnson (August 10, 1905) in *Mother Earth, 6,* 182.

117. Shioda Shōbei, *Kōtoku Shūsui,* p. 406.

118. Cole, *A History of Socialist Thought, 3,* part 2, 793–97.

119. Kōtoku, "San Furanshisuko yori" (From San Francisco), *Hikari,* reprint, pp. 40, 44, 52, 60, 81, 86, and 102.

toku, just returned from six months abroad studying the new tendencies of Socialist parties, came back to Japan carrying a bombshell, his talk about 'direct action' as opposed to parliamentary [methods]."[120] After the meeting Japanese Socialists began to absorb the staggering idea that Kōtoku, their leading intellectual, believed that Marxist social democracy was outmoded and that the wave of the future was direct action and anarcho-communism.

After his speech Kōtoku, whose health was bad, went to the country to recuperate and did not return to Tokyo until September. Once back, though still ill, he threw himself into the socialist movement. Although he joined with Sakai, Nishikawa, and others in their plans to publish a daily newspaper supported by all socialist factions, he attacked their two main policies, agitation for adult suffrage and for economic help to the workers and unemployed. He gave several speeches in which he argued fiercely and effectively for "direct action" and anarcho-communism, and reinforced his image as a man in touch with the latest European trends by publishing a letter to him from Kropotkin himself.[121]

In January 1907 the political and Christian wings of the socialist movement came together to found the new daily *Heimin shimbun,* and for the first time the Japanese socialist movement was united under one party with one journal. However, the annual meeting of the Japanese Socialist Party in February revealed the divisions that were rending the movement. The chief motion before the conference was one put forward by the Executive amending three points in the party constitution, the most important being the proposed change of Article I from "We advocate socialism within the limits of the law" to "Our aim is the realization of socialism."[122] This radical departure from Social Democratic legality illustrates the great changes that had taken place in the party. But Kōtoku was not satisfied, and in "one of the great orations of our time" he demanded an explicit renunciation of parliamentary methods, and that the party should openly support direct action and a general strike. A moderate proposed a countermotion asking the party to state that "parliamentarianism is the tacit direction of the Japanese socialist movement."[123] He received 2 votes, the Executive

120. Tanaka, *Kōtoku Shūsui,* p. 315. See also Shioda, *Kōtoku,* p. 457, and Nishio Yōtarō, *Kōtoku Shūsui* (Tokyo, 1959), p. 159.

121. *Hikari* (November 25, 1906), pp. 3, 221.

122. Tanaka, *Kōtoku Shūsui,* p. 336.

123. See Kublin, *Sen Katayama,* p. 195.

28, and Kōtoku 22. Thus by February 1907, 60 out of the 62 delegates were no longer Social Democrats and 22 out of 62 were anarcho-syndicalists. After the party's repudiation of authority it was immediately banned by the police, and *Heimin shimbun* did not long survive it. In the situation of semilegality that followed, anarchism continued to flourish until, by 1908, Kōtoku and his ideas completely dominated the Japanese Socialist movement.

Kōtoku's personality and oratory together with his convincing claim to be in touch with the latest Western trends were largely responsible for the rapid change of ideas in the winter of 1906–07. However he was effective only because many of his colleagues, particularly the newer and younger members, shared his dissatisfaction with social democracy—its emphasis on voting and moderation, its slow, staged progress toward socialism, and above all its faith in the proletariat and its contempt for youth. Furthermore, they were strongly moved by the non-Marxist aspects of the Russian Revolution, which was by no means over in the autumn of 1906. But violence alone was not sufficient; to be attractive it had to be applicable to Japan, modern, and scientific. The concept of direct action satisfied all three requirements. According to Kōtoku it was possible in countries where parliamentary progress was blocked but in which conditions were not yet ripe for revolution. Furthermore, it was backed by Kropotkin's theoretical anarchism which, from a basis in Marxist economics and Darwinian evolution, had developed them into something more modern and "scientific." Moderate and old-fashioned, Marxist social democracy had no hope against the new and radical "direct action" and anarchism.

Kōtoku was not completely unaided in his conversion of the Japanese Socialists to anarchism. In November 1906, a favorable account of anarchism appeared under the title of *Ō-Bei no museifu shugi* (Anarchism in Europe and America). This book, installments of which had been published earlier in the year in *Shakaishugi kenkyū (The Study of Socialism)*, was by Kutsumi Ketsuson, a journalist and an old friend of Kōtoku who in 1906 was working in Nagasaki. He was a contributor to the socialist journals in Tokyo and a member of the local branch of the Heiminsha. Before 1906 Kutsumi had the reputation of being "a kind of anarchist" and by that year he had become extremely interested in anarcho-communism.[124] His sympathies with anarchism and populism must

124. Nishida Nagashi, Introduction to reprint of *Hikari,* p. vii.

have been strengthened by his contact with a small group of Russian Social Revolutionaries based in Nagasaki. In May 1906 he wrote in *Hikari* enthusiastically describing a Captain Wadezki who had just founded a revolutionary magazine in Russian called *Volia*. He also stated that a Dr. Russel was involved.[125]

Kutsumi was not the only Japanese to have contact with the Russian group. The ultranationalist Black Dragon Society (Kokuryūkai) also sent its agent to meet and encourage the revolutionaries.[126] The aims of the society, which had been founded in 1900, were to spread Japanese influence to the Amur River (Kokuryū or Hei-lung-chiang) area and eventually to drive Russia from eastern Siberia. Since 1902 its members, many of whom were interested in social reform at home, had seen the potential of the Russian revolutionary movement and had considered ways of helping it in order to weaken the Tsarist regime.[127] It is unlikely, however, that they made any personal contact with the revolutionaries before the war.

In the 1890s the extreme nationalist groups, aiming toward a reformed East Asia under Japanese leadership, were interested primarily in Korea and China. Such societies as the East Asia Common Culture Society were set up with official encouragement partly in order to train young men in Chinese language and culture so that Japan would have capable agents there.[128] Apart from spying, the chief activities of these enthusiastic young men—zealous patriots (*shishi*)—were to encourage Chinese reformist and revolutionary movements, which they supported both for their intrinsic worth and for the opportunities that such changes would give to Japan.[129]

After 1900 the defeat of the Chinese reformists and revolutionaries and the Russian occupation of Manchuria caused most of the ultranationalists and their influential backers to turn their attention toward the dangers and opportunities coming from Rus-

125. *Hikari* (May 20, 1906), p. 2, reprint, p. 92. The life of Russel, whose real name was N. K. Sudzlovski (1858–1930), is too fantastic and eventful to give here. See S. L. Tikhvinsky, *Sun Yat-sen* (in Russian) (Moscow, 1964), note on pp. 92–93.

126. Tanaka, *Kōtoku Shūsui*, p. 366.

127. See D. M. Brown, *Nationalism in Japan: An Introductory Historical Analysis* (Berkeley, 1955), p. 114.

128. The history of this movement and its relations with China are well described and analyzed by M. B. Jansen, *The Japanese and Sun Yat-sen* (Cambridge, Mass., 1954).

129. Ibid., p. 52; Brown, p. 136.

sia.[130] At the same time the Japanese government began to see the possibilities of advantageous cooperation with the Manchu regime. However, Miyazaki Torazō and a small group of patriots (*shishi*) who had become deeply involved in the Chinese revolutionary movement retained their interest in China and their support for Sun Yat-sen despite coldness and discouragement from the Japanese authorities.[131]

For the group, and for Miyazaki in particular, 1901 to 1904 were years of depression.[132] In 1905 affairs brightened, and like revolutionaries everywhere the patriots were greatly encouraged by events in Russia. Furthermore the group helped bring about the meetings between the revolutionary Chinese students in Tokyo and Sun Yat-sen, and the foundation of the Revolutionary Alliance with Sun as its leader. Miyazaki, Hirayama Shū, and others became closely associated with the new society, though not fully accepted by all the Chinese students.[133] Sun however retained complete confidence in his Japanese friends and in the summer of 1906 he went with a retired officer named Kayano Nagatomo on a journey to Southeast Asia.[134] On the way south their ship called at Nagasaki, and through the local Black Dragon Society agent they were introduced to Russel, who came on board and had a two-hour conversation with Sun.[135] Their talk concerned the revolutionary movement in both countries, and as Russel was a trained chemist and a specialist in the manufacture of explosives, there was almost certainly some discussion of assassination techniques. After this meeting Sun and Russel maintained their friendship through correspondence.[136]

This was not the only instance of Miyazaki's group trying to link the Russian and Chinese revolutions. That same summer, probably inspired by the existence of *Min-pao* and the newly founded *Volia,* they decided to create a new journal entitled *Kakumei hyōron* (*Review of Revolutions*). Kayano stated the factors behind this decision:

130. Jansen, p. 108; Brown, p. 136.

131. Jansen, p. 107.

132. Ibid., p. 112.

133. Feng, *Chung-hua* (2 vols. 1954), *1,* 309.

134. *KFNP, 1,* 163.

135. Tanaka, *Kōtoku Shūsui,* p. 367.

136. Two letters from Sun to Russel in November 1906 are reprinted in A. N. Kheifet, "Revolyutsonye svasi Narodov Rossii i Kitaya v Nachale XX Veka" (Revolutionary Contacts between the Russian and Chinese Peoples at the Beginning of the Twentieth Century), *Voprosi Istorii* (1956), no. 12, pp. 91–100. Neither letter touches on revolutionary techniques.

> At that time, we Japanese who were members of the Revolutionary Alliance believed that China and Russia were the two great autocracies and that their repression was a block to freedom. We also believed that for the advance of civilization it was necessary to overthrow these autocracies. As a change in their regimes was necessary we launched a bimonthly magazine called *Kakumei hyōron* to help the revolutions in China and Russia.[137]

Miyazaki's devotion to the Chinese revolution was not simply for the purpose of allowing Japan to expand into China. He was genuinely in favor of social justice everywhere, although he thought it possible to achieve this in Japan by reform alone. He sympathized with or shared his brother Tamizō's ideas of land nationalization or distribution, and Tamizō collaborated with the patriots (*shishi*) on the new magazine. Other radicals also joined the group, the most notable being the future fascist leader Kita Terujirō, better known as Kita Ikki.[138] Kita was a member of the National Socialist Party led by Yamaji Aizan and founded in August 1905.[139] Yamaji denied that his party was as moderate as the German State Socialists, and it does seem to have been more radical in its attitude toward property. However it went even further than the latter in its proposals to strengthen the power of the Emperor at the expense of the rich in order to protect the workers and increase national unity.[140]

In 1905 Kita wrote a book entitled *Kokutairon oyobi junsei shakaishugi* (The Orthodox Myth and Pure Socialism) expressing similar national socialist views. Because of its critical interpretation of the official historical legend, the book was immediately banned. However, two sections of it were published in June and July 1906. Although Kita's "pure socialism" as expressed in his writings was passionately nationalistic and in favor of the increase of state

137. Kayano Nagatomo, *Chūkaminkoku kakumei hikyū* (Secrets of the Chinese Revolution) (Tokyo, 1941), p. 85, quoted in the introduction to "Tokyo shakaishugi shimbun, Kakumei hyōron," in *Meiji shakai shugi shiryō shū*, p. 9.

138. Apart from the Miyazakis and Kita the group consisted of Hirayama Shū, Kayano Nagatomo, Ike Kyōkichi, Wada Saburō, and Kiyofuji Kōshichirō. For information on Kita see Tanaka Sogorō, *Nihon fasshizumu no genryū, Kita Ikki no shisō to shōgai* (The Origins and Development of Fascism in Japan, as seen in the Life and Opinions of Kita Ikki) (Tokyo, 1949), and G. Macklin Wilson, "Kita Ikki, Okawa Shumei, and the Yuzonsha: A Study in the Genesis of 'Showa Nationalism,'" Harvard University, East Asian Research Center, *Papers on Japan, 2* (Cambridge, Mass., 1963).

139. Tanaka, *Kita Ikki*, p. 27.

140. Ibid.

power, many aspects of his ideas were closer to anarcho-communism and populism than to social democracy. He used the term communist anarchism (*kyōsan museifushugi*) for what Marx simply called communism and was very close to Kropotkin in his description of social democracy as a mere stop-gap:

> a necessary stage on the way to communist anarchism . . . While the communal property of the communist-anarchist period is appearing, some aspects of existing society will remain and social democracy will maintain the equal division of property for a time.[141]

Kita was a constant critic of parliament, the chief hope of the Social Democrats, and he described the Japanese proletariat, the class upon which they relied, as men "who are sleeping like unselfconscious slaves, with no trace of [the spirit of] class struggle."[142] Thus although the historian Tanaka Sogorō is not entirely convincing when he claims that Kita was the pioneer of anarcho-communism in Japan, many of Kita's arguments disparaged social democracy and praised anarcho-communism as the ultimate and purest form of socialism.[143]

Kita's writings were a great success. It reveals either eclecticism or naïveté that some socialist leaders, like Katayama Sen and Kawakami Hajime, received them with rapture.[144] The Miyazaki group was also impressed and invited Kita to join them. Kita, believing that the patriots' action abroad could have the same results in Japan that Lafayette's activities in America had had in France, accepted their invitation.[145] He had in fact been interested in China since August of the previous year when he had seen a curious claim by Sun Yat-sen that there were fifty-four socialist newspapers in China.[146]

After some delay, the first issue of *Kakumei hyōron* appeared on September 5, 1906. Its contents were listed in English on the front page as follows:

141. Ibid., p. 50.

142. Ibid.

143. Ibid., pp. 50–51.

144. G. Macklin Wilson, p. 148.

145. Tanaka, *Kita Ikki*, p. 117.

146. *Chokugen* (August 6, 1905), p. 3, reprint (cited in n. 108 above), p. 213. The interview was first published in the Flemish socialist journal *Vooruit*, and was reprinted in *Le Peuple* (May 20, 1905), p. 1. For Kita's reaction see Tanaka, *Kita Ikki*, p. 27.

> Announcement of the New Edition of Kakumei-Hyōron or the Review of Revolutions; Current topics on the western Revolutionary movements: 1) Torpidinous [sic] measure of Revolution, 2) Open confession of Sasanof, 3) Secret bomb factories, 4) Glimpse of the boiling Russia, 5) Anarchism in Spain, 6) The Tsar's Iron Hell; Modern Revolutionary problem of China . . . ; Epitome of Revolutionary Heroes—Michael Bakunin; "Crossing the Threshold"—a novel [by Turgenev]; The Chinese Students in Japan; Appendix: Report of the Society of Equal Land.[147]

Throughout the journal's existence—the tenth and last issue came out on March 25, 1907—almost all the articles in it concerned assassination and the violent aspects of the Russian and Chinese revolutions. There were also articles on Western Anarchist activities and Anarchist leaders including the nonviolent Kropotkin, firmly linking them in the reader's mind to the Russian movement. The writers' belief in this false connection was undoubtedly consolidated by the increasing Japanese interest in anarchism after Kōtoku's return. It is not certain how much contact the patriots had with Kōtoku at this time, but Miyazaki Tamizō did have two long conversations with him early in September, and it is very likely that Kita Ikki too was seeing him.[148]

After the journal's foundation the patriots continued their efforts to put Sun in touch with Russian revolutionaries. In the middle of November 1906, Gregori Gershuni, the founder of the Social Revolutionary Party's "battle group" or assassination squad, and perhaps the party's most famous leader of the time, escaped from Siberia to Japan.[149] Members of the Miyazaki group contacted him, and on November 15, two days before his departure, they arranged a meeting with Sun, and the two talked through the night. Gershuni also gave an interview to *Kakumei hyōron* in which he described his adventures, the progress of the Russian Revolution, and the Social Revolutionary Party.[150]

Throughout the autumn and winter of 1906 the patriots kept up their close contact with the Chinese students. *Kakumei hyōron*

147. *Kakumei hyōron* (September 6, 1906), p. 1, reprint, p. 123.

148. Shioda Shōbei, *Kōtoku Shūsui*, p. 408, and Tanaka, *Kita Ikki*, p. 124.

149. B. I. Nikolayevsky, *Aseff the Russian Judas*, trans. G. Reavey (London, 1934), p. 202.

150. Wada Saburō, "Gershuni the Epitome of a Revolutionary Hero," *Kakumei hyōron* (January 25, 1907), p. 6, reprint, p. 198.

and *Min-pao* frequently advertised each other and the calligraphy for the Japanese journal's front page title was done by Chang Ping-lin, *Min-pao's* editor.[151] Writers for *Kakumei hyōron* were very much in evidence at the *Min-pao* anniversary meeting in December, which received extensive coverage in their journal.[152] From Sung Chiao-jen's diary it is clear that at least he and his Hunanese friends were in close and constant contact with the Miyazaki brothers and Kita Ikki.

There is little doubt that *Kakumei hyōron* was successful in its attempts to influence and inspire the Chinese students. Again we can rely on Sung's diary:

> 9/6/06 Cloudy . . . received a copy of *Kakumei hyōron*. . . . When I examined it, I saw that it contained articles about political and social revolution, novels, and news, though it emphasized the Chinese revolutionary movement. . . . It contained a section on the Chinese students in Japan and it talked of the flourishing Chinese revolutionary movement, and it said that the students in Japan should not be insulted. . . . There were also accounts of Wu Yüeh and Ch'en T'ien-hua and their self-sacrifice for their country. . . . I was so moved that without being aware of it I cried for a long time.[153]

The chief effect of *Kakumei hyōron* on the Chinese students in Japan was to consolidate the link that already existed in their minds between the Russian revolutionary tradition and the situation in China. In addition, two important side effects were the creation of an imaginary identification of anarchism with populist terrorism, and the establishment of Bakunin and Kropotkin as heroes of the Russian Revolution.

The Change from Marxism to Anarchism in China, July 1906–July 1907

In his article on the introduction of Marxism to China, the modern Chinese historian Jung Meng-yüan states: "From 1907 the

151. Kayano Nagatomo, p. 85.

152. Hu Han-min and Wang Ching-wei, "Chi shih-erh yüeh erh-jih pen-pao chi-yüan-chieh ch'ing-chu ta-hui-shih chi yen-shuo tz'u" (Record of the Meeting Held on December the 2nd to Celebrate the First Anniversary of our Journal and the Speeches Given), *Min-pao, 10*, 81–114.

153. Sung Chiao-jen, p. 203. In fact the sections on Wu Yüeh and Ch'en T'ien-hua did not appear until the seventh issue in January 1907, pp. 6–7. This means that Sung did not write up his diary immediately, which, if anything, strengthens his report of the impact of *Kakumei hyōron*.

articles in *Min-pao* introducing socialism became very scarce, while the articles introducing anarchism increased."[154] Analysis of the contents of *Min-pao* shows him to be substantially correct. In the first five issues—November 26, 1905 to June 26, 1906—there were ten favorable articles on social democracy and Western theories of land nationalization, and none on anarchism.[155] The following four issues—July 25, 1906 to December 20, 1906—contained two articles on socialism and anarchism favoring socialism, and two on anarchism alone, one neutral and one hostile.[156] After the eleventh issue, January 25, 1907, there were no further articles concerning social democracy but more than ten favoring anarchism or populist terrorism.[157]

Thus it seems convenient to divide the series into three periods: the first half of 1906, when there was interest in and sympathy for social democracy, the second half of that year when there was interest in anarchism, and finally 1907 when there was both concern and sympathy for anarchism. The periodization is made less distinct by the fact that two articles on the Russian Revolution appeared in the first period and one in the second. One of these was a translation from the first issue of *Volia* in Nagasaki, and the other two were general descriptions of the activities of Russian liberals and Socialists as well as of the terrorists.[158] It is also impossible to discern any trend in the journal's illustrations. At no

154. Jung Meng-yüan, p. 7.

155. See above, nn. 47–67.

156. The general articles were: "She-hui chu-i shih ta-kang" (An Outline of the History of Socialism), trans. Liao Chung-k'ai (under the pen name Yüan-shih) from W. D. P. Bliss, *A Handbook of Socialism*, ch. 4, in *Min-pao, 7*, 101–11; and "Wu-cheng-fu chu-i yü she-hui chu-i" (Anarchism and Socialism), trans. Liao Chung-k'ai, from *A Handbook of Socialism*. The neutral article was Liao Chung-k'ai, trans., "Wu-cheng-fu chu-i chih erh p'ai" (Two Schools of Anarchism), *Min-pao, 8*, 131–38, from Kutsumi Ketsuson, *Ō-Bei no museifu shugi* (Anarchism in Europe and America). Kutsumi's article first appeared as a chapter in *Shakai shugi kenkyū, 2* (April 15, 1906). The hostile piece was Meng T'ieh-sheng (Yeh Hsia-sheng), "Wu-cheng-fu-tang yü Ko-ming-tang chih shuo-ming" (Explanation of the Relationship between the Anarchist Party and the Revolutionary Party), *Min-pao, 7*, 111–23.

157. These included: sections from *Kinsei museifu shugi* (Modern Anarchism), trans. Liao Chung-k'ai, 2 parts, *Min-pao, 11*, 89–109, and *17*, 121–48; Wu-shou, "Su-fei-ya chuan" (Life of Sophia Perovskaya), *Min-pao, 15*, 119–25; "Pa-k'u-ning chuan" (Life of Bakunin), *Min-pao, 16*, 109–23; and T'ai-yen (Chang Ping-lin), "Wu-cheng-fu chu-i hsü" (Introduction to Anarchism) (an introduction to Chang Chi's pamphlet, "Wu-cheng-fu chu-i" [Anarchism]), *Min-pao, 20*, 129–30.

158. Pien-chien (who was not Hu Han-min), "O-kuo ko-ming-tang chih jih-pao" (The Daily Newspaper of the Russian Revolutionaries), *Min-pao, 4*, 93–95; "1905 nien Lu-kuo chih ko-ming" (The Russian Revolution of 1905), translated by Sung Chiao-jen from an article in *Tokyo nichi-nichi shimbun*, part 1, *Min-pao, 3*, 1–9, part 2, *Min-pao, 7*, 63–74.

time were there any portraits of social democrats, while pictures of populists, anarchists, and their victims appeared throughout the life of the magazine.[159] This discrepancy can be explained by the fact that socialism was only of peripheral interest to the revolutionaries, while the illustrations reflected their central concerns with nationalism, political liberty, and violent revolution. Furthermore, although interest in the Russian terrorists increased during 1906–07 the Chinese students had known about them and sympathized with them at least since 1902.

The new elements that appeared between July 1906 and July 1907 were the association of interest in Russian terrorism with interest in anarchism, and an identification of anarchism with "true" socialism. On August 30, 1907, Liu Shih-p'ei and Chang Chi established the Society for the Study of Socialism (She-hui chu-i chiang-hsi-hui). At its foundation Liu proclaimed: "Our aim is not only to practice socialism, but to have anarchism as our goal."[160] From 1907 to 1911 a considerable number of advanced Chinese intellectuals believed that anarcho-communism was the essence of socialism. In June 1911, Sung Chiao-jen wrote: "If one advocates true (*chen-cheng*) socialism, it will not succeed unless you support anarchism (*wu-chih chu-i*) and communism; neither social democracy nor state socialism is worthy of respect!"[161]

The new tone was clearly set by the summer of 1907. The foundation of the Society for the Study of Socialism was preceded by the establishment in June of *T'ien-i pao* (Journal of Natural Justice), the first Chinese anarchist journal in the Orient.[162] The same month an unrelated group of revolutionaries in Paris founded another anarchist magazine, *Hsin shih-chi* (The New Century).[163] The reasons for this remarkable coincidence and for

159. See the list given in Man-hua (T'ang Tseng-pi), "T'ung-meng-hui shih-tai *Min-pao* shih-mo chi" (Full Record of *Min-pao* during the Revolutionary Alliance Period), reprinted in *HHKM*, 2, 455–59.

160. Liu Shih-p'ei quoted in "She-hui chu-i chiang-hsi hui ti-i-tz'u chi-shih" (Record of the First Meeting of the Society for the Study of Socialism), *T'ien-i pao*, *6*, reprinted in *SLHC*, 2, sect. 2, 944–47.

161. Sung Chiao-jen, "Lun she-hui chu-i" (On Socialism), reprinted in Chiang K'ang-hu, *Hung-shui chi* (Rampaging Waters) (San Francisco, 1914), p. 47. For the anarchist period as a whole see R. A. Scalapino and G. T. Yu, *The Chinese Anarchist Movement* (Berkeley, 1961), pp. 1–34.

162. See notes in *SLHC*, 2, sect. 2, 1074–75.

163. For some background to the foundation of *Hsin shih-chi* (New Century) see Wu Chih-hui, *Chih-lao hsien-hua* (Chats with Old Wu) (Taipei, 1952), pp. 27–29. See also Scalapino and Yu, pp. 2–5.

the establishment of *Hsin shih-chi* at this particular time are still obscure. They are probably connected to a worldwide trend toward anarcho-syndicalism, of which the East Asian trend after 1905 was only a part.[164] *Hsin shih-chi,* which survived *T'ien-i pao* by two years, was even more influential than the latter in the consolidation of anarchism among the Chinese students, but it did not initiate the swing toward it.

One of the reasons why many historians have failed to note the change from socialism to anarchism is that Liu Shih-p'ei and the other writers in *T'ien-i pao* continued and even developed Chinese interest in Marxism. Early in 1908, the journal published translations from the Japanese of Engels' 1888 "Introduction to the Communist Manifesto," the first chapter of the *Manifesto* itself and sections from Engels' *The Origin of the Family.*[165] This interest should not be misunderstood; East Asian Socialists wanted any information about the subject, however heterodox. Furthermore, anarchism is by definition eclectic; Kropotkin and the anarcho-communists respected Marx and Engels as the founding fathers of "scientific socialism," and accepted much of Marxist economics and sociology. They believed however that in many respects Marxism had been superseded by more modern and "scientific" theories.

This confusion notwithstanding, some historians have recognized and deplored the shift toward anarchism.[166] However, there have been few attempts to analyze the causes for this change. The most common explanation is that anarchism came in as an adjunct of individual terrorism, because of pessimism among the revolutionaries after repeated failures of assassination attempts.[167] There had been sporadic individual attempts since 1900, but there was a period of depression immediately before 1911 when attempted assassinations became more frequent. However, this depression only set in in 1908 or 1909, whereas interest in anarchism was

164. The syndicalist movement in France, the I.W.W. in the U.S.A., Tom Mann's activities in England, and perhaps even the soviets (syndicates?) in Russia, seem to make up a general pattern of radical reaction to social democracy, the contradiction only being resolved by Rosa Luxemburg and Lenin.

165. T'an Pi-an, "O-kuo min-tsui chu-i tui T'ung-meng-hui ti ying-hsiang," *Li-shih yen-chiu* (1959), *1,* p. 36.

166. Jung Meng-yüan, p. 11, and Tang Leang-li, *The Inner History of the Chinese Revolution* (London, 1930), p. 54.

167. See for instance Li Chu, "Lun she-hui chu-i tsai Chung-kuo ti ch'uan-po," *Li-shih yen-chiu* (1954), *3,* 1–21.

established in the spring of 1907, a season of relative optimism.[168]

A more convincing explanation of the transformation is that interest in anarchism began when Chang Ping-lin and his group took control of *Min-pao* and the student revolutionary movement in Japan, replacing Sun and his Cantonese supporters, Wang Ching-wei, Hu Han-min, and Chu Chih-hsin. This theory is supported by the fact that aside from Chang Chi, who had been interested in the subject since 1903, the leading champions of anarchism in Tokyo were Chang Ping-lin's close associate Liu Shih-p'ei and Liu's wife Ho Chen. Moreover Chang Ping-lin himself was clearly sympathetic toward it.

The following points may explain these sympathies. To appreciate Marxism and social democracy, one must have a knowledge of and curiosity about Western economics and institutions. For this, Cantonese like Sun and his supporters—or Liang Ch'i-ch'ao, for that matter—with their cosmopolitan outlook were uniquely qualified among Chinese of the day. On the other hand, the simplicity of anarchism and its emphasis on morality, together with its total rejection of Western society, were appealing to men from more traditional North and Central China like Chang Chi, Chang Ping-lin, and Liu Shih-p'ei. Furthermore, Sun and his followers from the crowded counties around Canton and Hong Kong and having connections with Chinese communities all round the Pacific were the only Chinese not completely repelled by the Marxist emphasis on towns, industry, and the proletariat. Chang and Liu, with more rural backgrounds, naturally preferred the rustic idyll of anarchism and its appeal to the people as a whole, including peasants and intellectuals.

There are a few drawbacks to this scheme. First, interest in social democracy was not confined to the Cantonese. Sung Chiao-jen, for instance, from tradition-bound Hunan, translated extremely technical articles on the subject.[169] Second, while Liu was preeminently interested in China, he also wrote about Hobbes, Rousseau, and Darwin.[170] Moreover, he published advanced Marxist texts. Third, one should not overemphasize the backwardness of

168. For the beginning of the period of depression see Chün-tu Hsüeh, *Huang Hsing*, p. 56. For some of the many revolutionary activities of early 1907, see pp. 62–67.

169. Ibid.

170. Liu Shih-p'ei and Ho Chen, "Lun chung-tsu ko-ming yü wu-cheng-fu ko-ming chih te-shih" (The Pros and Cons of Racial and Anarchist Revolutions), reprinted in *SLHC, 2*, sect. 2, 947–59.

Liu's home on the Yangtze between Shanghai and Nanking, or of Chang Ping-lin's just outside Hangchow.[171]

There is however no doubt that generally speaking Chang and Liu were culturally and psychologically more susceptible to anarchism than the group around Sun. For some years they had been intensely interested in terrorism. This seems to have come mainly from the Chinese heroic tradition but it was at least indirectly influenced by Russian activities. Although Chang was in prison when the Restoration Society was founded early in 1904, he was very much involved with the members of this society, which was founded by his son-in-law Kung Pao-ch'üan (Wei-sun) specifically as an assassination group.[172] The society also developed to its highest extent in China the populist technique of intellectuals establishing relations with and control of secret societies.[173] Liu Shih-p'ei, also a member of this society, had been known for the violence of his views at least since 1904, when under the pen name of The First Extremist he had written an article on "The Advantages of Extremism."[174]

Chang Ping-lin became editor of *Min-pao* immediately after his release from prison in Shanghai and his arrival in Japan in July 1906. The beginning of his editorship marked the change from the period of interest in social democracy to that of interest in anarchism. The spring of 1907, when the interest in anarchism turned to support, was the season in which Sun and his followers left Tokyo. It was also the one in which Chang and the newly arrived Liu Shih-p'ei took complete control of *Min-pao*. The seeds were sown for the schism between Chang and Sun later that year.[175]

It is on the question of chronology that one comes up against difficulties. Granted that Chang and Liu were susceptible to anarchism, why did they become interested in it only at this point? The indications are that although they took part in the change from 1906 to 1907, they were not wholly responsible for it. Chang Ping-lin began writing articles in *Min-pao* immediately after becoming its editor, but members of Sun's entourage like Wang Ching-wei and Hu Han-min continued contributing frequent

171. Liu Shih-p'ei was born at Icheng and Chang Ping-lin at Yühang.

172. Shen Tieh-min, "Chi Kuang-fu-hui erh-san shih" (Recollections of Two or Three Things about the Restoration Society), *HHKMHIL, 4,* 131–42.

173. T'ao Ch'eng-chang, "Che-an chi-lüeh" (A Brief Account of the Chekiang Case), reprinted in *HHKM, 3,* 1–22.

174. In *Chung-kuo pai-hua pao,* reprinted in *SLHC, 1,* sect. 2, 887–90.

175. Feng, *I-shih, 1,* 56.

articles until the end of 1906, while Liao Chung-k'ai and Chu Chih-hsin were still writing for it in 1907. The students who were interested in socialism were not forbidden to write. They simply stopped writing about social democracy, either because the editors and readers had lost interest in it, or because they themselves had done so. Tang Leang-li stated that as it was Chu Chih-hsin who introduced socialism, when Chu left Tokyo to take up revolutionary activities in China people gave up studying it.[176] In fact Chu stopped writing on socialism nine months before he left Japan, and after his return to China in the spring of 1907 he found time to write two articles on Revolutionary Alliance land policies but not on Western socialism.[177] Another indication that Chu had lost enthusiasm for social democracy is the statement by his younger brother that Chu was "clearly influenced by anarchism" in the years before 1911.[178]

Thus it would seem that although anarchism might not have found such active champions if Sun's group had remained in control of the revolutionary movement in Japan, the loss of interest in social democracy and the capture of the word "socialism" by anarchism would still have taken place.

What then were the fundamental causes of the transformation? Primarily they were the increase of interest in Russian terrorism stemming from the activities of the Social Revolutionaries and the conversion of the Japanese Socialist movement to anarchism, which itself had the same origins.[179] The chief reasons why the Chinese students in Tokyo became particularly aware of the Russian terrorists in the year from July 1906 to July 1907 were the establishment of *Kakumei hyōron* in September 1906, and Sun's meetings with Russel and Gershuni, which for the first time brought Chinese and Russian revolutionaries into personal contact. In April 1907 Chang Ping-lin brought out a special supplement to *Min-pao* entitled "T'ien t'ao" which made a great impact. The pamphlet featured the writings of Wu Yüeh with their emphasis on the Russian historical scheme of the three stages of revolutionary litera-

176. Tang Leang-li, p. 54.

177. See "Hu Han-min tzu-chuan," p. 393. The articles were "T'u-ti kuo-yu yü ts'ai-cheng" (Land Nationalization and Finance), part 1, *Min-pao, 15,* 67–99; part 2, *Min-pao, 16,* 33–72.

178. Chu Chih-ju, "Chu Chih-hsin ko-ming shih-chi shu-lüeh" (A General Narration of Chu Chih-hsin's Revolutionary Activities), *HHKMHIL, 2,* 422–29.

179. This last point seems to be confirmed by the fact that the first half of 1906 was the high point of interest in social democracy in both Japan and China.

ture, agitation, and assassination. The publication also reminded the students of the heroism of this leading Chinese follower of the Social Revolutionaries. All these factors drew attention to Russia and made the activities of the German Social Democrats and Anglo-Saxon land reformers seem very tame and uninteresting.

After his return to Japan in June 1906, there is no evidence that Kōtoku met any Chinese before April 1907.[180] However it is certain that some students listened to his speeches and were aware of his ideas before then.[181] In March 1907, for example, Chang Chi and Chang Ping-lin begged Kita Ikki to introduce them to his old friend Kōtoku.[182] By August enough contact had been established for Kōtoku to address the inaugural meeting of the Society for the Study of Socialism.[183] Kōtoku's campaigns removed social democracy's chief attraction in Chinese eyes: its claim to represent the most advanced and scientific thinking in Europe.

After the autumn of 1906 the Russian terrorists became attractive not only for their courage and fervor, but also because of their alleged possession of the "modern," "scientific" theory of anarchism. No longer did Chinese radicals interested in Western theories have to worry about such aspects of Marxist social democracy as class conflict, the need for China to pass through capitalism, the hegemony of the urban proletariat, or the achievement of social justice by parliamentary means. All of these could now be bypassed by anarchism, the "true" socialism. For the less radical the identification of socialism with anarchism led to a retreat from both. Sun's difficulties in persuading people to accept his social policies increased from 1907 to 1911.[184]

It cannot be overemphasized that the subject of this paper was peripheral to the Chinese revolutionaries themselves. Their interest in socialism of any sort was subordinate to their concern over national, constitutional, or even personal issues. However, the fact that socialism was later to play a crucial role in Chinese history gives this topic wider relevance. Aside from their intrinsic interest, the changes examined here contain at least three points of more general significance. They help to explain how, although

180. See Shioda Shōbei, *Kōtoku Shūsui.*

181. See for instance the description of one of Kōtoku's meetings by Ching Mei-chiu in *Tsui-an,* sections of which are reprinted in *HHKM,* 2, 253–56.

182. Tanaka, *Kita Ikki,* p. 124.

183. "She-hui chu-i chiang-hsi hui ti-i tz'u k'ai-hui chi-shih," p. 946.

184. For the dropping of the principle of Equal Land Rights by revolutionary organizations after 1907, see Feng, *I-shih, 3,* 214.

Marx was hardly mentioned in China after 1907, by 1919 several Chinese thinkers had absorbed Marxist concepts; they must have done this either before 1907 or indirectly through Marxist elements in the more "modern" theories in the decade that followed. They indicate why after relatively promising beginnings the study of Marxism should have been aborted until the 1920s. They also show the essential irrelevance of pre-Leninist Marxism to China.

3. The Constitutionalists

P'eng-yüan Chang

During the last years of the Ch'ing dynasty, two opposing movements sought to renovate China, the revolutionary groups and the constitutionalists. Because the Revolution of 1911 resulted in the overthrow of the Ch'ing dynasty and the establishment of a republic, the revolutionaries have been regarded by some as champions of China's salvation, and the constitutionalists as conservatives and stubborn reactionaries who placed obstacles in the way of the revolutionary movement. Today's orthodox Nationalist Chinese historians generally use the term "constitutionalist" derisively, neglecting or distorting the contribution of this group to the Revolution of 1911.

The significance and identity of the constitutionalists have long been obscured by prejudice and neglect. Generally speaking, they comprised loosely organized groups favoring the adoption of a constitutional monarchy by peaceful means. Such groups might include government officials who memorialized in favor of the adoption of a constitution, a news editor who wrote articles discussing the way to establish a constitution, or a merchant who occasionally joined in the petitions for the convening of a parliament. Since the character of a political group is determined by its ideology, organization, and activities, we will briefly examine the constitutionalists from these three aspects, as well as their historical development.

In both theory and practice, the so-called constitutional movement was a continuation of the Hundred Days' Reform led by K'ang Yu-wei in 1898. Marking the beginning of China's constitutional renovation, K'ang's program included the convening of parliament,[1] although he did not consider it the basis for all other

1. See K'ang's memorials presented to the Kuang-hsü Emperor: *Wu-hsü pien-fa* (The Reform of 1898) (Shanghai, 1953) 2, 123–267; S. Y. Teng and J. K. Fairbank, *China's Response to the West: A Documentary Survey, 1839–1923* (Cambridge, Mass., 1954), pp. 147–64, 195.

reforms. In light of his endeavors of 1898, K'ang deserves to be called a reformer; indeed, his career is generally considered to merit that label. The constitutional movement, however, differed ideologically from K'ang's attempts in its primary emphasis on the convening of parliament. Furthermore, the ideological leadership shifted from K'ang Yu-wei to Liang Ch'i-ch'ao. It was no coincidence that when Liang, after several years of radical activities, turned toward a constitutional movement as China's salvation, the Ch'ing court decided at the same time to renovate its political system; Liang's theory greatly influenced the Ch'ing decision.[2] Most important, many Chinese accepted Liang's idea as the best means of dealing with the danger facing their country and offered their support.

After formulating their ideological goal, the constitutionalists had to try to combine their efforts. Early in 1906 a number of constitutional organizations appeared. The Constitutional Preparatory Association in Shanghai, the Constitutional Government Association in Hunan, the Constitutional Government Preparatory Association in Hupeh, the Self-Government Association in Kwangtung, as well as the nearly nationwide Political Information Institute were all organized in the same year.[3] Most of these organizations were either local in character or too weak to be nationwide associations. Moreover, their right to exist was not recognized by law; at any time the Ch'ing government could force them to disband. After repeated disappointments, they came to see the need for strong legal organization.

The provincial assemblies and the Provisional National Assembly were organized in 1909 and 1910, respectively. The establishment of these quasi-representative organizations gave the constitutionalists an excellent opportunity to unite. They managed to be elected as representatives and turned the assemblies, which the government dared not dissolve arbitrarily, into legal forums where they could express their opinions.

Before the organization of the assemblies the constitutionalists

2. For Liang's political thought and activities after the coup d'état of 1898, see Chang P'eng-yüan, *Liang Ch'i-ch'ao yü Ch'ing-chi ko-ming* (Liang Ch'i-ch'ao and the Revolutionary Movement in the Late Ch'ing Period) (Taipei, 1964), chaps. 4–6, and Joseph R. Levenson, *Liang Ch'i-ch'ao and the Mind of Modern China* (Cambridge, Mass., 1953).

3. For more information about these organizations, see Samuel Chu, *Reformer in Modern China, Chang Chien 1853–1926* (New York and London, 1965), p. 65; Chang P'eng-yüan, *Liang Ch'i-ch'ao*, pp. 177–93.

in local associations petitioned for the calling of a parliament,[4] but their petitions and admonitions were discounted by the Ch'ing court as "noisy voices." When the Manchu princes who controlled the central government felt offended, they had the power to retaliate. The Political Information Institute organized by Liang Ch'i-ch'ao, for instance, was arbitrarily closed in 1908.[5] Now the constitutionalists had to decide on their next move: Should they merely petition and admonish, or should their protest take a more active form?

In brief, the constitutional movement may be divided into two stages: gestation and development. The establishment of the provincial assemblies in 1909 marked the division between these two stages. The meaning of constitutionalism was vague in the first stage but became clearer and more concrete in the second. Before the organization of the assemblies the constitutionalists had been scattered in small groups. When they became the representatives of the people, they organized more broadly and united in the struggle for the realization of their goals.

This chapter will be confined to the developmental stage of the constitutional movement from 1909 to 1911—the period which determined whether China would undergo peaceful renovation or bloody revolution. Although the constitutional movement itself failed, its relation to the Revolution should be considered. Did the constitutionalists change any of their attitudes before and after the Wuchang uprising? What was their influence on China as a whole? If these questions can be answered, the problem of whether the constitutionalists were obstacles to the Revolution or whether they contributed something to it will be illuminated.

The Emergence of Leaders

The Ch'ing government, with the intention of staving off its final collapse, promulgated an edict on August 27, 1908, outlining steps to be taken during a nine-year period preparatory to establishing a constitutional monarchy. In the third year of preparation, the Revolution broke out and ended with the overthrow of the dynasty. However, although the preparations had failed to set up an actual constitution, they did yield some positive results. The unprecedented local elections (February through June 1909) in all the provinces were among its accomplishments. The people's first

4. See Chang P'eng-yüan, *Liang Ch'i-ch'ao,* pp. 191–93.
5. Ibid.

representative organizations, provincial assemblies, were established after the elections; and half of the two hundred delegates to the National Assembly were elected from the provinces.

The Ch'ing government decided to establish twenty-one assemblies for twenty-two provinces.[6] The number of representatives for each province was determined not by the population but by a proportion of 5 percent of the number of scholars who had passed the traditional examinations, and by the tax rolls. The quotas were fixed for each province as follows:

Fengtien	50	Kirin	30	Heilungkiang	30
Chihli	140	Kiangsu	121	Anhwei	83
Kiangsi	93	Chekiang	114	Fukien	72
Hupeh	80	Hunan	82	Shantung	100
Honan	96	Shansi	86	Shensi	63
Kansu	43	Szechwan	105	Kwangtung	91
Kwangsi	57	Yunnan	68	Kweichow	39

The following persons were considered to be qualified as candidates: those who had successfully been engaged for at least three years in teaching above the primary level or in some other occupation contributing to the public welfare; those who had graduated from a middle school or school of corresponding level in China or abroad; those who held the old literary degree of senior licentiate (*kung-sheng*) or higher; those who had held any official post of the seventh rank of the civil service or fifth rank of the military service or higher and had not been demoted or impeached; and those who had any business valued at 5,000 *yüan*. Persons who did not meet the qualifications required for candidacy included those involved in turbulence or law-breaking; convicted criminals; those engaged in any disreputable business; those under suspicion of business irregularities; opium users; the insane; any member of a family engaged in a disreputable pursuit; the illiterate; those guilty of misdemeanors in office; soldiers; police officers; students; Buddhist or Taoist priests or religious teachers of other sects; teachers in primary schools.[7]

The requirements for voters were the same as those for candi-

6. Originally the Ch'ing government planned to establish twenty-three assemblies for twenty-two provinces; Kiangsu would have had two. Later, the people there requested that only one be established; this was approved. The establishment of an assembly in Sinkiang was postponed because the educational standard of the province was too low to operate one. It was reported that among 5,000 Sinkiang people, only one could read Chinese. See *TFTC* (1909), no. 1, pp. 16–17.

7. For the regulations of the assemblies, see *TFTC* (1908), no. 8.

dates except in regard to age. Male adults over twenty-five could vote, while candidates had to be over thirty. The election was indirect. Qualified voters first elected a fixed number of representatives to be members of an electoral college, which subsequently elected the assembly members. For instance, the Assembly of Shensi was to consist of sixty-six members (including three Bannermen). In the primary election voters elected ten times (660) the number of representatives to form electoral colleges from which the fixed quota for the Assembly was elected. The administrative divisions of a province formed the basic electoral units.[8]

The regulations and procedures of the elections had, of course, many defects which cannot be enumerated here.[9] Of interest, however, is the underlying atmosphere of the elections. It is strange that few people paid attention to this unprecedented event. Limited information can be obtained from official records and Westerners who were in China at the time. According to several fragmentary reports, the prevalent attitude toward the elections throughout the country was one of apathy.[10] First of all, most Chinese knew nothing about an election, since they had never experienced anything like the Western democratic system. Second, transportation difficulties discouraged many from going to the voting stations —each district had only one station and most people had to walk many miles to vote.[11] Third, qualified wealthy people were "unwilling to give to the registrars the real value of their property, being suspicious lest there might be something else behind their questioning."[12] People were unenthusiastic even in the coastal provinces, which had already been exposed to Western influence.[13]

If, on the one hand, the elections suffered from the indifference of most Chinese, they were also the victims of another serious de-

8. *Hsü-hsiu Shen-hsi t'ung-chih kao* (Supplementary Gazetteer of Shensi Province) (1931), chüan 43. Hereafter *Shen-hsi t'ung-chih.*

9. The subject is dealt with in Meribeth E. Cameron, *The Reform Movement in China 1898–1912* (Stanford, 1931), pp. 101–35.

10. *NCH* (Feb. 18, 1910), p. 358; USDS, 893.00/351/2.

11. See Governor-general Chang Jen-chün's memorial, *Cheng-chih kuan-pao* (Imperial Gazette) (Peking), HT 1/6/21 (Aug. 6, 1909); *TFTC* (1909), no. 5, pp. 241–42.

12. *NCH* (June 12, 1909); USDS, 893.00/351/2. But others reacted in the opposite way. According to a sarcastic novel entitled *Yü-pei li-hsien* (Preparation for a Constitution), many people thought that a representative would become a government official. They bought land and houses right away in order to qualify as candidates. See *Yüeh-yüeh hsiao-shuo* (Monthly Novels) (Shanghai, 1906–09), 1909, no. 10.

13. USDS, 893.00/351/2.

fect—bribery. A report from the American consulate general in Canton said: "Dishonesty characterized the balloting; . . . the count of the votes was not accurate, and bribery was resorted to in a number of instances, the prices of single votes ranging from H. $100 to $500 or G. [U.S.] $40 to $200."[14] Another report from the American legation in Peking stated: "These elections excited no popular enthusiasm and [only] a small proportion of those qualified to vote actually cast ballots. The official influence in the choice of assembly members was very strong, in some of the provinces, notably the three Manchurian provinces, amounting almost to the appointment of the members by the officials."[15]

This was the first time that China had put into operation a Western system of election. A feeling of distrust was inevitable in this country of limited education.[16] But there are some favorable reports on the assemblies in coastal provinces and in a few inner provinces. We know, for example, that the election in Chihli was one of the best conducted. The American legation reported that the members chosen were "generally respectable." The people there had been stimulated by the introduction of Western ideas since the middle of the nineteenth century. Tientsin, the seaport of Chihli, had had a Municipal Council since 1907. Under the governorship of Yuan Shih-k'ai, the council had been exposed to the Western system. This had given the local population practice in limited self-government before the establishment of their Provincial Assembly. Thus the Municipal Council not only laid a foundation for the Assembly; it also enhanced the leadership of the constitutionalists from Chihli province.[17]

Kiangsu, another coastal province, had a well-organized Assembly from the beginning of its preparation. Under the leadership of Chang Chien, the Kiangsu people operated their Assembly in an orderly way.[18] They even asserted that there had been little bribery in the election.[19] The operation of their Assembly became the model for other provinces.[20]

14. Ibid.

15. Ibid., 893.00/492.

16. *NCH* (Feb. 18, 1910), p. 358.

17. For more details on the Tientsin Municipal Council, see "Shang jen Chih-li tsung-tu Yüan tsou T'ien-ching shih-pan tzu-chih ch'ing-hsing che" (Memorial on the General Condition of the Practice of Self-government in Tientsin by Governor-general Yuan Shih-k'ai), *TFTC* (1907), no. 10.

18. For more details about the Kiangsu Assembly, see Chang Chien, *Se-wang tzu-ting nien-p'u* (Chronological Autobiography of Chang Chien) (Shanghai, 1935), p. 63.

19. *HHKM, 4,* 160–62.

20. *Shen-pao* (Shanghai Daily News) (Shanghai), HT 22/8/2 (Sept. 25, 1910).

In Shansi and Shensi, two interior provinces, the establishment of assemblies was praised as a "conspicuous success." A reporter for the *North China Herald* who had visited these two assemblies said he was "much impressed with the session spirit."[21]

Although the 1909 elections had the greatest impact on the coastal provinces, they had, as well, some effect on the Chinese people as a whole by introducing them to the Western system of self-government. Let us look at the results of the elections. First we must determine how many people were qualified and in what proportion they represented the whole population of each province. Then we will consider the backgrounds of those who emerged as leaders of the constitutionalists.

Since there were strict requirements the proportion of qualified voters to the whole population was low. From the figures in Table 3.1, we can see that the highest percentage was in Chihli (.62%); the lowest in Kansu (.19%) and Heilungkiang (.23%). The average was only .42 percent, a figure which roughly corresponds to the observation of an American official.[22]

Who was chosen by the four voters out of each 1,000 of the population? According to the limited materials available, most assembly members were civil degree holders. Table 3.2 shows the backgrounds of those elected in five provinces. Assuming these five provinces to be indicative of a nationwide trend, the figures in Table 3.2 show that 89 percent of the representatives were degree holders; the other 11 percent included large taxpayers and some men of unknown status.

Further analysis of these materials in conjunction with local and provincial gazetteers and additional details about the levels of the degree holders are shown in Table 3.3. Unfortunately, detailed materials available at present are limited to these five provinces.[23] Nevertheless, existing figures do show that a large proportion were of the gentry class, among whom higher-level gentry were the most numerous (50.5%), while the lower level constituted almost two-

21. *NCH* (Feb. 18, 1910), p. 359.

22. The report of the American consulate in Canton says: "That of every three hundred inhabitants, but one is entitled to vote" (USDS, 893.00/351/2).

23. *Hei-lung-chiang t'ung-chih kao* (Heilungkiang Provincial Gazetteer) (1932) includes the names of the Assembly members with their backgrounds. Apparently, because of the low educational standard, only 11 out of the 30 members were listed as *sheng-yüan* degree holders; none of those listed held a degree higher than that. (See chüan 50, pp. 26b–28a.) Among the 72 Fukien Assembly members, I find 2 with *chin-shih* degrees and 17 with *chü-jen* degrees. Further data are not available at present.

fifths (39.5%) of the total members.[24] Apparently, all the assemblies were controlled by the gentry.

It is interesting that the ninety-eight members of the National Assembly elected from the provinces were also largely of the gentry class. The distribution is: metropolitan degree holders (*chin-shih*),

Table 3.1. Proportion of Electoral Voters to Population[25]

Province	*Population*	*Electoral Voters*	*Percentage*
Chihli	25,932,133	162,585	.62
Fengtien	12,133,303	52,679	.43
Kirin	5,580,030	15,362	.27
Heilungkiang	2,028,776	4,652	.23
Kiangsu	32,282,781	162,472	.50
Anhwei	16,229,052	77,902	.48
Kiangsi	23,987,317	—	—
Chekiang	21,440,151	90,275	.42
Fukien	15,849,296	50,034	.39
Hupeh	25,590,308	113,233	.38
Hunan	27,390,230	100,487	.36
Shantung	30,987,853	119,549	.38
Honan	35,900,038	—	—
Shansi	12,269,386	53,669	.43
Shensi	10,271,096	29,055	.29
Kansu	4,989,907	9,249	.19
Szechwan	48,129,596	191,500	.39
Kwangtung	32,000,000	141,558	.44
Kwangsi	8,000,000	40,284	.50
Yunnan	9,466,695	—	—
Kweichow	9,665,227	42,526	.42
Average			.42

24. For differing criteria for determining the line between the upper and lower gentry, see Chung-li Chang, *The Chinese Gentry, Studies on Their Role in Nineteenth Century Chinese Society* (Seattle, 1955) and Ping-ti Ho, *The Ladder of Success in Imperial China, Aspects of Social Mobility, 1368–1911* (New York and London, 1962).

25. Sources: Population figures are quoted from D. K. Lieu, *The 1912 Census of China* (Institute of Pacific Relations, 4th Conference, Shanghai, 1931), Documents, no. 40b. The figures for Anhwei are taken from *An-hui t'ung-chih* (Gazetteer of Anhwei Province); the province had its first census in 1911. The figures for Kwangtung and Kwangsi are quoted from the 1910 estimate because Lieu did not include either these two provinces or Anhwei. The figures on electoral voters are from *TFTC* (1909), nos. 3–7. Figures for Heilungkiang are from *Hei-lung-chiang t'ung-chih kao* (Draft Gazetteer of Heilungkiang Province), chüan 50, p. 23b; Shensi and Kansu from *Cheng-chih kuan-pao,* HT 1/8/13 (Sept. 26, 1909) and 2/6/4 (July 10, 1910).

20; provincial degree holders (*chü-jen*), 37; senior licentiates (*kung-sheng*), 18; licentiates (*sheng-yüan*), 11; and others, 12. Details appear in Table 3.4.

The sources for these four tables inform us, although the precise figures are unreliable, that among the members of both the

Table 3.2. Proportion of Gentry to Other Members in Five Provincial Assemblies[26]

Province	*Members of Gentry*	*Others*	*Total*	*Percentage*	
				Gentry	*Others*
Fengtien	42	8	50	84	16
Shantung	96	7	103	93	7
Shensi	55	11	66	83	17
Hupeh	92	5	97	95	5
Szechwan	115	12	127	91	9
Total	400	43	443	89	11

Table 3.3. Distribution of Gentry Members in the Provincial Assemblies[27]

Province	*Chin-shih*	*Chü-jen*	*Kung-sheng*	*Sheng-yüan*	*Non-gentry*	*Total*
Fengtien	3	8	13	18	8	50
Shantung	5	19	23	49	7	103
Shensi	3	11	22	19	11	66
Hupeh	7	12	39	34	5	97
Szechwan	2	33	25	55	12	127
Total	20	83	122	175	43	443
Percentage	4.5	18.6	27.4	39.5	10	100

26. Sources: Fengtien from *NCH* (Feb. 18, 1910), p. 359; Shantung from *TFTC* (1909), no. 7; Shensi from *Shen-hsi t'ung-chih,* chüan 43; Hupeh from *Hsü-hsiu Hu-pei t'ung-chih kao* (Supplementary Gazetteer of Hupeh Province), chüan 10; Szechwan from *HHKMHIL, 3,* 145–52. The figures for Shantung, Hupeh, and Szechwan include reserves (alternates).

27. Sources: The same as those for Table 3.2 plus consultation of local gazetteers. For Fengtien Province see *Feng-t'ien t'ung-chih* (Gazetteer of Fengtien Province) and also *hsien* (district) gazetteers. Of course assemblymen were not exclusively gentry constitutionalists. According to the *HHKMHIL, 3,* 145–52, there were, for example, four delegates to the Szechwan Provincial Assembly who belonged to the Revolutionary Alliance, secretly of course. Obviously, there must have been secret Revolutionary Alliance members chosen from delegates to other provincial assemblies. We know that Kuo Chung-ch'ing (Hsi-jen), vice-chairman of the Shensi Provincial Assembly, was an important revolutionary. However, the total figure was probably very low.

local and central assemblies, a number had studied either in Japan or in other foreign countries.[28] During the last years of the Ch'ing dynasty, there undoubtedly were quite a number of degree holders who had studied abroad, although most of them were of the lower level. These people may have introduced some Western parliamentary procedures into China, but no complete record is available at present. A number of these elected representatives were part of the constitutional movement; moreover, among them were its most important leaders.

The majority of the chairmen of the provincial assemblies had

Table 3.4. Backgrounds of the Representatives from the Provinces in the National Assembly[29]

Province	*Chin-shih*	*Chü-jen*	*Kung-sheng*	*Sheng-yüan*	*Non-gentry*	*Total*
Fengtien		2		1		3
Kirin			1		1	2
Heilungkiang					2	2
Chihli	3	3	2	1		9
Kiangsu	2	3	1	1		7
Anhwei		4		1		5
Kiangsi	1	2	1		2	6
Chekiang	2	2	2	1		7
Fukien	2	1	1			4
Hupeh			5			5
Hunan	1	1		2	1	5
Shantung		3	1	2		6
Honan	4		1			5
Shansi	1	1	1		2	5
Shensi	2	1	1			4
Kansu	1	2				3
Szechwan		3		2	1	6
Kwangtung		5				5
Kwangsi		1	1		1	3
Yunnan	1	2			1	4
Kweichow		1			1	2
Total	20	37	18	11	12	98

28. Fengtien 4; Chihli 10; Kiangsu 9; Anhwei 1; Kiangsi 2; Chekiang 7; Fukien 3; Hupeh 5; Hunan 3; Honan 2; Shansi 4; Shensi 1; Szechwan 5; Kwangtung 2; Kwangsi 2; Yunnan 1; Kweichow 4.

29. Source: *Hsiu-chen chio-chih ch'üan-han* (Concise Government Ranks and Officials) (Peking, 1911), pp. 31b–33a. The quota was 100. Owing to the postponement of establishing self-government in Sinkiang, two representatives were missing.

the tremendous prestige of the metropolitan degree, as Table 3.6 shows. In the National Assembly, however, the most eloquent and popular leaders were of the lower gentry and had studied abroad. Some constitutionalists who demonstrated ability as leaders before and during the Revolution were Chang Chien of Kiangsu, T'an Yen-k'ai of Hunan, T'ang Hua-lung of Hupeh, and P'u Tien-chün of Szechwan, all chairmen of their provincial assemblies; Sun Hung-i, a member of the Chihli Assembly and the top leader during the petition period; and I Tsung-k'uei, Lo Chieh, Lei Fen, and Liu Ch'un-lin, the most eloquent in the National Assembly.

Constitutionalist Propaganda Before the Revolution

Before the Revolution, the constitutionalists propagated their ideal of a constitutional monarchy for China. Their goal remained constant, but their propaganda methods changed from time to time. This can be seen in Liang Ch'i-ch'ao's writings.

Liang was the theorist and leader of the constitutionalists. When he abandoned his radicalism in 1903, he turned to the constitutional movement and suggested means for the adoption of a constitution.[30] He wrote to several Ch'ing government officials, urging them to work to establish a constitutional monarchy;[31] at the same time, he wrote articles discussing steps toward its adoption. He took the adoption of the Meiji constitution as his model. He thought that the Meiji constitutional movement should be followed because the Chinese were a backward people; there was too much illiteracy for a constitutional government to function effectively. China needed a period of enlightenment similar to that experienced by Japan and the European countries. In "On Enlightened Autocracy"[32] and other articles (1906–07) attacking the

30. See Chang P'eng-yüan, *Liang Ch'i-ch'ao*, pp. 163–75.

31. In 1905 Liang corresponded constantly with Tuan-fang, an influential Manchu official; for the latter, he drafted memorials for the adoption of a constitution that "amounted to some 200,000 words." In 1907, Tai Hung-tz'u, minister of the Board of Justice, addressed Liang asking him to define the relationship between the Board of Justice and the Supreme Court. See *Liang . . . nien-p'u* (Taipei, 1958), pp. 215, 223. Important new material on the secret relations between the Ch'ing court and the constitutionalists is to be found in Ernest Young, "The Reformer as a Conspirator: Liang Ch'i-ch'ao and the 1911 Revolution" in A. Feuerwerker, R. Murphey, and M. C. Wright, eds., *Approaches to Modern Chinese History* (Berkeley and Los Angeles, 1967), pp. 239–67.

32. "K'ai-ming chuan-chih lun" (On Enlightened Autocracy), *HMTP* (1906), no. 74.

views of the revolutionaries,[33] Liang argued that raising the educational standards of the Chinese people was an important prerequisite for the establishment of a constitution.

How long should the period of enlightening China last? As long as ten or twenty years, Liang thought.[34] He was aware that Japan had adopted its constitution twenty-two years after the Meiji Restoration. China might be prepared in less than twenty-two years, but according to traditional Chinese thought, education is a long-range project. To wipe out illiteracy takes time.

Liang's views may well have influenced the Ch'ing government. In 1906, the same year that he was arguing the necessity of enlightened steps, the Ch'ing court announced that China was going to establish a constitutional monarchy; two years later, it promulgated its nine-year Preparation Program, in which education was heavily emphasized. Surprisingly, Liang objected to the slowness of this program, although it was to be carried out in a much shorter time than he had originally recommended. By 1907, however, he wanted to speed up the preparation even more. There were a number of reasons for this change. First, he feared that China might be divided at any time by foreign powers. He also felt that the Ch'ing government had not adopted as positive an attitude toward the preparation as the constitutionalists had hoped for, and that this appearance of procrastination might easily cause revolution at such a critical time. He was right. Internal dissent was mounting and externally, in her weakened condition, China was easy prey for any one of the great powers. She was saved from complete foreign domination only by the existence of contradictory aims among the powers themselves.

The attitude of the Ch'ing government toward the establishment of a constitution was apathetic, if not deliberately negligent. Liang could not bear to see how slowly the regime acted. He now stressed the urgency of the task. Before 1907 his slogan had been, "Construct a parliamentary system and set up a responsible cabinet." Afterward, he added the word "urgent" to the slogan. Liang subsequently wrote many articles calling for the early establish-

33. Especially "Ta mou-pao ti-ssu-hao tui pen-pao chih po-lun" (A Reply to the Fourth Issue of a Certain Magazine Which Argues with the New People's Miscellany), *HMTP*, no. 79. For more information, see Chang P'eng-yüan, *Liang Ch'i-ch'ao,* chap. 7.

34. See reference in n. 32, and Chang P'eng-yüan, *Liang Ch'i-ch'ao*, p. 239.

Table 3.5. Eloquent Orators of the National Assembly[35]

Name	*Native Province*	*Chin-shih*	*Chü-jen*	*Kung-sheng*	*Sheng-yüan*	*Study Abroad*
Lei Fen	Kiangsu				X	X
I Tsung-k'uei	Hunan				X	X
Lo Chieh	Hunan				X	X
Liu Ch'un-lin	Chihli	X				X
Shao Hsi	Chekiang			X		
Meng Chao-ch'ang	Kiangsu		X			X
Yü Pang-hua	Chihli				X	
Li Chin-jung	Chihli				X	
Chi Chung-yin	Chihli		X			X
T'ao Chün	Hupeh			X		
Wu Tz'u-ling	Kwangsi				X	

Table 3.6. Chairmen of the Provincial Assemblies[36]

Province	*Chairman*	*Chin-shih*	*Chü-jen*	*Study Abroad*	*Unknown*
Fengtien	Wu Ching-lien		X	X	
Kirin	Ch'ing-k'ang		X		
Heilungkiang	Wang Ho-ming				X
Chihli	Yen Feng-ko	X		X	
Kiangsu	Chang Chien	X			
Anhwei	Fang Li-chung	X			
Kiangsi	Hsieh Yüan-han	X			
Chekiang	Ch'en Fu-ch'en	X			
Fukien	Kao Teng-li		X		
Hupeh	T'ang Hua-lung	X		X	
Hunan	T'an Yen-k'ai	X			
Shantung	Yang Yü-ssu	X			
Honan	Tu Yen	X			
Shansi	Liang Shan-chi	X		X	
Shensi	Wang Heng-chin		X		
Kansu	Chang Lin-yen	X			
Szechwan	P'u Tien-chün	X		X	
Kwangtung	I Hsüeh-ch'ing	X			
Kwangsi	Ch'en Shu-hsün	X			
Yunnan	Chang Wei-ts'ung		X		
Kweichow	Yo Chia-tsao		X	X	

35. The sources for names and backgrounds are the same as those in n. 29. For the speeches see USDS, 893.00/482; also *TFTC* (1910), no. 12, pp. 175–77.

36. Sources: Names quoted from *Chung-wai jih-pao* (Universal Gazette) (Shanghai), HT 1/11/9 (Dec. 21, 1909).

ment of a constitution, most of which were published in the periodicals *Cheng-lun* (Discussion of Politics) and *Kuo-feng-pao* (National Trends).[37]

The constitutionalists adopted Liang's slogan to popularize and strengthen their movement. Liang's ideas for a parliament and cabinet put the Ch'ing government in a dilemma, for the regime had never explained the relation between a parliament and a cabinet. A parliament would be summoned after the period of preparation, but a "responsible" cabinet was, as Liang asserted, intentionally neglected. Although the Ch'ing preparation was to a certain extent influenced by Liang, elements of the Western system were distorted by the regime. Liang was enraged, and his criticism was severe.[38] Both openly and privately, he urged the constitutionalists to fight for both parts of his program. But though his criticism was severe, his actions were moderate. It seemed to him that if the constitutionalists admonished and petitioned continually, they would achieve their goal;[39] Liang believed the government would give in.[40] His advice was accepted by the constitutionalists, who repeatedly presented petitions, as we shall see.

Liang Ch'i-ch'ao, as theorist of the constitutionalists, had various propaganda organs. These were the well-known *Hsin-min ts'ung-pao* (New People's Miscellany), *Cheng-lun,* and *Kuo-feng-pao.*[41] But while Liang's works were read by the constitutionalists, the circulation of these periodicals was limited. The constitutionalists needed to reach the whole nation. Therefore, in addition to the periodicals edited by Liang, other propaganda organs were set up or permeated. The most important of these included *Tung-fang tsa-chih* (Eastern Miscellany), *Shih-pao* (Eastern Times), *Chung-wai jih-pao* (Universal Gazette) in Shanghai, and *Kuo-min kung-pao* (Public Opinion Daily) in Peking. These were the most influential constitutionalist organs during the last years of the Ch'ing

37. The important early articles: "Cheng-wen-she hsüan-yen-shu" (The Manifesto of the Political Information Institute); "Cheng-chih yü jen-min" (Politics and the People), *Cheng-lun* (1907), no. 1.

38. "Chiu-nien yü-pei li-hsien kung-pa" (An Epilogue to the Nine-Year Preparation for a Constitution), *KFP* (1910), no. 1.

39. "Tsa-ta mou-pao" (A Miscellaneous Reply to a Certain Magazine), *HMTP* (1907), no. 84.

40. "Lun cheng-fu tsu-nao kuo-hui chih fei" (On the Crime of the Government in Impeding Parliament), *KFP* (1910), no. 17; *Liang . . . nien-p'u,* chüan 17–19, passim.

41. For more detailed information about these three periodicals, see Chang P'eng-yüan, *Liang Ch'i-ch'ao,* pp. 286–304, 311–22.

dynasty. Generally speaking, they supported Liang's views. In addition to printing his articles, they reported on their own views and activities. These periodicals and daily newspapers did not merely represent in-group support of the constitutional movement. Most other publications of the time expressed similar positions, for example, the *Shen-pao* (Shanghai Daily News) which, founded in 1872, was China's oldest newspaper.

The widely circulated *Tung-fang tsa-chih* and *Shen-pao* were greatly influenced by Chang Chien, the top leader of the Kiangsu-Chekiang (Chiang-Che) constitutionalists. Chang, with the intention of using public opinion organs to spread constitutionalism, extended his influence in 1907 to *Shen-pao*;[42] his disciple Meng Sen, a well-known historian in the later years of his life, was appointed chief editor of the *Tung-fang tsa-chih*.[43] These two organs generally expressed the views of the constitutionalists.

The other two daily newspapers, the *Shih-pao* and the *Chung-wai jih-pao,* were also closely allied to the constitutionalists. Ti Pao-hsien, publisher of *Shih-pao,* was himself a member of the Kiangsu Provincial Assembly. Like his friend Liang Ch'i-ch'ao, he had been caught up for a time in the tide of radical thought and had joined in the uprising of the Independent Army in 1900. But like Liang, Ti changed his views and came to feel that China could not bear drastic change before the people had been educated and enlightened, and so he turned to the constitutional movement. We are variously informed that his daily newspaper was established with funds left by the Independent Army, or with a 30 percent

42. *Shen-pao* was first published in 1872 by Ernest Major, an American, as a commercial newspaper. For more than 30 years, it remained rather conservative with few readjustments of its opinions. Politically, it generally supported the Ch'ing government. In 1905 *Shen-pao* adopted a constitutional outlook by quoting Liang Ch'i-ch'ao's constitutionalist slogans on New Year's Day. In 1907 *Shen-pao* was sold to Hsi Tzu-p'ei, its former manager, who was very much influenced by Chang Chien. After that, *Shen-pao* supported strongly the constitutional movement. See Lei Chin, "*Shen-pao* chih kuo-ch'ü chuang-k'uang" (A Short Account of the Past of *Shen-pao*), Shen-pao kuan, *Tsui-chin chih wu-shih nien* (The Last Fifty Years) (Shanghai, 1922), part 3.

43. Meng Sen (1868–1937) held the minor traditional degree of *sheng-yüan*. He studied in Japan from 1901 to 1904. When he returned to China, he actively joined the constitutional movement. His ardent attitude was influenced by Chang Chien and Cheng Hsiao-hsü, directors of the Association to Prepare for the Establishment of Constitutional Government. Afterward, Meng was appointed chief editor of the *Tung-fang tsa-chih* (Eastern Miscellany). For more information about Meng, see Wu Hsiang-hsiang, "Wo ti yeh-shih Meng Hsin-shih hsien-sheng" (My Teacher Meng Sen), *Chuan-chih wen-hsüeh* (Biographical Literature) (Taipei, 1962–), *1*, 1.

investment from K'ang Yu-wei and Liang Ch'i-ch'ao,[44] who in fact claimed that *Shih-pao* would not have been able to maintain its operation without their continuous financial support.[45] This suggests that Ti was for a long time closely associated with both K'ang and Liang. He was also a friend of Chang Chien. When Chang went to Shanghai, the two often met in the Hsi-lou study at the *Shih-pao* office.[46]

Wang K'ang-nien, publisher of the *Chung-wai jih-pao,* was an "old" constitutionalist. Even before the Reform Movement of 1898, Wang had been an active comrade of the K'ang-Liang group. Firm in his conviction that China's salvation lay in peaceful reform, Wang sought to bring his views to a wider public through journalistic activity. We can trace the origin of his *Chung-wai jih-pao* to the Reform Movement of 1898.[47] Wang consistently held to his views as a newsman and a constitutionalist.[48] He also maintained his friendship with the K'ang-Liang group.

It is worth pointing out here that such newspapers and periodicals as these took a common stand on contemporary political issues. Given their close relationship to the constitutionalists, it is not mere coincidence that they used the same slogans and propaganda. The *Tung-fang tsa-chih* is a good example. The questions discussed and emphasized seem almost a copy of Liang's *Hsin-min ts'ung-pao*. The former, a monthly magazine, appeared in 1904. In the first year of its publication, since there was little open talk about the adoption of a constitution, the magazine did not touch

44. *Chung-kuo chin-tai ch'u-pan-shih tzu-liao* (Historical Materials on Modern Chinese Publishing), ed. Chang Ching-lu (Shanghai, 1953–54), p. 87; *HHKMHIL, 4,* 86–88.

45. According to a letter from K'ang Yu-wei to Liang Ch'i-ch'ao, during the period from 1903 to 1908, K'ang had sent Ti at least $200,000 to cover *Shih-pao's* operating expenses. Liang also stated in a letter that he had invested $10,000 in the newspaper. See *Liang . . . nien-p'u,* pp. 286, 299.

46. *HHKMHIL, 1,* 62–63.

47. The earliest form of the newspaper was not a daily but a ten-day periodical, the well-known *Shih-wu pao* (Chinese Progress); for political reasons, *Shih-wu pao* changed its name to *Ch'ang-yen pao;* it then reorganized as *Shih-wu jih-pao;* finally it adopted its present name. See Ko Kung-chen, *Chung-kuo pao-hsüeh shih* (History of Chinese Journalism) (Peking, 1955), p. 140.

48. Wang sold the newspaper to a government official, Ts'ai Nai-huang, in 1909. Because of Ts'ai's conservative policy, the paper was lifeless and stopped publication after the Revolution in 1911. See Hu Tao-ching, "Wu-hsü cheng-pien wu-shih-nien-chi yü *Chung-wai jih-pao*" (The Fiftieth Anniversary of the Coup d'État of 1898 and the Universal Gazette), *Pao-hsüeh tsa-chih* (Journal of Journalism) (Shanghai, 1948–49), *1,* 8–10.

upon the question. In 1905 the question of the constitution arose. An editorial said that China's salvation lay neither in a constitutional monarchy nor in a democratic republic; the only path to salvation was "enlightened autocracy."[49] In essence, this was no different from Liang's statements in *Hsin-min ts'ung-pao.* In 1906, *Tung-fang tsa-chih* agreed to the establishment of a constitution and also propagandized the urgent need for education for all.[50] But in 1907 it abandoned all its previous views, arguing that such educational goals could not be achieved without a constitutional monarchy.[51] Therefore China needed a constitution immediately. This was also Liang's point of view in the last issues of *Hsin-min ts'ung-pao* in 1907 and in the newly published *Cheng-lun.*

In addition, Meng Sen, the chief editor of *Tung-fang tsa-chih,* contributed a special feature to the periodical, the Constitutional Chapters, which reported on every aspect of the constitutional movement.[52] The widely circulated monthly reproduced important constitutional articles from newspapers and periodicals, especially those of Liang. *Tung-fang tsa-chih* was quite influential during the period of constitutional preparation and furthered the cause of the constitutional movement.

Shen-pao, Shih-pao, and *Chung-wai jih-pao,* three important daily newspapers in Shanghai, adopted almost the same attitude as *Tung-fang tsa-chih.* Here I quote a few lines of a *Shih-pao* editorial of June 1907 which I consider representative of these papers:

> China today is in a period of transition from autocracy to constitutionalism. Our editorials and other important articles will not fail to explain and compare the advantages and disadvantages of each. Our target is autocracy. We shall not cease our attack before its elimination. We encourage and hope for a constitution. We shall make every effort to have the government and our people understand what a constitution means,

49. "Li-yung Chung-kuo chih cheng-chiao lun" (On the Use of Official Exhortations to Keep Order in China), *TFTC* (1905), no. 4.

50. "Lun li-hsien yü chiao-yü chih kuan-hsi" (On the Relation Between the Adoption of a Constitution and Education), *TFTC* (1905), no. 12.

51. "Jen-min ch'eng-tu chih chieh-shih" (An Interpretation of the Educational Standard of the People), *TFTC* (1907), no. 2 (Constitutional special edition).

52. *TFTC* (1909), nos. 1–7, 12; (1910), nos. 1–2, 4–5. It is interesting to note that Meng's articles first appeared with his surname; after he was elected a member of the Kiangsu Provincial Assembly, he wrote under the pseudonym Hsin-shih. When the constitutionalists were accused of "having secret connections with newspapers," Meng's articles appeared in the section of "National Affairs" without his name.

> be willing to have one, and be on the way toward having one. To initiate such an attitude is our responsibility and our hope. Can we solve China's problems? That depends upon whether we get a constitution. Let us not forget that a constitution is the foundation of politics.[53]

Finally, the *Kuo-min kung-pao* in Peking should be mentioned. Unfortunately, no file of this paper is available. Some information is supplied by its chief editor Hsü Fo-su, from which it is clear that the paper was an important organ of the constitutionalists in North China.[54] In 1909, the constitutionalists decided to organize a daily paper in Peking. Hsü was invited to be the chief editor. *Kuo-min kung-pao* began publication in July 1910. Liang Ch'i-ch'ao and many other constitutionalists supplied articles. During the period of the publication of *Kuo-min kung-pao,* the constitutionalists who gathered in Peking to present their petitions to the government frequently met in its office. It was the only organ which served as an opinion center of the constitutionalists in the North and according to Hsü's record had wide influence in the capital. Because it often attacked the Ch'ing regime, it was suspended briefly in December 1910.[55]

Petition and Protest

The constitutionalists had established their leaders and their principles. In 1910 they began to take action. It was Chang Chien, the chairman of the Kiangsu Provincial Assembly and one of the group's most important leaders, who initiated a conference in Shanghai to discuss united action. Fifty-one representatives from sixteen provinces[56] arrived in Shanghai after the first yearly assembly session in November 1909. Many among the representatives were chairmen and vice-chairmen of their local assemblies. In light

53. *Shih-pao* (Eastern Times) (Shanghai, beginning in 1904), KH 33/5/16 (June 26, 1907); also reproduced in *TFTC* (1907), no. 7.

54. Hsü was originally a member of the Society for China's Revival of the revolutionaries. When he got acquainted with Liang Ch'i-ch'ao in Japan, he turned to the constitutionalist group. Several of his articles were published in *Hsin-min ts'ung-pao* in 1907. He returned to China as Liang's liaison representative to the constitutionalists. For more information on Hsü, see Chang P'eng-yüan, *Liang Ch'i-ch'ao,* pp. 205–06, n. 42.

55. For more details on *Kuo-min kung-pao* (Public Opinion Daily), see *Liang . . . nien-p'u,* pp. 313–14; *Who's Who in China* (Shanghai, 1926), under Hsü Fo-su.

56. The sixteen provinces were Kiangsu, Chekiang, Anhwei, Kiangsi, Hupeh, Hunan, Fukien, Kwangtung, Kwangsi, Shantung, Honan, Chihli, Shansi, Fengtien, Kirin, and Heilungkiang. See *Chung-wai jih-pao,* HT 1/11/9 (Dec. 21, 1909).

of China's critical condition the constitutionalists decided to petition for the early convening of parliament, which seemed to them the best means to achieve China's salvation. They immediately proceeded to Peking; a series of three petitions followed in the next year.

These petitions, presented on January 26, June 22, and October 3, 1910, were carefully worked out. According to the constitutionalists 200,000 people signed the first petition, 300,000 the second, and 25,000,000 the third.[57] This was the first time that large numbers of Chinese under the leadership of the constitutionalists had spoken out. This "mass movement" was an unprecedented event, for not only was it an endeavor in which able leaders personally participated, but it was also an action which profoundly affected the development of subsequent events. Its course deserves a brief account.

First we should consider how the constitutionalists mobilized the intellectuals, if not the masses, to support this movement. Members of the local assemblies, who considered themselves the representatives of the people, presented the first petition under the name Petition Association of the Provincial Assemblies. When they received a cold reply they realized that their group of 200,000 would have to be expanded if the Ch'ing court was to be aroused. They then appealed to those who saw the urgent need for a parliament, and the associations of education, commerce, agriculture, railroads and mining, the Bannermen, the Overseas Chinese, and the residents of Peking sent representatives to join them. On June 22, they petitioned again under a new name, Petition Association for the Early Convening of Parliament, this time with approximately 300,000 signatures. Although the second petition was much stronger than the first, the Ch'ing regime still turned a deaf ear. The petitioners were warned that further petitioning would be reprimanded.[58]

But the constitutionalists were not silenced by threats from arrogant princes. They concerned themselves with expanding their strength still further. Having already incorporated all possible support of civic associations they then appealed to the governors and governors-general. The provincial administrative chiefs were

57. The figures are based on Huang Hung-shou, *Ch'ing-shih chi-shih pen-mo* (General History of the Ch'ing Dynasty) (Shanghai, 1925), chüan 77; *KFP* (1910), no. 16, p. 5; *NCH* (July 25, 1910), p. 205.

58. *NCH* (July 8, 1910), p. 103.

urged to memorialize in favor of the early convening of parliament when the constitutionalists submitted their third petition, allegedly with 25 million signatures, on October 3. The National Assembly, which held its first formal session at the same time, was also requested to extend its support.[59]

The constitutionalists organized themselves efficiently. Those who were able to write prepared the texts of the petitions; those who were eloquent spoke to the masses in large cities. The petitioners, most of them between the ages of thirty and forty and having some knowledge of modern political science, took responsibility for the practical work. They conferred together before each step. They improved with experience. The second petition was better organized than the first; the third was more colorful than the second. In 1910 the attention of the whole nation seemed to be attracted by the petitioners.

Sun Hung-i was one of the ablest and most ardent leaders throughout the petitioning. A provincial degree holder (*chü-jen*), he had studied in Japan and was a member of the Chihli Provincial Assembly. He was chosen by the conference in Shanghai to lead the petition movement. Before Sun went to Peking to take up his duties, he swore that "if the petition failed, he would prefer to die at the gate of the palace rather than leave the capital."[60] He uncomplainingly devoted his full time to the petitions, the parades, and the pleading, seldom participating in social activities.[61]

The constitutionalists cited three reasons for the immediate convening of parliament. First, China's international position was very dangerous because the foreign powers had been threatening partition; only a parliament which showed national unity could prevent the catastrophe of the nation's downfall. Second, China was on the brink of bankruptcy, and the outbreak of revolution was imminent; only a parliament which lent popular support to the government could prevent such disasters. Third, the present

59. *TFTC* (1910), no. 6, p. 86.

60. *KFP* (1910), no. 2, literature section, pp. 1–2. In Peking, Sun Hung-i once more assured his comrades of his determination, saying, "Since we have assumed responsibility on behalf of our countrymen, we are trusted by the whole nation. Until we realize our aim, I shall not leave the capital, even if every one of our representatives has left." See *Shen-pao*, HT 2/6/11 (July 17, 1910).

61. For more details about Sun's career, see *Who's Who in China* (1926), under Sun Hung-i.

government officials had not devoted themselves to their duties; only a parliament could force them to be responsible.[62]

In basic content the petitions were similar; in tone, however, the three texts differed greatly. At first, the constitutionalists tried moderation, quoting such Western theories as the separation of the legislative, executive, and judicial functions, and putting emphasis on the importance of a parliament. When they discussed how internal affairs could be better conducted, for instance, they stated: "The parliament is one of the most important institutions of a constitutional country. When there is a parliament [run by the people's representatives], the government can be urged to function in the right way for the people's benefit."[63] When they talked about solving the financial difficulties of the government, they again stressed the need for a parliament: "The parliament is a solemn place in which the people's representatives engage in deliberation on political affairs. This right must be guaranteed. If the government needs to raise taxes to solve any difficulty, the people's representatives should be consulted."[64]

The second and third petitions grew progressively stronger. The constitutionalists no longer discussed the people's rights on a theoretical basis. They began to warn and curse the princes and ministers responsible for government corruption. In the third petition, presented to the Regent, the constitutionalists accused the government of being just as corrupt as a hopeless, dying regime:

> Your Excellency may have observed the results of the [constitutional] preparation in the past two years. Though edicts have repeatedly been sent down to enforce its practice, when finance is mentioned the present condition is as confusing as it has always been; when education is talked of, it is as rotten and pedantic as it has always been; as far as the police are concerned, they are as remiss as usual. Furthermore, regarding

62. See the texts of the first and third petitions, *TFTC* (1910), nos. 1, 11. The original texts of the second petition, which were not published, are in the archives of the National Palace Museum (Taiwan). An article "Kuo-hui ch'ing-yüan t'ung-chih-hui i-chien shu" (Prospectus of the Association of Comrades to Petition for a Parliament), which I suspect to have been written by Liang Ch'i-ch'ao, contains the opinions of the second petition. See *KFP* (1910), no. 9.

63. Text of the first petition, *TFTC* (1910), no. 1.

64. Ibid.

> military construction, [economic] enterprises, and all other national affairs, nothing whatsoever has been accomplished to satisfy the people's will. Foreign observers seeing this corrupt situation have only pity for us, marching blindly in the dark; there is no hope at all.[65]

They demanded that parliament be called immediately. Otherwise, they warned, the histories of the English and French people, who in struggling for constitutional government had overthrown and guillotined their kings, might be repeated in China. They threatened the outbreak of revolution.[66] They quoted lofty and bold words from Chinese history:

> Liu Hsiang once warned the Han Emperor Chen-ti, saying: "When the people turn to keeping silent about the government, the throne is in a very dangerous situation. Your Excellency is the descendant of the imperial family which you have the obligation to preserve. If your imperial throne should be removed and replaced, you could not escape the miserable fortune of becoming a slave of others. If you are not concerned about yourself, you must in any case remember that you cannot ignore your obligation to preserve the shrine of your imperial ancestors." These are truly bitter and bold words. When we read it a thousand years later, we cannot refrain from shedding tears. But we wonder why a ruler whose situation is just as dangerous pays little attention to these bold but honest words. Perhaps he knows that the appeal is well-intentioned but trusts it not; instead he sits idle until he is placed under the guillotine, when he will be laughed at by the people. It is a pitiable thing, and we know it is not because heaven has no pity on him, or that he is out of reach of salvation. The ruler did not listen to this honest warning. It is he himself who is to blame.[67]

Trying every means of persuading the Manchu court, the constitutionalists hoped their pleas would be given a fair hearing. But the reward they received was a mere three-year reduction in the preparation period. Another edict was sent down at the same time, on November 4, 1910, ordering the petitioners to dissolve their

65. Petition presented to the Regent, *TFTC* (1910), no. 11.
66. The second petition and the prospectus, see n. 62 above.
67. Petition through the National Assembly, *TFTC* (1910), no. 11.

organization; no more petitioning would be allowed.[68] A vigorous movement ended abruptly.

The petition for a parliament was led almost entirely by the constitutionalists of the local assemblies. It was clear that it was useless to talk about a responsible cabinet before the establishment of parliament, but the constitutionalists in the National Assembly, who considered themselves parliamentary members, emphasized in their deliberations that a cabinet which would be responsible to the Assembly must be organized.

The National Assembly was a provisional organization of two hundred members, half appointed by the Emperor and half elected by the representatives of the local provincial assemblies. It was formally inaugurated on October 3, 1910, the same day the petitioners were launching their third petition. It is interesting that the representatives, many of whom had taken part in the first and second petitions, boldly moved that the whole Assembly support the petitioners. And when the third petition was over, they immediately took up the question of responsible government. A whole session, which lasted for more than three months, spent most of its time deliberating this subject.

How was it possible that the Assembly, with an apparent majority of imperial representatives, spent most of its sessions on a single question which manifestly was opposed by the conservative Ch'ing court, when the latter had no intention of establishing a cabinet responsible to a deliberative body organized on a provisional basis? The answer to this strange question is simple. The representatives from the provinces ran the whole Assembly.

To explain briefly, there were two factors which gave the people's representatives the upper hand. First, there was the nature of the Assembly's organization. The Ch'ing court thought that the appointed president and one hundred members appointed by the Emperor would control the decisions. But in fact, not all the imperial appointees wholeheartedly supported the interests of the government. It was reported that some appointed princes and dukes from the dependencies, for example, inclined to the people's side.[69] In addition, some Chinese hereditary nobles differed with

68. For the reply edicts to the three petitions, see *TFTC* (1910), nos. 1, 6, 11.

69. *KFP* (1910), no. 26, "Chinese Affairs"; USDS, 893.00/482, "The Constitutional Assembly," enclosure 7; *TFTC* (1910), no. 13, p. 255.

the government.[70] Thus the imperially appointed representatives, in theory the majority, became de facto the minority.

Second, there was a contrast of ability and forbearance. Generally speaking there were able men among both the imperial and the people's representatives who recognized the weaknesses of the government. In the sessions, however, the imperial appointees often kept silent, fearing to speak against the government lest their criticism endanger their future official careers. On the other hand, the representatives from the provinces, mostly young men with some knowledge of Western ideas and less at stake personally, were quick to speak and criticize. Among them, Lei Fen of Kiangsu, I Tsung-k'uei and Lo Chieh of Hunan, and Liu Ch'un-lin of Chihli were the most influential and eloquent orators. Lei, "gifted with the talent of analyzing details," I, "the sharpness of his voice penetrates the whole room," and Lo, "a bold critic," were praised as three heroes of the National Assembly. Liu Ch'un-lin, a metropolitan degree holder and a Confucian armed with Western knowledge, was a learned scholar-politician and his speeches were always respected by his comrades.[71]

Of course, the basic problem was that the Ch'ing regime was too weak to withstand the representatives' criticism. There were several proposals from the provincial assemblies which led the representatives to criticize the government. The sale of local bonds in Hunan led the constitutionalists to criticize the government's breaking its own law;[72] the rise in the price of salt in Yunnan and the need for a revision of the school regulations in Kwangsi[73] enraged the constitutionalists and led them to denounce the princes and ministers "who had insulted" the Assembly. This was the turning point at which the constitutionalists became hostile to the Ch'ing regime. After the eighteenth session, there were furious attacks on the princes and ministers. One accused them "of deceiving the throne and the people by not giving the proper advice"; another denounced them for having violated the law of the land, "for they changed the regulations of the Assembly at their will"; a third accused them "of committing a crime because they had

70. Marquis Tseng (Tseng Kuang-luan) spoke denouncing the government. See USDS, 893.00/482. Also see Young, "The Reformer as a Conspirator."

71. For further information about these people, see I Tsung-k'uei, *Hsin shih shuo* (The World Made New) (Hsiangt'an, 1922), chüan 2, p. 25; *KFP* (1910), no. 26, pp. 97–98; *Who's Who in China* (1926).

72. USDS, 893.00/482.

73. USDS, 893.00/492; *TFTC* (1910), no. 12, pp. 170–77.

attempted to defeat the aims of the constitutional movement of the nation."[74]

The constitutionalists in the National Assembly launched a formal protest against the Grand Councillors by submitting to the throne a memorial which listed the faults of the princes and ministers, a gesture of open hostility toward the government. There could be no compromise except, the constitutionalists asserted, through establishment of a cabinet responsible to the National Assembly. The key section of the protest reads:

> Facing the present dangerous situation of the nation—internal anxiety and external disorder—the people suffer from intense poverty; finance is confronted with difficulties. We do not know what the end will be. The Grand Councillors, who are granted the Emperor's highest favor, occupy the top positions among the officials. They should be cautious and encouraging. They should try to show their loyalty faithfully and strive together in order to recompense the great favors they have received. But, on the contrary, they are neither responsible about their duty, nor do they have the intelligence for administration; they advance and retire together with pretended interest and sympathy. They have no will either to return the [obligatory] grace to the imperial family or to pay any attention to the suffering of the people. Holding high positions and enjoying large salaries, they guard their own private affairs and ignore those of the public. They look like strangers who care nothing about the peace and danger of the nation, the joy and sorrow of the people. They have no heart.[75]

The memorial was rejected by the government. The representatives were reprimanded and told that they were forbidden to interfere with "the appointment of government officials, which is the absolute right of the court."[76] Although some of the constitutionalists ventured to criticize the Regent, the belligerence between the National Assembly and the government came to an end. There were no more stormy attacks launched by the representatives.[77]

74. See notes 72, 73.

75. *TFTC* (1910), no. 12, pp. 172–74.

76. Ibid., p. 163.

77. The second yearly session took place in October 1911, when the Revolution broke out. Some 80 to 90 members, mostly imperial appointees, attended the session. Their decisions received no contemporary attention so we shall not discuss the matter. For further information, see USDS, 893.00/790, 892; *Liang . . . nien-p'u,* p. 350.

The constitutionalists were disillusioned. With this the development of China's current affairs completely changed direction.

Loss of Aim and Change in Attitude

As we have seen, the Ch'ing government had promised on November 4, 1910, to reduce the projected period of preparation by three years but simultaneously ordered that the petitioning organization be disbanded and that no more petitions be presented.[78]

According to a report in *Shen-pao,* the constitutionalists obeyed the order of the government and disbanded their petitioning organization.[79] There were no more petitions, except for a few local protest demonstrations. *Shen-pao* reported nothing unfavorable to the interests of the government. But this was a mere facade. Some recently available materials show that the constitutionalists did not simply disband their organization and go home. Instead they drew up further plans in secret before leaving Peking.

According to Hsü Fo-su, chief editor of *Kuo-min kung-pao* and the liaison between Liang Ch'i-ch'ao and the constitutionalists, the attitude of the petitioners changed greatly:

> In the third petition, strong words appeared. The summary sentences say: "If the government has no sympathy toward its people's suffering, and will do nothing to prevent revolution or chaos, and is determined not to call a parliament immediately, we, the representatives, can only return home to report to the people that the government was disappointing. We will beg no more." As I understand them, these rather radical words expressed not only the indignation of the representatives, but also indicated that if the government refused them again, they might turn to revolution. The Ch'ing court was very angry after reading the third petition. An edict was sent down which ordered the representatives to depart immediately from the capital and return home. The representatives were also angry. The evening after receiving the edict, they all gathered together in my office [of the *Kuo-min kung-pao*] and secretly decided: "Let us go back home and report the hopeless political condition of the government to the provincial assemblies. We here decide that we shall lead rev-

78. For the edict, see *TFTC* (1910), no. 11.
79. *Shen-pao,* HT 2/10/24 (Nov. 25, 1910).

> olution secretly. All the comrades of the assemblies will form the body of the organization. If there is any event in the future which could lead to an uprising, comrades in each province will respond by proclaiming independence immediately." When the secret decision had been made, they left Peking the next day. The Ch'ing court, knowing nothing about the decision of the representatives, was delighted to see their peaceful departure. The court took it for granted that there would be no more disturbances; but the fool's paradise would not last long.[80]

Wu Hsien-tzu, who was a petition representative of the Overseas Chinese in America, makes a similar statement:

> On the day the petition representatives were ordered to leave the capital, they had a secret meeting. They would proclaim provincial independence in demanding a constitution. That T'ang Hua-lung, P'u Tien-chün, and many others who had been petition leaders and had attended the secret meeting seized the opportunity [to proclaim their provinces' independence] is no trivial incident.[81]

I question Hsü's statement that "if the government has no sympathy toward its people's suffering . . . we will beg no more," and Wu's assertion that the petitioners would proclaim provincial independence in demanding a constitution. I doubt that they recorded the precise facts. But attention should be centered on whether or not the constitutionalists really changed their attitude at all. Judging from the text of the third petition, the radical words recorded by Hsü might have appeared in an early draft, but were omitted or revised in the final statement; although the third petition was much stronger than the first two, we find nothing of the tone recorded by Hsü. Based on the statements of Hsü and Wu we can be sure the secret meeting was held, but the decision that was reached remains a mystery.

It is possible that the constitutionalists grew hostile toward the government when they received the order to leave Peking immediately. Some materials supply supporting evidence. First, the "Message to Fellow Countrymen" from the constitutionalists should be noted. The significant portions follow:

80. *Liang . . . nien-p'u,* pp. 314–15.

81. Wu Hsien-tzu, *Chung-kuo min-chu hsien-cheng tang tang-shih* (A History of the Chinese Democratic Party) (Hong Kong, 1952), p. 16.

> Our Dear Fellow Countrymen: We have been entrusted with the responsibility of petitioning for a parliament in the capital since last year. We have used all our efforts to pray for an early calling of parliament. It was very lucky that we obtained the support of both the governors and members of the National Assembly who memorialized to back up our prayer. Princes and ministers seemed to be touched and to change their minds. But a decision was not made until they had held several procrastinating meetings. Now the court has proclaimed that parliament shall be called in 1913 [three years ahead of the original schedule]. You can see that this three-years reduction [in delay] is not what we struggled for, although we have made every effort. It is a pity that our strength is not as great as the firmness of our will. It is painful to tell the bitter result. We are very sorry that we have to report to you what is contrary to what we wished. We are ashamed to say that we have failed.[82]

The message went on to express concern about what might happen in the future, as the government, in the hands of a few incompetent princes and ministers, was weak. The constitutionalists feared that China's very destiny was at stake. The concluding sentences state:

> Now that the decision has been made by the court, and judging that the further offering of a few people's prayers would be useless, we are hesitant about what our future steps should be. We need your direction. What you decide, we will follow.[83]

The words are ambiguous, but they express at least the feeling that a change was needed.

For additional evidence, let us turn to Liang Ch'i-ch'ao. In a speech which recalled his writings a year before the Revolution, Liang said that since the tenth month of the second year of Hsüan-t'ung (November 2–December 2, 1910) he had "proclaimed war against the government almost every day." He thought the *Kuo-feng pao,* his organ during this period, was much more radical than the earlier *Ch'ing-i-pao* had been:

> I remember during the high tide that the people of the whole nation petitioned for a parliament, the government was trying to procrastinate and evade [the will of the people] by a false

82. *TFTC* (1910), no. 11, "Current Affairs."
83. Ibid.

> promise. I was really very angry. I shouted with desperation that if the government did not try to change its attitude, there would be no such date as "the fifth year of Hsüan-t'ung" in history.[84]

When we examine his writings, we find nothing radical immediately after the Ch'ing court had proclaimed the three-year reduction in the period required for constitutional preparation.[85] Violent words came some three months later. He attacked the government for seeking an unlawful foreign loan and denounced the corruption of the government as an incitement to revolution.[86] What caused him once again to become so hostile to the Manchu regime? Here a letter from Liang to Hsü Fo-su is relevant. Dated March 13, 1911, it reads:

> In recent months this kind of thought [revolution] enters my mind several times almost every day. But I prefer not to change my words again. It is not that I fear being laughed at for having a character as changeable as the weather. I know that I truly do not have that kind of cleverness. I cannot do that any more. It is beyond my ability. If you want to return to the old idea, there is nothing wrong with you. Only I do not understand whether you adopt it as an end [as the revolutionaries do]; [if so] further discussion would be worthwhile. Otherwise, I absolutely cannot agree with your doing things insincerely. Nevertheless, this question cannot be decided without our seeing each other. I earnestly hope that you can come.[87]

This letter reveals that Hsü had informed Liang of the indignation and the intentions of the constitutionalists. Apparently Hsü, also disillusioned, intended to return to his earlier and more radical ideas.[88] Liang indicates that until he received Hsü's news of the constitutionalists in Peking he had simply been following the

84. Liang Ch'i-ch'ao, *Yin-ping-shih wen-chi* (Shanghai, 1915), chüan 57, p. 3. The fifth year of Hsüan-t'ung (Feb. 6, 1913–Jan. 26, 1914) was the date on which the government proposed to convene parliament. In fact, what would have been the fifth year of the Hsüan-t'ung reign became the second year of the Chinese Republic.

85. See Liang's "Tu shih-yüeh-ch'u-san shang-yü kan-yen" (My Feeling after Reading the Edict of October Third), *KFP* (1910), no. 28.

86. "Wu-hu! hsin-wai-chai, ching-ch'eng" (Alas! The New Foreign Loan), *KFP* (1911), no. 9.

87. *Liang . . . nien-p'u,* p. 333.

88. It must be remembered that Hsü was once in the revolutionary camp.

usual propaganda line; his position had not changed. Thus his writings remained moderate, discussing how to organize a parliament and how a responsible cabinet should function, among other things. Though he denied it later, during this period Liang seems to have tolerated the three-year reduction.

Hsü's letter, which is not available, apparently asked Liang to initiate a change in public opinion toward revolution. But that was not possible for Liang in March 1911, though he was derided as a changeable man. He had quarreled and severed relations with the revolutionaries long before. It was impossible for him to rejoin them now. He could however write and condemn the Ch'ing regime. Though he tried to refrain from expressing radical thoughts, he severely criticized the government. He apparently sympathized with revolution. After the March 29 uprising in 1911 in Canton, there appeared an article which shows that Liang had taken the same stand as the constitutionalists. In the article, he says:

> The longer [the present government] lasts, the more *yüan-ch'i* or power of evolution we lose. Death by decay and committing suicide by taking poison are the same. However . . . deadly poison sometimes cures disease. We would rather try [some poisonous medicine] to have a hope of living than merely sit waiting for death by decay.[89]

The study of Liang's letter to Hsü Fo-su and his change in outlook reveals the position of the constitutionalists. When they were ordered to leave Peking, the leaders evidently had a secret meeting. Radical discussion inevitably took place. Some decision not confined to the previous course of the movement may have been reached orally. This may explain why those constitutionalists in the National Assembly, which was still in session, now criticized the Ch'ing regime without reserve.

The attitude expressed by the constitutional newspapers further helps to explain the situation. After the third petition their editorials were often radical in tone and frequently denounced the Ch'ing government. A few lines of the *Shen-pao* of February 1911 illustrate the general tendency:

> Alas! The slovenly mask of the new politics of our government is clearly off. Angry at those who petitioned for parliament, an

89. "Yüeh-luan kan-yen" (My Feeling about the Uprising in Canton), *KFP* (1911), no. 12.

> order was issued to drive them out of the capital; angry at the members of the National Assembly who demanded an extraordinary session, another order was almost issued. . . . Everyone knows that a constitution is the brain of a country; that the National Assembly is the foundation of our parliament. But the government hates both. How strange it is.[90]

An earlier editorial was sarcastically critical:

> The Europeans petitioned for their parliament with blood; we Chinese pray for ours with ink and brush. How superior our culture is to that of the West! But their petition succeeded, our ink has failed repeatedly. . . . A word from the editors: weapons of war are ominous; sincerity cuts through metal and stone. A certain petitioner said that petitions will not stop until the calling of parliament. But when will you gain your end? If you gain your end, our Western forerunners will be surprised and say, "They are really cultured people. We Westerners cannot compete."[91]

The constitutionalist organ now urged that they "not waste valuable time by waging an empty war of tongues."[92]

Criticisms of this sort are too numerous for us to include them all. The general feeling is clear: the will of the constitutionalists was not as firm as before; their confidence in achieving their aim had been shaken. Hsü Fo-su recorded the truth, though in exaggerated form. Other material sheds further light. The constitutionalists' attitude changed with the tide of the Revolution. We turn now to their activities during the Revolution.

Constitutionalist Support of the Revolution

As a result of their disillusionment with the government, some constitutionalists decided to join in revolution, should it break out. Sun Hung-i, the petition leader, and T'ang Hua-lung, T'an Yen-k'ai, and P'u Tien-chün, all provincial assembly chairmen, led the group that would not compromise with the Ch'ing government. Although they had organized the Constitutionalist Friends Club on June 4, 1911, with the aim of forcing the Ch'ing regime to call parliament immediately, their thoughts soon turned toward revolution. Their background made it impossible for them to lead an uprising, but they could accept the fact of revolution. Since

90. *Shen-pao,* HT 3/2/24 (March 24, 1911).
91. Ibid., HT 2/6/1 (July 7, 1910).
92. Ibid., HT 2/12/3 (Jan. 3, 1911).

these four men represented four different provinces, we will examine their activities individually.

P'u Tien-chün and the Szechwan Railroad Struggle

Szechwan was the last of the fourteen provinces to declare independence in response to the Wuchang uprising. After its declaration of independence, P'u Tien-chün, the Provincial Assembly chairman, was chosen as governor (*tu-tu*). Why did Szechwan declare its independence so late?

The Szechwan railroad struggle was under the leadership of P'u Tien-chün.[93] The significance of the railroad struggle as an added stimulant to the outbreak of the Wuchang uprising is well known, but we are sometimes given a distorted picture of who the actual leaders in this crisis were.[94] The railroad company was controlled by a small group of P'u's men. When P'u was studying in Japan, he had already declared that the Szechwan railroad should be commercially managed. Probably he had invested some capital in the railway's construction. He tried to control the Board of Directors, of which seven out of thirteen members were his men.[95]

P'u and his followers declared that civilized or peaceful struggle for the railroad (*wen-ming cheng-lu*) was their guiding principle. But although the principle was peaceful, their actions were provocative. It is interesting to note that on the one hand, the petitioners in Peking denounced the government for perversely clinging to the words of old edicts, thus creating delays in convening parliament.[96] On the other hand, in Szechwan, they contradicted themselves by quoting past edicts to support their own arguments.

93. P'u obtained his metropolitan degree, the highest civil honor, simultaneously with T'ang Hua-lung and T'an Yen-k'ai in 1905. He also studied in Japan, where he became acquainted with Liang Ch'i-ch'ao. P'u's schoolmate Hsiao Hsiang was also elected as vice-chairman of the Szechwan Assembly. Teng Hsiao-k'o, the chief editor of *Shu-pao* (Szechwan News), was another of P'u's schoolmates and a good friend. They led the Railroad Struggle together.

94. On this, see Ichiko Chūzō, "Shisen horo undō no shunōbu" (The Leaders of the Railway Protection Movement in Szechwan in 1911), *Ochanomizu daigaku jimbun kagaku kiyō*, *6* (1955), 161–73.

95. For more details of the Szechwan Railroad Company, see *HHKMHIL*, *3*, 158–59.

96. In reply to their first two petitions, the Ch'ing government quoted the edict of the Kuang-hsü Emperor that promulgated the nine-year constitutional preparation and said that the projected program could not be altered. The petitioners argued that times change quickly, and that the government should adjust its policy to the changed situation; it was not good to hold on too strongly to past edicts. For details, see the texts of both the edict and petition in *TFTC* (1910), nos. 1, 6, 11.

They protested that the government had forgotten the edict of the Kuang-hsü Emperor promising that "the government should respect the people's opinion in public affairs; and the railroad would be allowed to be commercially managed."[97] They wrote the two phrases in parallel form and used them to decorate the Kuang-hsü Emperor's shrines, which the Szechwanese now built at crossroads and main streets. Wherever there was a shrine of the late Emperor, P'u's followers gave speeches to arouse the people's support. In addition, some distance from the shrines they posted another sign which read, "Officials get out of sedan chairs; officers dismount from horses." Supposedly the spirit of the late Emperor was there. Therefore, any government official passing by should be on foot.

The arrogant officials had been shown up by the clever Szechwanese, and conflicts were inevitable. When some Szechwanese issued the "Ch'uan-jen tzu-pao shang-chiao shuo" (A Discussion of Szechwanese Self-Protection), Chao Erh-feng, the Szechwan governor-general, took it as a declaration of rebellion. In autocratic China, such a discussion was considered very serious. P'u and eight of his followers were arrested. A peaceful struggle had turned into a bloody upheaval.

In effect, the railroad crisis was a rebellion, as well as showing P'u's hostile attitude toward the Ch'ing government. Since he was supported by the Szechwanese, however, the government dared not condemn him to death and had to release him. And finally, Chao Erh-feng, who had arrested P'u, had to turn the local government over to him as the Provincial Assembly chairman.

T'ang Hua-lung and the Wuchang Uprising

When the Wuchang uprising broke out, T'ang Hua-lung, chairman of the Hupeh Provincial Assembly, announced that he had "agreed to the Revolution a long time ago."[98] It was said that the revolutionaries had intended to offer him the leadership before they found Li Yüan-hung, an army colonel, to lead them. It was also said that T'ang had refused the offer, for he was not the military man needed in the early stage of the uprising.[99] Nevertheless,

97. *Ssu-ch'uan pao-lu yün-tung shih-liao* (Documents of the Szechwan Railroad Protection Movement) (Peking, 1959), pp. 183–84; *HHKM, 4,* 410–13; *HHKMHIL, 3,* 162.

98. *HHKM, 5,* 129, 176.

99. *Wan Yao-huang hui-i-lu* (Memoir of Wan Yao-huang) (Ms, Academia Sinica, Taipei, 1963); *Liang . . . nien-p'u,* pp. 376–77.

he was chosen first as general adviser and then as civilian executive chief of the revolutionary government in Wuchang.

T'ang cooperated positively with the revolutionaries. Here I quote a few lines of the speech he delivered at his inauguration as general adviser.

> The [Provincial] Assembly is a representative organization of the people. It has the responsibility to revive [the local province and] the nation. Now I thank you for having chosen me [as general adviser]. I will devote all my efforts to fulfilling my responsibilities. If we succeed, we shall regain our dignity; if we fail, I am afraid that chaos will never come to an end. The destiny of the Han people depends upon the outcome of this event. Will they distinguish themselves or will they be extinguished? I wish only one thing of you—do not slaughter your own people.[100]

T'ang gave hope to the Wuchang uprising. He immediately organized an administrative body which sent telegrams to other provinces asking them to declare independence.[101] He also stated that the future government should be a republic.[102]

T'ang's contribution to the Wuchang uprising was twofold: he provided financial support to the revolutionary government,[103] and he successfully negotiated with the foreign consuls in Hankow, securing their governments' recognition of the Chinese revolutionary force as a belligerent group and gaining assurance of foreign neutrality in the uprising.[104] T'ang's actions stabilizing the revolutionary situation in the first few days of the uprising almost make us forget that he was a constitutionalist.

T'an Yen-k'ai's Influence

T'an Yen-k'ai, chairman of the Hunan Provincial Assembly, was elected governor of his native province ten days after its independence. But it seems he had been expected to lead the province ever since the Wuchang uprising. The murder of the revolutionary governor Chiao Ta-feng brought the chaotic situation in Hunan to an end. When T'an succeeded Chiao as provincial governor, he

100. *HHKM,* 5, 176–77.
101. Ibid., p. 203.
102. Ibid., p. 200.
103. Ibid., p. 178.
104. Ibid., pp. 226–27.

tried to restore local order, as well as contributing financial support to the revolutionaries.[105]

T'an believed that the Revolution should be "civilized." It should be different from a mob uprising; order was very important.[106] When Chiao Ta-feng planned to kill some Ch'ing officials, T'an stopped him, saying, "Our purpose is to capture power, but not by killing officials."[107] His influence prevented slaughter in Hunan.

Some of his followers asserted that T'an's greatest contribution to the Revolution was that he persuaded some Hunanese to declare independence in response to the Wuchang uprising. According to a contemporary memoir, encouraged by T'an, Ts'ai Ao in Yunnan, Sun Tao-jen in Fukien, and Shen Ping-k'un in Kwangsi all declared their provinces independent.[108] We know that during the first month after the uprising the Wuchang government very anxiously awaited the response of other provinces. Although Hunan declared its independence immediately after the uprising, the situation in the province was confused. When T'an became governor, T'ang Hua-lung in Wuchang wrote him saying that only T'an could maintain order in Hunan, the nearest province to the revolutionary government in Hupeh with which it could expect to stand shoulder to shoulder.[109] T'an's influence was indeed what the revolutionaries hoped for.

The Chihli Constitutionalists

Finally, we will briefly consider the constitutionalists of Chihli province. In view of the able leadership of Sun Hung-i during the petition period, it is clear that he and his comrades would not be idle when the Revolution broke out.

According to a revolutionary source, the Chihli people positively supported the Revolution.[110] The story concerns General Chang Shao-tseng, who protested against the Ch'ing government and

105. Shang Ping-ho, *Hsin-jen ch'un-ch'iu* (A History of 1911–12) (Shanghai, 1924), chüan, 5, p. 2.

106. Ibid., p. 1.

107. Ibid.

108. *HHKM, 6,* 154–58; some three other minor figures were mentioned also. Ts'ai Ao was a student of Liang Ch'i-ch'ao; Sun Tao-jen was the son of the famous Hunan general, Sun K'ai-hua, follower of Tseng Kuo-fan. Shen Ping-k'un was the incumbent governor of Kwangsi.

109. *HHKM,* 7, 159.

110. *HHKMHIL,* 5, 403–04.

urged it to promulgate the outlines of the constitution. General Chang decided to remodel the government by a coup d'état. This he could do only if his troops could pass through Tientsin[111] and obtain adequate financial support. A special envoy was sent to consult with the Provincial Assembly in Tientsin. The envoy's statement reflects the attitude of some assemblymen:

> On October 25, I arrived in Tientsin. . . . I visited the Assembly chairman, Mr. Yen Feng-ko . . . and Delegate Mr. Sun Hung-i and others . . . They were very glad to hear our plan. . . . Mr. Wang Fa-ch'in and Mr. Sun Hung-i were sent as representatives to Luanchow to meet General Chang Shao-tseng. They said that if General Chang's troops—the Twentieth Division—declared an uprising and organized a government in Tientsin, the local Assembly would definitely supply all military necessities in time.[112]

General Chang was a little too timid. He did not act in time. The expected events did not occur. However, the story reveals the Chihli people's attitude.[113]

The Trend Toward Revolution

The Remaining Constitutionalists

There were constitutionalists in other provinces who were also important though comparatively less active than the four "radical" figures discussed above. In Yunnan, the Provincial Assembly chairman, Chang Wei-ts'ung, joined hands with the military leader, Ts'ai Ao, to take over the local government from the Ch'ing governor-general.[114] In Kwangsi, the vice-chairman, Huang Hung-hsien, worked out the declaration of independence together with the incumbent governor, Shen Ping-k'un.[115] In Kweichow, chairman T'an Hsi-keng, joined by other assemblymen, demanded that the governor declare a peaceful independence.[116] In Chekiang,

111. According to the peace treaty of 1901, the Chinese army was not allowed access to the port city, Tientsin.

112. *HHKMHIL*, 5, 403–04.

113. It seems to me that North China was more or less controlled by the Ch'ing government. Although the assemblymen of Chihli would have preferred a drastic change, it was not an easy thing for them, simply because they were very near to the capital.

114. *HHKM*, 6, 246.

115. *HHKMHIL*, 2, 460–64.

116. T'an Hsi-keng succeeded Yo Chia-tsao, becoming chairman in 1910. See *HHKM*, 6, 447–48.

Chairman Ch'en Fu-ch'en and Vice-chairman Shen Chün-ju pressed the Manchu governor to turn the local government over to T'ang Shou-ch'ien, a constitutionalist, although he was not on the list of the local assembly.[117] In Anhwei, Chairman Tou I-chio tried to maintain order in the province and arranged the election of the incumbent governor, Chu Chia-pao, to continue the functioning of local government.[118] In Honan, many assemblymen tried to make contact with the Wuchang Revolutionary Government and attempted independence, but they were suppressed by the Manchu governor.[119] In Shansi, Chairman Liang Shan-chi worked in cooperation with the newly elected governor, Yen Hsi-shan, to maintain peace and prevent slaughter in the province.[120] In Fengtien, Chairman Wu Ching-lien, who later came to Nanking to join the new government, attempted to persuade the governor-general not to support the Ch'ing government.[121]

Although the role of these eight constitutionalists was not as prominent as that of the four "radicals," their importance cannot be neglected. Without their participation a chaotic situation with serious consequences might have resulted.

We know little about the rest. But since we find no one who openly opposed the Revolution, we may assume that they approved or at least maintained a neutral attitude.[122]

Chang Chien, A Special Case

The case of Chang Chien, one of the leaders of the Kiangsu-Chekiang group, is a curious one. Chang was a constitutionalist from the beginning.[123] He had not changed his view even a month

117. *HHKMHIL, 1,* 139–40. T'ang Shou-ch'ien, like Chang Chien, resigned from all official government positions and became a businessman; he had been general manager of the Shanghai-Hangchow Railroad Company before the Revolution. He, Chang Chien, and the Kiangsu governor, Ch'eng Te-ch'üan, were three influential figures during the Revolution. The three formed the Kiangsu-Chekiang group.

118. *HHKM,* 7, 173–75.

119. *HHKM,* 7, 352–56.

120. Shang Ping-ho, chüan 6, p. 2.

121. *Chung-kuo ko-ming-chi* (Records of the Chinese Revolution) (Shanghai, 1911–12), 7, 2.

122. I have some reservations about Chairman Chang Lin-yen of the Kansu Provincial Assembly, who was reported to be opposed to the Revolution. See Huang Yüeh, *Lung-yü kuang-fu-chih* (The Revolution of 1911 in Kansu) (1912), pp. 1–12.

123. In 1901, Chang wrote *Pien-fa p'ing-i* (A Calm Discourse on Reform), which suggests that China adopt a parliamentary system. When he visited Japan in 1903, the idea became stronger; later on he discussed from time to time with high officials how to reform China as a constitutional monarchy. He urged Chang Chih-tung, Yuan Shih-k'ai, and other influential figures to memorialize the government for an

after the Wuchang uprising. He had initiated the parliamentary petition and was content with its results. While Sun Hung-i and others were to readjust their future position, Chang and his comrades from the Kiangsu-Chekiang area set off firecrackers to celebrate the concession of the Manchu court.[124] Chang would not accept any suggestions that he change his attitude toward the establishment of a constitution. In 1911 he did not join the Constitutionalist Friends Club, although some of his disciples participated.[125] On the day the Revolution broke out in Wuchang, he was in Hankow across the river from the revolutionary city. Apparently he did not try to watch the beginning of the uprising. He immediately hurried back to his native province. He urged the commander in chief of the Manchu forces at Nanking, T'ieh-liang, and the Liang-Chiang governor-general, Chang Jen-chün, to send reinforcements to suppress the "rebellion."[126] In Soochow, where he met the provincial governor, Ch'eng Te-ch'üan, he joined him in memorializing the court to convene a parliament, hoping thereby to stem the tide of revolution.[127] He did not give up his idea of a constitutional monarchy.

However, on December 23, 1911, Chang abruptly changed his attitude. He cut off his queue to show that he was a republican, sent telegrams to the Mongolian people and to the army asking them to accept the birth of the Republic, and wrote many articles discussing its goals. His actions reflected a complete shift in position.[128]

---

early adoption of a constitution. He printed the Meiji constitution, which was presented to the court with his comments in 1904. When the Constitutional Mission sent by the government in 1905 to investigate foreign constitutions was threatened by a revolutionary bomb, he angrily denounced the assassination squad as rebels. He wrote another book on the constitutional history of Japan and organized the Association to Prepare for the Establishment of Constitutional Government, the first constitutionalist club, the same year; later he called on the constitutionalists to petition for an early convening of parliament. By studying Chang's constitutional thought, we find that he was to some extent a conservative among progressives.

124. *Shih-pao,* HT 2/10/19 (Nov. 20, 1910). But according to a report of the American legation in Peking, this was instigated by the Ch'ing government. See USDS, 893.00/482.

125. Sun Hung-i informs us that Chang Chien and some of his disciples had differences with the other constitutionalists. See *Liang . . . nien-p'u,* p. 397.

126. Chang Chien, *Tzu-ting nien-p'u,* p. 70.

127. Ibid.

128. For more details, see Chang Chien, *Tzu-ting nien-p'u,* pp. 70–71; "Cheng wen lu" (Political Writings), *Chang Chi-chih chiu-lu* (Complete Works of Chang Chien) compiled by his son, Chang Hsiao-jo (Shanghai, 1931), chüan 3, pp. 39–44.

The news organs under Chang's influence also changed in tone. During the first few weeks, his papers treated the Revolution as a rebellion or as a mere local disturbance. But "suddenly all of them turned to the stream of revolution."[129]

This seemingly strange and sudden change can be explained. First, we must consider the fundamental ideal of the constitutionalists. Liang Ch'i-ch'ao had often emphasized that if there were a parliamentary system including a responsible cabinet, any form of government would be acceptable.[130] This was a flexible doctrine. To be sure, the constitutionalists preferred peaceful reform to drastic change; they hoped that revolution could be avoided. But once the Revolution broke out and its forward motion could not be halted, they were forced to reexamine the slogans which the revolutionaries had propagandized. It seemed to the constitutionalists that there was no basic difference between the two political groups in their ideal of representative government. Since the goal for which they had struggled had yet to be achieved, they felt it might be wise to follow the new trend.[131]

Furthermore, the constitutionalists did not wish to witness a China divided and in chaos. They were fearful that if order could not be maintained their country faced the danger of being devoured by the foreign powers.[132] Therefore they tried to help the government suppress rebellions. Even P'u Tien-chün had claimed that the Szechwan railroad struggle was a "peaceful struggle."

However, while stopping the uprising was beyond their power, preventing it from spreading seemed an easy task to the constitutionalists. Their attitude of cooperation and compromise with the Revolution may have sprung from the hope of restoring peace as soon as possible. Taking this as a premise, it is easy to see why Chang Chien was busy discussing the maintenance of order with the local leaders. T'ang Hua-lung and T'an Yen-k'ai also gave this idea serious consideration. They demanded an early settlement of the situation.

Finally, it was apparent that the constitutionalists intended to

129. Yao Kung-ho, "Shang-hai pao-chih li-shih" (History of Newspapers in Shanghai), *Hsiao-shuo yüeh-pao* (Fiction Monthly) (Shanghai, 1910–31), *8*, 1 (1917).

130. Liang, *Yin-ping-shih wen-chi*, chüan 57, p. 4.

131. In the early Republic, former constitutionalists who organized a party continued to fight for their long-held ideals.

132. Their fear was not groundless; several of the contemporary powers were ready to interfere if the situation deteriorated. See John G. Reid, *The Manchu Abdication and the Powers, 1908–1912* (Berkeley, 1935); USDS, 893.00/650-750, passim.

control the situation themselves. The traditional Chinese gentry class saw themselves as the rightful leaders of the country. They refused to accept the role of idle bystanders watching the actions of the revolutionaries. And so the constitutionalists participated in public affairs. On the one hand, they urged a positive response to declared independence for the purpose of maintaining order, and on the other, they urged an early organization of a new government. Their influence was widespread. Nine out of the fourteen independent provinces were largely in their hands.[133] Chang Chien's influence was impressive. He was connected both with the revolutionaries and the Peking government, which was then in the hands of Yuan Shih-k'ai. Chang also became a key figure between the North and the South, and between the conservatives and the radicals. The peace negotiation envoys came to ask his opinion. The new government obtained his support. At his suggestion, the doomed Manchu court received polite compensation.[134]

Because of its ultimate failure, the constitutional movement in the late Ch'ing period has been criticized as too conservative, or even reactionary. But research into the ideals and activities of the movement reveals that both contributed to the success of the 1911 Revolution.

In summary, let us once more pose the question: Who were the constitutionalists? A look at the organization of the assemblies provides the answer. The leaders who came to the forefront after the establishment of the provincial assemblies were mostly the last generation of the traditional gentry. Though they were often wrongly abused as rotten Confucianists who cherished a broken and worn-out tradition, they saw bitterly that their country needed a change. They were young, on the average between thirty and

133. The nine provinces were: Hunan, Kiangsu, Chekiang, Fukien, Kwangsi, Yunnan, Kweichow, Shantung, and Szechwan. Based on *Chung-kuo ko-ming chi, 17,* 12–14.

134. Ti Pao-hsien's Hsi-lou and Chao Feng-ch'ang's Hsi-yin-t'ang (both private studies) were two places where the constitutionalists and revolutionaries met with one another. The private peace talks were often held there also. See Chang Chien, *Tzu-ting nien-p'u,* p. 71; *HHKMHIL, 1,* 62–63; *6,* 261–65; *HHKM,* 544; *Hsi-yin t'ang hsin-hai ko-ming-chi* (Chao Feng-ch'ang's Notes on the Revolution of 1911), quoted in Lu Yao-tung, "Hsin-hai ko-ming ch'ien-hou Chang Chien ti chuan-pien" (Chang Chien's Attitude before and after the 1911 Revolution), *CHS ts'ung-k'an, 1,* 223–24; Hupeh Provincial Philosophical Society and Scientific Society, ed., *Hsin-hai ko-ming wu-shih-nien lun-wen chi* (Essays in Commemoration of the Fiftieth Anniversary of the 1911 Revolution) (Peking, 1962), pp. 408–25.

forty, and they persevered in the pursuit of the ideas which had been provided by their theorist, Liang Ch'i-ch'ao. Their struggle, though it did not achieve its goals, undermined the Manchu government and gave impetus to the outbreak of the revolution.

During the petitioning period the constitutionalists backed up their demands with democratic slogans, which the revolutionaries also proclaimed. Both attacked the corruption of the government, although the constitutionalists sought legal rather than violent solutions. Hence the propaganda of the constitutionalists was able to spread to all parts of the country, while that of the revolutionaries could only be circulated secretly. Indeed, at one time people claimed that Liang Ch'i-ch'ao was the "spokesman" of the revolutionaries. Only after the establishment of the local representative system did the revolutionaries have other spokesmen to spread the doctrines which both parties cherished. If the tide of revolution was stirred by the revolutionaries, the constitutionalists were an indispensable aid.

But most important of all, we have to consider whether the constitutionalists really had a change of attitude when their petitions were finally rejected. Although at present sufficient documentary material to give positive proof of the changed attitude of the constitutionalists is unavailable, their activities during the Revolution proved where they stood. Without their opposition, the imperial system might have been preserved and renovated. On the other hand, without their leadership of the Revolution, there might have been more and bloodier local upheavals, leading to more sweeping revolutionary change. That compromise was possible and China was not fragmented is the constitutionalists' great achievement.

4. Political Provincialism and the National Revolution

John Fincher

Scholars of the Revolution of 1911 have been preoccupied with revolutionaries and their parties. Few have analyzed the role of the Ch'ing government and its bureaucracy, and little has been offered to make possible an understanding of either the constitutionalists or the army.

This essay tries to sketch in the missing parts of the picture needed to answer general questions about state and bureaucracy and their relationship to society and gentry from about 1909 to 1913. The answers are, however, stated in terms different from those of the original questions. Thus we speak of polity and society rather than state and society. Here "polity" includes a great deal that is reserved to "society" in most state-society schemes. Here "polity" covers not only the official government apparatus but also the informal structure of the Chinese sociopolitical matrix that performed public welfare and other functions at the local level. Since the gentry occupied most of the positions in this informal structure, a scheme like this, which focuses directly on the borderline between the gentry and other groups, is useful in examining the considerable changes in gentry cohesion and character and in the relationship of the gentry to the official apparatus after the abolition of the Examination System in 1905.

Polity is, along with society and economy, one of three complementary aspects of the same phenomenon; its description as a separate system eases the difficulty of explaining political process and political change.[1] For the period 1909 to 1913, the acceleration of

1. For a recent version of the concept of "polity" see Gabriel A. Almond, "A Developmental Approach to Political Systems," *World Politics, 17* (1965), 183–215. This article, which contains many bibliographical leads, supersedes much of Almond and Coleman, eds., *The Politics of the Developing Areas* (Princeton, 1960). A compre-

change was itself a distinguishing feature: different *rates* of response to events figured as much as different *ways* of response in distinguishing groups within the polity. Thus many "constitutionalists" differed from "revolutionaries" mainly in their slower acceptance of republicanism rather than in a preference for monarchy, which might, for example, be attributed to their Confucianism.

Out of the massive pile of data the Ch'ing bureaucracy deposited at the doorstep of students of modern Chinese history, the fragments introduced[2] and analyzed in this essay offer only illustrations, not proofs, of hypotheses about the drift of events. In 1908, the Manchu court announced a vast nine-year program of administrative reforms designed to bring the entire polity under greater central control than ever before. The reforms included the establishment of representative consultative bodies at the national, provincial, and local levels that, if successful, would have largely assimilated the informal local power structure into the official apparatus dominated by the bureaucracy. In fact, the establishment of provincial representative institutions in 1909 initiated a staged breakup of the central civil administrative apparatus. The task of reorganizing and rationalizing the local power structure was too great to be handled by the personnel or financial resources of a single administrative center, especially one so badly ravaged by time. The following section of this chapter discusses how these representative institutions broke the throne's monopoly on legitimacy with the tacit support of provincial governors (*tu-fu*)[3] and went on

---

hensive bibliography listing many case studies in the "political development" vein is "Political Development: a Bibliography, 1960–1964" (External Research Paper 159, August 1964, External Research Staff, Department of State, Washington, D.C.). Perceptive critiques include Samuel P. Huntington, "Political Development and Political Decay," in *World Politics, 17* (1965), 386–430, and Hugh Tinker, *Ballot Box and Bayonet: People and Government In Emergent Asian Countries* (London, 1964).

By far the most comprehensive and relevant example of the utility of structuralist approaches for the historian of China is S. N. Eisenstadt, *The Political Systems of Empires* (Glencoe, Ill., 1963).

2. I owe a great debt to Esther Morrison's monumental work on "The Modernization of the Confucian Bureaucracy" (unpublished Ph.D. dissertation, Department of History and Far Eastern Languages, Radcliffe College, 1959—hereafter referred to as Morrison). Professor Morrison's work is the most detailed and comprehensive analysis yet produced on Ch'ing administration.

3. The best translation of *tu-fu* is "governor-general and/or governor," as Chinese statutes of this period rarely specify further. I do not take up the question of the relationship of the two offices here and therefore translate the term *tu-fu* as "governor."

themselves to become legitimizers of the governments established during the 1911 Revolution. The third section explores in detail the relationship of the provincial assemblies to the bureaucratic structure and their contribution to a transformation of that structure that radically increased the power of the provincial apparatus at the expense of the central government. The fourth section deals with the sociopolitical changes the elections of the provincial assemblymen reflected and the new tone these changes imparted to politics. The final section concludes that the 1911 Revolution was part of the "Devolution of 1909 to 1913" which restructured the polity and introduced a new form of provincialism (the provincialism of residence rather than of native place) that was transitional to nationalism.

Numerous studies have distinguished the official apparatus of the metropolitan empire from the substructure of localities and have sought to explain the composition of, and relations between, the official hierarchy dominating the former and the informal hierarchy of gentry dominating the latter. In discussing these complex and controversial questions, two distinctions are helpful.[4] The first distinction is between the official bureaucratic apparatus—an official hierarchy of positions or functions reaching down to the district magistracies, and the local power structure—a relatively informal hierarchy of positions or functions reaching up from the villages and market towns. The second distinction is between two parts of the leisured class or elite: the bureaucratic elite—a higher elite who hold or can hold (at any given time the

4. In addition to Chung-li Chang, *The Chinese Gentry, Studies on Their Role in Nineteenth Century Chinese Society* (Seattle, 1955), which provides the most detailed study of the gentry's local functions, the distinction between the official and local structures is studied in T'ung-tsu Ch'ü, *Local Government in China Under the Ch'ing* (Cambridge, Mass., 1962); Hsiao-t'ung Fei, *China's Gentry* (Chicago, 1953); Kung-ch'uan Hsiao, *Rural China* (Seattle, 1960); C. K. Yang, "Some Characteristics of Chinese Bureaucratic Behavior" in Nivison and Wright, eds., *Confucianism in Action* (Stanford, 1959), pp. 134–64; and Franz Michael, "State and Society in Nineteenth-Century China," *World Politics*, 7 (1955), 419–33.

The scheme stated here draws largely upon that outlined very briefly by G. William Skinner in "Compliance and Leadership in Rural Communist China, a Cyclical Theory" (paper prepared for the 1965 Annual Meeting of the American Political Science Association, Washington, D.C.), p. 34; and in "Marketing and Social Structure in Rural China, Part 1," *JAS*, *24* (1964), 20, 30, 35, 40 ff. It meets some of the problems raised by Maurice Freedman in his review of Chung-li Chang, *The Chinese Gentry*, in *Pacific Affairs*, *29* (1956), 78–80, and by Ping-ti Ho, *The Ladder of Success in Imperial China, Aspects of Social Mobility, 1368–1911* (New York and London, 1962), pp. 30–32 and passim.

majority are out of office) positions in the official apparatus by virtue of having certain higher degrees, and the nonbureaucratic elite—a lower elite who may have certain lower degrees, but none of whose degrees is high enough for them to be entitled to positions in the official apparatus. The first distinction pertains to the political system—the higher and the lower polity, and the second to the social system—the higher and lower elites in society.[5] The two sectors were linked by the Examination System, which determined the particular individuals in the social system who were to hold particular positions in the political system. Ordinarily the official hierarchy was manned by the higher elite exclusively and the informal hierarchy of the local power structure manned by both the lower elite and, increasingly in its upper reaches, the higher elite while out of office. The law of avoidance insured that the official apparatus was always manned by individuals serving away from their native places; the organization of the local power structure was just the reverse.[6] The collapse of a dynasty involved the breakup of the upper polity but did not seriously disrupt the local power structure. The reestablishment of political unity under a new dynasty became at once a less impossible task and predictable in form.

Interpenetration of the local and central power structures over time was in general confined to the zone between the district magistracy and the provincial governorship. The stability of the gentry and ultimately of the whole polity suggest that, as the central apparatus retreated and even disappeared during periods of dynastic decline, the local power structure invaded this zone. At these times, the never completely clear line between the higher and lower elites was further blurred since it depended so much on the

5. Some questions about the difference between social classes and stratification could be raised here; the problem, I believe, turns on the extent to which political organizations "pervade" or "are pervaded" by the social and economic environment. This will be discussed in my conclusion. Eisenstadt, *Political Systems,* prefers the category "stratification" to "class" in his analysis of historic bureaucratic empires, a preference shared by most who stress, as I do here, the autonomy of the political segment. For a succinct comment on the difference between "strata" and "classes" in Ch'ing times, see Jonathan Spence, "On the Chinese Upper Class in Early Ch'ing," in *Ch'ing-shih wen-t'i* (mimeographed bulletin issued by the Society for Ch'ing Studies, New Haven and St. Louis), Issue 1, no. 1 (1965), 12–16. On the question of "pervasiveness" see Amitai Etzioni, *Modern Organizations* (Englewood Cliffs, 1964), chap. 7.

6. Access to the local power structure by resident nonofficial outsiders was, however, a critical qualification of the "localism" of this structure. See concluding section below.

parts of the polity controlling the granting of degrees.[7] The establishment of a new dynasty thus became a process of administrative reconquest.[8]

By the time of the 1905 abolition of the Examination System, and partly because of it, the local power structure was invading the domain of the central apparatus. The reforms of 1909 and events of the 1911 Revolution accelerated the process. At the same time, the take-over process itself was transformed and the character of the local structure changed from what it had been in past periods of dynastic decline and fall. This change served the cause of republicanism rather than that of restoration of monarchy.

Representative Institutions as Legitimizers

For more than two millennia before 1911, the legitimacy of the Emperor's rule was the most important bond holding the Chinese polity together. An important and to some extent unique component of this legitimacy was the popular sovereignty implied in the Mandate of Heaven. The strand of popular sovereignty was sometimes strong enough to shake the monarchy, but dynasties were traditionally toppled by other means. In the late Ch'ing popular sovereignty was becoming strong enough to pull an Emperor down. Previously the Emperor had merely been informally ac-

7. The point at which the line is drawn between the higher and the lower elite depends on judgments about the "pervasion" of society by the polity, since the point is determined by a degree (e.g. *kung-sheng* as the bottom of the higher elite) granted by the central bureaucratic apparatus (the upper polity). To the extent that money, education, and residence or place of family origin, etc., figure in the conferring of degrees and are controlled by social and economic factors, the line also measures the "pervasion" of the polity by the society and economy. Chang, *The Chinese Gentry,* pp. 7–8, marks the bottom of the "upper gentry" by the regular *kung-sheng* degree; thus his "upper gentry" and "lower gentry" fit the higher and lower elites respectively of the present scheme if the *kung-sheng* degree is used as the line. It would take more examination of what he calls (p. 111) the "marginal gentry" as well as the "lower gentry" to confirm or refute his thesis that economic and social factors conferred little autonomy on these two groups in their relations with the upper polity. It is apparently this conviction that leads him to group holders of purchased *kung-sheng* degrees with "lower gentry" (pp. 132–34). Ch'ü also downgrades purchased degrees, but for different reasons. The examination of "marginal" and "lower" gentry and of the influence of nongentry groups is particularly critical to the understanding of transition periods. See Ho, *Ladder of Success,* pp. 30–32; Ch'ü, *Local Government,* pp. 172, 176–77, notes on 313–14, 318–21.

8. This was essentially a process of civil rather than military conquest. As the dynastic histories generally indicated, *wen-chih*—civil achievements—usually reached a peak only some time after *wu-kung*—military achievements. See L. S. Yang, "Towards a Study of Dynastic Configurations in Chinese History," in his *Studies in Chinese Institutional History* (Cambridge, Mass., 1961), pp. 1–17.

countable[9] to the Confucian bureaucracy and other groups among the people and had depended on them for some of his strength. Then, in 1909 and 1910, the creation of provincial and national representative assemblies[10] greatly strengthened these popular elements; eventually the representative assemblies themselves threatened the throne's monopoly on legitimacy.

Though intended by the court to mobilize the resources of all localities under centralized control, the provincial assemblies often allied themselves with the powerful provincial governors and used the National Assembly to help isolate the Manchu court from the rest of the polity. During the 1911 Revolution the provincial assemblies helped organize provisional military governments (Lin-shih chün-cheng-fu) upon which they conferred legitimacy. Their role as a source of legitimacy was fortified by their cooperation in organizing, under republican banners, a second national assembly in Nanking. The Nanking Assembly began as a rival of the National Assembly that had been convoked in Peking by the Emperor, and finally became a rival to the Emperor himself. Thus the groundwork was laid for the abdication in Peking on February 12, 1912, when the Emperor turned his claim to legitimacy over to the Republic.

The provincial assemblies' claim on legitimacy dated back to elections held in 1909 under the provisions of the Ch'ing proclamations of 1908. In September and October 1907, the country had been promised a national assembly, provincial assemblies, and various local assemblies which were to have mixed legislative and executive duties and powers in preparation for eventual "self-government" (*tzu-chih*) at all levels. In August 1908, the Ch'ing promulgated a program designed to complete constitutional reform in nine years. The program called for popular elections of provincial assemblies in 1909. These assemblies were to provide half the members of the National Assembly, scheduled to convene in Peking in 1910; the Emperor was to appoint the other half pri-

9. See Eisenstadt, *Political Systems,* pp. 19–20, on "accountability" in traditional empires.

10. For the purposes of this paper it is sufficient to use the terms Provincial Assembly and National Assembly to cover the several different Chinese names for the institutions at these two levels over the period in question; the only further distinction I will make in English is between the rival Peking Assembly and Nanking Assembly, both of which were national assemblies in late 1911 and early 1912. Occasionally I have inserted the precise Chinese term in parentheses when the context requires it.

marily from metropolitan officials and court circles. "Self-government" in cities, towns, and villages was to be completed in 1914 and in prefectures, departments, and, most important, districts (*hsien*) in 1915. Finally, a parliament elected by the people in special elections was to convene in 1917.[11]

The members of the 1910–11 National Assembly who were elected from the provincial assemblies quickly and completely dominated that institution. Events of the 1911 Revolution showed the progress of their home provincial assemblies toward becoming potentially independent sources of legitimacy. In almost all cases, the provincial assemblies played a critical role in the smooth transfer of authority from the imperial to the revolutionary governments. In Hupeh, where the revolutionary explosion had begun, Li Yüan-hung became chief of the revolutionary military government (*Chün cheng-fu tu-tu*) with the endorsement of the Provincial Assembly as well as of the revolutionary soldiers. The regular commander of the secret revolutionary forces, Chiang I-wu, was absent when the imperial government fell and Governor-general (*tsung-tu*) Jui-cheng fled.[12] Chiang's successor to the captaincy of the rebel soldiers, Wu Chao-lin, accepted the invitation of the chairman of the Provincial Assembly, T'ang Hua-lung, to a meeting on October 11 in the Assembly Hall, where the two persuaded Li to accept the leadership. T'ang Hua-lung then became head of civil affairs, a subordinate but distinct position approximating that of the regular governor (*hsün-fu*), with the concurrence of the rebels obtained through Wu Chao-lin.[13] Only in Fukien does the Revolutionary Alliance appear to have met alone formally to

11. For a general account see Meribeth E. Cameron, *The Reform Movement in China 1898–1912* (Stanford, 1931) and Hou Shu-t'ung "Ch'ing-mo hsien-cheng yün-tung kang-yao" (An Outline of the Constitutional Movement of Late Ch'ing), in *Keng-wu lun-wen chi* (vol. 5 of *Yen-ching ta-hsüeh cheng-chih-hsüeh ts'ung-k'an*) (Yenching University, Political Science Series, Peiping, 1931).

12. Chang Kuo-kan, *Hsin-hai ko-ming shih-liao* (Historical Materials on the 1911 Revolution) (Shanghai, 1958), pp. 1, 2; Chang Yü-k'un, "Wen-hsüeh-she Wu-ch'ang shou-i chi-shih" (Record of the Wuchang Uprising of the Literary Institute), in *Chung-kuo chin-tai-shih tzu-liao hsüan-chi* (A Collection of Selected Materials on Modern Chinese History) (Peking, 1954), pp. 645, 648.

13. Chang Yü-k'un, pp. 649, 651–53; Chang Kuo-kan, pp. 71, 82–83; Yang Yü-ju, *Hsin-hai ko-ming hsien-chu chi* (An Account of the Beginnings of the 1911 Revolution) (Peking, 1958), p. 61; Ts'ao Ya-po, "Wu-ch'ang ch'i-i" (The Wuchang Uprising) in *HHKM, 5* (Shanghai, 1957), pp. 130, 131. For an account of the activities of revolutionary groups in Hupeh up to 1911, see Josef Fass, "Revolutionary Activity in the Province of Hu-pei and the Wu-ch'ang Uprising of 1911" (in English), *Archiv Orientalni* (Prague), *28* (1960), 127–49.

organize a revolutionary government. There the Alliance eventually not only supported reconstituting a provincial assembly, but also refused special provisions for its representation as a party in the assembly and did not exercise party control, as such, over the provincial government.[14] In other provinces, excepting perhaps Yunnan, Revolutionary Alliance members appear to have accepted the role of provincial assemblies, variously constituted, as the legitimizing organs whose concurrence was necessary, if not sufficient, to establish a republican government.

The relative autonomy of the provincial assemblies helped the anti-Manchu struggle during 1911 even in such supposedly loyal provinces as Fengtien. There the Assembly made no declaration of independence from the imperial government as had its counterparts in the revolutionary provinces, but it was at the center of the organization of a Society to Protect the Peace that absorbed most of the principal officials of the province, including the governor-general, into an unofficial hierarchy paralleling the official apparatus. This society ran the province behind the facade of the official government, at once preserving its loyalty to the Emperor and reserving the possibility of a smooth revolt.[15] Kirin and Heilungkiang imitated Fengtien, and a similar device was used by Shantung, which first declared support for the Revolution and then returned to the imperial government within a period of weeks.[16] The metropolitan province itself, Chihli, and nearby Honan housed provincial assemblies full of republican sympathizers. Their geographical position precluded a response to the Revolution like Fengtien's, but they sent delegates to the Nanking Assembly.[17]

During the 1911 Revolution, the provincial military governments showed some disposition toward autonomy, and in this the provincial assemblies had a hand. Szechwan, the "fuse of the Revolution," though the first to protest with wholesale violence against the Peking government, was the last to declare allegiance to the Republic. In no other province did the provincial assembly play as large a role in organizing rebellion and providing the prisoners for

14. Shelley H. Cheng, "The Revolutionary Activities of Fukien Republicans, 1901–12" (paper prepared for Research Colloquium on Modern China, The Sino-Soviet Institute, George Washington University, March 31, 1966), pp. 10–12.

15. Chang Kuo-kan, *Hsin-hai ko-ming shih-liao,* pp. 262 ff.

16. Ibid., pp. 249–51.

17. As did Fengtien. See Ku Chung-hsiu, *Chung-hua min-kuo k'ai-kuo shih* (A History of the Founding of the Chinese Republic) (Shanghai, 1914), p. 35.

imperial jails as well as leaders of the provincial republican government.[18] Kwangtung provided Sun Yat-sen and many other of the most prominent national leaders of the Revolutionary Alliance, but it also produced tendencies toward autonomy, expressed in Provincial Assembly plans for organizing the postrevolutionary government. These were overcome only by the vigorous intervention of Revolutionary Alliance members in Hong Kong.[19] Even in Kiangsu, home of the Nanking national republican government, the Provincial Assembly strained against the republican government in such matters as the appointment of officials to head the provincial government and the Nanking local government.[20] The strain was exacerbated by the financial burden of supporting the Nanking government, felt more immediately in Kiangsu, and the ambiguity of the attitude of Chang Chien, a former leader of the Provincial Assembly, toward the Revolution.[21]

The interest the assemblies showed in provincial autonomy, however, was more an assertion of their power as provincial legitimizers than a desire to exercise autonomy. None of the provinces that declared independence remained independent; independence was unanimously treated as transitional to the organization of a national republic. The provincial assemblies cooperated fully in the organization of a national assembly. While the legitimacy of the new national government depended on them, they also increased their own legitimacy by participating in a republican resolution of the succession crisis. The first republican national assembly (Ko-sheng tu-tu-fu tai-piao lien-ho hui) was convoked in Shanghai and Hankow in November by the duly constituted provincial military governments, and moved to Nanking in December in a compromise with the Wuchang military government's aspirations to national leadership. This assembly was succeeded on January 28, 1912 by a more regularly organized assembly (Lin-shih ts'an-i-yüan) of delegates from all the "independent" revolutionary and most of the "loyal" provinces. Regulations allowed provinces to choose their delegates in several ways: appointment by the chief

18. Chūzō Ichiko, "The Railway Protection Movement in Szechwan in 1911," *Memoirs of the Research Department of the Tōyō Bunko, 14* (Tokyo, 1955).

19. Message from Viceroy Chang to U.S. Consul Bergholz, November 9, 1911 (Chinese original), enclosure in Canton dispatch of 11/14/11, USDS, 893.00/779. See also Canton dispatch of 10/27/11, USDS, 893.00/709.

20. Dispatches from Nanking of 1/2/12 and 1/11/12 in *PP China No. 1 (1912)*, pp. 176, 178.

21. See supra Chang.

of the military government, election by the provincial assemblies, direct election by the people, or a combination of these methods. The delegates from provinces still "loyal" to Peking were elected by the provincial assemblies, but otherwise the majority were appointed rather than elected. This compromised the Nanking Assembly somewhat in the competition with the Peking Assembly for the role as *the* national source of legitimacy, but insured it more power through the direct backing of the powerful governors (*tu-tu*).

By late 1911 the provincial assemblies enjoyed a privileged relationship to both the Peking and the Nanking governments through the national assemblies of each. In contrast to both national assemblies, the provincial assemblies were the product of special popular elections and the most explicit source, by that token, of legitimacy. The Nanking Assembly enjoyed some independent claim to legitimacy through its connection with the Revolutionary Alliance, which more than any group could boast of its part in the Revolution as evidence of a special relationship to the people; it still depended, however, on the support of provincial governments legitimized by the provincial assemblies. The Peking Assembly's only claim to legitimacy independent of the provincial assemblies was its special relationship to the throne. This element, however, was only enough to make monarchy a possible rather than a probable option to the solution of the succession crisis. Only in Szechwan did monarchy retain loyalists among rebels themselves, and there it was the Kuang-hsü, not the Hsüan-t'ung Emperor who was honored by demonstrators nostalgic for a monarch who could be used against the reigning faction.[22] With Assembly leadership, the Szechwan rebels felt free to attack the reigning Emperor, and it was but a short step from there to an attack on the throne as an institution.

By the time of the abdication on February 12, 1912, then, contending claims to inheritance of the throne's legitimacy had been institutionalized in the assemblies of the Peking and Nanking governments. Yuan Shih-k'ai headed the Peking government by the authority of the throne's compliance on November 2, 1911 with the Peking Assembly's demand that the throne substitute Yuan for Prince Ch'ing (I-k'uang) as Premier. Sun Yat-sen became President of the Nanking government by vote of the Nanking Assembly on

22. Ichiko, "Railway Protection Movement."

January 1, 1912. The contention resolved itself into a debate over the procedure of the abdication and the location of the capital. Sun pressed in the first place for the immediate abdication of the Emperor in favor of the Republic, which would then elect Yuan as its Premier, offering his own resignation in return. The abdication came, but it was made in favor of Yuan as the prospective organizer of a republic and present Premier of the Assembly of the imperial government. Yuan thus did not, as Premier, have to become a simple citizen of the new Republic before he was elected its President. The drama of the transition to a republic was thus minimized.

On February 14 Sun nonetheless obtained the Nanking Assembly's endorsement of the change. He had thus been forced into a de facto compromise, essentially by problems of timing. Yuan's great advantage, once abdication seemed inevitable, was in knowing better when it was most likely to occur and therefore what the procedure would be even if he couldn't—given the problems in his relationship with the court—control the abdication. He could thus play on the fact that the intensity of Nanking's desire for the abdication of the Manchus limited concern over its form. A Nanking ultimatum demanding the abdication appears to have crossed, on its way to Peking, the announcement of the abdication coming from Peking. This made it too late to negotiate further about the form of the abdication.[23]

The Nanking government thus had nothing more—short of resumption of hostilities—to bargain with but the location of the capital. The demand that Yuan come to Nanking was essentially part of the bargaining over the precise relation of the Nanking Assembly to the new republican President and to the "republicanized" remnants of the Peking Assembly who owed allegiance to Yuan as their old Premier. On February 14, however, the Nanking Assembly voted 20 to 8 to move to Peking. Severe pressure from Huang Hsing reversed the vote immediately. In the following weeks, the Nanking Government was thus better able to bargain over the conditions of the move to Peking but was unable to prevent it. Nanking republicans had broken ranks in a way that prejudiced future debate with Yuan over the composition of cabinets and the provisions of the constitution. The opportunity to draw clear lines in future challenges to the legitimacy of Yuan's title as

23. See report of 2/16/12 from Nanking of conversation with Wang Ch'ung-hui, *PP China No. 3 (1912)*, p. 204.

President passed with Sun's formal resignation and Yuan's inauguration in Peking on April 1, 1912. Political agitation from then until the "Second Revolution" of mid-1913 centered around efforts to emphasize the "provisional" nature of Yuan's presidency and the National Assembly of his government, rather than challenges to their legitimacy.

At the time, the February 14 vote to move to Peking was excused by some as the result of confusion among delegates as to whether they were voting on the question of the permanent or the provisional capital.[24] Later interpretations blamed a combination of republican naïveté (or its converse, Yuan's treachery) and Northern military superiority. However, recent studies have discredited the military explanation.[25] Some contemporary commentators criticized the "unrepresentative" character of the Nanking Assembly that made the decision, pointing to the fact that most of its delegates were appointed, not elected, and that attendance was not complete.[26] Such criticisms, however, tended to discredit the Nanking government as much, if not more, than the Peking government, while pointing to the need for elections.

A more careful decision about the transfer of legitimacy as it was worked out between February and April 1912 could only have been made by referring the question back to the provincial assemblies; they had underwritten the legitimacy of the two national assemblies that had to make the decision. Another alternative was entirely new elections for a national convention; however, this alternative had been discredited (during earlier bargaining) by Peking's proposal that a convention be called to decide whether the government should remain a monarchy or become a republic. Extensive preparations for any elections could too easily be used to buy time for the revival of the central government's bureaucratic apparatus and its use against the republican cause. The truce un-

24. Ibid., p. 208; 2/22/12 from Nanking on conversation with Wang Ch'ung-hui.

25. See supra Young, and Shelley Cheng, "The T'ung-meng-hui: Its Organization, Leadership, and Finances, 1905–1912" (unpublished Ph.D. dissertation, University of Washington, 1962).

26. See U.S. Department of State, *Foreign Relations of the United States* (hereafter referred to as *For. Rel.*) (*1913*), pp. 88–92, for a memorandum on the composition of the Nanking Assembly. According to unpublished portions of a letter of 2/4/13 from Secretary Knox to Sen. Cullom (USDS, 893.00/1529a) the memorandum was based on a report prepared March 19, 1912, by a discontented participant in the Nanking Assembly which reached U.S. representatives through official channels. See also *PP China No. 3* (*1912*), pp. 1–23, dispatch from Peking of 4/3/12 on "popular criticism" of the National Assembly as unrepresentative.

der which negotiations took place was too fragile to survive any more thorough electoral process. The most plausible explanation of the decision to move to Peking is that the provincial interests represented in the Nanking Assembly genuinely preferred the compromise to the available alternatives.

The range of choices was finally limited by the governors, as in the case with earlier critical decisions over the relationship between Peking and the provinces. Although the provincial assemblies between 1909 and 1911 gradually had acquired control of the power of legitimation, the governors from the beginning had had a monopoly on military power and an influence over civil matters limited only by their desire or ability to use force. Thus only the gradual emergence of a tacit alliance between the provincial assemblies and the governors against Peking insured the influence of the provincial assemblies throughout the national polity.

This alliance was most clearly demonstrated in the movement to force the Ch'ing government to agree to an earlier opening of parliament than that called for in the 1908 timetable. Shortly after the end of their first sessions in late 1909, representatives from the various provincial assemblies met in Shanghai as the Delegation to Petition for a Parliament on the initiative of Chang Chien, chairman of the Kiangsu Provincial Assembly. In January 1910, nine months before the 1910 National Assembly was to open, the delegation went to Peking to submit a petition for a parliament. In April, rebuffed and rebuked by the central government, they established the Association of Comrades to Petition for a Parliament in Peking and returned to their provinces to agitate and stimulate unsuccessful petitions. When the National Assembly opened in October 1910, the Association made its petition through the Assembly. At this point the governors joined force with the petitioners and jointly recommended the early convocation of a parliament to provide more efficient resolution of disputes interfering with the progress of the constitutional and other reforms. Unlike the assembly representatives, the governors skirted the issue of the formation of a cabinet. In November, the government announced that parliament would open in 1913—as it actually did—and that a cabinet would be set up prior to its opening—as was done in April 1911.

Although the provincial assemblies played the leading role in forcing the central government to accelerate its reform timetable, the governors played the deciding role. The situation in February 1912 was similar. The position of the assemblies depended in part on their special relationship to the governors and other parts of the bureaucratic apparatus. Their growing control of the institutionalized processes of legitimation by no means meant that popular sovereignty had won the day, as the fate of parliamentary government in later years was to demonstrate. In order to appreciate the effect of these institutions on the polity between 1909 and 1913 and in subsequent years, their relationship to the administrative system must be examined more closely.

New Channels of Information and Control in the Bureaucracy

The central government intended the self-government measures announced in 1908 as a supplement to official administration where the latter was ineffective, particularly in the mobilization of new forms of material and human resources. In January 1909 it explicitly denied that assemblies had independent authority, rebuking those who had taken political advantage of the 1908 measures.[27] Reformers with political ambitions within the new institutions therefore had to carve out whatever power base they could by going against the official bureaucracy. The assemblies provided new channels for the flow of information (ideas as well as data) and control which bypassed or diverted those of the regular administrative apparatus. Operating through these channels, the assemblies became far more than glorified reform bureaus with subordinate administrative status. They were increasingly valuable to the governors in implementing the central government's numerous reforms. The usefulness of the assemblies provided the basis of a tacit alliance between governor and assembly in opposition to Peking over critical matters, particularly national finance, and sometimes caused the governors to have divided loyalties. Not only did the provincial assemblies play the governors off against Peking, but they also used Peking against the governors. In addition to creating new vertical channels within the administrative apparatus, the assemblies had stimulated the horizontal flow of information and control, a tendency that was useful to the governors only up to the point where it began to threaten their maintenance of discipline. The governors further recognized the danger to themselves as well as to Peking in the tendency of provincial assembly members to operate outside the bureaucratic apparatus.

27 Edict of 1/18/09. See translation in *For. Rel. (1909)*, p. 129.

The memorial accompanying the 1908 regulations for the election and organization of the provincial assemblies noted their critical role as the new link between the central and local governments.[28] It betrayed no suspicion, however, that the chain of local, provincial, and national assemblies might open a new channel in the administrative apparatus for the upward flow of power as well as information.

Traditional administrative procedures carefully prescribed access to power by creating one distinct channel—memorials—for the upward flow of information and another—edicts—for the downward flow of power. Although a memorializer had the "power" to withhold or distort information, the system and all its supporting features worked to deprive him of the right to speak even for other officials, not to mention "the people." He or whoever else would agree to sign the memorial stood, so to speak, alone before the Emperor; there was no provision for him to represent any group in the figurative confrontation. The Emperor alone could presume to speak for "the people" or to read their true desires, and the power conferred on officials charged with execution of his edicts came only from above.[29]

The new assembly regulations provided that issues over which the governor and the provincial assembly were deadlocked be referred to the National Assembly for resolution. At the same time, advisory councils to be established at the local level were entitled

28. *Tzu-i-chü chang-ch'eng chi hsüan-chü chang-ch'eng chieh-shih hui-ch'ao* (Compilation of Explanations of Provincial Assembly Regulations and Election Regulations—hereafter referred to as Regulations) (edited and published by the Constitutional Government Commission [Hsien-cheng pien-ch'a-kuan] in seven sets from June 1908 to April 1910), no. 1, KH 34/6/12 (July 10, 1908); also *Kuang-hsü hsin fa-ling* (New Laws and Decrees of the Kuang-hsü Period) (Shanghai, 1909), ts'e 2, 2b–24a.

29. I see "access" to power as involving some degree of control of, or influence over, decisions about the exercise of power; this may mean a direct hand or participation only through the decision maker's concern over an individual or group's possible reaction (see Eisenstadt, *Political Systems*, pp. 19–20 on "accountability").

My understanding of specific features of the traditional "memorial-edict" system is derived largely from Morrison (see esp. pp. 317, 701, 1074 ff.), E-tu Zen Sun, *Ch'ing Administrative Terms* (Cambridge, Mass., 1961); Pao-chao Hsieh, *The Government of China* (Baltimore, 1925); H. S. Brunnert and V. V. Hagelstrom, *Present Day Political Organization of China* (Shanghai, 1912); J. K. Fairbank and S. Y. Teng, *Ch'ing Administration* (Cambridge, Mass., 1961); and Charles O. Hucker, *The Traditional Chinese State in Ming Times* (Tucson, 1961). An important new work which, on this topic, supersedes these was published after the completion of this essay: Silas Hsiu-liang Wu, "The Memorial Systems of the Ch'ing Dynasty (1644–1912)," *Harvard Journal of Asiatic Studies*, 27 (1967), 7–75.

to refer their deadlocks with the officials to the provincial assembly for resolution in consultation with the governor (*hsün-fu*). Here the danger to the throne was that new provisions for the upward flow of information might disrupt the downward flow of power. Several tactics were used to conform the new institutions to the memorial-edict system. The ritual forms of address prescribed for provincial assemblies put them below the governor's chief assistants, the commissioners (*ssu-tao*) in the official hierarchy, much to the distaste of the assemblymen.[30] Also the list of duties largely confined the assemblies to local matters, though they were given control of many new provincewide projects and welfare functions traditionally accorded the gentry.

Limitations on the assemblies' authority betrayed a fear that in the end "self-government" could not fit the memorial-edict system. For many years the inviolability of this system had delayed other permanent reforms of the government apparatus. Until about 1905, such innovations as the Tsungli Yamen had been accepted only on an ad hoc basis.[31] Although the ten new ministries which replaced the six ancient boards of the metropolitan government in 1906 were permanent, in the case of representative institutions a new tactic was used: constant insistence that the assemblies were only preparatory—somewhat in the manner of "acting" officials—and that the exercise of parliamentary functions would have to await the convening of a true parliament.

The National Assembly which convened in Peking in October of 1910 was in a sense but an enlarged and strengthened version of the Constitutional Government Commission (Hsien-cheng pien-ch'a-kuan), which at its own inception had been compared to the compilation and statistics bureau attached to the Japanese cabinet.[32] Much of the same unflattering attitude existed toward the new assembly, whose officers had been named long before it was convened.[33] The establishment of the Constitutional Government

30. Regulations, no. 1, p. 2, KH 34/6/26 (July 24, 1908); see also concern over opening rituals, relations with governors' staffs, and conventions of correspondence in *Feng-t'ien tzu-i-chü ti-i-tz'u pao-kao shu* (The First Report of the Fengtien Assembly) (hereafter referred to as *Feng-t'ien pao-kao*) *1*, 5–13, passim.

31. The transition from ad hoc to semipermanent to permanent administrative innovations is a dominant theme of Professor Morrison's periodizations of Ch'ing administration: 1850–1901, 1901–06, 1906–11. Morrison, pp. 367, 684, 968 ff.

32. *Yü-che hui-ts'un,* KH 33/7/5 (Aug. 13, 1907); *Kuang-hsü cheng-yao,* chap. 33, 72b–73b.

33. *Kuang-hsü-ch'ao Tung-hua-lu,* KH 33/8/20 (Sept. 27, 1907), *5*, 5736.

Commission in August 1907 had been accompanied by the stipulation that the Grand Council was to supervise the commission pending the formation of a national assembly.[34] Finding itself between the council and the commission, the new assembly could easily have been hamstrung.

Given its duty to see that abuses as well as deficiencies of government were remedied, the National Assembly might have performed as a censorate as well as a reform bureau. Its principal officers had the right to memorialize the throne if high officials abused it or its laws.[35] Unlike the traditional censor, however, the petitioning officer of the National Assembly would be backed by a two-thirds vote of the membership in his confrontation with imperial authority. In a potentially radical departure from the memorial-edict system, provision was thus made for an institution rather than an individual official to approach the throne. The right to memorialize was, for those members of the National Assembly who came from provincial assemblies, a license to realize the disruptive potential of the national institution.

The ease with which the elected provincial delegates from the provinces dominated the appointed metropolitan delegates in the National Assembly[36] derived from the growing power of the provincial government apparatus. By the time of the 1906 reforms of the metropolitan apparatus, it was already too late to put the central government at the head rather than the tail of change. Consequently the 1906 reforms increased the number of reform plans rather than the capacity of Peking to coordinate such plans and to help the provinces fulfill them. The 1906 central reorganization cleared the way for the long overdue administrative reorganization of the provinces announced in July 1907, and made a start toward the long-discussed "self-government" reforms designed to improve the "official system" (*kuan-chih*). Intended to centralize civil administrative power, the reforms actually accelerated the drift of responsibilities and power into provincial capitals, downward from Peking as well as upward from the districts (*hsien*).

By 1906 a host of new specialized bureaus (*chü*) had been established at the provincial level to fulfill new, and manage the reform of old, functions traditionally the responsibility of the nonspecial-

34. *Kuang-hsü hsin fa-ling,* ts'e 1, p. 19a.

35. Article 21 of the organization regulations is translated in *For. Rel.* (*1910*), p. 334.

36. See supra Chang.

ized district magistracies. The provincial apparatus thus assumed duties beyond its traditional task of supervising other officials performing these tasks and policing the lines of communication and control between Peking and the districts. The new bureaus were first used during the creation of the New Army, and included officers in charge of training and subsections attending to various technical matters. A new educational commissionership oversaw lower-level offices in charge of running elementary, middle, and technical or higher schools. Other new bureaus in the provincial capitals and larger cities handled likin, minting, and other fiscal duties; "official-supervision merchant-management" enterprises; commercial affairs; arsenals; and police protection.[37]

Administrative reorganization after 1906 further upgraded the provincial apparatus by abolishing territorial circuits (*tao*), an intermediate geographical subdivision directly below the province. The change increased provincial centralization of reforms, but also added to the load on the Empire's governors (*tu-fu*)—the nine governors-general (*tsung-tu*) and the nineteen civil governors (*hsün-fu*). Two new provincewide commissioners (taotais) for police and industry in addition to the five commissioners of education, justice, finance, foreign affairs, and salt reflected the scope of their superiors' duties. The growing governor's yamen was reorganized to include an officially authorized yamen staff (Mu-chih-yüan) under a private secretary and ten section chiefs corresponding to the ten ministries recently established in Peking. Finally, the governor's establishment came to include an executive council (Hui-i-t'ing) appointed from the yamen staff, selected local officials down to district magistrates, and local notables and members of the provincial assembly.

On numerous issues, particularly local reforms, the provincial assembly and governor cooperated closely and effectively. In Fengtien, supposedly the model for provincial administrative reorganization, the fifteen items of the 1910 Assembly agenda prepared by the Assembly itself differed from the nineteen prepared by the

37. *Ch'ing-kuo hsing-cheng-fa* (Ch'ing Dynasty Administrative Law) (Shanghai, 1906), pp. 330–32. [There is a Chinese work of this date translated by Ch'en Yu-nien, Liang Chi-tung, and Cheng Ch'ih. Possibly the translators drew on the monumental *Shinkoku gyōsei hō,* ed. Oda Yorozu. This was a project sponsored by the Research Bureau on Chinese Customs of the office of the governor-general of Taiwan (Taiwan sōtokufu, rinji kyūkan chōsakai) (Tokyo and Kobe, 1910–14) and was being compiled in Taiwan at the time this unidentified Chinese work was published.—ed.]

governor's yamen less in substance than in the priority assigned the items. The Assembly preferred to take up constitutional questions, such as relations with the governor's staff, first, while the governor preferred them last.[38] Often, as had been hoped, the assemblies functioned smoothly where official administration was ineffective. One of the items on the Fengtien agenda was a proposal to promote mining. Another concerned raising capital from Overseas Chinese who might be interested in China in view of the discrimination and hostility then prevailing in their host countries. Two problems prevented a direct approach by officials of the governor's yamen: the size of the job, which would include setting up a special office, and the suspicion Overseas Chinese merchants felt toward officials in general, given past experience with "official-supervision merchant-management" schemes. The solution was the establishment of a special committee of the assembly that would first solicit funds from resident businessmen for its own support and then approach Overseas Chinese capitalists, promising special treatment of their investments.[39]

The simultaneous growth of assembly authority and autonomy and of the governor's power involved more than cooperation between assembly and governor; the critical element was the nature of their agreements to disagree. The regulations allowed the governor to ask Peking for permission to dissolve the assembly. Governors were reluctant to exercise this power, however, because of their dependence on merchant and gentry help, particularly in financial aspects of the reform programs. During disagreements the assembly, taking advantage of the governor's caution, would often threaten to disrupt official business by dissolving *itself*. The most common tactic of the governor was to avoid communicating on an issue, often provoking provincial assembly complaints to the National Assembly.[40] To avoid such standoffs, the regulations specified joint reference of deadlocks to the National Assembly for decision. Such action preserved the machinery for cooperation between the two parties. Often it also implied a conviction that the division between the provinces and Peking was, on certain issues, deeper than that between assembly and governor. The tacit alliance of assemblies and governors against Peking that the 1911 Rev-

38. *Feng-t'ien pao-kao, 1*, 2–5.
39. Ibid., *3*, 56–68.
40. *TFTC*, *7* (1910), no. 11, 87–94.

olution brought into the open emerged from such situations, the most important of which had to do with budget-making.

From 1908 to 1911 the Ministry of Finance strove mightily to reassert its control over the revenue of the Empire, beginning with an effort to account in detail, and by modern methods, for income and expenditures. A temporary Committee for the Reorganization of Finances was established in Peking in 1909 along with similar bureaus in the provincial capitals. Together they completed in the fall of 1910 a national trial budget for the coming year of 1911. The budget was divided into national and local expenditures, the former to be approved by the national and the latter by the provincial assemblies.[41] The governor-general of the three Eastern Provinces, concurrently governor of Fengtien, Hsü Shih-ch'ang, seized the occasion to increase local control over revenues by proposing to the Provincial Assembly that a distinction (similar to that made between national and local expenditures) be made among various Fengtien sources of revenue. He was, in effect, refusing to wait until the Ministry of Finance determined which revenues were national, as it had tried to do for expenditures. The governor-general justified his proposal as a necessary "clarification" of the financial situation. His real intention was betrayed, however, by his favorable reference to the fact that in Japan locally collected and expended taxes exceeded national taxes by 60 percent.[42]

The Fengtien Provincial Assembly vetoed the measure, nominally because the governor-general did not clearly itemize the types of taxes included in each category. It is unlikely, however, that it genuinely opposed what amounted to an increase in local control of finances: in the explanation of its veto the Provincial Assembly also opposed any increase in taxation without popular supervision.[43] It apparently agreed with the governor-general on the merits of local control as long as the Assembly's own supervisory powers were increased.

The dispute was therefore referred to the National Assembly in what amounted to a veiled request by both governor-general and Assembly for more local control as well as a request by the Assembly for more popular supervision of finances. At the same time, both sides, by putting technicalities first in their arguments, seemed to have been exercising a kind of "legislative restraint." Neither

41. Morrison, pp. 1182 ff.

42. *Feng-t'ien pao-kao, 3,* 59.

43. Ibid., *3,* 61–62.

insisted on a substantive decision on the question of distinctions between local and national finances.

Similar problems appeared all over the Empire and the trial budget mainly dramatized the inadequacy of the nation's resources as they were then organized to the reform tasks the central government was setting for itself. This demonstration of financial incompetence paralleled the demonstration of military weakness in the Sino-Japanese War of 1895. The alliances of assemblies and governors against Peking became stronger as, by 1911, governors found themselves responsible to Peking for reform goals far beyond Peking's resources. Thus although Peking planned improved communications and finances, the new budget revealed that Peking would have to use such means as railroad nationalization and foreign loans that would incur opposition from those elements of the population on which the governors relied for funds.

Increasingly, the duties of office were placing the governors-general and governors in positions which fostered divided loyalties in conflicts between the assemblies and the central government. The 1911 Railway Protection Movement in Szechwan provided the classic example of this dilemma. The officers and members of the Szechwan Provincial Assembly played key roles in the movement. The acting governor-general, Wang Jen-wen, vacillated so long that Peking sent Chao Erh-feng to replace him. Even Chao was unable at first to decide how to handle the issue, waiting until news arrived that Tuan-fang was leading a punitive expedition before he arrested the president and vice-president of the Assembly and other leading figures of the Railway Protection League. Central authority had not yet been openly challenged; had this incident been one of the last rather than the first of the 1911 Revolution, divided loyalties might have induced Wang Jen-wen to side openly with the protesters or to ignore them with impunity. The fact that from 1908 through 1911 the annual turnover rate of provincial officials in the top four or five jobs increased from about 33 percent to 300 percent higher than that for similar level personnel in the central ministries[44] provides a rough index of the difficulty posed by such dilemmas.

After the repudiation of the Emperor in 1911, enmity with Peking had disadvantages as well as advantages for the provincial assemblies in their relations with the governors (*tu-tu*). In using both

44. Morrison, p. 1141.

provincial and national assembly channels, the provincial assemblymen had been playing both ends against the middle. They approached the throne through the National Assembly as—to put it in terms of the memorial-edict system—groups of censors backed in their remonstrances by a novel alliance with the provincial governors. They approached the governors, however, as a special group of the Emperor's privileged subjects. Their membership in the assemblies had the effect of commissioning them as a special class of censors to impeach provincial officials; in this capacity they had the Emperor's permission (through edicts prescribing elections) to share his right to speak for the people. The assembly members had won much of their autonomy in dealing with the Emperor and the governors only at the price of accepting a system still headed by an emperor. As long as *an* emperor existed, they could pose not only as his censors, but also, to an extent, as his regent; undoubtedly the death of the Kuang-hsü Emperor in 1908 and his replacement with a child Emperor and Regent eased the transition to republicanism. The connection of the provincial assemblies with the Emperor could hardly survive their participation in the legitimation of revolutionary governments even though these connections had made possible their function as legitimizers.

We shall again see, in the next section, that the assemblies' role as legitimizers in 1911 showed they had sources of legitimacy and autonomy outside the bureaucracy that survived the Emperor. First, however, we must examine their contribution to the increased horizontal distribution of information and power within the bureaucracy, which complemented their exploitation of new upward and downward channels. Horizontal modifications of the bureaucratic hierarchy had begun long before 1909 and had accelerated with the abolition of the Examination System in 1905. The elections of 1909 were in a sense but one of the new forms of recruitment of personnel at the provincial level after 1905. Residence, property, and education all figured among the qualifications for both electors and candidates. All three were measured by the provincial apparatus. Academic degrees, the formal requirement for government employment and the most important qualification for election, were conferred by schools controlled by the commissioners of the new offices of education serving the governors and the assemblies.[45]

45. Wolfgang Franke, *The Reform and Abolition of the Traditional Chinese Examination System* (Cambridge, Mass., 1963), pp. 65–67.

The whole tone of administration was changing at the provincial level along with the changes in the educational system. The first change had been in the governor's yamen, where specialists in "practical" subjects like finance and engineering had first found employment. In the traditional bureaucracy of mid-Ch'ing described by Wang Hui-tsu and others, relations had conformed to a strict official hierarchy. Relations between the bureaucracy and outside society had been largely confined to the district level, and there to interactions with an informal but relatively strict social hierarchy.[46] The entire polity, in other words, operated through carefully maintained vertical channels. The crises of the Taiping Rebellion forced the governors charged with suppression of rebellion to rely increasingly on informal yamen staffs. In the years following the Rebellion, the central government only partially succeeded in controlling appointments, either by suppressing the growth of such staffs or by absorbing them into officially authorized structures.[47] The establishment after 1906 of official yamen staffs with ten section chiefs each, and of executive councils, was the last in a series of such control measures attempted by the central government. Earlier ones, established at the provincial level in the nineteenth century, had included the General Board of Reconstruction (Shan-hou tsung-chü) and the General Military Supplies Board (Chün-hsü tsung-chü).[48] The provincial assemblies contributed greatly to this process by their relations with the governors via the executive councils. The executive councils included two separate sections, one composed entirely of administrative officials from commissioners down to magistrates and charged with such administrative functions as drawing up orders, the other including a mixture of administrative officials from the same level, local notables, particularly those learned in the law, and members of the provincial assemblies, and charged primarily with planning rather than executing reform.[49]

The members of the provincial assemblies were therefore part of

46. C. K. Yang, "Bureaucratic Behavior," pp. 136 ff.

47. Kenneth E. Folsom, "Li Hung-chang: Friends, Guests, and Colleagues" (unpublished Ph.D. dissertation, University of California, Berkeley, 1964), pp. 52, 106–07. [Since published under the title, *Friends, Guests, and Colleagues; the Mu-fu System in the Late Ch'ing Period* (Berkeley and Los Angeles, 1968)—ed.]

48. Brunnert and Hagelstrom, p. 418.

49. G. Pernitsch, "Das Beratungsamt," *Mitteilungen des Seminar für Orientalische Sprache, 16* (University of Berlin, 1913), 61–65, translates and discusses the regulations.

a new category of officialdom, recruited from the provinces according to standards controlled after 1905 largely by the governors. The effectiveness of the assemblymen was increased by their acceptance of the framework provided by the assemblies and the modified memorial-edict system. The assemblymen were heirs to much of the prestige of traditional officials; like these, the assemblymen were not merely functionaries (*kuan*) but Confucian ministers (*ch'en*) vis-à-vis the governor and the Emperor. Their special relationship to the Emperor and, with imperial endorsement, to the people set the assemblymen apart from other officials. It thereby reduced the governor's and his senior officials' share of power. Thus the governors needed the assembly members, and could and did cooperate with them. But the autonomy of the assemblies was also *limited* by their members' acceptance of this system, and their position vis-à-vis the other "new" officials of the provincial apparatus was insecure. The organization of the Executive Council reflected the degree to which the governors and their subordinate officials shared the central government's fear and suspicion of the new institutions. Though the final selection of officials was the governors' prerogative, the assemblies, unlike other groups represented in the executive councils, chose their own candidates for positions. The candidates, however, were relegated to the bottom rung of administrative power in these organs: representing the outside authority of the provincial assembly, they were not trusted with more than a small share of responsibilities in the planning section.[50]

The governors rightly feared that the administrative horizontalization, to which the assemblies were contributing so much, might go too far, and that the system might become too egalitarian. Assembly members showed their independence by organizing on their own, forming groups outside the individual provincial assemblies to deal with provincial matters and outside the National Assembly to deal with national matters. Such behavior reflected the realization that the election of 1909 had conferred on them not only more than the status of special protectors of the Emperor's interests but also more than a position in the new officialdom recruited by and for the provincial apparatus. The governors tol-

50. Joseph Levenson, *Confucian China and its Modern Fate* (Berkeley, 1964), 2, 124–28, develops the distinction; it resembles that involved in analyses of "official," "formal," and "informal" hierarchies in James G. March and Herbert A. Simon, *Organizations* (New York, 1958).

erated but the Emperor disapproved the creation in Shanghai of the Association of Provincial Assembly Representatives, which agitated for earlier convening of parliament and creation of a cabinet. The Emperor tolerated but the governors disapproved the tendency of assemblymen from one province to enlist support of those from other provinces in confrontations with their governors. Both the Emperor and governors feared the irregular meetings convened by a majority of the provincial assemblymen in the National Assembly; such meetings attempted to deal with proposals which were the concern of the governors, for example, the organization of militia.[51]

The 1909 elections of provincial assembly members had, as the legitimation process during the 1911 Revolution suggests, ramifications in areas outside both provincial and central government. This fact becomes clearer when the 1909 elections are examined in the light of the elections of late 1912 and early 1913 and the general changes in the polity from 1909 to 1913. In such an examination a clear distinction must be made between the assemblymen as a group and the assemblies as organizations, and the relationship of the electoral process to each must be noted.

The Expanding Electorate and the New Tone of Politics

Between the 1909 elections for the provincial assemblies and the 1912 elections for new provincial assemblies (Sheng-i-hui) and a House of Representatives (Chung-i-yüan), the registered electorate in China expanded from about 1 percent to about 20 or 25 percent of the adult male population.[52] This vast quantitative change in the electorate was accompanied by even more important qualitative changes. The expansion of the electorate injected a new tone into politics that was to survive the waning of the parliamentary institutions brought into existence by the 1912 elections. The new tone was characterized by the emergence of a wide array of political interest groups and by the nationalization of local politics. This signified the fragmentation and political retreat of traditional elements and the rise of a new political class, a public, educated by republicanism into a disregard for the administrative ritual that up to this time had governed the behavior of the gentry and offi-

51. *Chih-sheng tzu-i-chü i-yüan lien-ho-hui pao-kao shu* (Report of the League of Provincial Assembly Representatives) (no publication date or place), proceedings of 5/14 (presumably June 10, 1911).

52. See supra Chang.

cial classes. The provincial assemblies had prepared the ground for the new political interest groups. Their members, as a special variation of gentry and official, joined the vanguard of the new public from which constitutionalists, revolutionaries, and other types of republicans were drawn. The membership of the provincial assemblies thus constituted the leading sector in the modernization of the polity.

The 1909 and 1912 elections are the closest thing to general elections ever held in China. The condition of the central government apparatus has never since been combined with sufficient local interest in the electoral process to produce more than what might be called partial plebiscites. The first genuinely national elections since 1913 were those for the First National People's Congress of 1954. By this time, however, one-party government had transformed the nature of the electoral process.[53]

Apart from their results, therefore, the 1909 and 1912 elections were impressive achievements simply as efforts to overcome those obstacles, such as the size of the country and poor communications, that made any event requiring nationwide participation difficult. No census statistics existed then, or exist now, adequate to support a precise quantitative description of the elections. The increase of the electorate from 1909 to 1912, however, suggests some gross changes.[54]

Out of a population of very roughly 400 million, approximately 160 million or 40 percent were men over the age of twenty-five, the minimum voting age in 1909. Over 1.6 million of these were included on the electoral lists in 1909; voters therefore totaled some 1 percent of the males over twenty-five years of age and .4 percent of the total population, and represented through their families a possible 2 percent of the population, or 8 million. In 1912, however, the electoral lists included over 40 million, representing from 20 to 25 percent of the adult male population and 10 percent of the total population.[55]

53. William Li Tung, *The Political Institutions of Modern China* (The Hague, 1964), pp. 61, 79, 136, 212, 218, 259, 288.

54. For reasons too detailed to give here, I believe the very distortions (and they were great) built into population and voting statistics of 1909 and 1912 strengthen my general thesis of vast quantitative and qualitative changes in the polity between those dates.

55. 1912 electorate figures are from *Cheng-fu kung-pao* (Government Gazette) (Jan. 5, 1913), "T'ung-kao" section.

Chang P'eng yüan's population figures (Table 3.1, p. 150) total precisely

The increase followed a lowering of the education requirement from a secondary to only an elementary or "equivalent" school education, and of the property qualification from ownership of business or property worth $5,000 ($10,000 for non-natives) to ownership of real estate worth only $500 or annual payment of at least two dollars in direct taxes. Meeting these qualifications entitled a person to vote provided he was a male over twenty-one years of age (lowered from twenty-five years in 1909), had resided in his district for at least two years (lowered from ten years), and was not disqualified by certain crimes, and so on. The changes in requirements, however, are not explanations in themselves; they were the result of a change in attitude toward elections. The change involved genuine interest in the elections, reflected by the fact that, according to Western officials, up to 75 percent of the qualified voters participated in the elections.[56]

This quantitative change in the electorate is in turn a measure of qualitative changes in the way the polity functioned between 1909 and 1912, of which the very establishment of elections was itself an example. The impact of the provincial assemblies of 1909, 1910, and 1911 on the procedures of the bureaucracy far ex-

---

410,123,175. To facilitate rough comparisons between 1912 figures and the figures for the Taiping period of the nineteenth century in Chung-li Chang, *The Chinese Gentry*, p. 164, I have rounded this off to 400 million. Rounding off Chang P'eng-yüan's percentage of electorate from .42 to .40 thus brings a conservative total of about a 1.6 million electorate. (This is compared further on in the text with Chung-li Chang's figures for nineteenth-century gentry population: families are here taken to have an average of five individuals in them in both periods.) The percentage of adult males in the population is a very rough estimate based on W. W. Rockhill's conclusion from 1910 census figures ("The 1910 Census of the Population of China," reprinted Leyden, 1912, from *T'oung Pao, 13*, 5) that "able-bodied men" are about 40% of the population. The category theoretically (see Ping-ti Ho, *Studies on the Population of China, 1368–1953* [Cambridge, Mass., 1959], p. 35) includes men from 16 to 45; I feel justified in using it for all men over 25 by rough extrapolation from the estimates that the population under 16 years of age was 15% of the total (see Rockhill, p. 8, n. 1). In 1912, for voting purposes "adult" meant over 21 rather than over 25 as in 1909; hence my speaking of the electorate as 20–25% rather than saying 25%.

56. See, for example, USDS, 893.00/1528 and –/1529, estimating a 60% turnout for Fengtien and a 75% turnout for Kiangning Hsien (Nanking) respectively. The accuracy of voting figures, like those of eligible voters, is, of course, very suspect. They do, however, indicate that very high levels of participation in the elections were reached at widely scattered points and therefore perhaps through very large areas. The observation seems the more valid as they are often accompanied in Western sources by a tendency to fasten on examples (admittedly common) of "corruption" and to compare the elections very unfavorably to those of the contemporary West.

ceeded, as we have seen above, what might have been expected, considering the small electoral base of 1909. The surprising strength of this impact came not merely from coincidence with changes within the bureaucracy, but also from changes in the polity as a whole. The latter can best be seen in the preparations for assembly elections, and in the activities of the elected members outside as well as within the provincial assembly itself and related parts of the governmental apparatus.

The new tone of politics saw the emergence of new political interest groups and a more thorough mixture of local and national affairs. Before turning to this, we must note the appearance of a modern public where previously the dominant group (apart from incursions by various rebels) had been the gentry.

The dilution and fragmentation of the gentry class had been under way for several decades before the 1905 abolition of the Examination System insured its radical transformation and eventual breakup. The government's mobilization efforts during the Taiping period had enlarged the gentry by about 34 percent, though it increased the proportion of gentry who obtained their degrees irregularly by sale and other nonexamination routes.[57]

In the absence of a thorough census, traditional examination and tax lists were used to prepare the 1909 electorate lists, and as a result assemblies included a very high proportion of degree holders. The 1909 electorate was a somewhat larger proportion of the population than the post-Taiping gentry.[58] Quantitatively it therefore appears that the 1909 electorate represented a new mobilization of gentry elements that was rather less successful than the anti-Taiping effort.

The new public, however, measured by the electoral franchise, reflected qualitative changes in the gentry and the polity already apparent at the time of the 1909 elections. Insofar as the members of the assemblies from 1909 to 1911 were still gentry, they can be said to have been dominated by the lower—in terms of traditional degrees—ranks. But biographical data on assemblymen show the dominant pattern to be a *combination* of traditional and modern educational and career experiences.[59] The careers of men like Chang Chien[60] and the behavior of assemblymen in the Szechwan

57. Chang, *The Chinese Gentry*, pp. 140–41.

58. See supra Chang.

59. E.g. *Feng-t'ien pao-kao* 2, 13–34.

60. See Samuel C. Chu, *Reformer in Modern China, Chang Chien 1853–1926* (New York and London, 1965).

Railway dispute and other disputes and enterprises prove that traditional credentials, mainly acquired at least five years earlier and not always by traditional methods, were no sure bar to modern behavior. At the same time, the proliferation of government-sponsored reform committees and associations inflated modern titles and degrees until they easily obscured position and education based on traditional ways. The new public thus blended new and old strains in a novel manner and changed the tone of the political process.

The most important feature of the emerging public was the complicated mixture of roles played by its members. The elasticity of the concept of "gentry" must be strained beyond the breaking point to comprehend this variety. On the other hand, it cannot be subsumed under such categories as the "bourgeoisie" and the "intelligentsia"; strong elements of both existed, but they had to coexist with more traditional patterns that still survived, particularly in the interior.

Nourished by a burgeoning private and official press, the new public provided an arena for a form of politics in which old class lines were constantly crossed and new ones distorted. The articulation and proliferation of political interest groups in a wide variety of organizational forms was the most characteristic feature of this new tone.[61]

Though radical, K'ang Yu-wei's recommendation in 1895 to expand the privilege to memorialize expressed essentially traditional conceptions of the political process.[62] In essence K'ang planned to give even district officials the privileges previously reserved for the highest provincial and metropolitan officials, while granting, with some improvements, to all "scholars and commoners" the privileges previously enjoyed by lower officials. At best, the reform would have, in traditional terms, made censors of all, but could have left them, in modern terms, standing as individuals or perhaps heads of families before the court. K'ang's own difficulties in being heard suggest that the diffusion of the direct or indirect right to memorialize had already made that right less meaningful. If the channels of the memorial system were already clogged by 40,000 individual officials with this privilege, how much worse

61. See David B. Truman, *The Governmental Process* (New York, 1951) and also more recent theorists of "interest group" politics listed in the bibliographic paper by Bernard E. Brown, "Interest Groups and Parties in Comparative Analysis" (paper delivered at American Political Science Association meeting, New York, September 1963).

62. *Wu-hsü pien-fa* (The 1898 Reform Movement) (Shanghai, 1953), 2, 199.

would the situation have been if all one and one-half million or so degree-holding gentry, not to mention commoners, had the privilege?[63]

K'ang's suggestion, however, forcefully made the point that "the people" of the Empire had the right to be heard. This encouraged the emergence of organizations that eventually insured some access to the polity's policy makers, even when the latter did not want to hear.[64] In the years surrounding the 1898 reform attempt, pressure for reform was largely in the hands of organized groups of public-minded men, many of whom had been office holders. These groups, however, were primarily private and operated more often with the suspicious tolerance or opposition of officials than with their encouragement. Usually educational in character, they often associated themselves with schools. Though they at times provided cover for radical and even revolutionary activities, their idea of action usually meant drafting petitions and publishing discussions on the need for reform in their numerous new magazines. Liang Ch'i-ch'ao listed many of these groups in his discussion of reform associations, noting the preponderance of scholars among the Hunanese and of merchants among the Kwangtung groups.[65] The departure for and return from Japan of thousands of Chinese students stimulated the growth and activism of such organizations, especially after 1905.

Gradually the government gave special encouragement to groups with an interest in the specific reforms being undertaken by the numerous new provincial reform bureaus. Eventually it established organizations to take up the work of these groups, though at first only in relatively apolitical areas, for example the agricultural guilds (*nung-hui*) and chambers of commerce (*shang-hui*).[66] In August of 1907 the government entered explicitly political areas and ordered the governors to establish societies to instruct the people in self-government. Classes were begun to train teach-

63. This is but one estimate of the number of individual office holders at any given time, that of C. K. Yang, "Bureaucratic Behavior," p. 145. An estimate several times this number, or conversely one much smaller, would serve the present point about as well.

64. On K'ang's awareness of the importance of the earliest of such organizations, see John Schrecker, "The Pao Kuo Hui: A Reform Society of 1898," Harvard University, East Asian Research Center, *Papers on China, 14* (1960), 50–70.

65. Liang Ch'i-ch'ao, *Wu-hsü cheng-pien chi* (Record of the 1898 Coup) (reprinted Taipei, 1964), pp. 292–97, 299.

66. Brunnert and Hagelstrom, pp. 358 and 362.

ers in the ways of self-government, and meetings were organized in which these teachers and sometimes foreign guests participated. In Szechwan the process resulted in the establishment of 127 instructional offices which eventually trained over 1,000 instructors.[67]

On a locality by locality basis,[68] the transition from various types of reform group agitation and education at large to the sessions of the newly elected provincial assemblies was a very gradual process. First came the government's shift of emphasis from educational efforts to the Provincial Assembly Preparations Bureaus (Tzu-i-chü ch'ou-pan-chü), which actually prepared electoral lists and arranged for the supervision of the 1909 balloting.[69] The drama of a modern Western campaign followed by a day or two of anxious waiting for results of one day's balloting was lacking. Thus it is easy to overlook the genuine interest and participation through a structure of groups with wide connections. The elections themselves were in two stages, each of which could last days or even weeks, depending on local conditions. Geographic conditions made it difficult to bring voters together and political conditions determined how many votes were required to elect a particular candidate. The first stage named the electors who in the second stage voted for the actual members of the provincial assemblies. Not surprisingly, a number of governors confused the complicated formal functions of the preparations bureaus with the substantive functions of the assemblies. They therefore applied provincial assembly procedures, such as the election of chairmen and parliamentary procedure, to these bureaus. Peking objected lest such actions give the preparations bureaus a status that might too rapidly increase expectations.[70]

The development of political interest groups entered a new stage when the provincial assemblies assimilated many pre-1909 political groups. Locally, there were even lobbies on some issues. In one instance Kwangtung merchants telegraphed groups in the province urging them to exert pressure on assemblymen concerning a gambling law up for debate.[71] Nationally there was of course the movement to petition for an early parliament. This

67. Chang Hui-ch'ang, "Li-hsien-p'ai jen ho Ssu-ch'uan tzu-i-chü" (The Constitutionalists and the Szechwan Provincial Assembly), *HHKMHIL, 3* (Peking, 1962), 152.

68. Regulations, passim.

69. Ibid., no. 1.

70. Ibid., pp. 2–3, Kuang-hsü 34/7/3 (7/30/08).

71. *TFTC,* 7 (1910), no. 11, 8.

movement was paralleled by a national Convention of Educators, a central Chamber of Commerce, and various special purpose organizations, such as the one to suppress opium. Although the educators formed a body sponsored by the central government,[72] their group and the others like it served as a precedent for national organization on a functional or professional basis, a phenomenon of increasing importance after the 1913 dissolution of the assemblies.

It was, however, the combination of a national issue with strong local economic interests, producing a well-organized and powerful political interest group genuinely independent of the government, that was the distinguishing mark of the new tone of politics. The Szechwan Railway Protection League best reflected this blend.[73] This organization functioned like a powerful shadow provincial government, but, unlike the Fengtien or Shantung Societies to Protect the Peace, was not in itself adequate to govern the province.

The most powerful civil political interest groups were generally the chambers of commerce. During the 1911 Revolution and the efforts of 1912 to reconstruct civil government, these organizations proved capable of growing into efficient local, if not provincial, governments. Not composed of merchants alone, they became the principal bulwark of civil order in one locality after another during 1911 and 1912. Funds were needed not only for local welfare functions but for demobilizing or bribing marauding soldiers and bandits; chambers of commerce became important in these money-raising campaigns. Local duties were mixed with duties (such as troop maintenance and interregional railway construction) more naturally the concern of national government. Occasionally the task of dealing directly with foreign representatives was added to this mixture, bringing the chambers to the peak of their influence. Originally organized by the government to promote commerce and industry, the chambers had been gradually reorganized after 1900 into a more independent form. They had grown strong enough not only to assert considerable autonomy, but, by 1912, even to substitute for the government itself in many localities.

In Kwangtung the complex debates and group maneuverings over the course of action to be followed by the province in the

72. Brunnert and Hagelstrom, p. 135.

73. *PP China No. 1 (1912)*, pp. 15–16, translates the organization's regulations.

Revolution of 1911 suggest that the Provincial Assembly was actually *primus inter pares* among groups like the Chamber of Commerce, the Agricultural Society, and political reform organizations. This tendency was confirmed after the Revolution in other provinces that, like Kwangtung, added representatives of various commercial, artisan, educational, agricultural, professional, and political or military groups to the original provincial assembly members. In Kwangtung even women were represented.[74] The new political freedom led to the blossoming of scores of public-spirited and politically minded organizations. In such an environment, the provincial assembly often functioned more as the heir to the more powerful political reform societies and bureaus, private and official, than as a new arena in which these various groups were represented and contended. Its general representative features, however, did allow it to transcend local issues more easily than any other group, particularly through its direct connections with the National Assembly. Thus national orientations easily became the basis for distinctions even at a local level between two examples of a new type of group to emerge during the 1912 elections, the Nationalist Party and the Republican Party—that is, political parties.

Thus the provincial assemblies after 1912 served as the institutional forum for emerging groups in the polity just as standard Western parliaments have. However, in a context where political groups had been half summoned into the polity by the government and were half invaders of the polity from the economy and society, pure parliamentary institutions were unlikely to develop and were, to some degree, even redundant; this is one reason the 1914 dissolution of the assemblies was not more disruptive.

The provincial assemblies, then, reflected the new tone of politics between 1909 and 1913: the emergence of interest-group politics cutting across class lines and the new integration of national and local politics. Accompanying the new tone, however, was an ominous undertone of violence and militarism which placed many governments "at the mercy of military mobs" and led in 1912 to occasional attacks on provincial assemblies intended to intimidate their members. Rapid and radical changes had loosed large armies across the country and the story of efforts to reestablish civil au-

74. Chinese Imperial Maritime Customs, *Decennial Reports, 1902–11, 2* (Shanghai, 1913), 143; *1, 2, 3* passim: *Feng-t'ien t'ung-chih* (Gazetteer of Fengtien Province) chap. 142, p. 56.

thority throughout 1912 is mostly the search for funds to demobilize troops and send them home with pay in their pockets—assuming they still had homes.

Two intermingling parts of the new public not discussed directly above—the revolutionaries and the military officers—had combined to mobilize and use soldiers, but had not proven they could prevent their disintegration into mobs. In 1912 even officers were reduced to the status of a political group whose main immediate interest was some more glorious employment than, for example, service by the score as nominal aides to governors or even railroad conductors. The elections of late 1912 and 1913 produced assemblies that met in the provinces and Peking in the spring of 1913 with high hopes of organizing civil governments capable of handling these problems. Ominously, however, at the same time another solution was being tried: the rearming of provincial forces under various commanders who had attained prominence in the Revolution.

Provincialism and the Devolution of 1909–1913

During the Taiping and other rebellions of the nineteenth century, the central government's Board of War permanently lost its ability to exert direct control over the major military forces of China.[75] This power devolved instead upon various high provincial officials who mobilized the resources, men, and money for the armies they organized and led in suppression of the rebellions.[76] Thenceforth central government control over military matters was exercised through the military leaders of the major regions of China. The restoration of central government's authority depended primarily upon its ability to manipulate the loyalties of these regional leaders, who were usually imperially appointed governors-general (*tsung-tu*), and to limit their military power by tighter control of the centralized civil administration within which they still operated.

By 1909, the growth of new economic resources around the periphery of the traditional central apparatus and the increasing use of personnel not subject to traditional controls had increased the power of the provincial governors-general. The central govern-

75. Mary C. Wright, *The Last Stand of Chinese Conservatism* (Stanford, 1957), p. 206.

76. Franz Michael, "Introduction" to Stanley Spector's *Li Hung-chang and the Huai Army* (Seattle, 1964).

ment held its ground principally by the inertia of the civil administrative structure, which assured it a large though relatively diminishing proportion of the Empire's resources. In contrast to the governors-general, however, whose principal advantage lay in their military power, the central government's advantage was a monopoly on legitimate authority. The central government combined this monopoly with its share of economic resources to maintain a balance that delayed, if it did not for long reverse, its decline.

The balance was upset when one part of the upper polity, the central government, tried not only to restore but to increase its power. During this effort, it entered a kind of competition with another part, the provincial governors-general and governors, for the direct allegiance of the lower polity. The provincial representative institutions played key roles in this competition not only because they were located near the center of the struggle, but also because they came closest to institutionalizing the most genuinely new elements in the whole equation, popular sovereignty and a new form of provincialism. The element of popular sovereignty, reinforced by the emergence in the polity of new social and economic groupings, was critical in ending the central government's monopoly on legitimacy. With this monopoly broken, the central government was powerless to prevent the draining off of civil administrative authority to an increasingly complex provincial administrative apparatus. What began as an effort to centralize civil administrative power through sweeping reforms ended with the "devolution" of central administrative authority upon the provinces.

Devolution has usually meant revocable authority conferred by a national legislature upon provincial legislatures to handle problems that seem more manageable at the local level.[77] However, a de facto delegation of authority took place from 1909 to 1913, suggesting a case of inadvertent or poorly controlled devolution. The central government reformers had hoped that the assemblies would increase the efficiency of central government. They did not foresee that circumstances would make it virtually impossible to retrieve the authority conferred on the provinces. Conceived as a technique for tightening up and mobilizing the polity, the reform only

77. Wan-hsuan Chiao, "Devolution in Great Britain" (unpublished Ph.D. dissertation, Columbia University, 1926).

drew authority out of the central apparatus and into the new provincial governmental institutions.

During the Devolution of 1909–13, these provincial institutions could have become the captives of the local, the subprovincial power structure as in previous dynastic interregnums and the country fallen into a parochial disunity. The disunity of the warlord period is often interpreted in a like manner, and as a result, 1917 to 1928 is usually regarded as the nadir of modern Chinese history and the 1911 Revolution as essentially but an incident in the secular decline of the polity. The 1911 Revolution then seems but a dynastic fall. It did result in considerable local advances for the "marginal" and "lower" or even the "disreputable" gentry, judging from the still very limited data on the backgrounds of members of local assemblies.[78] It is important, however, to note the extent to which the gentry had been fragmented and its elements transformed by events in the polity during the 1911 Revolution. It is the new, growing public that replaced the gentry that explains the large size of the registered electorate in 1912, the response to the 1913 "Second Revolution," the reaction to the Twenty-one Demands of 1915, opposition to the Restoration of 1916, and finally the background of the May Fourth Movement of 1919.

The provincial institutions that emerged during the Devolution of 1909–13, despite the danger of parochialism, expressed a form of provincialism oriented to the national polity both through and outside the bureaucracy and therefore transitional to rather than an obstacle to nationalism.

Provincialism's orientation toward the national polity is less surprising when certain features of the traditional society from which it grew are examined. Chinese society has long been regarded as having a particular genius for intricate organization of its social life in clans, welfare societies, name associations, and the like. Usually, however, the social system containing such organizations has been contrasted sharply with the strong, centralized, and inflexible forms of the polity. The social groups are usually considered fairly simple in structure and limited in extent and are identified with localism or parochialism, while the state is regarded as a prime example of complex and almost universal organization and is identified with centralism and national integra-

78. See infra Ichiko; in fact, Ichiko's thesis does not so much describe gentry advances as the frustration of the peasant masses.

tion. The way has thus been left to depict traditional Chinese society as, like its central state, essentially uniform with no politically significant pluralism possible in the country because of the anarchic particularism of the social groups. However, a look at a particular type of organization, the *hui-kuan,* which lay close to the society's boundary with the polity, suggests otherwise. *Hui-kuan* were associations of people from one province residing for one reason or another in some city of another province. Usually they have been regarded as contributing to localism and community exclusiveness, and indeed they would have, had they functioned primarily in the native places of their members. In fact, however, they contributed to the national integration of Chinese society and economy at the local level in several ways: first, by greatly facilitating regional emigration; second, by preserving the cosmopolitanism of the host province in a way the presence of unorganized immigrants could not; and third, by giving outsiders an organization for contact with the political processes of the local power structure.[79]

In a sense, the *hui-kuan* functioned as the natural complement in the lower polity to the law of avoidance in the upper polity. The law of avoidance insured that the officials serving in the bureaucratic apparatus of each province would always be outsiders, thereby achieving a high degree of national integration in the upper polity. The *hui-kuan* meanwhile insured outsiders a prominent role in the economy and society of each province. As suggested above, however, while the local power structure was manned by natives of each province, it was also much more directly affected by social and economic factors than the upper polity. Through their roles in the economy and society of their host province, nonofficial outsiders therefore achieved a degree of influence over the local polity. This influence betrayed a degree of national integration, paradoxically, of local power structures. The *hui-kuan* thus measured the degree of national integration of the lower polity as well as of the integration of the society and economy of China.

As long, however, as the *hui-kuan* and similar institutions were denied, or did not assume, political status, the political content of provincialism was largely negative. The province was something an official could *not* represent; it was something that he supervised and whose claims to existence as a separate community he officially

79. Ping-ti Ho, *Chung-kuo hui-kuan shih-lun* (An Historical Survey of "Landsmannschaften" in China) (Taipei, 1966), esp. pp. 101–17.

resisted. The provincial chief was in general more an administrator than a leader. Historically, the province was a more purely administrative division than the county. Located at the level where lines between the throne and the county were policed and formal tasks performed, provincial officials, in contrast to county magistrates, traditionally conducted most of their business in the official world: county magistrates supervised the people, higher officials supervised other officials.[80] Contact between provincial officials and local gentry on official business was closely regulated at all levels. Out in the provinces, contact with members of the local power structure was to be social in character. When both happened to be in Peking, virtually all contact was to be avoided.[81] Similarly, officials participated in *hui-kuan* only in their capacity as outsider gentry residents of a province, avoiding official involvement and not holding *hui-kuan* offices, presumably to avoid direct contacts with the local power structure.[82]

The provincialism of the *hui-kuan* was thus to a large degree apolitical, both by design and by historical accident. In only one aspect then was provincialism political in content: cliques among traditional officials were most often based on connections developed during the long period of preparation for and participation in examinations.[83] The law of avoidance was but one device to restrict the feeling of provincial fellowship and community which the Examination System itself automatically fostered among examination "classmates." Provincial sentiments of community were confined as much as possible to a cultural mold by the law of avoidance working in combination with competition among provinces for successful scholars; provincialism in this sense was a special form of China's "Great Tradition."

The increase in economic and social integration of China during Ming and Ch'ing, however, was related to population growth and movements and eventually had a major impact on the nation's political structure.[84] The provincial representative institutions

80. Wei-chin Mu, "Provincial-Central Government Relations and the Problem of National Unity in Modern China" (unpublished Ph.D. dissertation, Princeton University, 1948), passim, and Wang Hui-tsu, cited in C. K. Yang, "Bureaucratic Behavior," p. 136.

81. Ch'ü, *Local Government*, p. 323 and n. 55, p. 323; n. 177, p. 338.

82. H. B. Morse, *The Guilds of China* (London, 1909), p. 37.

83. Ch'ü, p. 176.

84. Ho, *Chung-kuo hui-kuan shih-lun,* has demonstrated the significance of the *hui-kuan* as a measure of internal migration and an index to national economic and social integration.

had by the early Republic gone far toward absorbing outsiders into the provincial government structure and formalizing the local power structure generally. In 1909 the first stipulation for voters had been that they be natives of the province in which they voted. Special provision was made for outsiders to vote if, and only if, they had twice the business or real property demanded of qualified natives. Unlike natives they could not substitute education or other qualifications for the property qualification. They also had to have ten years' residence in the province. In 1912 two years' residence was the basic qualification for *all* voters, after which small property or educational qualifications were required of all. No special provisions were made, as had been the case in 1909, for natives who did not meet property or educational qualifications but who either had for three years taught or been in some other occupation "conducive to the public good" or had held military or civil posts above a certain rank.[85] At the same time, the hegemony of the provincial capital over the province was increased by new procedures for electing delegates from outlying counties: the provisional provincial assemblies that met during the months from the October 1911 uprising to the December 1912 elections frequently provided for the representation of such counties through groups of their citizens normally resident in the provincial capital.

Gradually, then, a provincialism of native place confined largely to cultural manifestations was overlaid and replaced by a new provincialism of residence with political significance. Provincialism during the Devolution of 1909–13 involved the organization and institutionalization of some of the most complex allegiances and loyalties that had existed in the traditional society and been latent in the traditional polity. The change worked only in combination with the emergence of political interest groups and organizations that could provide a concrete social and economic content for the abstract political forms of the new representative institutions. The process required the further politicization of numerous groups upon which the traditional structure of the lower polity had always depended, but against which the upper polity had discriminated in its own sphere while tolerating and even indirectly encouraging them in the lower polity. Scholarly concentration on the upper polity has led to the picture of a monolithic China with a strong state and a weak—albeit complex—society. In actuality, as the sudden development of provincial politics re-

85. See translations of regulations: *For. Rel. (1908)*, p. 184; *China Year Book, 1914* (Shanghai), p. 484.

vealed, in China a strong state *and* a strong society combined to create, if not a pluralistic, at least a polylithic polity.[86]

Through the cultivation of such abstract loyalties as allegiance to large territorial limits and to a people viewed as voting citizens, Chinese provincialism facilitated the rise of nationalism. It arose from a traditional society whose complexity easily matched that of modern ones. In the process, new loyalties did not so much immediately replace as gradually overlay and displace old loyalties to an Emperor and a people understood in terms of family ties and the five Confucian relationships. These changes were not so completely worked out by 1913 as to allow a new structuring of the upper polity that could have prevented the disunity of the warlord period. The residue of regional militarism that had accompanied the fall of the Ch'ing had yet to be overcome.

An institutional product of the 1911 Revolution and of the 1909–13 Devolution was, as in other modern revolutions, the mob. For special reasons—including the sheer size of the country and the history of military-civil relations—China's revolutionary mobs were a curious kind of "military mob."[87] These mobs, when they ransomed county magistrates or presidents of local chambers of commerce, were not the anomic gatherings of some revolutions. As mobs they were curiously calculating, showing more regimentation than spirit. When they attacked loyalist troops as part of

86. A strong state and a strong society are conceptually compatible if one recognizes, as Parsons has suggested, that politics is not a "zero sum" game. Talcott Parsons, "The Distribution of Power in American Society," *World Politics, 10* (1957), 139. See also the critique of the "scarcity theory" of power in Robert S. Lynd, "Power in American Society as Resource and Problem," in Arthur Kornhauser, ed., *Problems of Power in American Society* (Detroit, 1957), pp. 9–10. While not eschewing definitions of political power as "over others," as do these theorists, I prefer the concept of "compliance" worked out by Etzioni, *Modern Organizations.*

On Chinese pluralism, the most recent comment is found in Franklin W. Houn in *Chinese Political Traditions* (Washington, D.C., 1965). Professor Houn draws extensively on Hsiao's *Rural China: Imperial Control in the Nineteenth Century* (Seattle, 1960). See also Hsiao's *Political Pluralism* (London, 1927), particularly his views on the relationship of politics to economics in chap. 5, especially pp. 124–25; also pp. 75–76.

87. I have taken the expression from the summary of the Hunan political situation made in late December 1911 by British Consul General Giles in Changsha: "The government is at the mercy of a military mob." I believe it catches very well the texture of the Revolution—its patterns of action—conveyed by the Chinese, Japanese, and Western eyewitness accounts I have examined. Some connotations of Giles' word "mob" are unfortunate. However, I hesitate to substitute the neutral term "bands" as it conveys none of the scene's color and action. The topic deserves extended treatment. *PP China No. 3 (1912)*, pp. 63–65.

the republican army at Hankow and elsewhere they rarely showed as much discipline as most revolutionary armies. In the armies of the time, soldiers had shown unusual sprit but little regimentation. The telegraph had rapidly brought news of the Wuchang uprising to every part of the country and hundreds of new newspapers had spread the word to crowds waiting outside their offices. Over a dozen governments of provinces larger than most countries had been organized or reorganized in a few weeks (more in a couple of months) and armies mobilized and sent across a continent-sized country.

The issue of monarchy versus republic was decided too rapidly, however, for other questions to be decided finally. The problem of demobilization of the armies overtook provincial governments almost before they had solved the problem of mobilization. In the meanwhile, troops that had marched on the telegraph's word of revolution cut up the telegraph wire for shot to feed their cannon.[88] In the absence of roads to the battlefield police action was long delayed even where there were forces to carry it out. The problems of control were beyond the strength of the new provincialism and the reach of the even newer nationalism.

The provincial sense of community was further taxed in its struggle for order by the need to cultivate the foreign powers. The nation needed foreign loans to pay its soldiers. Apparently these could be had only by asking the new public to turn from provincialism to internationalism without an intervening period of nationalism. The formula was not alien to many who felt the similarities of internationalism to the cultural cosmopolitanism of the traditional elite even in the provinces; however, nationalism was needed to calm the soldiers once they had been paid off. The old regional militarism was an alternative that generals like Chang Hsün were trying again. The changes in the polity had gone far enough, however, to preclude forever the reestablishment of general unity through military means alone. The emergence of the lower polity had produced a public which called for more than a retreat to T'ang dynasty solutions (or even a combination of T'ang, Sung, Ming, and Ch'ing solutions). The problem was not only how to control the mobs but also how to control the apparatus for controlling the mobs while resisting foreign enemies. It would take a special blend of military and civil politics to satisfy national

88. Dispatch from Chungking, 10/12/11, USDS, 893.00/682.

pride and demands both for social order and for social justice. Yuan Shih-k'ai had only some of the answers. Parliaments—provincial, national, local—figured in most prescriptions. The demands of the members of the parliaments, as well as of the rest of the public, would necessitate, it was commonly acknowledged, new forms of army and party organization.

As the ideas of model province and base area suggest, however, the provincialism of these parliaments and their public was still to have a role in national movements. For a long time it was the best possible adjustment of ideals to a reality shaped by the declining but resilient monarchy and bureaucracy.

PART II

Sociological Aspects of the Revolution

5. The Role of the Bourgeoisie

Marie-Claire Bergère

The importance of the events that ended an imperial regime that had been in existence for two thousand years, ushered in a period of instability in which rebellion followed uprisings, and culminated finally in the establishment of communism in China, can hardly be denied. Yet the play of social and economic forces underlying the movement, and indeed the very nature and significance of the movement as a whole, are far from clear.

Was the Revolution of 1911 a rebellion of the traditional type that had so often brought about the fall of dynasties? Certainly the events that followed the fall of the Manchu dynasty—the spread of peasant unrest, the role played in it by secret societies, the gentry's participation, and the attempted restoration of the empire by Yuan Shih-k'ai—have many analogies in the past. Or should the events of 1911 be regarded as a revolution of the Western type, similar to the bourgeois revolutions in England and France, in which a new class, the commercial bourgeoisie, was determined to seize power in order to introduce a political system better suited to its own interests? A situation to some extent parallel to that found in Europe a century or two ago did indeed exist in China in 1911, with some sections of the economy undergoing a comparatively slight, yet real, process of modernization, with the appearance of a commercial bourgeoisie, and with the spread of an ideology in which nationalist ideas (the unity and independence of China) were combined with, and given new vigor by, liberal doctrines (abolition of privileges, democracy, liberty of the individual). Or should comparisons with the past be left aside? Turning instead to those countries of Africa, Asia, and Latin America whose recent history might throw light on the slightly earlier events in China, should the 1911 Revolution be described as a revolution of a new kind, similar to those that for the past few decades have been shaking the countries of the Third World?

In recent years Chinese Communist historians have emphasized the importance of the role of the bourgeoisie.[1] They regard the 1911 movement as a revolution led by the bourgeoisie, whose members were nationalist, democratic, and to a very slight extent socialist in outlook. But this bourgeoisie was only partially successful in having its demands met. As far as its nationalism was concerned, the Communist theory is that it got rid of the Manchus only to capitulate to Western imperialism; its democracy failed to reverse the absolutism of the imperial regime, and the establishment of a republican regime merely gave rise to a new kind of personal power. This semi-impotence and partial failure are attributed to two main causes: first, the numerical weakness of the bourgeoisie and its lack of political maturity, which made it incapable of choosing the right allies in the struggle and led it to rely on the gentry rather than on the peasant masses; and second, the deep hostility shown by the foreign powers toward the republican movement and the aspirations of the bourgeoisie, whose expansion could only take place at the expense of the imperialist powers with vested interests in China. These theories, which provide the basis of many recent Chinese books and articles, necessarily form the point of departure for a study of the bourgeoisie. They cannot be accepted uncritically, but neither can they be rejected out of hand.

The Bourgeoisie at the Outbreak of the Revolution

Exactly what section of society did the Chinese bourgeoisie represent just before the outbreak of the Revolution? What were its economic activities? What were the indications of its existence as a distinct class? What were its relations with other classes, its manner of life, its political ideas?

Before attempting to find answers to these questions, a definition must be given of what is understood here by the word "bourgeoisie." Throughout this chapter, the word is used in the most restricted sense of the term—that is, in the technical meaning of commercial bourgeoisie, a group comprising entrepreneurs in the modern, or more or less modern style, businessmen, financiers, and industrialists—and not in the more general sense of "middle class," which would include intellectuals, landowners, and members of the liberal professions, as well as people belonging to business circles.

1. M. C. Bergère, "La révolution de 1911 jugée par les historiens de la République Populaire de Chine," *Revue Historique*, no. 230 (1963), 403–36.

This narrow definition is adopted primarily because of certain features of Chinese society at the time. It was neither a hierarchical society in the strict sense (that is, legally constituted as such, despite the existence of a dwindling hereditary Manchu aristocracy), nor a class society based on the differentiation of economic functions. The power of the ruling group rested on land ownership, civil service examination qualifications, and participation in the administrative system, these factors being capable of many different combinations and permutations. Hence the bourgeois class has to be defined in terms of the occupations of its members, however unsatisfactory a criterion this may be, if its essential nature is to be appreciated. A further justification for this narrow definition of the term "bourgeoisie" lies in the fact that businessmen and entrepreneurs have often been regarded as the most dynamic element of the middle class—its "progressive wing." Finally, there is a more technical reason for its adoption, namely that the study of the "commercial" bourgeoisie is greatly facilitated by the fact that documentation includes both Chinese and Western sources.

If one word had to be chosen to characterize the Chinese bourgeoisie at the outbreak of the 1911 Revolution, it would be *weakness.* This weakness was directly linked with the economic backwardness of China. I do not want to enter here upon the well-worn argument about the "germs of capitalism" (*tzu-pen chu-i meng-ya*),[2] but let us assume that even if certain embryonic forms of mercantile capitalism had existed since Ming times, it was not until the twentieth century that a commercial bourgeoisie came into existence as the result of changes that occurred in some sections of the Chinese economy.

Economic Change at the Turn of the Century

The economic consequences of the "opening up" of China in the middle of the nineteenth century have already been described

2. A. Feuerwerker and S. Cheng, "The 'Capitalist Bourgeois' Controversy," *Chinese Communist Studies of Modern Chinese History* (Cambridge, Mass., 1961), pp. 181–89; the book contains a short essay and a bibliography of Chinese works. A. Feuerwerker, "From 'Feudalism' to 'Capitalism' in Recent Historical Writing from Mainland China," *JAS, 18* (1958), 107. On the question of the existence of a Chinese bourgeoisie before the twentieth century, see Louis Dermigny, *La Chine et l'Occident; le commerce à Canton au 18e siècle, 1719–1833* (3 vols. and 1 album, Paris, 1964). The author is of the opinion that, despite their wealth, the merchants of Canton did not become capitalists, because there was no real accumulation of capital and therefore no proper system of credit.

by a number of historians.[3] They stress the efforts made by the Chinese to create a modern industry, the difficulties encountered in this attempt, and the frequent failure to carry it through. Without retracing a process that has already been studied in such detail, I feel that certain special features of the Chinese economy at the beginning of the present century need to be emphasized here.

Although in the economic sphere the Chinese reaction to Western aggression was a fairly serious, adroit, and successful effort to industrialize, the main aim of the foreign powers in opening up the country was to promote the expansion of trade. In this they succeeded, and during the second half of the nineteenth century the volume of foreign trade in China increased continuously, fed by the flow of imports of such manufactured products as textiles, sugar, and kerosene, and the export of such primary, mainly agricultural, products as tea and silk. But the balance of trade was thereby disturbed, for the value of imports increasingly exceeded that of exports, and China was forced to make up her trade deficit in cash. From the Western point of view, the tendency at this time was to regard the Chinese market more as an outlet for manufactured products than as a source of supply for primary products; and contrary to what was happening at that time in other colonial countries such as Egypt and Cochin-China, the effect of these new channels of trade on the Chinese economy was an increase in the sale of foreign products rather than an increase in the supply of local agricultural products for export.

The trade was conducted in the main treaty ports—Tientsin, Canton, and above all Shanghai—which served as transit centers between foreign countries and the Chinese interior. Control of this trade was unequally divided between foreign and Chinese businessmen. The Western and Japanese firms and banks established in the treaty ports had complete control over the circulation of capital and goods between China and the importing and exporting countries. It was not until the First World War that China attempted to develop direct contact with foreign countries.

3. See A. Feuerwerker, *China's Early Industrialization* (Cambridge, Mass., 1958); Yoshihiro Hatano, *Chūgoku kindai kōgyōshi no kenkyū* (Studies on the Industrialization of China) (Kyoto, 1962); D. K. Lieu, *China's Industry and Finance* (Peking, 1927); Suzuki Tomoo, "Shinmatsu minsho ni okeru minzoku shihon no tenkai katei" (The Process of Development of Native Capital During the Late Ch'ing and Early Republic), in *Chūgoku kindaika no shakai kōzō, 6* (Tokyo, 1960), 45–71; Yen Chung-p'ing, *Chung-kuo mien-fang-chih shih-kao* (History of the Chinese Cotton Industry) (reissued Peking, 1955).

Because foreigners were hampered by their ignorance of the language and customs of the country and by the restrictions placed on their movements by the international treaties, in China itself commercial transactions, regarding both imports and exports, between the treaty ports and the interior were usually relegated to Chinese merchants. They, however, had no alternative to foreign banks for effective financing of their activities. The financing was done chiefly through Chinese establishments called native banks (*ch'ien-chuang*), which were granted very short-term loans known as chop-loans, the unusual feature of which was that they were not covered by any real guarantee. The annual total in loans of this kind contracted by the native banks of Shanghai amounted to as much as around ten million taels in 1910.[4] In addition, on orders with immediate delivery, foreign banks usually accepted payment in promissory notes known as *chuang-p'iao,* payable on maturity, issued by the native banks. Thus, in the absence of a central bank or a sufficient number of modern Chinese private banks, the native banks which financed the Chinese brokers and wholesalers were themselves financed by foreign banking firms.[5]

Since the Chinese economy was still partitioned into regional or even local units, with a resulting chaotic diversity of monetary systems, it is perhaps difficult to envisage the possibility of a national market developing. Nevertheless new forms of financial and commercial organization connected with the expansion of the export trade were beginning to be superimposed upon the old. They were still in the early stages, still tenuous and incomplete, but that they existed is shown by the occurrence of such national crises as that of 1910. This was caused not by any natural calamity affecting farming, but by Chinese speculation in the world rubber market, and within a few weeks it had brought many commercial and industrial concerns throughout the country to bankruptcy.[6] That this emerging national market was essentially an extension of the export trade, operating for foreign requirements, cannot be overemphasized. Unprotected by any effective tariff legislation, it began simply as a sector of the international market. The unifica-

4. In 1910 and throughout the revolutionary period the haikwan tael was roughly equivalent to $4.65 in U.S. gold dollars. In the text, "dollars" unless otherwise specified means the Mexican or Carolus silver dollar.

5. See M. C. Bergère, *Une crise financière à Shanghai à la fin de l'ancien régime* (Paris, 1964), pp. 5, 32.

6. Ibid.

tion of the Chinese economy accompanied its expropriation—it was in fact simply a by-product of that process.

The first real advances toward modern industrial development took place at the very end of the nineteenth century, and were mainly a secondary result of the new channels of trade. Since they were authorized to do so by the Treaty of Shimonoseki in 1895, the foreign powers had established factories, chiefly for cotton spinning and weaving, in the treaty ports, which supplied goods for the trade with the Chinese interior. Thus, attracted by the supply of cheap labor and the low price of local raw materials, the entrepreneurs sought to increase their profits by manufacturing in China the goods that had formerly been imported from the West or from Japan. Thereafter the importation of capital either supplanted or complemented the importation of goods.

The Chinese tried to take part in this development, but although force of circumstances had enabled them to collaborate with foreigners in operating the import-export cycle, when it came to industrial expansion collaboration gave way to direct competition, in which the Chinese entrepreneur, handicapped from the outset by the absence of any effective tariff protection, had little chance of success. In the textile industry, for instance, one of the industries in which expansion was most apparent, the success of the industrialist Chang Chien in the early years of the twentieth century was the exception that proves the rule.[7]

This development of trade and industry depended upon the erection of the necessary buildings, carried out largely by the foreigners for their own concerns, and the provision of means of transport (steamships and railways) and communication (telegraph lines). Meanwhile the growth of urban development led to the destruction of ancient walls and the construction of new business districts, and even—in Tientsin, for instance—to the application of a policy of town planning.[8]

Clearly these changes had very little effect on Chinese economic life as a whole, in which traditional methods of agriculture remained the predominant feature. The vast majority of the population continued to live within what was for all intents and purposes

7. Cf. Yen Chung-p'ing, pp. 126–27; Samuel Chu, *Reformer in Modern China, Chang Chien, 1853–1926* (New York and London, 1965). (Hereafter cited as S. Chu, *Reformer*.)

8. See *TR* (1904), part 2, Report from Tientsin, p. 53; *TR* (1907), part 2, Report from Tientsin, pp. 56–57; *NCH* (Aug. 17, 1906), p. 417.

a closed economy. The commercial exploitation of such primary products as silk, cotton, and tea, and the supply of manufactured goods for the domestic market were still on such a small scale that they only ranked as secondary features of the Chinese economy. Production of this kind was centered in a few key areas or in places served by modern means of transport.

The interior was only to a limited extent affected by the activities in the treaty ports. According to Albert Feuerwerker, the area affected by the new metropolis of Shanghai lay in the Yangtze Valley and scarcely extended beyond the province of Hunan. Even in areas where new channels of trade were developing, the existence of the treaty ports probably did little to make any appreciable change in the rhythms of life or in methods of production. The decline of handicrafts that did in fact occur in certain sectors of industry was by no means general. On the contrary, the growth of industrialized spinning and the extension of the consumer market for foreign imports sometimes stimulated handicraft production. This is confirmed by the amazing achievements of the traditional handicraft industries, such as the textile, sugar, and dyeing industries, during the First World War, when they filled the void in production caused by the withdrawal of Western industrialists far more effectively than the modern Chinese-owned factories.

Similarly, with regard to trade, G. William Skinner has shown that there was no change in the market structure during the first years of the twentieth century except in the big cities served by modern transport and communications and in the areas immediately surrounding them. It is true that, under the stimulus of the growth in foreign trade, the number of markets increased, but owing to such factors as the transport difficulties occasioned by impassable roads, the role of fairs, and so on, they retained their traditional character. The requirements of foreign trade and the new demand may have intensified trade, but its pattern still followed the old models. This is what Skinner calls "false modernization."[9]

Thus the extent to which modernization, in any real sense of the term, had been introduced into the Chinese economy prior to 1911 was limited in the extreme. Nevertheless, however slight its effect in practical economic terms, modernization certainly had important consequences in social and political matters. The trade channels connected with the export trade, with Shanghai as their

9. G. William Skinner, "Marketing and Social Structure in Rural China," *JAS*, *24*:1 (1964), 3–43; *24*:2 (1965), 195–228.

starting point, did not stop at Hunan, but penetrated as far as Szechwan, and in fact extended to all parts of China. Certainly the further the distance from the coast, the more tenuous and intermittent they were, and the more negligible from the economist's point of view. But they did exist, and that, I believe, is the important point.

Unlike the long-distance channels of trade of the medieval West, to which they have sometimes been compared, these channels in China brought together two completely different worlds: the backward Chinese interior with its medieval economy, and the treaty ports and their Concessions with their modern Western business methods and advanced techniques. The movement of capital and goods between these two worlds, even on a very limited scale, offered remarkable opportunities for introducing the Chinese to new ways and new awareness. Although their first experiences with these new ways may have been something of a shock, as for example in the case of the leading Szechwanese who entrusted their ingots to the native banks of Shanghai and then found themselves nearly ruined after the Stock Exchange crash of 1910, their introduction was nonetheless significant.

In short, the modernization of China's economy at the beginning of the twentieth century must be judged not merely quantitatively, but also qualitatively. And here the decisive role played by foreigners is undoubtedly the vital factor. The Chinese, of course, also played their part in introducing changes, but their role was always a secondary one, and in no way creative. Most of their entrepreneurial activities were merely an extension of those conducted by the foreigners, and more often than not they confined themselves to exploiting the opportunities for making money created by the opening up of China.

Thus speculation was the realm where the Chinese businessman was king: land for building in rapidly expanding suburbs; in stocks and shares on the Shanghai Stock Exchange, where the absence of strict control encouraged the taking of the wildest risks; in variations in exchange rates between the various provincial monetary systems; in fluctuations in the price of silver in relation to gold, which often made foreign trade operations a real gamble; and also in the world market, in railway companies, in copper currency, and so on. At best, these Chinese capitalists may be regarded as auxiliaries in the modernization of the Chinese economy; at worst, as parasites. Either way, the levers of economic control escaped their grasp, although they did not lack opportunities for getting rich quickly or for initiation into the ways of the modern world. In these conditions, at the turn of the last century, a new class arose in China: the commercial bourgeoisie.

The Rise of the Commercial Bourgeoisie

It was because modernization was an innovation, and because the Chinese economy was only partly affected by it, that the commercial bourgeoisie was so limited in size. But there is little hope of arriving at a figure for the number of its members from the documents available at present. All that can be determined is that however many there were, they were very unevenly distributed geographically, the main concentration being in the treaty ports, with a thin scattering in the interior. The term "treaty port" designates a legal status and applied to several towns deep in the interior—Chungking in Szechwan, for example; yet it was in the coastal towns, where there was direct and constant contact with foreigners, that the bourgeoisie congregated. The chief centers were Tientsin, Canton, and above all Shanghai, for the Yangtze delta was the only part of China where economic change had really gone deep enough to enable the new Chinese bourgeois class to expand its activities.

This new bourgeois class was still far from homogeneous at the outbreak of the Revolution; its members were drawn from a number of diverse groups—compradores, merchants, bankers, industrialists, and Overseas Chinese—and still retained some of the particular characteristics of whichever group they had come from.

The compradores had long since ceased to be the somewhat seedy individuals who had provisioned the ships riding at anchor outside the port of Canton during the first decades of the nineteenth century,[10] nor can they be denounced as servile intermediaries (*nu-ts'ai*), as certain historians have done.[11] Many of them ranked among the wealthiest and most highly respected of promi-

10. See Huang I-feng, "Kuan-yü chiu Chung-kuo mai-pan chieh-chi ti yen-chiu" (Research Concerning the Compradore Class in China from 1840 until 1927), *Li-shih yen-chiu* (1964), *3*, 89; Yoshihiro Hatano, pp. 150 ff.; K'uang Yung-pao, "The Compradore: His Position in the Foreign Trade of China," *Economic Journal* (December 1911); Negishi Tadashi, *Baiben seido no kenkyū* (Research on the Compradore System) (Tokyo, 1948), pp. 34–74.

11. Huang I-feng, "Ti-kuo chu-i ch'in-lüeh ti i-ko chung-yao chih-chu: mai-pan chieh-chi" (An Important Support for Imperialist Aggression in China: the Compradore Class), *Li-shih yen-chiu* (1965), *1*, 55.

nent citizens. Their wealth was ostensibly derived from services rendered to foreign firms; but they had already been wealthy when first taken on by these firms. Foreign firms made it a rule to recruit their compradores from the established, wealthy merchants, who were likely to be trustworthy and also to be trusted in Chinese business circles.[12] Indeed, in some respects the compradores seem to have acted as partners in the firms they worked for rather than as employees—the compradore for the Chartered Bank of Hankow, for instance, was apparently authorized to sign documents on behalf of the bank over a period of more than thirty years.[13] They have been regarded by some as particularly glaring examples of subservience to foreign interests, but as entrepreneurs they may not have been any more subservient than other Chinese bourgeois. To counterbalance their dependence, their day-to-day experience had given them a special knowledge of the realities of the new political and economic situation. They seem to have been a small, rather closed group (the post of compradore was often a hereditary one)[14] which exercised a great deal of influence.

The big merchants were for the most part engaged in the import-export trade. They lived in the treaty ports, from which, in command of the network of distribution and supply, they controlled the circulation of goods in the interior; but whether brokers or independent merchants, their function remained an auxiliary one.

In the early years of the century the moneychangers of Shansi no longer did most of the banking in China, for now that international trade was beginning to supplant interprovincial trade, new forms of financing operations were required. Bankers were now found in the increasing number of native banks, their primary role being to extend to Chinese clients the credit supplied by foreign banks.

Merchants and bankers were probably in the majority among the ranks of the bourgeoisie, whereas industrialists formed a very small minority. It is often difficult to distinguish industrialists from merchants in the sense that their manufacturing activities

12. See *NCH* (June 10, 1910), p. 593: "As a class, Chinese compradores enjoy a fine record of fair dealing. Entrusted with large transactions and possessing a large degree of independence they . . . have won for the Chinese nation a deservedly high reputation for commercial rectitude."

13. *NCH* (Jan. 20, 1905), p. 140.

14. *NCH* (Feb. 8, 1913), p. 418: legal proceedings concerning the inheritance of the compradore of the Hongkong and Shanghai Bank. The position of compradore is considered by the heirs as a part of the inheritance.

were frequently no more than an extension of their commercial dealings, an early form of vertical integration.

Finally, the Overseas Chinese who became entrepreneurs were a somewhat marginal group. For three centuries these "colonials," who had formerly been suspected of favoring restoration of the Ming dynasty, had not been allowed to take part in the activities of the metropolitan centers. But at the end of the nineteenth century the Manchu government encouraged them to renew contact with the mother country in order to give it the benefit of their experience abroad. From then on the Overseas Chinese began to assume an increasing role in Chinese economic affairs, often with great success: for example, the Sunning Line in Kwangtung was the only purely Chinese-owned railway that showed an overall profit.[15] They also began to play a part in politics.

In spite of the diversity of its component parts, is it possible to speak of a "bourgeois class"? There do not in fact seem to have been any barriers between the various groups mentioned above. On the contrary, it was customary for a man to belong to more than one group—for the compradore to be at the same time a merchant, and the banker an entrepreneur. In addition he was bound by many kinds of personal ties, such as kinship or regional loyalties, all of which helped to reinforce cohesion in the new class. Thus within Chinese society as a whole the bourgeoisie had already begun to display unity and its own particular characteristics.

The bourgeoisie had also begun to be differentiated from other classes. It was distinguished from the peasantry by its wealth and by the very nature of its activities; from the artisans by the scale of its enterprises and by the leading role it had assumed in the various forms of mercantile capitalism it had developed.[16]

However, its relations with the gentry were both closer and more ambiguous. Sometimes, in fact, the two classes seem to have been regarded as one, since Chinese writers of the time did

15. *NCH* (Jan. 16, 1908), p. 76.

16. *TR* (1907), part 2, Report from Changsha, p. 175 (concerning the silk embroideries manufacture). Report from Nanking, p. 586, concerning firecracker manufacture: "in this trade numerous small and bigger shops are engaged . . . the greater part of the work connected with this industry is not carried out in the various hong but given to outside people to be done in their homes." *TR* (1906), part 2, Report from Canton, p. 398: the same type of organization is found here for matting manufacture; friction was frequent between the dealer-employers of Canton and the manufacturers living outside the city. Concerning the same problems, but for a later period, see also H. D. Fong, *Rural Weaving and the Merchant Employers in a North China District* (Tientsin, 1935).

not hesitate to class them together under the single term merchant-gentry (*shen-shang*). Doubtless the reason for this change lies in the weakening of the position of the gentry, which had depended on land ownership, examination degrees, and participation in the administrative system. However, for more than fifty years the imperial government had been selling to rich men the titles formerly won only in the civil service examinations, and with the growing deficit in public finances, this practice grew to such an extent that toward the end of the nineteenth century more than half of the body of scholar-officials had achieved their legal status by buying their credentials; among them there were, of course, many wealthy merchants. This process reached its conclusion with the abolition of the traditional Examination System in 1905. Meanwhile the bourgeoisie had begun to invest in land in the areas surrounding the main treaty ports, particularly in the hinterland of Canton and Shanghai, thus striking a blow, if only locally, at the virtual land monopoly of the gentry.

In political and administrative functions, the gentry still reserved for themselves the highest offices at the national level. Rarely did a merchant or a businessman hold a ministerial post; at the most, a few of them played comparatively subordinate roles as advisers to leading statesmen—Cheng Kuan-ying's role, for example, in the entourage of Li Hung-chang. But merchants were playing an increasingly important part in local affairs, in which the interests they defended often coincided with those of the gentry. That the collaboration thus established was capable of further development is shown by the formation in 1908 of experimental provincial assemblies which acted as forums where the gentry and merchants could make joint demands.

Thus the gentry, whose social position had become less clearly defined with the decline of the Manchu government after 1870 and the abolition of the Examination System in 1905, and the nascent bourgeoisie who had not yet attained a clearly defined social position, merged to form the merchant-gentry, a class composed of the influential people of each locality, closely connected with land ownership, but not above taking the opportunity to derive profit from investment in modern business ventures.

The degree of amalgamation seems, however, to have differed in different regions, being greater, curiously enough, in such regions as Szechwan and Hunan in the interior, where traditional methods of agriculture were still predominant and the gentry had maintained their prestige, and lesser in the coastal regions, where there was constant contact with foreigners and where investment in land had taken new forms, such as speculation in suburban real estate and reclamation of land by large commercial companies. In Canton and Shanghai it was more a question of an alliance than of an amalgamation between the bourgeoisie and the gentry, an alliance in which the bourgeoisie was very conscious of its social status and its own particular role—witness the case of the merchants of Canton who, in 1905, demanded the abolition of all the humiliating formalities that until then had marked their relations with the gentry.[17]

This increasing "bourgeois" awareness of having a place in society also found expression during the same period in the formation or further development of special organizations. Many chambers of commerce came into being from 1904 on. They had been formed on government initiative, Sheng Hsüan-huai's original idea being to use them as a mechanism of administrative and political control over the local business communities and of contact between these communities and the central government. In the smaller centers the chambers of commerce only partially succeeded in emancipating themselves from the control of government officials, but in the main treaty ports, particularly in Shanghai, they very soon achieved a considerable degree of autonomy, and it became their primary aim to act in the interests of the merchants whose spokesmen they were. At the same time the merchants felt the need for direct protection and formed the well-known Volunteer Corps. These were militia composed of young men recruited exclusively from business circles, and sometimes of mercenaries hired by the guilds or the chambers of commerce. Their arms and equipment were paid for by special contributions made by business concerns. Their ostensible task was to protect shops and offices in times of unrest, but in fact they provided the merchants with what amounted to an independent army of intervention. The first merchant Volunteer Corps was formed in Shanghai in 1905.[18]

Finally, the bourgeoisie was distinguished from other classes by its beliefs and its manner of life, which were influenced by Western ideas and customs. It was mainly through Anglo-Saxon business circles that Chinese merchants were initiated into the spirit-

17. *NCH* (Jan. 20, 1905), p. 149.

18. *NCH* (May 18, 1906), p. 40; (May 25), p. 441; (July 13), p. 69; (July 16), p. 83; (July 27), p. 181. *NCH* (Jan. 4, 1907; Jan. 25; June 21, etc.).

ual and material refinements of modern civilization, and this accounts for the fairly general (although perhaps superficial) adoption of Protestantism among them, their belief in the health-giving qualities of sport, and their enthusiasm for social work, for clubs, and for such organizations as the Y.M.C.A.[19] A growing number of them learned to speak English, and their sons learned it at an early age in the schools of the Concessions and later perfected their mastery of the language at English and American universities. All innovations, whatever they might be, whether Western-style clothing, multistoried houses, the launching of ships with champagne, or driving an automobile, were eagerly welcomed by the Chinese bourgeoisie.[20]

Here, then, was a class that was economically dependent, small in numbers, socially heterogeneous, and not yet fully differentiated. Nevertheless during the decade preceding the 1911 Revolution a number of ideas and political demands usually associated with the full maturity of the bourgeoisie began to arise and to spread. What were these ideas, and how were they able to take root in China at this time?

Bourgeois Ideology

First, I use the term "bourgeois ideology" here to span the whole development of bourgeois thought in Europe, from the ideas of the Enlightenment formulated by, among others, the French philosophers of the eighteenth century, to the nationalist ideas which reached their peak in the mid-nineteenth century. By the beginning of the twentieth century Chinese political thought and writings were permeated with ideas from both these poles of bourgeois ideology. This whole stream of thought is familiar to all students of modern Chinese history and has been studied in great detail; there is no need for further elaboration here. The question for discussion is whether the Chinese bourgeoisie could itself have produced ideas that coincided with those expounded in Western bourgeois ideology. Were these ideas a reflection of Chinese experience? The small size of the class that had newly arisen in China would seem to rule out such a possibility. It could, of course, be argued

19. Concerning the good relations between the YMCA and some of the most important merchants of Shanghai, see *NCH* (May 18, 1906), pp. 364–65.

20. Many illustrations of this can be found in the files of the *NCH,* and in memoirs and biographies, such as Emily Hahn, *The Soong Sisters* (London, 1942).

that because the bourgeoisie was concentrated in the treaty ports, possessed great material wealth, and was in contact with the modern world, it enjoyed a favorable position for influencing political opinion; but despite these advantages, there are many counterarguments to show that it had not yet reached an advanced enough stage in its development as a class to produce such advanced ideas. In Europe, the political ideas propounded by Voltaire and Rousseau, for example, marked the culmination of a process of change that had begun several centuries earlier; but in China these ideas sprang up before the bourgeois class had even come into existence. The first manifestos of Sun Yat-sen appeared before 1900, and in 1902–03 Liang Ch'i-ch'ao reached one of the high points of his career as a writer and journalist when the collection of articles entitled *Yin-ping shih ch'üan-chi* was published. But it was not until 1905, during the first national boycott, that the Chinese bourgeoisie made its entry on the political scene. Nationalist feelings arose from the general resentment in China at the presence of the imperialist powers, long before there was a united China or a national market; and the bourgeoisie seems to have been much more concerned about foreign control of the market than about its unification.

The fact that China was now threatened by foreign conquest may explain the rapid adoption of nationalist attitudes. There is, however, a vast difference between the attitudes adopted in face of this threat and the primitive xenophobia which culminated in the Boxer Rebellion; the new nationalist demands were couched in terms of advanced political ideas, suggesting that these political ideas were borrowed from abroad. The political writings of the time confirm this impression. Most of them give much more space to Western theory and practice than to any possible application to the Chinese situation. It so happened that at the same time that the circulation of ideas, along with goods and capital, was accelerated, the Chinese were brought into direct contact with coherent ideological systems developed abroad over several centuries.

It was the young intellectuals, together with some of the officers in the New Army (many of them recent graduates), who were mainly responsible for the importation of the new ideas. They had, of course, affiliations with the main social classes (peasantry, gentry, or bourgeoisie), but at this particular juncture they seem to have formed a separate social group with a certain independence of political outlook. Despite the largely marginal character of this group, it nevertheless served as a channel of communication for the imported ideology, and the new ideas spread throughout China without any firm class basis to support them. There thus seems to have been a certain lack of harmony between the social and economic aspect of events and the political and ideological aspect.

This detachment perhaps helps to explain certain features of the Chinese version of the bourgeois ideology that existed at the outbreak of the Revolution. What is immediately striking about it is its inherent theoretical weakness. It was a construct of ideas that had very little relevance to the realities of the Chinese situation. The construct itself was far from satisfactory, because of the difficult circumstances in which it had been worked out and because Chinese intellectuals were still badly equipped for their task. Most of them were unable to read the writings of foreign authors in the original, and since few of these works had been translated into Chinese, they had to rely on Japanese popularized versions. Thus misunderstandings piled up one after another. A similar lack of maturity was shown in the clash between the reformist and revolutionary factions that divided Chinese "progressive" intellectuals, and which were based on personal loyalties (followers of Liang Ch'i-ch'ao versus followers of Sun Yat-sen) rather than on any real or profound differences of theoretical approach.

Another feature of this Chinese version of the bourgeois ideology resulting from its lack of class basis was the diluted form in which it reached the various sections of society. The spreading of an ideology so incoherent in its main principles only led to a weakening of the ideas it contained, thus making them politically ineffective. New words came to be used for old situations, and the imported ideology served as a cover for traditional ways of expressing opposition. Nationalism was translated into terms of anti-Manchu feeling; democracy into terms of local magnates defending their privileges against the central government. It is noteworthy that a leader like Sun Yat-sen did nothing to counteract this ambiguity. On the contrary, whether because of inexperience or a clumsy kind of Machiavellianism, he seems to have encouraged this confusion.

Naturally the bourgeois ideology also spread among the nascent Chinese bourgeoisie. Did it meet with any more comprehension there than elsewhere, and did its new demands meet the fundamental needs of the bourgeoisie better than it met those of other sections of society? In order to answer this question, the various political attitudes and views of the bourgeoisie at the outbreak of the Revolution must be examined in more detail.

Political Attitudes at the Outbreak of the Revolution

Before examining the various ways in which the bourgeoisie became involved in politics, I should like to emphasize the difficulties they encountered in doing so, particularly the psychological ones. Chiefly holding them back was that common phenomenon, the persistence of old mental attitudes. Deeply rooted habits of thought concerning the social isolation and separate way of life of the merchant class had to be overcome before a new attitude toward participation in public affairs and a desire to promote the interests of the country as a whole could develop.

For centuries the merchants had been looked down on and prevented from taking part in public affairs. Tolerated rather than socially integrated, they had lived in a world apart, with their own professional skills, their own code of honor, and their own corporate organizations, where making money was the main purpose in life, and where having anything to do with the government (which usually meant having to pay exactions) was a calamity to be avoided. It was a closed world, contained within the solid framework of closely interwoven ties of kinship and of regional and professional loyalties. Being self-sufficient, it went on its way almost completely out of contact with the outside social environment. This enabled emigrants to form communities overseas without greatly altering their way of life.

Thus at the beginning of the twentieth century, at a time when the Chinese economy was, willy-nilly, becoming integrated into the world economy, the merchants were as hesitant as ever to become integrated into the society that surrounded them within their own country. This hesitancy showed itself in quite trivial situations. In the plague epidemic of 1911, for example, the merchants of Mukden demanded to have an isolation center reserved exclusively for them.[21] But it also appeared in more significant ways. There may have been a hidden nationalist purpose, as some people were inclined to suspect, behind the formation of the merchant militias, but to most people, including perhaps those who were dubious of nationalist motives, it appeared primarily as a safety precaution.[22] The merchants often seemed concerned not so much with public

21. *NCH* (March 3, 1911), p. 483; the same attitude is found among the Shanghai merchants, who insisted on starting an independent plague hospital to avoid having to mix with other classes. Cf. *NCH* (March 3, 1911), p. 504.

22. This, for example, was Yü Hsia-ch'ing's attitude; he was in favor of amalgamating the Chinese Volunteer Corps with the foreign Shanghai Municipal Volunteer Corps. Cf. *NCH* (Jan. 4, 18, 1907).

safety as with having a private police force to protect their own interests.[23]

They also seemed less anxious to promote a new form of central government, however advantageous that might be for them, than to be allowed to go their own way, creating small islands of security where peace would prevail and modernization could be introduced, without interference from politicians and the rest of society. Hence their preference for exercising their influence in local and municipal affairs. Businessmen founded schools, opened up new streets, and installed running water and electricity in the districts where they lived.[24] The wealthiest among them even built model towns, as Chang Chien did at T'ungchow.[25] They seem mainly to have adopted a secessionist attitude toward the imperial government—many of them had long been ardent advocates of local or provincial autonomy.[26] Model towns and well-run provinces each reflected the hope entertained by many Chinese merchants of perpetuating in the twentieth century the separate world their forebears had lived in. The bourgeoisie, combining an atavistic distrust of politics with a philanthropic utopianism, seemed to think that it could change its own way of life without making any change in the lives of the rest of the Chinese people, and furthermore that one province could be modernized without entailing the modernization of China as a whole. In short, the bourgeoisie believed that China's revival could be achieved by nonpolitical means, that is, by practical actions which had no need of an accompanying ideology.

Nevertheless, however devoutly Chinese merchants may have hoped to escape the realities of the political situation, these realities were forced upon them, affecting even strictly business matters. As a result of the relations that circumstances obliged them to have with the imperial government and the foreign powers, they gradually began to acquire a new self-awareness. The political attitudes adopted by the Chinese bourgeoisie were a crystallization of experiences undergone in dealing with Manchu officials and Western businessmen.

The relations of the bourgeoisie with the Manchu government were ambiguous, ranging from close collaboration to fierce compe-

23. *NCH* (Feb. 23, 1906), p. 397.

24. *TR* give many details on this "urbanism" movement in the various ports for the period 1905–10.

25. See S. Chu, *Reformer*, pp. 162 ff.

26. This local autonomist trend was particularly strong in Canton.

tition or even outright hostility. At the local level, personal factors played an especially important part, since, with the disintegration of imperial power, local government officials enjoyed an increasing degree of autonomy; from this it followed that the situation was largely determined by the personality of the officials concerned. As a general rule, Chinese businessmen expected aid and protection from the government, and they sought to obtain exemptions, privileges, and monopolies for their enterprises.

The government did all it could to accommodate businessmen. For instance, one of the first Chinese industrial enterprises, the Shanghai Cotton Cloth Mill (Shang-hai chi-ch'i chih-pu chü), established in 1890, which admittedly was a semiofficial concern, was given a production monopoly and exemption from the likin (the internal customs tax) for a ten-year period. The government went even further in introducing measures designed to promote the interests of the Chinese bourgeoisie. In 1903 it established a Ministry of Commerce; in 1904 it drafted a bill containing legislation for the transformation of private companies into limited liability companies; and in 1905 it promulgated a bankruptcy law.

The setting up of foreign factories in China after the Treaty of Shimonoseki in 1895 prevented the central government from granting production monopolies to Chinese, administrative chaos weakened the effectiveness of tax exemptions, and all attempts at reform were made futile by the impotence of the imperial government. Nevertheless, even if the Manchu government showed itself incapable of offering anything more than pledges of goodwill, at least it did not stand in the way of the bourgeoisie in its efforts to find appropriate means for strengthening its position. The chambers of commerce were initiated by the government,[27] and the formation of the merchant militias received encouragement and approval from Peking, because the government wanted to give the impression that it regarded the bourgeoisie as its ally in a united front against the foreign powers. When the Mixed Court incident occurred in Shanghai in 1905, Imperial Army soldiers in civilian dress took part in the riots shoulder to shoulder with shopkeepers and members of the bourgeoisie.[28] Again in Shanghai, two years later, government officials and merchants took joint action in an attempt to form a tramway company financed purely by Chinese

27. See A. Feuerwerker, *China's Early Industrialization*, pp. 70–71.
28. *NCH* (Dec. 22, 1905), pp. 671, 673.

capital, in order to prevent foreign financiers from doing so.[29] On a more modest scale, taotais, such as Hsü Ting-ling at Wuhu, carried out a policy of active encouragement of commerce, and had streets widened and public markets built. On the day when Taotai Hsü retired from his post, the merchants of the town expressed their gratitude by raising a commemorative stele in his honor in front of the offices of the Chamber of Commerce.[30]

Friendly relations of this kind were frequent. Often they were founded on a shared hostility toward foreigners and a shared feeling of impotence in taking action against them. They were strengthened by the need for practical collaboration in the management of local affairs and economic enterprises. But sometimes they sprang from less disinterested motives, for in these relations, as in many others, bribery and corruption also played a part.[31]

The merchants often found it necessary to buy the goodwill of government officials because the alliance between the bourgeoisie and the imperial government was always fragile and superficial. It was inevitable that the bourgeoisie should become disillusioned by the totally ineffective measures of protection introduced on its behalf by the government. Fiscal exemptions might be granted, but the paralyzing likin system continued to exist; patriotic feelings might be encouraged, but at times of crisis, such as the Stock Exchange crash in 1910, the Chinese state unhesitatingly sacrificed the interests of its nationals and contracted new debts in order to safeguard foreign loans.[32] Clearly there had been ulterior motives behind the apparently benevolent intentions in founding the chambers of commerce. More than once government officials had attempted to influence the decisions made by these bodies and even to misappropriate their funds.[33] Collaboration between the state and the bourgeoisie in the running of commercial enterprises had been fraught with difficulties: often the officials had abused their positions of authority and the merchants had refused to advance capital. The critical situation that arose from 1905 on concerning the railway companies indicates that there was far more distrust and rivalry between the two parties than effort to coop-

29. *NCH* (June 7, 1907), p. 586.
30. *NCH* (Jan. 6, 1905), p. 23.
31. *NCH* (Feb. 11, 1910), p. 302.
32. M. C. Bergère, *Une crise financière,* p. 39.
33. *NCH* (July 1, 1911), p. 25.

erate.[34] And although the merchants, in their fight against officialdom, may have been chary of giving vent to open criticism of the central government, they did not hesitate to make direct attacks on local government, accusing it in public meetings of corruption and inefficiency.[35] Accusations of this sort were no light matter, for often the magistrate concerned either was dismissed or had to shoulder the blame.

It is clear, therefore, that at first the bourgeoisie, as a class, was not in direct opposition to the imperial government. To some extent, its own particular organizations, especially the chambers of commerce, might be regarded as part of the machinery of government. In the conduct of daily affairs businessmen went out of their way to obtain the goodwill of officials so essential to the success of their enterprises. But necessary though it might be, experience soon showed that goodwill was not enough. It failed to provide adequate protection against foreign encroachment, and the privileges granted were rendered ineffective by the breakdown in the administrative system. In these circumstances it was only natural that, despite the good relations which the merchants were sometimes able to establish with local officials, feelings of distrust and hostility toward the imperial government became widespread.

Relations between the bourgeoisie and the foreigners living in China were also marked by great contradictions. Many Chinese historians distinguish between a "national" bourgeoisie, operating with purely Chinese capital and nursing a lively hostility toward foreigners, and a "compradore" bourgeoisie, completely foreign-dominated in both economic and political matters. The distinction is superficially obvious, but surely rather artificial. In early twentieth-century China with its semicolonial economy dominated by the presence of the imperialist powers, there could be no such thing as independent national enterprises. One way or another, whether from the aspect of finance, supply, equipment, or distribution, all Chinese businesses of any size operated within a context of foreign domination. When in 1910 the big foreign banks in

34. *TR* (1905), part 2, Report from Canton, p. 402 (Canton-Hankow line). *NCH* (Jan. 24, 1906), p. 177; (June 22), p. 691 (Canton-Hankow line). *TR* (1907), part 2, Report from Kiukiang, p. 237. *NCH* (Sept. 16, 1910), p. 672 (Chekiang line); (Oct. 7), p. 27. *NCH* (Feb. 11, 1910) (Szechwan and Canton-Hankow lines); (Apr. 1), p. 39.

35. *NCH* (Oct. 5, 1906), p. 13 (Incidents in Kiangyin).

China decided to cut off the loans to the native banks and no longer accepted the "native orders" in lieu of ready money, all Chinese businesses were threatened. In these circumstances, "national capital" is meaningless as an economic term. It can be said that in all relations established with the foreigners, the Chinese bourgeoisie was in a position of total economic dependence.

However, economic dependence did not, as some have argued, automatically rule out the adoption of independent political attitudes.[36] On the contrary, it was much more likely to foster particularly lively feelings of resentment and sensitive nationalism. As far as nationalism was concerned, the Chinese merchants, including the compradores, set an example for all. No one kept a more vigilant watch than they over the sovereign rights of their country, or grew more indignant when in 1905 the Mixed Court of the Shanghai International Settlement went beyond its treaty rights in condemning an accused Chinese woman to imprisonment in the Settlement's municipal jail.[37] Nor did anyone make demands with greater insistence than they for Chinese participation in the management of affairs in the foreign Concessions,[38] in the administration of the Imperial Maritime Customs,[39] and in working out a tariff system.[40] Again it was they who put up the most energetic resistance to a further extension of the foreign Concessions,[41] and who were the most disturbed by the prospect of the partition of national territory. For these businessmen were in the best position to know the inner workings of foreign domination. It was they who first realized the dangers of accepting certain loans, and it was the injury to their patriotic feelings just as much as jealousy of a suc-

36. Huang I-feng, "Ti-kuo chu-i ch'in-lüeh," in *Li-shih yen-chiu* (1965) *1*, 57–76.

37. *NCH* (Dec. 22, 1905), pp. 653, 671, 673.

38. *NCH* (Feb. 16, 1906), p. 347; Chinese merchants asked to be represented on the Municipal Council. They chose seven leaders to form a special committee. Among them were Wu Shao-ch'ing, chief compradore of Messrs. Arnhold Karberg & Co., Yuh P'ing-han, president of the Piece Goods Guild, Yü Hsia-ch'ing, compradore of the Netherlands Bank, Hsieh Lun-hui, president of the Chinese Bankers Guild, and Chu Pao-san, president of the Sundries Goods Guild. Cf. also many *NCH* references for February, March, and April 1906.

39. *NCH* (July 20, 1906), p. 151.

40. *NCH* (Aug. 2, 1907), p. 265: Report of a meeting held in the Chinese part of the city by members of the Chinese Mercantile Association and of the Chinese Chamber of Commerce to discuss the necessity of presenting petitions "in which the merchants of this port demand the right of having their wishes consulted in future commercial or tariff treaties with foreign powers."

41. *NCH* (Jan. 14, 1910), p. 81.

cessful rival that made them resent Western control over mines and railways.[42]

The merchants gave practical expression to their nationalist leanings by joining the gentry in campaigns for the recovery of railway and mining concessions.[43] They also undertook to advance capital for the creation of a modern navy,[44] and payment of the country's heavy foreign loan.[45] This was a forlorn hope, for however large the resources of Chinese businessmen might be, they could not possibly meet the national deficit. Moreover subscribers were reluctant to contribute to this patriotic fund, distrusting the central government's ability to administer it. Meanwhile the campaigns for the recovery of concessions continued, but they lacked coordination and progress was hampered by quarrels between the merchants and the gentry. As often as not the funds disappeared without a trace.[46]

The bourgeoisie also played a leading role in the movements of public protest against foreigners, which were becoming more and more frequent. In 1907, merchants aided by students organized public meetings,[47] and in Shanghai during March 1910 they helped to found an Association for the Preservation of Chinese Territory.[48] Sometimes the bourgeoisie employed its own methods. The merchant militias, formed to protect the business districts in case of trouble, were trained for direct military intervention against the foreigners in the event of China's partition[49]—no doubt a somewhat unrealistic plan, but one which indicated highly patriotic motives. To be taken more seriously was the adaptation for nationalist purposes of that traditional and specifically bourgeois form of resistance, the boycott.

It had long been customary for the Chinese guilds to use the boy-

42. *NCH* (May 27, 1910): Translation of a manifesto published by the Hupeh merchants in the *Chung-Hsi pao* the 4th day of the 4th lunar month (May 2, 1910).

43. See Li En-han, *Wan-Ch'ing ti shou-hui k'uang-ch'üan yün-tung* (The Recovery of Mining Rights Movement at the End of the Ch'ing) (Taipei, 1963).

44. *NCH* (Jan. 28, 1910), p. 175.

45. *NCH* (Jan. 14, 1910), p. 73; (Feb. 11), p. 316.

46. A large part of the funds raised for the building of the Szechwan-Hankow line, for instance, were lost during the Shanghai financial crisis of 1910.

47. *NCH* (Nov. 22, 1907), p. 454; (Dec. 20), pp. 706–07.

48. *NCH* (March 17, 1911), p. 636.

49. See the telegram sent by the Chinese community of Malaya to the National Merchants Volunteer Corps, etc.: "The powers planning partition . . . Kindly train citizen army to support foreign policy . . . We emigrants will help as best as we can." Quoted in *NCH* (Apr. 22, 1911), p. 240.

cott as a means of exerting pressure, either on merchants who had infringed corporation rules, or on the government if it was thought to have abused its powers. It was an effective weapon that soon brought the refractory to heel and often acted as a curb on the power of the central government. Traditionally its use was confined to dealing with an individual case involving a particular trade or craft or affecting the interests of a particular guild. But during the first decades of the twentieth century it became one of the main forms of struggle against foreign domination, and its whole nature changed.

When in 1905 the Chinese businessmen in all the big treaty ports, as represented by their guilds and chambers of commerce, decided to stop importing and selling American goods, a movement began in which for the first time the whole of the bourgeois class was involved.[50] Another new feature of this boycott was that it was essentially political in character. The merchants intended it as a protest against the racial discrimination the Chinese in America had encountered under the immigration laws. The honor of the Chinese nation was at stake. Thus the boycott of 1905 shows what a remarkable widening of horizons had taken place. Loyalties were no longer confined to a particular corporation or region; from now on they included national loyalty. For the first time, apparently, the Chinese bourgeoisie had consciously asserted itself as a class and given voice to political aims.

The use of the boycott spread during the years that followed, sometimes occurring on the national level, as with the anti-Japanese boycott of 1908, and sometimes affecting only a region or a town, as in Kirin at the end of 1909,[51] or Shanghai and Hangchow in 1910,[52] but on whatever scale it operated, the movement as a whole was antiforeign. The boycott had become the method habitually adopted by the bourgeoisie for organizing nationalist protest, whether the cause of protest was a serious diplomatic incident like the *Tatsu Maru* affair in 1908, a local quarrel between Chinese

50. Concerning the boycott of 1905, see C. F. Remer, *A Study of Chinese Boycotts* (Baltimore, 1933); Margaret Field, "The Chinese Boycott of 1905," in Harvard University, East Asian Research Center, *Papers on China, 2* (1957), 63–98; and E. J. Rhoads, "Nationalism and Xenophobia in Kwangtung (1905–06); the Canton Anti-American Boycott and the Lienchow Anti-Missionary Uprising," Harvard University, East Asian Research Center, *Papers on China, 16* (1962), 154 ff.

51. *NCH* (Feb. 11, 1910), p. 296.

52. *NCH* (Feb. 18, 1910), p. 381.

and Japanese merchants,[53] or a scuffle between coolies and the English police.[54] The aims were political, but the means—the refusal of all collaboration in order to strike at foreign interests—were economic.

On a short-term basis the boycott could be effective, since to some extent the Chinese merchants were indispensable adjuncts of imperialism.[55] In the long run, however, there was no hope of success. Chinese entrepreneurs were too dependent on foreign capitalists and too much involved in foreign trade to withstand the effects of a decline in imports and exports, the difficulty in getting rid of goods, and the consequent accumulation of stocks. The defining characteristic of the Chinese commercial bourgeoisie was that it belonged to the system of imperialist exploitation, and any attempt to protest this system was bound to be self-destructive. At the beginning of the century economic self-sufficiency was for China as much of a utopian dream as national independence, and the boycott served the Chinese bourgeoisie more as a means of self-expression than as a means of exerting pressure.

The real contradiction lies not between a "national" and a "compradore" bourgeoisie, but between the economic dependence of the entire bourgeoisie and its unanimous nationalist aims.

The complex relations which the bourgeoisie was forced to enter into with the powers surrounding it—namely, the imperial government and the foreign powers—led to its adopting antigovernment and antiforeign political attitudes. These attitudes corresponded to the principal themes of the newly imported ideology, so that before the Chinese bourgeoisie had become fully aware of its own aims, it found them already formulated in the programs of political parties. It is doubtless this peculiar feature of the situation that explains the political precocity of the Chinese bourgeoisie which contrasts so strangely with its economic weakness and its as yet undefined place in society. At a very early date it gave its support to the main opposition parties, and although these parties had

53. *NCH* (Apr. 8, 1910), p. 88; on the *Tatsu Maru* case and other boycotts, see also Akira Iriye, "Public Opinion and Foreign Policy: The Case of Late Ch'ing China" (a paper originally prepared for the 1965 Conference on the Revolution of 1911, from which the present volume emerged), in A. Feuerwerker, R. Murphey, and M. C. Wright, eds., *Approaches to Modern Chinese History* (Berkeley and Los Angeles, 1967), pp. 216–38.

54. See n. 52.

55. See *TR*, Reports of the various ports in 1905 and 1906.

been brought into being by the intellectuals, for the most part it was the merchants who provided them with a solid backing.

Both the reformist and the revolutionary parties benefited from this support. Attempts have been made to divide reformist and revolutionary elements among the bourgeoisie according to the division between its upper and lower, or its national and compradore sections,[56] but this seems too mechanical a procedure. At a time when everyone was groping toward an ideology, and when the impact of a powerful personality sometimes had more persuasive effect than the often vague outlines of a political program, there can scarcely have been any hard and fast dividing lines. Merchants militated now for reform, now for revolution, according to the time and the place, and sometimes an incident like Liang Ch'i-ch'ao's visit to Hawaii in 1900 was enough to bring a whole community from one camp to the other.[57] The main political leaders were well aware of this floating allegiance, and some of them, such as Sun Yat-sen, K'ang Yu-wei, and Liang Ch'i-ch'ao, became traveling salesmen for their own particular brands of political ideas.

In general, it can be said that reformism seems to have found most favor during the early years of the century and to have been the preference of the mainland bourgeoisie, while revolutionary doctrines seem to have come to the fore just before 1911 and to have been more widely adopted among merchants overseas. In China, the commercial bourgeoisie still had close links with the gentry, and they shared both a desire to maintain the social status quo and a realistic assessment of the stage of development reached in the country as a whole. The Overseas Chinese, on the other hand, had no direct knowledge of what was happening at home, but wanted China to have what they considered the most modern forms of political and economic organization so that it could become a nation of the first rank.

Merchant allegiance to the reformist cause was expressed, from 1900 onward, by the support given to the Society to Protect the Emperor. Founded in Japan in 1898 with money advanced by the

56. See Chang K'ai-yüan and Liu Wang-ling, "Ts'ung hsin-hai ko-ming k'an min-tsu tzu-ch'an chieh-chi ti hsing-ko" (Character of the Chinese National Bourgeoisie As Seen in the Revolution of 1911), in Hupeh Provincial Philosophical Society and Scientific Society, ed., *Hsin-hai ko-ming wu-shih chou-nien chi-nien lun-wen-chi* (Essays in Commemoration of the Fiftieth Anniversary of the 1911 Revolution) (Peking, 1962), p. 12.

57. Joseph R. Levenson, *Liang Ch'i-ch'ao and the Mind of Modern China* (Cambridge, Mass., 1959), p. 65

Chinese merchants of Yokohama,[58] the society was the first of the reformist organizations. In 1900 the Chinese community in Honolulu contributed more than 100,000 dollars to it which helped to finance the Hankow uprising in the following year.[59] In 1903 Liang Ch'i-ch'ao had similar success with the communities in the United States and Canada.

These episodes are well known. But less well known, though equally important, are the ways in which the bourgeoisie participated in the reform movements in China itself. The imperial edict of September 1906, promising to give the country a constitution, was enthusiastically received by the bourgeoisie. The Shanghai Chamber of Commerce sent telegrams to the chambers of commerce in all the provinces telling them the news, and asking them to hold meetings for the purpose of providing information and to organize demonstrations to celebrate the occasion. Celebrations were held in Swatow,[60] in Canton,[61] and in Kiangyin, where the Emperor Kuang-hsü was acclaimed, but not the Dowager Empress Tz'u-hsi.[62] The chambers of commerce and leading members of business circles drew up a commercial code, thus expressing their willingness to collaborate in the drafting of future constitutional laws.[63] When the provincial assemblies began functioning in 1909, their members included a number of wealthy entrepreneurs, such as Chang Chien in Kiangsu.[64] In 1910 merchants played an active part, either as members of the Federation of Provincial Assemblies which met in Peking[65] or simply as representatives of certain business interests,[66] in the agitation for the convocation of a national assembly.

58. Ibid., p. 62.

59. Concerning the struggles of the revolutionary and reformist parties in the Chinese overseas communities, see Tuan Yün-chang, et al., "Hsin-hai ko-ming ch'ien tzu-ch'an chieh-chi ko-ming p'ai ho kai-liang p'ai tsai Hua-ch'iao chung ti tou-cheng" (The Struggle between the Reformist and the Revolutionary Groups among the Overseas Chinese Bourgeoisie Prior to the Revolution of 1911) in *Hsin-hai ko-ming wu-shih chou-nien chi-nien lun-wen-chi,* pp. 619 ff.

60. *NCH* (Sept. 28, 1906), p. 746.

61. *NCH* (Sept. 28, 1906), p. 748.

62. *NCH* (Oct. 5, 1906), p. 13.

63. *NCH* (Aug. 30, 1907), p. 495.

64. See S. Chu, *Reformer,* pp. 66 ff.

65. *NCH* (Jan. 14, 1910), p. 119. After the delegates of the provincial assemblies met in Peking, they elected three presidents, one of whom was a merchant.

66. *NCH* (May 27, 1910), p. 509. The Shanghai merchants sent a special delegate, Shen Man-yün, assistant manager of the Sin Chun Bank, to Peking to present a petition urging the speedy establishment of a national assembly.

Relations between the bourgeoisie and the revolutionaries were just as close, and it is upon these that stress has been laid in recent times.[67] In Honolulu in 1895 Sun Yat-sen founded his first major political party, the Society to Restore China's Prosperity, and his first followers were the Chinese traders of that town who were friends of his brother.[68] During the years that followed, members were recruited from the Chinese communities in Yokohama, Hong Kong, Singapore,[69] and to a lesser extent, China itself.[70] When the Revolutionary Alliance was formed in 1905, the inclusion of Huang Hsing's group and the rapprochement with Chang Ping-lin extended Sun's political audience among intellectuals, but did not interfere with his close ties with the merchants.[71]

A curious aspect of the active participation of businessmen in the revolutionary movement was that it thereby acquired a certain mercantile character. For example, to anyone who provided him with funds Sun gave an IOU for 300,000 dollars and a promise that his investment would be doubled if he came to power.[72] In his program he stressed the points likely to cement the merchants' allegiance to him, such as total condemnation of the Manchu dynasty (which had never been popular with the overseas communities, with their reputation for having been supporters of the Ming), modernization of the political system, and development of the Chinese economy in collaboration with the foreign powers while at the same time safeguarding China's independence. Socialist aims, particularly proposals for agrarian reform, which had always been rather vague, were given second place,[73] and the newspaper *Min-*

67. The Chinese mainland historians currently present the Revolutionary Alliance as the political expression of the national bourgeoisie.

68. See Feng, *I-shih* (reissued in Taiwan, 1953), *1*, 11; Tsou Lu, *Chung-kuo kuomin-tang shih-kao* (Draft History of the Chinese Kuomintang) (3rd ed. Chungking, 1941), p. 16.

69. Ibid.

70. In April 1911, 60 followers of Sun Yat-sen were arrested in Peking, among them several merchants (cf. *NCH* [April 22, 1911], p. 197); cf. Feng Tzu-yu, "Hsing-Chung-hui ch'ien pan-ch'i chih ko-ming t'ung-chih" (Revolutionary Members of the Society to Restore China's Prosperity During the First Half of its Existence), *HHKM, 1*, 141–72. Feng established that 75 new members joined the Society to Restore China's Prosperity between 1895 and 1900. Twenty-five of these new members were merchants, half of them being Overseas Chinese living in Yokohama.

71. See Chün-tu Hsüeh, *Huang Hsing and the Chinese Revolution* (Stanford, 1961), pp. 35–37.

72. See *NCH* (Oct. 19, 1912), p. 176.

73. Harold Schiffrin, "Sun Yat-sen's Early Land Policy," *JAS, 16* (1957), 549–64; R. Scalapino and H. Schiffrin, "Early Socialist Currents in the Chinese Revolutionary Movement," *JAS, 18* (1959), 321–42.

pao (People's Report), which in its first numbers had devoted a large number of articles to socialist doctrines and their possible application to China, became increasingly discreet on this subject as the years went by.[74]

The collaboration established between the bourgeoisie and the "progressive" intellectuals within the new "parties" shows how well the political slogans borrowed from the West fitted the aims and aspirations of the class that had come into being as a result of the partial modernization of the economy. The advanced ideas and the nationalist views imported by the intellectuals met with a deeper understanding and a more genuine acceptance among the bourgeoisie than they did among the other classes. Through its inheritance of the earlier experience of Western bourgeoisies, the Chinese bourgeoisie, still in the process of formation, still economically weak and uncertain of its place in society, had a whole arsenal of political and ideological weapons at its disposal. The inheritance might be patchy and incoherent and the weapons imperfect, but the fact that they existed at all gave a peculiarly dynamic force to the actions taken by the bourgeoisie.

The central question is, to what extent did the advantages of this ideological overcompensation balance the economic weakness and ill-defined social status of the bourgeoisie? What was the part actually played by the bourgeoisie in the events which shook China between 1911 and 1913?

The Bourgeoisie During the Revolution

The Revolutionary Turmoil of October–December 1911

In many ways the events of 1911 look more like a conservative than a revolutionary movement. The overthrow of power was almost always instigated by men in high positions in the civil or military hierarchy. Sometimes the imperially appointed governor proclaimed the independence of the province in his charge, as did Ch'eng Te-ch'üan, governor of Kiangsu (who joined the movement November 3, 1911), Chang Ming-ch'i, governor-general at Canton (proclamation of October 24, 1911), and Sun Pao-ch'i, governor of Shantung. The underlying motive differed in each of these three cases. For Ch'eng it was his adoption of revolutionary ideas; for Chang Ming-ch'i it was a desire to keep control of the situation,

74. Nearly all the important articles concerning the socialist "aims" of the revolutionary party were published during the period 1905–07.

which he failed to do, and he was forced to flee from Canton at the beginning of November; and for Sun Pao-ch'i it was merely opportunism, and on November 17 he annulled the declaration of independence and changed back to the central government side. Such changes in allegiance on the part of high officials of the Manchu dynasty played no small part in increasing the speed with which the unrest spread during the autumn of 1911. An equally important factor was the establishment during the month of October of a network of contacts between army officers for the purpose of finding out each other's aims and intentions, in order to further common action.

It was the winning over, not without a certain reluctance on his part, of Li Yüan-hung (still wearing his pigtail) just after the Wuchang uprising that gave the go-ahead to the Revolution; and it was because Chang Hsi-yüan changed sides during the first days of the uprising that the insurgent troops of Wuchang were able to avoid an encounter with the Hunanese contingents that had been sent against them.[75] In the Northwest, it was the defection of the Twentieth and the Sixth Regiments in Chihli and Shansi that offered a threat to Peking at the very moment when Yuan Shih-k'ai, at the end of October, was about to carry out the reconquest of Hankow in the name of the imperial government; and the rapid return to calm after Yuan Shih-k'ai had the leading rebel officer, Wu Lu-chen, assassinated, shows that it was the choice of allegiance on the part of the officers concerned that determined their anti-monarchical move.[76]

Another conservative feature of the movement was the major role played in it by the local gentry and the members of the provincial assemblies. These were the people to whom the insurgents immediately turned in order to consolidate their position, for without their support the revolutionary leaders could not hope to survive. In Hunan, Chiao Ta-feng lost his life on account of his quarrel with the Provincial Assembly.

A final point is that from the beginning the revolutionaries adopted a conciliatory attitude toward foreigners. A note of October 13 sent by the military government of Wuchang to the foreign consulates promised to recognize the treaties and loans that had been negotiated by the Manchu dynasty. Wu T'ing-fang, in his

75. Ts'ai Chi-ou, *Ou-chou hsüeh-shih* (Tragic History of Hupeh) (Shanghai, 1958), p. 98.

76. Ibid., p. 128.

"Manifesto to the Foreign World" of November 17, once more took up the themes of respect for foreign interests and for international obligations, and of collaboration between New China and the West.

None of these events—the transfer of allegiance on the part of governors and generals, the taking over of power by provincial assemblies, the rapprochement with the foreign powers—were particularly revolutionary in themselves. But the vocabulary used was something quite new. Such words as revolution, democracy, republic, which had been thrown about in a highly confused way during the preceding years, now sounded everywhere. The gentry out to defend their privileges, army officers trying to establish military governments, intellectuals hoping to lay the foundations of a new political system—all, paradoxically, spoke the same language. The language had been borrowed from the West and had perhaps lost some of its significance and effectiveness in being transposed to a Chinese context.

In a movement so full of ambiguities, what was the political role of the bourgeoisie? The Wuchang uprising of October 10, 1911 was a military operation in which the merchants did not participate directly. Nevertheless they had not stood aside during the troubles preceding the outbreak of the Revolution. They took an active part in the fierce campaign against nationalization of the railways that occurred in Szechwan at that time and helped to form the Railway Protection League, placing at its disposal the premises of their own organizations, the guilds, which served as offices for local branches of the League.[77] In Chungking the Chamber of Commerce even recruited several hundred unemployed under pretext of raising men for the merchant militia, but in fact as an armed force for the League.

Some of the bourgeoisie were disturbed by this militancy. About the middle of September the businessmen who were members of the local branch of the League at Paoning, in the north of the province, criticized the extremism of the Chengtu leaders and refused to have anything further to do with these "bandits" (*t'u-fei*) who were sowing the seeds of disorder.[78] In Chungking the merchants refused to organize a proposed boycott. First the cotton wholesalers declared that, in spite of their sympathy with the

77. FO 228/2497, British Consular Correspondence (hereafter BCC), Dispatch No. 25 (Sept. 14, 1911) from Chungking.

78. FO 228/2497 BCC, Dispatch No. 59 (Sept. 28, 1911) from Chengtu.

League's activities, they would never bring trade to a standstill. Their decision was then endorsed by the Bankers' Guild, and then by other guilds.[79]

Such reservations could not, however, halt a movement that clumsy measures of repression, such as calling upon the support of Tuan-fang's troops, had only served to aggravate. By the beginning of October the unrest had spread to the middle Yangtze Valley. Following the meetings that took place in Shanghai between Yang Yü-ju and Chü Chio-sheng, and the amalgamation of the Progressive Association and the Literary Institute, the insurrection began at Wuchang on October 10 with the revolt of the Eighth Regiment of the Engineers Corps. By the end of the night the town was in the hands of the rebels. The operation was an entirely military one, with rifle fire, artillery fire, pillaging of armories, and blowing up of government buildings. But the merchants were no mere passive spectators. The story goes that when Wu Chao-lin, who was in charge of the attack against the yamen of the governor-general, ordered the surrounding districts to be set on fire in order to guide the aim of his artillery, enthusiastic tradesmen themselves, without thought of future indemnity for losses sustained, brought drums of oil to start the fires.[80]

During the following weeks, taking advantage of the respite afforded them by the efforts of the imperial armed forces to regroup, the insurgents began to form a new government, which at once brought about a close collaboration with the bourgeoisie. On October 12 a military proclamation announced: "Those who treat merchants unfairly will be beheaded. Those who interfere with commerce will be beheaded. Those who attempt to close the shops will be beheaded. Those who maintain the prosperity of commerce will be rewarded."[81] In exchange for this protection, the merchants agreed to help maintain order. They organized militia and helped the fire brigade fight fires and prevent looting.[82] Ts'ai Fu-ch'ing, president of the Chamber of Commerce, was even made Chief of Police, with 600 men under him.[83] The bourgeoisie also provided the revolutionaries with much-needed financial support. The Chamber of Commerce immediately granted a loan of 200,000

79. FO 228/2497 BCC, Dispatch No. 25 (Sept. 14, 1911) from Chungking.
80. Ts'ai Chi-ou, *Ou-chou*, p. 87.
81. *Hankow Daily News* (Oct. 12, 1911).
82. Ts'ai Chi-ou, *Ou-chou*, p. 100.
83. *Hankow Daily News* (Oct. 13, 1911).

taels,[84] and to prevent panic and devaluation, the members of the professional and regional associations (*pang*) set up a "Bureau of Conversion" (Tui-huan-so) to guarantee the cashing of paper currency.[85]

Although the merchants neither instigated nor directed the revolutionary uprising, they were quick to extend practical help to the army insurgents, and during the week when victory was still doubtful and crucial decisions were being made about choice of allegiance to the revolutionary or the counterrevolutionary side, their cooperation was invaluable to the military government (chün-cheng-fu) of Wuchang.

In this short essay it is impossible to examine in detail the part played by the bourgeoisie in all the Chinese provinces during the three months of revolutionary turmoil at the end of 1911, but a few examples may serve to show how varied were the methods, the effectiveness, and the aims of bourgeois intervention.

In the Northeast, Manchuria was predominantly conservative. At the local level the merchants, pending a solution of the national political crisis, collaborated with the remaining government officials in the maintenance of public order. In Mukden, for example, they helped organize, in the beginning of November, the Society to Protect the Peace, of which Governor-general Chao Erh-sun was president.[86] In their anxiety to prevent unrest at all costs, they were tempted to appeal to the foreigners for help, and they even proposed joint action for the purpose of raising a Volunteer Corps.[87] In Yingkow the Chamber of Commerce itself took over the administration. Its headquarters already housed the local branch of the Society to Protect the Peace, and its president had become the directing power behind the newly formed society. So now the Chamber of Commerce was responsible for the pay of the taotai's guard while at the same time it organized the recruitment of 500 volunteers among the town merchants. The aim of this recruitment was clearly stated in a circular put out by the local branch of the society (Ying-k'ou ti-fang pao-an-hui): "no matter what alarms and movements may arise elsewhere our town of Yingkow shall unite its forces for the assurance of peace."[88] The situation at Newchwang

84. Ibid.

85. Ts'ai Chi-ou, *Ou-chou*, p. 100.

86. FO 228/2834 BCC, Dispatch No. 41 (Nov. 13, 1911) from Mukden.

87. FO 228/2834 BCC, personal letter from the consul in Newchwang to Sir John Jordan, enclosed in Dispatch No. 44 (Nov. 16, 1911).

88. FO 228/2834 BCC, Dispatch No. 44 (Nov. 16, 1911) from Newchwang.

was almost identical, but it should be noted that in this port a rival, and much more radical, society had been formed, the Association of Comrades for Peace,[89] which also had ties with the Chamber of Commerce. But the two leagues for the maintenance of peace finally amalgamated and together formed the Volunteer Merchants' Corps.[90]

Thus in provinces where the revolutionary movement was comparatively weak, businessmen pursued a "wait and see" policy and confined their activities to maintaining public order. But in Chihli and Shantung the merchants, or some of them at least, played a much more active role and were involved in organizing the insurrection and in setting up provisional military governments. After the terrible reprisals following the first uprising there at the end of 1911, the revolutionaries concentrated their forces in Tengchow in Shantung. Two of their staff officers were prominent merchants of the town. Ch'iu P'ei-chen, a member of one of the leading families in eastern Shantung and a graduate of a Japanese military school, largely financed the movement.[91] And on January 14, 1912, when Tengchow fell into the hands of the insurgents, a banker named Liu Yü-ping was put in charge of the finances of the provisional government.[92] The revolutionary army of Tengchow was finally crushed after a few transitory victories and Ch'iu P'ei-chen was executed in 1913. His younger brothers, who were also members of the Revolutionary Alliance and had taken part in the Tengchow uprising, remained faithful to the Revolution. One of them later became an officer in the Northern Expedition (*Pei-fa*) of 1926–28.

In Central China there were many merchants who likewise sided with the revolutionaries, and with more success. In Shanghai on November 3, Ch'en Ch'i-mei led the attack against the Kiangnan Arsenal that gave the republicans control of the town. Ch'en, a native of Chekiang, had begun his career as a pawnshop employee. He then came to Shanghai, and entered the silk trade. In 1907 he gave up his business in order to devote himself exclusively to po-

89. The word *pao-an* has the sense of maintaining law and order. *Ho-p'ing*, especially in conjunction with "comrades," suggests peace following a successful revolution.

90. FO 228/2834 BCC, Dispatch No. 45 (Nov. 27, 1911) from Newchwang.

91. Yin-k'o, "Hsin-hai kuang-fu Pi-lai chi-shih" (Factual Account of the Revolution in Pi-lai District), in *Chin-tai shih tzu-liao* (Materials Concerning Modern History), *4* (1957), 15–21.

92. Ibid.

litical activities.[93] But he retained many contacts in the commercial world, which no doubt accounts for the generous way in which the businessmen of Shanghai subsidized the revolutionary movement. In the beginning of November the president of the Chamber of Commerce pledged 50,000 taels. Many others followed suit,[94] while various firms undertook to furnish supplies of food and munitions on credit to the republican troops. It cost approximately 7 million dollars to bring the revolutionary movement in Shanghai to final victory, and most of this money was provided by Shanghai's businessmen.[95]

In Hangchow, after the officials quit at the end of October, the merchants took the situation in hand and organized a Volunteer Corps to prevent panic and disturbances. In Chinkiang the leading merchants also played an important part. Their representative, the president of the Chamber of Commerce, acted as intermediary between the revolutionaries and the imperial army and negotiated the surrender of the garrison. A decision in support of the Revolution, reached at a general meeting, authorized the establishment of a military government.[96]

Meanwhile in the middle Yangtze Valley the revolutionary movement continued to spread from Wuchang outward. Hankow fell on October 19, and the merchants of the town prepared a triumphal welcome for the insurgent troops; the Chamber of Commerce even held a feast for them.[97] On the other hand, in the dramatic events which led to the independence of Hunan, the main protagonists seem to have been the army and the Provincial Assembly, and the main groups involved the gentry, the secret societies, and army officers.

The Cantonese bourgeoisie also took a keen interest in political

93. Concerning the role played by the merchants of Shanghai in the revolutionary events there, see Kojima Yoshio, "Shingai kakumei ni okeru Shanhai dokuritsu to shōshinsō" (The Movements of the Merchant Class of Shanghai while the City was Independent during the Revolution of 1911), *Tōyō shigaku ronshū, 6* (1960), 113–33. On the career of Ch'en Ch'i-mei, see *NCH* (June 15, 1912), p. 783.

94. *NCH* (Nov. 11, 1911), p. 350.

95. *NCH* (Dec. 16, 1911), p. 723; (March 1, 1913), p. 650.

96. Chang Li-ying, "Chen-chiang kuang-fu shih-liao" (Historical Materials Concerning the Revolution in Chinkiang), in *Chin-tai shih tzu-liao,* 6 (1957), 75–81. For the Soochow merchants' role in the Revolution, see "Ch'ing-mo Su-chou shang-wu tsung-hui tang-an" (Archives of the General Chamber of Commerce of Soochow at the End of the Ch'ing), in *Hsin-hai ko-ming Chiang-su ti-ch'ü shih-liao* (Materials Concerning the History of the Revolution in Kiangsu) (Nanking, 1961).

97. Ts'ai Chi-ou, *Ou-chou,* p. 116.

events. At first the news of the October 10 uprising was received in the town with no more than somewhat cautious sympathy. But at a mass meeting held on October 25, organized by the merchants together with members of the gentry, those present decided to break with the imperial government. Pending the establishment of a central republican government the Cantonese ran their own administration, and for this reason they kept their tax revenue and did not send aid either in money or in troops to any of the neighboring provinces. The governor-general, who had remained at his post, was put at the head of the autonomous administration under the control of a governing council.[98] It is clear that certain sections of the gentry and the bourgeoisie in Canton, while giving their approval to the revolutionary movement in progress further north, had no intention of taking part in it, preferring to take advantage of the situation in order to realize their long-cherished plans for autonomy.[99] But public opinion became impatient. The cautious attitude of the governor-general irritated even the merchants, one of whom declared: "If His Excellency could only declare himself openly on one side or the other . . . this exasperating uncertainty would soon be ended."[100]

On October 30 the Seventy-two Guilds of Canton hoisted the revolutionary flag, and on November 12, at a meeting held on the premises of the Commercial Association of Canton, it was decided, in the presence of delegates from Hong Kong, to establish an independent government in the form of a republic.[101] Immediately money flowed in from Hong Kong and from Canton itself totaling 1,500,000 dollars, and there were promises of 10 million dollars from the Overseas Chinese.[102] A few weeks later the Chamber of Commerce organized a big reception in honor of the republican governor-general, Hu Han-min, and his ministers.[103] But official rejoicings could not dispel the anxiety of the Cantonese merchants over the spread of banditry and piracy and the republican government's proposal to arm 30,000 vagabonds as a countermeasure.

With the support of the corporations of Hong Kong, the Seventy-two Guilds and the Nine Charitable Associations approached Gen-

98. *SCMP* (Oct. 27 and 28, 1911).
99. Ibid.
100. *SCMP* (Oct. 30, 1911).
101. *SCMP* (Nov. 9, 1911).
102. *SCMP* (Nov. 18, 1911).
103. *SCMP* (Dec. 7, 1911).

eral Lung Chi-kwong (kuang), who despite the Revolution had remained at his post, and requested him to stay in the town at the head of his troops, whose pay they promised to provide.[104] Fifteen days later the Cantonese bourgeoisie decided to take further precautions and formed a Volunteer Corps. Cham Lin-pak (Ch'en Lien-po), the well-known compradore of the Hongkong and Shanghai Bank, himself took command.[105] On December 20, upon discovery of a reformist plot, the republican government embarked upon a fierce campaign of reprisals. The militant members of the Society to Protect the Emperor were hunted down and finally discovered hiding in the premises of certain business firms.[106] Thus although power had been seized very quickly in Canton by a remarkably homogeneous group of republicans (Governor-general Hu Han-min and his assistant Ch'en Chiung-ming were both members of the Revolutionary Alliance), it was also in Canton that some of the big merchants suddenly switched their allegiance at a very early date.

Despite the varying nature of bourgeois participation in the Revolution from one province to another, it is nevertheless possible to make certain generalizations about the methods used and about the significance of the part played by the bourgeoisie.

The uprisings were seldom instigated by the bourgeoisie. The revolutionary leaders were usually army officers (as in Wuchang), or members of secret societies (as in Changsha), or militant members of the Revolutionary Alliance (as in Canton), and scarcely ever merchants. The role played by the bourgeoisie usually developed in reaction to local political situations created by other groups, and thus varied widely from place to place.

Yet although the bourgeoisie was seldom responsible for initiating revolutionary activities, it was sympathetic once they had started, and it is quite remarkable that no serious economic crisis ever arose as a result of such activities. The difficulties that arose were due to the interruption of communications between the interior and the treaty ports, or to a lack of liquid capital—a chronic problem that tended to paralyze the Chinese economy, and was now accentuated by the large payments made to the revolutionaries.[107] But although there are records of runs on the local banks, and even

104. *SCMP* (Dec. 4 and 6, 1911).
105. *SCMP* (Dec. 20, 1911).
106. *SCMP* (Dec. 20 and 25, 1911).
107. FO 228/2197 BCC, Dispatch No. 59 (Sept. 28, 1911) from Chengtu.

on the foreign banking houses in Shanghai, Tientsin,[108] and Peking, there was very little panic and the big depositors remained calm. These financial difficulties naturally led to a decline in trade and industry during the first weeks. But by mid-December the situation in Shanghai began to improve.[109] This rapid recovery was no doubt due to the fact that from the beginning the difficulties had been primarily technical, while the basis of the whole fragile edifice—the confidence of the merchants—remained unshaken.[110]

Preventing an economic crisis was not, however, the only way in which the bourgeoisie showed its sympathy toward the Revolution. At times it even became enthusiastic enough to throw off its traditional reluctance to take part in politics, and actively engage in revolutionary activities. The merchant militias sometimes fought side by side with the insurgent troops—as did, for instance, the Volunteers who patrolled the Kiangnan Arsenal in Shanghai after the fall of the imperial garrison. But more often the merchants provided financial support. For although in Wuchang, because a monetary reform was in progress at the time, the rebels had the good fortune to seize a well-stocked Provincial Treasury,[111] in Shanghai and Canton, with none of the normal fiscal revenue coming in and the Customs receipts confiscated by the foreigners, it was the businessmen who filled the revolutionary coffers.

Some historians have suggested that the bourgeoisie underwent a sudden revulsion of feeling;[112] that its members, having gone into action along with the young intellectuals and the revolutionary army officers, became alarmed by the extent of the changes involved and beat a hasty retreat, thereafter aligning themselves with the gentry in order to safeguard their own class interests. The change in attitude of the Szechwanese merchants, who began as active members of the opposition but whose reservations increased with the spread of unrest, might be cited in support of this hypothesis.

Attempts have also been made to polarize the contradictions within the bourgeoisie with regard to the two main currents of opposition by distinguishing between an upper reformist stratum

108. *NCH* (Oct. 21, 1911), pp. 147, 150; (Nov. 25, 1911), p. 501; *SCMP* (Oct. 17, 1911).

109. *NCH* (Dec. 30, 1911), p. 858; *SCMP* (Oct. 20, 1911).

110. *NCH* (Oct. 21, 1911), p. 151.

111. Ts'ai Chi-ou, *Ou-chou,* p. 104.

112. This idea is often expressed by historians of mainland China at present.

and a middle and lower revolutionary stratum. A division of this kind, relating political views to social status, does seem to have existed in some areas, particularly in Canton, where at the end of December the republican government put down a reformist plot hatched by a number of businessmen. But in general it is scarcely possible to make such cut-and-dried distinctions. The whole situation was far too confused to allow for any clear declaration of political allegiance, and the weakness and muddled thinking of the parties added to the difficulties. The Chinese bourgeoisie was as blind as anyone else to the dichotomy between the conservative nature of the uprisings and the revolutionary ideas they embodied. Thus while favoring the seizure of power by men from the higher ranks of society to which they themselves belonged, the bourgeoisie at the same time seemed to assume that this would result in effecting a revolutionary program. Their attitude, in the situation that existed in China in 1911, cannot simply be dismissed as one of duplicity or treason: it resulted from their profound immaturity in political and ideological matters.

To sum up, China's October Revolution was not made by the merchants, but it aroused their liveliest sympathy. They went so far as to abandon their traditional reluctance to take part in politics and gave their support to the insurgents, and by preventing an economic crisis, they affirmed their faith in the future. Doubtless their vision of the future, combining the return of former privileges and the triumph of revolutionary ideas, was vague and inconsistent; but anxious to make it come true and encouraged by the rapid success of the first uprisings, they did not hesitate to take further political action.

The First Bourgeois Ventures into Local Administration

In 1911 the bourgeoisie had merely provided followers of the revolutionary movement or played the part of commissariat, but during the first months of 1912 its role was greatly altered. It became one of the main political forces in the country and occupied a position of power it would hardly ever attain again during the first half of this century.

Its first approach to power toward the end of 1911 occurred in the peculiar circumstances of the time. The Emperor and his court were still in Peking, but they no longer governed the country. The revolutionary government established under the leadership of Li Yüan-hung at Wuhan after the October uprising was in serious trouble as a result of the counterattacks of Yuan Shih-k'ai's troops, and its control did not extend beyond the area of the middle Yangtze Valley. There was in fact no central government at all. The provinces that had declared their independence were running their own governments. In some places (as in the Northeastern provinces) the former administrative machinery still remained, but the officials no longer recognized the Peking government. In Central and South China new provincial governors (*tu-tu*) had appeared, but the whole system of provincial control was still breaking down. In Kwangtung, for example, Canton had almost completely lost control of the eastern part of the province. Particularism reigned everywhere, and there was a general parceling out and distintegration of political power. In Szechwan, which already had two rival provincial governments, one at Chungking and the other at Chengtu, there had in addition grown up innumerable small "autonomous states" and "independent communes."[113] The same was true of Shantung and many other provinces. This breakup of Chinese unity determined the ways in which the bourgeoisie began to intervene in political affairs, leading on the one hand to a general assumption of the everyday business of local affairs, and on the other to an attempt to establish a national government.

Toward the end of 1913 a foreign observer who had witnessed the course of events during the Revolution wrote: "With the downfall of the Manchu regime . . . the government of almost every city in China was for months virtually carried on by the chambers of commerce and associated guilds."[114] In order to be able to exert its influence, the bourgeoisie sometimes seized hold of a key post in local government. Thus a "businessman turned official" named Lian (sic), from the prefecture of Tengchow in northern Shantung, got himself elected provisional governor of the province in 1912, although he never really exercised control beyond his own prefecture.[115] In Swatow in eastern Kwangtung a Chinese merchant named Goe,[116] who was a naturalized American citizen and manager of the American and Chinese Trading Company, played an

113. CCF, Rapport de Tchentou (Chengtu) (March 10, 1912).

114. *NCH* (Nov. 1, 1913), p. 352.

115. CCF, Rapport de Tchefou (Chefoo) (March 15, 1912).

116. CCF; an anonymous essay, probably written by an official at the Quai d'Orsay, entitled "La Révolution Chinoise jusqu'à la proclamation de la République," dated March 17, 1912, in the file labeled "Chine, politique intérieure, 1912." I have been unable to locate the characters for Goe's name; thus I can only follow the rendering in the French document cited.

active part in the revolutionary movement and then tried to seize power for himself at the end of December. His plans were foiled by the hostility of the Hakka troops, and he finally made way for another businessman, Kao Ping-chen, a former president of the Swatow Chamber of Commerce, who became "Commander in Chief of the District of Shaochowfu."[117]

But the bourgeoisie was not often in direct control of the local governmental machinery. Usually either the actual organs of government in the towns, districts, and provinces stayed in the hands of the mandarins of the old regime who had remained at their posts, as in Manchuria and a number of places in Szechwan;[118] or they were taken over by members of the Revolutionary Alliance, such as Hu Han-min and Ch'en Chiung-ming in Canton; or by military leaders whose claims were based in varying proportions on membership in the revolutionary organizations, on the power wielded by a local clan, or simply on force. In its dealings with these de facto governments, the nature of which varied according to local circumstances, the bourgeoisie endeavored to influence the march of events. Its political influence was thus usually indirect.

During the formation of the new local governments the bourgeoisie continued to play the essentially secondary role it had during the Revolution itself. Thus, faced with a fait accompli, it had to deal with whatever government had arisen as the result of the local insurrection. In addition there were probably psychological reasons preventing the bourgeoisie from occupying the forefront of the political scene. The reluctance to do so, stemming from traditional attitudes, was emphasized by foreign observers. Maybon, speaking of the "commercial magnates," remarks: "They had too big an interest in the control of public opinion for them to refrain from taking part in party and personal struggles for power, but, anxious to avoid being compromised and sparing of their time, they usually employed agents . . . to do the job of paying the bribes and carrying out the shady deals which, for the Chinese, is the essence of politics."[119]

This method of indirect political control obviously had its drawbacks and its risks. Whether greater or lesser, the potentates who had been brought to power by the insurrections were sometimes little inclined to have their conduct of affairs dictated by an as-

117. CCF, Rapport de Swatow (Jan. 13, 1912).
118. CCF, Rapport de Tchentou (Chengtu) (Jan. 10, 1912).
119. Albert Maybon, *La République Chinoise* (Paris, 1914), p. 140.

semblage of merchants. They usually had powerful coercive means at their disposal, never having disbanded the troops, regular or otherwise, whose support had given them victory several weeks earlier. Their power was based on naked brute force, and they did not hesitate to use it. The least of the ills that threatened the wealthy merchants were abusive demands for loans, forced imposts, and various other exactions. Kidnappings, blackmail, and mysterious deaths were frequent occurrences.[120] When serious conflict between the local government and the merchant community broke out, sometimes the garrison troops launched an attack on shops, warehouses, banks, and dwellings. On these occasions the police would join in the operation which, although conducted primarily to intimidate the merchants, had the extra advantage of providing a rich harvest of loot which might compensate for irregular pay.

Although the bourgeoisie sometimes suffered from terroristic measures and persecution of this kind, it had effective methods for bringing pressure to bear on local government. In the first place, the bourgeoisie was not alone in its stand against the various governments that had been established. At its side stood the gentry, including mandarins who had not been too much involved with the old regime, landowners, and literati. The close ties between the still undifferentiated bourgeoisie and the well-established gentry have already been noted. In the Chinese provinces that had declared their own independence after the fall of the Manchu government, the solidarity between the two groups became stronger.

The first attempts of the bourgeoisie to enter into politics and to exercise control over local government took place behind a common front of local men of influence. In Szechwan, for instance, the gentry and the merchants of Chengtu joined forces in obliging the new governor (*tu-tu*) to permit the establishment of an assembly. In the beginning of February 1912 they met in a provisional provincial assembly consisting of 300 members; but the governor refused to recognize it on the grounds that it was not representative. A compromise was then reached, and a committee was appointed for preparing the convocation of a provincial assembly, thirty of its members being nominated by the regional associations (*hsiang-hui*) of Chengtu.[121]

120. For incidents in Chefoo, see *NCH* (Feb. 17, 1912), p. 439, and CCF, Rapport du vice-consul de Tchefou (Jan. 29, 1912); for incidents in Kweiyang, see *NCH* (Aug. 10, 1912); and in Foochow, see CCF, Rapport de Foochow (Feb. 6, 1912); etc.

121. CCF, Rapport de Tchentou (Chengtu) (Feb. 20, 1912).

In Canton, where the election of a provincial assembly was achieved at the end of December, the conflict turned upon the extent of its powers. The deputies made insistent demands to be shown accounts and estimates that the revolutionary government was no more able than willing to provide, thus making public the questionable honesty of the first republican governor, Hu Hanmin.[122]

Thus the commercial bourgeoisie, along with other groups of local notables, sought to establish official organizations of a kind that would enable them to keep the local governments under strict supervision. Most effective, however, were the more specifically "bourgeois" means by which the merchants ensured that their voice would be heard. Since there was a scarcity of ready money in China at the time, the commercial bourgeoisie held a trump card, being the group that could most easily liquidate capital and realize large sums with the least delay. This was especially valuable in view of the fact that many governments were short of funds, since taxes either had been abolished or could only be collected irregularly and with difficulty. Maritime Customs duties had been seized by the foreign powers on the ground that they were assigned to the central government and the nonexistent central government could no longer provide help. The funds supplied directly by the merchants were often the only means available for paying the officials and the troops. In Chengtu, for instance, "despite the disappointments and the destruction, the new regime is encouraged and supported; it has no difficulty in obtaining voluntary subscriptions, for the merchants, although they have suffered greatly, eagerly offer their cooperation."[123] Emigrants, many of whom were merchants established overseas, contributed to the raising of funds by sending money to their native provinces. These lay in the southeastern coastal districts, where the money received from the Netherlands

122. CCF, Rapport de Canton (Feb. 25, 1912). The Assembly demanded that a budget be introduced. On January 11, President Ch'en Chiung-ming sent a telegram to the director of the Department of Finance asking for a statement of accounts of receipts and expenditures since the establishment of the autonomous government. On January 12 the Assembly, to which the statement had been submitted, expressed dissatisfaction with it, pointing out that from November 9 to December 31, 1912, expenditures had risen to 6 million dollars, while the Subscriptions Office received barely 600,000 dollars a month, and that there was thus a considerable deficit. The Assembly declared that it was not prepared to help the government make up the deficit until it had received full details justifying the expenditure.

123. CCF, Rapport de Tchentou (Chengtu) (Jan. 10, 1912).

East Indies was collected into a central fund at Foochow, "whence the amounts required were sent to the provincial officials."[124]

Yet however useful the money contributed by the bourgeoisie may have been, it was not usually sufficient to cover the costs of administration, which included the pay of the police and of the local troops; thus local governments were forced to issue paper money that often had no backing or guarantee. When this stage was reached, the cooperation of merchants and bankers was absolutely vital if normal circulation of notes of this kind was to be ensured. In Chengtu, where relations between the government and the bourgeoisie were fairly good, 2 million piastres[125] were issued in this way, and the paper money was accepted everywhere at its nominal value.[126] In Canton, on the other hand, the distrust with which the bourgeoisie viewed the republican government was expressed by its refusal to accept the notes that had been hastily printed to meet the enormous deficit in public funds. The small ten-dollar bills were used to provide the soldiers' pay, but the soldiers were unable to use this worthless currency. As a result, toward the end of January such incidents as brawls between soldiers and restaurant proprietors or pawnbrokers led to the closure of a large number of shops.[127] Ch'en Chiung-ming's decree of January 25, making acceptance of the currency compulsory, did nothing to improve the situation.

The terroristic methods occasionally used to extort large sums from merchants were obviously not the best way to gain their confidence. Yet it was precisely their confidence that was required if the government in power wanted to achieve financial stability, upon which its stability as a government rested. Hence a certain state of equilibrium was usually reached between the local governments, with force at their disposal, and the merchants, with money at theirs. Thus although indirect, the control of the bourgeoisie over the de facto governments thrown up by the Revolution was firm enough to ensure the defense of its class interests.

The impact of the new revolutionary ideology was much weaker in the interior than in the open coastal ports like Shanghai and Canton. Therefore, Chinese merchants in the provinces felt no

124. CCF, Rapport d'Amoy (Jan. 2, 1912).

125. The piastre was the dollar issued in Indochina by the French in 1895. For practical purposes this is also equivalent to the U.S. dollar and to the Chinese yüan.

126. CCF, Rapport de Tchentou (Chengtu) (Jan. 31, 1912).

127. CCF, Rapport de Canton (Feb. 1, 1912).

need to proclaim liberty or equality in order to defend their interests. For them the Revolution meant primarily the abolition of the old Confucian doctrines, and the possibility of starting from scratch to create not so much a new political system as a social hierarchy and an economic organization that would conform with their aims and aspirations.

In the task of social reorganization, the bourgeoisie and the gentry followed much the same line. Both classes had the same end in view: the maintenance of order. Safeguarding the lines of communication was vital to the merchants, and this was part of the same operation as preventing unrest in the countryside, which acted in the interests of the landowners, since banditry and piracy had increased with the flight from the land. So the bourgeoisie and the gentry made common cause to put society in order again. But it seems to have been the bourgeoisie who played the major role in this alliance, perhaps because the merchants' interest in ensuring free circulation for their merchandise made their concern for the restoration of order and public safety extend beyond local boundaries.

Increasingly the merchants intervened more or less directly for the "preservation of peace" (meaning order)—*pao-an*. Sometimes they demanded military protection from local governments for the main trade routes. It was in answer to one of these demands that the government of Canton provided an escort for a certain number of convoys coming down the Sikiang and its affluents through a region infested with pirates. In cases of more direct and more immediate danger, the merchants often used monetary pressure. This happened in Canton in April 1912, when violent street fighting broke out between about 30,000 regular troops and the militia that had been recruited from "pirates" and were unemployed during the revolutionary uprising, and which the authorities were now attempting to disband. The merchants managed to stop the fighting by exerting very strong financial pressure on both the government and the troop commanders. In addition, by offering a preliminary gratuity, they succeeded in disbanding about 50,000 militiamen.[128]

Pirates, brigands, and undisciplined troops were not the only disorderly elements. The presence of more organized factions, some recently formed and some of long standing, offered a further threat

128. *NCH* (April 20, 1912), p. 163.

to social order. First and foremost were the secret societies, which, although historians still disagree as to the social strata from which they were recruited—poor peasants or landless and otherwise displaced persons—constituted by their very existence a questioning of the established order. In Chengtu, for example, during the first months of 1912, the Elder Brother Society had succeeded in establishing headquarters in the various districts of the city, and their officers constituted a sort of shadow municipal government. Some of their activities were distinctly disreputable. The district offices were turned into gambling dens where gambling and opium smoking went on a big scale, bringing in a large profit to the Brothers who collected a handsome rake-off from these debauches. Whether such societies were a form of embryonic democratic organization or more a mafia type of tyranny, their activities constituted a threat to the order desired by the bourgeoisie. Thus with the combined support of all the groups of influential people, the governor at Chengtu conducted a vigorous and successful campaign to rid the city of the Elder Brother Society.[129]

Lastly, as soon as the first signs of working-class protest appeared, the bourgeoisie found the existing governments to be docile and effective allies. When on January 25, 1912 the workers at the Chengtu Arsenal attempted to strike for higher wages and shorter hours, Governor Yang (possibly Yang Wei) intervened in person. The two leaders of the movement were beheaded and the men returned to work immediately.[130]

Thus in the task of social reorganization that was necessary after the revolutionary uprisings, the bourgeoisie made no special contribution of its own. It simply formed part of the great coalition of the "haves," all of them anxious to preserve their wealth and their privileges. The fact that within this coalition the bourgeoisie played a particularly active role is no doubt explained by a contemporary comment: "Of all the factors constituting the complex organism of Chinese society, the mercantile element is at once the soundest and the most conservative."[131]

While there is little to distinguish the bourgeoisie from the gen-

129. CCF, Consular reports from Tchentou (Chengtu) (January, February, and March 1912).

130. CCF, Rapport de Tchentou (Jan. 31, 1912). The source gives only Governor Yang's surname. At this time, Yang Wei was not governor but chief of police at Chengtu. Later in the summer of 1912, Yuan Shih-k'ai appointed him governor but whether he filled the post is not known.

131. *NCH* (Nov. 1, 1913), p. 352.

try and other influential persons in the matter of social reorganization, the same does not hold true of economic reorganization. In this sphere the bourgeoisie, by virtue of the very nature of its specific functions, had definite plans and every intention of putting them into effect without delay. It wanted freedom from medieval restraints and assurance that the measures necessary for commercial expansion would be introduced.

The great movement for the abolition of the likin, which immediately after the uprisings spread throughout all China, is a striking illustration of the desire for liberation and emancipation that animated the bourgeoisie. The spontaneous and widespread nature of the movement, springing as it did not from any initiative received from the central government but from the multitude of autonomous governments that had come into being, provides supplementary evidence of the existence and influence of the commercial bourgeoisie in China. In Hangchow "one of the first acts of the authorities was to abolish the likin."[132] In Wenchow the tax was likewise abolished during the first days of coming to power,[133] and "Soon after Fukien became incorporated in the revolutionary area, in November 1911, all the likin stations were closed and the tax was declared abolished."[134]

In Canton the merchants were just as much opposed to the likin, but they were unable to get it abolished because the former governor-general Chang Ming-ch'i had pledged the receipts from this tax as guarantee for a 5-million-dollar loan he had contracted with such big foreign banks as the Banque de l'Indochine, the Hongkong and Shanghai Bank, and others. On December 28, 1911 the Provincial Assembly demanded that the republican government give them full details about the transaction, and expressed the desire to have the loan secured by other means, so that the likin could be abolished throughout the province.[135]

The existence of internal customs hindered the circulation of goods. The existence of town walls hindered the growth of the big economic centers—Chinese towns were being strangled by the stone corset that had become too tight for them; and during the first exuberant days of freedom, the merchants made a concerted attack on these age-old walls. In Shanghai whole sections of the city wall

132. *TR* (1911), part 2, Hangchow, p. 536.
133. *TR* (1912), part 2, Wenchow, p. 593.
134. *TR* (1912), part 2, Amoy, p. 645.
135. CCF, Rapport de Canton (Jan. 10, 1912).

were knocked down to make way for a main thoroughfare.[136] In Hangchow the walls enclosing the western area of the town disappeared.[137] In Canton on January 13, President Ch'en Chiung-ming announced that expropriation procedures had been started to authorize the expulsion of owners of houses built against the town wall and the destruction of the wall.[138] Surely the demolition of these walls was symbolic. Might it not be said to mark the liberation of the commercial sector of society that had for so long been scoffed at under the old regime?

The bourgeoisie had taken action in a remarkably unanimous if unconcerted way to remove from its path some of the obstacles the imperial government had been neither able nor willing to remove. It remained to be seen whether, with the path now clear, the bourgeoisie would be capable of organizing its forces in a constructive way. The Chinese merchants were undoubtedly well aware that if economic expansion was to be achieved, special measures needed to be taken. On February 5, 1912 the Industrial Association (Shih-yeh-t'uan) of Kwangtung wrote to the provincial government denouncing the inaccuracy of the weights and measures in use as "harmful both to industrial and general scientific advance and to commercial prosperity,"[139] and recommending the adoption of the French metric system. In another communication, dated February 6, the same association demanded the establishment of a bank in Kwangtung for financing industrial enterprises, and a code of law based on the French one.[140]

The Canton government did not by any means remain deaf to suggestions of this kind, and occasionally introduced measures designed to act in the interests of the commercial bourgeoisie. For example, on January 13, 1912, President Ch'en announced that the tael as a measure of weight in silver was henceforth abolished, and that all commercial accounting must now be carried out in terms of *yüan* (dollars), in order to bring about uniformity of currency.[141]

But by their very nature all these proposals for the standardization of weights and measures, currency, and laws made no sense

136. *TR* (1912), part 2, Shanghai, p. 447.
137. *TR* (1912), part 2, Hangchow, p. 569.
138. CCF, Rapport de Canton (Jan. 25, 1912); *SCMP* (Jan. 18, 1912).
139. CCF, Rapport de Canton (Feb. 17, 1912), where the announcement is quoted.
140. Ibid.
141. CCF, Rapport de Canton (Jan. 25, 1912).

unless they were carried out, not on a local or provincial basis, but at the national level. This was the explanation given by the deputies of the Kwangtung Provincial Assembly when on January 13 they rejected a plan submitted by the government for the abolition of the likin, for which a stamp duty was to be substituted. The Assembly stated emphatically that however desirable in itself the abolition of the likin might be, it would be useless unless coordinated with measures taken by a central government to increase maritime customs duties on imports and to establish civil and commercial law codes.[142]

Thus the limitations of the management of affairs on a local basis soon became evident. What of the successes obtained? Up to a point the bourgeoisie, with the support of the gentry, was successful in its efforts to restore social order. It made a stand against the mounting chaos and lawlessness by which its social position and very existence was threatened, and also against the workers' movement, which was not yet well enough organized to constitute a direct threat. The Revolution of 1911 was a gigantic process of political disintegration, in the course of which the bourgeoisie had managed to preserve a certain degree of continuity and stability at the local level. It had also attempted to open the way for economic advance by abolishing outworn structures that for several decades had paralyzed or retarded commercial expansion, and suggesting the establishment of suitable commercial and industrial institutions.

These efforts soon met with insoluble difficulties and sometimes ended in complete failure. Unrest persisted and spread as, with the increasing difficulty of providing regular pay for the troops, many of them joined bands of brigands. In Kwangtung, which Jean Rodes, correspondent of *Le Temps,* nicknamed the Pirates' Republic,[143] the presence of these bands made the use of roads and rivers impossible. In the autumn of 1912 the boats of the China Merchants' Steam Navigation Company that plied between Ningpo and Shanghai had to be accompanied by gunboats for protection against pirates.[144] The financial situation remained very precarious. Manchuria went through an acute monetary crisis when paper

142. CCF, Rapport de Canton No. 27, entitled: "La Révolution à Canton du 13 au 20 janvier."

143. Jean Rodes, *Scènes de la vie révolutionnaire en Chine, 1911–14* (3rd ed. Paris, 1917), p. 117.

144. *NCH* (Dec. 7, 1912), p. 661.

money was no longer accepted and there was not enough specie to go round.[145] In Canton during the spring and summer of 1912, the notes issued by the government had a maximum exchange value of only 70 or 80 percent of their nominal value, and not always as much as that.[146] Finally the internal customs duties, which in the first days of the Revolution merchants everywhere had abolished, gradually began to reappear. In April 1912 they were reestablished in the province of Fukien under the name of merchant contributions (*shang-chüan*).[147] In Wenchow[148] and Hangchow they reappeared under the term general contributions (*t'ung-chüan*).[149]

It is fairly easy to see why the bourgeoisie and the gentry were in the end unable to manage local affairs. The main reason was the almost universal lack of funds. In the absence of all regular tax revenue, the merchants, however wealthy they might be, could not possibly supply all the money required to cover public expenditures. It was impossible to provide regular pay for the soldiers and this often drove them to revolt. The lack of funds also necessitated repeated issues of paper money that underwent a steady devaluation, and led to the reestablishment of the likin because it was a tax easy to collect and yielded a good profit. A further reason for failure was the lack of coordination between local governments, which both hindered the task of "pacification," since a band of brigands that had been bought off in one area simply moved to another, and paralyzed all attempts at economic unification.

These difficulties reflect the fundamental weaknesses of the whole effort. Since the influence exerted by the leading groups did not extend beyond local affairs, both the means at their disposal and the results obtained were of a limited nature. This particularism was partly due to the fact that since the time of the autumn uprising in 1911 there had been no central government; but it was also a typical feature of Chinese political practice. According to Confucian doctrine it was the responsibility of the gentleman to look after public welfare, security, and peace in his locality, and there was a curious echo of this tradition of direct participation in local affairs in the modern utopian ideals of the bourgeoisie, with its dreams of creating model regions or provinces. Thus the region-

145. *TR* (1912), part 2, Mukden, p. 66; Antung, p. 72.
146. *NCH* (Sept. 14, 1912), p. 769; (Jan. 25, 1913), p. 233.
147. *TR* (1912), part 2, Amoy, p. 645.
148. *TR* (1912), part 2, Wenchow, p. 593.
149. *TR* (1911), part 2, Hangchow, p. 536.

alism imposed by events corresponded to already existing attitudes. This may have made it easier for the bourgeoisie and the gentry to take action in the first place, but was a fatal stumbling block to a successful outcome.

Once the imperial administrative system had broken down, the gentry had no alternative to purely local action. But what about the bourgeoisie? Were its members under the illusion that, without any change in the form of the central government, an alliance with the gentry would be enough to ensure the maintenance of the status quo and simultaneously the creation of the economic revival they so much desired? Had they forgotten the revolutionary ideas of the movement with which they had been associated before 1911? Or did they simply not feel strong enough to break away from their common front with the gentry and adopt instead a wider political outlook more in accord with their own interests? Was it merely the means that were lacking, or did they lack ambition and imagination? The weakness of the provincial bourgeoisie was particularly conspicuous. There were too few of them and they were too little differentiated from the gentry to be able to free themselves from subordination to them. The two groups shared the same conservative views on social matters, but their views on economic expansion were quite different.

If the bourgeoisie had been stronger, would it have tried to find other means of political expression? The experiment carried out in the region of the lower Yangtze by the Shanghai bourgeoisie may to some extent supply an answer to this question.

The First Bourgeois Ventures into National Politics

The provinces of Kiangsu, Chekiang, and Anhwei are situated in the area where the lower reaches of the Yangtze open out into the plain. This highly favorable location makes them a key economic area, and here the bridgehead of foreign imperialism and the bastion of Chinese capitalism, so closely linked with imperialism, were to be found. This was in fact the only region where the bourgeoisie attained a sufficient degree of class consciousness and power to enable it to make an attempt to establish a government capable of looking after bourgeois interests.

The Chinese Republic was proclaimed at Nanking on January 1, 1912, with Sun Yat-sen as its President. The government had been voted into being by the seventeen provincial delegates, and it hoped to extend its authority over all the regions where revolutionary governments had been established. Although not all its members were revolutionaries, it was a product of the Revolutionary Alliance, to which three of the new ministers belonged. The vice-ministers were also all from the ranks of the Revolutionary Alliance.

As soon as it was constituted, the Nanking government set itself up as a rival to the government that had been established for nearly three months at Wuhan. Neither Li Yüan-hung and his circle in Wuhan nor the revolutionaries who supported them, consisting for the most part of men who had belonged to revolutionary groups in the army or to the Progressive Association, had ever recognized Sun's authority. The Revolutionary Alliance had played no part in organizing the Wuchang uprising and only later attempted to gain control of events. Huang Hsing's mission to Wuhan in October-November 1911 is evidence of this attempt—and of its failure. The Revolutionary Alliance then turned its back on the battles in which the fate of the Revolution was determined and, having succeeded in arranging for the transfer of the provincial delegates from Wuhan to Shanghai, decided to set up a second major revolutionary center in Kiangsu. Thus, as had happened so often in China, the struggle for power was fought on a geographical basis, taking the form of a proliferation of revolutionary areas and displacement of the center of gravity from one to the other.

In withdrawing to the lower Yangtze area and establishing their base there, Sun and the Revolutionary Alliance obviously hoped to take advantage of the support of the upper bourgeoisie of Shanghai, which since the beginning of November had been in direct control of all the Chinese districts in the metropolis. The Provisional Government that had been installed after the attack on the Kiangnan Arsenal on November 2 included several of the city's leading businessmen. Yü Hsia-ch'ing, an eminent compradore, occupied the post of Assistant Director of Foreign Affairs, and also administered the Chapei district; and Chu Pao-san, one of the leaders of the Ningpo Guild, to which the most influential bankers belonged, was in charge of finance.[150] After the imperial government officials had disappeared from the scene, close relations were established between the Chinese Chamber of Commerce and the consular corps for the regulation of day-to-day matters.[151] Further-

150. See F. McCormick, *The Flowery Republic* (London, 1913), p. 459; *NCH* (Jan. 20, 1912), p. 153.

151. *NCH* (Nov. 1, 1913), p. 352.

more, the governor, Ch'en Ch'i-mei, although no longer a businessman, had several years earlier established connections with business circles, having been first employed in a pawnshop and then by a silk merchant before entering politics.

In Shanghai, as elsewhere in China, the bourgeoisie in the hour of its triumph began by demolishing the city walls,[152] and then proceeded to abolish the likin. By December 6 the internal tariff walls throughout the province were also down. But the bourgeoisie did not stop there. It concentrated all its forces in support of the proposals put forward by the Revolutionary Alliance for the establishment of a republican government. It has been estimated that the business community of Shanghai advanced more than seven million dollars to the revolutionary party.[153] Later, the Chamber of Commerce officially requested Yuan Shih-k'ai to repay the three million taels that the merchants had provided to pay the troops during the first months of 1912, one million of which had been a direct loan from the businessmen of Shanghai, the rest having been borrowed by the Board of Managers of the Chamber of Commerce from the (German?) Diederichsen Company.[154] As a foreign observer commented, "the merchants at first contributed voluntarily and gladly."[155]

During this period the bourgeoisie lent all its influence toward helping Sun Yat-sen to triumph over the last efforts at resistance put up by Yuan Shih-k'ai and the Manchu court. Contacts were established with the foreign chambers of commerce that had the successful result of inducing the British Chamber of Commerce of Shanghai, ignoring the neutrality status of its home government, to send telegrams to the ex-Regent, Prince Ch'un, and to Yuan Shih-k'ai, expressing the need for an immediate abdication on the part of the dynasty and for a "democratic" solution of the crisis.[156] (This of course horrified the protocol-minded British Foreign Office.) The support of the Chinese merchants must likewise have been behind the Manifesto of January 5, 1912 issued by the new republican government, which threatened to boycott any foreign power that consented to make loans to the imperial government.[157]

152. *TR* (1912), part 2, Shanghai, p. 447.

153. *NCH* (March 1, 1913), p. 650.

154. *NCH* (July 13, 1912), p. 109.

155. *NCH* (Jan. 20, 1912), p. 160.

156. CCF, Rapport de Shanghai (Jan. 19, 1912). Also mentioned in Anatol M. Kotenev, *New Lamps for Old* (Shanghai, 1931), p. 55.

157. Kotenev, *New Lamps*, p. 63.

Thus the establishment of the republican government in Nanking was very largely due to the financial and political support of the Shanghai bourgeoisie. Yet few businessmen actually formed part of the government personnel. Even Chang Chien's post as Minister of Industry was not a true exception, since besides being a wealthy industrialist and entrepreneur, he was also an eminent scholar whose contacts with officialdom had always been as close as his relations with the business world. It would further seem not only that no businessmen were included in the government, but that they did not even exercise any direct control over the appointment of ministers or other high government officials. The Guild of Cantonese Merchants in Shanghai did its best to have its own candidate, Wu T'ing-fang, appointed as Minister of Foreign Affairs, even going so far as to threaten to withdraw the subsidy of 400,000 taels it had promised to the National Assembly if he were not appointed.[158] But the Guild failed in its efforts (which had been repudiated by Wu T'ing-fang himself), and I have come across no record of any other instance of pressure of this kind being exerted. Nevertheless, to infer, as some historians have done, that the Nanking government was not a bourgeois one because none of its ministers were primarily merchants, would seem to be a rather hasty conclusion. For the facts show that the Shanghai bourgeoisie, using all the money and influence at its command, had brought to power a group of politicians in whom it had confidence and whose program met its own needs.

The program of the new central government broadly followed the lines of the principles upheld by the Revolutionary Alliance, although now that the Revolution had actually taken place, the pressure of events added certain nuances and refinements to the original proposals. After becoming President, Sun continued to insist on the abdication of the Manchu dynasty. He called for the reunification of China under a republican government, and undertook to promote economic expansion. It should be noted that no further mention was made of plans for the agrarian reform that had so often been advocated by Sun and his followers a few years before. No doubt the omission was not entirely unintentional.

The program presented coincided with the views of the upper bourgeoisie of Shanghai, now deeply hostile to the imperial re-

158. *NCH* (Jan. 13, 1912), p. 96.

gime, although it had often been content to compromise in the past. In Sun's indictment of the "obscurantist" Manchus he almost seems to be pleading the case of the bourgeoisie as he mentions the "privileges and monopolies" created by the Manchus, and complains that: "They have levied irregular and unwholesome taxes upon us without our consent, have restricted foreign trade to the treaty ports, placed likin embargoes upon merchandise in transit, and obstructed internal commerce."[159] While conducting negotiations with Yuan Shih-k'ai in January, Sun stipulated that the abdication of the dynasty was a preliminary condition for any agreement they might reach. The Shanghai bourgeoisie had meanwhile found a spectacular way of demonstrating its final rupture with the Empire: at a big reception given by the Chinese Commercial Association and the Shanghai Chamber of Commerce, held on January 19 at the Temple of the Queen of Heaven, it was announced that only those not wearing a pigtail would be admitted.[160] This question of hair styles may appear trivial, but it was of deadly importance at the time, since the queue was the detested symbol of subservience to the Manchu dynasty.

Thus the bourgeoisie opted for the Republic out of hatred for the Empire. What the new regime would be like, what its power structure would be, and how its functions would be coordinated, were problems that do not seem to have been of direct concern to the businessmen who financed the setting up of the Nanking government. No doubt they regarded a republic as the most modern, the most emancipating, and the most effective form of government, to which the powerful positions attained by such Western countries as France or the United States were due. They left it to the politicians to work out the administrative details. The debate then taking place between Sun, who upheld the presidential form of government, and Sung Chiao-jen, who argued for parliamentary government, does not seem to have aroused much interest in the guilds or in the Shanghai Chamber of Commerce.

The question of the reunification of China was another matter. Here Sun's views were fully shared by his bourgeois supporters, who were deeply committed to the idea of Chinese unity. In the eyes of the President, to whom the idea of nationhood was all-important, the most urgent task following the abdication was the

159. The Manifesto is quoted and translated in a number of works; in particular, see McCormick, *The Flowery Republic*, p. 457.

160. *NCH* (Jan. 20, 1912), p. 153.

creation of a central pan-China government. On January 1, 1912, the very day he took office, Sun sent Yuan Shih-k'ai a telegram offering him the presidency if he would support the Republic. This self-effacement on the part of a man like Sun, in whom modesty cannot be said to have been a striking characteristic, is surprising. Of course the power balance was not favorable to Sun and he must have known this. But it is possible that the desire to see China reunited speedily and peacefully also motivated his withdrawal. The priority of the idea of national unity is constant in his political ideology.

This faith in the Chinese nation was in accord with the view of a certain section of the bourgeois class. As soon as the unifying force of Confucianism had declined and the empire based upon its doctrines had disappeared, the pan-Chinese sentiments formerly entertained by the scholar-officials of the old regime weakened. At the same time these sentiments were growing in strength among the wealthiest and most advanced section of the bourgeoisie, whose members had discovered in their professional activities the potential existence of a national market, even if it was still in the very early stages.

It is true that many members of the Shanghai bourgeoisie entertained the particularist tendencies so evident among the provincial bourgeoisie. But after all, Shanghai was China's most important economic center, with a hinterland which, even if it has been described as containing a tenuous network of trade with a very irregular flow of goods, nevertheless covered the whole of China. If the Shanghai businessmen were to make sure of their profits, it was essential that peace should reign throughout the whole of the lower Yangtze area, and that ease of communications be maintained, both with the provinces of the North that supplied cotton and tobacco, and with those in the South that produced silk and tea. The resources of the country as a whole were concentrated on the Shanghai market, and thus the import-export trade replaced Confucian doctrines as the school in which the bourgeoisie learned the principle of national unity.

The Nanking government finally adopted the program of expansion advocated by the Chinese bourgeoisie. In his Manifesto of January 5, Sun Yat-sen made the following promises: "We will remodel our laws; revise our civil, criminal, commercial and mining codes; . . . abolish restrictions to trade and commerce . . ."[161] He

161. Sun's Manifesto, as translated in McCormick, *The Flowery Republic.*

very soon attempted to translate these promises into action. He gave his support to the Society for the Development of Industry in the Chinese Republic, whose statutes were published in the Official Journal of the Provisional Government of Nanking on February 20, 1912.[162] A preamble to the text of the statutes has a clarion call about industrial development as the best means of improving mass welfare (*min-sheng*). These themes, so often developed by Sun, reappear in some of the decrees of the Minister of Industry, Chang Chien. On February 15, for example, the governors were asked to create "Bureaus of Industry" in the provinces to back up the actions taken by the ministry.[163] On February 29, Chang Chien made the same point again, stressing the need to coordinate economic activities throughout the country so as to foster industrial development and ensure prosperity for the people.[164] Chang was trying to inject a little order into the wild rush of enthusiasm with which new ventures were being started. Requests for incorporation and for loans poured into the ministry from every kind of company—insurance companies, companies for land reclamation, for opening mines, for building railways; in fact all sectors of the economy seemed to be full of a new energy.[165] The Overseas Chinese also took part in this development drive.[166]

The fact that capital was coming in from overseas was due largely to the efforts of Sun himself, aided by some of the more active members of the Revolutionary Alliance. Together they often helped to arrange for the collaboration of merchants abroad with merchants at home. Perhaps the most striking example of this collaboration was the Chinese Industrial Bank (Chung-hua shih-yeh yin-hang), established to finance the industrialization of China. Its shareholders met officially for the first time in May 1912. Most of the capital (five million out of six million dollars) had been subscribed by Overseas Chinese. Shen Man-yün, one of the directors, had raised this sum by touring Southeast Asia, visiting Singapore, Java, and Rangoon, and making use everywhere he went of introductions given him by Sun Yat-sen. Sun even agreed to become

162. The text of the Official Journal of the Provisional Government of Nanking (*Lin-shih cheng-fu kung-pao*) is included in a special number of the journal *Chin-tai shih tzu-liao, 1* (1961), devoted to the 1911 Revolution, and entitled *Hsin-hai ko-ming tzu-liao*. For no. 12 of the Official Journal (OJ), see p. 96.

163. OJ, *8* (Feb. 15, 1912), ibid., p. 58.

164. OJ, *25* (Feb. 29, 1912), ibid., p. 201.

165. OJ, *15* (Feb. 14, 1912), ibid., p. 111; OJ, *16* (Feb. 15, 1912), ibid., p. 121; OJ, *28* (Mar. 3, 1912), ibid., p. 223.

166. OJ, *34* (Mar. 10, 1912), ibid., p. 261.

Chairman of the Board in order to gain the confidence of shareholders overseas. The bank was established as a limited liability company. A steering committee was appointed to decide upon the terms and conditions of long-term (twenty-year) loans to mining and industrial enterprises, and other matters. Significantly enough the committee included, in addition to overseas members, the Revolutionary Alliance militants Sung Chiao-jen and Ch'en Ch'i-mei, and several leading citizens of Shanghai, such as Chou Chin-chen, the president of the Chamber of Commerce.[167]

The men who had seized power in Nanking were intellectuals and politicians, all of them either trusty or newly converted revolutionaries. But behind them, and hoping to use them as a mouthpiece, stood the upper bourgeoisie of Shanghai, with all its energy, its hopes, and also its weaknesses, not to mention its illusions. The Nanking government lasted only a few weeks. The manner of its fall shows as clearly as the way in which it had been set up the profound influence of the bourgeoisie on these events.

On February 12, 1912 three edicts were promulgated proclaiming the abdication of the Manchu Emperor. On February 14, Sun Yat-sen handed in his resignation and backed Yuan Shih-k'ai's candidacy for the presidency on certain conditions: he was to promise to uphold republican principles, to respect the constitution, and to transfer the capital to Nanking. On February 15, a senate consisting of representatives of the seventeen provinces met at Nanking and elected Yuan President. Sun did not actually retire from office until April 1, but he still had not obtained Yuan's promise to leave Peking. This meant defeat.

Why did the Nanking government fall so soon? Was it because the bourgeoisie wavered in its support? Or because its support was not strong enough? There is no doubt that as the weeks went by, relations between the bourgeoisie and the republican government became more difficult. There were numerous quarrels, the root of the trouble almost always being demands for money on the part of the government. The French consul recorded on January 13: "The bankers and the wealthy wholesalers and compradores have all had to contribute and there is no doubt that many of them are beginning to find the new regime very burdensome."[168] The *North*

167. *NCH* (Dec. 14, 1912), p. 728; (May 10, 1913), p. 179. See also Shen Yün-sun, "Chung-hua shih-yeh yin-hang shih-mo" (History of the Chinese Industrial Bank), in *Chin-tai shih tzu-liao, 6* (1957), 120–39.

168. CCF, Rapport de Shanghai (Jan. 13, 1912).

China Herald of the same date records that money was being hoarded at an increasing rate.[169] Bank withdrawals increased, and the approach of the Chinese New Year—the traditional date for settling accounts in financial and business circles—was not enough to explain the very low figure of deposits in both the foreign and the Chinese banks in Shanghai. The total sum on October 13, 1911 was 8,400,000 dollars, 24,400,000 taels, and 5,900 silver ingots. On January 19, 1912 there were only 6,800,000 dollars, 17,800,000 taels, and 1,836 ingots.[170] At the beginning of February it was rumored that the Chinese banks no longer felt able to protect their funds against government demands, and preferred to return deposits to their clients.[171]

Most of these banks were on territory belonging to the International Settlement. But that did not prevent republican agents from trying to procure money from them. "There have been several mysterious kidnappings of wealthy financiers and a good many attempts at extortion [in the International Settlement]," the French consul explained in his report. "The Municipality has complained to the Consular Corps, which has taken up the matter with the Ministers of the Republic."

These shady dealings were no doubt carried out by such minor officials as Hsiu Che-chiang, the superintendent of the Shanghai Office of the Ministry of Foreign Affairs. Hsiu, who was replaced on January 13, had a dubious reputation. He was in close touch with the Italian lawyer Musso, a well-known troublemaker, and the two formed links in a chain of dubious relationships, at one end of which was the Italian vice-Consul Ros and at the other Ch'en Ch'i-mei himself.[172] Ch'en, the military governor of Shanghai and an important figure in the republican party, was a friend of Ros, whom he never failed to invite to official ceremonies at the Town Hall of Nantao, the Chinese part of the city.[173] Thus the backwash of the scandal touched Ch'en, and he came under grave suspicion. The French consul, although he had no decisive proof, formally accused Ch'en of having been the instigator of a mysterious crime committed during the night of January 15 at the Sainte-Marie Hospital of the Jesuit Mission.[174] Some of the leading

169. *NCH* (Jan. 13, 1912), p. 121.
170. *NCH* (Jan. 20, 1912), p. 197.
171. *NCH* (Feb. 3, 1912), p. 292.
172. CCF, Rapport de Shanghai (Jan. 13, 17, 1912).
173. CCF, Rapport de Shanghai (Jan. 17, 1912).
174. Ibid.

citizens of Shanghai were agitating for his dismissal, and on January 17 seven hundred of them met in the offices of the Volunteer Corps at Tongkadou. Chu Pao-san, a wealthy and very influential merchant, formerly Director of Financial Affairs in the Shanghai Provisional Government, attended the meeting. An indictment was drawn up accusing Ch'en Ch'i-mei of misappropriation of funds, nepotism, and extortion. The French consul commented: "These leading citizens of Shanghai hoped at the very least for his [Ch'en's] dismissal. They held him responsible—and in my opinion, justly—for the acts of extortion by blackmail and other criminal acts which have recently been committed much to the exasperation of all Chinese merchants and proprietors."[175]

In this oppressive atmosphere the storm over the foreign loans affair broke out. The government, at the end of its resources, decided at the beginning of February to turn to the foreign powers for help. But in order to preserve, at least in appearance, the neutrality of the foreign powers, negotiations were conducted through such big companies as the China Merchants' Steam Navigation Company (Chung-kuo lun-ch'uan chao-shang chü), which undertook to contract a foreign loan guaranteed by its own assets, and to then turn the money over to the government.[176] The plan immediately met strong opposition from the shareholders, among whom were such leading personalities as Chou Chin-chen, president of the Chamber of Commerce.[177] The shareholders' committee held a protest meeting to denounce the use of armed force, which almost certainly would be required to carry through the company's plan of mortgaging its assets.[178] Their stand was supported by the Nanking Assembly, whose members reproached Sun for his foreign loans policy, which not only went against the interests of the bourgeoisie but also offended their national pride. In the end the government had to give up the idea of negotiating a loan through the China Merchants' Steam Navigation Company and several similar projects as well.[179]

Thus collaboration between business circles and the republican government very soon met serious obstacles. Only a very few weeks after Sun had become President, the merchants and finan-

175. CCF, Rapport de Shanghai (Jan. 18, 1912).
176. *NCH* (Feb. 10, 1912), p. 356.
177. *NCH* (Aug. 17, 1912), p. 458.
178. *NCH* (Feb. 17, 1912), p. 438.
179. CCF, Rapport de Shanghai (March 2, 1912).

ciers of Shanghai realized that they were neither willing nor able to be the sole suppliers of financial support to a government that proclaimed itself and aspired to be a national government, but which would probably have to conquer most of China by armed force in order to extend its control over the whole country.

Yet the conflicts that took place in Shanghai at that time do not seem to have been of the same order as those that were fought out in the 1920s between the Cantonese bourgeoisie, firmly committed to provincial particularism, and the Kuomintang government, which wanted to bring the whole country under its control, even at the cost of the difficult Northern Expedition. The Shanghai bourgeoisie, which was in a strong position economically, apparently shared Sun Yat-sen's ardor for national unity. But hopes had probably been entertained that the Nanking government, which owed its establishment to the Shanghai bourgeoisie, would rapidly extend its authority and, in so doing, find other means of support throughout the country. Realization of how illusory these hopes were was not long in coming.

As soon as the republican government began to lose the support of business circles, it found itself in an extremely isolated position. The provincial delegates of the Nanking Assembly, who had legitimatized Sun's authority, became increasingly indifferent and even hostile. Many of them, more aware of the local interests they represented than of the need for a national policy, had tried to enter into direct negotiations with the foreign capitalists of Shanghai to borrow large sums of money, for which the guarantee offered was the revenue from the taxes on the businesses in their own provinces. Sun and his Foreign Minister had made themselves very unpopular by opposing transactions of this kind, and by insisting that all loans should be negotiated through the government.[180] The attitude of the delegates reflected that of the provincial gentry with whom the bourgeoisie was associated; its ties with them never had been broken except, perhaps, in Shanghai—and there only partially. Regional loyalties still took priority over class loyalties; hence Sun could not expect to find much political support even in those provinces which in theory had rallied to his government. Thus, against Sun's express wishes, the Nanking Assembly voted to keep the capital in the North, thereby depriving the republicans of all hope of being able to exercise effective pressure on Yuan

180. Ibid.

Shih-k'ai after his accession to the presidency. Under strong pressure from the cabinet the Assembly voted again, this time in favor of the transfer of the capital south. This did little to improve relations between the delegates and the government.[181]

The Nanking government not only lacked a wide enough basis of support, but also had no efficient party machine behind it. The Revolutionary Alliance had always been very loosely organized. This gave it a flexibility that enabled some of its members to join other revolutionary groups as well. For instance, quite a number of its members belonged to the Progressive Association, and they had managed to stay on in Wuchang under Li Yüan-hung. At the beginning of January, however, they had to leave because the Wuchang government brought pressure to bear on the Progressive Association, and it broke up. Its Revolutionary Alliance members returned to Nanking and the rest formed the People's Association, which from then on gave exclusive support to Li Yüan-hung.[182] Soon other splits occurred. On February 21 Wang Ching-wei held a meeting at Tientsin in the hope of consolidating all the various splinter groups that had been formed under the aegis of the Revolutionary Alliance; but his attempt was not very successful and the Alliance, never noted for its unity, now tended increasingly to consist primarily of Sun's immediate entourage.

Meanwhile, as the power of the republicans disintegrated, the reactionaries and the conservatives were reorganizing their forces. The alliance between Yuan Shih-k'ai and Li Yüan-hung was translated into practical terms. In the reorganization of the army of Hupeh, whose revolt had been the signal for the Revolution, most of the new officers were men from the north, from the military entourage of Yuan Shih-k'ai. The Nanking government, supported —and not too well supported—by only the most advanced sections of the bourgeoisie, could not hope to compete with this Peking-Wuchang axis, which had the major part of the regular armed forces at its command, and which enjoyed the support of the traditional gentry. No doubt it was Sun's realistic awareness of the weakness of his position that made him voluntarily hand in his resignation without even demanding a ministerial post in the government to be headed by Yuan. The report of the French consul in Shanghai, dated February 8, states: "Sun wants to efface himself completely. He has absolutely refused to be given a portfolio, and

181. Ibid.

182. Ts'ai Chi-ou, *Ou-chou,* pp. 194–206.

is said to have expressed his willingness to accept the modest post of Director of Commerce and Industry, if such a post were created."[183]

Doubtless the actual alignment of forces is sufficient explanation of Sun's self-effacing gesture. Nevertheless the alacrity with which he retired from the presidency remains astonishing in view of the fact that he had always had such a high opinion of himself and of his mission. It may well be that he believed Chinese unity would be more easily attainable under Yuan Shih-k'ai and that it was therefore his duty to resign in order to prevent further prolongation of the divisions within the country. But the question arises as to whether Sun perhaps thought that, with the fall of the Manchu dynasty and the establishment of a republican regime, his main task was completed. His feebleness in action would thus be a result of the inconsistency of his ideas; and it is perhaps only to be expected that a revolutionary movement that for years had played around with words should end up in a government that was content with appearances. Or had Sun succumbed to the temptation of adopting the purely "economistic" approach that was the permanent standpoint of the Chinese bourgeoisie? Did he perhaps think that he would make a more effective contribution to the development of the country by direct intervention in economic matters rather than by confining himself to problems of political organization? Perhaps he had failed to see the forest for the trees.

In any case, not only was the support of the Nanking government confined to a very narrow, and essentially local, sector of society, but also the government seems to have been lacking, even at the top, in political and ideological vigor. The combination of the weaknesses inherent in a revolutionary movement inspired mainly by intellectuals full of new, utopian, and non-Chinese ideas with those of a numerically inadequate bourgeoisie, very unevenly distributed geographically and still a marginal social group, resulted in the brief life of the experiment carried out by the Nanking government, which was doomed to early failure from the start.

Thus the bourgeoisie's first ventures into politics during the spring of 1912 ended in defeat, at both the local and the national levels. It had, it is true, been able to make its weight felt. In the provinces it had helped greatly to maintain some degree of public

183. CCF, Rapport de Shanghai (Feb. 8, 1912).

order, and to ensure the dispatch of day-to-day affairs. By its support of the Nanking government it had prevented a counterattack by the Manchu dynasty and had contributed toward the introduction of the idea of a republic, if not its translation into practice. But in the end it had proved incapable of setting up the type of political organization required for the expansion of its activities. It had not yet acquired a social identity adequate to the task of carrying out a program in the provinces distinct from that of the gentry. Moreover its numerical weakness came into play, for Chinese businessmen obviously could not by themselves provide the necessary support for a national government. The inevitable conclusion is that the bourgeoisie, torn between utopian ideas for regional development and the subtleties of Western ideas about constitutional rights, failed to attain its aims because of its inadequate ideological equipment.

This failure was heavy with consequences for the future of the bourgeoisie and, indeed, for China as a whole. The Peking Republic was a government of monarchist reactionaries and conservative gentry, as represented by Yuan Shih-k'ai and Li Yüan-hung—a mere mask for dictatorship and a facade for anarchy. The bourgeoisie gradually detached itself from the republican cause, and only took part in politics from a distance. Yuan did all he could to bring it round to his side. He promised to put an end to disorder, he included the main demands of the merchants in his program, and he undertook to reimburse the money advanced by business circles to the revolutionaries. He also encouraged former leaders of the Revolutionary Alliance to retire from politics by making Sun Yatsen and Huang Hsing responsible for certain economic matters—of a quite unrealistic nature—in his new administration. So it is perhaps not surprising that the bourgeoisie, disillusioned by its recent experiences, chose to follow the path thus indicated, not only by Yuan Shih-k'ai but by the revolutionary leaders themselves. It was a path that gave every appearance of being the one best suited to its particular vocation, especially as all its energies were now engaged by an unprecedented trade boom. In 1912 foreign trade, profiting from a good harvest and a favorable rate of exchange, broke all records, and the resultant euphoria spread to the industrial sphere, where new enterprises sprang into being every day.

Political disillusionment, the removal of the republican leaders, and economic prosperity together brought about a rapid loss of interest in politics on the part of the bourgeoisie. Yuan Shih-k'ai's assassination of two republican generals, Chang Chen-wu and Fang Wei, in August 1912, excited no reactions,[184] and the dismay felt in the business circles of Shanghai in April of the following year after the murder of Sung Chiao-jen, the last of the revolutionaries to continue the struggle in the political field, seems to have been more a matter of anxiety over the prospect of unrest than of indignation against Yuan Shih-k'ai's treason.[185]

Yet during the spring of 1913 the bourgeoisie was far from having completely come round to Yuan's side. Although it was apathetic to the ups and downs of parliamentary infighting and the accompanying violence, it was nevertheless extremely hostile to the policy being followed by the government of capitulation to the foreigners. In particular the so-called Reorganization Loan negotiated with the International Consortium in January 1913 aroused sharp criticism among the merchants. Thus it was only grudgingly that the bourgeoisie accepted Yuan. But it did accept him, and when in July 1913 a revolutionary movement began in the central and southern provinces, it aroused nothing but disquiet and anxiety in business circles. It was rare indeed to find a merchant coming out in open sympathy with this uprising. Most of them oscillated between outright hostility and the opportunism required for the maintenance of order or, in places where the insurgents had managed to seize power, for the safeguarding of their interests and their lives.

This "Second Revolution" of 1913, far from gaining the support of the bourgeoisie, brought it much further into the camp of Yuan Shih-k'ai than it had probably ever intended to go. The main effect of the disorder and unrest was a revival of old isolationist attitudes. The social particularism bred by centuries of ostracism, which always tended to reappear at times of crisis, became stronger than ever, sweeping away the most cherished hopes. But the failure of the Second Revolution cannot really be accounted for by the hostility of the bourgeoisie. In 1913, as in 1911, the real struggle was between the high officials and the military leaders. The leaders of the republican movement, disillusioned by the failure of the Nanking government and the disastrous attempt to introduce a parliamentary regime, now renounced all ideology and brought the battle down to its real issue: armed conflict. They became "con-

184. *NCH* (Aug. 24, 1912), p. 555.
185. *NCH* (May 10, 1913), p. 427.

dottieri" in a good cause. The reign of the warlords had begun. Bourgeois support does not seem to have weighed any more heavily in deciding the events of 1913 than it had in 1911. Whether for or against revolution, the role of the bourgeoisie remained a subsidiary one.

The Revolution of 1911 provided the bourgeoisie with an opportunity for making its first attempts at political participation, and gave it its first taste of the disparity between hopes and reality—a disillusioning experience that led to a return to exclusively economic activities and to a narrow social particularism. The actual carrying out of the Revolution—the armed uprisings, led by the military and the gentry—was beyond the province, beyond the competence, of the bourgeoisie. In all this, it could play no more than an auxiliary role; and when, after the uprisings had succeeded, it attempted to take control, it met with immediate failure. The bourgeoisie had neither instigated the Revolution nor been in control of events while it was in progress, and the typically "bourgeois" ideology imported from the West, with all the "confusionism" resulting from this process, had done nothing to change either the balance of forces concerned or the actual political facts of the situation. Thus it can scarcely be said that a "bourgeois revolution," in the classic, or at least the Western, sense, had taken place.

Nevertheless it is equally difficult, despite the role played by conservative elements, to regard the 1911 Revolution simply as a traditional rebellion bringing about the fall of one dynasty and the founding of another. This revolution, although it followed the traditional pattern, had a new set of slogans, such as democracy, liberty, and national independence. Their use, owing to the reigning ideological confusion, may have been illegitimate; yet Yuan Shih-k'ai had only been able to seize power in the capacity of President of the Republic—a title which was no doubt devoid of meaning for him and for many members of his entourage. It is, of course, no easy matter to decide what significance words may have when divorced from the reality they are supposed to represent, or to assess what influence they may exert and what hopes and aspirations they may inspire. But even if the meaning of the words was distorted, does not the fact that they were used at all in the China of 1911 constitute a new and irreversible phenomenon?

We should not, therefore, be misled either by the similarity in the vocabulary of the 1911 Revolution and that of the English and French revolutions, or by the analogies between the fall of the

Manchu dynasty and that of former dynasties. The 1911 Revolution has every appearance of being a typical twentieth-century revolution, with marked similarities to contemporary revolutionary movements in Africa and in other parts of Asia. It took place in a colonial context, and was therefore predominantly nationalist in character. It made use of philosophical concepts borrowed from the West, and the groups—primarily the intellectuals and to a lesser degree a number of army officers—that brought these ideas into circulation thereby attained a position of importance quite out of proportion to their actual strength. As a result the imported concepts were often so ill-adapted to the realities of the situation that movements of traditional, conservative, or reactionary forces were able to take cover under the new revolutionary slogans. Yet these slogans, despite their misuse, despite the fact that they were inapplicable to the actual political situation, had a certain magic power of their own, and awakened responses which bore fruit in the later stages of the Chinese revolutionary movement.

If the 1911 Revolution is regarded in this way, it can be seen that the part played by the bourgeoisie was by no means unimportant, if only because it provided a link between the imported ideology and the actual facts of China's situation. But the link was a fragile one; and since the bourgeoisie had not yet attained its full strength as a class, its role could not be anything but subsidiary.

6. The Role of the Gentry: An Hypothesis

Chūzō Ichiko

The Definition, Background, and Function of the Gentry

The gentry I discuss here are men who held the metropolitan (*chin-shih*), provincial (*chü-jen*), or licentiate (*sheng-yüan*) degrees and who lived in their native places. Although they nominally entered the gentry class in order to become government officials, I assume that the primary aim of many was to secure prestige and to protect their property from exploitation by government officials, yamen clerks, and runners and their lives from attacks by bandits, vagabonds, and poor peasants.

Although the gentry had little intention of becoming government officials, they were expected to take an active part in local administration and in this they were greatly interested. The head of the district, or the district magistrate (*chih-hsien*), was called the "parent-official," but his contact with his "children"—the common people—was limited to taxation and maintenance of public order. The gentry functioned between these government officials and the common people as intermediaries or buffers; through them governmental orders came down to the people and public opinion went up to the government. Furthermore, the management of such affairs as irrigation, local self-defense, mediation in personal disputes, mutual aid, recreation, and religious activities, was left in the hands of the gentry. Therefore the gentry had quite a powerful voice in the administration of their native regions.

The gentry and the government officials were mutually dependent. Although the gentry were influential in local administration it did not occur to them to oppose the government officials, since these officials firmly controlled the national Examination System upon which the status of the gentry was based, as well as finance and military power. The gentry thought it wise to depend on the officials to protect their own lives and property, and therefore curried their favor. Conversely, the gentry were important to the government officials since the common people were generally under their influence. They realized that without gentry support they could not successfully govern the districts for which they were responsible and that their own positions would then be in danger, and therefore they were careful not to offend the gentry. For these reasons the governmental authorities and the gentry were interdependent. If the balance between the gentry and the government officials could be adequately maintained, all was well.

This interdependency was particularly apparent in taxation. If the officials went too far, the gentry, who were legally obliged to pay taxes just as the general public did, might lead the common people to revolt. In China, where the people accepted the idea that even the Emperor could be murdered if he was without virtue, no authority was ever secure. Riots were the most direct and dangerous expression of popular distrust of officials. The best way for the officials to prevent them was to lighten the taxes imposed on the gentry who, in return for the favor, would endeavor to appease the discontented people. Thus, in practice the gentry enjoyed privileges far greater than those permitted by law. For instance, the gentry in nineteenth-century China were allowed to pay only 70 or 80 percent of the legal tax, whereas the common people had to pay two or three times the assessment.

It should be remembered that the functions of the gentry in local administration were based on tradition rather than on written laws. The relationship between government officials and gentry was determined by custom and lubricated by diplomacy and compromise. The gentry worked behind the scenes, under the fiction of being the spokesmen of the common people. Yet, although they utilized their position for selfish purposes, they also wielded a restraining influence upon the officials in order to prevent them from being too ruthless and thereby provoking a popular uprising.

The balance of power between the gentry and government officials became unstable early in the nineteenth century. Although there were innumerable starving and homeless people everywhere and riots broke out frequently, the government was powerless to ameliorate conditions. Government officials at the time were interested primarily in increasing their own property, and paid little attention to local administration. The gentry realized that whenever the officials could not protect local lives and property, they themselves must form self-defense corps consisting of farmers directly under their influence. Since, under such circumstances, there was no need for the gentry to obey governmental authority, the balance between the gentry and government officials collapsed.

The Opium War and the Taiping Rebellion hastened the downfall of the authority of the Ch'ing government. Although the government was able to suppress the Taipings and maintain control for another half century, the powers that conquered the Taipings were not the traditional armies but the new regionally based armies. These militia were organized and commanded by the gentry, who raised funds and recruited soldiers on their own initiative from their own native villages and towns. Once the gentry had seized the powers of collecting new taxes and recruiting soldiers, their status in local administration was greatly elevated.

Only one factor on the late nineteenth-century scene was unfavorable to the gentry: the entry of Western civilization. From the middle of the nineteenth century, Chinese civilization was forced to retreat step by step in face of the incursions of Western civilization. Because of their Confucian education, the gentry were the incarnation of traditional Chinese civilization. Thus the gradual retreat of Chinese civilization meant the retreat of the gentry as well. Since the modernization movement of Tseng Kuo-fan and Li Hung-chang aimed at introducing only the material aspects of Western civilization, such as machinery, instruments, science, and technology, it did not constitute a great threat to the gentry. However, the reform movement started by K'ang Yu-wei and Liang Ch'i-ch'ao endeavored to adopt not only the material aspects but also the political and economic institutions of Western civilization. The new reformers drew up a plan to abolish the civil Examination System. Since the position and prestige of the gentry were derived from the fact that they had passed the traditional examinations rather than from their property or their lineage, the abolition of the system meant the destruction of the source of their influence. Similarly, the movement to centralize government power constituted a threat to the gentry because their authority depended upon a fair degree of local autonomy.

For these reasons, the gentry were opposed to the reform movement of K'ang and Liang. Among the various reasons for the failure of the 1898 reform movement, one of the major factors must have been the opposition or at least the noncooperation of the gentry, who were the influential elite in the local areas.

Despite the opposition of the conservative Manchus and the

reluctance of the gentry, the political situation, both domestic and foreign, after the Boxer Rebellion of 1900 forced the Ch'ing government to take steps to modernize traditional political institutions. The government decided to prepare for a constitutional system and, as the first step, announced the abolition of the Examination System in 1905 and ordered the establishment of provincial assemblies and local self-government in 1908.

What, then, was the effect on the gentry? Before proceeding to this question, let us first consider the fate of the reform movement of K'ang and Liang. The movement continued even after 1905. But once the Ch'ing government had announced its own plan for constitutionalism, the reformists could do nothing more than expedite its inauguration. Consequently, the revolutionaries felt that Liang's movement was nothing but a defense of the Ch'ing, and attacked it violently. On the other hand, to the frightened Ch'ing government, the mild reform movement seemed as threatening as the revolutionary movement, whose aim was to overthrow the Ch'ing dynasty.

Liang's movement was thus attacked on all flanks and had its power broken. However, the defeat of the movement did not mean that other constitutional movements were wiped out of existence. Constitutional theorists like K'ang and Liang lost much of their influence but, from about this time, more down-to-earth movements demanding the immediate implementation of constitutionalism arose as powerful forces. It was the gentry and the rich merchants who supported this new type of constitutional movement because they now saw in the assemblies an even more effective means than the examinations for assuring their own status and power. They organized such groups as the Constitutional Preparatory Association of Kiangsu, the Constitutional Government Association of Hunan, and the Self-Government Association of Kwangtung, and appealed to the government to convene parliament immediately. They had, of course, been influenced by K'ang's and Liang's ideas but, unlike these pioneers, they were more deeply concerned with provincial matters and their own businesses than with national interests. Their goal seemed to be, "Our native province governed by ourselves."

In 1909, during the first provincial assembly election, the gentry and merchants saw a chance to achieve this objective. The qualifications for the candidates for membership were:

1. Male, native of the province, over twenty-five years of age, belonging to one of the following categories: (a) Those who had served in educational or other public service in the province more than three years. (b) Graduates of middle or high school in China or overseas. (c) Persons with degrees higher than licentiate (*sheng-yüan*). (d) Those who had held ranks higher than the seventh degree in the civil service, or higher than the fifth rank in the military service. (e) Those who possessed more than 5,000 *yüan* of working capital or of real estate;[1] or

2. Males who were not natives of the province, but were over twenty-five years old, had resided in the province for over ten years, and possessed more than 10,000 *yüan* of operating capital or of real estate.

Assemblies thus constituted offered the gentry new instruments of expression and influence. They ran as candidates for membership and ultimately dominated all of the provincial assemblies.

Most of the new constitutionalists were members of the upper gentry class, and some of them might be called industrial capitalists. Under the influence of these gentry were a great many members of the lower gentry class who were generally holders of the licentiate degree, located in their native cities, towns, or villages, and concerned only with the security of their own lives and property. As they were conservative by nature and disliked any kind of social change, they had looked askance at the constitutional movement of K'ang and Liang, particularly at the proposal to abolish the traditional examinations. However, once the Examination System had definitely disappeared and the inauguration of local self-government had been announced, they were forced to consider the effect of these measures on the local power situation. And probably detecting that the constitutional reforms could be used to preserve or even to strengthen their position in local administration, the gentry, or at least the politically minded and rather unscrupulous elements among them, suddenly changed their attitude and sought to take the lead in the constitutional reforms scheduled by the Ch'ing government. As soon as they discovered that graduates of the Western-style schools would be accorded the traditional degrees, they became enthusiastic about establishing new schools with Westernized curricula, for the purpose not of creating an

1. The Chinese silver dollar (*yüan*) was roughly equivalent in value to the U.S. dollar at this time.

opportunity for their sons and grandsons to learn about Western civilization, but of giving them an opportunity to acquire gentry status and privileges. At the same time, like the upper gentry at the provincial level, the lower gentry ran for election to the assemblies at the local level. As a result, most of the important posts in local self-government, such as chairman and vice-chairman of the assembly, mayor of the town, and village headman, were virtually monopolized by the lower gentry. In this way they could succeed not only in maintaining their traditional functions and authority in local administration, but also in giving them a legal basis for the first time. It was no longer necessary for them to curry favor with corrupt local officials.

Thus, with the abolition of the Examination System, the gentry did not lose their influence but instead, by a sharp about-face, utilized the change for their own advantage and expanded their influence. At the same time it was evident that they were to face opposition on new fronts.

First there was opposition from the common people. Since the gentry belonged to the same social stratum as the government officials, at times they had had to face popular revolts; but most of these riots had hitherto been started in opposition to the government officials, and had sometimes been instigated by the gentry themselves. However, toward the end of the Ch'ing dynasty there were numerous revolts in which the positions of the officials and the gentry were reversed. The gentry became the primary object of popular discontent, and at times the government officials sympathized with the masses. Previously, it had been government officials who collected taxes, embezzled money, and ordered the common people around. Now it was the gentry, as they became responsible for all the phases of new local self-government: building schools and railways, establishing self-government offices, and conducting censuses and local elections. Under these pretexts, they levied new taxes called contributions (*chüan*). There were undoubtedly cases where they actually needed money to build schools and railways and spent it for these purposes. Generally speaking, however, the gentry who held the local self-government posts were conservatives and not at all interested in Westernization. They were only interested in constitutional reforms for their own self-preservation, so very often they collected taxes in the name of self-government and pocketed the revenue. It was the common people who suffered from constitutional reforms. Many anticontribution or antireform revolts broke out, and school houses, self-government offices, and the homes of the gentry were attacked by the common people. The government officials, who had lost out to the gentry and therefore were not favorably inclined toward them, often sided with the masses in these revolts.

However, this did not mean that the gentry, who in the past had closely controlled the common people, completely lost their support. Although there were frequent revolts, the gentry maintained their popular influence.

Secondly, the gentry also had to meet the opposition of the central government. As I remarked earlier, the constitutional movement led by K'ang and Liang had tried to strengthen the central government's authority, and the administrative reforms introduced by the Manchu government at the end of the Ch'ing dynasty far exceeded the degree of centralization that had been advocated by K'ang and Liang. For instance, in 1906 the Manchu government tried to reduce the authority of governors-general and governors to the level of Japanese prefectural governors. The failure of this attempt was due to the opposition of Yuan Shih-k'ai, governor-general of Chihli at the time. In the next year, 1907, the Manchu government promoted Yuan and Chang Chih-tung, governor-general of Hupeh and Hunan, to the Grand Council. This was a promotion in name only since, in fact, governors-general at that time held actual power in military, civil, and financial affairs far exceeding that of Grand Councillors. The Manchu government took this step because it wanted to deprive these governors-general of their influence over the local gentry and commoners. In the following year, 1908, the Emperor Kuang-hsü died, and the child Emperor Hsüan-t'ung ascended the throne. Soon after this succession the Regent, Prince Ch'un, father of the new Emperor, forced Yuan to retire to Honan, since his influence in the Chihli area had not waned significantly even after his promotion to the Grand Council. The Regent then tried to fill most of the high ranking posts in the central government with Manchus, especially his own kinsmen, and thus to centralize political power in the hands of the Manchu aristocrats. The gentry, who were inclined to decentralization, naturally were not pleased by this kind of centralization. They tried to stop this tendency by forcing the Manchu government to implement a constitutional system immediately.

The greater the degree of centralization the Manchu government tried to enforce, the deeper the schism between the Manchu government and the gentry became.

Gentry Control of the Revolution of 1911

The conflict between the gentry and the Manchu government reached its climax in 1911 when the government issued an order to nationalize the trunk railways, trying to buy up the Szechwan-Hankow and Canton-Hankow lines, hitherto privately operated. The railway rights and interests had previously been in the hands of foreigners, but it was the gentry who had recovered them from the foreigners. The gentry were indignant at the government's plan to nationalize the railways by means of a foreign loan, and they called the step "taking the rights and interests away from the natives in order to give them to foreigners." At the gentry's instigation, riots occurred in Szechwan and the other provinces involved.

But, however wide the cleavage between the gentry and the Manchu government, the gentry never supported the revolutionary movement, which planned to overthrow the government. Certainly as far as the gentry were concerned, there was no advantage to being governed by the Manchu Emperor. They felt quite estranged from Manchu authority, especially at the end of the Ch'ing dynasty, when it became even more centralized and dictatorial. The Manchus could very well be overthrown. However, the gentry were afraid of the disturbances that would ensue after the outbreak of revolution. They were well aware that the masses would eventually turn around and attack them, even if the revolt was started at the gentry's guidance and instigation. It was for this reason that they wanted to maintain the status quo and could not side with the revolutionary movement. For example, although the riots in Szechwan were instigated by the gentry, the gentry suppressed them, though with great difficulty, when they realized that these riots were spreading beyond the scale they had originally anticipated.

The Revolution erupted in Wuchang on October 10, 1911, at a time when the revolts in Szechwan had not yet subsided. It was inevitable that the disturbances would spread to other places. Seeing this, the gentry reversed their position, just as they had in 1905 when the civil service Examination System had been abolished. They were afraid that the Revolution might turn against them, and they therefore decided to side with the revolutionaries. The conservative gentry, in order to protect themselves, led the Revolution.

The following characteristics in the development of the Revolution up until the Yuan Shih-k'ai regime was established in Peking in 1912 are to be noted:

1. There were fifteen provinces that became independent before the end of 1911: Anhwei (November 8), Chekiang (November 4), Fukien (November 9), Hunan (October 22), Hupeh (October 10), Kiangsi (October 31), Kiangsu (November 5), Kwangsi (November 7), Kwangtung (November 9), Kweichow (November 4), Shansi (October 29), Shantung (November 13), Shensi (October 22), Szechwan (November 27), and Yunnan (October 30).

2. In six of these provinces—Hupeh, Hunan, Kweichow, Shansi, Shensi, and Yunnan—soldiers of the New Army started their revolutionary war under the leadership of the revolutionaries. But in three of these six provinces—Hupeh, Shensi, and Shansi—members of the provincial assemblies and the gentry held the reins of civil administration by strongly cooperating with the revolutionaries. In Hunan, where the revolutionaries first seized control of the government, assembly members, with the aid of the gentry and rich merchants, staged a coup d'état ten days after the declaration of independence and took over the government from the revolutionaries. Almost the same process occurred in Kweichow.

3. In nine of the fifteen provinces, the gentry and rich merchants, led by the members of provincial assemblies, gathered at assembly halls and declared the independence of their provinces, as it was anticipated that soldiers of the New Army, influenced by the revolutionaries, might revolt very soon. These were Anhwei, Chekiang, Fukien, Kiangsi, Kiangsu, Kwangsi, Kwangtung, Shantung, and Szechwan. As a result, the gentry kept political power entirely in their own hands in these provinces.

4. In nine provinces—Anhwei, Chekiang, Kiangsi, Kiangsu, Kwangsi, Kwangtung, Kweichow, Shansi, and Shantung—high-ranking Ch'ing officials (e.g. governors-general, governors, and commissioners) were nominated by the revolutionaries or provincial assembly members as governors or heads of provincial military governments (*tu-tu*). In five out of these nine provinces, namely, Anhwei, Chekiang, Kiangsu, Kwangtung, and Shantung, they took up the posts.

5. In Fukien, Hupeh, Kiangsi, Kweichow, Shansi, Shensi, and

Yunnan, the posts of the governors were taken by military officials of the New Army, five of them holding high ranks as commanders of divisions, brigades, and regiments. In Chekiang, Kwangsi, and Szechwan, civilian governors were very soon replaced by military officials.

6. Graduates of the Japanese military academies governed Fukien, Kweichow, Shansi, Shensi, and Yunnan at the first stage of the Revolution, and later they also governed Chekiang, Kiangsi, Szechwan, and Yunnan. The civilian governors of Kwangtung and Anhwei had also been educated in Japan.

7. In seven provinces—Chekiang, Hunan, Kwangtung, Shansi, Shensi, and Szechwan—the governors were natives of their provinces. Among the provinces that were originally governed by outsiders, Anhwei, Kiangsi, Kwangsi, and Shantung were later to be governed by natives.

8. In every province, the New Army and the older provincial forces (*hsün-fang-tui*) were rivals.

These eight points account for the fact that although the Revolution of 1911 was touched off by the revolutionaries, it soon came under the control of the gentry, who had suddenly become supporters of the Revolution. The success of the Revolution of 1911 in overthrowing the monarchy was in large measure the work of the gentry. One of the reasons the Revolution of 1911 could be accomplished almost bloodlessly was that it was guided and brought to victory by the gentry, who controlled the common people or at least, through their proximity to them, were well informed about popular feelings and attitudes. At the same time, the fact that the gentry took the lead in the Revolution played a major role in determining the characteristics of the Revolution. During the initial stage, the revolutionaries established a Provisional Government at Nanking with Sun Yat-sen as President. But, after a short period of power struggle with Yuan Shih-k'ai, they were forced to succumb to Yuan's demands, whereupon Sun Yat-sen was replaced by Yuan Shih-k'ai as President, and the Provisional Government was removed from Nanking to Peking. This was the natural consequence of the Revolution of 1911, and the fulfillment of gentry hopes.

In these circumstances, the gentry could not possibly have favored Sun Yat-sen, who was the top leader of the Revolutionary Alliance. Indeed, the gentry who supported the Revolution in order to prevent it from proceeding to a more advanced and destructive stage, could find no better leader than Yuan Shih-k'ai; Yuan had caused the failure of the reforms proposed by K'ang and Liang; he had been an ardent supporter and promoter of the local self-government system and a vigorous opponent of the recentralization of the Manchu government; moreover, he had sufficient military power to overcome the revolutionary forces and to suppress mass uprisings. In view of the character of the Revolution it could do nothing more than abolish the Ch'ing dynasty and free the gentry from traditional restraints.

One of the conspicuous changes seen in the postrevolution society of China was that for the first time a Chinese official gained the freedom of choosing the location of his post. The gentry had long cherished the ideal of conducting local government by themselves. Even though they had almost approached this ideal of self-government in the late Ch'ing period, they had never been able to secure the coveted post of district magistrate (*chih-hsien*), because there had been a rigid stipulation prohibiting an official from serving in his native province. Now the gentry, through the success of the Revolution, could reach their goal at last.

The Gentry Turn Against Yuan Shih-k'ai, 1912–1913

Having seized power in their native places, the gentry supported the military governors of their provinces. The governorships were in many cases taken over by the provincial military authorities, whose forces were composed of native soldiers. Thus, a military clique made up of and supported by fellow provincials was established in each province.

However, once Yuan Shih-k'ai assumed central power, events did not proceed exactly the way the gentry anticipated. Contrary to their expectation, Yuan behaved like a dictator and strove to centralize power in his own hands. Trunk railways were nationalized by his order. When the House of Representatives was created, he ignored it. Since these developments were against their interests, the gentry lost confidence in Yuan and gradually became anti-Yuan. The reason the Kuomintang, the opposition revolutionary party, won the overwhelming majority in the first House of Representatives election in 1913 was that the conservative gentry had now become an anti-Yuan force. They supported the Kuomintang only to oppose Yuan's centralizing measures.

Despite this opposition, Yuan pushed ahead with his dictatorship, and finally tried to make himself Emperor. He was unable to succeed, however, and died in frustration in 1916 in the midst of campaigns against his imperial regime. One of the reasons an imperial regime could not be restored, even under Yuan's influence, was that the gentry, who were influential in local areas and who had been responsible for the overthrow of the Ch'ing, would not permit the restoration of a strong central authority.

The Dilemma of the Gentry in 1911

The role of the gentry in the Chinese Revolution of 1911 may be summarized as follows. The gentry were the local leaders of the old Chinese society. They tended to maximize their influence at the end of each dynasty, when the ruling power of the central government waned. It was not strange, therefore, that they increased their strength at the end of the Ch'ing dynasty. However, in the case of the Ch'ing there appeared, at the same time, a new factor quite unfavorable to the gentry—the advance of Western civilization. Since the prestige of the gentry was based upon traditional Chinese civilization, the modernization of China at the last stage of the Ch'ing inevitably endangered the power of the gentry in local administration.

Caught thus between one force that strengthened their influence and another that weakened it, the gentry dealt with this situation very cleverly. Although they encountered crises time and time again, each time they quickly reversed positions and overcame the crisis, thus utilizing it to their own advantage and expanding their own influence. The first crisis was the Hundred Days' Reform in 1898, when the abolition of the traditional examinations was proposed. But this was a simple matter for the gentry, because they were able to merge with the other conservative forces and to tide over the crisis easily. The second crisis was the abolition of the Examination System in 1905. This time they made a quick change and switched over to the constitutionalists. The third crisis was the Revolution of 1911. The gentry, making another quick reversal, unexpectedly became the leaders of the Revolution, rendering it nothing but a dynastic revolution, or a racial revolution of the Han Chinese against the Manchus.

Thus in overcoming these three crises, the gentry virtually took the lead in modernizing China, and for several years after the birth of the Republic their influence was at its peak. They could not disguise themselves forever and continue to increase their influence after the First World War, but they did maintain it, even under the control of the Kuomintang, until the emergence of the People's Republic of China in 1949. The tenacious strength of the gentry's influence was deeply rooted in traditional Chinese society. Modernization should have destroyed them, but instead it gave them a chance to expand their influence.

My interpretation of the Revolution of 1911 has been challenged by several Japanese scholars who argue that I do not recognize the importance of foreign pressure as a cause of the Revolution, and that I underestimate the role of the bourgeoisie.[2] I do not attach much importance to foreign pressure because I believe that, if one compares the political, economic, and social conditions in China from the late eighteenth century until the Opium War with the history of past dynasties, it is clear that the Ch'ing dynasty was doomed to destruction sooner or later, even if there had been no pressure from abroad. I thus view foreign pressure merely as a force that hastened the inevitable collapse of the Ch'ing dynasty.

Such a view, however, gives rise to certain problems. If my hypothesis is correct, then the 1911 Revolution becomes a dynastic revolution that did no more than topple the Ch'ing government. If the Chinese Revolution of 1911 is instead to be called a bourgeois democratic revolution, there must have been a newly rising bourgeois class. But was there really such a class that could be called a bourgeoisie in late Ch'ing China? Conceding for argument's sake that there was, I would ask three basic questions: 1. Did the revolutionary movement begin as a movement of the bourgeoisie? 2. Did Sun's Three Principles of the People (*San-min chu-i*) express the aspirations of the bourgeoisie? 3. How many bourgeois joined the revolutionary movement under the banner of the Three Principles of the People?

1. Although there are various theories as to when Sun Yat-sen first conceived of revolution, it is certain that it was 1894 at the latest, the time of the founding of the Society to Restore China's Prosperity. It is thus clear that it was not for the sake of the bourgeoisie that Sun set his mind on revolution. There is no doubt that

2. Nakamura Tadashi, "Shingai kakumeishi kenkyū o megutte; tokuni sengo no kenkyū dōkō." (Review of Japanese Studies of the 1911 Revolution, with Special Reference to the Works of Iwamura Michio, Hatano Yoshihiro, and Ichiko Chūzō), *Tōyō gakuhō, 14*:4 (1963), 113–24. Kikuchi Takaharu, "Chūgoku shihon shugika no tokushitsu; taigai boikotto undōshi yori mite." (Characteristics of the Capitalization of China: Evidence from the Study of Anti-foreign Boycotts in Modern China), *Rekishi kyōiku, 11*:1 (1963), 5–12.

Sun, like K'ang Yu-wei, was urged to revolution by feelings of nationalism and patriotism.

2. Granted that the bourgeoisie sought popular sovereignty (*min-ch'üan chu-i*), was mass welfare (*min-sheng chu-i*) really for their benefit? For Sun, mass welfare was a means to make inequality of wealth less severe in the future. If one takes the term at face value, it literally aimed at securing the "livelihood of the people" (*min-sheng*), and it would be farfetched to claim that this meant "for the sake of the bourgeoisie."

3. Who rallied to the revolutionary cause in response to the cry of the Three Principles? The peasants at the time were suffering many hardships and small uprisings were breaking out everywhere. But because Sun's principle of mass welfare did not aim at giving land to the peasants, they did not join the revolutionary cause, and the revolutionaries for their part made no attempt to aid them. The gentry, students, the New Army, and the secret societies account for many of the recruits to the Revolution. Some scholars claim that the students and the personnel of the New Army were bourgeois, but this has not been proved. It may be true that since such people went to school, they tended to be rich, and because they were literate, they tended not to be very poor. But it is illogical to say that they were bourgeois simply because they were educated and literate. There may have been bourgeois who did in fact enter the revolutionary movement. But it would be unreasonable to claim that the revolutionary movement as a whole was carried out on behalf of the bourgeoisie. One should notice here that the factor which attracted students, secret societies, and officers and soldiers of the New Army to the Revolution was neither popular sovereignty nor mass welfare, but simply the anti-Manchu racism called nationalism (*min-tsu chu-i*).

It is clear that Sun sometimes envisioned a new China modeled on the bourgeois democratic countries of the West, such as America, France, and England. But it would be wrong to conclude that Sun's movement was therefore one of bourgeois democracy, because the revolution that Sun conceived was for the sake of the nation and not for the sake of the bourgeoisie. His plan for a bourgeois democracy was no more than a means to make China strong, and if socialism or communism would accomplish the same end, then they would serve just as well. Sun's Three Principles, although they seem to have Western-style democracy as their aim, were in fact a complex mixture of ideological elements, including many which were very different from bourgeois democracy. This complexity did not stem from an attempt to make the ideology conform exactly to actual conditions in China, but came rather from a confused selection of Western ideas and techniques. It is impossible to term such a movement "bourgeois democratic."

One argument that the 1911 Revolution was bourgeois-democratic in character runs as follows: The 1911 Revolution was carried out by the revolutionaries, but as soon as it occurred, the constitutionalists joined the revolutionary forces whom they had previously opposed and the Revolution was carried to a successful conclusion. Since the constitutional party was composed of bourgeois, it is possible to term the 1911 Revolution a "bourgeois revolution." I cannot accept a logic that terms the constitutionalists bourgeois because at first they opposed the Revolution, and from this concludes that because they were bourgeois, it was a bourgeois revolution.

My own interpretation nevertheless has several points in common with some of the other interpretations by Japanese scholars.[3] For example, I agree with their emphasis on the role of the constitutional party in the Revolution, taking care, however, to distinguish among three different types within the constitutional party:

1. The members of the Self-Strengthening Society, the Society to Protect the Emperor, and the Political Information Institute, of whom the most notable were K'ang Yu-wei and Liang Ch'i-ch'ao.

2. Members of the provincial assemblies and men who had formerly been officials and had entered business in their native provinces, such as Chang Chien, T'ang Shou-ch'ien, and T'an Yen-k'ai. The establishment of provincial assemblies had been the most important of the constitutional reforms of the Ch'ing government in the period after the Russo-Japanese War, and it was to stimulate such reforms that these men founded such societies as the Constitutional Preparatory Association, the Constitutional Government Association, and the Kwangtung Self-Government Association.

3. People associated with the structure of local self-government, which had been instituted as part of the government's constitutional reforms.

In my view, the *gentry* were the common thread joining all three groups within the constitutional party. The members of the first groups were largely of gentry origin, but because they were

3. Ibid.

active on a national scale, not remaining in their own provinces, they had already ceased to function as gentry. The second group was composed of members of the upper gentry and was active on the provincial level. Many of them had formerly been officials, or held honorary posts in the Manchu government. A good number of this group lived in large cities and took an interest in industrialization. Those in the third group were active at the prefectural, district, and village levels, living in their home towns. Generally speaking, their status as gentry was lower than those in the second group, their wealth less, and their interest in industrialization not as keen. The first group was strongly nationalistic, patriotic, and politically conscious, while the second and third groups had fewer such feelings and tended to be conservative. But it is the role of these last two groups, especially the third, in the 1911 Revolution that I wish to emphasize. Within this third group, there were many who took advantage of the constitutional reforms of the Ch'ing government to make money, thus inviting frequent attacks from the peasantry. Social order at the end of the Ch'ing was extremely unstable, so that uprisings were likely to break out at the slightest agitation, no matter what the slogan of the agitator. The second and third groups were thus opposed to revolution, not out of loyalty to the Manchu dynasty, but rather from a fear of the social change which the upheavals of revolution would bring. The flames of revolution were already rising at Wuchang, and they feared that the disturbance would spread to their own provinces. But they lacked sufficient military strength of their own to prevent this, and the troops of the Ch'ing government were unreliable. They therefore hastily switched over to the side of the revolutionaries and proclaimed the independence of the provinces. While thus trying to protect themselves by nipping any disorder in the bud, they managed to seize the real political power in the provinces and strengthen their own political voice.

My reason for thus stressing the role of the second and third groups within the constitutional party is that it neatly explains how the exchange of political power was effected with almost no bloodshed. Finally, I contend that, even if those in the second group were largely bourgeois, as many people claim, it is still more appropriate to view the Revolution of 1911 as a dynastic revolution. According to many scholars, the bourgeoisie of the late Ch'ing was composed of former officials, landowners, and merchants, who, utilizing their special rights and position as members of the ruling class, eagerly devoted themselves to swelling their fortunes. If this definition is valid, then these bourgeois would be unwilling to upset the existing social order, and their only ambition would be to rise to higher positions within the present social order. Then did not their actions represent merely a power struggle within the ruling class? In these terms, the Revolution of 1911 turns out to be a dynastic revolution. This supposition is supported by two facts. One is that what attracted students, secret societies, and officers and soldiers of the New Army to the Revolution was nothing more than the anti-Manchu racism in Sun Yat-senism. The other is that no great economic and social changes can be detected between the periods before and after the Revolution. Of course, there was some progress in industrialization, but this may be explained as natural growth rather than the result of the Revolution.

Table 6.1. A Table of Governors (*tu-tu*) During the Revolution from October 1911 to March 1912

Province and Date of Revolution	*Governor*	*Background**
Hupeh (Oct. 10)	Li Yüan-hung	1) October 11 2) Hupeh 3) Tientsin Naval Academy 4) Brigade Commander
Hunan (Oct. 22)	Chiao Ta-feng	1) October 23 2) Hunan 3) Changsha High School 4) Kung-chin-hui
	T'an Yen-k'ai	1) October 31 2) Hunan 3) *chin-shih* 4) President, Provincial Assembly
Shensi (Oct. 22)	Chang Feng-hui	1) October 23 2) Shensi 3) Japanese Military Academy 4) Battalion Commander
Kiangsi (Oct. 24) (Oct. 31)	Ma Yü-pao (Kiukiang)	1) October 24 2) Anhwei 3) Peiyang Military Academy 4) Regiment Commander
	(Feng Ju-k'uei)	1) October 31 2) Hunan 3) *chin-shih* 4) Governor
	Wu Chieh-chang	1) November 2 2) Kiangsu 3) Kiangsi Military Academy 4) Brigade Commander
	P'eng Ch'eng-wan	1) November 12 2) Kiangsi 3) Japanese school 4) Revolutionary Alliance
	Ma Yü-pao	1) December 8
	Li Lieh-chün	1) March 1912 2) Kiangsi 3) Japanese Military Academy 4) Teacher, Yunnan Military Academy

Table 6.1 (*cont.*)

Province and Date of Revolution	*Governor*	*Background**
Shansi (Oct. 29)	(Li Sheng-to)	1) October 29 2) Kiangsi 3) *chin-shih* 4) Commissioner for Judicial Affairs
	Yen Hsi-shan	1) October 29 2) Shansi 3) Japanese Military Academy 4) Brigade Commander
Yunnan (Oct. 30)	Ts'ai Ao	1) October 29 2) Hunan 3) Japanese Military Academy 4) Brigade Commander
Kweichow (Nov. 4)	(Shen Yü-ch'ing)	1) November 3 2) Fukien 3) *chü-jen* 4) Governor
	Yang Chin-ch'eng	1) November 5 2) Szechwan 3) Japanese Military Academy 4) Regiment Instructor
	T'ang Chi-yao	1) March 2, 1912 2) Yunnan 3) Japanese Military Academy 4) Supervisor, Military Academy
Kiangsu (Nov. 4) (Nov. 5)	Ch'en Ch'i-mei (Shanghai)	1) November 4 2) Chekiang 3) Japanese school 4) Revolutionary Alliance
	Ch'eng Te-ch'üan	1) November 5 2) Szechwan 3) *lin-sheng* 4) Governor
Chekiang (Nov. 4)	(Tseng Yün)	1) November 3 2) Mongol 3) *fu-sheng* 4) Governor

Table 6.1 (*cont.*)

Province and Date of Revolution	*Governor*	*Background**
	T'ang Shou-ch'ien	1) November 4 2) Chekiang 3) *chin-shih* 4) Chief Manager of the Chekiang Railway Company
	Chiang Tsun-kuei	1) 1912 2) Chekiang 3) Japanese Military Academy 4) Brigade Commander in Canton
Kwangsi (Nov. 7)	Shen Ping-k'un	1) November 7 2) Hunan 3) *chien-sheng* 4) Governor
	Lu Jung-t'ing	1) February 8, 1912 2) Kwangsi 3) *chün-kung* 4) Commander in Chief
Anhwei (Nov. 8)	Chu Chia-pao	1) November 8 2) Yunnan 3) *chin-shih* 4) Governor
	Sun Yü-yün	1) November 28 2) Anhwei 3) Japanese school 4) revolutionary
Fukien (Nov. 9)	Sun Tao-jen	1) November 9 2) Hunan 3) *yin-sheng* 4) Division Commander
Kwangtung (Nov. 9)	(Chang Ming-ch'i)	1) November 8 2) Shantung 3) *chü-jen* 4) Governor-general
	(Lung Chi-kuang)	1) November 9 2) Yunnan 3) *chün-kung* 4) Commander in Chief

Table 6.1 (*cont.*)

Province and Date of Revolution	*Governor*	*Background**
	Hu Han-min	1) November 9 2) Kwangtung 3) Hosei University, Japan 4) Revolutionary Alliance
Shantung (Nov. 13)	Sun Pao-ch'i	1) November 13 2) Chekiang 3) *yin-sheng* 4) Governor
	Chou Tzu-ch'i	1) February 2, 1912 2) Shantung 3) T'ung-wen-kuan 4) Government official
Szechwan (Nov. 22) (Nov. 27)	Chang P'ei-chüeh (Chungking)	1) November 22 2) Szechwan 3) Chengtu High School 4) revolutionary
	P'u Tien-chün	1) November 27 2) Szechwan 3) *chin-shih* 4) President, Provincial Assembly
	Yin Ch'ang-heng	1) December 8 2) Szechwan 3) Japanese Military Academy 4) Supervisor, Primary Military School

* Explanation of Background Data

1) Date appointed or recommended.
2) Native province.
3) Academic background.
4) Former occupation.

The names in parentheses are those who were recommended but did not take office.

7. The Revolutionary Movement in Chekiang: A Study in the Tenacity of Tradition

Mary Backus Rankin

The early revolutionary movement in Chekiang was shaped by a group of intellectuals, mostly members of the Restoration Society, who succeeded in establishing pervasive contacts with secret society leaders. The movement gradually emerged from the reform movement after 1900 and began to be organized during 1904, partly under the influence of radical student centers in Tokyo and Shanghai. Revolutionaries then attempted to establish bases in the provincial towns and villages. However, in 1907 the promising organization which they had built up was badly shattered by the premature uprisings led by Hsü Hsi-lin and Ch'iu Chin, and never regained its effectiveness. Ultimately the overthrow of the government in 1911 was effected by a more conservative coalition of gentry, members of the provincial assembly, army officers, and somewhat different revolutionary allies in the Revolutionary Alliance.

Although the early revolutionary movement in Chekiang failed in the end, a study of its course reveals a great deal about the character of the radical intellectuals who led it and the problems of launching the kind of revolution they wanted in the interior of China. The Restoration Society revolutionaries, most of whom genuinely strove for sweeping social and political change, appeared isolated and ineffectual in their time. However, they initiated a radical, nationalistic trend in Chinese politics which was to continue into the Republic. The students who participated in the May Fourth Movement, those who protested against failure to resist Japanese aggression in the early 1930s, and those who finally turned to communism were following in the footsteps of the radical intellectuals of the last decade of the Ch'ing.

If one looks at the early revolutionary movement in Chekiang, it seems quite clear that despite their new Western-inspired radicalism, the Restoration Society intellectuals remained traditional in many ways. They were caught between two worlds, and their consequent inability to master either contributed to their failure. The ideology of their most admired leaders, such as Hsü Hsi-lin and Ch'iu Chin, was permeated by their versions of Western-inspired nationalism, anarchism, and individualism, but their psychology was shaped by the traditional concept of the self-sacrificing hero. Restoration Society radicals interpreted Western anarchism and terrorism in the light of their own traditions. Russian tragic-heroic figures, such as Sophia Perovskaya who helped assassinate Alexander II, could be easily assimilated to the list of Chinese romantic heroes. The revolutionaries' romanticism was further intensified by the frustrations inevitably suffered by a small number of intellectuals who sought to overthrow a large bureaucratic government and remake a slow-changing society. All three influences pushed the radical intellectuals toward assassinations and other individualistic, self-sacrificing acts. Both Ch'iu Chin and Hsü Hsi-lin were concerned more with their moral images than with the immediate effect of their behavior on the party organization. They believed that ultimately they would be vindicated by the righteousness of their cause.

The same traditional-modern ambiguity is reflected in the institutions the revolutionaries used. These were partly products of the movement for reform and modernization, partly revolutionary fronts, and partly in the familiar mold of such old-style instruments of protest as the Tung-lin Academy. Socially, many student revolutionaries had begun to acquire some characteristics of a Russian-type intelligentsia, and held vague ideas of a freer and more egalitarian society which was incompatible with the existing gentry-dominated countryside. Yet many came from scholar, gentry, or merchant families themselves, and when they began to organize for an uprising they behaved much like traditional scholar rebels, seeking alliances with both secret society leaders and the established gentry, and founding schools and militia as vehicles for their activities.

The history of the early movement in Chekiang illustrates some of the channels open to revolutionaries seeking to penetrate areas outside the major treaty ports. Cooperation of revolutionaries with modernizing members of the local elite anticipated the widespread cooperation between these two groups in 1911. The pre-1908 period also shows the weaknesses of the transitional organizations established by revolutionaries and the limits to the support afforded by their allies. The revolutionaries successfully managed to penetrate both the established elite level of the local social structure and the secret societies, but they failed to dominate or change either. They were thus frustrated in efforts to marshal enough force to achieve their aims and fell back on self-destructive and essentially symbolic gestures. The revolutionaries' difficulty in surviving long in one place again foreshadowed the situation in 1911, when the gentry and others cooperated with the revolutionaries within limits but by this very cooperation were usually able to prevent them from making basic changes in the local power structure.

Revolutionary Antecedents in Chekiang

Secret Societies

The oldest elements in the background of the Chekiangese revolutionary movement were the secret societies. Most important societies in the province were associated with the Triads that had originated in Chekiang and Fukien during the Manchu invasion. After the middle of the K'ang-hsi reign in the late eighteenth century, however, the Triads no longer actively opposed the dynasty. Moreover, although the total number of members gradually increased, they were fragmented into many small societies.[1] Apparently the new groups, founded for a variety of purposes, made use of the general Triad rituals, banners, ranks, and terminology. These esoteric rituals helped to attract recruits and to maintain superficial solidarity among members. However, there was no overall Triad organization, but rather an illegal or quasi-legal world of independent bands which sometimes cooperated and sometimes fought. Included were avowedly bandit groups, secret societies whose main purpose might waver between fraternity and rebellion depending on the current situation, and semiprivate gangs formed by an individual to enhance his local power. The boundaries between legal and illegal organization were not always clear. For instance, militia raised to keep order might on occasion shift to banditry or rebellion.

1. T'ao Ch'eng-chang, "Che-an chi-lüeh" (A Brief Account of the Chekiang Case), reprinted in *HHKM, 3,* 18; Feng, *Chung-hua, 1* (Shanghai, 1928), *2* (Shanghai, 1930), and *3* (Chungking, 1944), *2,* 6.

The term secret society used here actually covers a variety of organizations which had affiliated themselves with the locally dominant tradition in the world beyond the law. Unity under such circumstances was difficult to achieve, even under the impact of the mid-nineteenth-century Taiping Rebellion. The Taiping Rebellion, however, did revive secret society militancy and resulted in the emergence of a number of new groups that made use of the Triad heritage.

Besides this fresh antidynastic stimulus, the secret societies with which the revolutionaries developed contacts were shaped by a number of post-Taiping social and economic changes. A special legacy of the rebellion was the resettlement of large areas of uncultivated land, particularly in northern Chekiang, by immigrants (*k'o-min*) from other parts of Chekiang and from other provinces. The influx of new settlers, vagrants, and disbanded soldiers who were often not natives of the province led to disturbance and frequent banditry. Conflicts over property rights, exacerbated by cultural and linguistic differences, followed.[2] This, like the tension between the Hakka and native inhabitants of Kwangtung, favored the recruitment of secret society members. In addition, Chekiang recovered slowly from the devastation of the Taiping Rebellion,[3] a factor which intensified the usual late dynastic problems of official exactions, poor harvests, and famines. Finally, xenophobic reaction to Western encroachment in the form of hostility to Christian missionaries is evident in the frequency with which attacks on missionaries were associated with the history of the secret societies.

The secret societies with which the revolutionaries cooperated were fairly recently established Triad groups of up to 10,000 or 20,000 members. They have been most thoroughly described by T'ao Ch'eng-chang, who was their most active revolutionary organizer.[4] The Chung-nan Society (Chung-nan-hui) was the oldest

2. Feng, *Chung-hua, 2,* 11–12. Immigrants often used force against competitors for property. On the other hand, because they were a disruptive element, officials came to treat them unsympathetically, so there were legitimate grievances on both sides.

3. Ping-ti Ho, *Studies on the Population of China, 1368–1953* (Cambridge, Mass., 1959), pp. 243–44, 246.

4. T'ao, pp. 18–21, 52–76. Pages 18–21 contain short descriptions of each society and pages 52–76 contain biographies of revolutionaries and secret society members that provide additional information. Unless otherwise stated the information on the societies is from this source. T'ao is unquestionably the best-informed writer on the Chekiangese secret societies. However, his reliability is difficult to determine because

of these and produced many offshoots, including the Double Dragon, Crouching Tiger, and Dragon Flower groups. It had been brought from Hunan to Kiangsi and from there to Fukien and Chekiang. Probably it entered southern and western Chekiang immediately following the Taiping Rebellion. The White Cloth Society was first established in Wenchow during the Taiping Rebellion. After a brief decline it moved northwest to Chuchow and Yenchow. The salt smugglers also flourished in the disrupted post-Taiping years. The revolutionaries had closest connections with those who operated in the Chekiang-Kiangsu border area. The Double Dragon and Crouching Tiger societies were probably founded during the 1890s in Chuchow and Taichow respectively. The youngest organizations were the P'ing-yang and Dragon Flower societies, which were established about 1900 or 1901. The former was located in Chenghsien, south of Shaohsing, and the latter centered in Kinhwa, in the middle of the province.

The social composition of the societies is difficult to determine because of lack of biographical data. Rank and file members were presumably drawn from the usual assortment of peasants, villagers, and vagrants. A large number were immigrants. They formed the basis of the White Cloth Society and were a significant element in some of the bandit bands that had alliances with the more formally organized societies.[5]

The leaders on whom there is information include ex-soldiers, pugilists,[6] and educated men, some of whom were or claimed to be degree holders. Certain local merchants had high-level connections

---

other authors have often taken their information from him, particularly, e.g., the section on the Chekiang case in Feng, *Chung-hua*, 2. Accounts of secret society uprisings and missionary incidents in the *North China Herald* are generally roughly compatible with T'ao's account. Where I have found differing interpretations they will be indicated in the notes.

5. One such bandit band was formed by the brothers Kao Ta and Kao K'uei, who had moved from Taichow to Kinhwa. After getting in trouble with yamen underlings they fled to the mountains where they organized a bandit band. It became powerful enough to become a worthwhile ally and eventually the brothers reached agreements with several secret societies. Through these connections they were introduced to revolutionaries, frequented the Ta-t'ung School, and were finally killed in one of the unsuccessful uprisings after Ch'iu Chin's death in 1907.

6. In this context, pugilists or boxers were men who practiced ancient calisthenics and prescribed rituals of Buddhist-Taoist derivation. Through these they gained a harmony of mind and body that led to supernatural powers. As is well known, they had expected to be impervious to Western bullets in the Boxer Rebellion of 1900.

in the societies, but they usually remained in the background.[7] The original leader of the Chung-nan Society in Chekiang and his chief lieutenant had both belonged to Tseng Kuo-fan's Hunan Army. A branch leader who led a rebellion in 1900 was an ex-soldier whose chief assistants were a boxer and an elementary school teacher. The organizer of the Double Dragon Society was a poor itinerant boxer and watchman who had the backing and protection of his wealthy employer, who wanted a force available to seek revenge in a personal quarrel. The two salt smuggler leaders with whom the revolutionaries had the closest contacts were also, not surprisingly, from a low element of society. Before joining smuggling bands both had been drifters, had been in trouble with the law for gambling, and had served briefly in governmental armed forces.

Among the more highly educated leaders was the founder of the Double Dragon Society, who was a licentiate (*sheng-yüan*). The White Cloth Society had originated in militia established about 1860 for protection against the Taipings by the younger brother of the well-known official and scholar Sun I-yen. This group was chiefly used to suppress the Gold Coin Society which had risen in the Jui-an area south of Wenchow. When Tso Tsung-t'ang's imperial forces recaptured Chekiang, the younger Sun failed to stay on good terms with Tso and the White Cloth Society had to be disbanded.[8] However, some of the members who later migrated northwest brought the society with them and in Yenchow found a new leader in P'u Chen-sheng, a wealthy senior licentiate by

7. One such merchant secret society member was Lü Hsiung-hsiang, a friend of the Dragon Flower Society leaders. Through them he was introduced to the revolutionaries and was active in the Wen-T'ai-Ch'u Guildhall and the Ta-t'ung School, and later in the 1911 Revolution. Feng, *I-shih* (Shanghai, 1945–47), *3*, 114.

8. According to T'ao Ch'eng-chang, the White Cloth Society was founded by Sun I-yen himself. T'ao says Sun was contemplating rebellion, but disbanded the society when Tso Tsung-t'ang's troops approached Hangchow because it was then clear that any chance for an uprising was past. T'ao, p. 19. If true, this would be very interesting not only because Sun was a prominent official, but because during these years he was serving under Tseng Kuo-fan in campaigns against the Taipings. Since he must have been away from home most of the time it is difficult to see when he could have organized and supervised the society. The Communist author Wei Chien-yu says the society was founded by Sun I-yen's younger brother to help suppress the Gold Coin Society. This account seems more probable and I have followed it here. See Wei Chien-yu, "Hsin-hai ko-ming ch'ien-yeh ti Che-chiang hui-tang huo-tung" (Activities of Chekiangese Secret Societies on the Eve of the 1911 Revolution), in Hupeh Provincial Philosophical Society and Scientific Society, ed., *Hsin-hai ko-ming wu-shih chou-nien chi-nien lun-wen chi* (Essays in Commemoration of the Fiftieth Anniversary of the 1911 Revolution) (Peking, 1962), *2*, 542–43.

seniority (*sui-kung-sheng*) who held an official or quasi-official supervisory position over immigrant affairs. Because of his efforts on their behalf he became very popular with the immigrants and thus gained control of the White Cloth Society.

Some of the leaders of the two newest societies, the Dragon Flower and P'ing-yang, appear to have been intermediate figures between the student revolutionaries and the traditional scholars, gentry, and merchants who joined or founded societies. They began with traditional careers, but also had been exposed to Western ideas in modern schools. It is possible that their association with secret societies was an expression of their discontent, but they do not appear initially to have been founding protorevolutionary organizations. They did, however, have a good deal in common with the student revolutionaries, who developed their closest contacts with these groups. The founder of the P'ing-yang Society was Chu Shao-k'ang, a licentiate (*sheng-yüan*) and the son of a prosperous doctor. He originally established the society to avenge his father's murder, but came to work very closely with the revolutionaries. Even after the movement fell apart in mid-1907 he maintained his revolutionary contacts and after the Revolution eventually reached the rank of lieutenant-general. His chief assistant, Wang Chin-fa, was a military graduate under the old Examination System who had then studied in Japan. His relations with the revolutionaries were even closer than Chu's. After 1907 he continued to promote the interests of the Restoration Society in Chekiang and also aided T'ao Ch'eng-chang abroad. In the end he became closer to the revolutionary movement than to the secret societies.

One of the Dragon Flower leaders, Chang Kung, was also an intermediate figure.[9] He had been a member of two other societies before the Dragon Flower. In 1900 he was a student in Hangchow where he met reformist and radical intellectuals and promised to support T'ang Ts'ai-ch'ang's Hankow uprising. In 1903, although already a secret society leader, he obtained the provincial (*chü-jen*) degree. Not long after he also founded a short-lived radical

9. The two other major leaders of the Dragon Flower Society probably were not gentry. Shen Jung-ch'ing came from a well-to-do family but had been imprisoned. He has been described as a *hao-chieh* in Feng, *I-shih, 3,* 114. There is no information on Chou Hua-ch'ang's family. One of the Dragon Flower branch leaders, Chiang Lo-shan, had studied at the Hangchow Tzu-yang Academy in 1900 and he as well as Chang Kung had promised to support T'ang Ts'ai-ch'ang's uprising. He was the one who introduced Ch'iu Chin to Chang Kung. Yü Chao-i, *Ch'iu Chin nü-chieh* (The Heroine Ch'iu Chin) (Hong Kong, 1961), p. 51.

paper in Kinhwa. Chang continued contacts with the revolutionaries after 1907 and in 1909 was arrested and imprisoned.

The large number of societies of recent origin was indicative of a continuing surge of discontent following the Taiping Rebellion. Smaller bandit bands and some of the societies engaged in open robberies and there were instances of clashes between competing groups. Regardless of the specific causes for which they were founded, the secret societies came by degrees to oppose the established order. In 1900 the Chung-nan Society staged an uprising in southwest Chekiang under a leader who assumed a kingly title and established a court ritual.[10] The following year P'u Chen-sheng began to organize the members of the White Cloth Society into militia on the pretext of protecting the countryside against bandits. In late 1902 he seized upon the opportunity created by trouble between Catholic converts and the rest of the Yenchow populace to start an uprising under the guise of suppressing Christianity.

Anti-Christian sentiment was another product of the prevailing unrest. During the Boxer Rebellion there was a rash of attacks on Christians in Chekiang, although where secret societies were responsible they were not usually those with whom the revolutionaries later cooperated. Conflicts with Catholics in Yenchow, which formed the background for the 1902 White Cloth Society uprising, were not primarily caused by that society. Nonetheless, one account does indicate that rivalry existed between Christian converts and secret society members.[11] In contrast, the Crouching Tiger Society had been specifically created to oppose Westerners and it instigated a series of antimissionary incidents in 1900, in 1901, and again in 1903. After that year it was strongly influenced by the revolutionaries' anti-Manchu propaganda. However, it probably did not entirely abandon its antagonism to Christianity.[12]

T'ao Ch'eng-chang points to a general reduction of attacks on missionaries after 1904 and attributes this change to the success of

10. T'ao, pp. 50–51; *NCH, 45*:570 (Sept. 12, 1900); *45*:1107–08 (Nov. 21, 1900).

11. *NCH, 69*:1288 (Dec. 24, 1902); *70*:58 (Jan. 14, 1903).

12. T'ao, pp. 18–19; *NCH, 71*:882–83 (Oct. 23, 1903). T'ao states that the Crouching Tiger Society abandoned anti-Christian activities for anti-Manchuism. However, certain reports in the *North China Herald* that may be interpreted as referring to the Crouching Tiger Society indicate the conversion may not have been as complete as T'ao claims. See *NCH, 74*:541 (Mar. 17, 1905); *75*:13 (Apr. 7, 1905); *76*:276 (Aug. 4, 1905).

revolutionary propaganda in diverting the secret societies to antidynastic activities. Without belittling the revolutionaries' efforts, it seems possible that the shift may partly illustrate the sort of anti-Christian/antidynastic ambiguity in secret society attitudes which had been evident early in the Boxer Rebellion. In Chekiang it seems that as dissatisfaction increased and became more political, xenophobic opposition to Western Christianity was easily transformed into opposition to the Manchus as foreign rulers.

The secret societies in Chekiang presented an opportunity for the revolutionaries to move in and take advantage of an existing situation. Potentially discontented elements of the populace were already partially organized in relatively politically minded groups. There were many precedents for dissatisfied members of the educated classes to organize and make common cause with secret society or gangster bands. Such an alliance in the mid-nineteenth century is recorded in a verse repeated at initiation meetings that was preserved in a gazetteer of T'ung-ch'uan prefecture in Szechwan.[13] The Taiping rebels, who had many characteristics of a secret society or sect, had a number of educated men among their leaders besides Hung Hsiu-ch'üan.[14] The contemporary Nien rebels, a remnant of the White Lotus Sect, were joined by a number of lower gentry, and many of the leaders were drawn from members

13. This verse reads:

> "The happy ties of brethren are with incense
> fire solemnized;
> After burning the incense can there still be
> barriers between you and me?
> Officials, scholars—all into the fold are
> received;
> Yamen runner, servants, soldiers—none is barred."

Kung-ch'uan Hsiao, *Rural China: Imperial Control in the Nineteenth Century* (Seattle, 1960), p. 472. This verse was quoted by Hsiao from *T'ung-ch'uan fu-chih* (1897 ed.), 30 chuan, 17/42b.

14. Hung failed the examinations for the district (*hsiu-ts'ai* or *sheng-yüan*) degree several times. Wei Ch'ang-hui was a landlord and a pawnshop owner, an educated man who had experience in dealing with local officials. Shih Ta-k'ai had studied for some time, but had no examination degree and had turned to farming because of his lack of success. Among Wei Ch'ang-hui's adherents were merchants, a few rich farmers, and well-educated people. Some other scholars, such as Wang T'ao, Yung Wing, and possibly Ch'ien Chang, approached the Taipings after their initial successes and when rebuffed aided the government instead. Ssu-yü Teng, *New Light on the Taiping Rebellion* (Cambridge, Mass., 1950), pp. 29–34, 51–52, 58–59, 73.

of large clans who were men of local wealth and influence even when not degree holders.[15]

Clearly certain members of the local elite found it advantageous at times to supplement their influence (or make up for the lack of it) by founding or joining an illegal society. In times of disorder and breakdown of government control the likelihood that these groups would turn to rebellion increased.[16] A number of the societies with which the revolutionaries cooperated had been founded or taken over by members of the educated classes for their own purposes. When the revolutionaries began to operate in Chekiang they sought to do the same thing. The possibilities for cooperation may have been enhanced because a few of the secret society leaders came from backgrounds fairly similar to the revolutionaries' own.

Intellectual Circles

Chekiang had long been noted for its academies and libraries and for producing a large number of scholars. After the Sino-Japanese War of 1894–95 this provincial intellectual tradition began to develop along lines that eventually fed the revolutionary movement. During the 1890s interest in reform was particularly evident in the promotion of modern education rather than in industrial development or army modernization. Hangchow was the first center of modern thought, where such papers as the *Ching-shih-pao* (Journal of Statecraft), established in 1897, helped spread Western ideas among the educated classes.[17] Such "modern schools" as the Ch'iu-shih Academy were founded by progressive

15. Some gentry who joined the Nien enhanced their influence by bringing with them their own armed forces, which had originated as local militia raised according to imperial orders. Other gentry became independent leaders of bandit bands also based on militia. In the end they usually joined the Nien because both were in defiance of the government. Chiang Siang-tseh, *The Nien Rebellion* (Seattle, 1954), pp. 14, 45–54, contains interesting information on members of the local elite who joined the Nien.

16. The examples I have cited are all from the nineteenth century. However, this was not a new development. Yuji Muramatsu states that most of the "egalitarian leaders" who rebelled against the T'ang and Sung were actually from well-to-do landlord families or the merchant class. Among these were Chung Hsiang and Yang Yao, who were Taoist-Manichaean preachers and sorcerers as well as wealthy landowners. Yuji Muramatsu, "Some Themes in Chinese Rebel Ideologies," in Arthur Wright, ed., *The Confucian Persuasion* (Stanford, 1960), p. 259.

17. Ko Kung-chen, *Chung-kuo pao-hsüeh shih* (A History of Chinese Journalism) (Peking, 1955), p. 125.

gentry to teach both traditional Chinese and Western subjects.[18] The educational movement was not limited to the provincial capital of Hangchow, but spread to most of the sizable towns in the province. For instance, in Shaohsing the Chinese and Western School (Chung-Hsi hsüeh-t'ang) offered Western languages even though the teaching of Western ideas was discouraged.[19] The prominent scholar and educator Sun I-jang was said to have contributed to the founding of over three hundred primary and middle schools in the southeastern prefectures of Chuchow and Wenchow during the latter half of the 1890s.[20]

The spread of reform ideas caused an increasing number of young men to develop a serious interest in current events, which led them toward radical ideas. Many evidently traveled to Hangchow where they met in schools or reformist associations. One of the first groups to be organized was the Chekiang Society, which was founded in 1899 or 1900 to discuss current problems.[21] It was a transitional reformist organization, symptomatic of the growing concern over China's future which was soon to push some of the reformers toward revolutionary ideas. Its members came from all parts of the province. Some did not remain radicals, but a number of others were to play significant revolutionary roles in Chekiang or among Chekiangese students in Japan. Members of particular relevance to this study were Sun I-chung, Ch'en Meng-hsiung, Ao Chia-hsïung, and Chang Kung.

That incipient discontent might be translated into action was evident as early as 1900 when T'ang Ts'ai-ch'ang's younger brother visited Hangchow. Antigovernment feeling had recently been inflamed by the execution of two Chekiangese officials in Peking for advocating suppressing the Boxers.[22] Some students at such long

18. The Ch'iu-shih Academy later became Chekiang College (Che-chiang ta-hsüeh-hsiao) and finally the Chekiang Higher School (kao-teng hsüeh-hsiao). T'ao, pp. 10–11; Sheng Lang-hsi, *Chung-kuo shu-yüan chih-tu* (The System of Chinese Academies) (Shanghai, 1934), p. 239.

19. Ts'ai Yüan-p'ei as told to Huang Shih-hui, "Ts'ai Chieh-min hsien-sheng ch'ing-nien shih-tai" (The Youth of Ts'ai Chieh-min), *KKWH, Ko-ming chih ch'ang-t'ao yü fa-chan, Hsing-Chung-hui,* 2, 364. Ts'ai briefly directed this school in 1898 and 1899, but had to resign because of his support of two reformist faculty members.

20. Arthur W. Hummel, ed., *Eminent Chinese of the Ch'ing Period* (Washington, D.C., 1943–44), p. 678. Sun I-jang was the son of Sun I-yen.

21. T'ao, p. 68; Feng Tzu-yu, *Chung-kuo ko-ming yün-tung erh-shih-liu nien tsu-chih shih* (Twenty-six-Year Organizational History of the Chinese Revolutionary Movement) (Shanghai, 1948), p. 53.

22. Hummel, pp. 312, 945.

established schools as the Tzu-yang Academy promised support for T'ang's Hankow uprising, although his rapid failure prevented them from actually taking action.[23]

The chief academic center of early radical activity in Hangchow, however, was the Ch'iu-shih Academy,[24] which in both the period of its existence and the composition of its faculty bridged the transition from the reform movement. Such men as Ch'en Fu-ch'en, who was to be president of the Chekiang Provincial Assembly in 1911, reinterpreted the Confucian classics in their lectures to justify modern ideas. At the same time Chang Ping-lin had briefly given anti-Manchu lectures in 1898 before fleeing to Taiwan.[25] Radical ideas current in the school finally brought a clash with the governmental authorities in 1901. Sun I-chung, then lecturing on Chinese literature at the Academy, wrote an essay "On Abolishing the Queue" ("Tsui-pien wen") for a student literary society. A student changed Sun's straightforward term "this dynasty" to "the bandit Ch'ing" (*tsei-Ch'ing*). News of the manuscript eventually reached the governor. In the end no disciplinary action was taken, but Sun had to leave Hangchow.[26] Not long after, he and a number of others from the school went to Japan where they were among the founders and members of radical organizations there. In particular, they formed the nucleus of the staff of the radical *Che-chiang-ch'ao* (Tides of Chekiang).

These early radical centers were not yet revolutionary and were not of great importance except as indications of an indigenous intellectual ferment which by 1903 seems to have penetrated many of the main towns of Chekiang. This penetration was on a small scale, but it antedated the first significant influx of radical students returning from Japan in late 1903 and 1904. The way was thus eased

23. T'ao, p. 20; Yü Chao-i, *Ch'iu Chin* (Hong Kong, 1956), p. 118. The Tzu-yang Academy later became the Jen-ho district elementary school as part of the imperial government's plan to reorganize and modernize education. Sheng Lang-hsi, p. 239. It is not to be confused with the academy of the same name in Soochow, Kiangsu.

24. Chou Ya-wei, "Kuang-fu-hui chien-wen tsa-i" (Miscellaneous Recollections of Experiences in the Restoration Society), *HHKMHIL, 1,* 624. Near the Ch'iu-shih Academy on the same street was the Wu-pei hsüeh-t'ang, a military academy to which the first revolutionary ideas in the Chekiangese army have been traced.

25. T'ao, p. 11; Ma Hsü-lun, "Wo tsai hsin-hai che-i-nien" (My Experiences During the Year 1911), *HHKMHIL, 1,* 170, 176. Chang Ping-lin was a friend of Ch'en Fu-ch'en, who warned him he was in danger of arrest. It seems possible that acquaintances developed or furthered in this school contributed to revolutionist-constitutionalist cooperation in 1911.

26. T'ao, pp. 10–11; Feng, *Chung-hua, 2,* 3; Ma Hsü-lun, pp. 176–77.

for a rapid organization of revolutionary forces by intellectuals who had acquired or intensified their radicalism in Japan and Shanghai.

The Restoration Society

Most of the important figures in the revolutionary movement in Chekiang spent some time either studying in or frequenting student circles in Tokyo or Shanghai. They were thus exposed to the nationalistic, antiauthoritarian, and radical atmosphere which predominated in many of the student organizations. Student radicalism was intensified in the spring of 1903 during the agitation over Russian refusal to make a scheduled withdrawal of troops from Manchuria without additional concessions from China. The break between the government and the radical intellectuals was then dramatized early in the summer by the arrest of six people connected with the revolutionary newspaper *Su-pao*.[27] By mid-1903 the revolutionary movement had consequently emerged as a distinct entity from more vaguely defined reformist and radical currents. Almost immediately it began to shift away from open verbal propagandistic attacks on the government toward more clandestine active attempts to organize its overthrow. The most significant developments for the revolutionary movement in Chekiang were the decision in late 1903 of several Chekiangese students in Japan to work for an uprising against the Ch'ing government and the founding of the Restoration Society in Shanghai in late 1904.

In the fall of 1903 about ten members of the Chekiang students' provincial club resolved to form a revolutionary organization. They consulted Kung Pao-ch'üan, Wei Lan, and T'ao Ch'eng-chang, other Chekiangese radicals then in Japan. In December 1903 or January 1904 they decided that T'ao and Wei should go to Chekiang and Anhwei to make contacts with secret societies. Kung was to go to Shanghai and two other students were to establish connections with Huang Hsing in Changsha.[28]

In Shanghai the Restoration Society was partly an outgrowth of radical activity in that city during 1902 and 1903, and partly an

27. Y. C. Wang, "The *Su-pao* Case: A Study of Foreign Pressure, Intellectual Fermentation, and Dynastic Decline," *Monumenta Serica, 24* (1965), 84–129. The draft of this article was first discussed at the Conference on the Revolution of 1911 from which the present volume emerged.

28. T'ao, p. 17; Shen Tieh-min, "Chi Kuang-fu-hui erh-san shih" (Recollections of Two or Three Things about the Restoration Society), *HHKMHIL, 4,* 131–33. Shen was one of the students who went to Changsha.

attempt to answer the need for more effective organization in the face of growing revolutionary activity. Despite the setback caused by the suspension of the intensely nationalist newspaper *Su-pao,* radicals had quickly reassembled in Shanghai. To the old group were added other revolutionaries who had returned from Japan to agitate in China. Kung Pao-ch'üan established an assassination corps (*an-sha-t'uan*) in Shanghai.[29] Revolutionaries active in other provinces, including T'ao Ch'eng-chang and Huang Hsing, used the city as a meeting place, a source of arms, or a place of refuge.[30] When T'ao Ch'eng-chang came to the city in the fall of 1904, he and Kung Pao-ch'üan discussed organizing a society along the lines originally contemplated in Tokyo. Ts'ai Yüan-p'ei was then the best known revolutionary figure in Shanghai and, while T'ao remained temporarily in the background, Kung invited Ts'ai to head the group.[31]

The party's members were drawn mainly from young intellectuals of Chekiang, Kiangsu, and Anhwei, many of whom had studied in Japan. In Chekiang a particular effort was made to bring secret society leaders into the party. During the first half of 1907 Ch'iu Chin went even further by attempting large-scale enrollment of secret society members.

The Restoration Society was originally conceived as a highly secret group. New recruits took a blood oath to be faithful to the revolutionary cause and were not supposed to know the identification of others in the party until they received orders to carry out some joint task.[32] However, the party was actually weakly led, loosely disciplined, and far from exclusive. Not all radicals who worked intimately with members in Chekiang were willing or allowed to join.[33] In other cases, such members as Wu Yüeh inde-

29. Feng, *I-shih, 5,* 61.

30. T'ao, pp. 23–24; Chün-tu Hsüeh, *Huang Hsing and the Chinese Revolution* (Stanford, 1961), p. 20. T'ao made at least two trips to Shanghai during 1904. Huang Hsing also used the city as a contact point, a source of arms and ammunition, and briefly as a refuge when his plans for a November uprising in Hunan failed.

31. Shen Tieh-min, pp. 133–34. According to Shen, T'ao and Kung were the main architects of the Restoration Society, but T'ao hesitated to approach Ts'ai Yüan-p'ei because of Ts'ai's high scholarly reputation. Therefore, Kung and Ts'ai established the society, and it was arranged that Ts'ai would personally ask T'ao to join.

32. Ch'en Wei, "Kuang-fu-hui ch'ien-ch'i ti huo-tung pien-tuan" (Miscellany about the Activities Preceding the Founding of the Restoration Society), *HHKMHIL, 4,* 127.

33. For instance, Ao Chia-hsiung refused to join and Wei Lan was mistrusted by Ts'ai Yüan-p'ei and discouraged from joining. T'ao, p. 17.

pendently pursued their own schemes. Although widely respected for learning and character, Ts'ai Yüan-p'ei was an ineffectual revolutionary leader. Members did not look to him as the real authority in the party.[34] Without strong central direction, the scene of the party's activities was determined by where its more forceful members developed their own groups. T'ao Ch'eng-chang and Hsü Hsi-lin soon emerged as the real leaders. Because they already had a network in Chekiang, the center of Restoration Society activities almost immediately shifted away from Shanghai to the towns of that province.

Organization of the Revolutionary Movement in Chekiang

The development of the revolutionary movement in Chekiang can be roughly divided into three periods. 1904 and 1905 were years of intense activity in establishing contacts with secret societies and founding schools and other organizations. The establishment of the Ta-t'ung School in Shaohsing was the culmination of this phase. During 1906 the leading revolutionaries diverted their attention to other projects, dissensions arose, and the Restoration Society organization in Chekiang threatened to disintegrate. Toward the end of 1906 a new impetus was provided by plans for an uprising to support the Revolutionary Alliance revolts in Hunan and Kiangsi. Although this project proved abortive, the momentum thus generated led directly into a final phase of planning for a major uprising centered in Chekiang under the leadership of Ch'iu Chin in cooperation with Hsü Hsi-lin in Anking. Failure in July 1907 was followed by sporadic secret society uprisings during the rest of the year, but these were scattered and anticlimactic, without significant effect.

The three outstanding figures among the Chekiangese revolutionaries during these years were T'ao Ch'eng-chang, Hsü Hsi-lin, and, during 1907 only, the woman revolutionary Ch'iu Chin. All three were in their late twenties or early thirties at the time. They all came from well-educated or lower gentry families[35] and had re-

34. Ch'en Wei, p. 127.

35. T'ao came from a family that had lived in Kuei-chi district of Shaohsing prefecture. He had an uncle who was probably a licentiate (*hsiu-ts'ai*). Hsü Hsi-lin's father was a merchant who may have held a low degree. A cousin was an ex-governor. Ch'iu's father had a low degree and served as a legal secretary and minor official. Her grandfather was a prefect.

Most of my biographical information on T'ao comes from Chang Huang-ch'i, "Kuang-fu-hui ling-hsiu T'ao Ch'eng-chang ko-ming shih" (The Revolutionary

ceived traditional educations as youths. In various ways each had partially set aside classical studies for modern subjects.[36] All had gone to Japan where their previous discontent had been concretely channeled into revolutionary activity.

Despite these similarities, T'ao was much more conservative and cautious than the other two. Information about him is scarce, but he seems to have been less influenced than Ch'iu and Hsü by new Western ideas. After 1908 he joined Chang Ping-lin in opposition to Sun Yat-sen and in 1910 they revived the Restoration Society to combat the Revolutionary Alliance in Southeast Asia and Japan. Very probably his views were rather similar to those of Chang, with whom he was able to cooperate until the Revolution brought him back to Chekiang. Although T'ao was an excellent organizer with a good ability to assess practical possibilities, his reserved temperament set him somewhat apart from many of the other Chekiangese revolutionary intellectuals. He was unable to continue to work with many of them after 1906; this made his future activities in the province ineffective and deprived the movement in Chekiang of his much needed steadying influence.

Hsü Hsi-lin and Ch'iu Chin, who happened to be distant cousins, were revolutionary romantics with compelling personalities and a flair for dramatic action. Both had been pushed toward revolution by family problems as well as by concern for China's future. Hsü was in constant conflict with his conservative father. Ch'iu, after enjoying an exceptionally indulgent upbringing, was particu-

---

Activities of the Restoration Society Leader T'ao Ch'eng-chang), *HHKM, 1*, 521–29. Information on Hsü is from T'ao, pp. 55–58, and Chinese Kuomintang, Central Executive Committee, Committee for the Compilation of Materials on Party History, comp., *Ko-ming hsien-lieh chuan-chi* (Biographies of Revolutionary Martyrs) (Chungking, 1941), pp. 183–208. In contrast to the relatively scarce amount of information about T'ao and Hsü there are numerous biographies of Ch'iu Chin, although they are mostly highly uncritical. Among them are Ch'iu Ts'an-chih, *Ch'iu Chin ko-ming chuan* (A Revolutionary Biography of Ch'iu Chin) (Taipei, 1953); P'eng Tzu-i, *Ch'iu Chin* (Shanghai, 1941); *Ko-ming hsien-lieh chuan-chi* (Biographies of Revolutionary Martyrs), pp. 209–30. Ch'iu's poems and essays have been printed in many collections. The most complete is *Ch'iu Chin chi* (The Collected Works of Ch'iu Chin) (Shanghai, 1960).

36. T'ao was said to have become interested in "new books" as a youth. Hsü preferred mathematics, astronomy, and geography to literary studies and later became interested in Western subjects. Ch'iu enthusiastically studied Western history, science, and philosophy after leaving her husband. As far as I know, however, none knew any Western language and their knowledge of the West was rather superficial. All had received fairly good traditional educations as youths and never completely rejected this inheritance.

larly distressed by marriage to a husband less talented and much more conventional than she. Ch'iu, at least, never lost her love for Chinese history and poetry and it seems likely that Hsü, too, remained attached to much of Chinese tradition. Both, however, did make decisive breaks with their past life and were decidedly influenced by Western ideals of liberty and equality.

As part of this break Ch'iu and Hsü turned from the orthodox Confucian morality. Nonetheless, they did not find their main substitute in Western beliefs, but in the equally traditional, if less officially sanctioned, idea of the hero. They were adventurers (*chieh*) pursuing new goals. This influence can be seen in the few surviving examples of Hsü Hsi-lin's writings and in his testimony after he assassinated the Manchu governor of Anhwei, En-ming.[37] It is explicit in many of Ch'iu's poems.[38] She wished singlehandedly "to rescue the ancestral country." Her ambition could not "decay" and at the "war drums' sound" fury welled up in her heart.[39] Along with exhilarating gifts of personality and morality, Ch'iu also saw herself sharing the isolation which was traditionally the hero's lot. Fated to a painful role, she had deserted friends, wealth, and honor to requite her ancestors.[40] The only reason to preserve her life was so she might sacrifice herself for her country. The rewards would come from the personal satisfaction of proving that she was worthy of being included among the ranks of heroes,[41]

37. E.g. in "Ch'u-sai" (Crossing the Frontiers), in Hsiao P'ing, ed., *Hsin-hai ko-ming lieh-shih shih-wen hsüan* (Selected Writings of Martyrs of the 1911 Revolution) (Peking, 1962), p. 129. Hsü Hsi-lin's testimony has been printed in numerous standard sources. See T'ao, pp. 80–81.

38. The motif of the hero is obvious in many of Ch'iu's poems. Sometimes it is applied directly to herself, sometimes to others—as to the Dragon Flower Society branch leader Chiang Lu-shan, and sometimes as part of the general association of the revolutionary movement with a world of dragons, tigers, and raging seas where only the brave might prevail. Ch'iu makes frequent reference to great figures of Chinese mythology, history, and historical fiction, particularly those in *The Romance of the Three Kingdoms.* It is possible to match roughly Robert Ruhlman's description of the traditional ideal hero with excerpts from her various writings. See Robert Ruhlman, "Traditional Heroes in Chinese Popular Fiction," in Arthur Wright, ed., *The Confucian Persuasion* (Stanford, 1960), pp. 151–52. Ch'iu also assumed some of the external trappings of a hero. She was proud of her abilities to ride horseback, use a sword, and drink wine. She often carried a short sword in her belt.

39. Ch'iu Chin, "Pao-tao ko" (Sword Song), in Hsiao P'ing, p. 140.

40. Ch'iu Chin, "Chi Hsü Chi-ch'en" (To Hsü Chi-ch'en), in Hsiao P'ing, p. 143.

41. Ch'iu Chin, Letter to Wang Shih-tse, in *Ch'iu Chin chi,* pp. 44–45. Ch'iu's preoccupation with self-sacrifice was also connected with her feminism. Superior men had already died for the revolutionary cause, but no woman had done so. This was a disgrace she might remedy.

and from whatever honor might be awarded her after death.[42] It would not matter if she died without achieving her revolutionary aims. More important than immediate practical success was the moral victory which would come from unswerving self-sacrifice. Since Ch'iu and Hsü shaped the course of the attempt to initiate revolution in 1907, their attitudes were to have a strong influence on the future of the whole revolutionary movement in that part of China.

Establishment of Secret Society Contacts

When the revolutionaries began to plan for an uprising in Chekiang their initial efforts were directed toward the secret societies. Since the societies were illegal, secret, and esoteric, the revolutionaries needed personal introductions from mutual acquaintances in order to approach their members. Once a few contacts had been established, further introductions followed and a network of relationships could be constructed. Revolutionaries were then established as a cooperating rather than a competing group on the extralegal local scene.

T'ao Ch'eng-chang and Wei Lan were mainly responsible for the initial success of this policy, which required much traveling and talking. An example of their efforts was an extensive tour of the province which they undertook early in 1904. Through the returned student Sun I-chung they were introduced to the White Cloth Society leader P'u Chen-sheng who was jailed in Hangchow because of his 1902 uprising. P'u gave them a list of names and introductory passes to those places where his society was strong. With this help T'ao and Wei traveled upriver from Hangchow as far as Chü-chou. They then turned east toward the coast making contacts in the prefectures of Chuchow, Wenchow, and Taichow. In the late spring T'ao returned to Hangchow and Shanghai. Meanwhile, Wei Lan successfully established relations with the leaders of the Dragon Flower, Double Dragon, and Crouching Tiger societies. The immediate goal was an uprising in November in conjunction with the Society for China's Revival in Hunan. This attempt never materialized, but these contacts provided a foundation for a broad plan of organization and indoctrination.[43]

The Chekiangese societies were so fragmented that it was neces-

42. Ch'iu Chin, "Tui-chiu" (To Wine), in Hsiao P'ing, p. 142.

43. T'ao, pp. 23–25, 54–55; Chang Huang-ch'i, pp. 522–23; Feng, *Chung-hua*, 2, 9–10.

sary to try to impose some order if the revolutionaries were to rely on them as an effective fighting force. Revolutionaries, therefore, attempted to establish their own organizations that would be intermediate between the secret societies and the revolutionary party. Brief accounts of two such efforts by T'ao Ch'eng-chang and Ch'iu Chin survive. Both organizations remained largely paper schemes with little practical consequence. In addition, it is uncertain whether T'ao wrote his regulations in 1904 or 1905 or during 1908 in a later attempt to organize secret societies along the Yangtze Valley.[44] However, they are still worth considering here because T'ao's methods of dealing with the societies were probably constant and they illustrate the more traditionalistic facet of the revolutionaries' approach to the problem.

T'ao's technique was to attempt to establish a society of his own which also used the name Dragon Flower Society. The new organization was devised from a mixture of traditional secret society and bureaucratic forms. T'ao took great pains to show that the new system meant no sharp break with the traditional Triad hierarchy and each society was to keep its old slogans, ceremonies, and passwords. Organization was along military lines. The field command was divided into five armies under grand commanders (*ta-tu-tu*). Below were nine grades ranging down to rank and file members. T'ao based his titles on T'ang and Ming official titles and equated each with the corresponding Triad and smugglers' terms. Traditional incentives and punishments were promised, even to the ex-

44. T'ao Ch'eng-chang, "Lung-hua hui chang-ch'eng" (Regulations of the Dragon Flower Society), *HHKM, 1*, 534–44. There is no date on these regulations. It has generally been believed that they were written during the 1904–06 period when T'ao was most active in organizing the secret societies. E.g. the date 1904 is given in Wang I-sun, "Hsin-hai ko-ming shih-ch'i tzu-ch'an chieh-chi yü nung-min ti kuan-hsi wen-t'i" (The Question of Relations between the Bourgeoisie and the Peasantry During the Period of the 1911 Revolution), in *Hsin-hai ko-ming wu-shih chou-nien chi-nien lun-wen chi, 1*, 128.

However, the date 1908 is given in Hirayama Shū, Commercial Press Translation Bureau, trans., *Chung-kuo pi-mi she-hui shih* (A History of Chinese Secret Societies) (Shanghai, 1912), p. 80. Wei Chien-yu argues that the regulations were written in 1908 mainly on the grounds that the association was obviously distinct from the original Dragon Flower Society and that the second article of the regulations uses both the names Revolutionary Association and Dragon Flower Society. Revolutionary Association (*ko-ming hsieh-hui*) was the name generally given to the group in which T'ao tried to unite secret societies from Kiangsu, Chekiang, Fukien, Anhwei, and Kiangsi in 1908. Wei Chien-yu, pp. 538–39. T'ao was also appointed Grand Commander (*ta-tu-tu*) in 1908 and the five armies in the regulations correspond to the five provinces. These points are still not conclusive, however, especially since T'ao might have made use of earlier ideas in 1908, and the question remains open.

tent of offering rewards or threatening vengeance once a new dynasty was established.

Along with the problem of organization went the question of ideological appeal. T'ao's particular approach, which presumably reflected his own views as well as a deliberate strategy, stayed close to traditional lines of thought. In an essay preceding the regulations of his Dragon Flower Society, T'ao sought to revise the traditional attitude toward rebellion to encourage greater initiative in translating popular grievances into an attempt to overthrow the dynasty. By quotations from Confucius and Mencius, he rather laboriously justified the people's right to rebel against oppressive rule without reliance on the will of heaven. The distinction between essentially cyclical traditional rebellion and fundamental Western-inspired revolution remains thoroughly unclear, however. Generally there is little evidence that T'ao had assimilated Western ideas or acquired new images. He held out the promise of a traditionally utopian society characterized by common land ownership, light taxation, few soldiers, and ample food and shelter for all. On the other hand, no picture of the future form of government emerges. A republic, it seems, would ensure able and popular governors reminiscent of the legendary era of Shun and Yao. If the evils inherent in hereditary monarchy were avoided it would not particularly matter what alternative type of organization was chosen.

T'ao's approach was not typical of that used by many of his associates. During 1904 and 1905 the student revolutionaries, with secret society aid, began to flood the province with standard revolutionary works: the writings of Tsou Jung and Ch'en T'ien-hua, periodicals published by student groups in Japan, and radical newspapers from Shanghai.[45] These were apparently used to attract recruits to the secret societies as well as directly to the revolutionary movement.[46]

Nonetheless, the main effort was to bring the secret society members closer to the revolutionaries rather than to accommodate the

45. T'ao, p. 25.

46. That some success was achieved in spreading revolutionary propaganda is indicated by a case that occurred in the middle of 1906. A boxer named Ts'ao sought to enter the Dragon Flower Society, and Chang Kung gave him a copy of a famous radical pamphlet "Meng hui t'ou" (About face!) to read. Ts'ao kept the book with him, read it many times, and lectured on it. One day he lost it in a scuffle with some cattle robbers, was denounced to the authorities, and executed. This case provided good publicity for the book and increased its circulation in the Kinhwa villages. T'ao, pp. 12–13; Feng, *Chung-hua,* 2, 5.

revolutionary movement to the Triad tradition. When Ch'iu Chin sought to unite the secret societies in 1907, her method was to enroll their members in the Restoration Society, which she reorganized into sixteen grades of membership to better embrace the secret society hierarchy. She did not, however, use traditional titles, but designated grades either by letters of the English alphabet or by characters from a four-line verse she composed to reflect anti-Manchu aims.[47] Similarly, Ch'iu devised a Restoration Army in which the ranks were based on the Japanese modern military hierarchy with a number of additional titles and somewhat altered terminology.[48]

In the preface to her Restoration Army regulations, Ch'iu's ideas reflected Tsou Jung and Ch'en T'ien-hua, not Confucius and Mencius. Under the twin pressures of Manchu tyranny and Western aggression (for which the Manchus were held responsible) a critical point had been reached. Now the Chinese race could escape annihilation only if individuals were willing to risk death for the revolutionary cause and, conversely, individuals could not long survive if the race as a whole were obliterated. The long history of slavish subservience to the Manchus had only brought debasement of the Chinese character. A corrupt and oppressive government extracted taxes, but gave the people no voice in political affairs. Constitutional proposals were not remedies, but merely devices to increase Manchu power at the expense of the Chinese. The time, therefore, had come to wipe out over two hundred years of humiliation by overthrowing the dynasty.

Ch'iu Chin and T'ao Ch'eng-chang chose two possible approaches to the problem of devising contacts with secret societies that could be translated into support for the revolutionary cause. Both, however, chose to use the societies as their channel for relations with the rural populace and so remained within the traditional framework of political power. The secret societies were not class organizations, but embraced men of a wide variety of social backgrounds including some scholars, gentry, and merchants, peasants, vagrants, and others who were essentially *déclassé* in

47. T'ao, p. 62.

48. Ibid., pp. 77–79. Ch'iu's regulations for the Restoration Army appear in numerous other sources, including the Grand Council archives on the Ch'iu Chin case in *HHKM, 3,* 206–10; *KMWH, 1,* 136–39; *KKWH, Ko-ming chih ch'ang-tao yü fa-chan, T'ung-meng-hui, 3,* 267, 269–72. The Japanese ranks appear in H. S. Brunnert and V. V. Hagelstrom, *Present Day Political Organization of China* (Shanghai, 1912), pp. 293–94.

terms of the conventional classifications.[49] The revolutionary intellectuals were not "going to the people" in the Russian populist sense; nor were they moving toward a peasant-based strategy such as the one later adopted by the Maoist wing of the Chinese Communist Party. They were not influenced by any mystique of the people similar to the original essence of populism, or by any Rousseauist fervor for the simple life such as inspired the Russian student movement to the people in the mid-1870s. The Russian populists who did have some influence on the radical intellectuals were those for whom terror had become an end in itself. The "populism" of the group that assassinated Tsar Alexander II must have been indistinguishable from anarchism and terrorism to the young Chinese intellectuals. Certainly they did not believe that the key to a future better life lay in traditional peasant institutions and values. On the other hand, unlike the Maoists, they did not seek to remold the village social structure and use peasant grievances as a dynamic force to propel themselves to power.

When the Restoration Society intellectuals turned to the secret societies they were partly simply following in the footsteps of local elites who had traditionally cooperated with the societies when it suited their purposes. To this partnership the partially modernized revolutionaries brought new aims. They were "foreknowers" concerned with the problems of how to save, strengthen, and reform the nation and society as a whole. To achieve their hopes they had to use, lead, and educate the people, but they did not seek to bridge the social gap and identify themselves closely with the attitudes and problems of the peasantry.

Legal Front Organizations

The other half of the revolutionaries' activities in Chekiang centered about efforts to develop their own bases from which they might strengthen contacts with the scattered secret societies, build up a party cadre, and provide some rudimentary military training. Several of the revolutionaries arrived at the idea of establishing schools, militia, or guilds as blinds behind which they could pursue such aims—a type of activity distinct from merely spreading propaganda to win new converts. In following this course of action the radicals were simultaneously taking advantage of opportunities afforded by the modernization movement and of the relative

49. For a brief description of *déclassé* elements in secret societies see Yuji Muramatsu, pp. 255–56.

degree of immunity enjoyed by those who were part of or associated with the gentry and other members of the local elite. By 1904 and 1905 the founding of modern schools had become commonplace throughout the province, so it was possible for revolutionaries to found an ostensibly reformist institution without attracting unusual attention and very possibly with official support. It is also striking that Chekiangese revolutionaries often established their organizations in or near their home towns rather than in the main urban centers. In their native areas radicals from prestigious families enjoyed the advantages of influential connections and greater knowledge of the local situation. The upper layer of society in the towns was composed mainly of a mixture of degree-holding gentry, scholars, and merchants. Occupational lines were often indistinct, but there did exist a layer of educated and influential men who were accustomed to dealing with one another and with officials. These men were often active in community affairs and enjoyed a certain freedom of action based on prestige and influence even when they were not backed by the formal legal privileges granted to gentry. When the Restoration Society revolutionaries sought to establish themselves in Chekiang, they associated themselves with the local elite, founding schools and establishing connections with local officials.

China's defeat in the Sino-Japanese War of 1894–95 and the cataclysm of the Boxer Rebellion in 1900 had shaken some of the local elite as well as the radical students in new schools. Some became interested in strengthening China by borrowing selectively from the West. Common interest in and promotion of modernizing projects created a bond between revolutionaries and progressive scholars, merchants, and gentry. The Chekiang revolutionaries began their projects with the interest and support of reformers in the community. What emerged was a spectrum of revolutionary and progressive elements within the educated elite classes not separated by any distinct lines. At one end were the professional revolutionaries. Next were such men as Ao Chia-hsiung who gradually moved from reformist to revolutionary positions, became acquainted with the professional revolutionaries, and took part in some of the revolutionary organizations, but who did not entirely cut their ties with their traditional backgrounds and might or might not remain active in the revolutionary movement until 1911. One step further removed were scholar, gentry, and merchant sympathizers who provided funds and protection for the revolutionaries, but did not otherwise play an active role. Finally, there were progressives (constitutionalists) who might be acquainted with the revolutionaries and who themselves, for different reasons, were promoting modernizing projects similar to those used by the revolutionaries. They and the revolutionaries were brought closer together when local officials were clumsy in suppressing a revolutionary organization and appeared to be persecuting needlessly and indiscriminately threatening all modernizing ventures.

An example of progressive support for those involved in revolutionary work occurred in 1906–07 when Ch'en Meng-hsiung, a radical returned student, was tried for dispensing revolutionary propaganda at a girls' school he had founded in his home town in Wenchow. A local scholar reported the existence of radical literature at the school to gain revenge in a personal quarrel. The magistrate, already annoyed by Ch'en's radicalism in another instance, sent soldiers to close the school who plundered in the process. Ch'en fled to Japan, but returned to Hangchow for trial to protect his friends, including Ao Chia-hsiung. The high-handed behavior of the magistrate and soldiers had brought protests from local scholars and gentry and interrogation failed to produce damaging evidence against Ch'en. He was guaranteed by Sun I-jang and other Wenchow gentry. Among those who spoke for Ao Chia-hsiung was the son of a former governor-general of Kwangtung and Kwangsi. In the end the case was dropped and the magistrate transferred.[50]

50. T'ao, pp. 13–14; Feng, *Chung-hua*, 2, 41, mainly paraphrases T'ao's account. A fuller, but largely similar, account is given by Chou Ch'i-wei, who was a middle school student at Lo-ch'ing in 1906. According to Chou, Ch'en's family had cooperated with the Taipings when they occupied the area so Ch'en was heir to an antigovernment tradition. Ch'en and a Buddhist monk established a Monks' and People's School (Seng min hsüeh-t'ang) at which military drill was taught and revolutionary works were studied. Among these was the Song of New Mountain (*Hsin-shan ko*), which Chou claims was written by Ch'en and T'ao says was written by Ao Chia-hsiung. Ch'en then founded his girls' school where *Hsin-shan ko* was also used. The magistrate was already angry with Ch'en because students at the Monks' and People's School had disrupted a meeting of local students and scholars, called to prepare for the beginning of constitutional government, by reciting *Hsin-shan ko*. Sun I-jang had met Ch'en before this case. He helped him escape after the school was closed. When Ch'en returned to Hangchow, Sun went there to see the governor, and Lo-ch'ing scholarly circles also sent a representative to Hangchow. After his release Ch'en went to Java to do educational work among Overseas Chinese. In his second year there he became ill and died. After the Revolution a memorial was erected on West Lake to him, Ao Chia-hsiung, and three others. Chou Ch'i-wei, "Lo-ch'ing hsin-hai ko-ming shih-liao" (Historical Materials on the 1911 Revolution in Lo-ch'ing), *HHKMHIL*, *4*, 188–91.

The first major front organization was the Wen-T'ai-Ch'u Guildhall founded by Ao Chia-hsiung in October or November 1904.[51] Ao was one of the more interesting of the lesser figures in the Chekiangese revolutionary movement because of his ambiguous position. He was part revolutionary, part independent radical, and part disreputable lower gentry. He was the son of a prosperous merchant of P'ing-hu in northeastern Chekiang. After passing the district (*sheng-yüan*) examinations he briefly studied tax accounting. Disliking this work, he turned to reform projects, joining the Chekiang Society in Hangchow and in 1900 supporting a variety of reformist institutions with other progressive scholars and students in Kashing. Early in 1903 he entered the Patriotic School (Ai-kuo hsüeh-she) in Shanghai. After the *Su-pao* case he returned to Kashing, where he organized a revolutionary debating club and an educational society. When these were closed by local officials, Ao traveled to southeastern Chekiang and then returned to establish his Guildhall. While it was operating Ao was in close contact with the revolutionary movement, but refused to join the Restoration Society. After it closed he maintained his acquaintances in revolutionary and secret society circles, but no longer played an important part in the movement. It is not clear whether his murder in 1908 at the age of thirty-four was for private or political reasons.[52]

Ao's intention in establishing the Guildhall was to use it to organize and finance militia that would serve as the basis for a revolutionary army. There were a large number of unruly immigrants from the southeastern prefectures of Wenchow, Taichow, and Chuchow in the Kashing area. Ao's plan was to obtain permission for a guildhall to act as a tax collecting agent for the government. The people would pay taxes to the Guildhall, thus avoiding the exactions of the yamen clerks. Instead of turning the money over to the officials, the Guildhall would use it to buy military provisions and supplies to finance an uprising. Ao supplied the initial funds and won gentry and official support for the scheme by presenting it as a means to control the immigrants. Local gentry were

51. Information on the Guildhall is from T'ao, pp. 25, 69–72; Chang Huang-ch'i, p. 523; Feng, *Chung-hua, 2,* 11–13. Wei Chien-yu is a secondary Communist source. Feng, *I-shih, 3,* 113–15, gives brief biographical information on some of those connected with the Guildhall.

52. T'ao, pp. 68–71; Shen Tieh-min, p. 135. Ao Chia-hsiung's last important political act was in keeping with the role of a member of the local gentry with secret society connections. When the salt smugglers rebelled and threatened to take Kashing in the fall of 1907, Ao persuaded them to bypass the town.

legally prohibited from collecting and transmitting taxes although it was not an uncommon practice.[53] Still, official approval of this plan seems extraordinary and was probably indicative of weakening government control.

Ch'en Meng-hsiung was one of those who helped Ao establish the Guildhall. Among others who worked for it were a number of students and merchants originally from southeast Chekiang who might establish rapport with the immigrants. These students evidently had not studied abroad and at least some of them and the merchants had secret society connections. Very soon a number of the professional revolutionaries were added to the group. T'ao Ch'eng-chang had previously met Ao in Shanghai. He introduced Wei Lan, whom Ao accepted as director of the Guildhall, and Wei brought two of his relatives and some revolutionary associates.

For a time during the first half of 1905 the Guildhall became the center of the revolutionary movement in Chekiang. Ao provided the funds to enable cadres to travel about northern Chekiang strengthening contacts with secret societies and recruiting militia among the villagers. Evidently the Guildhall was presented to the peasantry as a secret or quasi-secret society. Ao decided that the best way to attract members was through the superstitious, debased Buddhist-Taoist religion of the countryside. He therefore devised an Ancestral Sect (Tsu-tsung-chiao) complete with sacred texts, incantations to assure longevity, secret slogans, and passwords.

Ambitious plans were laid for an uprising. These were never tested, however, because after June 1905 Ao Chia-hsiung was plagued by family and business difficulties and could no longer continue to support the Guildhall. The man Ao had chosen to head the Ancestral Sect was jailed at about the same time. Without a source of funds and with official suspicions aroused, the revolutionaries could no longer continue their activities in Kashing and soon turned elsewhere.

About the time the Wen-T'ai-Ch'u Guildhall ran into difficulties, Hsü Hsi-lin independently laid the groundwork for establishing the Ta-t'ung School, which was to become the new revolutionary center. By the spring of 1905 Hsü had joined the Restoration Society and had made contacts with secret society members in

53. T'ung-tsu Ch'ü, *Local Government in China under the Ch'ing* (Cambridge, Mass., 1962), pp. 187, 333.

Shaohsing and Kinhwa prefectures.[54] The founding of the school was precipitated by the arrival in April of Ts'ai Yüan-p'ei's younger brother, who had a scheme to raise party funds by robbing local banks. Hsü approved and bought guns and ammunition in Shanghai. Permission to transport the arms was obtained from the Shaohsing prefect, under whom Hsü had once served, by saying they were to be used for drill in various schools in the area. The revolutionaries then decided to establish a school of their own where they could keep the weapons and hide stolen funds.[55]

The bank robbery idea was eventually abandoned as impractical, but that summer T'ao Ch'eng-chang visited Hsü and told him of the decline of the Guildhall. Hsü suggested replacing it with a school in Shaohsing. Official permission was obtained to use an empty storehouse in Ta-t'ung, just outside the west gate of the town, and the school formally opened in September.

Although Hsü Hsi-lin initiated the school and had the necessary connections with local officials, scholars, and gentry, T'ao Ch'eng-chang seems to have done the most to shape its organization and activities.[56] T'ao petitioned the provincial Commission for Educational Affairs for permission to establish a special six-month military course at the Ta-t'ung School. Upon graduation students were to return to their villages and organize militia, thus giving the people military training that would lay the basis for a national army.[57] The petition was approved, thereby obtaining innocent official sanction for a scheme that had obvious advantages for building revolutionary forces.

Once the revolutionaries had decided to use the school as part of such a long-range plan, every effort was made to gain the goodwill of officials and respectable members of the educated community. Leading local figures were invited to opening and closing exercises. Diplomas were awarded by the prefect and bore the prefectural

54. T'ao, p. 26.

55. Ibid., pp. 26–27.

56. Ibid., p. 27; Feng, *Chung-hua, 2,* 23. Hsü's initial plan for the school was to celebrate opening day by killing all the officials invited to the ceremonies and starting an uprising—an interesting anticipation of his eventual assassination of En-ming at the graduation exercises of the Anking Police Academy. T'ao, who was convinced that a revolution could not succeed in Chekiang without support from Nanking and Anhwei, dissuaded him from this plan.

57. T'ao, p. 27; Feng, *Chung-hua, 2,* 23.

seal.[58] Most of the financial support came from Hsü Chung-ch'ing, a wealthy merchant who was a friend of Hsü Hsi-lin. It is not clear how far his sympathies for revolution extended or whether he was fully aware of all the uses to which his contributions were put. However, he was willing to provide considerable sums for a variety of purposes.[59]

Although military drill was emphasized in the curriculum of regular students as well as those taking the special course, the school offered a full range of the history, science, and language courses normally found in modern schools. According to the recollections of one student there were not many outward signs of revolutionary intent. However, before summer vacations the head of the school met individually with each student to ascertain his views and urge him to engage in revolutionary work during the holidays.[60] With such a respectable backing and muted approach, the school was at first relatively immune to attacks even though there was some murmuring against it.

Under the guise of a typical product of the modern education movement, the Ta-t'ung School actually marked a significant advance in relations between revolutionaries and secret societies. Certain of the well-educated secret society leaders such as Chu Shao-k'ang and Wang Chin-fa shared in its management. Secret society leaders were urged to send their followers for military training and travel expenses were offered to any who came.[61] Since most of those who studied there joined the Restoration Society,[62] secret

58. T'ao, p. 28; Feng, *Chung-hua, 2,* 24.

59. Ch'en Wei, p. 128, summarizes Hsü Chung-ch'ing's contributions. T'ao refers to him at several points throughout his text. Hsü employed Ts'ao Ch'in-hsi as a tutor in his household and Ts'ao was instrumental in persuading Hsü to make contributions. Later Ts'ao served as head of the Ta-t'ung School. He was a competent scholar, but neither familiar with secret societies nor an effective head of a revolutionary organization. T'ao, p. 58; Feng, *I-shih, 3,* 113–14.

60. Chu Tsan-ch'ing, "Ta-t'ung shih-fan hsüeh-t'ang" (The Ta-t'ung Normal School), *HHKMHIL, 4,* 144–45, 147; Ch'iu Chin, Letter to a reporter of *Nü-tzu shih-chieh* dated June 17, 1907, *Ch'iu Chin chi,* p. 49.

61. T'ao, pp. 27–28. T'ao, Kung Pao-ch'üan, and the merchant secret-society member Lü Hsiung-hsiang traveled to invite secret society recruits immediately after the founding of the school. They had covered Kinhwa and Chuchow prefectures when they returned to to Shaohsing to develop new plans. Consequently most of the secret society members who came to the school were from those two prefectures or from Shaohsing, and these areas were the ones mainly involved in the plans for an uprising in 1907.

62. Ibid., p. 28.

society members were thus bound more closely to the revolutionary movement than they would have been by simple alliances between the party and an entire society.

Weaknesses and Defeat

Despite the promising beginning, certain weaknesses in the Chekiangese movement were not overcome and eventually led to fatal results. The top leaders were not content to remain long in Shaohsing, but soon began to search for new areas of activity. Revolutionary fronts outside the treaty ports were in a very exposed position, which increased the difficulty of balancing legal activities necessary to prevent discovery against genuine subversive purposes. Despite their many contacts with the revolutionaries, the secret societies remained a scattered, poorly armed, and weakly indoctrinated force. Finally, the leaders who ultimately planned the uprisings in 1907 were in a mood to risk their party organizations in desperate and almost hopeless gambles.

Conflicts over Alternate Courses of Action

T'ao Ch'eng-chang now believed that control of regular New Army troops as well as of militia would be necessary for revolutionary success. Therefore, he, Hsü, Kung Pao-ch'üan, and a number of others connected with the Ta-t'ung School resolved to go to Japan for military study. Upon graduation they intended to become officers and thus gain command of a significant force.[63]

Aside from hopes of eventual practical results, perhaps the decision to study further in Japan reflected the attraction major urban centers and the life of radical student circles had for the revolutionaries. To facilitate this plan, however, they turned again to traditional methods: the purchase of titles, bribery of officials, and reliance on influential family connections. Hsü Hsi-lin visited a cousin who was a former governor with a wide acquaintance among Ch'ing officials. His cousin gave him an introduction to Shou-shan, commander in chief of the Manchu forces in Chekiang, who was then acting governor. Hsü went to see Shou-shan and, finding him corrupt, bribed him, with the result that the revolutionaries received permission to study in Japan and a letter of recommendation to the Chinese minister in Tokyo.

63. Ibid., pp. 28–29; Chang Huang-ch'i, p. 524; Ch'en Wei, pp. 129–30. Ch'en was one of the five to hold a purchased title and seek to enter military school in Japan.

After arriving in Japan in late 1905 or early 1906 they were, nonetheless, unable to gain admission to military school.[64] With their plans thus blocked, T'ao and Hsü quarreled over what their next step should be. The tensions were aggravated by personality differences and led to a complete break between the two.[65] Hsü Hsi-lin returned to China, where he persistently pursued an official post with the aid of more introductions from his cousin. After several failures he was employed by the Anhwei governor En-ming,[66] thus paving the way for the governor's assassination in July 1907.[67] T'ao meanwhile stayed in Tokyo until mid-1906 when he fell ill and returned to Chekiang. He did not, however, work again at the Ta-t'ung School, which he believed had outlived its usefulness, and played no part in the main events of 1907.[68]

The departure of the top leadership left a vacuum at the Ta-t'ung School, and weakened its contacts with the Restoration Society. The man whom Hsü appointed to direct the school when he

64. In Japan T'ao, Hsü, and the others were frustrated by a combination of official suspicions and lack of qualifications. The superintendent of students suspected them because they did not hold provincial scholarships. These were procured with the aid of Hsü's cousin. Their entry into military school was still delayed, however, and when they finally were allowed to take the physical entrance examinations all five failed to pass. Hsü was nearsighted; I do not know on what grounds the others were rejected. T'ao, p. 29; Ch'en Wei, p. 130.

65. T'ao, p. 29; *Ko-ming hsien-lieh chuan-chi,* pp. 192–94. Hsü argued that they should return to China and try to infiltrate the police. T'ao believed it essential to control the army. He believed the Ta-t'ung School should be abandoned after the first class had graduated to prevent its purpose from being discovered, and emphasis placed on forming and training militia. Hsü believed the school should continue to produce as many graduates as possible. T'ao joined the Revolutionary Alliance in Japan. Because of their quarrel he joined without Hsü, who decided not to join at all. At his interrogation after assassinating En-ming, Hsü made a disparaging remark about Sun Yat-sen. Besides intellectual snobbishness and provincial differences, the fact that T'ao had joined the Revolutionary Alliance may have influenced Hsü's attitude. When Hsü began to plan an uprising in Anking, T'ao believed he was motivated by a desire for personal glory and refused to have anything to do with the venture. T'ao had a talent for usually being right, but also for ending up on the outside.

66. En-ming had once served under Hsü's cousin when the latter was governor of Shansi.

67. T'ao, pp. 29–30. Considering the split between the two men, T'ao's account of Hsü's activities during this time is quite dispassionate, and fuller than his account of his own. Once when Hsü was in Peking looking for a job, he considered assassinating T'ieh-liang, the Minister of War and a powerful figure in court circles, and also made a trip to Manchuria to make the acquaintance of a bandit chieftain there.

68. Chang Huang-ch'i, p. 524. There is little information about T'ao's activities during 1906–07 after he left the Ta-t'ung School. At least part of the time he was active in the middle and lower Yangtze areas.

left was a reputable progressive scholar, but had no contacts with secret society circles. He was unable to cooperate closely with the secret society leaders associated with the school, who in turn had no close ties with scholars and students in the town of Shaohsing. Conflict came into the open after the graduation of the first class in the spring of 1906 when a new group of secret society members were invited to attend the school. Disagreement in the administration was then reinforced by a cleavage which developed between students from Shaohsing and those from other parts of the province. The director finally resigned and was succeeded by several others, none of whom could control the situation. Quarrels degenerated into actual fighting among the students which spilled over into the streets. Naturally the school began to acquire a bad name.[69]

When Ch'iu Chin came to Shaohsing in February 1907 the problem of leadership was solved, but that of relations with the community exacerbated. Her revolutionary enthusiasm and strong feminism were just the combination to provoke further hostility among gentry and officials. One of her favorite schemes was a national women's army, so she ordered girl students to practice military drill. Many in the town were shocked at such impropriety. The girls, too, were largely opposed and the idea had to be abandoned. Ch'iu attracted even more unfavorable attention by riding horseback astride and dressing in Western male clothing. One day she rode into town so dressed and some conservatives incited a small riot. Ch'iu was rescued by students from the school, but bad feeling remained.[70] Thus, as the school became more openly radical under Ch'iu's influence the chances of premature exposure increased. The school was searched in April or early May. Community hostility came to a climax in early July when the head of the prefectural Education Bureau, a relatively conservative returned student whose views Ch'iu had criticized in Japan, reported to Prefect Kuei-fu that she and P'ing-yang Society leaders were planning an uprising.[71]

Behind the conflicts within the school and the deteriorating re-

69. T'ao, pp. 30–31, 34, 58.

70. T'ao, p. 31. It is not clear whether the girls in question were attending the Ta-t'ung School or the Ming-tao Girls' School of which Ch'iu was then headmistress. Probably they were at the latter.

71. Telegram of Kuei-fu to Governor Chang Tseng-yang, in T'ao, p. 43; Wang Shih-tse, "Hui-i Ch'iu Chin" (Recollections of Ch'iu Chin), *HHKMHIL, 4,* 227.

lations with influential members of local society lay problems that were also evident in a number of other front organizations established by the revolutionaries, including the Patriotic School, Patriotic Girls' School, and the Chinese Public Institute (Chung-kuo kung-hsüeh) in Shanghai.[72] If the school was to continue to serve as an effective cover it had to offer a convincing educational program to justify its existence. Moreover, the revolutionaries sincerely believed in the need for modern, Westernized education to lay the basis for a regenerated China and could not treat the curriculum as a mere facade. By offering any substantial education, however, the school attracted students, teachers, and financial supporters who, though progressive, were not revolutionaries. These might help to camouflage the school's real purpose, but would also hinder its functioning as a revolutionary instrument. Eventually a critical point would be reached where the school would have to split, disband, or decide between a revolutionary and nonrevolutionary course.

At the Ta-t'ung school the issue was early resolved in favor of revolution by the arrival of Ch'iu Chin. However, this decision sharpened other issues. In Shaohsing the school's safety depended considerably more on community acceptance than did that of similar institutions in Shanghai. The revolutionaries had to maintain the goodwill of the local elite, and so could not overtly stray too far from the path of respectability without risking exposure. In the absence of a general abandonment of faith in the existing government such as occurred in 1911, revolutionary fervor had to be kept in check to maintain the secrecy necessary for the organization's survival.

72. In the Patriotic School there was disagreement between faculty who felt that more time should be devoted to education and those who wanted to emphasize revolutionary activism, although this particular conflict was overshadowed by others that caused the split between the school and the Chinese Educational Association (Chung-kuo chiao-yü hui). The Patriotic Girls' School, after several changes in fortune, ended up in 1907–08 as a nonrevolutionary institution partly supported by official funds. Chiang Wei-ch'iao, "Chung-kuo chiao-yü hui chih hui-i" (Recollections of the Chinese Educational Association), *HHKM, 1,* 492–96. The Chinese Public Institute started in 1906 as a radical institution similar to the Patriotic School. Within a year it was hard pressed for funds and a new administration tried to impose more conventional discipline on the students in hope of attracting official and additional private support. Students' objections eventually resulted in mass withdrawals and the establishment of a New Chinese Public Institute in 1908. The new school was characterized by strong esprit de corps and weak finances. At the end of 1909 it merged back into the old school under moderate and conventional leadership. Many of the students were disappointed and unwilling to return. Hu Shih, *Ssu-shih tzu-shu* (Autobiography at Forty) (Hong Kong, 1957), pp. 63–65, 81–88.

Such secrecy carried the risk of encouraging safe inaction which might allow the organization to come under the control of moderates favoring a reformist approach. More immediately it conflicted with the psychological need to affirm the dedication felt by many of the more radical members of the party. The founders of revolutionary fronts inherited some of the style and technique that characterized such historic Confucian opposition groups as the Tung-lin Academy of the late Ming period.[73] They too were engaged in a moral crusade and, convinced of their own superiority, found it difficult to resist openly denouncing the evil degeneracy of their opponents. Also like the Tung-lin group they were drawn to quixotically attack antagonists stronger than they. The recognition won by such moral courage gained support for their general cause, but the consequent attrition of their forces weakened the specifically revolutionary character of the opposition to the government.

Inability to Control the Secret Societies

Equally dangerous to the revolutionaries at the Ta-t'ung School was premature activity by secret society allies. The immediate problem was insufficient discipline both of local leaders over their followers and of Ta-t'ung leaders over the local leaders. Ch'iu Chin's reorganization of the Restoration Society and regulations for the Restoration Army were very elaborate, but were largely paper schemes. In practice they merely confirmed the existing situation. Since the Chekiangese secret societies were still highly fragmented, a hierarchical organization did not necessarily result in effective lines of command.

In addition, revolutionary propaganda had influenced but not remolded the secret societies so their interests and those of the revolutionaries were not completely identical. Some of the Ta-t'ung graduates who returned home and some of the secret society branches became involved in local personal, economic, or political conflicts divorced from the main aims of the Restoration Society. In a town in Chuchow, one Ta-t'ung graduate forced the dismissal and flight in disguise of a magistrate who had tried to prevent him from organizing militia.[74]

A more general source of discontent stemmed from the disas-

73. On the Tung-lin Academy see Charles O. Hucker, "The Tung-lin Movement of the Late Ming Period," in John K. Fairbank, ed., *Chinese Thought and Institutions* (Chicago, 1957), pp. 132–62.

74. T'ao, pp. 32–33.

trous floods and famine in Central China during the winter and spring of 1906–07. Chekiang was outside the worst area, but it, too, suffered.[75] At least ten rice riots or related uprisings of significant proportions occurred in Chekiang between the beginning of March and the end of June.[76] Even though two of these riots occurred in Shaohsing, the student revolutionaries seem to have remained generally aloof. The middle grade secret society leaders, however, were much closer to the peasant discontent. One of the Dragon Flower branch leaders, for instance, led his followers in harassing grain and tax collectors and fought with government troops sent to restore order.[77]

His connection with the Ta-t'ung School was not discovered; but as the date set for Ch'iu Chin's uprising approached, the secret societies became still more difficult to control. Periodic postponements contributed to the confusion and increased the likelihood of disclosures. At the end of June and during the first week of July several premature uprisings and other incidents occurred that alerted officials to the probability of trouble. Still worse, one man who was captured implicated the Ta-t'ung School under torture.[78]

Heroism and Sacrifice

Despite the other problems, the attempted uprisings in 1907 would not have so greatly damaged the revolutionary movement if it had not been for the particular nature of the leadership of Ch'iu Chin and Hsü Hsi-lin. Exactly opposite to the Leninist type of revolutionary, their efforts ended in personal testimonies of faith in revolution with no thought for preserving the party organization. Although Hsü and Ch'iu must be considered as individuals, they also embodied a type much admired by many of the radical students in the Restoration Society.[79] The attraction of heroic self-sacrifice seems to have been a general characteristic of the revolutionary movement, at least in that part of China.

The final phase of the early Chekiangese revolutionary movement began in February 1907 when Ch'iu became directress of the Ming-tao Girls' School in Shaohsing. She also taught at the Ta-

75. Edict to the Grand Council dated Nov. 18, 1906, *Ta-Ch'ing li-ch'ao shih-lu* (Veritable Record of Successive Reigns of the Ch'ing Dynasty), KH 565/3b.

76. Kuo T'ing-i, *Chin-tai Chung-kuo shih-shih jih-chih* (A Daily Chronology of Modern Chinese History) (Taipei, 1963), 2, 1271–79.

77. T'ao, p. 33.

78. Ibid., pp. 34–36, 64–66, 74–75; Kuo T'ing-i, 2, 1279.

79. Ch'en Wei, p. 127.

t'ung School and became its real leader. Not long before, Hsü Hsi-lin had succeeded in winning Governor En-ming's confidence and had been placed in charge of the newly established Police Academy at Anking. He and Ch'iu soon began planning a joint uprising.

Ch'iu already knew many of the secret society leaders and during the spring made two trips to Kinhwa and Chuchow to reach further agreements.[80] She was also acquainted with some of the members of the recently formed second New Army regiment in Hangchow. From it she enlisted the aid of a few of the officers to organize a gymnasium. This new group was appended to the Ta-t'ung School to provide military training for a larger number of secret society members.[81] During that spring she also reorganized the Restoration Society and Restoration Army and procured additional arms from Shanghai.

The groundwork laid by Hsü in Anking was much less thorough than that in Chekiang. He had made little contact with students or secret societies in Anhwei. Revolutionaries in the 31st Mixed Brigade of the New Army stationed outside Anking knew of Hsü's intentions, but were not notified by him before he actually attempted his coup and so could not give help.[82] Even the students at the Police Academy, who were to form the main force of the uprising, had not been much indoctrinated with revolutionary ideas or considered trustworthy enough to be informed of Hsü's plans.[83]

80. T'ao, p. 34; Feng, *Chung-hua*, 2, 29.

81. The revolutionaries in the New Army in Hangchow were also going to support Ch'iu's uprising in July, but never acted because government troops closed the Ta-t'ung School before the date set for the uprising. Ch'iu had become acquainted with members of the New Army in 1906 when she had visited Hangchow to recruit party members and lay the groundwork for an uprising in Chekiang in conjunction with the P'ing-Liu-Li uprising in Hunan and Kiangsi at the end of the year. These plans were canceled when the Hunan-Kiangsi uprising failed. Chou Ya-wei, pp. 626–27; *KKWH, Ko-sheng kuang-fu* (The Revolution in the Provinces) (Taipei, 1962), 2, 132; T'ao, p. 88.

Chu Tsan-ch'ing, pp. 146–47, estimated that 80 or 90 came to the gymnasium. Chiang Chi-yün testified that 60 attended. T'ao, p. 88.

82. Tsou Lu, *Chung-kuo kuo-min-tang shih-kao* (A Draft History of the Kuomintang) (Shanghai, 1938), pp. 764–65.

83. Feng, *Chung-hua*, 2, 21. It seems very strange that Hsü had not tried to indoctrinate the police students more thoroughly. He had held Sunday meetings where patriotic speeches were given. However, he had only tried to introduce modern Western ideas and excite interest in free discussion. Although the principle of race was introduced unobtrusively, revolutionary ideas were not clarified. Prudence was not one of Hsü's chief characteristics, so it seems unlikely that he was motivated by fear of outside discovery. One possibility is that the police students were not very good revolutionary material. In many places the first "modern" police

Actually his only accomplices were two other returned students whom he had persuaded to join him in Anking.[84]

The dates selected for the joint insurrections had to be postponed several times. In the end the Anking uprising took place slightly before schedule because a list of Restoration Society party members that included Hsü's alias had been captured in Shanghai and because En-ming insisted that graduation at the Police Academy take place on July 6 instead of two days later. Neither of these factors significantly altered the outcome, however. When officials were assembled for the graduation exercises, Hsü announced that the Revolution had started and he and one of his associates began shooting at En-ming. Unfortunately they proved very bad shots. The governor was fatally wounded, but not killed outright. Other officials were able to carry him back to his yamen where they raised the alarm. Meanwhile, Hsü was able to coerce only 30 or 40 of the 280 astounded police students to follow him to the provincial armory. There they were soon surrounded by loyal troops and captured after a few hours. Hsü was executed the next day and his heart cut out as a sacrifice to the dead governor.[85]

Hsü's connection with the Ta-t'ung School was soon discovered by government officials, and on top of the evidence that had been accumulating in Chekiang virtually guaranteed that troops would be sent to close the school. Ch'iu also realized that the secret societies in Kinhwa could no longer be relied upon because of premature uprisings there. However, she decided to continue to plan

---

forces were staffed by the less degenerate members of the Green Army, which was by then scheduled for dissolution. To ease the problem of disbandment an effort was made to retain and use in other capacities those younger soldiers who might give passable service. If this was true in Anking, Hsü's students probably were not a very progressive group.

84. Hsü's associates were Ch'en Po-p'ing and Ma Tsung-han, both returned students in their mid-twenties. Ch'en was killed during the uprising and Ma executed one and a half months later.

85. Hsü's uprising is described in T'ao, pp. 38–40; Feng, *Chung-hua, 2,* 42; Ts'ao Ya-po, *Wu-ch'ang ko-ming chen-shih* (A True History of the Wuchang Revolution) (Shanghai, 1930), *1,* 220–22. Official telegrams dealing with the case are reprinted in *HHKM, 3,* 112–77, and a smaller number appear in *KKWH, Ko-ming chih ch'ang-tao yü fa-chan, T'ung-meng-hui, 3,* 207–16.

Not all the police students who started for the armory arrived there. The first government troops to come up were New Army forces, which did not seriously try to attack the armory. The old-style provincial forces (*hsün-fang-tui*), which arrived slightly later, had no sympathy with the revolutionaries and quickly suppressed them. The police students captured with Hsü and Ma Tsung-han were not punished.

for an uprising in Shaohsing and Hangchow on July 19. On the evening of July 12 government troops arrived outside Shaohsing and moved against the Ta-t'ung School about the middle of the next day. Ch'iu had been forewarned by military students in Hangchow, and in any case still had had ample time to escape after she knew troops had arrived in the vicinity. Most of the students at the school had already left for summer vacation or fled when they heard the news. There was no hope that an attack could be repulsed, but Ch'iu chose to put up a token resistance. She and seventeen others were quickly captured.

Although interrogated three times and moderately tortured, she refused to admit her revolutionary connections. Captured documents, however, made her intent clear. Kuei-fu, the prefect, recommended her execution, which was authorized by Governor Chang Tseng-yang. She was then beheaded promptly to forestall any further revolutionary attempts.[86]

Both Ch'iu Chin and Hsü Hsi-lin had deliberately sacrificed themselves to dramatize the revolutionary cause. Hsü had only the most quixotic plan for any action beyond the assassination of En-ming.[87] At his interrogation he freely admitted his revolutionary views and claimed that he had killed the governor to further the abstract principle of anti-Manchuism even though En-ming had been a good official and a generous sponsor.[88] In Chekiang Ch'iu had been deeply depressed by what she realized was the imminent failure of her hopes. There had seemed to be no road open ahead and the only possible course was to prove she had the moral convic-

86. T'ao, pp. 41–42, 63–64. Documents dealing with the Ch'iu Chin case appear in *HHKM, 3; KMWH, 1; KKWH, Ko-ming chih ch'ang-tao yü fa-chan, T'ung-meng-hui, 3;* Ch'iu Ts'an-chih, pp. 127–45. There is considerable duplication. The *HHKM* collection is from the Grand Council archives only, while the other sources print documents from the Shaohsing prefectural archives. This accounts for differences between certain items found in both *HHKM* and the Taiwan publications.

As in the Anking case, those captured with Ch'iu were treated leniently. None were important. One was jailed for three years, two received one-year sentences and the rest were released.

87. Hsü's plans had originally called for assassination of any other government official attending the graduation who would not surrender. The police students would then seize the armory, telegraph bureau, and other important government buildings. After gaining control of Anking, the revolutionaries would march on Nanking. In view of the small force available to Hsü this plan seems rather optimistic. Testimony of Ma Tsung-han in T'ao, p. 82.

88. T'ao, pp. 80–81; Feng, *Chung-hua, 2,* 44–46; Tsou Lu, pp. 737–38; Ts'ao Ya-po, *Wu-ch'ang ko-ming,* pp. 221–22.

tion to die for her beliefs. Her duty would thus be fulfilled and others might be inspired to carry on the task of eliminating the Manchus.[89]

Ch'iu Chin's execution marked the end of effective wide-scale revolutionary activity in that part of China until shortly before 1911. Many Restoration Society members fled abroad and joined the Revolutionary Alliance in Japan. Certain individuals continued to promote revolution in Chekiang, but the party as originally constituted almost went out of existence. The revived Restoration Society was used for very different purposes abroad in 1910 and 1911, and when revolution came it did not have a strong base in China.

The revolutionaries' secret society allies also suffered badly. A series of uprisings occurred after Ch'iu's death and continued into the early months of 1908, but these were scattered and sporadic. The closing of the Ta-t'ung School not only ended any possible chance for coordination, but also undermined the influence of revolutionary ideas among the societies. Restoration Society slogans and trappings seem to have been conspicuously used in only one of the uprisings. The chief result of these uprisings was that those societies that had been closest to the revolutionaries were most weakened because they were the ones that resisted the Ch'ing most strongly.[90] After 1907 the secret societies were never again the main force of revolution in Chekiang.

Paradoxically, the aftermath of the Chekiang case made a tangible contribution to weakening the government. As a martyr Ch'iu Chin was an instantaneous success. Her sex, her steadfast behavior during interrogation, and doubts about whether she was really guilty all disposed public opinion in her favor. Right after her execution the story spread that in jail before she died she asked for paper and wrote "The autumn wind and the autumn rain will make me die of sorrow" (*Ch'iu-yü ch'iu-feng, ch'ou sha-jen*), a poem which since has become inseparable from her revolutionary

89. Shortly before she was captured, Ch'iu wrote a poem to a friend in Shanghai expressing these sentiments. Ch'iu Chin, "Chin Hsü Hsiao-chu chüeh-ming tz'u" (Poem to Hsü Hsiao-shu in Contemplation of Death), in Hsiao P'ing, p. 156; Hsü Shuang-yün, "Chi Ch'iu Chin" (Memories of Ch'iu Chin), *HHKMHIL, 4,* 218.

90. T'ao, p. 21. The Dragon Flower Society was nearly broken down and the P'ing-yang Society considerably weakened. The Crouching Tiger, White Cloth, and Double Dragon societies continued to flourish, especially the last.

image.[91] Reformist and radical newspapers were generally sympathetic to Ch'iu.[92] By the end of 1907 the first edition of her poems had probably been published and the Ch'iu Chin myth was well under way.

Sympathy for Ch'iu was greatly increased by maladroit official handling of the case. During the previous eight months revolutionaries had been involved in several uprisings and assassination attempts in various parts of China. Officials, therefore, had good reason for alarm. As a Manchu and potential victim, Prefect Kuei-fu had particular cause to favor strong measures. He and Governor Chang hoped that with Ch'iu Chin out of the way they would be able to arrest other leaders and then win back the secret society rank and file by lenient treatment.[93]

This was a standard course of action, but the mistake was to alienate much of public opinion by unnecessary arrests and extortions. Two other schools in Shaohsing were searched and plundered by soldiers. Students were arrested, as were a number of prominent local gentry and merchants. Among them were Sun Te-ch'ing, a landlord and a former director of the Ta-t'ung School, Hsü Chung-ch'ing, a wealthy merchant, and Hsü Hsi-lin's impeccably conservative father Hsü Feng-Wu. It was widely believed that those arrested had to pay large sums to procure their freedom

91. That the poem was widely publicized just after the execution is shown by a telegram from Chang Tseng-yang to Kuei-fu asking if Ch'iu had really written such a poem. Telegram of Chekiang Governor to Shaohsing Prefect dated July 30, 1907, *KMWH, 1,* 112. T'ao, p. 42, says the poem was actually written by a supporter and attributed to Ch'iu. Whether or not she did write it is rather immaterial since it was generally accepted that she did and the poem's significance lay in its propaganda effect. The plays on words—*ch'iu* meaning her surname or autumn, *ch'ou* meaning melancholy and containing the character for *ch'iu,* and *feng* and *yü* meaning wind and rain with the implication of sighs and tears—all appear in earlier poems that she did write.

92. The *North China Herald* criticized official handling of the case and suggested Ch'iu was innocent. *NCH, 84:*205 (July 26, 1907). The *Chung-wai jih-pao* and *Shih-pao* (*Eastern Times*) were both strongly critical of the hasty execution and the behavior of troops. Even *Shen-pao* (Shanghai Daily News) suggested that although there may have been justification for executing Ch'iu, officials had blundered by alienating public opinion at a time when the government was preparing for constitutionalism. See articles from these papers in Ch'iu Ts'an-chih, appendix, pp. 1–4, 16.

93. "Memorial of Chekiang Governor reporting on the Chekiang case dated September 24, 1907," *HHKM, 3,* 213; *KMWH, 1,* 115; *KKWH, Ko-ming chih ch'ang-tao yü fa-chan, T'ung-meng-hui, 3,* 289.

and that official avarice was a governing motive behind their arrests.[94]

It appeared that a general purge of new schools and all those connected with Ch'iu and Hsü was under way. Alarm was widespread and rumors prevalent.[95] Guarantors came forward to aid those arrested. Protest petitions were sent to the governor. Gentry complaints received support from the Shan-yin magistrate and from a deputy sent from Hangchow to investigate. When word reached Peking, Yuan Shih-k'ai, Prince Ch'ing, and Prince Su opposed what they considered the excessive harshness of the provincial authorities.[96]

Under pressure from above and below, the authorities had to moderate their approach. By then, however, it was too late to eradicate the hostility which had been aroused. The evidence of Ch'iu Chin's treason, which was certainly strong had the government presented it properly, was overlooked by much of the literate public in their animosity toward Kuei-fu and Governor Chang. Since the chief villain, Kuei-fu, was a Manchu it was easy for criticism to take an anti-Manchu turn. Before the end of autumn he and Chang Tseng-yang had been transferred to different posts, but a residue of distrust remained.

Ultimately, therefore, the Chekiang and Anking cases contributed to the success of the Revolution by undermining public faith in the government. At the same time the results worked against control of the Revolution by the radical intellectuals. Their party was weakened while the spectrum of revolutionary support tended to widen beyond the point where the Restoration Society could assume leadership over all the diverse elements.

A brief look at events of 1911 in Chekiang again shows not only

94. Feng, *Chung-hua, 2,* 65; *KKWH, Ko-ming chih ch'ang-tao yü fa-chan, T'ung-meng-hui, 3,* 282–83.

95. Even on the day after Ch'iu was executed, Kuei-fu felt compelled to deny that all schools would be closed and that the prefectural government was suspicious of education in general. Ten days later he repeated this assurance in a second proclamation and denied that irresponsible accusations would be heeded and that Hsü's father's property had been seized. Proclamations of Shaohsing prefect dated July 16, 1907, and July 26, 1907, *KMWH, 1,* 103, 108–09.

Widespread arrests had also occurred in Anking as a result of En-ming's assassination. These affected the members of many influential families throughout the lower Yangtze area. Thus the outcry against the government was not limited to Chekiang. *NCH, 84:*208, 222 (July 26, 1907).

96. *NCH, 84:*205 (July 26, 1907); *KKWH, Ko-ming chih ch'ang-tao yü fa-chan, T'ung-meng-hui, 3,* 189. The handling of the case was also criticized by a deputy sent from Hangchow to investigate and by the Shan-yin magistrate who resigned.

some similar opportunities for cooperation between revolutionaries and moderates, but also the continued weakness of the Restoration Society organization and leadership and limits to radical influence on politics. The allegiance of reformist and constitutionalist scholars, merchants, and gentry to the Ch'ing dynasty had been further weakened by disputes over the financing and management of the Shanghai-Hangchow-Ningpo Railway and struggles to speed constitutional government. After the Revolution began in Wuchang, Ch'en Ch'i-mei in Shanghai and other members of the Revolutionary Alliance took the initiative in planning the Chekiangese declaration of independence with certain members of the provincial assembly and radicals in the New Army. There was some overlap and many personal ties between members of these groups, so cooperation was relatively easy.[97] Revolutionary planners were generally careful not to antagonize moderate opinion, as was evident in the selection of T'ang Shou-ch'ien, a gentry-merchant and recent hero of the railway disputes, as provincial military governor.

Old members of the Restoration Society and secret society members, a more militant group, were relegated to an auxiliary role. Their dare-to-die corps supplemented the revolutionary forces provided by the New Army, but they were outside the circle that determined policy. They were not, for instance, informed of the choice of T'ang Shou-ch'ien until a general meeting of revolutionary representatives was called after Hangchow had fallen and T'ang had arrived there from Shanghai. T'ang was most unacceptable to Restoration Society members, who suspected he had advised in favor of executing Ch'iu Chin in 1907, but Wang Chin-fa's protests were unavailing.[98] T'ao Ch'eng-chang did not return to Chekiang from abroad until after the Revolution and was never powerful in the new government. The last chance for the Restora-

97. For example, the Assembly president Ch'en Fu-ch'en was a constitutionalist but had friends who were revolutionaries, as did Shen Chün-ju, one of the vice-presidents. Many members of the New Army were members of the Revolutionary Alliance, Restoration Society, or both. One of these, the second military governor, Chiang Tsun-kuei, was also a relative of the constitutionalist Chiang Chih-yu. Ch'u Fu-ch'eng was both a member of the Revolutionary Alliance and the Chekiang Provincial Assembly, and played an important part in discussions leading to the Chekiangese declaration of independence. Shen Chün-ju, "Hsin-hai ko-ming tsa-i" (Miscellaneous Recollections of the 1911 Revolution), *HHKMHIL, 1,* 138; Ch'u Fu-ch'eng, "Che-chiang hsin-hai ko-ming chi-shih" (An Account of the 1911 Revolution in Chekiang), *HHKM, 7,* 153–54, 156; Chang P'eng-yüan, oral communication.

98. Ch'u Fu-ch'eng, *HHKM, 7,* 156.

tion Society to reassert authority ended when T'ao was assassinated in January 1912.[99] After T'ang resigned subsequent governors were chosen from the New Army.

Outside of Hangchow, the Restoration Society and secret society members Wang Chin-fa and Lü Hsiung-hsiang headed the prefectural military governments in Shaohsing and Chuchow. From the beginning, however, local scholars, gentry, and ex-Ch'ing officials retained political influence. More important, Wang and Lü's authority was not backed by strong organizations of their own. Wang was often in Shanghai, and when prefectural governments were abolished throughout the province in mid-1912 he did not return to Shaohsing. Lü took part in the unsuccessful "Second Revolution" of 1913 and died while fleeing arrest. What remained of the pre-1911 radical group in the old prefectural city then dissolved.[100]

Why should only a small number of arrests and executions have so badly shattered the organizational structure which the revolutionaries had carefully built up during the previous three and a half years? One possible answer is that despite their vague radical aims and new Western-derived theories, the revolutionaries themselves remained largely within the confines of traditional roles and values. Moreover, despite the use of certain new institutions such as modern schools and newspapers, they did not succeed in breaking away from the local social and political structure, which was resistant to radical alterations. Intellectual and institutional changes had already begun in the provincial towns, and the revolutionaries were able to take advantage of the existence of a conservative modernization movement as a cover for their subversive activities. However, change had not proceeded far enough to undermine the grip of the gentry-merchant secret-society elite which dominated the local social and political scene under the official level. Much of this local organization was informal and extremely flexible, leaving room for a wide variety of relationships and many gradations of legal and illegal activity. Although it was relatively

99. T'ao Ch'eng-cheng's assassination was almost certainly arranged by Chiang K'ai-shek at the behest of Ch'en Ch'i-mei and was the result of power rivalries in the Shanghai-Chekiang area. See Ma Hsü-lun, "T'ao Ch'eng-chang chih ssu" (The Death of T'ao Ch'eng-chang), *HHKM, 1*, 520.

100. Ch'en Hsieh-shu, "Shao-hsing kuang-fu shih chien-wen" (Experiences at the Time of the Revolution in Shaohsing), *Chin-tai shih tzu-liao* (Materials on Modern History) (1958), no. 1, pp. 107–08; Mao Hu-hou, "Hsin-hai ko-ming tsai Li-shui" (The 1911 Revolution at Li-shui), *HHKMHIL, 4*, 201–02.

easy for the revolutionaries to enter this picture, the same flexibility made it difficult for them to fundamentally change it. Scholar rebels had traditionally been able to find allies among dissatisfied members of established gentry and secret society leaders, and in this role the revolutionaries enjoyed some success. However, their aims were far enough removed from those of traditional rebels to create a gap between their interests and those of their allies. The revolutionaries could not thoroughly control the organizations they had created.

Nor did their backgrounds, temperaments, and aspirations suit them for the long-term task of building an organization entirely their own based on the existing discontent of the lower classes. They lacked any clear image of oppositional political organization beyond the *tang* or the secret society. As part of the educated elite they had little real sympathy with the peasantry. Moreover, they had absorbed enough modern, radical, Western ideas to make it difficult for them even to enter completely into the traditional secret society world. They were too urban, too oriented toward the life of "student circles" to find a long struggle in isolated areas congenial. Rather they wanted quick results that would open opportunities to become part of a modern world of national power, individual liberty, and scientific achievement.

The key to these goals seemed to be in the large cities rather than in the villages of Chekiang. Therefore, once the movement was checked, the basis for cooperation with local political elements easily weakened and many revolutionaries withdrew. The strongest of the remaining nonofficial political leaders were gentry who could operate from a socially entrenched and legally protected position. As they became increasingly hostile to the government they made new alliances with opponents of the Ch'ing who had to accept their local hegemony.

PART III

Military Power in the Genesis of the Revolution

8. The New Armies

Yoshihiro Hatano

Leaders of the Revolution of 1911 came chiefly from the lower strata of the literati and rich merchant class.[1] Before the Sino-Japanese War of 1894–95, these men would have been candidates for the traditional government examinations. After the defeat of 1895, however, increasing numbers of them were aware of China's precarious international position. Many supported reform movements within the imperial system. Others, especially after the Boxer Rebellion of 1900, became nationalist revolutionaries.

The educational reforms undertaken by the Manchu government after 1901 fed the new anti-Manchu currents of thought. Many new schools with modernized curricula were founded and students were encouraged to study abroad, especially in Japan. Most important of all, in 1904 the government announced that the traditional Examination System would be abolished by degrees over the next eight years, and then, stimulated by Japan's victory over Russia, abolished it in one stroke in 1905. Henceforth officials were to be drawn from students in the modern schools and those who had returned from study abroad.

The new nationalists did not believe that Manchu reforms could strengthen China enough to withstand the onslaught of foreign powers. They argued that the Manchus would always compromise with foreigners, sacrificing Chinese national interests to preserve the Manchu dynasty. Thus Chinese nationalists became anti-Manchu revolutionaries in order to clear the way for strengthening China through modernization.

The revolutionaries founded one organization after another; in 1905, these were incorporated into the Revolutionary Alliance.

1. The upper strata, who were closely connected with official circles, were too satisfied with their social position and too preoccupied with preserving it to conceive of new ideas for dealing with changing conditions, while those with fewer vested interests could meet the demands of the new age with fewer preconceptions.

The establishment of this first nationwide organization indicates that the revolutionaries were beginning to develop a national perspective. However, most of the rank and file retained provincial prejudices and failed to unite for common causes. This provincialism, which characterized the late Ch'ing and early republican periods, may be traced to the following causes:

1. Increased economic differentiation among the provinces, accentuated in the years after the Taiping Rebellion. Differences became more pronounced as a result of modernizing policies carried out by a number of enlightened provincial officials after the Sino-Japanese War.

2. Fostering of provincial consciousness by students, especially those who had studied in Japan, where students often formed groups on the basis of provincial origin. They published such journals as *Hu-pei hsüeh-sheng chieh* (Hupeh Student World), *Chiang-su* (Kiangsu), and *Che-chiang ch'ao* (Tides of Chekiang). These were designed not only to introduce new thought and scientific knowledge to their provinces, but also to arouse provincial consciousness for the purpose of uniting the people of the province as a step toward national cooperation.[2] The number of news-

2. For example, the Hupeh student group wrote:

> Victory belongs to the superior and defeat to the inferior, as ordained by natural law. Firstly the battle is won by those who unite, secondly by those who unite intensively. Because they did not unite, innumerable races and states have been annihilated and ruined in history. Today this natural law is operating with such force that those who cannot unite firmly will not survive on the earth. . . . It is owing to the lack of national cooperation that we the Chinese, descendants of the Yellow Emperor, have been reduced to such a miserable situation by the most ruthless natural selection. We who have studied abroad and witnessed world affairs have come to the conclusion that China will not be able to survive in the evil stream of the struggle for existence unless the people unite and cooperate. National cooperation must be brought about step by step, built on smaller units of cooperation. Love of the country must therefore start from love of the home province.

From "The Origin of the Association of Hupeh Fellow Provincials," in the initial number of *Hu-pei hsüeh-sheng chieh* (Tokyo, 1903), pp. 121–23.

"If the strength of the several tens of millions of people in the province is united, it will surely have sufficient power to exert an influence upon the whole country, and the united strength of the several hundreds of millions of the whole country will be so powerful as to influence the whole world. Alas! Our nation has been too accustomed to esteem personal intelligence and courage to pay heed to educating and encouraging the people. In the modern countries, on the contrary, it is essential to depend on the intelligence and courage, not of individuals, but of the whole country. . . . It is not strange that we have not won battles of war and commerce and have remained poor and weak." From an editorial in *Chiang-su,* no. 3 (Tokyo, May 1903), p. 13.

Many students were under the influence of Social Darwinism, as introduced into

papers and magazines published in the treaty ports and provincial capitals greatly increased after the Sino-Japanese War and contributed to the same ends.[3] Their influence grew rapidly with the increase in literacy, a result of the establishment of modern elementary schools.[4]

3. Increased interest in provincial affairs stimulated by railway development. After the Russo-Japanese War many provinces began constructing railways, and natives of the province either voluntarily or involuntarily became shareholders.

4. Organization in many provinces of the New Armies (Hsin-chün), that is, modernized armies. Except in Chihli, where Yuan Shih-k'ai had earlier organized six divisions, provincial modernized armies were founded after the Russo-Japanese War. Provincial prejudices and interests were reinforced in these armies, as will be seen in detail below.

5. Aroused political consciousness of the literati who were active in the constitutional movement and the provincial assemblies. Provincial assembly members, especially the chairmen, became powerful enough to exert great influence upon provincial politics. They reflected the provincial interests of the literati and often opposed the central government's policies.

6. Reaction against the Ch'ing centralization policy. The major

---

China by a translation of Huxley's *Evolution and Ethics* (Yen Fu's *T'ien-yen-lun*), emphasizing the importance of national cooperation starting with cooperation of people in each province. On the introduction of Darwinism into China, see Onogawa Hidemi, "Shinmatsu no shisō to shinkaron" (Late Ch'ing Thought and the Theory of Evolution), *Tōhō gakuhō,* no. 21 (1952), pp. 1–36.

3. According to the second of the *Decennial Reports (1892–1901)* of the Chinese Imperial Maritime Customs Service (*1*, 106), there were 12 Chinese newspapers published in the country in 1894, but in October 1898, 15 newspapers were published in Shanghai alone. As for magazines, in 1895 only 8, relating to missionary activities, were published, but by October of 1898 the number had increased to 35, of which 25 were published in Shanghai. According to the *Decennial Reports,* none of the 1898 newspapers or magazines was conservative. According to Ko Kung-chen, *Chung-kuo pao-hsüeh shih* (A History of Chinese Journalism) (Peking, 1955), pp. 113–19, the number of Chinese newspapers after 1895 rose to 170, including 12 published in Hong Kong and one in Macao. The number of Chinese magazines rose to 81, excluding 34 published in Tokyo, 4 in Yokohama, and one in Macao. The number of publications increased even more rapidly after the Boxer uprising.

4. According to Yüan Hsi-t'ao's "Wu-shih nien-lai Chung-kuo ch'u-teng chiao-yü" (Chinese Elementary Education in the Last Fifty Years) in Shen-pao kuan, *Tsui-chin chih wu-shih-nien* (The Last Fifty Years) (Shanghai, 1923), the number of pupils in elementary schools was several thousand in 1902; it increased sharply to 895,000 in 1907, 1,153,000 in 1908, and 1,481,000 in 1909. By the autumn of 1911 the number of boys and girls in elementary schools must have been no less than two million.

part of a provincial official's income was usually derived from bribery and embezzlement. The imperial government, financially hard pressed after the Boxer incident, tried to increase its revenue by checking these practices.[5] In 1908 a Committee for the Reorganization of Financial Affairs (Ch'ing-li ts'ai-cheng ch'u) was established in Peking, with a branch office (Ch'ing-li ts'ai-cheng chü) in each province. Both the chief and the associate chief of each branch were appointed by the central government.[6] Provincial officials, as expected, vehemently opposed these measures; the literati also expressed concern, since they too had profited by officials' peculation. Because provincial officials had to follow the central government's orders, the literati were alienated from the provincial officials as well as from the central government. These factors not only account for the growing provincialism of the late Ch'ing but also suggest why the literati, students, merchants, and journalists united against provincial officials as well as the central government.[7]

Origin and Development of the Modern Armies

The organization of new military forces sprang from a background in which secret societies had been a main channel of opposition to government, along with the peasantry, who formed the great reservoir of manpower. The secret societies constituted the oldest and strongest strain of anti-Manchu sentiment in China. They continued to reiterate the perennial slogan, "Destroy the Manchus, restore the Ming." Further, in Fukien, Kwangtung, and Kwangsi there usually were connections between the secret societies and the organizations of the Overseas Chinese, since these provinces were the birthplace of both. However, the anti-Manchu feeling of these societies was motivated by a traditional Chinese

5. An imperial instruction of January 6, 1904 ordered the Board of Revenue to draft means of prohibiting embezzlement in order to increase governmental revenues without disturbing the lives of the people. The board recommended ten specific methods, including strict inspection of the collection of the land tax; see *Kuang-hsü ch'ao Tung-hua-lu*, pp. 5121, 5133–39. The following year each province was ordered to prepare a detailed account of the land taxes. Ibid., p. 5198.

6. *Hsüan-t'ung cheng-chi*, *5* (Jan. 11, 1909), 10a–15a; *8* (March 21, 1909), 36a; *9* (April 4, 1909), 36a–37a.

7. The provincial viewpoint lies between the traditional district or prefectural viewpoint and the national one. At this time, it was mainly the enlightened literati and modern intellectuals who could deal with matters from the point of view of the province. Some of them were already advanced enough to have a national point of view, but provincial standpoints were still prevalent.

ethnocentrism, springing from the periodic intrusion of nomads into China, and therefore it differed from the anti-Manchuism of the revolutionaries, which was predominantly a reaction to Western imperialism.

This distinction is illustrated by the difference in outlook between Sun Yat-sen's Society to Restore China's Prosperity, on the one hand, and the Society for China's Revival and the Restoration Society on the other. The former represented many secret societies; Sun's anti-Manchuism was first fed by his secret society friends, and the original members of the Society to Restore China's Prosperity had previously belonged to secret societies in southern China and Hawaii. Though Sun himself advocated more than the overthrow of the dynasty, the nationalism of the Society to Restore China's Prosperity differed from that of the Society for China's Revival and the Restoration Society, whose anti-Manchuism grew out of an awareness and fear of imperialist aggression. These two types of nationalism were fused in the republican revolutionary movement led by the Revolutionary Alliance.

The late Ch'ing reforms alienated peasants as well as literati, although in different ways. Peasants throughout China became restive under what appeared to them to be the burden of modernization. For instance, the ban on the cultivation of opium had taken away one of their most important cash crops in certain provinces. Poor peasants loathed the new schools, for which they had to pay but to which few of them could afford to send their own children. They had no liking for local self-government, as it implied further exactions. But the revolutionaries were themselves modernizers and hence unable or unwilling to capitalize on this source of discontent.[8]

There is only one explicit reference to the problems of the agricultural population in the proclamation of the Revolutionary Alliance. It is the principle of Equal Land Rights (*P'ing-chün ti-ch'üan*). The Program of the Revolution (*Ko-ming fang-lüeh*) explains it as follows: The benefits of civilization should be equally enjoyed by all; to this end a land survey should be made to determine the value of each parcel of land; any increment in land values resulting from progress after the Revolution should be claimed by

8. See my "Shingai kakumei chokuzen ni okeru nōmin-ikki" (Peasant Uprisings Immediately before the Revolution of 1911), *Tōyōshi kenkyū, 13*:1, 2 (1954), 77–106.

the state as national property.[9] This was a vision of a socialist state in which every citizen lived in comfort and contentment. Some members of the Revolutionary Alliance opposed this policy and attempted to delete it from the party proclamation, but Sun Yat-sen was determined to retain it.[10] He believed that the increase in land values would provide the state sufficient revenue to meet its expenses. Burdensome taxes could then be abolished, and landlords would be discouraged from increasing their holdings at the expense of the poor peasants. This would minimize the evils of capitalism from which Europeans were suffering. Sun might have used this principle to appeal to peasants burdened by oppressive taxes. But even on this point he seems to have given little thought to gaining peasant support. It was simply a pet idea he had picked up in his reading. In any event the principle was difficult even for Revolutionary Alliance intellectuals to grasp; peasants could hardly have been expected to understand it, and the revolutionary leaders never directly attempted to solicit their support.[11] Neither the revolutionaries' new nationalism nor their land program won peasant support. The revolutionaries concentrated exclusively on organizing members of the existing secret societies. In the end, some farmers and peasants joined the Revolution. It was not, however, directly in response to revolutionary appeals, but as participants in the modernized armies being created in the provinces.

Toward the end of the Sino-Japanese War, China began to organize modern armies equipped with modern arms and trained by German officers. The first of these were Chang Chih-tung's Self-Strengthening Army (Tzu-ch'iang-chün) in Nanking and Yuan Shih-k'ai's Newly Established Army (Hsin-chien lu-chün) in Chihli.

9. According to *Tōa senkaku shishi kiden,* published by Kokuryūkai (Tokyo, 1935), 2, 381, *Ko-ming fang-lüeh* was printed and distributed secretly by Sun Yat-sen and Huang Hsing in 1906. Feng Tzu-yu states that it was edited by the headquarters of the Revolutionary Alliance in Tokyo in 1906 and was originally mimeographed. Feng, *Chung-hua* (Taipei, 1954), *1,* 213.

10. Sun may have taken this idea from Henry George's *Progress and Poverty,* but it seems more likely that he obtained it directly from John Stuart Mill's original, which in turn had been quoted and discussed in George's book. See my "Shoki ni okeru Son Bun no 'heikin chiken' ni tsuite" (On Sun Yat-sen's Principle of Equalization of Land Rights at the First Stage of its Development), *Shakai-keizaishigaku, 21:* 5, 6 (1956), 59–82.

11. The greatest difference between the Revolution of 1911 and the two following revolutions is the fact that the importance of the peasants was not recognized by republican revolutionary leaders.

These armies were intended for protection against the advancing Japanese forces, but they were never used.

The way in which Chang Chih-tung, then acting governor-general of Liang-Chiang, organized his army is of special interest.[12] Chang was sharply critical of the existing armies, which dated from the Taiping period and had been crushed by the Japanese in 1895. He wrote that they were disorderly crowds whose rank and file had no permanent home and therefore no basis for judgment. There were no fixed numbers of troops, and the ranks were filled with vagrants. Officers embezzled funds earmarked as payments to the rank and file, with the result that the latter were constantly destitute while the former lived in luxury. These traditional officers had no interest in or understanding of modern arms and neglected to train their forces. They adhered to the old-fashioned manner of fighting and had no knowledge of planning battles on maps; hence they could resist internal bandits but were helpless against foreign enemies.

When Chang organized the Self-Strengthening Army, he took steps to remedy these defects. Recruits were to be men between sixteen and twenty years of age, from farm families in areas near Nanking so that their references could be checked. They were to be vouched for by their neighbors and by the clan and village heads and examined by a foreign doctor before admission to the army. Although it is unlikely that all soldiers of the New Army met these standards, Chang's emphasis on them is worth noting.

Similar efforts were made when Yuan Shih-k'ai modernized the Chihli forces after the Boxer Rebellion. His recruiting officers were assisted by local officials in selecting soldiers from settled peasant families. The new recruits were registered at their respective district offices. Yuan ordered that part of the men's salary be sent to their families, who were to be exempted from government labor.[13]

With a view to modernizing the entire country's military institutions, a Commission for Army Reorganization (Lien-ping-ch'u) was established in late 1903. The commission was presided over by

12. Chang Chih-tung, "Hsüan-mu hsin-chün ch'uang-lien yang-ts'ao che" (Memorial on Recruitment and Western Training for the New Army), Dec. 27, 1895, in *Chang Wen-hsiang kung ch'üan-chi* (The Complete Works of Chang Chih-tung) (Peking, 1928), "tsou-kao," *40*, 1a–5b.

13. *Kuang-hsü ch'ao Tung-hua-lu,* Feb. 23, 1902, pp. 4827–28.

Prince Ch'ing, and Yuan Shih-k'ai and T'ieh-liang were appointed senior and junior minister respectively.[14] The commission issued new regulations concerning the organization and salaries of the armed forces. These regulations were patterned after those Yuan Shih-k'ai had already instituted in his army. They decreed that the modernized army of each province was to be manned by provincials. Recruits were to be men of good health between the ages of twenty and twenty-five, selected from settled peasant families; each candidate was to present a certified statement concerning his family's domicile for three generations, and to be fingerprinted. They must have no past record as criminals or opium smokers. The village head was to prepare registers of the new recruits in advance, to be checked by district officials. A certificate was to be issued to the recruit's family, to guarantee the payment of a part of his monthly salary accumulated from the fourth month after entrance into the barracks; commissioners were to be dispatched every six months to personally deliver the money to each family. Finally, a family whose member proved competent in the army was exempted from as much government labor as was ordinarily imposed on farm land or thirty *mou*.[15]

In each province the commission established a Training Director's Office (Tu-lien kung-so) responsible for the organization and training of the army. Although the governor-general, governor, or general in command of the Banner forces was named superintendent (*tu-pan*), real power belonged to the director (*ts'an-i-kuan*), appointed by the commission. Interestingly, most of the directors at this time were graduates of the Officers' School in Japan. The Chinese government planned to have one, two, or in some exceptional cases three or four modern divisions in each province, amounting to thirty-six divisions in the whole country. By

14. Ibid., Dec. 4, 1903, p. 5108. Hsü Shih-ch'ang was named chief of the Military Administration Department, Tuan Ch'i-jui chief of the Military Command Department, and Wang Shih-chen chief of the Military Education Department. Ibid., Dec. 27, 1903, p. 5118. All were Yuan's friends and subordinates. Although Yuan was the country's leading expert in training a modern army, his own army may have served exclusively to enhance his personal power. It has been said that Yuan's portrait was hung in the barracks to indoctrinate the soldiers to be loyal to him. See *Yüan shih-k'ai i-shih, hsü-lu* (Shanghai, 1916), 2, 32; Jordan to Grey, *PP China No. 1 (1912)*, p. 22.

15. *Te-tsung shih-lu, 534*, 2a, Sept. 12, 1904. For the full text of the regulation see *Ta-Ch'ing Kuang-hsü hsin fa-ling*, section on military administration, pp. 58a–59a.

1906, six divisions were already in existence, under the command of Yuan Shih-k'ai and stationed mainly in Chihli.[16]

Traditionally, military men lacked status in China and talented young men had sought civil office. However, the situation had changed dramatically after the Sino-Japanese War, when many discerned the military and economic threats of the foreign powers. At this time nationalism drove many able Chinese youths to enroll in military schools.

Military Schools

The first military school in China was founded at Tientsin in 1885 by Li Hung-chang to train officers of the Huai Army. After the Boxer uprising, Yuan Shih-k'ai, governor-general of Chihli, established a military academy at Paoting. However, the first large-scale attempt was made in the autumn of 1904. The Commission for Army Reorganization, under the stimulus of the Russo-Japanese War, adopted Regulations for Military Schools (*Lu-chün hsüeh-t'ang chang-ch'eng*) which provided for four levels of military training. Each province was to establish a three-year elementary military school with students to be drawn from graduates of senior elementary schools. Two-year middle-grade military schools were to be established in Chihli, Shensi, Kiangsu, and Hupeh; and in Peking a military academy with a term of a year and a half and a military college with a two-year term were to be established.[17] It should be noted that even at the lowest level, officers would be drawn from landlords, rich farmers, and prosperous merchants, because only these could afford to send their sons through senior elementary schools.

In addition to these new military schools, many Chinese students also studied in Japan. The number of Chinese in military schools in Japan increased after the Boxer uprising and even more after Japan's victory over Russia.[18] The Seijō gakkō, a prepara-

16. The Commission for Army Reorganization was eventually incorporated into the newly reestablished Ministry of War headed by T'ieh-liang, Shou-hsün, and Yin-ch'ang, all Manchus. Control of the army was officially transferred to the ministry, with the exception of two divisions that remained under Yuan Shih-k'ai until he was appointed Grand Councillor and Foreign Minister a year later.

17. The full text of the regulations is in *Ta-Ch'ing Kuang-hsü hsin fa-ling*, section on military administration, pp. 1a–3b.

18. See names of Chinese graduates from the Military Officers' School arranged according to the year of enrollment in the appendices to *Saishin Shina kanshinroku* (Record of Contemporary Chinese Officials and Gentry) (Peking, 1916), pp. 397–401.

tory school, originally for Japanese students who intended to enter the Military Officers' School, also accepted Chinese students. It limited admission to Chinese students on government scholarships after the Shinbu gakkō, another preparatory school, was founded in 1903. A third private preparatory school, the Tōhin gakudō, was founded in 1903 for Chinese students who were suspect in the eyes of their government and hence barred from government support.[19] Since students who were not on government scholarships tended to be revolutionary, in 1903 the Manchu government forbade such students to enter the Military Officers' School,[20] and in 1904 forbade them to enter any military school.[21] It was difficult to enforce this ban and in any event many of the students the government financed in the Military Officers' School became revolutionaries.[22] Their later influence in the new provincial armies and military schools was significant.

The education and training of soldiers as well as officers of the new armies were far superior to those of the older armies. The regulations[23] stipulated that one-fifth of the recruits for a battalion should be literate; that these should be trained for five months; that the best of these should then be promoted to the rank of corporal (*fu-mu*), and the remainder to the rank of regular private (*cheng-ping*). The corporals and privates were to train the remainder of the battalion for three months, whereupon the corporals were to become sergeants (*cheng-mu*) and the privates to become corporals. For new recruits a comparable and continuing program of training and promotion was provided. Available case histories indicate how literate soldiers were able to become first noncommissioned and then commissioned officers.[24]

19. Sanetō Keishu, *Chūgokujin Nihon ryūgaku-shi* (History of Chinese Students in Japan) (Tokyo, 1960), pp. 68–71.

20. *Ta-Ch'ing Kuang-hsü hsin fa-ling, 14,* 4b–5a.

21. Ibid., "Hsüan-p'ai lu-chün hsüeh-sheng yu-hsüeh chang-ch'eng" (Regulations for Selecting Military Students to be Sent Abroad for Study), and Nagai Kazumi, "Iwayuru Shinkoku ryūgakusei torishimari-kisoku no seikaku" (On the Nature of the Japanese Government's Regulations for the Control of Chinese Students Studying in Japan), *Shinshu daigaku bunri-gakubu kiyō, 2.*

22. According to Li Shu-ch'eng, who used the name of Ting Jen-chün and was one of the fifth-term students in the Military Officers' School, there were 75, 58, and 198 Chinese students in the 4th, 5th, and 6th terms respectively in 1908 (?), of whom more than 100 were members of the Revolutionary Alliance. *HHKMHIL, 1,* 193.

23. *Ta-Ch'ing Kuang-hsü hsin fa-ling, 14,* 59a–b.

24. For example, Huang Chia-lin became a soldier upon graduation from senior elementary school, was later promoted to noncommissioned officer, and then to

In the years after the Russo-Japanese War, many literati and intellectuals enrolled in military schools and even enlisted as soldiers.[25] Some of them remained in the rank and file to encourage revolutionary activity among the troops; others were sent to military schools and were promoted to lower officer rank. These soldiers, noncommissioned officers, and lower commissioned officers became the core of the expanding revolutionary activity in the army.

The officers and men of the new armies were in the main natives of the province in which they served. The junior officers and many of the men had had some schooling and could read, and they had a strong sense of provincial loyalty. Those senior officers who had gone to military school in Japan shared this provincial loyalty and more often than not were sympathetic to the revolutionary cause.

The Case of Kwangtung

The modern armies of Kwangtung and Hupeh best illustrate these points. Revolutionaries like Chao Sheng, Huang Hsing, Hu Han-min, and I Ying-tien were active in the Kwangtung Army. The first three were leaders of the Revolutionary Alliance, while the fourth had been a junior officer in the modern army of Anhwei.[26] These four men operated from a base in Hong Kong, and their efforts, especially I Ying-tien's, resulted in the creation of a revolutionary organization in the Kwangtung Army. The nucleus of the organization consisted of noncommissioned officers.[27] They planned to rise in revolt on February 10, 1910, which was the first day of the Chinese lunar New Year. On the preceding day I Ying-

lower commissioned officer after graduating from the Hupeh Military Academy (Hu-pei chiang-wu hsüeh-t'ang); see Huang's biography in Chang Nan-hsien, *Hu-pei ko-ming chih-chih lu* (A Record of the Revolution in Hupeh) (Shanghai, 1946), p. 176. Similarly, Ts'ai Chi-min became a soldier at the age of nineteen; after graduating from a "special school" (*t'e-pieh hsüeh-t'ang*), he was promoted to noncommissioned officer and then to section commander; Ts'ai's biography, ibid., pp. 204 ff.

25. According to the memoirs of Ch'en Hsiao-fen, *Hsin-hai shou-i hui-i-lu* (Reminiscences of the 1911 Uprising), *1*, 68, when he enlisted in the Hupeh army there were 36 holders of lower examination degrees among the 96 volunteers at Huang-p'o hsien. Ho Sui states that when he was a leader of the Ninth Division at Nanking, there were 34 literati, including one provincial degree holder in his company of 126 men; ibid., *1*, 161.

26. I Ying-tien had tried to organize a revolutionary coup among his men, but had been removed just before the revolt of 1910 staged by Hsiung Ch'eng-chi.

27. Wang Chan-k'uei and Chiang Yün-ch'un were special sergeant-majors; Yu Lung-piao and Huang Hung-k'un were commanders of squads.

tien and other revolutionary leaders became involved in a petty squabble between a group of soldiers and the police. Within two days, they attempted a revolt that was suppressed shortly. There were many casualties, including I Ying-tien; seven or eight hundred men surrendered, and about a thousand deserted the barracks.[28]

The response to this incident by the peasants, merchants, literati, and provincial officials is revealing. The peasants, it is said, provided the revolutionary deserters with food, lodging, clothes, and money. As the soldiers of the Green Standard and the Huai Army had robbed the people mercilessly, the peasants now were agreeably surprised that such was not the case with the revolutionary soldiers.[29] Members of the gentry, journalists, members of the education and self-government committees as well as charitable societies, took it upon themselves to look after the deserters. They presented a memorial to Governor-general Yüan Shu-hsün requesting that he deal leniently with the deserters, according to the rule of "no punishment of forced followers." A petition was also sent to Li Chun, commander of the Kwangtung Navy, requesting that the authorities cease to call the incident a revolution and the soldiers "rebel soldiers."

Public opinion forced Yüan Shu-hsün to permit the return of the soldiers to their native places under controlled conditions. A list of soldiers returning home was to be prepared for each county. They were to be given travel allowances and escorted by an official and ten policemen in groups of no more than thirty. Police who had fought the rebels were to be excluded from the escort. The soldiers were to be lectured on proper behavior and told stories of historical figures who had gone astray but later reformed and gained fame. On arrival home, they were to be secretly watched, and the county magistrate was to report to the police on their conduct. Those who lived for three years without giving offense were to be returned to normal status. Any who were discovered to have been

28. For a detailed description of the revolutionary revolt of the modern army of Kwangtung, see *TFTC,* 7:2 (1910) "Chung-kuo ta-shih-chi" (Chronology of Major Events in China), 15–21; no. 3, "Chung-kuo ta-shih-chi pu-i" (Supplement to the Chronology of Major Events in China), 1–4; and no. 4, "Chung-kuo ta-shih-chi pu-i," 10–11. The report of an official inquiry by Chang Jen-chün, governor-general of Liang-Chiang, is also found in *TFTC,* no. 5. See also Ch'en Ch'un-sheng's account in *HHKM, 3,* 347 ff.

29. "Chung-kuo ta-shih-chi," *TFTC,* 7:2, 20.

ringleaders of the revolt were to be jailed, but coercion was not to be used to extract information.[30]

The General Chamber of Commerce, the Red Cross, and various charitable and other organizations petitioned the governor-general to relax these conditions. They argued that the provisions for a police escort and for a three-year probation would disgrace and shame the soldiers; it would be better to let them go home freely or under the escort of merchant and charitable organizations. Moreover, they pointed out, certain artillery, engineering, and transport units had been trained for years. Instead of being disgraced they should be recalled for service in the Kwangtung division just then being completed.[31]

The Kwangtung Merchants' Self-Government Association (Yüeh-shang tzu-chih-hui) held a meeting to demand the recall of the deserters to military duty. Many segments of society were represented, and speeches were made blaming the brigadier for the incident and exonerating the soldiers. They stated that these men all came from good families and had joined the army from patriotic motives; most of them were well educated. They had never troubled peasants or merchants; they had never robbed the peasants of even a tree or an herb, and they would not have troubled them even if they were starving. They had been welcomed everywhere by the peasants.[32]

Governor-general Yüan resisted the clamor, saying the soldiers had clearly intended to start a rebellion; this was proved by their disobeying orders, breaking into brigade headquarters, plundering arms, money, vessels, and utensils, and trying to compel the regimental commander to rise with them.

> How could I strain the law to protect these rebels? Certainly not! There were allegedly many who had been forced to join the revolt; I took measures for their return to their native places and provided travel expenses so that they could find ways to reform themselves. People looked up to them as soon as they learned that they were soldiers of the modern army and did not pay any attention to their rebellious acts. Could I allow these young fellows to become bolder and to rebel

30. Ibid., pp. 19–20.
31. Ibid., p. 21.
32. Ibid., no. 3, "Chung-kuo ta-shih-chi pu-i," 3–4.

> again? Certainly not! It is true that some of them had been forced to join the revolt, but it is wrong to claim that all of them were men of good character.[33]

The incident reveals certain characteristics of military modernization at this time. Soldiers of the modern army in Kwangtung were mostly men of good background and education. At least they were not robbers. They shared the interests and outlook of the farmers, merchants, and literati of the province. This is why they were defended against the governor-general's accusations. Popular resentment against the Manchus was translated into indignation against the governor-general and other officials who were believed to represent hostile interests. Far from condemning the revolutionary uprising, the literati and merchants lauded it.

In these circumstances, the governor-general could not rely on the New Army to enforce the execution of Manchu policies. He had to turn to other less effective forces—the provincial forces (*hsün-fang-tui*) and the constabulary (*hsün-ching*). The latter were quasi-military police forces organized in 1907, whose members were drawn from the older armies. Most of them had no settled residence in Kwangtung and were of doubtful character. They resented the modern army, which was favored by the people, and were willing tools of the governor-general.

Kwangtung was not unique. The pattern was repeated in Szechwan, where the modern army of Szechwanese natives enjoyed good relations with the people, and the acting governor-general Chao Erh-feng had to rely on the old-style provincial forces.[34]

The Case of Hupeh

The modern army of Hupeh was reorganized in 1901 from the old armies, and in 1904 was expanded to two divisions by the addition of recruits from settled peasant families.[35] T'ieh-liang, who inspected the army at the end of 1904, reported[36] that the first and

33. Ibid., no. 4, "Chung-kuo ta-shih-chi pu-i," 10–11.

34. A telegram from Sheng Hsüan-huai to Jui-cheng and Tuan-fang, August 29, 1911, quoting a telegram from Chao Erh-feng in *Yü-chai ts'un-kao, 80,* 12b. See also the dispatches of Wilkinson, the British consul general in Chengtu, *PP China No. 1 (1912)*, pp. 17, 51.

35. Chang Chih-tung's memorials on reforms in military training: "Ch'ou-pan lien-ping shih-i cho-i ying-chih hsiang-chang che," Oct. 31, 1902, *Ch'üan-chi,* "tsou-kao" *57,* 22b–25b; and "Ni pien Hu-pei ch'ang-pei chün-chih che," Aug. 28, 1904, *Ch'üan-chi,* "tsou-kao," *62,* 24a–35a.

36. T'ieh-liang's memorial of February 22, 1905, in *Kuang-hsü ch'ao Tung-hua-lu,* pp. 5289 ff. T'ieh-liang inspected the provinces of Central China to look for sources of revenue and to inquire into conditions in the modern armies.

the second divisions had completed only one brigade each, but the army was already rated one of the best in the Yangtze provinces. Most of the rank and file could read. Officers were graduates of the Military Academy (Wu-pei hsüeh-t'ang) or had studied abroad.[37] According to Chang Chih-tung, the grand total of the army's officers and men in late 1905 was 12,317, of whom 9,915 were from Hupeh province, 1,916 from other provinces, and 486 from the Banner garrison of Wuchang. Chang stated that men from other provinces would gradually be replaced by Hupeh natives.[38]

Wuhan had been a revolutionary center since 1900 when the Independent Army attempted an armed uprising under the leadership of T'ang Ts'ai-ch'ang; Fu Tz'u-hsiang and Wu Lu-chen, both graduates of the Military Academy of Hupeh, took part. In 1904 the Institute for the Diffusion of Science was established in Wuchang with the specific purpose of staging a revolution.[39] The central figure of the institute, Liu Ching-an, was secretary of the cavalry battalion under the command of Li Yüan-hung. Liu's efforts to form a revolutionary nucleus in the army were foiled and his institute was destroyed.[40]

The institute's collapse was followed by the emergence of the Society for Daily Improvement. Originally a missionary society, in early 1906 it was transformed into a revolutionary organization by Liu Ching-an, who had become its manager. This organization also collapsed at the end of the year owing to the failure of an uprising by Liu Tao-i in Hunan with whom the society was closely allied.[41] Liu Ching-an, Chang Nan-hsien, Li Ya-tung,[42] and others were arrested.

37. Ibid., p. 5301.

38. See Chang's memorial of December 7, 1905, on this subject: "Tsun-chao hsin-chang kai-pien ying-chih hsiang-chang ping she tu-lien san-ch'u che," *Ch'üan-chi,* "tsou-kao," *65,* 3a–13b.

39. The organizers were Chang Nan-hsien and Hu Ying, both intellectuals who had enrolled in the Wuchang modern army, Lü Ta-sen, a student at the Military High School (reorganized from the former Hupeh Military School), and Sung Chiao-jen, a student at the Civil High School.

40. Chang Nan-hsien, "K'o-hsüeh pu-hsi-so shih-mo" (An Account of the Institute for the Diffusion of Science), in *Hu-pei ko-ming chih-chih lu,* pp. 55–57. Interesting memoirs of members of various revolutionary organizations who had been active in the modern army of Hupeh and were still alive were compiled in *Hsin-hai shou-i hui-i-lu* (3 vols. Wuhan, 1957–58). Also see Li Lien-fang. "Wu-ch'ang shou-i ch'ien chih ko-ming t'uan-t'i" (Revolutionary Organizations Prior to the Wuchang Uprising), in *KKWH, Ko-ming chih ch'ang-tao yü fa-chan, Wu-ch'ang shou-i* (Taipei, 1961) *1,* 388 ff. and passim.

41. Ts'ao Ya-po, *Wu-ch'ang ko-ming chen-shih* (A True History of the Revolution in Wuchang) (3 vols. Shanghai, 1930), pp. 129 ff. According to "Jih-chih-hui shou-ling Liu Ching-an," Feng, *I-shih, 2,* 62, Liu Ching-an was converted early to

In the summer of 1908 a revolutionary organization called the Hupeh Military Revolutionary Alliance was founded by Huang Shen-hsiang and Li Ya-tung. After the authorities became suspicious its name was changed to the Society for the Study of Popular Government. It collapsed, however, when its attempt to take advantage of the rice riots in Changsha in the spring of 1910 was discovered.[43] In the summer of that year a new society, the Institute for the Restoration of Martial Spirit, was organized to intensify revolutionary activity within the modern army. Li Yüan-hung became aware of these activities; he dismissed Fan K'ang-shih, a company commander and a member of the society, along with the central revolutionary figures in each company.[44] Chiang I-wu, Chan Ta-pei, and others then reorganized the society into the Literary Institute in January 1911.[45] This time their experience with revolutionary propaganda paid off, and the organization expanded rapidly.

Only a few members of the Institute for the Diffusion of Science and the Society for Daily Improvement were from the modern army, and they were mostly officers. But the number of soldiers and noncommissioned officers increased in the successor organizations, and the Literary Institute consisted entirely of members from the rank and file, except for a few lower officers.[46] Higher officers were not invited for fear they might inform the authorities.[47] Most members of the Literary Institute were joining a revolutionary organization for the first time. Each company, battalion, and regiment elected a responsible representative to the organization.[48]

Christianity, transformed the Society for Daily Improvement into a revolutionary organization, and then entered the barracks under the command of Li Yüan-hung in order to enlarge the revolutionary organization. He seems to have received his entire education from his father and literati, not in any modern school. His biography is included in Chang Nan-hsien, pp. 73 ff.

42. Li Ya-tung was from Hsinyang, Honan, a graduate of the Hupeh Officers' School (Hu-pei chiang-pan hsüeh-t'ang). He had been a captain in the modern army but was dismissed because of revolutionary activities. Chang Nan-hsien, p. 100.

43. "Hu-pei chün-tui t'ung-meng-hui chih shih-mo," and "Ch'ün chih hsüeh-she chih shih-mo" in Chang Nan-hsien, pp. 145 ff.

44. "Chen-wu hsüeh-she chih shih-mo" in Chang Nan-hsien, pp. 152 ff.

45. "Wen-hsüeh-she chih shih-mo" in Chang Nan-hsien, pp. 158 ff.

46. *Wu-ch'ang shou-i*, p. 60.

47. "Ch'ün-chih hsüeh-she chih shih-mo" (Account of the Society for the Study of Popular Government) in Chang Nan-hsien; Kita Ikki, *Shina kakumei gaishi* (An Unofficial History of the Chinese Revolution) (Tokyo, 1921), p. 66.

48. Organizing methods are described in Ts'ao Ya-po, *Wu-ch'ang ko-ming, I*, 380–81. It seems that pressure and special incentives were used to enlarge the organi-

The Progressive Association was a specialized organization of the Revolutionary Alliance organized by Chiao Ta-feng to work on the secret societies. In the spring of 1909 it moved its headquarters to Hankow and cooperated with the Literary Institute in agitation within the army. However, Revolutionary Alliance activities were still concentrated on acquiring a base in southeast China. It was only after the failure of the attack on the Kwangtung government at the end of April 1911 that its attention turned to the development of revolutionary organizations in Wuhan. At the end of September 1911, the Literary Institute and the Progressive Association united to stage a revolutionary uprising in Wuhan, and in an attempt on October 10 they finally succeeded in bringing down the Hupeh government.

Concerning the revolutionary movement within the Hupeh army, the following points are clear:

1. A number of intellectuals such as Chang Nan-hsien and Hu Ying had voluntarily joined the army in order to propagate the Revolution.[49]

2. Soldiers of the modern army were generally of good character and education. They were responsive to revolutionary propaganda circulated in pamphlets, journals, and magazines. It is said that such propaganda as Ch'en T'ien-hua's "Meng hui t'ou" (About Face!) and "Ching-shih chung" (Alarm to Warn the World) was hidden in the soldiers' beds while they were out training.[50]

3. Many lower officers and all noncommissioned officers were promoted from common soldiers.

4. Although there is no evidence to indicate that the modern army of Hupeh was as esteemed by peasants, literati, and merchants as the Kwangtung Army, it may well have been.

---

zation. According to Ts'ao Ya-po, 30% of the members were active, 30% were sitting on the fence, and the rest had been forced to join the organization. In the Kwangtung modern army, those who had canvassed ten members were awarded a superior order and those who had brought in a hundred an extraordinary order. (Feng, *I-shih, 1,* 207.) This fact is mentioned in the testimony of Wang Chan-k'uei, a special sergeant-major and one of the central figures of the revolutionary organization of the Kwangtung modern army.

49. Chang Nan-hsien and Hu Ying seem not to have been educated in a modern school. They may be called enlightened lower literati. According to *Hsin-hai shou-i hui-i-lu, 1, 2, 3,* and the biographies in Chang Nan-hsien, the following became soldiers after having been educated in modern schools: Chiang I-wu: higher elementary school, normal school; Chiang Kuo-kuang: higher elementary school; Hsieh Ch'u-heng: higher elementary school; Huang Chia-lin: higher elementary school; Li Chi-ch'en: higher elementary school; Liu Hua-ou: Chung-kuo kung-hsüeh; Ts'ai Ta-fu: normal school; Wang Shih-chieh: higher elementary school.

50. Liu Ching-an's biography in Feng, *I-shih, 2,* 62.

The preceding account suggests the following general conclusions about the revolutionary era. The provincialism that became dominant in the late Ch'ing period was stimulated by China's modernization and by Chinese nationalism in response to imperialist aggression. This provincialism should therefore be viewed as a stage in the development of nationalism, not as a retrogressive stage. It was a phenomenon accompanying the growing self-awareness of the Chinese people, especially the enlightened literati, rich merchants, and modern intellectuals.

The development of provincialism and a strong modern army were interrelated phenomena. Soldiers of the modern armies were usually recruited from peasant families in the province; they were respectable men trusted by the people of the province. Noncommissioned and lower officers were likewise natives of the province. All the officers and many of the soldiers were educated and interested in provincial affairs. They responded readily to revolutionary propaganda and sympathized with the developing nationalism of the enlightened literati, rich merchants, and modern intellectuals.

In these circumstances, the governor-general or governor, who was an outsider, could not depend on the modern army to enforce Manchu policies. He had to turn to the provincial forces or the constabulary, who were uneducated and disreputable and seldom had firm roots in the province.

The republican revolutionaries concentrated their attention on secret societies and the army, and failed to capitalize on popular unrest. They never approached the peasants, who bitterly opposed the modernizing policies of the Manchu government. Paradoxically, it was one of the products of those policies—the modern armies—that successfully channeled peasant discontent into organized, revolutionary form.

9. The First Week of Revolution: The Wuchang Uprising

Vidya Prakash Dutt

The Revolution of 1911 was sparked by the revolt of New Army units in Wuchang in October 1911, which enabled the revolutionaries to make their first successful bid to overthrow Manchu rule. Since the turn of the century they had made a number of abortive attempts, each of which was suppressed with much bloodshed. The pattern followed in Wuhan was significantly different from the general one. First, all earlier revolts had relied heavily on secret societies; in Hupeh the primary reliance was on subversion of the New Army (Hsin-chün). While the need for mobilizing the army was recognized by revolutionaries everywhere, in most other areas the revolutionaries' main strength still lay in the secret societies, and normally if they won over adherents in the army units, these army groups were merely expected to respond to the uprisings led by the secret societies. But in Hupeh, particularly in the Wuhan area, the revolutionaries decided early to concentrate on the New Army and to make the army itself lead the revolt against Ch'ing rule. Perhaps this was essential because, aside from the metropolitan province of Chihli, the New Army was centered in Hupeh.

Second, the role of ordinary soldiers in the Wuchang uprising was a striking characteristic of the Revolution in Hupeh. The leaders were unpretentious men in uniform who worked with the single-minded purpose of bringing down the Manchu dynasty. Third, they had only a tenuous link with revolutionary bodies elsewhere and with the central revolutionary organization, the Revolutionary Alliance. The core leadership of this purely military organization—which sprang up under one name after another each time it was discovered and suppressed by the authorities, and whose final name was the Literary Institute—had little to do with outside organizations. It did finally join forces with one of the subsidiary organizations of the Revolutionary Alliance known as the Progressive Association, but the connection was superficial and partial. The successful uprising in Wuhan was the result of the conversion of large numbers of soldiers of the New Army to the cause of revolution. This, as we shall see later, was both a strength and a weakness.

Revolutionary Activity in Hupeh

Revolutionary activity in Hupeh dated back to 1900, when one of the reformist leaders, T'ang Ts'ai-ch'ang, in league with secret societies, fomented revolts in the Yangtze area.[1] Although the revolts were quickly put down, for a time revolutionary attention was centered on Kwangtung. But the Yangtze Valley revolutionaries did not give up their work. Ironically, Governor-general Chang Chih-tung's decision to create a New Army in Hupeh considerably facilitated the work of the rebels and the spread of revolutionary ideas. The dispatch of large numbers of students to Japan for military training also exposed them to radical ideas and helped spread the seeds of revolution among them. In 1900 a Hupeh student, Wu Lu-chen, who later rose to be a general in the New Army and a leading revolutionary, was sent to Japan; by this time students had begun to organize reading rooms and publish papers secretly to propagate revolution. In 1901 Wu Lu-chen graduated, and upon his return from Japan was appointed an instructor in the New Army by Chang Chih-tung. By then Wu had been converted to the cause of revolution and began discussing it with friends in the army.[2]

In the meantime Huang Hsing, later a major leader of the revolutionaries second only to Sun Yat-sen, first became a student at the Liang-Hu Academy and then was sent to Japan by Chang Chih-tung. In Tokyo, Huang soon became busy with fellow students from Hupeh and Hunan in support of revolutionary activities, publishing papers like the *Hu-pei hsüeh-sheng chieh* (Hupeh Student World) and translating materials on nationalism and popular rights. When the Russians penetrated Manchuria (1902–03), Huang Hsing, Lan T'ien-wei, Ch'en T'ien-hua, Feng Tzu-yu, Li Shu-ch'eng (Ting Jen-chün), and others organized the Independent

1. Chang Nan-hsien, *Hu-pei ko-ming chih-chih lu* (A Record of the Revolution in Hupeh) (Shanghai, 1947), pp. 19–26.

2. Hu Tsu-shun, *Wu-ch'ang k'ai-kuo shih-lu* (Record of the Founding of the Republic at Wuchang), 1 (Wuchang, 1949), 8–9.

Army. They decided that for China to have a nationalist revolution, the army and students must be mobilized, and Huang was selected to go back to the mainland and organize a rebellion. He returned to Hupeh in June 1903 and after making an inflammatory speech at the Liang-Hu Academy proceeded to Changsha in Hunan. In December 1903, Huang Hsing, Wu Lu-chen, Ch'en T'ien-hua, Sung Chiao-jen, Chang Chi, Hu Ying, T'an Jen-feng, Liu K'uei-i, and others met in Changsha and established the Society for China's Revival. Huang was elected leader and preparations were intensified for a rebellion against Ch'ing rule.[3]

In 1904, at the same time, some of the leading revolutionaries of Hupeh, including Liu Ching-an, Ts'ao Ya-po, Hu Ying, Chang Nan-hsien, Lü Ta-sen, Chu Tzu-lung, and Ho Chi-ta, gathered in Wuchang and decided after consultation that unless the Revolution spread from the army itself, it would have little chance of success.[4] Therefore, Hu Ying and Chang Nan-hsien infiltrated the Engineers Corps and the others managed to smuggle themselves into other New Army units.[5]

The same year they formed the Institute for the Diffusion of Science, with Lü Ta-sen as head and Hu Ying, Sung Chiao-jen, Ts'ao Ya-po, and Liu Ching-an among the other officers.[6] The Wuhan revolutionaries forged a common front with their counterparts in Hunan and prepared to respond to the revolt being organized there by the Society for China's Revival. However, the Hunan revolt came to grief because of the leakage of plans. The Hunan governor informed Governor-general Chang Chih-tung about the nature of the Institute for the Diffusion of Science, and the organization was suppressed in October 1904.[7]

Hu Ying hid himself in Hanyang while Liu Ching-an took refuge in the American Church Mission. Liu managed to smuggle himself into the Hupeh cavalry commanded by Li Yüan-hung, who shortly afterward was made commander of the Mixed Brigade there, and became Li's secretary. In 1905 a letter from Huang Hsing to Liu Ching-an was intercepted and Li Yüan-hung became

3. Liu K'uei-i, "Huang Hsing chuan-chi" (Biography of Huang Hsing), *HHKM*, *4*, 275–77.

4. Chang Kuo-kan, *Hsin-hai ko-ming shih-lu* (History of the Revolution of 1911) (Wuchang, 1949), p. 9.

5. Ibid.; Yang Yü-ju, *Hsin-hai ko-ming hsien-chu chi* (An Account of the Beginnings of the Revolution of 1911) (Peking, 1958), p. 41.

6. Hu Tsu-shun, p. 9.

7. Chang Nan-hsien, p. 56.

suspicious of Liu's activities and forced him to resign. Liu became a Christian and joined the American Church Mission, leading to the formation of the next revolutionary organization, the Society for Daily Improvement.[8] This society was started by the American Church Mission to propagate Christianity, but Liu Ching-an secretly started propagating revolution[9] and popularizing Ch'en T'ien-hua's writings, such as "Meng hui t'ou" (About Face!) and "Ching-shih chung" (Alarm to Warn the World).[10] Meetings were held every Sunday and were well attended by radically inclined students and army elements. All those who had been in the Institute for the Diffusion of Science joined the Society for Daily Improvement, many becoming well known in the revolutionary movement. Among the active workers were Ch'a Kuang-fo, Lan T'ien-wei,[11] Ts'ai Chi-min, P'eng Ch'u-fan, Wu Chao-lin,[12] Li Ya-tung, and Wang Hsien-chang.[13]

The Society for Daily Improvement became affiliated with the Revolutionary Alliance and spread its net far and wide. In Kiukiang the organization's workers established a reading room with books containing revolutionary ideas. The students, the military, and even many merchants and members of the gentry class, came under their influence. They established an office in Huangchow for printing revolutionary materials for secret distribution in the army and effective use was made of patriotic songs that became popular in military circles. The Society for Daily Improvement also organized, in nearby Huang-kang, a Military Training Institute (Huang-kang chün-hsüeh-chieh chiang-hsi-so) where lectures were delivered on nationalism and people's rights, as well as on provincial autonomy.[14]

At this time, Sun Yat-sen established contacts with the French authorities, and the French army was willing to lend a helping hand. A French army officer deputed to inspect the party organization in Hupeh arrived in Wuhan on June 29, 1906 and addressed a

8. Hu Tsu-shun, pp. 9–10.

9. Ibid., p. 10.

10. Ts'ao Ya-po, *Wu-ch'ang ko-ming chen-shih* (True History of the Wuchang Revolution) (Ch'ien-pien) (Shanghai, 1930), p. 12.

11. At the time of the Wuchang uprising in October 1911, Lan T'ien-wei was commander of the Mixed Brigade at Mukden.

12. Wu Chao-lin was destined to play a central role on the fateful night of October 10 when the Wuchang uprising broke out, as I shall indicate below.

13. Hu Tsu-shun, p. 10.

14. Ts'ao Ya-po (Ch'ien-pien), p. 136.

meeting of the Society for Daily Improvement, attended by many hundreds of people at Kao-chia-hsiang in Wuchang. He delivered a militant speech about the inevitability of, and the imperative need for, revolution in China. However, an agent of the imperial government had smuggled himself into the meeting.[15] According to some revolutionary accounts this agent was Chang Piao himself, commander of the Eighth Division at Wuhan.[16] In any case, the authorities learned of the developments and became extremely watchful of the activities of the society.

Shortly afterward the P'ing-hsiang uprising in 1906 occurred, greatly affecting the fortunes of the Society for Daily Improvement. Government officials decided to swoop down on the society's leaders. Hu Ying, Li Ya-tung, Chang Nan-hsien, and many others were arrested and jailed. Liu Ching-an escaped initially but was later betrayed by an agent and also jailed. Despite considerable efforts by American missionaries, Liu Ching-an's release could not be secured and he remained in prison.[17] The Society for Daily Improvement was dead.

Although an overall organization for the army units no longer existed, a number of small secret groups continued to lead a perilous existence. Then in July 1908, a new unified organization for military men, the Army Revolutionary Alliance, was set up by Yang Wang-p'eng, Huang Shen-hsiang, and other revolutionaries in army circles. Government suppression forced them to adopt a more innocuous name and in December it became the Institute for the Study of Popular Government.[18] This was in fact the first real revolutionary organization of the New Army of Hupeh. An indication of the new winds blowing about the New Army was the rapid development of this organization. The Forty-first, Forty-second, Thirty-second, and Eighth Regiments were all successfully infiltrated and there was a rapid increase in membership.[19] The new organization was supported almost entirely by the resources of the members; the regulations provided that each contribute one-tenth of his salary to its funds.[20] The remarkable headway the new or-

15. Ibid. At the time of this writing the French archives were not available for consultation. [They have since been organized and opened.—ed.]

16. Hu Han-min, ed., *Tsung-li ch'üan-chi* (Complete Works of Sun Yat-sen) (Shanghai, 1931), (Tzu-chuan) (Autobiography), p. 11.

17. Ts'ao Ya-po, pp. 140–62.

18. Yang Yü-ju, p. 18.

19. Ibid.

20. Ibid.

ganization had made and its insight into the requirements of a successful revolution were evident in its decision to include soldiers of all ranks, as well as officers.[21] There is no doubt that without the support of the rank and file the Wuchang uprising would have met the same fate as previous uprisings.

About this time a talented young Hunanese, Chiang I-wu, who soon rose to be an important revolutionary leader in the New Army, came to Hupeh and joined the Forty-first Regiment. He made the acquaintance of Ch'a Kuang-fo, a member of the Society for the Study of Popular Government, and became a leading member of the organization. Together they started the *Shang-wu-pao* (Journal of Commerce) to carry the message of revolution.[22] Since this was a period of considerable unrest in the South, the imperial authorities hesitated to resort to severe repression. Thus the organization escaped immediate suppression and carried on its work of propaganda and training for almost two years.[23]

The revolutionaries tried to make use of the Changsha rice riots of April 1910 in which thousands of famine-stricken people of Hunan demonstrated before the governor's office and set fire to it, burning some missionary institutions as well. The agitation spread. The Hupeh revolutionaries decided to stage a revolt which, it was determined, would be started by the Forty-first Regiment. Huang Hsiao-lin was sent to Hunan and Lin Chao-tung to the Szechwan border to aid rebels in these areas. Just when the preparations were being completed the news came that the Hunan revolt had been quelled. The troops could not be called out; the secret had leaked and the Manchu authorities clamped a strict curfew on the city. Huang Shen-hsiang fled to Shanghai and Lin Chao-tung to Szechwan. *Shang-wu-pao* was suppressed and the Society for the Study of Popular Government was dissolved.[24]

It was not long, however, before the army revolutionaries were again in action. In September 1910, Yang Wang-p'eng, Chiang I-wu, and others started another organization, the Institute for the Restoration of Martial Spirit. Despite the dissolution of the earlier organization, the old apparatus was intact and could thus provide the new organization with representatives from nearly every regiment and battalion. Yang Wang-p'eng headed the new society and

21. Chang Nan-hsien, p. 147.
22. Chang Kuo-kan, p. 22.
23. Chang Nan-hsien, p. 147.
24. Ibid., pp. 147–48.

a new paper called *Ta-chiang-pao* (Yangtze River Review) was started in Hankow. Once again information reached Li Yüan-hung, who forced Yang to resign from the army and struck a few other names from the rolls. There was strict surveillance in each military camp and the Institute for the Restoration of Martial Spirit had to be dissolved.[25]

In early 1911 the members again met to revive their activities but decided to change the name of the society to the Literary Institute in order to insure secrecy and avoid the attention of the authorities. The office of the Literary Institute was located in Chang T'ing-fu's house at 85 Hsiao-ch'ao-chieh or at 85 Hsiao-miao-chieh, both in the Russian concession at Hankow. Chiang I-wu was elected president of the organization and representatives were selected from various army units. Emissaries were dispatched to Shanghai, other parts of Kiangsu, Anhwei, Hunan, Kwangtung, Kwangsi, Shantung, and Manchuria to contact their comrades there.[26]

By now the revolutionary organization had representatives from all the New Army units except the cavalry. It became a major goal of the Literary Institute members to spread their network to this unit. Chang Yü-k'un was entrusted with this task and it was reported that very shortly there were nearly forty converts from the cavalry.[27] The influence and membership of the new organization spread rapidly and it became a powerful revolutionary organization in the Hupeh New Army, ready to strike at the roots of governmental authority and power in Wuhan. By the time of the outbreak of the Szechwan railway crisis, the Literary Institute already had some three thousand members.[28]

In the meantime the Progressive Association had been established in Hankow. In October 1908, the top elected leaders of its Tokyo office went back to China and divided their field of activity. In January 1909, Chiao Ta-feng arrived in Hankow and discussed with Sun Wu ways and means of conducting revolutionary activity in Hupeh and Hunan. In April 1909, the headquarters office was established in the French concession in Hankow, and later, with

25. Chang Kuo-kan, p. 26.

26. Hu Tsu-shun, p. 21.

27. Chang Nan-hsien, p. 158.

28. *Ch'ien Wen-hsüeh-she t'ung-jen kung-chi* (Deposition of Former Members of the Literary Institute), "Wu-han ko-ming t'uan-t'i Wen-hsüeh-she li-shih" (History of the Wuhan Revolutionary Corps, the Literary Institute), *HHKM*, 5, 5.

the financial assistance of two merchants, a branch office was established in Wuchang to make it more convenient for army and student circles there to meet and carry on their work. Progressive Association members began to work on the secret societies in the Yangtze provinces, which, as a result of their efforts, were united into a league called Chung-hua-shan.[29] Sun Wu, a graduate of the Hupeh Military Academy and an important party member, also got in touch with local revolutionaries like Huang Shen-hsiang to advance party work.[30]

According to Yang Yü-ju, a meeting was held in mid-1910 in Tokyo in which it was decided to shift attention to the Yangtze region. Chü Cheng had returned to Tokyo from Burma and Chao Sheng from Southeast Asia, and they called together the heads of eleven provincial branches of the Revolutionary Alliance, including Sung Chiao-jen, to hammer out future strategy. A sharp discussion took place on Sung Chiao-jen's suggestion for continued revolutionary activity on a regional basis, but Chao Sheng led the opposition by insisting on coordinated activity with one area as the base of operations, suggesting that this base could only be the Yangtze Valley. Finally, on the advice of T'an Jen-feng the policy of unifying decision-making power but dividing regional responsibility was adopted, and a central bureau was established in Shanghai. T'an Jen-feng was asked to investigate the situation in the Yangtze Valley. Following this meeting the associates left for their native places one by one. T'an Jen-feng and Sung Chiao-jen headed toward Shanghai, where they conferred with Ch'en Ch'i-mei and Chang Mu-liang on the strategy for the Yangtze region.[31]

In February 1911, Chü Cheng came to Hupeh as the representative of the Revolutionary Alliance in charge of Hupeh affairs. Chü was a leading member of the Alliance as well as of the Progressive Association. He was accompanied by T'an Jen-feng, who had also just visited Hunan. By that time Huang Hsing and Chao Sheng had already made plans for the capture of Canton, and T'an came to Hunan and Hupeh to coordinate plans with the Liang-Hu rebels for supporting the projected Canton revolt. T'an gave eight hundred dollars to the Wuhan rebels, with which a headquarters was established at 14 Pao-shan-li in the Russian concession.[32] Both

29. Chang Nan-hsien, p. 179.
30. Hu Tsu-shun, p. 16.
31. Yang Yü-ju, p. 31.
32. Hu Tsu-shun, p. 18.

the Progressive Association and the Literary Institute had made rapid progress, and Hupeh and Hunan revolutionaries were ready to answer the call from Canton. The Canton rebellion, however, failed and the Southern revolutionaries suffered heavy losses.

At the time of the defeat in Canton, most of the Progressive Association members were in Wuhan. Chiao Ta-feng, the Hunanese revolutionary leader, and some of his associates had also come to Wuchang to coordinate a response to the impending revolt in Kwangtung. The news of the disastrous defeat in Canton had just started coming in and rumor had it that even Huang Hsing and Hu Han-min had been killed. There was dismay in the revolutionary ranks, and a Progressive Association meeting was called on May 3, 1911 that was attended by Yang Yü-ju, Hu Tsu-shun, and Ch'a Kuang-fo among others. Highly emotional speeches were made expressing the determination of the revolutionaries from Hupeh and Hunan to concentrate on work in these two areas to bring about a revolution. "If there were no Kwangtung," Chiao Ta-feng asked rhetorically, "would there be no revolution?" Another member shouted passionately that the central provinces had no big names to boast of but that it was the turn of these unknown and nameless (*wu-ming*) revolutionaries to succeed when those with big names had failed. The meeting resolved to make Hupeh and Hunan the focus of a new effort and to depend upon the New Army in Wuchang to start an uprising in Hupei. It was also decided to seek the support of the Literary Institute for a new joint attempt at revolution.[33] The center of activity was finally and definitely shifted to Hupeh and Hunan.

Contacts between members of the Literary Institute and of the Progressive Association had been established earlier with the predecessor organization, the Society for the Study of Popular Government. In April 1909, when Sun Wu was in Wuhan developing the Progressive Association organization there, he met Huang Shen-hsiang of the Society for the Study of Popular Government and prevailed upon him to join the Progressive Association.[34] Thus a working relationship between the two organizations was established; but it was not characterized by close cooperation or mutual confidence. Rivalry was not infrequent, and each organization sought to increase its membership at the expense of the

33. Yang Yü-ju, p. 35.
34. Hu Tsu-shun, p. 16.

other.[35] The Progressive Association was a broader organization, for it had members in both army and nonarmy circles, whereas the Literary Institute and its predecessors included only army personnel. But since the Progressive Association also assigned a crucial role to the New Army, the activity of the two was centered on the same field, and a spirit of competition in extending influence and membership often bedeviled their attitude toward each other. The increasing tempo of revolutionary activity and the sharpening of the crisis in Wuhan brought to a head the question of their mutual relations, for a united effort by the two was an essential condition for the success of any attempt to overthrow the Manchu regime.

There were, however, skeptics on both sides. In the Progressive Association Liu Kung (Chung-wen) was dubious about the utility of this unity because the program of the Literary Institute lacked a revolutionary character,[36] while in the latter organization, when the suggestion for unity was debated, Chiang I-wu scoffed at the brilliant and prominent members of the Progressive Association.[37] But the general opinion of both was strongly in favor of unity, and on September 14, 1911 a meeting of the representatives was held to agree on the principles for unification of the two organizations.[38] Speakers from both sides enthusiastically welcomed the decision to unite forces and expressed their willingness to forget personal and temperamental differences for the sake of the Revolution.[39] The joint meeting elected Chiang I-wu as the Supreme Commander of the Revolutionary Army and Wang Hsien-chang (deputy chief of the Literary Institute) as vice-commander. Sun Wu was made chief of staff; Chang T'ing-fu, Ts'ai Chi-min, Liu Fu-chi (Yao-cheng), P'eng Ch'u-fan, and Hsü Ta-ming, among others, were chosen to supervise military affairs. The office of the commander in chief was located in Wuchang at the general headquarters of the Literary Institute.[40] For political affairs, the joint meeting decided to create a Political Preparatory Office and elected Liu Kung as director and Sun Wu, P'an Shan-po, and Li Chi-ch'en as members of the standing committee; Chü Cheng, Hu Ying, Li Ya-tung, Ch'a Kuang-fo, Liu Fu-chi, Yang Yü-ju, Yang Shih-chieh, Chan Ta-pei,

35. Yang Yü-ju, p. 30.

36. Ibid., p. 37.

37. Ts'ai Chi-ou, *Ou-chou hsüeh-shih* (Tragic History of Hupeh) (Shanghai, 1958), p. 56.

38. Yang Yü-ju, pp. 46–47.

39. Ibid.

40. Chang Kuo-kan, p. 60.

and ten others were elected members of this organization. The office was located at Pao-shan-li in the Russian concession at Hankow—which was also the office of the Progressive Association.[41] The method of selection makes the intention of the revolutionaries quite clear. The Literary Institute was essentially a military organization with simple and straightforward aims, while the political leaders were mostly in the Progressive Association. As a result the Literary Institute head was made commander in chief, and political matters were left largely in the hands of Progressive Association members.

The stage was now set for passing from the phase of organization and preparation to that of action. The necessary unity had been achieved and tension was mounting in the Wuhan area. The Szechwan railway crisis had gathered momentum and added fuel to the fire. The preparations of the revolutionaries were complete but they lacked the finances to start a revolt. The Wuhan revolutionaries did not include many well-known names and most of their organizations, particularly among the army, had been functioning on their own resources and consequently were short of ready funds.[42] The Progressive Association leaders had to address themselves to the urgent task of collecting money. Fortunately for them, Liu Kung had come to them with five thousand dollars. Liu came from a rich family that had given him this money to go to Peking and purchase an official post. His fiancée, also a party member, reported this to her comrades, who in turn asked Liu for financial aid. Since Liu had had no intention of proceeding to Peking, he willingly parted with the money.[43]

After the money had been collected, Chü Cheng and Yang Yü-ju were sent to Shanghai to contact Sung Chiao-jen and Ch'en Ch'i-mei about purchasing arms and ammunition, and also to persuade Sung Chiao-jen, Huang Hsing, T'an Jen-feng, and others to come to Wuhan to lead the impending uprising.[44] Both Sung and Ch'en were greatly pleased with the news from Wuhan, and Ch'en undertook to procure ammunition for the revolutionaries. Just at that time a secret letter came from jail from the well-known Hupeh revolutionary Hu Ying to Sung Chiao-jen, questioning the very idea of a successful uprising in Hupeh. Sung began to have doubts

41. Ibid.
42. Yang Yü-ju, p. 43.
43. Ts'ai Chi-ou, pp. 39–42.
44. Yang Yü-ju, p. 46.

about the exact state of affairs in Wuhan and delayed his departure.[45] In addition an emissary had been sent by Chü Cheng to Huang Hsing apprising him of the plans for the Wuhan uprising and urging him to come to Wuhan and lead the revolt. Huang Hsing sent the unexpected reply that he did not believe the Hupeh revolutionaries could succeed unless there were simultaneous uprisings elsewhere. He suggested putting off the Wuhan uprising by a month or more to allow time for coordinating plans with other provinces.[46] With their mission almost fruitless, Yang Yü-ju returned to Wuhan on October 1, leaving Chü Cheng behind in Shanghai to continue his efforts to buy arms and to persuade the leaders to come to Hupeh. Yang Yü-ju's report on his return amazed and angered his Wuhan comrades. Huang Hsing knew nothing about the Hupeh situation, they argued, and they were not prepared to accept his advice.[47]

Meanwhile, to meet the mounting railway crisis in Szechwan, the imperial authorities had transferred some of the New Army troops at Wuhan. Two battalions from the Thirty-first and Thirty-second Regiments of the Sixteenth Brigade were sent to Szechwan under the command of Tuan-fang, and one battalion of the Forty-first Regiment was ordered to Yüeh-chou on the borders of Hunan and Hupeh. Chiang I-wu was in the latter battalion and had to leave Wuhan. Sun Wu called a joint meeting of the Progressive Association and the Literary Institute at Hu Tsu-shun's house in Wuchang on September 24 to decide upon a new strategy. The meeting was attended by representatives of various companies of troops including Hsiung Ping-k'un and Ma Jung of the Eighth Engineers Corps and Ts'ai Chi-min of the Twenty-ninth Regiment, as well as representatives of the Progressive Association and the Literary Institute.[48] As a gesture of sincerity, Sun Wu proposed the retention of Chiang I-wu as their commander in chief. He himself was prepared to continue as chief of staff. The meeting also unanimously decided to fix October 6 as the day for the uprising.[49]

The first salvos of the Revolution were, however, sounded the same afternoon when a sergeant and another soldier belonging to the revolutionary group, who were on leave from their camp and

45. Ibid., pp. 52–53.
46. See text of Huang Hsing's letter in Chang Nan-hsien, pp. 245–46.
47. Ts'ai Chi-ou, pp. 63–64, 68.
48. Hu Tsu-shun, p. 22.
49. Ibid., pp. 22–23.

drinking with other comrades, were interrupted by their officer. The dispute developed into a stormy quarrel. Some of the revolutionaries present wanted to start a mutiny but were frustrated by the fact that the ammunition store was closed. They fled and the matter was referred up to Commander Chang Piao. Chang Piao ordered the cavalry commander, Yü Hua-lung, to catch the rebels, but Yü's unit included many party members, and so no one was arrested.[50] But the authorities had been alerted. Both the city and the military camps were now placed under strict surveillance, and nobody was allowed to enter or leave the camps without permission. In addition, Governor-general Jui-cheng took back most of the arms from the New Army unit and stored them at the Ch'u-wang-t'ai ammunition store in Wuchang.[51] According to one report, T'ieh-chung, chief of staff of the military training headquarters in Hupeh, wanted to station Bannermen to guard this important ammunition store but he was opposed by Li Yüan-hung, who minimized the strength of the revolutionaries and pointed out the misgivings and misunderstandings that such an action might cause among the Chinese troops. At his suggestion, the Eighth Engineers Corps was entrusted with the duty of protecting the ammunition store.[52] If this report is correct, Li Yüan-hung may be credited with unwittingly having aided the revolutionaries, because their capture of Wuchang gave them a valuable initial advantage in launching their revolt.

The uprising had been fixed for October 6 but Chü Cheng and Sung Chiao-jen had not yet arrived and the authorities were taking stringent precautions. Therefore the date was changed to October 9.[53] At the request of his comrades Chiang I-wu came back to Wuchang on the morning of the 9th,[54] but the same day an incident took place that precipitated the Wuchang uprising. Sun Wu and a number of his comrades were testing some ammunition in the office of the Progressive Association when, through the carelessness of Liu Kung's brother, who was smoking, a bomb exploded, injuring Sun Wu and making a terrific noise. Sun Wu was immediately

50. Ibid., pp. 23–24.

51. (Li) Chien-nung, "Wu-han ko-ming shih-mo chi" (Complete Account of the Revolution in Wuhan), *HHKM*, 5, 170.

52. Hsiung Ping-k'un, "Wu-ch'ang ch'i-i t'an" (On the Wuchang Uprising), *HHKM*, 5, 86.

53. Wu Hsing-han, "Wu-ch'ang ch'i-i san-jih chi" (A Record of Three Days of the Wuchang Uprising), *HHKM*, 5, 78.

54. Ts'ai Chi-ou, p. 67.

rushed to the hospital through a back door but a policeman on duty heard the noise and hastened to investigate its cause. The comrades scattered but the policeman found the membership register, seal, insignia, and other documents. Liu fled from the adjoining building but his wife and brother were taken into custody.[55] This event revealed almost everything about the revolutionary organization and made the explosion that followed the accidental bomb explosion inevitable.

The October Tenth Military Coup

At the time of the seizure of revolutionary documents in Hankow on October 9, Chiang I-wu was meeting with Liu Fu-chi (Yao-cheng), Chang T'ing-fu, P'eng Ch'u-fan, Ch'en Lei, and others at their Wuchang headquarters in Hsiao-ch'ao (miao)-chieh. Some of the Hankow comrades rushed to Chiang with the news. Hurried consultations followed on the next step to be taken. Chiang I-wu realized that it was a question of now or never, for if the rebels did not strike first, Jui-cheng would crack down with all his strength. They decided to call for an uprising for that night. Messengers were sent to the revolutionaries in various army units to convey Chiang I-wu's orders for the revolt. Chiang's plan was that the artillery at the South Lake (Nan-hu) would boom a signal at midnight and all the infantry, artillery, engineering, and transport units would revolt according to previous plans, with the engineering corps occupying the ammunition store at Ch'u-wang-t'ai.[56] As it happened, there was not a sound at midnight—only a creeping fear among the revolutionaries—and the revolt did not take place. According to one revolutionary account Chiang's orders were inadvertently delivered to Commander Chang Piao's office, thus exposing the secret.[57] The more probable explanation is that since all the city gates and the approaches to military camps were strictly guarded, the messengers carrying Chiang's instructions were unable to deliver them to the party representatives.[58]

Meanwhile Governor-general Jui-cheng and his officials were not idly sitting by. Jui-cheng was thoroughly alarmed at the large number of New Army soldiers among the register of names of the revolutionaries, and orders went out promptly for the arrest of all

55. Chang Kuo-kan, p. 63.
56. Yang Yü-ju, pp. 55–56.
57. (Li) Chien-nung, p. 169.
58. Wu Hsing-han, p. 78.

the members. The police raided the offices of the revolutionaries one by one. The raid on the office in Wuchang on Hsiao-ch'ao (miao)-chieh dealt a particularly severe blow. Chiang I-wu was present at the time of the raid, along with a number of other important associates. Liu Fu-chi (Yao-cheng) attempted to throw a bomb at the police but was injured and arrested. The police also arrested P'eng Ch'u-fan and Yang Hung-sheng. Chiang I-wu managed to escape by pretending to be an onlooker and fled to Ching-shan.[59] Liu, P'eng, and Yang were closely interrogated by T'ieh-chung but revealed nothing, and bravely went to the gallows proclaiming their faith in the Revolution and the awakening of the Han race against Manchu slavery.[60]

On the morning of October 10 at the drill grounds, Chang Piao's men took Chang T'ing-fu away from the Thirtieth Regiment, while some of his associates, such as Wu Hsing-han and Ts'ai Chi-min, representatives of the revolutionary organization from the Thirtieth and Twenty-ninth Regiments, looked on helplessly.[61] A large number of people, including two women, were arrested in those two days.[62] That same day Jui-cheng reported to the Board of War in Peking that he had suppressed an impending rebellion in Wuhan. He informed the board of the seizure of the documents indicating the revolutionaries' plans to make Hupeh the base of the projected revolt and to stir up trouble in the Yangtze provinces. But, Jui-cheng boasted, "without changing color" he had bravely met the situation, arresting and suppressing the revolutionaries.[63]

October 10 was a day of terror for the people of Wuhan. The authorities had apparently decided to resort to suppression in order to stamp out the rebels. The troops of Jui-cheng and Chang Piao were everywhere, arresting revolutionaries and suspected revolutionaries. A policy of indiscriminate arrests was pursued.[64] It was a field day for spies and self-proclaimed spies. Many who had old scores to settle and those who thought it a good opportunity to earn some easy money made loud claims of their "information" about party members. Fear and anxiety permeated the city. It was a situa-

59. Ts'ai Chi-ou, pp. 74–75.
60. Chang Kuo-kan, pp. 63–64.
61. Wu Hsing-han, p. 78.
62. (Li) Chien-nung, p. 170.
63. Ku-kung tang-an kuan (Imperial Archives, Peking), *HHKM*, 5, 289–90.
64. Chang Nan-hsien, p. 252.

tion not likely to endear Jui-cheng and the Manchu administration to the people. Most of those who had been arrested and taken away were natives of Hupeh; the severity of the repression was therefore deeply disturbing to the local people.[65] Jui-cheng had already nearly denuded the New Army of arms and ammunition and instead had armed the Patrol and Defense Troops, on whom he depended to rule Wuhan.[66]

The revolutionaries had their backs to the wall. They knew that the register of names was in the hands of Jui-cheng and that they would be taken to the gallows one by one unless they made a desperate attempt to overthrow the government in Wuhan immediately. Even if the revolt failed, it was better to make the attempt than wait for capture and execution.[67] What might have happened had Jui-cheng instead adopted a conciliatory policy, attempted to pacify the people, and shown more magnanimity toward the New Army units in Hupeh is open to speculation. It is not entirely impossible that the Wuchang revolt might have been postponed and the life of the dynasty prolonged.

The offices of the revolutionaries had been seized and their channels of communication closed. But still the hard core of the revolutionary organization in the New Army, built up by years of devoted work, remained intact, and this enabled them to fight back against heavy odds. During the afternoon various leading party members held consultations among themselves: Hsiung Ping-k'un (who was the chief representative of the Eighth Engineers Corps), Li Tse-ch'ien, and Lo Ping-shun in the Engineers Corps, and Wu Hsing-han, Ts'ai Chi-min, and Hsü Ta-ming from the Thirtieth and Twenty-ninth Regiments. Messages passed between them conveying the decision to revolt that night according to their previous plans.[68]

It is appropriate here to take a quick look at the troop situation in Wuchang on October 10. Inside the city were stationed the First and Second Battalions of the Twenty-ninth Infantry Regiment, the Thirtieth Infantry Regiment (consisting largely of Bannermen), the Eighth Engineers Corps, the Eighth Battalion of Military Police (also Bannermen), the Third Battalion of the Forty-first

65. Ts'ao Ya-po (Cheng-pien), pp. 1–2.

66. (Li) Chien-nung, p. 170.

67. As Hsiung Ping-k'un, chief representative of the revolutionaries in the Eighth Engineers Corps, put it: "If we fight, they will kill us; if we do not fight, they will still kill us." Hsiung Ping-k'un, p. 88.

68. Ibid., pp. 88–89; Wu Hsing-han, p. 79.

Infantry Regiment, and the eighty-odd students of the Institute of Draughtsmanship of the New Army (*lu-chün*). Among the troops guarding Jui-cheng's yamen were one battalion of drill troops, one of patrol and defense troops, and a company of cavalry.[69] It is obvious from these figures that the revolutionaries did not have a preponderance of military strength inside the city and that the attempt to stage an uprising was quite hazardous. On the outskirts of the city were the Second Battalion of the Thirty-second Infantry Regiment, the Eighth Cavalry Battalion, the Eighth Artillery Battalion, the Eighth Transport Battalion, the Twenty-first Cavalry Battalion, the Twenty-first Artillery Battalion, the Twenty-first Engineers, and the Twenty-first Transport Company.[70]

It was a rainy evening and a fierce wind blew as if to accentuate the agitation in the hearts of the revolutionaries. As the evening faded into darkness the wind whistled ever more fiercely. Shortly after seven o'clock, the tempest exploded. In the Eighth Engineers Corps one of the platoon commanders, T'ao Ch'i-sheng, noticing that Assistant Sergeant Chin Chao-lung and another soldier, Ch'eng Ting-kuo, were carrying arms, threateningly inquired from Chin Chao-lung whether he was going to revolt. "Yes. How about you?" came the reply. T'ao Ch'i-sheng tried to grab hold of Chin but was shot at by Ch'eng Ting-kuo. T'ao ran for his life and the battalion commander, mistaking him for the one who had started the revolt, shot him dead.[71] Thus the first shots were fired and the Wuchang uprising had begun.

For nearly half an hour the camp resounded with noise and gun shots. Sergeant Hsiung Ping-k'un led the revolt, opposed by Company Commanders Yüan Jung-fa, Huang K'un-jung, and Chang Wen-t'ao. All three were killed by the mutinous soldiers, as were most of the military officers in the Eighth Engineers Corps. The camp was in the hands of the revolutionaries.[72] The revolting troops now marched toward the Ch'u-wang-t'ai Arsenal. This strategy had been part of the earlier plans of the revolutionaries for an uprising in Wuchang.[73] The arsenal contained all the arms manufactured at the Hanyang Ironworks plus arms bought from foreign countries in previous years. It was, therefore, a rich storehouse of

69. Ts'ao Ya-po (Cheng-pien), pp. 28–29.
70. Ibid., pp. 29–30.
71. Hsiung Ping-k'un, p. 90.
72. Ibid.
73. See n. 56.

ammunition and its capture by the revolutionaries meant a significant addition to their strength.[74]

The Arsenal was being guarded that night by men of the Engineers Corps led by Wu Chao-lin, a graduate of the Hupeh Military Staff College and now a company commander. Wu had been a member of the Society for Daily Improvement but, after its disbandment, had not dared take further overt interest in the revolutionary organizations.[75] He was apparently a capable person, well versed in military science,[76] but he had ceased to be an active revolutionary out of fear of the consequences. When the troops of the Eighth Engineers Corps reached Ch'u-wang-t'ai, Wu Chao-lin's first reaction was to flee from the scene of trouble. He was, however, prevailed upon to return to Ch'u-wang-t'ai and was made provisional commander by Hsiung Ping-k'un, and others.[77] By this time more troops had revolted and arrived at Ch'u-wang-t'ai. Because the Thirtieth Regiment had a very large number of Bannermen and the Twenty-ninth Regiment was stationed nearby, it was extremely dangerous for the revolutionaries in these two camps to revolt. But Wu Hsing-han led the revolt in the Thirty-ninth Regiment and Ts'ai Chi-min and Hsü Ta-ming were the leaders in the Twenty-ninth Regiment. The Bannermen, apparently taken unawares and intimidated by the pitch of revolutionary frenzy, offered no opposition.[78] This enabled Wu Hsing-han and Ts'ai Chi-min to lead their people to Ch'u-wang-t'ai and join the other rebel troops there.

Wu Chao-lin was reluctant to accept command, partly perhaps because he was afraid of the consequences, but largely because of the extreme laxity of discipline among the troops at the time. The revolting troops had gathered at Ch'u-wang-t'ai and were behaving more like a mob than soldiers in the field.[79] There was utter confusion in their ranks and the noise and din was more reminiscent of mob violence than of a disciplined military coup. Wu Chao-lin accepted the command only after receiving assurance that his orders would be fully obeyed and that military discipline would be

74. Ts'ai Chi-ou, p. 83.

75. Chang Nan-hsien, p. 253.

76. Li Yüan-hung also paid a compliment to the ability of Wu Chao-lin. See Hsiung Ping-k'un, p. 92.

77. Ibid., p. 91.

78. Hsiung Ping-k'un, p. 90.

79. Wu Hsing-han, p. 81.

scrupulously observed.[80] Order was then restored and the troops reshaped into proper military formations.

Wu Chao-lin's role has excited much controversy. Was he an insignificant character in the revolutionary drama during the first three days when most of the well-known leaders were absent from the scene of action, or was it he who provided the leadership that led to the success of the Wuchang uprising, until others appeared on the scene a few days later and took charge of affairs? Ts'ao Ya-po has credited Wu Chao-lin with the energetic leadership and decisiveness necessary in those crucial hours.[81] On the other hand, Wu Hsing-han has claimed that Wu Chao-lin's role was of no consequence, condemning Ts'ao Ya-po as a "running dog of Wu Chao-lin."[82] Wu strongly suggests that it was he, along with Ts'ai Chi-min, Hsiung Ping-k'un, and Hsü Ta-ming, who made the decisions during that critical period, while Wu Chao-lin was there almost by sufferance. An analysis of the accounts of contemporary revolutionaries shows that although Ts'ao Ya-po somewhat exaggerated the role as well as the capabilities of Wu Chao-lin, Wu Hsing-han was guilty of belittling it to the point of blacking it out altogether. Nearly all revolutionaries except Ts'ao Ya-po—Hsiung Ping-k'un, Chang Nan-hsien, Hu Tsu-shun, Yang Yü-ju, and others—have acknowledged the role of Wu Chao-lin and his military leadership, particularly in the first two days when the revolutionary seizure of power at Wuchang was not yet a fully established fact. Wu Hsing-han's bias is apparent from the fact that he does not even mention that Wu Chao-lin was elected provisional commander of the republican troops on the night of October 10 and functioned in that capacity until Li Yüan-hung agreed to take over as military governor.

When Wu Chao-lin became commander, most of the New Army in Wuchang still had not risen in revolt and time was running out for the revolutionaries. If they were unable to capture the governor-general's yamen and seize the city by morning, their fate would be sealed, for Jui-cheng would by then be able to muster the troops that had not responded to the revolt and crush the revolutionaries.[83] Time was of the essence and the revolutionaries had

80. Hsiung Ping-k'un, p. 91.
81. Ts'ao Ya-po (Cheng-pien), pp. 1–45.
82. Wu Hsing-han, p. 83.
83. Ts'ai Chi-ou, p. 14.

to persuade other troops to join them. Wu Chao-lin made some astute moves. He sent troops to attack the Bannermen in the Thirtieth Battalion and the Military Police Battalion and thus secured his flanks. The Bannermen, who would have been the most determined foes of the revolutionary troops had they been able to join the governor-general's forces, were rendered ineffective. Wu Chao-lin sent emissaries to mobilize and bring into the city the artillery at the South Lake on the outskirts of the city, and he also ordered all telegraph lines[84] cut, so that Jui-cheng, Chang Piao, and Li Yüan-hung were deprived of communication with one another and kept uninformed of the progress of the revolt. Plans were also formulated for storming the governor-general's yamen.[85]

The Eighth Artillery Regiment at the South Lake responded to the call of the revolutionaries, and its arrival in the city greatly augmented the fighting capacity of the revolutionary troops, particularly their effectiveness in attacking Jui-cheng. In addition they were now joined by the Twenty-first Transport Battery from outside the city, by students of the Institute of Draughtsmanship, and later by some of the men of Li Yüan-hung's Third Battalion of the Forty-First Regiment.[86] Concerted action was now taken for a pincer attack on the governor-general's yamen.

It is unnecessary here to follow the details of the fighting that ensued.[87] Suffice it to mention that the revolutionary troops met with stiff resistance from the governor-general's troops and that had it not been for the lack of nerve shown by Jui-cheng, and to a lesser extent by Chang Piao, the victory of the revolutionaries would have been by no means certain. It is revealing, for example, to note that by the next morning, when the city had fallen to the revolutionaries, the only troops that had thus far risen in revolt inside the city were the Engineers Corps, one infantry battalion, and one infantry platoon, plus the students already mentioned; they had been joined from outside the city gates only by the Eighth Artillery Regiment and the Engineers and Transport Companies of the Mixed Brigade.[88] Jui-cheng's conduct was largely respon-

84. Ts'ao Ya-po (Cheng-pien), p. 14.

85. Hu Tsu-shun, pp. 41–3.

86. Ts'ao Ya-po (Cheng-pien), pp. 16–18; Ts'ai Chi-ou, pp. 83–85.

87. Almost all the accounts by revolutionaries contain a detailed report of the fighting in Wuchang that night.

88. Chang Nan-hsien, pp. 257–58.

sible for the government's debacle in Wuchang that night. As soon as the attack on his yamen began, he became frightened and showed little confidence in his troops' ability to hold out against the attack. When the first shells fell inside his yamen, he apparently panicked and reportedly asked the officials around him where he should take refuge. At the suggestion of Commander Ch'en Telung, he fled to the warship *Ch'u-yü* anchored in the river outside the city, leaving his troops discouraged and without a leader.[89] His flight made the capture of his yamen much easier.[90]

Chang Piao, commander in chief of the New Army in Wuhan, was at his Wen-ch'ang-men residence at the time. Upon receiving the news that the Eighth Engineers Corps had mutinied, he gave instructions by telephone to various army camps that strict discipline be maintained, but was thoroughly shaken upon hearing that the artillery at the South Lake had joined the revolt.[91] His fright took an extreme turn when the telephone wires were cut and he heard rumors that the entire army had revolted. Chang Piao was about to flee when he was joined by the Eighth Transport Battalion, which had remained loyal. This to some extent steadied his failing nerves and he conferred with the battalion leader, Hsiao An-kuo, but neither could muster the courage to give battle to the revolutionary troops. Finally they retired to Hankow to bide their time until reinforcements arrived from Peking.[92] The field was now clear for the revolutionaries.

Li Yüan-hung's position as commander of the New Army's Twenty-first Brigade differed only in that Li could not flee and was later made to play a role he had never dreamed of. Unfortunately for Li, most of his troops were camped outside the city gates, with only a battalion of the Forty-first Regiment posted inside the city near the Thirtieth Regiment.[93] When he learned of the mutiny by the Engineers Corps, he gave strict instructions for suppression of any trouble, and he himself went around to maintain his troops' loyalty. When one of the emissaries of the rebel troops came to request the support of his battalion, Li Yüan-hung took out a knife and killed him.[94] With the news of the revolt by the artillery

89. Ibid.

90. Regarding Jui-cheng's conduct, Ts'ao Ya-po's account is substantially similar to that of Chang Nan-hsien. Ts'ao Ya-po (Cheng-pien), p. 13.

91. Ibid., p. 14.

92. Ibid., pp. 14–15.

93. Chang Nan-hsien, p. 256.

94. Ibid.

and the seizure of the Ch'u-wang-t'ai depot, Li Yüan-hung became more and more anxious. Realizing that the situation was hopeless, he hid himself in the house of his staff officer.[95]

By the morning of October 11, the town of Wuchang, except for pockets of Bannermen, was in the hands of the revolutionaries. Wuchang had fallen rather easily despite the fact that the revolutionaries probably had only five battalions, while seventeen battalions remained aloof that night.[96] The revolutionaries had lost only a few score of men, while the Banner troops had suffered heavy casualties.[97] Most of the high civil and military officials had fled and Wuchang had been left virtually without an administration. The problem of the revolutionaries now was to create a new government and bring order out of confusion and chaos. Moreover, the men who had successfully hoisted the revolutionary flag at Wuhan were almost unknown. Their names had never been heard by the citizens of Wuhan or by the rest of the country. Units of the New Army had seized the city and had set the revolutionary steamroller in motion, but their leaders had been mostly petty officers—sergeants and platoon leaders—all the high officers having taken to their heels. The highest ranking officer to join the revolutionaries was Wu Chao-lin, a company commander. Having won the city of Wuchang for the republican cause, the revolutionaries then had to consolidate the gains and to win over public opinion. For this purpose they deemed it necessary to take shelter behind names that would be well known and acceptable to the people in Hupeh as well as in other areas.[98] Their insecurity about their own position clouded the deliberations of the revolutionaries for many days—and with far-reaching consequences.

The Organization of the Hupeh Military Government

Unfortunately for the revolutionaries none of the top leaders was at hand. Sun Wu, injured in the bomb explosion, was lying in a hospital at Hankow. Both Liu Kung (Chung-wen) and Chiang I-wu had fled on the eve of the uprising and were still untraceable. Chü Cheng had not yet returned from Shanghai and the arrival of such major leaders as Huang Hsing and Sung Chiao-jen was extremely uncertain. With this loss of front-rank leadership, the less

95. Yang Yü-ju, pp. 64, 73.
96. Chang Nan-hsien, p. 258.
97. Ts'ao Ya-po, p. 33.
98. Ts'ai Chi-ou, pp. 89–90.

important members of the Progressive Association and the Literary Institute were left to their own resources, and their first concern was to find a leader to lend respectability to the rebellion.[99] As soon as Li Yüan-hung's name was suggested, they seized upon it with an enthusiasm that surprised and even shocked some of the revolutionaries outside Wuchang.[100]

The case of Li Yüan-hung is a strange one, particularly when viewed with hindsight. Li had absolutely no sympathy for the revolutionary cause. He was, in fact, in the same tradition as Yuan Shih-k'ai. He tried to suppress the Revolution and to hide himself when he could not do so. He was trained in modern military science, as opposed to the old musket and arrow warfare, but that was about the extent of his claim to modernism or progressive ideas. He had never entertained any republican principles. He was very different from Wu Chao-lin, who was also tentatively approached to accept leadership on October 10. Wu was afraid to assume responsibility and, left to himself, would have kept away, but by conviction he was a republican and all his sympathies were with the revolutionaries. Li Yüan-hung, on the other hand, had no such convictions or sympathies.

The revolutionaries were, however, looking for a man with a well-known name, and Li Yüan-hung could provide that.[101] They thought this would help them to consolidate the Revolution in Wuchang and win public opinion elsewhere. Apparently, it was the anti-Manchu aspect which was uppermost in the minds of the Wuchang revolutionaries. They were not thinking in terms of a social revolution but only of ousting the hated Manchus. They believed that any Chinese would do, whether he believed in the Revolution or not, and since Li Yüan-hung was a Chinese with a reputation there was no harm in putting him at the top. For many of the revolutionaries the fact that a person belonged to the Han race was sufficient passport to office, as long as he did not oppose them.[102]

Exactly when Li Yüan-hung's name came up is not clear. It must have been suggested on the morning of October 11. According to one revolutionary account he had been considered as early as April 1911 when, at a meeting of New Army representatives, Chiang

99. Chang Nan-hsien, p. 266.
100. See n. 106.
101. Yang Yü-ju, p. 72.
102. Ibid.

I-wu suggested Li Yüan-hung as provisional governor of Wuhan. To an objection that Li was not a party man, Chiang reportedly replied that the revolutionaries were mostly ordinary soldiers, or at best sergeants, and lacked middle-rank officers, while Li was a knowledgeable person, well known everywhere. If only the Manchus were overthrown, the Revolution would be successful.[103] This account is, however, not supported by any other evidence. It is extremely doubtful that Chiang I-wu proposed Li Yüan-hung's name, and it becomes doubly doubtful when it is recalled that, at the joint meeting of the Progressive Association and the Literary Institute representatives in September, it had been decided to appoint Chiang I-wu as commander in chief, Sun Wu as chief of staff, and Liu Kung as director of a proposed Preparatory Office for Political Affairs.[104] No one had mentioned Li Yüan-hung in that meeting. Obviously his name came up on the morning of October 11 after the revolutionaries had been deprived of their own outstanding leaders.[105] Yang Yü-ju notes that he was at Ching-shan with Liu Ying when the news arrived of the capture of Wuhan and the selection of Li Yüan-hung as military governor. Liu Ying was amazed and exclaimed, "How could Li, who is not a revolutionary, be made the leader?" Yang suggested that it must have been due to the exigencies of the situation.[106]

Guards, led by Ma Jung, were sent to Li Yüan-hung's hiding place. Li was frightened but the soldiers told him that they wanted him to lead the great undertaking and forced him to accompany them to Ch'u-wang-t'ai. He was nervous and unwilling but in the end had little option but to accompany them.[107] Li's first advice to the revolutionaries was that they had already created enough trouble and should return to their barracks. The government, he said, would soon send reinforcements and there would be no hope for the revolutionaries. The Imperial Navy would blast them to bits.[108] Li was not concerned with loyalty to ideals or institutions, but with who was likely to win. Some of the revolutionaries lost patience with him. One pointed a gun at him, saying that although his comrades were willing to overlook Li's past, he would

103. Hu Tsu-shun, p. 144.

104. See section on "Revolutionary Activity in Hupeh."

105. Chang Nan-hsien, p. 266.

106. Yang Yü-ju, p. 98. Li Yüan-hung and Wu Chao-lin were graduates of the same academy and knew one another. Wu may well have suggested Li's name.

107. Hsiung Ping-k'un, p. 92.

108. Ibid.

not accept as leader a man who preferred to remain a Han traitor.[109] Wu Chao-lin and others restrained the potential troublemaker and at the same time advised Li to be more flexible.

In the afternoon the revolutionaries proceeded to the office of the Provincial Assembly, where they had also invited members of the gentry. Li was taken there against his will.[110] The meeting was significant for many reasons. A republic was proclaimed after thousands of years of imperial rule and the name of the country became the Central Florescent Republic (Chung-hua min-kuo). This was a signal victory for the republican cause, although the process begun at Wuchang was completed only after a republican government had been formed for the whole of China. The meeting also decided to form a military government and to elect Li Yüan-hung as military governor.[111] But Li was totally unwilling. One of the revolutionaries wrote a public declaration to reassure the people and asked Li to sign it. He refused, at which point others simply signed on behalf of Li while he looked on helplessly.[112] T'ang Hua-lung was elected chief of the civil government. T'ang, a constitutionalist, was elected chairman of the Provincial Assembly.[113] The elections of Li Yüan-hung and T'ang Hua-lung as the respective heads of the military and civil governments was a revealing fact. Power was virtually being handed over to those who had never belonged to the revolutionary camp. The republicans selected as their leaders men with little loyalty to the republican cause. Both reluctance to hold high position and concentration on the purely anti-Manchu aspect of their struggle were responsible for this. While this self-effacement spoke well of the dedication of the rank and file soldiers of the Revolution, it did not augur well for the propagation of the principles of the Revolutionary Alliance.

In view of Li Yüan-hung's unhelpful attitude, Ts'ai Chi-min suggested setting up a staff office (mou-lüeh-ch'u) to carry on the work of the military government. This staff office had about fifteen people in it, including Ts'ai Chi-min, Wu Hsing-han, Hsiung Ping-k'un, and their associates. They also selected Chang Ching-liang

109. Ts'ao Ya-po (Cheng-pien), pp. 34–35.

110. Hsiung Ping-k'un, p. 93.

111. Li Yüan-hung himself later gave an account of those days in a letter to Admiral Sa (Sah) Chen-p'ing, describing how he was forced to accept the military governorship but that he realized that he should serve the Han people.

112. Hsiung Ping-k'un, pp. 93–94.

113. Ts'ai Chi-ou, p. 12.

(commander of the Twenty-ninth Infantry Regiment) as chief of staff, and Wu Chao-lin and Yang K'ai-chia (commander of the Thirtieth Infantry Regiment) as deputy chiefs.[114]

The public declaration issued in the name of Li Yüan-hung proclaimed that he had staged the uprising to save the people, and not for any personal benefit. The people had been suppressed because of the despotic rule of another race. The declaration said that they could not allow thieves and traitors "to eat our flesh" and that their aim was the establishment of a republic. It appealed to the people not to lose sight of their goal and to keep the peace. At the same time it assured them that the military would help preserve order.[115] The declaration had a calming effect, especially since the republican army had behaved with exemplary discipline and restraint. Not a house had been broken into by any of the soldiers, nor had they indulged in looting, arson, murder, or rape. The changeover could almost be said to have been peaceful so far as the people were concerned. In a country where depredation by soldiers was a frequent phenomenon, the conduct of the revolutionary soldiers could not fail to elicit admiration[116]—particularly when contrasted with the general behavior of imperial soldiers. The sense of purpose and mission of the republican soldiers were chiefly responsible for their discipline and order. They were not mercenaries but were fighting for a cause. Strict orders had also been given for the protection of foreign concessions and foreign religious missions.[117]

By the afternoon the whole of Wuchang had been brought under the effective control of the republican forces. A large number of Manchus—particularly remnants of the Banner garrison—were either killed or arrested. The prison gates were opened and all the revolutionaries whom Jui-cheng had imprisoned were released, including Hu Ying, who brought out along with him all the ordinary prisoners from his jail. In the confusion and turmoil—which was heightened by the killing of Manchus—thieves and other antisocial

114. Chang Nan-hsien, p. 367.

115. Hu Tsu-shun, pp. 53–54.

116. Reporting the events in Wuhan, the British minister in Peking, Sir John Jordan, wrote in a dispatch to the Foreign Secretary, Sir Edward Grey: "The orderly manner in which the movement is being conducted and the marked consideration shown for foreign interests distinguish it from all previous risings of this kind and has enlisted for it a measure of sympathy amongst the Chinese which the Manchu dynasty can no longer claim to command." *PP China No. 1* (1912), p. 21.

117. Hu Tsu-shun, p. 54.

elements tried to take advantage of the situation. The next day was a troubled one as discipline relaxed slightly and some looting took place.[118] The merchants and the gentry asked the military government to preserve strict order and a security bureau was organized. They also requested the military government not to send troops to search private houses for Manchus. The military government was unwilling to accept this demand and explained that the discipline of the soldiers was of a high order, in contrast to the past, and that Manchu Bannermen had to be arrested. The military government—which in effect was a group of about fifteen revolutionaries from the New Army—gave orders for a close watch at the city gates and shooting of any undesirable elements. The night was relatively calm and the next day shops opened as usual.[119]

Li Yüan-hung was still unwilling to serve the revolutionaries. According to the account of Ts'ao Ya-po, the issue raised a sharp controversy among the revolutionaries themselves. Not all of them were enthusiastic about Li Yüan-hung. One of them, Chang Chen-wu, said that since the rebels had not killed any high official, they had not been able to arouse awe among the populace. He suggested public execution of Li Yüan-hung to create the proper respect for the revolutionary army, and the selection of Wu Chao-lin as military governor. Wu, however, would not hear of any such thing. His was not a famous name, he pleaded, and the Hupeh army, a large segment of which had not yet revolted, would not obey him. They must borrow Li Yüan-hung's name in order to elicit the respect of Chinese and foreigners alike. Ch'en Lei and Li Tso-tung interposed that Li Yüan-hung was not a revolutionary and could not exert himself for the good of the country; hence there was no point in trying to use him. Wu came forth with the interesting answer that, according to Chinese historical tradition, what mattered most in success or failure was a man's personality, and that moreover the Hupeh people would not want a fellow provincial to lead them.[120] Wu obviously had forgotten that Li Yüan-hung was also a native of Hupeh. In any case, Wu Chao-lin remained convinced of Li's usefulness and gave instructions to prevent him from escaping.[121]

On the morning of October 12, the rest of the country was ap-

118. Hsiung Ping-k'un, p. 94.
119. Ts'ao Ya-po, pp. 41–42.
120. Ts'ao Ya-po, p. 174.
121. Ibid., p. 43.

prised of the developments in Wuchang. Telegrams were sent in the name of Li Yüan-hung as head of the military government to other provinces as well as to local officials in Hupeh. The telegram to the "entire country" contained a severe indictment of the Manchus—the uncivilized tribe that had disturbed the natural law and had robbed and plundered the fair land of the Han people. A minority could not rule the majority, the telegram claimed. "Our people [fathers and mothers and brothers and sisters]" had suffered untold hardships and the Manchus had burned "our books and changed the Classics, proscribed written work and imprisoned innocent people." They had monopolized power and held all the important posts in their hands. The foreign danger was increasing. Under the attractive garb of constitutionalism, the Manchus were carrying on a policy of centralization of power. The military government (of Hupeh) had raised the standard of revolt and would soon be followed by Hunan, Kiangsu, and Kwangtung, as well as by Anhwei, Ningsia, Honan, and Shensi; Szechwan would also be liberated. The people of the eighteen provinces were urged to rise up and wipe out the shame of the country and establish a republican system forever. The opportunity must not be lost, for such an hour would not come again.[122] The telegram to the prefectural and district officials of Hupeh asked them to give their loyalty to the new government and to carry on work as usual. They were warned that all those who disobeyed would be punished.[123]

The revolutionary army was joined by a battalion of the Thirty-second Infantry Regiment and the Eighth Regiment's cavalry, as well as by the Cavalry Battalion of the Mixed Brigade.[124] By October 12, when the telegram was sent, the entire New Army of Wuhan—with the exception of one battalion of the Forty-second Infantry Regiment and the Service Corps of the Eighth Regiment (still with Chang Piao, who had now encamped near the Peking-Hankow Railway station commonly known as Kilometre 10)—had gone over to the new government. The Wuchang Revolution was an established fact. The office of commander (*tsung-chih-hui*) was abolished and only that of governor (*tu-tu*) remained.[125]

A communication was also sent on behalf of the Military Government of the Republic of China to foreign consuls at Hankow,

122. Chang Nan-hsien, pp. 268–69.
123. Ts'ao Ya-po, pp. 49–50.
124. Ibid., pp. 44–45.
125. Ibid., p. 70.

explaining to them the reasons for the Revolution and asking them not to aid the Manchus. It also stated that, while the military government accepted all the previous treaties between the Manchu government and the foreign powers, it would not recognize any new treaty arrived at between the two. The communication expressed the hope of increased cooperation with the friendly powers for the preservation of world peace and the happiness of mankind. It also assured the consuls that the property and rights of foreigners would be fully protected.[126] Three days later, after the whole of Wuhan was in the firm grip of the revolutionaries and their strict order and discipline had won general acclaim, the consuls sent a communication to the military government declaring the neutrality of the foreign powers in the civil war in China.[127]

The foreign powers declared neutrality, not support for the new regime. Most of them had been caught by surprise, and while their reactions differed, they were all watching and waiting. It was revolutionary propaganda which, perhaps deliberately, gave the impression of implicit foreign support when it was not really warranted by fact. Li Yüan-hung, for instance, expressed gratitude in a note to the acting British consul general at Hankow for his government's "impartial attitude" during the hostilities and for granting the republicans belligerent status, but as the British minister at Peking pointed out in a communication to the British Foreign Secretary, Li's claim was not correct.[128] The powers had merely declared their neutrality and had not gone beyond that. In point of fact, the first instructions to the British consul general at Hankow were to ignore the communication of the revolutionaries and to have no formal dealings with them.[129] Whatever communication took place subsequently between the two was solely for the purpose of safeguarding the lives and property of British nationals and the security of the foreign concessions.

The leaders—Wu Chao-lin, Ts'ai Chi-min, Wu Hsing-han, Hsiung Ping-k'un, and others—personally went to the treasury, mint, and other storehouses and took charge of the funds. A count of all the funds showed that the revolutionary government had at its disposal nearly forty million dollars.[130] The financial position

126. Chang Kuo-kan, pp. 101–02.
127. Ibid.
128. *PP China No. 1 (1912)*, pp. 64–65.
129. Ibid., p. 21.
130. Chang Nan-hsien, p. 274.

of Wuchang was thus quite sound, an important factor in the stability of the new regime. The republicans did not have to face a collapsing economy and thus gained much needed time to consolidate their position while waiting for uprisings in other places.

The confusion in the administration was by no means over. Another meeting of the military government in the afternoon further reorganized the administrative and military setup.[131] The armed strength of the new government was obviously in need of expansion—particularly in view of an inevitable attack by imperial reinforcements. It was decided to organize four brigades under the command, respectively, of Wu Chao-lin, Ho Hsi-fan, Ch'en Ping-jung, and Chang T'ing-fu. It was also decided to set up four ministries: a Staff Office, with Chang Ching-liang as chief of staff and Wu Chao-lin as deputy chief of staff; Military Affairs, with Sun Wu as chief and Chiang I-wu (who had fled to Ching-shan and not yet returned) as deputy chief; Government Affairs, with T'ang Hua-lung at the head; and Foreign Affairs, headed by Hu Ying.[132] The republican army continued to follow the system of the New Army, although gradually the troops newly raised began to be called the "new army" and older units of the New Army the "old army."[133]

The troops guarding Hanyang across the river rose on the morning of October 12, led by their representative from the Forty-second Regiment, Hu Yü-chen, and easily captured the city. Only one platoon commander was killed and the changeover was swift.[134] Hankow was less fortunate. On the morning of October 12 rumors had it that the paper currency could no longer be used, and the whole city was plunged into a state of uncertainty and near chaos. This was a great opportunity for lawless elements and Hankow was subjected to looting and arson on a large scale. It was only when the revolutionary troops from Wuchang crossed the Yangtze, moved into Hankow, and arrested some of the miscreants that order began to be restored. Stability returned to the city and the shops opened as usual on October 14.[135]

The whole of the tri-city of Wuhan had now fallen to the revolutionaries and the military government of Hupeh became an effective administration. Many officials, civil and military, came back

131. Ibid., p. 273.
132. Ibid.
133. (Li) Chien-nung, p. 177.
134. Chang Nan-hsien, p. 272.
135. (Li) Chien-nung, pp. 174–75.

and joined the new regime. In response to the enlightened policy of the new republican government in protecting trade and the lives and property of the people, and the commendable discipline maintained by their troops, the merchants and gentry of Wuchang and Hankow cooperated with the new government in maintaining order. In Wuchang the chief representative of the gentry, Ko Feng-shih, contributed 300,000 dollars and the Chamber of Commerce lent its services to the maintenance of normal conditions. At Hankow too, after order had been restored, the Chamber of Commerce offered to provide funds for one division, provided order and adequate security against pillage were maintained.[136]

Meanwhile Li Yüan-hung had still not yielded and the actual work was being done by Wu Chao-lin and his associates. On October 12 Chiang I-wu returned to Wuchang and shed tears over Li Yüan-hung's obstinacy.[137] Li had not eaten for two days; nor had he met anyone. On October 13 he was brought to the office of the Provincial Assembly, now the headquarters of the military government, and asked to decide whether he wanted to emulate Washington and Napoleon or whether he would force the revolutionaries to kill him as a traitor.[138] Li's resistance was now weakening and he was responding to the advice of Wu Chao-lin, Ts'ai Chi-min, and others. The success of the Revolution in Wuhan could not have failed to influence him, and for the first time he indicated his willingness to serve the new republican regime. A taunt by one of the revolutionaries incited Li to cut off his queue.[139] Li now became the real head of the Hupeh Military Government.

Suspicion among the Leaders

Li Yüan-hung's assumption of leadership and the formal organization of the military government marked the consolidation of the new order as well as the beginning of new troubles, not the least significant of them being the problem of personal relations and mutual suspicion. Surprisingly, the first alarm signal in this respect came from Chang Ching-liang, the chief of staff. Apparently, he believed that he had not got his fair reward and perhaps that he should have been put in Li Yüan-hung's place. As soon as Li Yüan-hung indicated his decision to accept the military governorship,

136. Ibid., pp. 174–75, 177.
137. Chang Nan-hsien, p. 274.
138. Ts'ao Ya-po, pp. 80–81.
139. Chang Nan-hsien, p. 278.

the leaders met to draw up a plan for attacking imperial troops at Kilometre 10. At this point Chang Ching-liang rushed toward Li with the obvious intention of killing him. He was held back by the other revolutionary leaders present and, according to the military code, would probably have paid with his life but for the fact that some of those present felt that he was not in his right mind. He was taken away and kept under watch.[140]

Within three days of Li's conversion, Liu Kung and Chü Cheng came back to Wuchang and joined the military government, but, contrary to the decisions made before the outbreak of the Revolution, they were not given top positions.[141] On October 17 the military government was formally reorganized and draft regulations of the new government were outlined. Two main departments—military and civil—were created under Governor Li Yüan-hung. Yang K'ai-chia was made chief of staff with Wu Chao-lin and Yang Hsi-chang as deputy chiefs, while Sun Wu took charge of the Department of Military Affairs. T'ang Hua-lung became the chief of civilian administration and Hu Ying, chief of foreign affairs. A General Supervisory Office was established and Liu put in charge. Under the civilian administration there were various civil departments. Among them, Ch'a Kuang-fo was put in charge of education, and Li Tso-tung in charge of finance.[142]

The problems of administration were complicated by inordinate mutual suspicion among the leaders, and by considerations of personal power. Apparently Chiang I-wu interfered at every turn and too often used his influence to fill important administrative posts with incompetent members of the Literary Institute.[143] This caused considerable discontent and eventually led to a three-way struggle for power within the Hupeh military government among Chiang I-wu, Sun Wu, and Chang Chen-wu. Mutual suspicion also marred the work of the military government. T'ang Hua-lung, for instance, was under a cloud because of his past record as a constitutionalist. Even Yang K'ai-chia was distrusted and not allowed to function properly, because he was supposedly a relative of one of ex-Governor-general Jui-cheng's men. The orders by Chiang I-wu and Chang Chen-wu to execute three revolutionaries because they

140. Tsou Lu, *Chung-kuo kuo-min-tang shih-kao* (Draft History of the Kuomintang) (Shanghai, 1948), *3*, 916.

141. See section on "Revolutionary Activity in Hupeh."

142. Chang Nan-hsien, pp. 285, 290.

143. Ts'ao Ya-po, p. 87.

were found huddled together and thus thought to be hatching a plot provides an extreme illustration of the rampant suspicion.[144]

The pattern of the Wuchang uprising was very different from that of most of the previous efforts led by Sun Yat-sen and even of those led by Huang Hsing. This time the secret societies, except for members in the army, played an insignificant role. Army men led the revolt and overthrew Manchu rule in Wuhan. Having won power, they turned it over to a well-known military leader and to the Provincial Assembly, which was dominated by the constitutionalists. Power thus passed into the hands of men without strong republican convictions. This process was repeated in province after province as the army overturned the government, declared independence of Peking, and joined the republican camp. Generally the commander of the army stationed in the province was selected as governor, and the Provincial Assembly was called into session to give legal sanction to the new government. Thus the army became an important factor in Chinese politics and divisions among army officers led to a power struggle.

But in one crucial aspect, the Wuchang result was a unique phenomenon—the role of the ordinary soldiers in bringing about the Revolution. Here it was not the commanders who led their troops to revolt; not the officers who influenced their men to be loyal to them and accept their decision to revolt. It was the rank and file soldiers along with some petty officers who defied their higher officers and marched out on the streets to rebel against the ruling dynasty. As mentioned earlier, the Literary Institute had a membership of 3,000, a majority of whom were rank and file soldiers.[145] When the rebellion took place, the highest ranking officer that the revolutionaries could attract was Wu Chao-lin, a company commander, and even he was a reluctant participant and only gave way under pressure of those who led the revolt that night—Hsiung Ping-k'un, Ts'ai Chi-min, Hsü Ta-ming, Wu Hsing-han, and others. None held a rank higher than sergeant. It was only after they had succeeded in overthrowing Manchu rule in Wuchang that they set about the task of coaxing, cajoling, and compelling their commanders to join them and take over the administration. Li Yüan-hung was literally compelled at bayonet point to accept the position of governor, and even Chang Ching-liang, com-

144. Ibid., pp. 87–88.
145. See p. 10.

mander of the Twenty-ninth Infantry Regiment, and Yang K'ai-chia, commander of the Thirtieth Infantry Regiment, were persuaded to join the revolutionaries only after the revolt had succeeded.

This core group of revolutionaries in the army in Wuhan had only a nebulous link with the central revolutionary organization, the Revolutionary Alliance, and with the leadership of Sun Yat-sen. There were two groups working within the army in Wuhan: the Progressive Association and the Literary Institute. The leading group in the Progressive Association had been actively associated with the Revolutionary Alliance, but owing to certain differences had established the Progressive Association in order to promote revolution in the Yangtze provinces. The Literary Institute had no contact with the Revolutionary Alliance, and worked independently. It was the result of the work done by this and its predecessor organizations, and the fact that their network remained intact even after the leakage of secrets, that the Revolution succeeded in Wuchang despite the arrest or flight of the leaders. The two organizations did finally unite in order to promote the Revolution, but this unity was achieved at the last minute and was neither organic nor enduring. These peculiar features and circumstances were to create many problems for Sun Yat-sen and the republican cause.

PART IV

The Limitations of Revolutionary Leadership

10. Yuan Shih-k'ai's Rise to the Presidency

Ernest P. Young

Interpretation of the 1911 Revolution has been bedeviled by the enormous discrepancy between the idealistic enthusiasm of the initial revolutionary leadership and the lackluster issue of the revolutionary struggle, the Yuan Shih-k'ai presidency. Every writer who has dealt with the events of 1911 and 1912 in China has had to attempt an explanation of this discrepancy. There have been several popular lines of resolution: for example, the organizational weakness of the Revolutionary Alliance and its lack of an "adequate" ideology; treachery within the revolutionary leadership or usurpation of leadership by nonrevolutionary forces; the military and financial inferiority of the revolutionary side; foreign imperialist support of the Peking government; the inhibiting effect on the Revolution of the risk of foreign intervention; or even the general insignificance of the events and the revolutionary forces producing them—that is, it wasn't much of a revolution to begin with.

I am interested in a remaining line of approach. One of the most enduring and least challenged explanations for the failure of revolutionary hopes has been the Machiavellian mind of Yuan Shih-k'ai and his manipulation of events. Yuan is supposed to have turned the Revolution to his own advantage, maneuvered the court and the revolutionaries into a situation in which they neutralized each other, and, exploiting his superior military strength and foreign support, emerged with the fruits of the struggle for himself as a first step in his scheme to become Emperor. Thus was achieved the ultimate irony: the first President of a unified Chinese Republic was neither revolutionary nor republican. The view that attributes a decisive role to Yuan's trickery has survived even in recent writings on the Revolution, despite an accumulation of evidence which undercuts some of its essential elements.[1]

1. See, for example, Wu Hsiang-hsiang, *Sung Chiao-jen: Chung-kuo min-chu hsien-cheng ti hsien-ch'ü* (Sung Chiao-jen: Precursor of Chinese Democracy and

Yuan did have a talent for political maneuvering and did engage in unscrupulous acts. But his opportunity to exercise supreme authority in China was not simply the result of his talent for intrigue, or his base of power in the Peiyang Army, or the favorable view of him held by foreign powers. Many factors contributed to Yuan's rise and the manner in which he took advantage of his renewed eminence in 1911 and 1912. I shall examine contemporary attitudes toward his assumption of power, the military realities that he faced as Prime Minister, his relations with the foreign powers, his "conversion" to republicanism, and the manner of his assumption of the presidency in Peking.

The Call to Office: Imperial and Republican

The notoriety among Chinese of various political complexions that Yuan has enjoyed since his death should not lead us to misconstrue his reputation in 1911. The single factor that best explains Yuan's rise during the Revolution is that many people, representing a wide range of opinion, in fact wanted him to bear responsibility for bringing China through the crisis precipitated by the Revolution.

The most conspicuous request that he assume leadership after the Wuchang uprising was the court's. Actually, even before the Revolution Yuan's talents had not been ignored. Despite his ignominious dismissal in January 1909, authoritative talk of Yuan's return to office had been current in Peking at least since August 1910.[2] As he observed the difficulties of the Manchu government growing more serious, however, Yuan could afford to wait until the need was so great that he could dictate the terms of his return. After the Wuchang revolt broke out, Sheng Hsüan-huai, formerly

---

Constitutional Government) (Taipei, 1964), pp. 114–21. A typical formulation is in Jerome Ch'en, *Yuan Shih-k'ai, 1859–1916: Brutus Assumes the Purple* (Stanford, 1961), p. 117: "The revolution was a sham; the independence of the provinces a farce. But Yuan would not destroy them lest he should deprive himself of an opportunity to play them off against the Imperial Court."

2. Max Müller, Chargé in Peking, to Sir Edward Grey, Foreign Secretary (Aug. 31, 1910), FO 405/201 (33924); Sir John Jordan, Minister to China, to Grey (Dec. 20, 1910), FO 371/1081 (574); Watanabe Atsushi, "En Seigai—Hokuyō-ha seiken dasshu no michi" (Yuan Shih-k'ai—the Path of the Seizure of Power by the Peiyang Clique) in *Rekishigaku kenkyū, 258* (1961), 32.

I am indebted to Harold Schiffrin for allowing me to use his copies of Public Record Office documents, which I have subsequently supplemented by use of microfilms of the Confidential Prints series and by my own investigations in the Public Record Office.

a rival for control of national policy, seems to have been the first to ask Yuan to return to government service in order to save the country.[3] On October 14, four days after the uprising, the court itself asked Yuan to join the fray on the government's side. At first he declined the appointment, but the court, in ever greater difficulties, enticed Yuan with ever-expanding powers. By November 15 he was installed as Prime Minister in Peking.

The view that Yuan was the only man who could resolve the domestic conflict arising from the provincial rebellion was not confined to the court but was also held with remarkable persistence by the revolutionary leadership. There were some in the South (that is, the revolutionary provinces, chiefly in South and Central China) who opposed surrendering ultimate authority to Yuan, but they were never successful in capturing a majority of any assembly of the revolutionaries, with only one or two exceptions, even at the provincial level.[4] Rather, it is striking how soon, after the Revolution broke out, Southern leaders turned to Yuan as the best hope for establishing a republic.

At first Yuan took the initiative in making contact. Offers of negotiation, even before he had reached Peking to assume the prime ministership, were extended to the Wuchang revolutionary government and rejected.[5] From that point on, however, the revolutionary camp persisted in offering Yuan the presidency of the Republic, with the obvious condition that he abandon his support of the Manchu monarchy. As early as November 12 a report was printed that Li Yüan-hung, governor (*tu-tu*) of the leading revolutionary province, had proposed to Yuan that he become the first President.[6] Sun Yat-sen telegraphed from Paris on the same day approving Li's proposal (as an alternative to Li's own candidacy).[7] Two or three days later, when emissaries sent by Yuan arrived for

3. Ch'en, *Yuan Shih-k'ai,* p. 111. Yoshino Sakuzō claims that Ts'en Ch'un-hsüan, another old rival, proposed Yuan's appointment at this time. Yoshino Sakuzō, *Chūgoku kakumei shōshi* (Short History of the Chinese Revolution) (Tokyo, no date), p. 38.

4. Bertram Giles, Consul in Changsha, to Jordan (Feb. 28, 1912: enclosed in Jordan to Grey, Mar. 31, 1912), FO 371/1317 (15689), which describes a mass meeting in Hunan's capital on Feb. 21, 1912, where it was decided to oppose Yuan's election as President. This forthright opposition was short-lived.

5. *Min-li pao* (Nov. 5, 1911, and Nov. 6, 1911); Jordan to Grey (Nov. 5, 1911), FO 371/1096 (47279).

6. *Min-li pao* (Nov. 12, 1911).

7. "Chung-hua min-kuo k'ai-kuo shih-ch'i shih-liao" (Historical Materials of the Period of the Establishment of the Republic of China), *KMWH, 1,* 1.

conferences in Wuchang, the offer seems to have been repeated by Li and Huang Hsing in the presence of Sung Chiao-jen.[8] On December 2, when representatives of the revolutionary provinces were formally gathered at Wuhan, they resolved that Yuan should be elected President if he changed his allegiance from the Manchus to the Republic.[9] On December 9, Huang Hsing cabled Wang Ching-wei, a revolutionary leader then in Peking, that the presidency would go to Yuan without question. The message was conveyed to Yuan through his supporter, Yang Tu.[10]

The Revolution was bigger than Yuan, and only a very few on the revolutionary side contemplated compromise on a constitutional monarchy with Yuan as Prime Minister—the goal he himself publicly espoused in this period. Support for Yuan had one unwavering condition: that he become a republican. But from mid-November onward, there seemed never to have been any serious doubt that, if he would arrange for Manchu abdication, he would be leader of the new republican order. Qualifications about constitutional limitations and sites for the capital were afterthoughts and were never urged with enthusiasm by the majority of Southern leaders. The republicans were not tricked into giving Yuan the presidency. Certainly he sought support in the South and worked strenuously at keeping channels of communication open.[11] But it

8. *Min-li pao* (Nov. 18, 19, and 20, 1911). In a detailed account to the *Times* correspondent, one of Yuan's emissaries implied that there was no firm offer. "Memorandum of a Visit from Ts'ai T'ing-kan, Nov. 16th, 1911," Morrison Papers (item 147). But from this and other documents it is clear that, at the least, a very cordial attitude toward Yuan was expressed, and the offer soon became firm, if it had not already been.

9. Li Shou-k'ung, "Min-ch'u chih kuo-hui yü tang-cheng" (National Assembly and Party Struggles in the Early Republic), *CHS ts'ung-k'an, 5* (Taipei, 1964), 89.

10. *Min-li pao* (Dec. 10, 1911); Chün-tu Hsüeh, *Huang Hsing and the Chinese Revolution* (Stanford, 1961), p. 134.

11. These efforts are described in Li Chien-nung, *The Political History of China, 1840–1928,* trans. Ssu-yü Teng and Jeremy Ingalls (Princeton, 1956), pp. 258–59. A recent addition to the standard accounts is: Hu Shih, "Pa Chung-yang yen-chiu-yüan li-shih yü-yen yen-chiu so ts'ang ti 'I-chün han-cha' chung ti Yüan K'o-ting kei Feng Kuo-chang ti shou-cha" (An Epilogue to a Letter from Yüan K'o-ting to Feng Kuo-chang, in the "I-chün han-cha"), deposited in the Oral History Institute of Academia Sinica, *CHS ts'ung-k'an, 1* (Taipei, 1960), 1–4. Allegations of Yuan's bribery of revolutionaries were current in the period after the abdication. Members of the Nanking Assembly and the Shanghai press were said to have been bought. David Fraser to G. E. Morrison (Nanking, Mar. 13, 1912), Morrison Papers (item 172), quoted in Cyril Pearl, *Morrison of Peking* (Sydney, 1967), p. 247, but erroneously attributed to Everard Fraser. Sun Yat-sen and, variously, T'ang Shao-i, Wu T'ing-fang, or the Revolutionary Alliance were reported to have received as a condition of the final settlement huge sums of money from Peking. F. E. Wilkinson, Consul in Nanking, to

is an unreasonable underestimation of the Southern leadership to suggest that their choice of Yuan for the presidency was not based on independent judgment about their cause and its needs. If more radical revolutionary forces which could not tolerate him were suppressed during the formation of the Republic, the suppression was performed by other "revolutionaries," not by Yuan.[12] An important reason for his becoming leader of the Republic was that, insofar as it could be determined, he was the "people's choice."

It should be added that the Southern appreciation of Yuan was not without doubts and moments of distrust. One could compile a long list of contemporary reports to the effect that his republican commitment was suspect: he did not share the outlook of the Southern revolutionaries; or he would restore the Manchus at the first opportunity; or he intended ultimately to enthrone himself. These hesitations were subordinated, however, to larger purposes, and another list of contemporary reports could be assembled, showing resolution or suspension of doubts and statements of confidence in Yuan's good intentions.

Because of his record as a reformer and his power struggles with certain leading Manchus, some Revolutionary Alliance members had hoped that he might support the revolutionary cause from the beginning.[13] Yuan was chiefly valued as the one man who could achieve the dynasty's abdication and at the same time retain national unity and keep the foreign powers at bay. Revolutionaries may have regretted that he was the leader who showed the most promise of attaining these aims, but they arrived at the conclusion on their own, not through trickery. Nor did the revolutionaries feel he was too strong to defeat, although they were conscious of his Peiyang Army support. The central fact was that most of them (or their dominant councils) were not eager for a showdown with Yuan: he was indispensable for the new polity.

The Military Prospects

After he accepted the reins of authority in Peking, Yuan's maneuverability was limited by military realities. It has sometimes

Jordan (May 19, 1912), FO 228/1836; Arthur Pope, General Manager, Shanghai-Nanking Railway, to Morrison (May 10, 1912), Morrison Papers (item 158). Certainly money changed hands in this period, but it was probably no more than a lubricant, not a determining factor.

12. The assassination of Wu Lu-chen remains an ambiguous case in this regard. See Li Chien-nung, p. 254, and the corresponding note, p. 512.

13. Li Chien-nung, p. 230.

been maintained that the Peking government, once Yuan had assumed control, was in a favorable military position throughout the Revolution. Yuan did not press the attack, it is asserted, simply because he needed the existence of the Revolution to force his will on the Ch'ing court. It is true that at various points in his career he seemed to prefer a political rather than military use of troops under his command. But in 1911, at least, this preference was reinforced by some unpleasant military facts. The revolutionary forces were stronger and more confident, and the imperial forces weaker and less cohesive, than is often supposed. Considerable contemporary testimony is available that suggests a military balance not to Yuan's advantage.

For example, in early November, two days after Yuan had agreed to lead the government forces, the acting British military attaché in Peking concluded that strategically, "the position of the Imperial Government at the present time would appear almost desperate . . ." and that, despite Yuan's appointment as Prime Minister, negotiations initiated by Peking could only end in the abolition of the Manchu dynasty.[14] On November 20 he reported: "So small a force of Luchun [New Army] as now remains in Chihli and the North could not possibly hope to bring the remaining provinces again into line, even if they remained loyal to the Imperial cause, and funds were forthcoming to pay and feed them. . . ."[15]

The example most commonly used in the argument that Yuan intentionally preserved the Revolution is the fighting in the Wuhan area in the second half of November. Before this, the only important battles between revolutionary forces and Northern divisions had been the revolutionary victories there in October, which resulted in the retreat of the government forces from all of Hanyang and most of Hankow, and the imperial counterattack of late October and early November, which regained Hankow. A concentrated Northern assault from November 18 to November 27 brought Northern troops back into Hanyang. At that point the assault ceased, and the commanding general, Feng Kuo-chang, was recalled to Peking before any serious attempt was made to take the neighboring rebel stronghold of Wuchang. Both then and later,

14. Report by Capt. M. Otter-Barry, enclosed in Jordan to Grey (Nov. 5, 1911), FO 371/1096 (47279).

15. Report by Otter-Barry, enclosed in Jordan to Grey (Nov. 20, 1911), FO 371/1096 (49155).

many believed that Yuan, had he pressed on and continued these assaults, could have crushed the Revolution.[16]

Opposing views were vigorously expressed by contemporary observers. The British minister emphatically disagreed that Yuan could have destroyed the Revolution by pursuing the attack on Wuchang. The only alternative to a truce and negotiations would have been, in his opinion, a long and bloody struggle, the outcome of which would have been by no means certain.[17] The well-informed Japanese observer Yoshino Sakuzō held that Yuan must have realized that, although he could probably win Wuchang, the revolutionary army as a whole could not be so easily smashed and that it was more important to consolidate in the North. For this purpose, Yoshino concluded, compromise with the South was necessary.[18] A source close to Yuan stated within a month after the event that the imperial troops had been restrained at Wuhan because they had engaged in too deep a salient and were threatened from the rear by the unsettled conditions in Shensi and Shansi.[19]

Certainly there was no disposition in the South to accept defeat. From early December on, preparations in that area were for offensive, not defensive, warfare. Many of the revolutionaries were confident that sentiment in much of the North was republican. Forces were being assembled in the Wuhan area, Nanking, and Woosung near Shanghai for a three-pronged attack on the government forces.[20]

Yuan's military difficulties did not lie only in Southern strength and enthusiasm. There were serious difficulties in Yuan's control of the Peiyang Army. These New Army (Lu-chün) divisions are generally considered to have been the principal source of Yuan's strength. They were certainly important, both in themselves and because they inspired respect in the country at large. Yet there were limitations to the reliability of the Peiyang Army in 1911.

Personal loyalty to Yuan, upon which his control over the army's

16. For example: Roger S. Greene, Consul in Hankow, to William J. Calhoun, Minister to China (Dec. 11, 1911), USDS, 893.00/953; Calhoun to Philander C. Knox, Secretary of State (Jan. 16, 1912), USDS, 893.00/1038; Ch'en, *Yuan Shih-k'ai,* pp. 116–17.

17. Jordan to Grey (Feb. 24, 1912), FO 371/1315 (11144).

18. Yoshino, p. 46.

19. Letter from Lan Kung-wu to Liang Ch'i-ch'ao, probably toward the end of December 1911, in *Liang . . . nien-p'u* (Taipei, 1958), pp. 357–58. Lan's source was Li Chia-chü.

20. Report by J. B. Murdock, commander in chief, U.S. Asiatic Fleet, enclosed in Secretary of the Navy to Knox (Feb. 15, 1912), USDS, 893.00/1075.

officers is said to have rested, must have been attenuated to some extent by his lack of administrative authority over them between 1907 and 1911. In addition, the group of officers trained under Yuan and his generals had been greatly augmented by large numbers of graduates of the Japanese Army Officers' Academy (Nihon rikugun shikan gakkō, sometimes called the Imperial Military College), open to Chinese since 1901 on the basis of a rigorous entrance examination. By 1910, there were 620 Chinese graduates.[21] Not all of them entered the Peiyang divisions upon their return, but a good proportion eventually did. They could not be expected to follow Yuan unswervingly. Further, the New Army generally, as the largest of any of the modernized institutions in China at the time—with a relatively high proportion of literacy, Western dress, a broad acquaintance with Western technology (both in weapons and in social organization), and a large number of foreign-trained officers—was responsive to political issues and difficult to control by traditional methods.

The Wuchang uprising itself was, of course, an expression of the political unreliability of the New Army. Then, at the end of October, after Yuan had been asked to join the government but before he had come to Peking, disaffection appeared even in the Peiyang divisions. On October 29, Chang Shao-tseng, commander of the Twentieth Division in control of forces stationed at Luanchow on the railway line between Peking and Mukden; Lan T'ien-wei, chief of the Second Mixed Brigade at Mukden; and other high-ranking officers submitted a petition to the throne. The petition consisted of twelve "requests" that amounted to a demand for a highly limited constitutional monarchy.[22] Both Chang and Lan (but not all their collaborators) were graduates of the Japanese Army Officers' Academy.

Another graduate of this school, Wu Lu-chen, was commanding the New Army's Sixth Division, one of the early Peiyang formations. Soon after the demands made by Chang, Lan, and others, Wu

21. Pekin Shina kenkyū-kai, ed., *Saishin Shina kanshin roku* (Record of Contemporary Chinese Officials and Gentry) (in two parts with separate pagination, Tokyo, 1918), 2, 392–405.

22. For a translation, see Li Chien-nung, pp. 251–52. In connection with the politicization which goes with modernization, it is interesting to note that the twelfth request was that military men should have the right to participate in the formulation of the constitution and the passage of parliamentary bills. A competing modern institution, the National Assembly, agreed to all of the requests but the twelfth. *Min-li pao* (Nov. 3, 1911).

and part of his division were transferred from Paoting to Shih-chia-chuang, the vital junction of the Peking-Hankow and Taiyuan railway lines. On November 4, instead of proceeding on his assigned task of suppressing the revolt in Shansi, he made secret arrangements with the revolutionary army of that province for joint action against Peking.[23]

The background of these two major defections in the Peiyang Army becomes more complicated the more one looks into it. Most accounts have stressed the Revolutionary Alliance affiliation of the three commanders and the revolutionary devotion of Wu and Lan especially. But this aspect has probably been exaggerated. Liang Ch'i-ch'ao was also deeply involved, and the most reliable contemporary evidence suggests a constitutionalist, rather than a revolutionary, anti-Manchu content to the immediate programs of these Northern commanders.[24] Still others claimed to have had a hand in these bold moves. Yuan Shih-k'ai's son, Yüan K'o-ting, assured the British minister on November 2 that the mutinous troops at Luanchow were "acting under Yuan Shih-k'ai's inspiration,"[25] while the Japanese adventurer Kawashima Naniwa, who was a police instructor in Peking, is said to have persuaded Wu Lu-chen to bar Yuan's return to Peking.[26] Wu, despite his reputed revolutionary inclinations, was in direct communication during this period with the imperial clansman Tsai-t'ao, who then controlled the imperial guards.[27] Although a great deal of mystery still surrounds these events, as well as Wu's assassination on the evening of November 6, they prove beyond a reasonable doubt that important elements of the Peiyang Army were not in fact totally committed to anyone.[28]

23. Chang Kuo-kan, *Hsin-hai ko-ming shih-liao* (Historical Materials on the Revolution of 1911) (Shanghai, 1958), pp. 197–202.

24. I have dealt with this question in "The Reformer as a Conspirator: Liang Ch'i-ch'ao and the 1911 Revolution," in A. Feuerwerker, R. Murphey, and M. C. Wright, eds., *Approaches to Modern Chinese History* (Berkeley and Los Angeles, 1967), pp. 249–59.

25. Jordan to Grey (Nov. 2, 1911), FO 371/1090 (43366).

26. Marius Jansen, *The Japanese and Sun Yat-sen* (Cambridge, Mass., 1954), p. 139.

27. Chang Kuo-kan, pp. 206–07. *KKWH, Hsin-hai ko-ming yü min-kuo chien-yüan, Ko-sheng kuang-fu* (Restoration in the Various Provinces) (Taipei, 1962), *3*, 248.

28. The most recent and extended attempt to sort out these events still relies heavily on later recollections and reconstructions, unfortunately unreliable. Chu Yen-chia, "Wu Lu-chen yü Chung-kuo ko-ming" (Wu Lu-chen and the Chinese Revolution), *CHS ts'ung-k'an, 6,* 161–232.

There is some evidence that even those generals considered to be the very crux of

Yuan gradually established control in the North. His military support, however, was never as certain as most accounts would imply. Part of the Twentieth Division engaged in revolutionary action and there was grave doubt about its reliability and that of other sections of the Northern army through January and into February of 1912.[29] The Peiyang Army's revolutionary elements were contained, but if faced with an attack from the South no one could be sure of their loyalty.

It is in the nature of unfought battles that the victor remains forever obscure. It seems fair to say, however, that there was less inevitability in the revolutionaries' deferring to Yuan and less choice for Yuan himself than is usually assumed. In other words, while on the one hand the rebel South chose Yuan in large part because they wanted him (or what he represented), Yuan for his part was compelled by the strategic situation to choose the Republic. Yuan handled this situation skillfully, but there was actually very little room for maneuver.

Yuan and the Foreign Powers

Yuan Shih-k'ai was much admired by most representatives of the foreign powers in Peking. Even the Japanese, who conceived a dislike of Yuan in the 1880s because of his role in Sino-Japanese rivalry in Korea, had learned to respect him, and in 1911 the Japanese minister, Ijūin Hikokichi, was an enthusiastic supporter.[30]

Yuan's control of the Peiyang Army, Tuan Ch'i-jui and Feng Kuo-chang, were not automatically obedient to him. Nagai Kazumi, "Shintei taii no keika ni kan-suru oboegaki—iwayuru jōkoku gozen kaigi o chūshin to shite" (Notes on the Process of the Abdication of the Ch'ing Emperor, Centering on the So-called Imperial Conferences for the Surrender of the Country), *Shinshū daigaku bunri gakubu kiyō, 12* (December 1962), 15–19; Watanabe, "En Seigai," p. 36; Chang Kuo-kan, p. 307.

29. Report by Lt. Col. M. E. Willoughby, enclosed in Jordan to Grey (Jan. 27, 1912), FO 371/1312 (6178). For accounts of the turbulence at Luanchow, see: T'ao Chü-yin, *Pei-yang chün-fa t'ung-chih shih-ch'i shih-hua* (Historical Tales about the Period of Rule by the Peiyang Warlords), *1* (Peking, 1957), 115–17; James E. Sheridan, *Chinese Warlord: The Career of Feng Yü-hsiang* (Stanford, 1966), pp. 44–47. Southern leaders professed to be convinced that there was serious disaffection in the Northern Army, which was held together, they thought, only by the pay it received. Report by Murdock, enclosed in Secretary of the Navy to Knox (Feb. 15, 1912), USDS, 893.00/1075.

30. Ijūin formed what he felt to be a close friendship with Yuan when they were both in Tientsin. Ikei Masaru, "Nihon no tai-En gaikō (Shingai kakumei-ki)" (Japanese Policy Toward Yuan During the Revolution of 1911), *Hōgaku kenkyū, 35* (1962), 83.

Putnam Weale, in his book on the early Republic, calls Yuan the "selected bailiff of the Powers,"[31] and indeed his return to the government was welcomed cordially by the leading imperialist power in China, Great Britain. Sir John Jordan, the British minister in Peking, had first met Yüan when they were both in Korea two decades previously, had renewed the acquaintance when Yuan was governor-general of Chihli and Jordan was stationed in Tientsin, and was known to consider himself a close friend of Yuan's. It was quite clear that the British hoped in October that Yuan would assume high office in Peking, and once he was installed they were inclined to endorse him. The influential *Times* correspondent, G. E. Morrison, was an ardent supporter. He urged the Southern leaders to make Yuan President (although they had already arrived at this decision independently) and was even rebuked by his London editor for his obvious enthusiasm for Yuan.[32] Sir Edward Grey, the British Foreign Secretary, observed on November 14, 1911 that there seemed to be "one good man on the side opposed to the revolutionaries, Yuan Shih-k'ai, whom we all respected, and under whom we believed that China was progressing, until the Manchu dynasty dismissed him."[33] Remarks such as these, uttered in circumstances where they would reach the ears of important Chinese, fortified the general belief that Yuan had foreign support, a belief that was, no doubt, a useful aspect of his authority in China.

On the other hand, the British were not ready to extend to the Peking government, or to Yuan personally, any material assistance. The British legation in Peking decided four days after the Wuchang uprising that the revolutionary movement "has enlisted for it a measure of sympathy amongst the Chinese which the Manchu dynasty can no longer claim to command."[34] G. E. Morrison concluded as early as October 13 that the "movement meets with almost universal sympathy" among educated Chinese. Before the end of the month, he observed that everyone he met privately expressed

31. B. Lennox Simpson (B. L. Putnam Weale, pseud.), *The Fight for the Republic in China* (New York, 1917), p. 20.

32. Morrison to D. D. Braham (Dec. 29, 1911); ibid. (Feb. 9, 1912), Morrison Papers (item 162).

33. Grey to Jordan (Nov. 14, 1911), FO 371/1095 (45661). This remark was made to an English arms manufacturer (Sir Trevor Dawson of Messrs. Vickers, Sons, and Maxim), who was representing Sun Yat-sen.

34. Jordan to Grey (Oct. 16, 1911), FO 371/1090 (42758).

a wish for the success of the Revolution. Moreover, this was based on experience not in the South but in Peking and on a trip to the headquarters of the imperial expeditionary forces![35] Gradually this British impression, at first unrelated to a judgment about Peking's military prospects, hardened into a conviction that the Manchu court was doomed.

With this view of the dynasty's lack of popular support and the view that the North could not claim a military advantage, the Foreign Office discounted the commonly held foreign opinion that a republic was an unsuitable form of government for China. British intervention against the republican forces, it was felt, would only provoke a reaction unfavorable to British interests. These interests, as the British minister had to remind his Japanese colleague, whose government urged intervention on behalf of the monarchy,[36] were largely in areas controlled by the revolutionaries. The extensive British trading interests in the Yangtze area would be jeopardized if London decided to give substantial aid to Peking and if the official British estimate of revolutionary strength was accurate. Further, the populations of Hong Kong and Singapore were overwhelmingly enthusiastic in their support of the Revolution, so that any British action against it would cause severe security problems in these important British colonies.[37]

The Japanese were not alone in their desire to provide Peking with tangible assistance. The American minister, William J. Calhoun, cabled Washington in the first part of December 1911 that Yuan was the only alternative to chaos and should be given financial support.[38] Willard Straight, the American representative in the five-nation banking consortium which had been negotiating a loan with Peking before the Revolution, was of the opinion that America and Germany should proceed on their own in aiding Yuan Shih-k'ai, "irrespective of our wobbling British friends. . . ."[39] The British, however, still held the diplomatic lead in China. Washington, more cautious than its diplomatic and financial representatives in Peking, vetoed independent action in support of Yuan. Despite its restlessness and its later feeling of

35. "Memorandum" (Oct. 13, 1911), "Notes" (Oct. 22, 1911), and Morrison to Braham (Oct. 17, 1911), Morrison Papers (items 147 and 131).

36. Ikei, "Nihon no tai-En gaikō," *Hōgaku kenkyū, 35,* 90–91.

37. Jordan to Grey (Dec. 28, 1911), FO 371/1310 (2021).

38. Calhoun to Knox (Dec. 6, 1911), USDS, 893.00/745.

39. Herbert Croly, *Willard Straight* (New York, 1924), p. 429.

betrayal, Tokyo valued maintenance of the Anglo-Japanese Alliance and was restrained by British unwillingness to consider intervention on the side of the monarchy.[40] The French, who urged that loans be granted to Peking, declined to act without the other powers.[41]

Although Yuan and his assistants tried repeatedly to obtain positive British support, Great Britain adhered scrupulously to a policy of neutrality. The most concise and authoritative statement of this policy was written personally by Grey, commenting on a dispatch from Peking: "We can only recognise what is accepted by the great majority of Chinese themselves. Intervention in any form before this is apparent must be dangerous and would I should think be prejudicial to the party on whose behalf foreign Powers intervened."[42]

The policy extended to loans. In the first week of the Revolution, Jordan formed the view that the Peking government should be denied foreign loans for the duration of the rebellion.[43] Though convinced that the Peking government was, in mid-December 1911, on the point of bankruptcy, the British government refused to approve any loans to Yuan Shih-k'ai unless the "revolutionary party" acquiesced![44] The Nanking authorities protested, of course, and no loans were approved by the British government for either the North or the South during the Revolution. The loans that were made over the opposition of the British government were, on the whole, more generous to the revolutionaries than to Peking.[45] Even Morrison assisted the Imperial Maritime Customs Service (that is, its foreign, predominantly British, management) in foiling an attempt by Yuan to get his hands on its reserve fund of three million taels.[46]

The British, then, did not assist Yuan in his contest with the revolutionary leadership until after he was declared President of the

40. Ikei, "Nihon no tai-En gaikō," *Hōgaku kenkyū, 35,* 81–92, and *35,* 50–82.

41. Sir F. Bertie, Ambassador to France, to Grey (Dec. 18, 1911), FO 371/1097 (50886).

42. Foreign Office memorandum appended to Jordan to Grey (Jan. 12, 1912), FO 371/1310 (1707).

43. Morrison to Braham (Oct. 17, 1911), Morrison Papers (item 131).

44. Grey to Sir Claude MacDonald, Minister to Japan (Dec. 11, 1911), FO 371/1097 (49348); Grey to Jordan (Dec. 12, 1911), FO 405/205 (50450).

45. For a comprehensive statement concerning loans, see: "Memorandum respecting China State Loans before, during, and after the Revolution of 1911–12" (Mar. 25, 1912), FO 371/1318 (19603).

46. "Memorandum" (Dec. 5, 1911), Morrison Papers (item 147).

Republic. And they succeeded in restraining Japan, the other power most interested and active in Chinese politics at that time. The presence of foreign powers in China was so entrenched and pervasive that nothing of importance could happen without being affected by it in some degree; or rather, the presence was an integral part of any large event. In this complicated fashion, the powers did influence the course of events in a way that was, on balance, inhibiting to the Revolution.[47] On the level of policy and conspicuous concrete acts, however, Britain held the ring against assistance to either side. If Britain had intervened in the interest of her trade and her colonies, she would more likely have done so in favor of the Revolution than against it.

Sir John Jordan was always ready to express the view, to the Japanese or to Yuan Shih-k'ai, that a constitutional monarchy was the best form of government for China. When it came down to more immediate advice, however, it sometimes seemed that the British legation was urging Yuan to accept a republic. In an interview on December 22, 1911, Jordan discussed with Yuan the proposal of T'ang Shao-i, "whose republican sympathies were well known . . . ," that the future form of government be left to a national assembly of delegates selected by the provincial assemblies. Undeterred by Yuan's pronouncements on the riskiness of a republican experiment and on the deep roots of the imperial institution in the habits and minds of the people, Jordan suggested that Yuan adopt T'ang's proposal. It was evident to both men that, given the number of provinces with revolutionary governments, a national

47. The American vice-consul in Nanking reported in the first week of the Revolution that it was his impression that the revolutionaries were delaying any action in Nanking until there were enough foreign gunboats in the area to intimidate the "rabble" that was bound to follow any disturbance. The revolutionaries were very anxious to avoid harm to foreigners and see that "no evil will attend any but the Chinese." Alvin W. Gilbert to Knox (Oct. 17, 1911), USDS, 893.00/692. Gilbert's impression may have been mistaken in this case, but there is no doubt that the timing and extent of revolutionary violence were checked by the mere presence of foreigners and foreign interests. Foreign interests, real or imagined, for which consular officials felt obliged to intervene against revolutionary action in Hankow during the first ten days of the uprising, are enumerated in a British report: the Asiatic Petroleum Company, the foreign superintendent of the telegraph administration and his Chinese employees, the foreign postal commissioner (the issue was revolutionary censorship), the concession grounds in Hankow, and the foreign Customs Inspector (the issue was the payment of the collections to the Hongkong and Shanghai Banking Corporation). Acting Consul General Goffe in Hankow to Jordan (Oct. 20, 1911), FO 371/1095 (45831). The British also intervened in a fashion that impeded the imperial troops.

assembly so constituted would decide on a republican form of government.[48] Ultimately the proposal was not adopted, but Yuan could be under no illusion that the British would help him retain the Ch'ing dynasty.

Although Yuan attempted to exploit his "foreign support" in negotiations with the South,[49] he must have known, after loans were denied and attempts to secure British support rebuffed, that he could not effectively use the powers against the republican movement.

Yuan Becomes Republican

What were Yuan's intentions during the months after the Wuchang uprising? There is no reason to doubt that he felt himself to be the indispensable man the leaders of both North and South considered him to be. Naturally, then, in his view of the future he saw himself in a key position. It is not surprising that his path of progress from retired official to provisional President is susceptible of being interpreted solely as a series of maneuvers designed to check his rivals and secure his own leadership over a reunified country. And he did indeed do everything in his power to achieve these objectives.

Whatever the path, however, the destination was one that not only he but most of the country seemed to desire. As we have seen, it was soon apparent that only a republican government could hope to reestablish central control over the Chinese provinces. Yuan's problem, then, if he was to lead a unified China, was to achieve the abdication of the Manchu dynasty as peacefully as possible. Southern republican leaders shared this objective, so that there was only adjustment, not conflict, between them and Yuan. (Of course, this overlapping of aims did not preclude the exchange of suspicion and vituperation between Yuan and the revolutionary leaders.)

Although it is said that Yuan's first reaction on hearing news of the Wuchang uprising was to abjure the revolutionary party for himself and his descendants, by October 23 he was assuring his followers that he held no harsh view of the revolutionaries.[50] As

48. Jordan to Grey (Dec. 28, 1911), FO 371/1310 (2021). T'ang Shao-i told Morrison that Yuan was fully aware of the republican implications of the plan. Morrison to Braham (Dec. 29, 1911), Morrison Papers (item 162).

49. Jordan to Grey (Dec. 23, 1911), FO 371/1098 (51476).

50. Wang Hsi-t'ung, "Hsin-hai chi-shih" (Recollections of 1911), *Hsin-hai ko-ming tzu-liao* (Materials on the 1911 Revolution) (Peking, 1961), pp. 517–18.

the British minister observed on October 30, the situation was so desperate that "Yuan may find himself obliged to espouse whatever cause stands the best chance of success in the stress and turmoil through which China is now passing."[51] Yüan K'o-ting, the Prime Minister's son, asserted privately in mid-November that it was almost impossible to save the dynasty; public opinion throughout the country demanded its removal; many of his father's old associates refused to cooperate in a government under the Manchus; and the rebel leaders at Wuchang had promised his father their full support for the presidency of a Chinese republic.[52]

The British legation concluded from this and other sources close to Yuan, including Ts'ai T'ing-kan, that virtually all Yuan's civilian entourage was in full sympathy with the Revolution and that T'ang Shao-i, who was openly working for a republic with Yuan as President, "enjoys the approval of the republican party here in Peking . . . and probably the acquiescence of Yuan himself."[53] Yuan, as was his wont with respect to his ultimate intentions, was silent about this early decision for a republican solution, if such it was. He had much to fear, including the wrath of the Manchus and the displeasure of the Japanese.

The peace negotiations between North and South, which were foreshadowed by Yuan's advances toward Li Yüan-hung's government in early November, got under way in December and were brought to fruition in January 1912. There was a brief break at the time of Sun Yat-sen's election as President of a separate Southern government in Nanking. Once terms were agreed upon, it was necessary for Yuan to get the acceptance of the court. This was done by February 2, and the abdication took place on February 12. Achieving a peaceful abdication was a considerable feat of persuasion that assumed a variety of forms, including threats and promises. Yuan's talent for intrigue was fully expressed in these intricate maneuvers in Peking in January 1912.[54] But it should not be supposed that he had any reasonable alternative.

During the period of parley with the revolutionaries, Yuan apparently feared that he might fall between two stools by prematurely antagonizing the court without securing the presidency of

51. Jordan to Grey (Oct. 30, 1911), FO 371/1095 (45829).

52. Jordan to Grey (Nov. 14, 1911), FO 371/1095 (45368).

53. Jordan to Grey (Nov. 17, 1911), FO 371/1096 (48411); Jordan to Grey (Nov. 19, 1911), FO 371/1095 (46299).

54. For a detailed description, see Nagai, "Shintei taii," pp. 1–24.

the new Republic.[55] Despite Sun's reassurance that his own election as President was temporary and that he would defer to Yuan as soon as negotiations were completed, Yuan reacted to the election with considerable suspicion. He seemed to feel this development represented a betrayal of promises and a tendency toward a permanent division of the country.

His marked concern for his own position in the new regime raises the matter of his sincerity, which is customarily questioned. Was he truly converted to republicanism during these months or was he merely striving for greater personal power? By the standard of long-term dedication, the depth of his conversion ultimately proved quite shallow.[56] In contrast to some in the South who held republicanism as an absolute principle, Yuan espoused a change in the polity as a pragmatic response to the balance of forces in the country and to the demands placed upon his leadership. After October 1911, no doubt many became republicans for similar reasons.

It is only fair to point out that in the short run Yuan adhered to the commitments made during the negotiations. As Sun demanded on January 22, 1912, he abolished the Ch'ing dynasty and declared to the world his support for republicanism. After his election he swore to observe the constitution prepared by the Nanking Assembly. For the first year of his presidency, Yuan maintained an adherence to the January agreements that even the Revolutionary Alliance considered tolerable, if not perfect.

The Revolution succeeded in its prime, if limited, objective: the end of the Manchu dynasty. Yuan played a prominent role in making that success so painless. Once it was clear that he would be the leading figure in the new Republic, as it was quite early, the security of his position and the firmness of his power were distinguished only with difficulty from the strength and unity of the new government. Certainly Yuan considered them to be the same thing. Others disagreed, though only a few to the extent of opposing his

55. F. E. Wilkinson to Jordan (Dec. 27, 1911), FO 371/1314 (9538). Ma Liang (referred to here by his *tzu,* Hsiang-po) is reported to have said that some of Yuan's men had asserted that Yuan was in favor of the revolutionary movement but would not declare himself unless absolutely sure of the presidency.

56. Yüan K'o-ting in mid-November 1911 mentioned to foreigners the possibility that his father would become Emperor. Jordan to Grey (Nov. 14, 1911), FO 371/1095 (45368); Morrison's Diary (Nov. 20, 1911), Morrison Papers (item 91). These comments are intriguing, but, if they were indeed trial balloons, they were shot down at this time and did not represent his father's immediate program.

presidency at this time. There was enough truth in Yuan's view for most of the country's leadership to support him in the first major controversy of the new regime, the location of the capital.

The Question of the Capital

Yuan was not formally inaugurated as President until March 10, 1912, and the members of the Nanking Assembly who were transferring to the new legislature at Peking did not gather there until April 10. Between February 12 and the beginning of April there were, in effect, two Presidents with their cabinets, two national assemblies (the Nanking Assembly and the old National Consultative Assembly in Peking), and one retired child Emperor, who retained his title but neither authority nor relevance. Much of this overlap was simply a result of the technical problems of succession and transition. But there were, for a while, points of dissension between Yuan and some Southern leaders.

Objection was first made to the manner in which the abdication was declared. A draft of an abdication edict was prepared by Chang Chien in the South and forwarded to Peking.[57] This draft was used by the court, but a paragraph was attached commissioning Yuan to arrange for unification with the revolutionaries. This approach to establishing a republic displeased the Southern leaders and seemed to undercut the agreement by which Yuan's new authority would stem from his election by the Nanking Assembly. The addition of the paragraph has been interpreted as early evidence of Yuan's presumption to be the inheritor of imperial power and of his own imperial aspirations. Whether he already harbored imperial ambitions or not, his behavior can be understood more concretely. If Sun Yat-sen's Nanking government did not hold to its agreement to resign and surrender authority to him, Yuan would have some legal basis on which to establish a government without the Manchus in the North. Morrison, the *Times* correspondent, was a principal advocate—perhaps the originator—of the abdication procedure followed. According to his discussions in late December and early January with Yuan's lieutenants, such as Ts'ai T'ing-kan, Liang Shih-i, and Chou Tzu-ch'i, the purposes it was designed to serve were: effecting the abdication while also removing from Yuan the stigma of disloyalty to his lord; insuring favorable treatment for the Manchus; and facilitating recognition of the

57. Samuel C. Chu, *Reformer in Modern China: Chang Chien, 1853–1926* (New York and London, 1965), p. 76.

new system by the foreign powers. Also, as the revolutionaries feared, there was undoubtedly the intention of reducing the dependence of the new regime on authority granted by Sun Yat-sen's government in Nanking.[58] But Yuan made no attempt to dispense with the proper revolutionary consecration. Almost immediately after the abdication, he sent a reassuring telegram to the Southern leaders. Within two days he was elected President by the Nanking Assembly in the fashion prescribed by the South.

The most awkward issue between the North and South, from the time of the abdication until the first republican cabinet under Yuan was established in Peking in April, was the location of the capital. The selection of a site for the capital of the new Republic was of symbolic significance. Retaining Peking would imply a continuation of the traditions of imperial conquest and East Asian hegemony. Nanking or Wuchang, sometimes suggested in the revolutionary South as possible capitals for the Republic, would signify a return to a more inward-looking tradition, as well as a symbolic acknowledgement of the revolutionary origin of the new regime.

The selection was also of immediate political significance. No matter who was President, a government located in any of the Yangtze provinces would be dominated by the Southern leaders. Yuan had little military control in that region. In Peking, on the other hand, the situation was reversed. Whatever his formal position in the government, Yuan's authority could not be ignored by appointed and elected officials.

On February 14, the day of Yuan's election as President, the Nanking Assembly passed by a vote of 20 to 8 a resolution making Peking the capital for the Provisional Government. Sun Yat-sen had formally registered objections as early as January 20 to establishing the Provisional Government in Peking. Now, already annoyed by the form of the Manchu abdication and its appearance of giving Yuan authority independent of election by representatives of the provinces, he and some of his immediate followers decided to make an issue out of the location of the capital and to insist that Yuan come to Nanking to be inaugurated. The assemblymen were

58. Morrison to Braham (Dec. 29, 1911), Morrison Papers (item 162); Diary (Dec. 31, 1911; Jan. 2, Jan. 10, Feb. 5, 1912), ibid. (items 91 and 92); "Conversation with Chou Tzu-ch'i" (Jan. 12, 1912), ibid. (item 147); "Conversation with Ts'ai T'ing-kan" (Jan. 15, 1912), ibid. (item 147). Pearl, *Morrison of Peking*, pp. 235–36, quotes from two of these documents.

forced to reverse their previous vote; Huang Hsing went so far as to threaten the Revolutionary Alliance members of the Assembly with arrest by military police if they did not conform. One Sun disciple declared he would commit suicide on the Assembly floor if the resolution in favor of Peking was not rescinded. The vote was reversed on February 15, 19 to 8 in favor of Nanking as capital.[59]

Sun's action was by no means popular, in either the North or South. The *Min-li pao,* a leading Revolutionary Alliance organ, had declared editorially only two days previously that "no informed person could disagree" that Peking should be the capital. Sung Chiao-jen and Chang Ping-lin, among others, held that considerations of national defense against Japan and Russia required that the capital not be moved to Nanking.[60] Among the governors (*tu-tu*) who during the next two weeks telegraphed in favor of retaining the capital in Peking were Lan T'ien-wei in Shantung, Lu Jung-t'ing in Kwangsi, T'an Yen-k'ai in Hunan, Chiang Tsun-kuei in Chekiang, Chuang Yün-k'uan in Kiangsu, and Chiang Yen-hsing in Kiangpei.[61] In short, Sun's government lacked anything like a general mandate to insist on Yuan's coming to Nanking. But it persisted and dispatched a delegation (including Sung Chiao-jen) to make arrangements with Yuan for his journey to the South.

While this delegation was still discussing the matter in Peking, a ferocious mutiny broke out among soldiers stationed in Peking and neighboring areas. Large parts of Peking were looted and burned. It has been commonly charged that Yuan Shih-k'ai instigated the rioting in order to dramatize to the Southern leaders the importance of retaining the capital in Peking and the impossibility of his going to Nanking.

There is no firm evidence, however, to support the accusation. Indeed, for several reasons it seems most improbable that Yuan instigated the Peking mutiny. In the first place, his national prestige depended considerably on his reputed talent for keeping order. It would have required an extremely serious emergency for Yuan to endanger both his reputation and his army by intentionally introducing anarchy in the North.

But the forces insisting on removal of the capital to Nanking were quite weak, as we have seen. On the day before the mutiny

59. Wu, *Sung Chiao-jen,* p. 123; Li Shou-k'ung, pp. 107–08.

60. Wu, *Sung Chiao-jen,* p. 123.

61. I Kuo-kan, et al., comps., *Li fu-tsung-t'ung cheng-shu* (Official Writings of Vice-President Li [Yüan-hung]), reprinted in *CHS ts'ung-shu,* pp. 98–99.

the British minister reported, obviously on the basis of authoritative sources, that Yuan and his entourage (specifically including T'ang Shao-i) believed Peking would remain the capital and that public opinion was increasingly supporting this position.[62] Clearly, the political situation did not demand anything so drastic as a manipulated mutiny in order for Yuan to have his way.

Also, as many Chinese pointed out at the time, any attempt to move the capital away from Peking would have met strenuous foreign opposition. When London learned of the Nanking Assembly's ruling that the provisional capital should be transferred south, the Foreign Office reaction was distinctly unfavorable. A memorandum was immediately prepared arguing that the removal of the capital from Peking would be "contrary to the spirit, if not the letter, of the international obligations . . ." that China had entered into under the Boxer Protocol of September 7, 1901.[63] Note was also taken in Washington of the discussion concerning the possible transfer of the capital, and it was observed that "it is not at all unlikely that we may be called upon at some later date to join the other powers in recommending to the Chinese that Peking be retained as the capital."[64] It seems doubtful that Britain and the other powers would have allowed Nanking to become the permanent capital, mutiny or no mutiny. Yuan was fully aware of this problem. As early as December 30, 1911, he had talked about the difficulties that would arise with the foreign legations if the capital were moved out of Peking. The virtual impossibility of moving the capital any great distance (closer sites were more seriously considered) was presented to him in detail in the period before the

62. Jordan to Grey (Feb. 28, 1912), FO 405/208 (8843). It is also true that after the mutiny both Ts'ai Yüan-p'ei, leader of the Southern delegation, and Yuan claimed that before the mutiny Yuan had been "very willing" to go to Nanking, once he found an appropriate caretaker for Peking. "Nan-ching lin-shih cheng-fu kung-pao" (Official Gazette of the Nanking Provisional Government), Mar. 6, 1912, in *Hsin-hai ko-ming tzu-liao,* pp. 258–59. It was reported in both Nanking and Peking on the eve of the mutiny that Yuan would agree to a brief trip, with careful insurance against assassination, to Nanking for inaugural ceremonies. F. E. Wilkinson to Jordan (Feb. 29, 1912), enclosed in Jordan to Grey (Mar. 8, 1912), FO 371/1315 (12648); Diary (Feb. 29, 1912), Morrison Papers (item 92). Yuan's going temporarily to Nanking for his inauguration was an issue of considerably less significance than that of the capital. Perhaps after all he had been intending to visit Nanking.

63. Minutes dated Feb. 16, 1912, appended to Jordan to Grey (Feb. 16, 1912), FO 371/1312 (6721); memorandum by Max Müller (Feb. 19, 1912), FO 371/1313 (8534).

64. Note from P. H. to Mr. Hengstler, dated Feb. 27, 1912, attached to a dispatch from the Nanking consul to State Department, Jan. 23, 1912, USDS, 893.00/1141.

mutiny.[65] If he was responsible for the military riots in Peking at the end of February, it was a work of supererogation.

An implicit assumption of the argument that Yuan instigated the riots is that a mutiny in the Peiyang Army would otherwise have been impossible. Actually, mutinies were extremely common in this period, particularly in the New Army divisions. Indeed, the New Army mutinies were generally the most severe. A series of these outbreaks began in 1908 and occurred sporadically in Central and South China into 1911.[66] In February 1912 and again in September 1912 there were violent uprisings in Hupeh.[67] Kiangsi troops in Nanking mutinied on April 11.[68] Chiang Kuei-t'i's Peiyang troops (although not New Army men) devastated the city of Tungchow, near Peking, in August 1912.[69] A spontaneous mutiny in the first year of the Republic was by no means inconceivable.

The troops who participated in the Peking rioting of February 1912—part of the Third Division and Yuan's bodyguard—had been conspicuous for some weeks previous to the outbreak for their agitated state, their lack of discipline, and a breakdown in the authority of their officers.[70] An unofficial study made in Peking soon after the mutiny concluded that its fundamental causes lay in such long-term defects as the inferior quality of the junior officers and the lack of discipline, aggravated by the excitement engendered by the Revolution and disappointment in being denied the rewards of plunder. More immediate considerations, according to this study, were the prospect of Yuan's going to Nanking (thus raising the soldiers' fears that they would not be rewarded for their services against the Revolution) and rumors of retrenchment and dismissals. It was reported that in the midst of their looting, the soldiers excused themselves by saying that their military careers were doomed and they were merely "borrowing" money for the trip home.[71]

65. Calhoun to Knox (Jan. 26, 1912), USDS, 893.00/1084; "Conversation with Ts'ai T'ing-kan" (Jan. 15, 1912) and Morrison to Ts'ai T'ing-kan (Feb. 19, 1912), Morrison Papers (items 147 and 172).

66. Ralph L. Powell, *The Rise of Chinese Military Power 1895–1912* (Princeton, 1958), pp. 268–71, 291–92.

67. Nakamura Tadashi, "Rei Genkō—Bushō hōki zengo" (Li Yüan-hung—in the Period of the Wuchang Uprising), *Rekishigaku kenkyū, 258* (1961), 27–31.

68. F. E. Wilkinson to Jordan (Apr. 14, 1912), FO 228/1836.

69. *National Review* (Shanghai, Aug. 31, 1912).

70. Wu, *Sung Chiao-jen,* p. 125. Calhoun to Knox (Mar. 1, 1912), USDS, 893.00/1215.

71. Kuo-shih hsin-wen she, ed., *Pei-ching ping-pien shih-mo chi* (Complete Record of the Peking Mutiny), reprinted in *CHS ts'ung-shu,* pp. 4–7. Wu Hsiang-hsiang, in

Although it is impossible to prove that Yuan had no responsibility for the mutiny, the evidence suggests that it could easily have occurred without his encouragement and that the mere fact of the mutiny was no proof of his complicity. Even if he or his henchmen did instigate the riot, as was immediately suspected in the South, the act had little effect on the main course of events, since there is no doubt that Peking was in any case to be the capital.

Yuan was inaugurated as provisional President on March 10 in Peking, according to a procedure hastily worked out with the Nanking authorities. All power was not concentrated in his hands, however. He prevailed in the question of the capital because certain forces—which he had not himself brought into being—were favorable to his position. Other forces, including the remaining strength of the revolutionaries in the South, militated against his free exercise of power. One measure of the confidence that some Southern leaders retained was the proposal, said to have been seriously made in Nanking after the Peking mutiny, that Huang Hsing lead troops north, under pacific pretenses, to destroy the Peiyang Army.[72] The proposal was rejected but reflected a truth: revolutionary military strength was left intact by the negotiated agreements with Yuan.

By mid-April, most participants in the new unified government had finally gathered in Peking, and the Republic of China, such as it was, was under way. Yuan Shih-k'ai was by no means the sole designer of the outcome, nor its only beneficiary. His contributions

---

his introduction to the reprinting of this volume and in his article, "Yüan Shih-k'ai mou-ch'ü lin-shih tsung-t'ung chih ching-kuo" (The Process by which Yuan Shih-k'ai Schemed to Obtain the Provisional Presidency), *CHS ts'ung-k'an, 1* (Taipei, 1960), 13–15, is the first historian to assert that Yuan and his associates were not responsible for the Peking mutiny. The British military attaché, in a report of March 4, 1912, FO 371/1316 (14452), attributed the mutiny to causes similar to those outlined in *Pei-ching ping-pien shih-mo chi,* including an army ministry announcement that the special wartime rates of pay were soon to be discontinued, a reduction of one tael per month. G. E. Morrison at first believed that the mutiny was "preconcerted" and suspected T'ang Shao-i of being responsible but later satisfied himself that this plot, at least, was only imagined. Morrison to Major Menzies (Mar. 2, 1912), Morrison Papers (item 172); Morrison to Braham (Mar. 5, 1912), ibid. (item 162).

72. Chü Cheng, *Hsin-hai ta-chi mei-ch'uan jih-chi ho-k'an* (Diary and Random Notes of 1911, Published in One Volume) (Taipei, 1956), p. 73. The Nanking government actually announced that it was dispatching troops to pacify the Peking mutiny and began preparations. The announcement stimulated strong British objection. Jordan to Grey (Mar. 11, 1912), FO 371/1316 (13313); David Fraser to Morrison (Mar. 5 and 8, 1912), Morrison Papers (item 172).

to the design were important, but his role should not be exaggerated.

The revolutionaries had decided at an early date that Yuan's cooperation was essential to their schemes. This decision was as important as anything Yuan himself did to obtain the presidency. His main assets were the Peiyang Army and his preeminence as a Chinese statesman. But he could not entirely depend on his military support, and he seems rather early to have envisaged ultimate cooperation with the revolutionaries. Britain was not disposed to help the court, even with Yuan as its Prime Minister. The only conceivable resolution of the civil conflict, if the country was to be unified, was a republic with Yuan as its leader. This view was widely held in both the North and the South.

Within about a month after the Wuchang uprising, the essential elements of the final amalgam had emerged. The months that followed saw a working out through adjustment and compromise of a formula that would encompass these elements in one political structure. The solution, when it was realized, did not mean that Yuan had triumphed completely. It did not give him control of the country. For over a year, in fact, Yuan was almost powerless in most of the recently revolutionary provinces. This limitation on his power was only natural: his rise to the presidency stemmed more from factors beyond his control than from his own maneuvers.

11. The Enigma of Sun Yat-sen

Harold Z. Schiffrin

The political style of Sun Yat-sen was the product of the interaction of personal temperament and unique social and historical circumstances. The period 1895–1911 in China had a revolutionary atmosphere about it: growing impotence and financial bankruptcy of the central government, disaffection of intellectuals, turbulence of the masses, and above all, the inability to resist foreign pressure. Fear and resentment of the foreign presence and power was the major theme of the Chinese political mood.

Sun Yat-sen shared the concern for China's survival, yet his response was affected by factors of social origin and education that set him apart from the great majority of modern Chinese political figures. He was born a peasant and lacked both gentry connections and training in the literary tradition which were part of the inheritance of most modern intellectuals. He was also unique as a product of missionary schooling, treaty port influences, and emigrant communities. No other Chinese leader has ever been so closely identified with foreigners.

His nongentry status cut him off from the only legitimate channels for political recruitment and action in traditional China. Even modern intellectuals were for a long time repelled by his lack of classical scholarship. Yet his social antecedents facilitated collaboration with the lower rungs of Chinese society at home and abroad, and his foreign upbringing made him ambitious. It gave him the assurance that he could contribute to China's modernization and mitigate the pressure of Western power, or even manipulate it to the advantage of revolution.

As for personality, Sun Yat-sen's outstanding trait was his incredible capacity for change and adjustment. Flexible, even impulsive, his style was an enigma of contradiction and improvisation. When is he rhetorical and when is he to be taken literally? The best we can do is to recognize this personality trait and view it as the hallmark of a politician or political entrepreneur.

But Sun's flexibility was not merely a necessity based on his weak personal position and the country's vulnerability. It was also a sign of strength. Improvisation came easily because of his supreme confidence that he could outmaneuver any individual and master any situation. Some of his attempted negotiations were not in keeping with the democratic, nationalist impulse he claimed to represent. But since he felt that he and his goals would somehow come out on top, it is easier to accuse him of overconfidence and naïveté than of insincerity. What was the source of his confidence? It was his faith in his destiny, a faith which seems to have crystallized after the London experience of 1896. It was also rooted in the conviction that despite the submissiveness dictated by her present position, China with her "multitude of 400 millions" would inexorably assert her rights and attain great power status.

The 1911 Revolution was the pivotal event in Sun's career. It ended his political apprenticeship. He had spent eighteen years prior to 1911 working for the Revolution and he spent the thirteen years following it trying to realize its unfinished tasks. Leadership of the renovated Kuomintang in the 1920s gave him more substantial power and influence. It was the Revolution, though, that turned him into a national political figure. This was the event around which the legend of the "Father of the Republic" and architect of China's regeneration was later woven. The Revolution assumed such importance in Sun's mind that he even claimed that it inspired the Russians to overthrow the Tsar.[1]

While the Revolution's positive achievements may be questioned, there is no denying that Sun's presence in Nanking when he held the presidency of the Republic in trust for Yuan Shih-k'ai marked a tremendous personal triumph. The ex-peasant, who eighteen years earlier had dejectedly left Li Hung-chang's yamen, now exchanged telegrams with Li's successor and helped decide the fate of the country. How did Sun get to Nanking and what did he represent? It is to these questions that this chapter is addressed. I shall attempt a profile of Sun's political personality for the two decades preceding the Revolution and try to determine why and under what conditions his leadership was accepted by the revolutionary movement.

The prerepublican political style of Sun Yat-sen evolved through four stages: reformism, initial activism, adjustment to the main-

1. *KFCC, 3* (July 17, 1917), 161.

stream of Chinese nationalism, and conditional leadership of a modern yet not cohesive revolutionary movement.[2]

THE REFORMIST PERIOD: 1890–1894

Sun's earliest manifestations of political interest reflect the composite legacy of his youth. Modern education had detached him from rural mores and the peasant mentality: the story of his smashing the village deity is illustrative. Yet the romantic tradition of peasant militancy continued to intrigue him. While studying in Canton and Hong Kong he is said to have admired Hung Hsiu-ch'üan,[3] castigated the Manchus, showed interest in the Triads, and even experimented with bombs in his medical school laboratory.[4] Although some of the stories may be apocryphal, there is no doubt that Sun was aware of the anti-Manchu tradition in the countryside—he was born only two years after the downfall of the Taipings—and that he even sympathized with it. But the thought of using his modern credentials to enter the privileged ranks of the literati initially proved more seductive. His overture to Li Hung-chang in 1894 is only the best known of these attempts to impress gentry reformers. While in medical school in Hong Kong (1887–92) Sun also submitted two essays to Cheng Kuan-ying,[5] and in 1890 he requested the patronage of Cheng Tsao-ju,[6] both natives of Hsiang-shan, his home district, and prominent in national affairs. In 1893 while practicing medicine in Canton, Sun tried and failed to get an interview with his reformist fellow provincial, K'ang Yu-wei.[7]

2. Discussion of the first three stages is based largely upon my *Sun Yat-sen and the Origins of the 1911 Revolution*, to be published by the University of California Press.

3. The now legendary leader of the Taiping Rebellion, 1850–64, and like Sun an anti-Manchu South Chinese.

4. *KFNP, 1*, 25, 35, 90; Ch'en Shao-pai, *Hsing-Chung-hui ko-ming shih-yao* (Outline of the Revolutionary History of the Society to Restore China's Prosperity) (reprinted Taipei, 1956), p. 2.

5. Lo Hsiang-lin, *Kuo-fu chih ta-hsüeh shih-tai* (Sun Yat-sen's University Days) (Taipei, 1954), pp. 61–64. See also Chou Hung-jan, "Kuo-fu 'Shang Li Hung-chang shu' chih shih-tai pei-ching" (Background of Sun Yat-sen's Letter to Li Hung-chang). *KKWH*, 1st series, *Ko-ming chih ch'ang-tao yü fa-chan, 9*, 274.

6. Ch'en Hsi-ch'i, *T'ung-meng-hui ch'eng-li ch'ien ti Sun Chung-shan* (Sun Yat-sen Prior to the Founding of the Revolutionary Alliance) (Canton, 1957), pp. 7, 24–25.

7. Feng, *I-shih, 1* (Taipei, 1953), 47; Yen-p'ing Hao, "The Abortive Cooperation between Reformers and Revolutionaries," Harvard University, East Asian Research Center, *Papers on China, 15* (1961), 93.

There was nothing unique about Sun's reformist proposals. His long statement to Li Hung-chang shows traces of Feng Kuei-fen's influence and close resemblance to arguments in Cheng Kuan-ying's famous *Sheng-shih wẹi-yen* (Words of Warning to a Prosperous Age).[8] What was unique was the attempt itself. Admitting his inability to write an "eight-legged essay," Sun still claimed a role in China's modernization by virtue of his foreign training. The approach to Li required courage, and after being turned down, it took even more courage to work for the overthrow of the dynasty.

One reformist influence which carried over to Sun's activist stage was that exerted by Ho Kai (Ho Ch'i) (1859–1914), a British-trained physician and barrister who achieved remarkable success in Hong Kong and taught in the medical school Sun attended.[9] Written with the help of a collaborator,[10] his essays were later translated into Chinese; Ho, like Sun, was more proficient in English. The distinctive feature of Ho's reformism was his unequivocal plea for foreign and especially British support. He urged Britain to "Come forward and . . . apply the requisite pressures" for China's reformation.[11] Even a rejuvenated China, he insisted, would pose no threat to the West.[12] This was the type of nationalism inherited by Sun Yat-sen when he first turned his full attention to politics.

The difference between Ho and Sun was the latter's readiness to sacrifice his professional training for the chance of becoming directly involved in China's future. Where Ho was generally content to lambast the mandarins in the Hong Kong press, Sun became a full-time conspirator. He turned to less respectable social elements, the Triads and peasant bandits, with whom Ho in his Hong Kong sanctuary had little affinity. Sun took for granted the latent anti-

8. Chou Hung-jan, "Kuo-fu 'Shang Li Hung-chang shu,'" in *KKWH,* 1st series, *Ko-ming chih ch'ang-tao yü fa-chan, 9,* 275–76.

9. For a biographical sketch of Ho, see Lindsay Ride, "The Antecedents," in Brian Harrison, ed., *The University of Hong Kong: The First Fifty Years, 1911–1961* (Hong Kong, 1962), pp. 11–12. See also Arnold Wright, ed., *Twentieth Century Impressions of Hongkong, Shanghai and other Treaty Ports of China* (London, 1908), p. 109; and Lo Hsiang-lin, *Ta-hsüeh shih-tai,* pp. 9–10.

10. Ho's collaborator was Hu Li-yüan, a prosperous Hong Kong merchant. See Lo Hsiang-lin, *Ta-hsüeh shih-tai,* pp. 9, 114, n. 10. For an analysis of their political writings, see Hsiao Kung-ch'üan, *Chung-kuo cheng-chih ssu-hsiang shih* (History of Chinese Political Thought), *6* (Taipei, 1961), 795–803.

11. See the letter by Ho and Wei Tyuk (Wei Yü) in Lord Charles Beresford, *The Break-up of China* (New York and London, 1899), p. 218.

12. See "Sinensis" (Ho's pseudonym), "Open Letter to John Bull" in the *China Mail* (Aug. 22, 1900).

dynasticism of his native Kwangtung and added some new ingredients to the old formula for peasant rebellion.

Initial Activism: 1895–1900

The merchants, peddlers, planters, laborers, and clerks of Hawaii and Hong Kong were the Chinese Sun knew best and the most likely financial backers of the Revolution. The Society to Restore China's Prosperity, formed by Sun in Hawaii and Hong Kong in 1894–95, consisted chiefly of these overseas supporters and a small leadership group composed of young men like himself: missionary-educated nonliterati from Hong Kong and Canton. (Even some of their internal correspondence was in English.) With a little over 150 members the organization as such was unimpressive,[13] but it was never meant to be a mass movement. The Canton plot of 1895 and the Waichow campaign of 1900 were the only occasions when it functioned, and both times it worked on the assumption that thousands of fighters would enter the field as soon as it made the initial spark. On neither occasion was the name Hsing-Chung-hui publicized. Sun and his friends were convinced not only that China was ripe for revolution but that traditional vehicles of anti-dynasticism—secret societies and bandit gangs (*lü-lin*)—would bear the brunt of the fighting. If a key yamen fell they assumed that the whole province would go and that others would fall in line. Instead of directly recruiting peasants the revolutionaries made temporary alliances with Triad and bandit chiefs or merely hired mercenaries. Primitive rebels[14] directed by a Westernized elite and subsidized by overseas merchants—this was the formula for the Canton and Waichow uprisings.

Sun and his friends also felt that no major political change could be carried out in China without the active assistance or friendly neutrality of foreigners. While respect for foreign power was universal, no group had more reason to seek external approval. Even if their revolutionary plans succeeded, they assumed that the foreign stamp of legitimacy would be needed as a substitute for in-

13. Feng Tzu-yu in *KMWH, 3,* 331–72, gives the membership of the Society to Restore China's Prosperity from 1894 to 1903. See also Chün-tu Hsüeh, *Huang Hsing and the Chinese Revolution* (Stanford, 1961), pp. 26–30.

14. I have taken the term "primitive rebels" from E. J. Hobsbawm, *Primitive Rebels: Studies in Archaic Forms of Social Movement in the 19th and 20th Centuries* (Manchester, 1959). Though he deals only with Europe, Hobsbawm's study of social bandits and millenarian movements provides many ideas pertinent to Chinese secret societies and *lü-lin*.

fluential connections at home. It is significant that both the Canton and Waichow plots were timed to exploit critical episodes in foreign affairs—after the Sino-Japanese War and while the Boxer settlement was pending—when increased intervention appeared likely.

Furthermore the conspirators were confident that foreigners also needed them. The European powers had been promoting missionary and commercial enterprises for half a century. Who were better equipped to further their interests than the Western-educated and Christian leaders of the Society to Restore China's Prosperity? No other group in China was so closely connected with the compradores and native pastors of Hong Kong and Canton.

This pro-European orientation was personified by Ho Kai. In 1895, while Sun organized his conspiracy in Canton and Yang Ch'ü-yün, his party rival, solicited merchants and mercenaries in Hong Kong, Ho was their foreign spokesman. Though he never joined the society he attended the first conspiratorial sessions. It was probably through him that the British editors of the *China Mail* and *Hongkong Telegraph* became the conspirators' confidants and mouthpieces.[15]

In March 1895, more than six months before the attack on the Canton yamen was scheduled, the *China Mail,* probably briefed by Ho Kai, disclosed that the reform party was planning to overthrow the Manchus and establish constitutional rule. Foreigners were advised not to repeat the mistake of supporting the dynasty, as they had done against the Taipings, because the new government would at last open China to Western trade and civilization. Printing a highly detailed version of the plotters' program, the *Mail* listed various institutional reforms and intimated that foreign advisers would help reconstitute the government. The collection of inland revenue, it suggested, would be placed in the hands of foreigners "under a similar arrangement to the Maritime Customs, until China is in a position to dispense with all foreign assistance."[16]

According to the *Mail* the rebels planned to replace the Manchus with a Chinese dynasty. What then is the significance of the Society to Restore China's Prosperity membership oath, which called for the establishment of a republic? Republicanism, I be-

15. See Tse Tsan Tai, *The Chinese Republic: Secret History of the Revolution* (Hong Kong, 1924), p. 9.

16. *China Mail* (March 12, 16, 1895).

lieve, represented their ultimate goal.[17] It was the most modern Western form of government and the logical model for avowed modernizers. Yet it was characteristic of Sun to avoid rigid programmatic formulas and to concentrate on the instrumental rather than the terminal aspects of revolution. He wanted to set the antidynastic forces into motion and was confident that he could do so. He was less confident of his ability to achieve quick success without catering to foreign preferences or even compromising with venal gentry like Liu Hsüeh-hsün, who toyed with the idea of using Sun to further his own imperial ambitions. What Sun wanted was freedom to maneuver without being tied down to a specific policy beyond that of overthrowing the Manchus and modernizing China's government. He had no audience for explicating ideological nuances at home. The rank and file of his potential fighters were motivated more by hunger and hatred of the authorities than by any programmatic aims.

For the Europeans, though, he had to show himself as a moderate and reasonable reformer and specify advantages for traders, manufacturers, and missionaries. Instead of insisting on a republic —which most foreigners considered an unrealistic goal—it was preferable to postulate a respectable transition to Chinese monarchical rule under foreign tutelage. Revolution, if it was to be approved of or permitted by foreigners, had to be carried out quickly, with a minimum of disorder and disruption.

In this first attempt Ho was the ideologist and Sun the conspirator. After its failure they temporarily parted. Ho returned to his civic duties in Hong Kong, and Sun, forced to flee from both China and Hong Kong, began a sixteen-year exile by trying to rebuild his network. After a brief stay in Japan, he returned to Hawaii and then went on to the United States.[18]

The campaign abroad was disappointing, and even Sun might have been permanently discouraged had he not been suddenly thrust into the limelight in London in the fall of 1896. The Manchus had taken Sun seriously, and it was their panic—seeing Sun as a Hung Hsiu-ch'üan marshaling the Overseas Chinese—which turned him into a much more dangerous adversary. His imprison-

17. For evidence of Sun's doubts concerning republicanism at this time, see Hsüeh, *Huang Hsing*, p. 29. I agree, however, with Wu Yü-chang, *Hsin-hai ko-ming* (The Revolution of 1911) (Peking, 1961), p. 15, that the conspirators were thinking of a federated republic based on the United States model.

18. Ch'en Shao-pai, *Hsing-Chung-hui*, p. 12.

ment in the Chinese legation in London made him famous and confirmed his faith in the Revolution and in himself. If he had not felt so previously, the outcome of the kidnapping episode led him to believe that he was destined to save China. It also reinforced his original conviction concerning the foreign role in the Chinese Revolution. Seeing the British public outraged over the Manchu attempt to spirit him out of London and subject him to the "slicing" punishment at home, Sun conjured up the vision of British support for the Revolution. He wrote letters of thanks to the newspapers and asserted that England represented the enlightened society he wanted to create at home.[19] He took great care to let the press know of his Christian affiliation and it was even reported that he would join a medical missionary venture.[20] Though he had ceased writing in Chinese he suddenly became very prolific in English. With the help of friends, in 1897, he published *Kidnapped in London,* a book that for a long time would remain his best known work, and in March 1897, again aided by a collaborator, Sun made a plea for British "benevolent neutrality" in an article in the *Fortnightly Review*.[21] Boasting that the Chinese army was to "a great extent leavened with sympathizers to the Reform Party," Sun echoed Ho Kai's attack on the mandarin system, which he claimed was buttressed solely by the Manchus. He dangled the promise of increased trade and access to China's mineral wealth. European advisers and administrative assistance would be invited to modernize the new regime. "The benevolent neutrality of Great Britain, and of the other Powers," he asserted, "is all the aid needed to enable us to make the present system give place to one that is not corrupt."[22]

Sun had already shown his ability to impress individual foreigners. His American missionary teachers helped him in Hawaii[23] and an American chemistry teacher from the Islands had joined the Canton plotters as an expert on explosives.[24] A Danish sailor

19. Sun Yat-sen, *Kidnapped in London* (Bristol, 1897), p. 133.

20. *The Globe* (Oct. 26, 1897).

21. Written with the assistance of one Edwin Collins, Sun's article, "China's Present and Future: The Reform Party's Plea for British Benevolent Neutrality," has not, as far as I know, ever appeared in any collection of Sun's works.

22. *Fortnightly Review, 61* (new series), no. 363 (1897), pp. 424, 440.

23. Chung Kun Ai (Chung Kung-yü), *My Seventy Nine Years in Hawaii* (Hong Kong, 1960), p. 107.

24. Ch'en Shao-pai, *Hsing-Chung-hui,* p. 11.

drilled Sun's recruits in a Hawaiian mission schoolyard.[25] British journalists had backed him in Hong Kong, and Portuguese friends had smuggled him out of Macao when the Manchus were after him.[26] His former teachers in Hong Kong, Dr. Cantlie and Dr. Manson—the latter convinced that Sun was a born Christian and not a convert[27]—had rescued him from the Chinese legation. And now Professor Giles of Cambridge translated his autobiography,[28] a member of Parliament raised a question on his behalf in Parliament,[29] and a British soldier, Rowland Mulkern, volunteered to join the next uprising against the Manchus.[30] More than ever Sun had reason to believe in his ability to win foreign sympathy for the Revolution.

Sun also took time out for intensive reading and study, mostly at the British Museum. Between December 1896 and June 1897, he visited the museum on fifty-nine days, spending hours on each visit.[31] Cantlie, with whom he was in close contact, testifies to Sun's wide range of interests covering scientific and political subjects.[32] Sun later claimed that this study period inspired the formulation of his famous Three Principles. This seems doubtful since it was five or six years before he began expressing these ideas.

25. Henry B. Restarick, *Sun Yat Sen, Liberator of China* (New Haven, 1931), p. 49.

26. While in Macao Sun had become friendly with the Fernandes family, and in 1893 contributed articles to the Chinese supplement of *O Eco Macaense,* published by Francisco Fernandes. Mr. J. M. Braga of Hong Kong, who knew Fernandes, kindly supplied me with information concerning Sun's relationship with this family, including their help to him in 1895.

27. See Dr. Manson's testimony in the report of the Treasury Solicitor, H. Cuffe, in FO 17/1718, p. 122. Cuffe's report is the authoritative version of Britain's role in the kidnapping episode.

28. *KFNP, 1,* 72.

29. In February 1897, Sir Edward Gourley raised a parliamentary question concerning the Chinese legation's actions. See FO 17/1718, p. 154.

30. Chin P'ing-ou, ed., *San-min chu-i tz'u-tien* (Concordance of the Three Principles of the People) (Taipei, 1956), p. 524, under "Mo-ken."

31. I am indebted to Professor C. Martin Wilbur of Columbia University, who informed me that a detailed account of Sun's visits to the museum can be found in *Chang P'u-ch'üan hsien-sheng ch'üan-chi (pu-pien)* (Supplement to the Collected Works of Chang Chi) (Taipei, 1952), pp. 204–06. The appendix to Lo Chia-lun's *Chung-shan hsien-sheng Lun-tun meng-nan shih-liao k'ao-ting* (A Critical Study of the Official Documents Concerning Sun Yat-sen's Kidnapping) (Shanghai, 1930) gives the reports of the detective agency that followed Sun's movements until he left England in the summer of 1897.

32. Quoted in Lyon Sharman, *Sun Yat-sen: His Life and its Meaning* (New York, 1934), p. 58.

Though the nine months—not the two years he subsequently claimed—spent in Britain had enabled him to learn more about contemporary political and social movements, Sun still showed no serious concern with political theory.

In the fall of 1897 he established his base in Japan and also looked for signs of Britain's "benevolent neutrality." He wrote to the Hong Kong Colonial Secretary demanding revocation of the banishment order issued against him in March 1896 and threatening to "appeal it to the English public and the civilized world." The reply informed him that the colony could not be used for conspiracies against a "friendly neighbouring Empire" and warned that he would be arrested if he set foot in Hong Kong.[33]

The rebuff was more than balanced by developments in Japan, where he was warmly welcomed by Miyazaki Torazō, Hirayama Amane (Shū), and their influential sponsor, Inukai Tsuyoshi (Ki). Quickly attuning himself to the mood of those pan-Asian Japanese sinophiles, Sun discarded the role he had played in London. Now he was no longer the churchgoing supplicant of Europeans but the would-be redeemer of humiliated Asians. Declaring his republicanism—something he had not done in Britain—he asked for Japanese help in "saving China's four hundred million people" and "wiping away the humiliation of Asia's yellow race."[34]

The Japanese were impressed with Sun, and their joint adventures, including the Philippine episode, are a delight in fanciful conspiracy.[35] They also present a remarkable study of Sino-Japanese comradeship. Yet even the Japanese could not overcome literati ostracism of Sun Yat-sen. K'ang Yu-wei and Liang Ch'i-ch'ao, in exile after 1898, won over the Overseas Chinese, and their friends in the Independent Army successfully competed for the allegiance of the secret societies.[36]

The summer of 1900, with the Boxer troubles, provided an ideal occasion for Sun to display his political style. The foreign powers were pitted against the Manchus, important governors-general were ignoring Peking, and literati reformers were acting

33. Sun's letter, undated, and Colonial Secretary Lockhart's reply of October 4, 1897, are enclosed in Black to Chamberlain, May 18, 1898, in CO (Colonial Office) 129/283. The five-year banishment order, later renewed, was issued on March 4, 1896. See Robinson to Chamberlain, March 11, 1896, in CO 129/271.

34. Marius B. Jansen, *The Japanese and Sun Yat-sen* (Cambridge, Mass., 1954), pp. 65–66.

35. Ibid., pp. 68–74.

36. See Hao, "Abortive Cooperation," pp. 91–114.

belligerent. Though preparations for his own Waichow uprising were under way, the opportunities for negotiating with these other foci of power were too good to pass up. Sun made a last, futile attempt to conciliate K'ang Yu-wei. He tried to induce Li Hung-chang to establish an independent Kwangtung-Kwangsi government, and calling once more upon Ho Kai, offered Britain and the other foreign powers temporary tutelary rule over China.[37] This too failed as did his fantastic negotiations with Li's lieutenant, Liu Hsüeh-hsün, whom he offered an emperorship or presidency in return for financing the Waichow uprising.[38]

Without receiving orders from Sun, who placed his final hopes on Japanese support from Taiwan, the Waichow fighters struck in early October. Under the leadership of Cheng Shih-liang, the Triads, Hakkas, and mercenaries, supported by peasants in the East River area, engaged the government forces in hard fighting for two weeks. Originally scheduled to attack Canton, where they had a sizable contingent of Christian-led followers, the rebels followed Sun's orders and turned toward Amoy where he was supposed to arrive with Japanese help. But the Japanese changed their minds and Cheng's makeshift army, now numbering about 20,000, was caught in a pocket and forced to disband.[39]

Waichow validated one of Sun's premises, that the Chinese countryside was sympathetic to revolution. It also exposed the weakness of his leadership. He had not prepared a self-contained movement for a sustained revolutionary campaign. What he contributed instead was a flurry of intrigues which left the fighters pursuing a dubious strategy.

The Waichow uprising, supplemented by the martyrdom of Shih Chien-ju,[40] grandson of a Hanlin scholar, was nevertheless impressive and redounded to Sun's fame as an activist precisely at the time when militancy was coming into vogue among the growing body of overseas students.[41] Yet almost five years passed

37. The Chinese version of Ho Kai's proposal to Governor-general Blake of Hong Kong appears in *KFCC, 5,* 16–19. I have not located the original English version.

38. Feng, *I-shih, 1,* 76–80; Chün-tu Hsüeh, "Sun Yat-sen, Yang Ch'ü-yün, and the Early Revolutionary Movement in China," *JAS, 19* (1960), 316.

39. The best sources on the Waichow campaign appear to be Ch'en Ch'un-sheng, "Keng-tzu Hui-chou ch'i-i chi" (An Account of the Waichow Uprising of 1900) in *HHKM, 1,* 235–44; and Miyazaki Tōten (Torazō), *Sanjū-sannen no yume* (The Thirty-three Years' Dream) (Tokyo, 1943), pp. 277–84.

40. On Shih Chien-ju, see Ch'en Ch'un-sheng, *HHKM, 1,* 235–36; Miyazaki, *Sanjū-sannen,* pp. 200–02.

41. See Hu Han-min, *Tzu-chuan* (Autobiography), in *KMWH, 2,* 377.

before Sun was accepted by the students, whose gentry prejudices never dissolved completely. Nor was Sun quick to contend for the loyalty of this group. Perhaps he felt uneasy in the presence of Chinese intellectuals. His earlier attempts at reaching literati through elegant essays had failed, and his impatience led him to seek faster ways of asserting himself. He assumed he was playing for higher stakes and scorned what he must have considered the inconsequential theorizing of youngsters who had only recently discovered George Washington and the French Revolution. His experience with Liang Ch'i-ch'ao in 1899–1900 left him with a deep suspicion concerning the reliability of literati even when they espoused revolution.

When his own formula for revolutionary conspiracy led to a dead end in the years following Waichow, Sun nevertheless found a way to reach the students. That he was able to suit his style to this new audience again attests to his versatility. This was not, however, simply a question of converting the students to revolution. Largely inspired by Liang Ch'i-ch'ao, they had been preaching a tough-minded nationalism which envisaged confrontation with a predatory Europe. This was the main current of Chinese nationalism and ran counter to the pro-Western protestations of Ho Kai, who until now had been speaking for Sun Yat-sen.[42]

The mainstream of Chinese nationalism originated with literati whose faith in the traditional system had been eroded in various degrees since 1895, when the system was discredited by Japan's victory. After the Boxer disaster this nationalist consciousness attained a high degree of sophistication among émigré intellectuals and the overseas students. Their anti-Manchuism flowed *directly* from the need for resisting foreign pressure when they became convinced of Manchu inability to perform this role.

As for Sun Yat-sen, anti-Manchuism derived *directly* from the need for a rapprochement with the West and was only *indirectly* concerned with resisting it. Sun's main enemy was outmoded, xenophobic government which he identified with Manchu rule. Why was Chinese sovereignty being violated? The student reply was that

42. My evaluation of the student mood from 1901 to 1904 is based upon the articles reprinted in *SLHC, I*. Detailed references can be found in my forthcoming book, *Sun Yat-sen and the Origins of the 1911 Revolution*, chap. 10. For Liang's contribution, see Chang P'eng-yüan, *Liang Ch'i-ch'ao yü Ch'ing-chi ko-ming* (Liang Ch'i-ch'ao and the Revolution in the Late Ch'ing Period) (Taipei, 1964); and Joseph R. Levenson, *Liang Ch'i-ch'ao and the Mind of Modern China* (Cambridge, Mass., 1953).

a deeply embedded impulse in modern capitalist society—this was their discovery of modern imperialism and its economic mainspring—was encouraged by Manchu appeasement tactics. Sun Yat-sen's reply, as far as we can discern, was that "Tartar" rulers were incapable of conducting civilized relations in the modern world. Western aggression, according to Sun, was a response to Manchu intransigence and obscurantism. Sun attacked the Manchus for blocking the beneficent influences of foreign trade and religion. The students attacked the Manchus for opening China to the imperialist incursions of missionaries and merchants. How were these contrasting attitudes reconciled?

First, it is quite obvious that these two approaches were aimed at different targets. The students were talking to the Chinese and Sun was addressing foreigners, the same missionaries and merchants who were anathema to the young intellectuals. And we know that Sun was quite adept at adjusting to his audiences. That he possessed unique powers of dissimulation and rarely hesitated to deceive foreigners is a matter of record. That he cherished more typically Chinese feelings is recorded by Miyazaki.

Nevertheless I feel that unless we consider Sun a complete rogue, it would be a mistake not to credit him with some degree of sincerity in his pro-Western orientation during this early period, and as far as that goes, until the end of his life. His Westernized background and education cannot be so easily dismissed. Though their governments consistently disappointed him, Sun's attitude toward foreigners in general can best be described as ambivalent rather than hypocritical or hostile.

What was required to bring him closer to the mainstream of Chinese nationalism was a mutual adjustment. Student anti-imperialism had to be diverted or softened, while Sun's attitude required a more sophisticated mode of expression and a touch of belligerence.

First, the young intellectuals changed; I think the adjustment was anticipated by Chang Ping-lin, the most traditional of the literati nationalists and an elder and respected figure amidst the student ferment of Tokyo and Shanghai. Heir to the traditional gentry anti-Manchuism of the Eastern Chekiang school, Chang had nevertheless been prepared to accept reformed Manchu rule as long as he saw the possibility of a joint Chinese-Manchu effort to resist the white invaders. By 1901 he despaired of the Manchus as defenders of Chinese sovereignty, and anti-imperialism tipped the balance in favor of militant anti-Manchuism in the pattern previously described.[43] In his famous rebuttal of K'ang Yu-wei in 1903[44]—one of the most significant documents in revolutionary literature—Chang intimated that there was really no immediate solution to the problem of imperialism. When K'ang asserted that revolution would invite further intervention, Chang replied that intervention could not be prevented no matter what China did. The foreign presence was already felt and was a fact which had to be taken into consideration. What was required was a realistic attitude. The revolution, he admitted, would have to go along with the foreigners, but if it enjoyed the massive popular support he anticipated, and if it quickly established effective government, foreigners would have no alternative but to recognize the new regime. Westerners, he asserted, would naturally seek self-aggrandizement should the Revolution be unsuccessful, but faced with a fait accompli they too would be realistic and make the best of the situation. In the crisis of Japan's response to the West, France had wanted to help the Shogun, he asserted, but the pro-imperial movement had had more support, and Japan's Meiji Restoration had succeeded.[45]

In the following years, though he continued to see the foreigners as the main danger to China, Chang became even more reluctant to clash with them. "From a political and social standpoint," he declared, "the West inflicts much more harm upon our race than the Manchus."[46] But contemporary China, he felt, was inadequate to this larger struggle against imperialism. The white race, "the most powerful in the world," would eventually be subdued by the colored people—"the black men and red men"—of the entire world.[47] China alone was too weak, and instead of openly proclaiming their anti-imperialist intentions, Chang argued that the revolutionaries had to remain silent and tread softly. Though "aware of the missionary evil and the merchant evil"[48] Chang in-

43. For an excellent summary of Chang's thinking, see Hu Sheng-wu and Chin Ch'ung-chi, "Hsin-hai ko-ming shih-ch'i Chang Ping-lin ti cheng-chih ssu-hsiang" (The Political Thought of Chang Ping-lin during the period of the 1911 Revolution), in Hupeh Provincial Philosophical Society and Scientific Society, ed., *Hsin-hai ko-ming wu-shih chou-nien chi-nien lun-wen chi* (Essays in Commemoration of the Fiftieth Anniversary of the 1911 Revolution) (Peking, 1962), ts'e 1, pp. 323–53.

44. "Po K'ang Yu-wei shu" (Letter refuting K'ang Yu-wei), reprinted in *SLHC* (Hong Kong, 1962), *1*, ts'e 2, 752–64.

45. Ibid., pp. 760–61.

46. *Min-pao, 22* (July 10, 1908), 49.

47. *Min-pao, 16* (Sept. 25, 1907), 29–30.

48. *Min-pao, 22* (July 10, 1908), 49.

sisted that the revolutionary army be restrained and tolerant. It was imperative not to give the foreigners the slightest provocation. Above all the revolutionaries had to prevent a Manchu–white man coalition.[49] As to the ultimate goal of Chinese nationalism, Chang had no doubts. Its aim was the complete recovery of Chinese sovereignty and elimination of foreigners' special privileges—the return of Weihaiwei and Shanghai's international settlement, abolition of spheres of influence, and so forth. "The foreigners," he cautioned, "had better not know this; otherwise their anger will be kindled . . . We must keep our mouths shut and not say a word."[50]

On the other hand, in 1903 Chang was convinced that any popular uprising—the Boxer uprising, T'ang Ts'ai-ch'ang's plot, the Kwangsi revolt—acted to increase the people's political consciousness and to prepare them for the greater struggle of the future.[51] These two concepts—the need for a temporary reconciliation with the foreign presence and the hope that a revolution would rapidly mature the Chinese political capacity—became crucial to militant nationalist thinking.

What happened was that even while elaborating upon the imperialist danger, the young intellectuals recoiled from the immensity of their task. Overthrowing the Manchus, establishing a republic, and at the same time belligerently redressing the wrongs committed by foreigners—this was too much to contemplate. Their mentor, Liang Ch'i-ch'ao, was convinced that revolution would invite further intervention. By 1903 he had repudiated his brief flirtation with revolution and pressed for institutional reform to strengthen national resistance. But the students shifted their focus to the easier hurdle. Avoiding the social and class implications of revolution, which they had touched upon tangentially in their writings, they elevated anti-Manchuism to the highest priority. Their predilection for heroic assassinations reveals their desperation.[52] They felt impelled to act, yet at least for the time being a collision course with the West had to be avoided.

With anti-Manchu revolution enshrined as the transcendent goal the way was paved for the oldest, most experienced, and most notorious revolutionary of the time. But it was not only that Sun Yat-

49. Ibid., p. 50.

50. Ibid., pp. 130–31.

51. *SLHC, 1,* ts'e 2, 759–60.

52. Infatuation with violence is especially noted in the writings of Tsou Jung, Ch'en T'ien-hua, Yang Shou-jen, Liu Shih-p'ei, and Lin Hsieh. See supra Bernal and Rankin.

sen had behind him a decade of revolutionary intrigue and well-publicized activism. More than anyone else he had combined revolutionary conspiracy with solicitation of foreign goodwill. No one else was as confident that he could guarantee the Revolution safe conduct past the foreign gunboats.

This shift in the student mood was matched by a corresponding adjustment on the part of Sun Yat-sen.

Transition and Adjustment

The two or three years following Waichow are among the most obscure in Sun's career. Until the fall of 1903 he spent most of his time in Yokohama, except for a short visit to Hong Kong in the beginning of 1902 and a longer trip to Hanoi toward the end of the year. With respect to the nationalist ferment among the Tokyo students and their colleagues in Shanghai, where the *Su-pao* case became a *cause célèbre,*[53] Sun remained on the periphery. It was mostly through long-standing Cantonese friends like Feng Tzu-yu and Wang Ch'ung-hui that tenuous contact was established. Sun contributed money to student publications like *K'ai-chih lu* (Record of Expanding Wisdom) and *Kuo-min pao* (National Journal) in 1900–01, but there is no evidence of any ideological contribution.[54] Several non-Cantonese students like Shen Hsiang-yün, Wu Lu-chen, and Ch'i I-hui were said to have been attracted to him as early as 1898–99,[55] but none were interested enough to join the Waichow enterprise and they instead devoted themselves to the Hankow plot of that same year. Among the older non-Cantonese intellectuals, Chang Ping-lin seems to have been one of the first to recognize Sun's talents as an exponent of anti-Manchuism. He had little regard, though, for Sun's attainments in foreign learning.[56] Both Chang and Liang undoubtedly contributed to Sun's knowledge of Chinese history and political thought in general.

Still unsure of the potential and trustworthiness of this new intellectual element, Sun preferred trying to revive the old Society for the Revival of China's Prosperity pattern of conspiracy. In

53. See Y. C. Wang, "The *Su-pao* Case: A Study of Foreign Pressure, Intellectual Fermentation, and Dynastic Decline," *Monumenta Serica, 24* (1965), 84–129. The draft of this article was first discussed at the Conference on the Revolution of 1911 from which the present volume emerged.

54. Feng Tzu-yu, in *KKWH,* 1st series, *Ko-ming chih ch'ang-tao yü fa-chan, 10,* 665–66.

55. Feng, *I-shih, 1,* 80–81.

56. Ibid., p. 54.

1902 he solicited French support and went to Hanoi to see representatives of the governor-general of Indochina. When negotiations lapsed he spent a desultory six months agitating among the local Overseas Chinese, and gained a handful of recruits while missing out on the student furor in Japan.[57]

At the same time the old Hong Kong–based combination was revived behind his back. Tse Tsan Tai, always closer to Yang Ch'ü-yün, Sun's early rival in the Society to Restore China's Prosperity (who had been eliminated by Manchu gunmen after Waichow), planned an attack on Canton in the beginning of 1903.[58] This plot, like that of 1895, was abortive but the attempt showed that Sun was drifting or being pushed away from his old base before establishing himself on new ground.

In the same year, with the Yokohama Overseas Chinese showing no more resistance to the K'ang-Liang appeal than Sun's former followers in Hawaii, Sun made his first tentative efforts toward creating a new combination among the overseas students. First was his unsuccessful attempt, backed by the Japanese, to provide students with military training. Though it closed down after several months and attracted only fourteen or fifteen cadets—all Cantonese except for two Fukienese—Sun's Yokohama school foreshadowed his new line of attack. By adding Equal Land Rights (*p'ing-chün ti-ch'üan*) to the principles of the Society to Restore China's Prosperity, he had the basis for an all-embracing political program. The oath administered to these cadets was the same as he would demand of the students in the Revolutionary Alliance two years later.[59]

Also indicative of Sun's new approach was his article in the student journal *Chiang-su* in November 1903.[60] The short essay, "On the Preservation or Dismemberment of China," was Sun's first contribution to the influential nationalistic press and his first article in Chinese since the petition to Li Hung-chang nine years earlier. It throbs with a militancy that carries him beyond Ho Kai and closer to the student tenor. Using the metaphors popularized by Liang Ch'i-ch'ao and the Tokyo-Shanghai firebrands, Sun acknowledged the imperialist motif in foreign policies toward China, praised the Boxers, and criticized the late Li Hung-chang's

57. Jansen, *Sun Yat-sen,* p. 115; Ch'en Shao-pai, *Hsing-Chung-hui,* pp. 60–61.
58. Tse Tsan Tai, *Secret History,* pp. 20, 22–23.
59. Feng, *I-shih,* *1,* 133–34.
60. Reprinted in *SLHC,* *1,* ts'e 2, 597–602.

failure to drive out the foreign invaders. After arguing that the Manchus were incapable of defending China, Sun warned foreigners that China would not easily submit to dismemberment: "Even though they may try to dismember, they will never be able to slaughter the majority of the Chinese people."[61] On the other hand, Sun pointed out that not all foreigners were motivated by imperialism. There were those who admired China's traditional civilization, her moral power, and her abhorrence of war. These men of goodwill wished to preserve China's territorial integrity, but as long as the Manchus remained, Sun argued, aggression would be invited.

It is significant that in this first public expression of his views to a student audience, Sun concentrated upon foreign affairs. His arguments were directed toward foreigners: warning the rapacious element and offering a reasonable approach to the friendlier segment. What he in fact was doing was showing the students that he possessed the expertise required to handle the foreign threat. Although he also hinted at his plan to create a new party, Sun did not remain in Japan. Before making a serious play for student support, he needed funds. Thus it was first necessary to recover his Overseas Chinese base.

The Sun Yat-sen who returned to Hawaii at the end of 1903 responded to Liang Ch'i-ch'ao's challenge with a new polemical style and displayed his mettle as a speaker and publicist.[62] He addressed thousands of Overseas Chinese at mass meetings and wrote newspaper articles defining his revolutionary, republican position. Liang had taken over not only the Overseas Chinese but the concept of revolution, and Sun proceeded to expose the contradiction between Liang's militancy and K'ang Yu-wei's unequivocal declarations of loyalty to the Emperor. He attacked gradualism in politics as comparable to using the earliest locomotive instead of buying the latest model. If a republic was admittedly the latest model of government, why settle for an absolete constitutional monarchy?[63]

Continuing the approach he had recently taken in Japan Sun also emphasized the external advantages of internal revolution: "If the people . . . could rise and overthrow the worthless . . . Manchu government, every country would respect [us]. . . . Would it

61. Ibid., p. 602.

62. *KFNP, 1,* 125–28.

63. *KFCC, 6,* 230.

then still be possible to carve us up like a melon?" This was the line the students were taking, and in castigating alleged Manchu appeasement policies, Sun no longer sounds like Ho Kai but like Yang Shou-jen (Yang Tu-sheng) and his associates: "The Manchu government not only signs treaties hacking at and mortgaging us, but pacifies the country for the foreigners and presents them with Kwangtung's Hsin-an district and Kwang-chow-wan."[64]

Though he recovered some lost ground Sun did not completely nullify Liang's success. The larger American Overseas Chinese community had likewise fallen under the reformer's spell. Armed with credentials from the Triads, whom he had joined in Honolulu, Sun undertook an ambitious coast-to-coast tour of the United States accompanied by the titular leader of the secret society. By the winter of 1904 he had reached New York. Again Sun found himself at a low point. Overseas Chinese audiences turned out to hear him but on the whole remained apathetic and the financial drive failed.[65] The need for a shift in tactics was obvious. While in New York Sun renewed his friendship with Wang Ch'ung-hui, then studying at the Yale Law School. With Wang's assistance Sun composed and privately printed his "True Solution to the Chinese Question."[66] This was his first direct appeal to the Americans.

Though it contained the same basic arguments he had used in his article in *Chiang-su,* there were tones reminiscent of the Ho Kai period. Instead of mentioning the recent imperialist conquest of the Philippines, he now recognized America as "one of the nearest neighbors of China," and called for American "Lafayettes" to join the struggle against the Manchus. Now he did not blame the Manchus for appeasing foreigners as he had done in Tokyo and Honolulu but charged them with cutting off the Chinese from foreign intercourse.

The pamphlet, said to have been circulated among influential foreigners, evoked no significant response.[67] However, news from the student front suddenly took a favorable turn. Student nationalists in Europe, mostly from Hupeh, invited Sun for discus-

64. Ibid., p. 227.

65. Feng, *I-shih, 2,* 123–24. Sharman, *Sun Yat-sen,* pp. 91–93.

66. Feng, *I-shih, 1,* 101; *KFNP, 1,* 134–35. The original English text of the pamphlet appears in *Tang-shih shih-liao ts'ung-k'an* (Serial Publication of Historical Materials on Party History) (Chungking, no date). I am grateful to the late Professor Shelley H. Cheng for lending me his copy.

67. Feng, *I-shih, 2,* 124.

sions and sent travel expenses. The young militants were looking for a leader and Sun eagerly grasped the opportunity.[68]

Leadership of the Revolutionary Movement

As a result of preliminary recruitment in Brussels, Berlin, and Paris, in the summer of 1905 Sun felt strong enough to submit his candidacy for leadership to the Tokyo hotbed of student activism. The resulting establishment of the Revolutionary Alliance in the summer of 1905 finally brought Sun to the forefront of the anti-Manchu revolutionary movement.[69] This predominantly student organization, representing almost every province in China, was actually China's first modern-style political party. It had a rudimentary organization, an ideology, and a program of propaganda and action. What it lacked was the cohesion and long-range staying power of a successful revolutionary movement.

Why was Sun chosen leader? I have already indicated that one of the crucial factors was the overriding concern with the foreign threat and Sun's purported ability to neutralize it. This impression is reinforced by Sung Chiao-jen's recollection of his first conversation with Sun in Tokyo. Sung did not remember all the details of their preliminary talk but he did recall Sun's assurance that China was in no danger of partition and that only an internal power struggle among the Chinese themselves would present foreigners with such an opportunity.[70]

Then too, the Japanese were his enthusiastic sponsors—living proof of his ability to gain foreign support.[71] Sun also had Overseas Chinese connections, which were required to finance revolution. And finally, he had cultivated the secret societies, which he continued to believe would provide the main fighting strength for the Revolution. (In his talk with Sung Chiao-jen, Sun noted the success of the Kwangsi Triads. They had tried to get in touch with him the previous year, he asserted, but were prevented by his ab-

68. *KFNP, 1,* pp. 137–38; Chu Ho-chung, "Ou-chou T'ung-meng-hui chi-shih" (Record of the Revolutionary Alliance in Europe), in *KMWH, 2,* 255.

69. Hsüeh, *Huang Hsing,* chap. 4, gives an informative account of the organization of the Revolutionary Alliance, its composition and leading personalities.

70. Sung Chiao-jen, *Wo chih li-shih* (My Diary), reprinted in *CHS ts'ung-shu,* p. 68.

71. Ibid., pp. 65–66. Three years previously, Miyazaki's publication of his *Sanjū-sannen no yume* with its glowing tribute to Sun did much to raise Sun's prestige among the young intellectuals. See Chang Shih-chao, "Su *Huang Ti Hun*" (Commentary on *Huang Ti Hun*), *HHKMHIL, 1,* 243–44. Chang's abridged translation of Miyazaki's book appeared in 1903, a year after publication of the original.

sence from Hong Kong.) Given educated leadership, as by the students, Sun insisted that the Triads were capable of overthrowing the dynasty.[72]

The result was purely instrumental or entrepreneurial leadership.[73] Sun was accepted because he appeared to be the most successful practitioner of revolution, and in particular a kind of revolution which could avoid a disaster in foreign relations. This was no ideological leadership. Sun was not accepted as the fountainhead of political wisdom. His appeal to the intellectuals lacked that element of personal authority without which the centralized organizational structure planned in 1905 could never be realized.

This is not to say that Sun did not attempt to assert ideological leadership. His reading and travels, the tutelage of Ho Kai, Japanese intellectuals, Russian revolutionaries, Chinese émigrés, and students all exposed him to the latest currents of foreign thinking as well as giving him insight into Chinese history. Now that he finally had an intellectual audience he rose to the challenge and presented a comprehensive program distilled from the fund of world knowledge. The substance of his famous Three Principles of the People (*San-min chu-i*) is too well known to require further elaboration. It is significant however that these principles, outlined in 1905 and given the collective term the following year, are so comprehensive that they include almost everything. "Nationalism, Democracy, and Socialism"—what is left? This much must be said for Sun Yat-sen: When he finally had to define his program, he made it all-inclusive. But its very comprehensiveness turned it into a generalized slogan. The Three Principles represented the universal main political trends, and had in various forms already been suggested by earlier Chinese writers.[74] All Sun was saying was that

72. Sung Chiao-jen, *Wo chih li-shih,* p. 69. On the Kwangsi uprisings, see Lai Hsin-hsia, "Shih-lun Ch'ing Kuang-hsü mo-nien ti Kuang-hsi jen-min ta ch'i-i" (Inquiry into the Great Popular Risings in Kwangsi during the Last Years of the Kuang-hsü Reign), *Li-shih yen-chiu, 11* (December 1957), 57–77. Some of Sun's followers attempted to establish contact with the Kwangsi Triad leader, Li Li-t'ing, in 1898. See Feng, *I-shih, 1,* 43.

73. On entrepreneurial leadership, see Joseph A. Schumpeter, *The Theory of Economic Development* (Cambridge, Mass., 1959), p. 88.

74. See Y. C. Wang, "The Influence of Yen Fu and Liang Ch'i-ch'ao on the *San Min Chu I,*" *Pacific Historical Review, 34* (1965), 163–84. Yang Shou-jen (Yang Tu-sheng) in his *Hsin Hu-nan* (New Hunan), published in 1903, had already listed *ko-jen ch'üan-li* (individual rights and privileges) and *min-tsu chien-kuo chu-i* (nationalism, or the principle of nations creating states) as the two universal principles discovered in the West and necessary for China's regeneration (see *SLHC, 1,* ts'e 2, 631). Another adumbration of Sun's Three Principles can be found in an

China was capable of incorporating and realizing these trends in a one-stroke revolution. Although he did suggest some improvements upon Western achievements, such as the "five-power constitution" and "equalization of land rights," he brought few new ideas to the revolutionary movement. It was precisely his innovations mentioned above that were least acceptable to his audience. Above all the striking characteristic of the Three Principles is their relative detachment from China's specific situation. The most pressing social problem—the agrarian question—is left in abeyance, and instead Sun's version of "social revolution" actually points to a way of preventing social injustice in China's future industrialized society. Of the inadequacies of traditional culture and society there is no mention. The essence of his position was that only the Manchu regime stood in the way of China's easy transplantation of the latest Western political institutions. True, Sun's subsequent suggestion of a nine-year hiatus before the final attainment of true representative government indicates recognition of the need for some sort of transition, a recognition perhaps forced upon him by Liang Ch'i-ch'ao's arguments. But the tutelary role of a revolutionary party required tighter control than he or any other party leader exercised; this was another of his innovations that would be forgotten by 1912.[75]

While the substance of Sun's program did not penetrate deeply into the revolutionary consciousness, the mood of his presentation was sufficiently attuned to student mentality to override the sober objections of Liang Ch'i-ch'ao. From 1905 to 1907 Liang, in his *Hsin-min ts'ung-pao* (New People's Miscellany), single-handedly took on a whole platoon of revolutionary scribes who defended the Revolutionary Alliance program in the *Min-pao* (People's Report). The significance of the debate[76] lies in its elaboration of the revo-

---

anonymously written *Hsin-min ts'ung-pao* article of the same year discussing the "Three Great Principles" of modern Europe: "Rights and privileges for majority of the people"; "Benefits from taxation"; and "National states" (see *SLHC, 1,* ts'e 1, 343–48). Furthermore, some of the ideas appearing in Sun's blueprint for democracy in China were expounded by Ho Kai between 1895 and 1900. These include the provision that all candidates for office undergo examination, that the capacity for self-rule was inherent in the Chinese people and could be awakened by stimulating local self-government, and that Yao, Shun, and the rulers of the Three Dynasties (at the dawn of history) were harbingers of democracy (*min-ch'üan*). See Hsiao Kung-ch'üan, *Chung-kuo cheng-chih ssu-hsiang shih, 6,* 795–803.

75. George T. Yu, *Party Politics in Republican China: The Kuomintang, 1912–1924* (Berkeley and Los Angeles, 1966), pp. 25, 80.

76. See supra Gasster. See also R. Scalapino and H. Schiffrin, "Early Socialist Currents in the Chinese Revolutionary Movement," *JAS, 18* (1959), 321–42.

lutionary values embodied in Sun's presentation. Among the values shared by Sun and the students was first of all the assertion of Chinese group-superiority. All their interpretations and commitments to action were in consonance with the hope of an early establishment of Chinese preeminence in the world. Secondly, there was a commitment to criteria of universal validity. Whenever possible, examples from the outside world, both past and present, were invoked in order to justify the revolutionary course. Yet their apparent submission to rational, universal criteria was always limited by their Chinese particularism. When Liang Ch'i-ch'ao pointed out that what they were attempting had no successful precedent in world history, they were quick to postulate a special road for China.

This brings us to the third value—elitism. Sun's frequent references to the interventionist, spearheading role of "men of determination" reflect his faith in a disciplined and enlightened elite. An elite that knew the course of world progress could transcend the social and cultural obstacles described by Liang Ch'i-ch'ao. And finally there was the emphasis upon speed. It was not only that China had to take her place among the major powers but that she had to do so quickly. Gradualism was rejected in favor of stage-skipping.

This value complex was implicit in Sun's first major speech to the students in 1905:

> Everything can be managed by men of determination. What the ordinary people do not understand will have to be introduced by [such] men. If the thoughts of [these] men are elevated, the people's qualifications will be elevated . . . It is incumbent upon us . . . to choose the most civilized form of government in the world . . . If in one transformation we can stir people's hearts, civilization will come in a hurry and in only ten years the word "independence" will be stamped on people's brains . . . We have decided not to follow evolutionary change [the way the rest of the world changed] but to pursue artificially induced change with its quick progress. I want you gentlemen to save China by choosing from the top . . .[77]

As a leader, then, I think Sun caught the young nationalist mood, and in catering to it won the battle with Liang even before

77. *KFCC*, 2, 5–6.

it began. Yet in promising everything so quickly and easily he was not laying the groundwork for long-term leadership. Sun was in a position where he had to produce tangible success immediately. He could not command the unswerving loyalty of his followers in a prolonged struggle preceded by intensive organization and agitation. The circumstances, as I have indicated, were conducive to the choice of a noncataclysmic but swift revolution. Only a truly Leninist-type leader, one commanding intellectual authority and possessed of extreme hardness of character, could have imposed his will completely upon the impatient band of students. Sun simply did not have such authority. In his speeches he perhaps asserted a demagogic sway over his listeners, but never real intellectual leadership. Compare, for example, Lenin's key editorial role in the Bolshevik organ, *Iskra,* with Sun's passive role in *Min-pao's* comparable internecine struggle with Liang.[78] By 1907 *Min-pao* was actually edited by Sun's party rivals who at that time began disputing his leadership.[79] In effect Sun never really overcame his original handicap. Lack of literary skill weakened his hold over followers who instinctively equated leadership with scholarship. And if the leader remained a functionary, the organization itself was only a temporary arrangement and not a chosen vehicle for the salvation of the country. The Revolutionary Alliance as an organization did not command that feeling of sacredness that characterizes the transcendent party, which is "Raised to the dignity of an end in itself, instead of remaining in the domain of ways and means."[80]

In action the Revolutionary Alliance for the most part extended and intensified the same pattern that Sun had evolved for the Society to Restore China's Prosperity. The difference, and this of course was crucial, was in the size and quality of the leadership echelon. The Revolutionary Alliance's social roots were not in the treaty ports and missionary institutions but in well-placed families from the interior of China. From 1907 to the spring of 1911 the organization sponsored eight unsuccessful uprisings, the first six of which (1907–08) relied chiefly upon secret societies and peasant

78. On Lenin and *Iskra,* see Bertram Wolfe, *Three Who Made a Revolution* (New York, 1948), p. 251.

79. See supra Bernal.

80. Maurice Duverger, *Political Parties: Their Organization and Activity in the Modern State,* trans. Barbara and Robert North (London and New York, 1959), p. 122.

dissidents. It was only in 1910 that it concentrated on subverting the army, whose ranks had by then been infiltrated by revolutionary sympathizers, many of them young officers trained in Japan.[81] After the failures of 1910 and the spring of 1911, this new strategy finally paid off at Wuchang. Though as with most revolutions, this successful uprising broke out unexpectedly, the Revolutionary Alliance's previous attempts, including the two undertaken by the Society to Restore China's Prosperity, had a cumulative, catalytic effect which weakened dynastic prestige and power and facilitated final victory. Though Sun's tactics failed, his original strategy of responsive revolt—that if one province fell the others would quickly fall in line—was largely validated by the events of 1911. Yet the very ease with which many provinces fell through negotiation with essentially nonrevolutionary elements precluded centralized party control. As Ernest Young points out in Chapter 10 of this volume, by the end of 1911 when they faced Yuan Shih-k'ai's Northern Army the revolutionaries were not in an inferior military position for continuing the struggle and bringing about a complete transfer of power. But it was soon apparent that they lacked the internal cohesion required for such an effort and were quite unprepared for a prolonged conflict. In most revolutions, as well as traditional Chinese rebellions, the crucial stage is the elimination of rivals after the ancien régime has been immobilized. The 1911 Revolution stopped short of this stage. The final transfer of power was less important to the Revolutionary Alliance than a negotiated replacement of traditional government by a third party without risking foreign intervention. Their leader lacked both the authority and the frame of mind required for such an all-out effort.

What exactly, then, was Sun's contribution to the Revolution? First there was his tangible role as fund-raiser, which was partly the result of circumstances. He was expelled from Japan in 1907 and a year later from Hanoi where he had joined the party's military strategists. There is no question, though, that his real milieu was among the overseas communities. He acted as the Revolution's spokesman among the Overseas Chinese, especially those of Southeast Asia and America.[82] The funds that Sun himself collected or

81. Hsüeh, *Huang Hsing*, chap. 5.

82. See Feng Tzu-yu, *Hua-ch'iao ko-ming k'ai-kuo shih* (History of the Overseas Chinese in the Revolution and the Establishment of the Republic) (reprinted Taipei, 1953); Feng Tzu-yu, *Hua-ch'iao ko-ming tsu-chih shih hua* (Discussion of the

which were remitted by others after he had laid the groundwork financed the Revolutionary Alliance's military engagements. It should be noted too that while tens of thousands of dollars flowed through his hands, Sun made no money out of the Revolution. Later, in the corruption-ridden republican era, this rectitude in financial matters helped substantiate the image of the patriotic national leader.

Sun's other specialty was his dexterous handling of foreigners. Yet though he tried vigorously, making bids to the Japanese, Americans, French, and again to the British, only a few individuals, not governments, responded.[83] Among these were some French officers at Hanoi,[84] the adventurous American Homer Lea,[85] the Russian social revolutionaries Russell and Gershuni,[86] and a hodgepodge of English socialists,[87] Old China Hands,[88] and devout Christians[89] who saw Sun as a Chinese Constantine. The British government hurt him the most, still keeping him out of

---

History of the Overseas Chinese Revolutionary Organizations) (Taipei, 1954); Huang Chen-wu, *Hua-ch'iao yü Chung-kuo ko-ming* (The Overseas Chinese and the Chinese Revolution) (Taipei, 1963), pp. 1–221; Huang Fu-luan, *Hua-ch'iao yü Chung-kuo ko-ming* (The Overseas Chinese and the Chinese Revolution) (Hong Kong, 1954), pp. 1–211.

83. Shao Chuan Leng and Norman D. Palmer, *Sun Yat-sen and Communism* (New York, 1960), pp. 29–30.

84. Ibid., p. 29; *KFNP, 1,* 193–94; Sharman, *Sun Yat-sen,* pp. 105–07.

85. Jansen, *Sun Yat-sen,* p. 127.

86. See supra Bernal.

87. See the letter sent by the Norwich branch of the Independent Labour Party to Sir Edward Grey, November 11, 1911, in FO 371/1095, no. 45240. The branch passed a resolution favoring the republican Revolution.

88. See J. Ellis Barker's letter to Asquith on October 13, 1911, in FO 371/1093, no. 40313. Barker, who had met Sun some months previously, strongly warned against British intervention on behalf of the Manchu government. See also the letters of Charles J. H. Halcombe to the *Daily Chronicle,* October 17, 1911, and to Sir Edward Grey on October 18, in FO 371/1093, both no. 4174. Halcombe was an honorary member of the China Reform Party (i.e. Sun's party) and a member of the Friends of China Society, said to have been formed in London in 1898 by Cantlie and Sun (who was not in London in 1898). Halcombe stressed the pro-Christian orientation of the rebels and pointed out that the Boxers too had been originally antidynastic, contending that it was only their realization that foreigners supported the Manchus that turned them against the West. He warned that pro-Manchu intervention would be fatal to continued British supremacy in the trade of West and South China.

89. See for example the letter sent to Grey by an English clergyman on December 30, 1911, in FO 371/1310: "Recognize, get Russia to recognize the super mensch Sun in China. 400 million human lives under a Christian President . . . The Missionary Societies . . . have spent at least one-half million a year to convert the world. In a day Sun has converted 400 million souls."

Hong Kong and in 1910 declaring him *persona non grata* in Penang, by then one of his strongest overseas bases.[90]

In the end, however, Sun's basic contention concerning foreign behavior was validated. By scrupulously respecting foreign privileges, the Revolution suffered no overt interference. It was not, however, that Sun had to restrain his followers. His rise, as we have indicated, was the result rather than the cause of moderation in foreign policy. It is true, nevertheless, that his personal followers, such as Wang Ching-wei and Hu Han-min,[91] showed less concern with the foreign threat than others like Chang Ping-lin, who by 1907 was questioning Sun's leadership on different grounds.[92] We can conclude that if the Revolution already tended to be moderate, Sun's influence strengthened this tendency.

Actually, though foreigners were pleased with the revolutionary restraint, they were also impressed with the Revolution's popular support and the fact that all except two treaty ports were in territory controlled by the rebels. While revolutionary generals were congratulating themselves on having obtained foreign neutrality, European diplomats and statesmen were sighing with relief at having found few signs of Boxerism. The fear of violence, in fact, was mutual rather than one-sided.[93]

Ultimately Sun's major contribution to the Revolution was his optimism. While even stalwarts like Huang Hsing, Hu Han-min, and Wang Ching-wei at times despaired of the Revolution's chances,[94] Sun continued to plug away, boosting the morale of the fighters with promises of funds and luring the Overseas Chinese with talk of imminent victory and promises of investment opportunities. Even with overseas supporters it was necessary to produce quick and tangible results. One gets the impression that military uprisings *had* to be undertaken in order to sell "patriotic bonds" which were to be redeemable at high premiums after the establishment of the Republic.[95] If Sun's unrestrained optimism did not

90. See Anderson to Harcourt, December 29, 1910, in FO 371/1086, no. 4028.

91. See for example Wang's article in *Min-pao, 6* (Jan. 10, 1907), 17–39; and Hu's, *6*, 41–63. See also supra Gasster.

92. Hsüeh, *Huang Hsing*, pp. 52–54.

93. This is based upon my reading of British diplomatic correspondence for 1911–12, available at the Public Record Office, London.

94. Hsüeh, *Huang Hsing*, pp. 75, 100.

95. See Wang Gung-wu, "Sun Yat-sen and Singapore," *Journal of the South Seas Society, 15* (December 1959), 55–68. See also the translated excerpt from Sun's speech in Penang (October 30, 1910), enclosed in Anderson to Harcourt, December 29, 1910, FO 371/1086, no. 4028. Sun declared that Western millionaires like Roosevelt, Rocke-

prepare his followers for a decisive struggle in 1911–12, it nevertheless energized their repeated attempts which eventually overthrew the Manchus. And when the Revolution did break out, he was recognized as "undoubtedly its prime mover."[96]

The circumstances that led Sun and his followers to propose Yuan for the presidency only a month after Wuchang are discussed elsewhere in this volume. I would only emphasize that Sun's attitude was based upon three factors: his fear of foreign intervention, his lack of unqualified organizational loyalty, and once more, paradoxically, his naïve confidence. If the Manchus were overthrown and Yuan converted to republicanism, the major revolutionary aims would be achieved. All that seemed to remain of his own program was "mass welfare" (*min-sheng*), which his followers had in any event discarded. The realization of mass welfare was exactly what he concentrated upon after the dust had settled in 1912, trying to convert both Yuan and the public.[97]

What of his personal ambitions? If it was still too early for a peasant to supplant the Son of Heaven, and if Chinese intellectuals still viewed him as the "skillful organizer of secret societies"[98] and not as presidential material, he nevertheless had the satisfaction of seeing his ideas ostensibly realized and himself universally acclaimed as a disinterested patriot. China and the rest of the world never praised him as much as when he exerted his influence for a peaceful solution and gave way to Yuan.[99]

There is some evidence, however, that immediately after Wuchang Sun entertained higher hopes. It is significant that his reaction to news of the uprising while in America had been to take the long way back to China through Europe. He apparently still felt

feller, and Morgan derived their wealth not from trade but from their "indirect assistance to . . . revolutionaries in the various countries." Instead of investing their money in other ways, the Overseas Chinese, Sun declared, could get one hundred times more profit by supporting the Revolution.

96. This was the opinion of the British minister, Sir John Jordan. See Jordan to Grey, Nov. 6, 1911, in FO 371/1095, no. 46946.

97. See Harold Schiffrin, "Sun Yat-sen's Early Land Policy," *JAS, 16* (1957), 554–57.

98. See the appraisals in the *Chinese Students' Monthly* (Boston), 7 (January 1912), 204; 7 (February 1912), 292; and 7 (June 1912), 655. While Sun is considered a patriotic conspirator, Li Yüan-hung is compared to Garibaldi and Yuan Shih-k'ai to Cavour.

99. For praise of Sun's "self-restraint" see the London *Times* (Feb. 27, 1912); and Li Yüan-hung's letter to Yuan Shih-k'ai and various officials on March 22, 1912, in *Li fu-tsung-t'ung cheng-shu* (Political Correspondence of Vice-president Li), reprinted in *CHS ts'ung-shu*, p. 112.

that the foreign attitude would be decisive not only for the Revolution but for his personal position. The Revolution could succeed if foreigners remained neutral and refused to advance funds to the Manchus. And active support by foreign governments could very well catapult him into supreme power. By this time he had less faith in the Japanese,[100] and concentrated upon Europe and especially the British.

Homer Lea and Sir Trevor Dawson of Vickers, Sons and Maxim acted on his behalf in London. The contact with the Foreign Secretary, Sir Edward Grey, was actually made through Trevor Dawson, who apparently hoped to obtain orders for munitions and armaments from Sun (who, he was led to believe, would be the "President of the United States of China"). In a statement signed by Sun and Lea and submitted to the Foreign Office by Dawson *after* Sun had left London for Paris, a number of proposals were made. Sun's party wished to make an alliance with Britain and the United States. Senators (sic) Knox and Root were interested, and prepared to lend the revolutionaries one million pounds if Britain agreed. Sun stated that he required Britain's friendship and support and promised to act under the advice of her government, whose nominee he would appoint as political officer. He further agreed that if his party came to power and he assumed the presidency, which he "believed to be a certainty," he would give Britain and the United States favored nation terms over all other countries and would place the navy under the command of British officers subject to his own orders. His attitude toward Japan would be determined by British advice. As for his support in China, Sun declared that no less than 30,000 to 40,000 of the country's "best educated students" had sworn under blood oath to serve him and that several secret societies with 35 million members backed him for the presidency.[101]

Sun Yat-sen's style, it appears, had not really changed very much since 1895–1900. This latest proposal was made at a time when he had already expressed privately extremely realistic and pessimistic views concerning possible support from the West. In 1906 he wrote

100. See Jansen, *Sun Yat-sen,* pp. 143–48. Through personal contacts with Mitsui officials and a flagrant disregard for Chinese national interests, Sun nevertheless got three loans from Japan. See Chang Chien's strong criticism in Samuel C. Chu, *Reformer in Modern China: Chang Chien, 1853–1926* (New York and London, 1965), pp. 78–79.

101. See Grey to Jordan, November 14, 1911, in FO 371/1095, no. 45661, and the enclosed memorandum of the previous day submitted by Sir Trevor Dawson.

Dr. Russel, whom he had met in Japan that year, that he did not think much of the Russian's efforts to gain capitalist support for the Chinese Revolution. How could you expect American capitalists to "commit commercial suicide" by helping China attain sovereignty and industrialization? he asked. If China showed the slightest sign of developing her industry, Sun asserted, the entire Western capitalist world would "scream about the so-called Yellow Industrial Peril." As for Russel's remark that China's revival would accelerate Western social revolutions—a prevision of Lenin's argument—Sun replied that the less Western capitalists knew of this, the better. Although he still believed that the "regeneration of one-fourth of the world's population would benefit all mankind," he was afraid that it would be a long time before Westerners had any sympathetic understanding of the Chinese problem.[102]

The British of course were not taken in by Sun's claims, though he actually invited them to check with Knox and Root. In the end all Sun got was permission to stop over briefly in British colonies, including Hong Kong, on his way back to China. Sun learned that the British would remain neutral—this was the result not of his diplomacy but rather of their appraisal of revolutionary strength and fear of great power rivalry—and would oppose making loans to either side. He also learned that the British considered Yuan Shih-k'ai the person best qualified to lead China.

Though this desperate bluff was made several days after Sun had already wired from Paris suggesting Yuan for the presidency,[103] it can be considered Sun's final long-shot gamble for personal success.[104] When Sun returned to Shanghai at the end of 1911 it was without the funds his followers had expected him to bring.[105]

102. The text I have used is a Chinese translation that appeared in the Hong Kong *Ta Kung Pao* (Nov. 17, 1956), p. 11. I am very grateful to Dr. T. C. Lau of Hong Kong for sending me the clipping. The Russian versions of these letters, originally written in English, are cited in Bernal, supra, n. 136.

103. On November 12 Sun wired from Paris proposing either Li Yüan-hung or Yuan Shih-k'ai for the presidency. See Kuo T'ing-i, *Chin-tai Chung-kuo shih-shih jih-chih* (A Daily Chronology of Modern Chinese History) (Taipei, 1963), ts'e 2, p. 1426.

104. I have no verified knowledge of purported negotiations with the French, including Clemenceau (*KFNP, 1,* 277). There was even a rumor, apparently circulated by Sun via the Japanese, that the Kaiser supported the Revolution. See Grey to MacDonald, Oct. 26, 1911, in FO 371/1094. Sun, according to the Japanese chargé d'affaires in London, had informed Japanese friends that his "special object" in going to Europe was to stimulate Chinese students in Germany. According to the record, however, the only continental country he visited was France.

105. Hsüeh, *Huang Hsing,* p. 131.

Given Sun's evaluation of the situation there was no option but to press for a peaceful settlement with Yuan.[106]

It has been said that there is no better way of bringing a decade or generation into focus than to ask what they were most afraid of and what they did about it. The Chinese of 1911 feared foreign conquest or dismemberment. What they did was to carry out a revolution characterized by unrevolutionary restraint and "sweet reasonableness,"[107] as a British observer so aptly phrased it. It was no accident, moreover, that such a revolution was led by Sun Yat-sen, who at that time was less concerned with seizing power for himself and his party than with the overthrow of the dynasty and preservation of Chinese unity.

That one of the aftereffects of the Revolution was the internal breakup of China into military satrapies is an historical irony, the discussion of which is beyond the scope of this paper. As for Sun Yat-sen, however, it should be pointed out that awareness of the Revolution's shortcomings led to one of his characteristic transformations. What he had learned was the significance and substance of power. After the failure of his "Second Revolution" of 1913, Sun Yat-sen in exile was no longer satisfied with being the entrepreneurial functionary of a loose revolutionary movement. In forming his new organization, the Revolutionary Party, in Japan in 1914, he insisted upon a new basis of loyalty, not the four-plank oath of the Revolutionary Alliance or the platform of the defunct Nationalist Party, but an oath of loyalty to himself.[108] He now saw the ideal party as a personally controlled conspiracy, a closed body of select personnel whose uniqueness consisted of its recognition of his personal and undisputed leadership. Less concerned with the foreign threat and fortified by his final attainment of national stature, Sun Yat-sen saw the creation of an instrument for the seizure of power as his main political task. Two years before the Bolshevik Revolution and eight years before his formal alliance with the Soviet Union, Sun was quoting Michels to the Southeast Asian secret societies in order to justify oligarchic party rule:

> The Italian, Dr. Michels, in his sociology of political parties, says that even the political parties most dedicated to pop-

106. See Sun's reply to Hu Han-min, who urged him to remain in Canton and fight for complete power, ibid., pp. 125–26, and Hu, *Tzu-chuan, KMWH, 3,* 426.

107. Memorandum of F. A. Aglen in H. B. Morse, *The International Relations of the Chinese Empire* (London, 1910–18), *3,* 402.

108. *KFNP, 1,* 370–71.

> ular rule have to be obedient to the will of one man in . . . their daily activities. It is apparent that no matter what the party, all must be obedient to the dictates of the party chief. And how much truer this is in the case of a revolutionary party which has to be obedient in carrying out military commands . . .[109]

Sun's style during his period of apprenticeship, however, did not foreshadow a future Chinese Lenin. It did contain the main ingredient of a populist-type leadership recently fashionable in Asia and Africa: a mystical belief that the leader personifies the nation and its aspirations, thus permitting grand improvisation in tactics and fluid generalization in ideology.

109. *KFCC, 3,* 177. The letter is dated July 1914 in this collection of Sun's works, but I have seen it dated a year later in other collections. I assume the later date is correct since the English translation of Michels' work, *Political Parties,* only appeared in 1915.

Appendixes

TABLE OF TRANSLATIONS OF POLITICAL BODIES

These disparate organizations are referred to primarily in English in this book. This table should identify them for specialists and, we hope, initiate a trend toward standardizing the terminology of Chinese politics in the early twentieth century.—M. C. W.

Army Revolutionary Alliance	Chün-tui t'ung-meng-hui
Association of Comrades for Peace	Ho-p'ing t'ung-chih-hui
Association of Comrades to Petition for a Parliament	Kuo-hui ch'ing-yüan t'ung-chih-hui
Black Dragon Society	Kokuryūkai
Chekiang Society	Che-hui
Constitutional Government Association	Hsien-cheng kung-hui
Constitutional Government Preparatory Association	Hsien-cheng ch'ou-pei-hui
Constitutional Preparatory Association	Yü-pei li-hsien kung-hui
Constitutionalist Friends Club	Hsien-yu-hui
Constitutionalists	Li-hsien-p'ai
Crouching Tiger Society	Fu-hu-hui
Delegation to Petition for a Parliament	Kuo-hui-ch'ing-yüan tai-piao-t'uan
Double Dragon Society	Shuang-lung-hui
Dragon Flower Society	Lung-hua-hui
East Asia Common Culture Society	Tōa dōbunkai
Eastern Socialist Party	Tōyō shakaitō
Elder Brother Society	Ko-lao-hui
Gold Coin Society	Chin-ch'ien-hui
Hupeh Military Revolutionary Alliance	Hu-pei chün-tui t'ung-meng-hui
Independent Army	Tzu-li-chün
Institute for the Diffusion of Science	K'o-hsüeh pu-hsi-so
Institute for the Restoration of Martial Spirit	Chen-wu hsüeh-she
Japanese Socialist Party	Nippon (Nihon) shakaitō
Kwangtung Merchants' Self-Government Association	Yüeh-shang tzu-chih-hui

Liberal Party	Jiyūtō
Literary Institute	Wen-hsüeh-she
National Assembly	Tzu-cheng-yüan
National Socialist Party	Kokka shakaitō
Nationalist Party	Kuomintang
People's Association	Min-she
Political Information Institute	Cheng-wen-she
Political Preparatory Office	Cheng-chih ch'ou-pei ch'u
Popular Rights Movement	Jiyū minken undō
Progressive Association	Kung-chin-hui
Provincial Assembly	Tzu-i-chü
Republican Party	Kung-ho-tang
Restoration Army	Kuang-fu-chün
Restoration Society[1]	Kuang-fu-hui
Revolutionary Alliance	T'ung-meng-hui
Revolutionary Party	Ko-ming-tang
Self-Government Association	Tzu-chih-hui
Self-Strengthening Society	Ch'iang-hsüeh-hui
Social Democratic Party	Shakai minshutō
Society for China's Revival	Hua-hsing-hui
Society for Daily Improvement[2]	Jih-chih-hui
Society for the Development of Industry in the Chinese Republic	Chung-hua min-kuo kung-yeh chien-she-hui
Society for the Education of a Militant People	Chün-kuo-min chiao-yü hui
Society for the Restoration of Land Rights	Tochi fukken dōshikai
Society for the Study of Popular Government	Ch'ün-chih hsüeh-she
Society for the Study of Socialism	She-hui chu-i chiang-hsi-hui
Society to Protect the Emperor	Pao-Huang-hui
Society to Protect the Peace	Pao-an-hui
Society to Restore China's Prosperity	Hsing-Chung-hui
Volunteer Corps	I-yung-tui
Volunteer Corps to Oppose Russia	Chü-O i-yung-tui
White Cloth Society	Pai-pu-hui

1. Restoration here means the recovery of China's territory and sovereignty. The term is revolutionary.

2. *Jih-chih* is an allusion to the *Analects* of Confucius. It means to study broadly, constantly adding to distilled wisdom. It has often been used in essay titles, the most famous of which is Ku Yen-wu's *Jih-chih-lu*. The revolutionary organization that used this name shielded itself behind Christian missionaries, but the name is not Christian in origin, despite the inevitably awkward translation.

Glossary of Characters for Selected Chinese and Japanese Names and Terms

The selection of characters to be included in this glossary is larger than usual, first for the convenience of Asian and European scholars and libraries, who do not use the Anglo-American system of romanization, and second because reference works are scarce in the new and chaotic field of early twentieth-century Chinese history. Characters are given for all personal names including the names of authors cited, except those that are very widely known or are drawn from Western documents in which we were unable to identify the person through Chinese-language sources. I have also included the names of most organizations, offices, and movements. I have excluded most book titles and many special terms because translation in conjunction with romanization makes the characters obvious.—M.C.W.

Abe Isō (Isoo) 安部磯雄
Ai-kuo hsüeh-she 愛國學社
An-sha k'ung-pu 暗殺恐怖
An-sha-t'uan 暗殺團
Ao Chia-hsiung 敖嘉熊

Ch'a Kuang-fo 查光佛
Ch'ai Te-keng 柴德賡
Cham Lin-pak. *See* Ch'en Lien-po
Chan Ta-pei 詹大悲
Chang Chen-hsün 張振勳
Chang Chen-wu 張振武
Chang Chi (P'u-ch'üan) 張繼(溥泉)
Chang Chien 張謇
Chang Chih-tung 張之洞
Chang Ching-liang 張景良
Chang Ching-lu 張靜廬
Chang Feng-hui 張鳳翽
Chang Hsiao-jo 張孝若
Chang Hsi-yüan 張錫元
Chang Hsün 張勳
Chang Huang-ch'i 張篁溪
Chang Hui-ch'ang 張惠昌
Chang Jen-chün 張人駿
Chang Kung 張恭
Chang Kuo-kan 張國淦
Chang Lin-yen 張林焱
Chang Ming-ch'i 張鳴岐
Chang Mu-liang 章木良
Chang Nan 張枏
Chang Nan-hsien 張難先
Chang P'ei-chüeh 張培爵
Chang P'eng-yüan 張朋園
Chang Piao 張彪
Chang Ping-lin (T'ai-yen) 章炳麟(太炎)
Chang P'u-ch'üan. *See* Chang Chi
Chang Shao-tseng 張紹曾
Chang Shih-chao (Hsing-yen) 章士釗(行嚴)
Chang T'ai-yen. *See* Chang Ping-lin
Chang T'ing-fu 張廷輔
Chang Tseng-yang 張曾敭

Chang Wei-ts'ung 張惟聰
Chang Wen-chu 章文著
Chang Wen-t'ao 張文濤
Chang Yü-k'un 章裕昆
Ch'ang-yen-pao 昌言報
Chao Erh-feng 趙爾豐
Chao Erh-sun 趙爾巽
Chao Feng-ch'ang 趙鳳昌
Chao Pi-chen 趙必振
Chao Shen 趙伸
Chao Sheng 趙聲
Che-chiang-ch'ao 浙江潮
Che-hui 浙會
Chen-wu hsüeh-she 振武學社
Ch'en Ch'i-mei 陳其美
Ch'en Chiung-ming 陳炯明
Ch'en Ch'un-sheng 陳春生
Ch'en Fu-ch'en 陳黻宸
Ch'en Hsi-ch'i 陳錫祺
Ch'en Hsiao-fen 陳孝芬
Ch'en Hsieh-shu 陳燮樞
Ch'en Hsü-lu 陳旭麓
Ch'en Lei 陳磊
Ch'en Leng-hsüeh 陳冷血
Ch'en Lien-po (Cham Lin-pak)
陳廉伯
Ch'en Meng-hsiung 陳夢熊
Ch'en Ping-jung 陳炳榮
Ch'en Ping-nan 陳炳南
Ch'en Po-p'ing 陳伯平
Ch'en Shao-pai 陳少白
Ch'en Shu-hsün 陳樹勳
Ch'en Te-lung 陳得龍
Ch'en T'ien-hua 陳天華
Ch'en Wei 陳魏
Ch'en Yü-nien 陳與年
Cheng-chih ch'ou-pei ch'u
政治籌備處
Cheng Ch'ih 鄭箎
Cheng Hsiao-hsü 鄭孝胥
Cheng Kuan-ying 鄭觀(官)應
Cheng-lun 政論
Cheng-mu 正目
Cheng-ping 正兵
Cheng Shih-liang 鄭士良
Cheng Tsao-ju 鄭藻如
Cheng-wen-she 政聞社
Ch'eng-hsien 嵊縣
Ch'eng Te-ch'üan 程德全
Ch'eng Ting-kuo 程定國
Chi Chung-yin 籍忠寅
Chi-ch'üan chu-i 集權主義
Ch'i I-hui 戢翼翬
Ch'i Ping-feng 亓冰峯
Chiang Chi-yün 蔣繼雲
Chiang Chih-yu 蔣智由
Chiang Fang-chen 蔣方震
Chiang I-wu 蔣翊武
Chiang K'ang-hu 江亢虎
Hung shui chi 洪水集
Chiang Kuei-t'i 姜桂題
Chiang Kuo-kuang 江國光
Chiang Lo-shan 蔣樂山
Chiang Lu-shan 蔣鹿珊
Chiang Tsun-kuei 蔣尊簋
Chiang Wei-ch'iao 蔣維喬
Chiang Yen-hsing 蔣雁行
Chiang Yün-ch'un 江運春
Ch'iang-hsüeh-hui 強學會
Chiao Ta-feng 焦達峰
Chieh (*hsia*) 俠(傑)
Chien-kuo yüeh-k'an 建國月刊
Chien-nung. *See* Li Chien-nung
Ch'ien-chuang 錢莊
Chih-sheng tzu-i-chü i-yüan lien-ho-hui pao-kao-shu
直省諮議局議員聯合會報告書
Chin Chao-lung 金兆龍
Chin-ch'ien-hui 金錢會
Chin Ch'ung-chi 金冲及
Chin I (Sung-ts'en) 金一(松岑)
Chin P'ing-ou 金平歐
Chin Sung-ts'en. *See* Chin I
Ching Mei-chiu 景梅九
Tsui an 罪案
Ching-shan 京山
"Ching-shih chung" 警世鐘
Ching-shih-pao 經世報

Ching-t'ien 井田
Ch'ing-i-pao 清議報
Ch'ing-k'ang 慶康
Ch'ing-kuo hsing-cheng-fa 清國行政法
Ch'ing-li ts'ai-cheng-ch'u 清理財政處
Ch'ing-li ts'ai-cheng-chü 清理財政局
Ch'ing, Prince (Ch'ing ch'in-wang, I-k'uang) 慶親王,奕劻
Ch'iu Chin 秋瑾
Ch'iu P'ei-chen 邱丕振
Ch'iu-shih shu-yüan 求是書院
Ch'iu Ts'an-chih 秋燦之
"Ch'iu-yü 秋雨
ch'iu-feng 秋風
ch'ou sha jen" 愁煞人
Chokugen 直言
Chou Ch'i-wei 周起渭
Chou Chin-chen 周金箴
Chou Hua-ch'ang 周華昌
Chou Hung-jan 周弘然
Chou Lai-su 周來蘇
Chou Pai-kao 周百高
Chou Tzu-ch'i 周自齊
Chu Chia-pao 朱家寶
Chu Chih-hsin 朱執信
Chu Chih-ju 朱秩如
Chu Ho-chung 朱和中
Chu Pao-san 朱葆三
Chu Shao-k'ang 竺紹康
Chu Tsan-ch'ing 朱贊卿
Chu Tzu-lung 朱子龍
Chu Yen-chia 朱炎佳
Ch'u Fu-ch'eng 褚輔成
Ch'u-wang-t'ai 楚望台
Ch'u-yü ping-ch'uan 楚豫兵船
Chuang-p'iao 莊票
Chuang Yün-k'uan 莊蘊寬
Ch'un, Prince (Ch'un ch'in-wang, Tsai-feng) 醇親王載灃
Chung-Hsi hsüeh-t'ang 中西學堂
Chung-hsing 種姓
Chung-hua-shan 中華山
Chung-i-yüan 衆議院
Chung-kuo ko-ming-tang 中國革命黨
Chung-kuo kung-hsüeh 中國公學
Chung-kuo lun-ch'uan chao-shang chü 中國輪船招商局
Chung-kuo pai-hua pao 中國白話報
Chung-nan-hui 終南會
Chung-teng she-hui 中等社會
Chung-wai jih-pao 中外日報
Chü 局
Chü Cheng (Chio-sheng) 居正(覺生)
Chü-O i-yung-tui 拒俄義勇隊
Ch'üan Han-sheng 全漢昇
Chün-fu-tang 均富黨
Chün-hsü tsung-chü 軍需總局
Chün-jen she-hui 軍人社會
Chün-kuo-min chiao-yü-hui 軍國民教育會
Chün-shih hsüeh-hsiao 軍事學校
Chün-tui t'ung-meng-hui 軍隊同盟會
Ch'ün-chih hsüeh-she 群治學社

En-ming 恩銘

Fang Li-chung 方履中
Fang Wei 方維
Feng Ju-k'uei 馮汝騤
Feng K'ai-chün 馮開濬
Feng Kuo-chang 馮國璋
Feng Tzu-yu 馮自由
Fu (Fourier) 傅
Fu-hu-hui 伏虎會
Fu-mu 副目
Fu-ping 副兵
Fu Tz'u-hsiang 傅慈祥
Fukui Junzō 福井準造

Hao-chieh (*hsia*) 豪俠(傑)
Hatano Yoshihiro 波多野善大
Heiminsha 平民社
Heimin shimbun 平民新聞

Hikari 光
Hirayama Shū (Amane) 平山周
Ho Chen 何震
Ho Chi-ta 何季達
"Ho-ch'ün chün-ch'an chih shuo" 合羣均產之說
Ho Hsi-fan 何錫藩
Ho Hsiao-liu 何曉柳
Ho Kai (Ho Ch'i) 何啓
Ho Ping-ti 何炳棣
Ho-p'ing t'ung-chih hui 和平同志會
Ho Sui 何遂
Hou Shu-t'ung 侯樹彤
Hsi-lou 息樓
Hsi-min 細民
Hsi Tzu-p'ei 席子佩
Hsi-yin-t'ang 惜陰堂
Hsiang-hui 鄉會
Hsiang-shan 香山
Hsiao An-kuo 蕭安國
Hsiao-ch'ao (miao) chieh 小朝(廟)街
Hsiao Hsiang 蕭湘
Hsiao P'ing 蕭平
Hsieh Ch'u-heng 謝楚珩
Hsieh Lun-hui 謝綸輝
Hsieh Tsuan-t'ai (Tse Tsan Tai) 謝纘泰
Hsieh Yüan-han 謝遠涵
Hsien-cheng ch'ou-pei hui 憲政籌備會
Hsien-cheng kung-hui 憲政公會
Hsien-cheng pien-ch'a-kuan 憲政編查館
Hsien-yu-hui 憲友會
Hsin-an 新安
Hsin-chien lu-chün 新建陸軍
Hsin-chien-she 新建設
"Hsin-min-shuo" "新民說"
Hsing-Chung-hui 興中會
Hsiu-chen chio-chih ch'üan-han 袖珍爵秩全函
Hsiung Ch'eng-chi 熊成基
Hsiung Ping-k'un 熊秉坤
Hsü Chung-ch'ing 許仲卿
Hsü Feng-ming 徐鳳鳴
Hsü Fo-su 徐佛蘇
Hsü Hsi-lin 徐錫麟
Hsü Shih-ch'ang 徐世昌
Hsü Ta-ming 徐達命
Hsü Ting-lin (ling) 許鼎霖
Hsü-wu chu-i 虛無主義
Hsü-wu-tang 虛無黨
Hsün-ching 巡警
Hsün-fang-tui 巡防隊
Hu Han-min 胡漢民
Hu Lan-t'ing 胡蘭亭
Hu Li-yüan 胡禮垣
Hu-pei chiang-pien hsüeh-t'ang 湖北將弁學堂
Hu-pei chiang-wu hsüeh-t'ang 湖北講武學堂
Hu-pei chün-tui t'ung-meng-hui 湖北軍隊同盟會
Hu Sheng-wu 胡繩武
Hu Tao-ching 胡道靜
Hu Tsu-shun 胡祖舜
Hu Ying 胡瑛
Hu Yü-chen 胡玉珍
Hua-hsing-hui 華興會
Huang Chen-wu 黄珍吾
Huang Chi-t'ing 黄吉亭
Huang Chia-lin 黄家麟
Huang Fu-luan 黄福鑾
Huang Hsiao-lin 黄孝霖
Huang Hsing 黄興
Huang Hung-hsien 黄宏憲
Huang Hung-k'un 黄洪昆
Huang Hung-shou 黄鴻壽
Huang-kang chün-hsüeh-chieh chiang-hsi-so 黄岡軍學界講習所
Huang K'un-jung 黄坤榮
Huang-p'o-hsien 黄陂縣
Huang Shen-hsiang 黄申薌
Huang Shih-hui 黄世暉
Huang Tsun-hsien 黄遵憲

Huang Yüeh 黄鉞
Hui-chi (K'uai-chi) 會稽
Hui-i-t'ing 會議廳
Hui-kuan 會館
Hung-men-hui 洪門會

I-cheng 儀徵
I Hsüeh-ch'ing 易學清
I Kuo-kan 易國幹
I Tsung-k'uei 易宗夔
I (Ni) Ying-tien 倪映典
I-yung-tui 義勇隊
Ichiko Chūzō 市古宙三
Ijūin Hikokichi 伊集院彦吉
Ike Kyōkichi 池享吉
Ikei Masaru 池井優
Inukai Tsuyoshi (Ki) 犬養毅
Iwamura Michio 岩村三千夫

Jiyū minken undō
自由民權運動
Jih-chih-hui 日知會
Jiyūtō 自由黨
Jui-cheng 瑞澂
Jung-lu 榮祿
Jung Meng-yüan 榮孟源

K'ai-chih lu 開智錄
Kakumei hyōron 革命評論
Kao Chia-hsiang 高家巷
Kao K'uei 高逵
Kao Liang-tso 高良佐
Kao Ping-chen 高秉貞
Kao Ta 高達
Kao Teng-li 高登鯉
Katayama Sen 片山潛
Kawajima Todanosuke 川島忠之助
Kawakami Hajime 川上肇
Kawakami Kiyoshi 河上清
Kawashima Naniwa 川島浪速
Kayano Nagatomo 萱野長知
Kemuyama Sentarō 煙山専太郎
Kikuchi Takaharu 菊池貴晴
Kinoshita Naoe 木下尚江

Kita Ikki (Terujirō)
北一輝(輝次郎)
Kiyofuji Kōshichirō
清藤幸七郎
Ko Feng-shih 柯逢時
Ko Kung-chen 戈公振
Ko-lao-hui 哥老會
Ko-ming chün-shih hsüeh-hsiao
革命軍事學校
Ko-ming hsieh-hui 革命協會
Ko-ming hsien-lieh chuan-chi
革命先烈傳記
Ko-sheng tu-tu-fu tai-piao lien-ho-hui 各省都督府代表聯合會
Kōbungakuin 宏文學院
Kojima Yoshio 小島淑男
Kokka shakaitō 國家社會黨
Kokuryūkai 黑龍會
Kōsaka Masaaki 高坂正顯
Kōtoku Shūsui 幸德秋水
K'o-hsüeh pu-hsi-so 科學補習所
K'o-min 客民
Ku Chung-hsiu 谷鍾秀
Kuang-chih shu-chü 廣智書局
Kuang-fu-chün 光復軍
Kuang-fu-hui 光復會
Kuei-fu 貴福
Kung-ch'an chih fa 共產之法
Kung-ch'an chün-fu chu-i
共產均富主義
Kung-chin-hui 共進會
Kung-ho-tang 共和黨
Kung Pao-ch'üan (Wei-sun)
龔寶銓(味蓀)
Kuo Chung-ch'ing (Hsi-jen)
郭忠清(希仁)
Kuo-feng-pao 國風報
Kuo-hui ch'ing-yüan tai-piao t'uan
國會請願代表團
Kuo-hui ch'ing-yüan t'ung-chih-hui 國會請願同志會
Kuo-min jih-jih pao 國民日日報
Kuo-min kung-pao 國民公報
Kuo-min-pao 國民報

Kuo T'ing-i 郭廷以
Kutsumi Ketsuson (Kesson) 久津見蕨村
Kyomutō 虛無黨
Kyōsan museifu shugi 共產無政府主義

Lai Hsin-hsia 來新夏
Lan Kung-wu 藍公武
Lan T'ien-wei 藍天蔚
Lei Chin 雷搢
Lei Fen 雷奮
Li Chi-ch'en 李濟臣
Li Chia-chü 李家駒
Li Chien-nung 李劍農
Li Chin-jung 李搢榮
Li Chu 黎澍
Li Chun 李準
Li En-han 李恩涵
Li-hsien-p'ai 立憲派
Li Li-t'ing 李立亭
Li Lieh-chün 李烈鈞
Li Lien-fang 李廉方
Li P'ing-shu 李平書
Li Sheng-to 李盛鐸
Li Shou-k'ung 李守孔
Li Shu-ch'eng 李書城
Li Tse-ch'ien 李澤乾
Li Tso-tung 李作棟
Li Ya-tung 李亞東
Li Yüan-hung 黎元洪
Liang Chi-tung 梁繼棟
Liang-Hu shu-yüan 兩湖書院
Liang Shan-chi 梁善濟
Liang Shih-i 梁士詒
Liao Chung-k'ai 廖仲愷
Lien-chün 練軍
Lien-ping-ch'u 練兵處
Lin Chao-tung 林兆棟
Lin Hsieh 林獬
Lin-sheng 廩生
Lin-shih chün cheng-fu 臨時軍政府
Lin-shih ts'an-i-yüan 臨時參議院
Liu Ching-an 劉靜庵(安)
Liu Ch'un-lin 劉春霖
Liu Fu-chi (Yao-cheng) 劉復基(堯澂)
Liu Fu-piao 劉福標
Liu Hsiang 劉向
Liu Hsüeh-hsün 劉學詢
Liu Hua-ou 劉化歐
Liu K'uei-i 劉揆一
Liu Kung (Chung-wen) 劉公(仲文)
Liu Shih-p'ei (Wei-i) 劉師培(韋裔)
Liu Ta-chün 劉大鈞
Liu Tao-i 劉道一
Liu Yao-cheng. *See* Liu Fu-chi
Liu Ying 劉英
Liu Yü-ping 劉雨屏
Lo Chia-lun 羅家倫
Lo Chia-tsao. *See* Yo Chia-tsao
Lo Chieh 羅傑
Lo Hsiang-lin 羅香林
Lo Ping-shun 羅炳順
Lo Ta-wei 羅大維
Lu Jung-t'ing 陸榮廷
Lu Yao-tung 逯耀東
Lung Chi-kuang (kwong) 龍濟光
Lung-hua-hui 龍華會
Lü Hsiung-hsiang 呂熊祥
Lü-lin 綠林
Lü Ta-sen 呂大森

Ma Hsü-lun 馬叙倫
Ma Jung 馬榮
Ma Liang (Hsiang-po) 馬良(相伯)
Ma Tsung-han 馬宗漢
Ma Yü-pao 馬毓寶
Mao Hu-hou 毛虎候
Meng Chao-ch'ang 孟昭常
"Meng hui t'ou" 猛回頭
Meng Sen (Hsin-shih) 孟森(心史)
Meng T'ieh-sheng (Yeh Hsia-sheng) 夢蝶生(葉夏生)
Min-ch'üan pao 民權報
Min-li-pao 民立報

Min-pao (*Minpo*) 民報
Min-she 民社
Min-tsu chien-kuo chu-i
民族建國主義
Min-tsui chu-i 民粹主義
Ming-tao nü-hsüeh 明道女學
Ming-te (School) 明德
Miyazaki Muryū 宮崎夢柳
Miyazaki Tamizō (Junkō)
宮崎民藏（巡耕）
Miyazaki Torazō (Tōten)
宮崎寅藏（滔天）
Mo-ken (Mulkern) 摩根
Mou-lüeh-ch'u 謀略處
Mu-chih-yüan 募職院
Murai Chishi 村井知至

Nagai Kazumi 永井算巳
Nakae Chōmin 中江兆民
Nakamura Tadashi 中村義
Negishi Tadashi 根岸佶
Ni Ying-tien. *See* I Ying-tien
Nihon rikugun shikan gakkō
日本陸軍士官學校
Nishida Nagashi 西田長寿
Nishikawa Kōjirō 西川光次郎
Nishikawa Michitetsu 西川通徹
Nishimura Shigeki 西村茂樹
Nishio Yōtarō 西尾陽太郎

Ōkawa Shūmei 大川周明
Ōkochi Kazuo 大河内一男
Onogawa Hidemi 小野川秀美
Ōsugi Sakae 大杉榮

Pai-hua-pao 白話報
Pai-pu-hui 白布會
P'an K'ang-shih 潘康時
P'an Shan-po 潘善伯
Pang 帮
Pao-an-hui 保安會
Pao-Huang-hui 保皇會
Pao-shan-li 寶善里
"P'ei tien pien" 悲佃篇

P'eng Ch'eng-wan 彭程萬
P'eng Ch'u-fan 彭楚藩
Pien-chien, pseud. 辨姦
P'ing-chün ti-ch'üan 平均地權
P'ing-hsiang 萍鄉
P'ing-hu 平湖
P'ing-Liu-Li 萍瀏醴
P'ing-yang-hui 平陽會
Po Wen-wei 柏文蔚
P'u Chen-sheng 濮振聲
P'u Tien-chün 蒲殿俊

Sa (Sah) Chen-ping 薩鎮冰
Sakai Toshihiko 堺利彦
San-ho-hui 三合會
San-tien-hui 三點會
Sanetō Keishū 實藤惠秀
Seijō gakkō 成城學校
Seng-min hsüeh-t'ang 僧民學堂
Shan-hou tsung-chü 善後總局
Shan-yin 山陰
Shang-chüan 商捐
Shang-hai chi-ch'i chih-pu chü
上海機器織布局
Shang-hai shang-wu tsung-hui
上海商務總會
Shang Ping-ho 尚秉和
Hsin-jen ch'un-ch'iu 辛壬春秋
Shang-wu-chü 商務局
Shang-wu-pao 商務報
Shang-yeh hui-i kung-so
商業會議公所
Shao Hsi 邵羲
She-hui chu-i chiang-hsi-hui
社會主義講習會
Shen Chün-ju 沈鈞儒
Shen Hsiang-yün 沈翔雲
Shen Jung-ch'ing 沈榮卿
Shen Man-yün 沈縵雲
Shen Ping-k'un 沈秉堃
Shen-shang 紳商
Shen Tieh-min 沈瓞民
Shen Yü-ch'ing 沈瑜慶
Sheng Hsüan-huai 盛宣懷

Sheng-i-hui 省議會
Sheng Lang-hsi 盛郎西
Shih Chien-ju 史堅如
Shih-pao 時報
Shih-wu-pao 時務報
Shih-yeh-t'uan 實業團
Shimada Saburō 島田三郎
Shimoide Hayakichi 下出隼吉
Shinbu gakkō 振武學校
Shinkigen 新紀元
Shinkoku gyōsei hō 清國行政法
Shioda Shōbei 塩田庄兵衛
Shishi 志士
Shizuno Matao 志津野又郎
Shou-hsün 壽勳
Shou-shan 壽山
Shu-pao 蜀報
Shuang-lung-hui 雙龍會
Somayama Sakutaro 杣山策大郎
Ssu-tao 司道
Su Man-shu (Tzu-ku) 蘇曼殊（子穀）
Su-pao 蘇報
Su P'eng 蘇鵬
Su, Prince (Su ch'in-wang, Shan-ch'i) 肅親王，善耆
Sun Hung-i 孫洪伊
Sun I-chung 孫翼中
Sun I-jang 孫詒讓
Sun I-yen 孫衣言
Sun K'ai-hua 孫開華
Sun Pao-ch'i 孫宝琦
Sun Tao-jen 孫道仁
Sun Te-ch'ing 孫德卿
Sun Wu 孫武
Sun Yü-yun 孫毓筠
Sung Chiao-jen 宋教仁
Suzuki Tomoo 鈴木智夫

Ta-chiang-pao 大江報
Ta-tu-tu 大都督
Ta-t'ung (shih-fan) hsüeh-t'ang 大通（師範）學堂
Tai Hung-tz'u 戴鴻慈
Tanaka Sōgorō 田中惣五郎
T'an Hsi-keng 譚西庚
T'an Jen-feng 譚人鳳
T'an Pi-an 譚彼岸
T'an Yen-k'ai 譚延闓
T'ang Chi-yao 唐繼堯
T'ang Hua-lung 湯化龍
Tang Leang-li (T'ang Liang-li) 湯良禮
T'ang Shao-i 唐紹儀
T'ang Shou-ch'ien 湯壽潛
T'ang Ts'ai-ch'ang 唐才常
T'ang Tseng-pi (Man-hua) 湯增壁（曼華）
T'ao Ch'eng-chang 陶成章
T'ao Ch'i-sheng 陶啟勝
T'ao Chü-yin 陶菊隱
T'ao Chün 陶峻
Te-shou 德壽
Teng Hsiao-k'o 鄧孝可
Ti Pao-hsien 狄葆賢
T'i hsüeh shih 提學使
T'i-tu 提督
T'ieh-chung 鐵忠
T'ieh-liang 鐵良
T'ien-i pao 天義報
"T'ien t'ao" 天討
T'ien-ti-hui 天地會
T'ien Tzu-ch'in (T'ung) 田梓琴（桐）
T'ien-yen-lun 天演論
Ting Jen-chün 丁人俊
Ting Wen-chiang 丁文江
Tōa dōbunkai 東亞同文會
Tochi fukken dōshikai 土地復權同志會
Tōhin gakudō 東斌學堂
Tou I-chio 竇以珏
Tsai-t'ao 載濤
Ts'ai Ao 蔡鍔
Ts'ai Chi-min 蔡濟民
Ts'ai Chi-ou 蔡寄鷗
Ts'ai Fu-ch'ing 蔡輔卿
Ts'ai Nai-huang 蔡乃煌

Ts'ai O. *See* Ts'ai Ao
Ts'ai Ta-fu 蔡大輔
Ts'ai T'ing-kan 蔡廷幹
Ts'ai Yüan-p'ei 蔡元培
Ts'an-i-kuan 參議官
Ts'ao Ch'in-hsi 曹欽熙
Ts'ao Ya-po 曹亞伯
Tse Tsan Tai. *See* Hsieh Tsuan-t'ai
Ts'en Ch'un-hsüan 岑春煊
Tseng Kuang-luan 曾廣鑾
Tseng Yün 增韞
Tsou Jung 鄒容
Tsou Lu 鄒魯
Tsu-tsung-chiao 祖宗教
"Tsui-pien-wen" 罪辯文
Tsung-chih-hui 總指揮
Tsung-tu 總督
Tu-fu 督撫
Tu-li chih ko-jen 獨立之個人
Tu-lien kung-so 督練公所
Tu-pan 督辦
Tu-tu 都督
Tu Yen 杜嚴
T'u-ti kuo-yu 土地國有
Tuan Ch'i-jui 段棋瑞
Tuan-fang 端方
Tui-huan-so 兌換所
T'ung-chüan 統捐
T'ung-i-tang 統一黨
T'ung-ling 統領
T'ung-meng-hui 同盟會
Tzu-cheng-yüan 資政院
Tzu-ch'iang-chün 自強軍
Tzu-chih-hui 自治會
Tzu-i-chü 諮議局
Tzu-i-chü ch'ou-pan-chü 諮議局籌辦局
Tzu-li-chün 自立軍
Tzu-pen (chu-i) meng-ya 資本(主義)萌芽
Tzu-yang shu-yüan 紫陽書院

Wada Saburō 和田三郎
Waichow (Hui-chou) 惠州
Wan Yao-huang 萬耀煌
Wang Chan-k'uei 王占魁
Wang Chia-chü 王嘉榘
Wang Chin-fa 王金發
Wang Ching-wei 汪精衛
Wang Ch'ung-hui 王寵惠
Wang Fa-ch'in 王法勤
Wang Heng-chin 王恒晉
Wang Ho-ming 王鶴鳴
Wang Hsi-t'ung 王錫彤
Wang Hsien-chang 王憲章
Wang Hui-tsu 汪輝祖
Wang I-sun 汪詒蓀
Wang Jen-chih 王忍之
Wang Jen-wen 王人文
Wang K'ang-nien 汪康年
Wang Shih-chen 王士珍
Wang Shih-chieh 王時傑
Wang Shih-tse 王時澤
Wang T'ao 王韜
Wang Te-chao 王德昭
Wang Ying-k'ai 王英楷
Watanabe Atsushi 渡辺惇
Watanabe Yoshimichi 渡部義通
Wei Ch'ang-hui 韋昌輝
Wei Chien-yu 魏建猷
Wei Lan 魏蘭
Wei Tyuk (Yü) 韋玉
Wen-ch'ang-men 文昌門
Wen-ming cheng-lu 文明爭路
Wen-T'ai-ch'u Guildhall 溫台處
Wu Chao-lin 吳兆麟
Wu Chieh-chang 吳介璋
Wu-chih chu-i 無稚主義
Wu Chih-hui 吳稚暉
Wu Ching-lien 吳景濂
Wu Hsiang-hsiang 吳相湘
Wu Hsien-tzu 伍憲子
Wu Hsing-han 吳醒漢
Wu Lu-chen 吳祿貞
Wu-pei hsüeh-t'ang 武備學堂
Wu Shao-ch'ing 吳少卿
Wu T'ing-fang 吳廷芳

Wu Tsung-yü 吳宗禹
Wu Tz'u-ling 吳賜齡
Wu-wei yu-chün 武衛右軍
Wu Yü-chang 吳玉章
Wu Yüeh (Meng-hsia) 吳樾(孟俠)

Yamaji Aizan 山路愛山
Yang Chin-ch'eng 楊藎誠
Yang Ch'ü-yün 楊衢雲
Yang Hsi-chang 楊璽章
Yang Hung-sheng 楊鴻盛
Yang K'ai-chia 楊開甲
Yang Shih-chieh 楊時傑
Yang Shou-jen 楊守仁(later name of Yang Tu-sheng, q.v.)
Yang Tu 楊度
Yang Tu-sheng (Yü-lin). 楊篤生(毓麟) *See also* Yang Shou-jen
Yang Wang-p'eng 楊王鵬
Yang Wei 楊維
Yang Yao 楊幺
Yang Yü-ju 楊玉如
Yang Yü-ssu 楊毓泗
Yao Kung-ho 姚公鶴
Yeh Hsia-sheng. *See* Meng T'ieh-sheng
Yen Chung-p'ing 嚴中平
Yen Feng-ko 閻鳳閣
Yen Fu 嚴復
Yüan ch'iang 原強
Yen Hsi-shan 閻錫山
Yin-ch'ang 蔭昌
Yin Ch'ang-heng 尹昌衡
Yo (Lo) Chia-tsao 樂嘉藻
Yoshino Sakuzō 吉野作造
Yu Lung-piao 尤龍標
Yu-shui shan-tung 游說煽動
Yü-chai ts'un-kao 愚齋存稿
Yü Chao-i 于肇怡
Yü-che hui-ts'un 諭摺彙存
Yü-hang 餘杭
Yü Hsia-ch'ing 虞洽卿
Yü Hua-lung 喻化龍
Yü Pang-hua 于邦華
Yü-pei li-hsien kung-hui 預備立憲公會
Yüan Hsi-t'ao 袁希濤
Yüan Jung-fa 阮榮發
Yüan K'o-ting 袁克定
Yüan-shih 淵實
Yüan Shu-hsün 袁樹勛
Yüan Sun 轅孫
Yüeh shang tzu-chih-hui 粵商自治會
Yūzonsha 猶存社

Contributors

MARIE-CLAIRE BERGÈRE, maître-assistant at the Ecole Nationale des Langues Orientales Vivantes, successfully defended her doctoral dissertation at the Faculty of Letters of the University of Paris in 1966. She has published a study of the financial crisis at Shanghai in 1910 and is presently working on the social and political consequences of the economic crisis in China in the early 1920s.

MARTIN BERNAL is Fellow and Assistant Tutor at King's College, Cambridge University, where he received his Ph.D. in 1966. He has also done graduate work at Harvard, the University of California at Berkeley, and Peking University (1959–60). His research interests are focused on the history of socialism in twentieth-century China.

P'ENG-YÜAN CHANG is a member of the research staff of the Institute of Modern History, Academia Sinica, now located in Taiwan. He received his M.A. in Chinese history from Taiwan Normal University in 1959 and has been a Visiting Scholar at Columbia and Harvard. His publications in Chinese include an important monograph on reform movements in the last years of the Chinese Empire.

VIDYA PRAKASH DUTT, Professor and Head of the Department of Chinese Studies at the University of Delhi, was previously head of the Department of East Asian Studies at the Indian School of International Studies. Educated primarily in India, he also did graduate work at Stanford and Harvard.

JOHN FINCHER is a doctoral candidate in Chinese history at the University of Washington, Seattle.

MICHAEL GASSTER is Associate Professor of History and Chairman of the Modern Chinese History Project at the University of Washington, Seattle, where he received his doctorate in 1962. He has recently completed a book on the origins of Chinese radicalism.

YOSHIHIRO HATANO, Professor of Oriental History at the University of Nagoya, received his Japanese doctorate from the University of Kyoto in 1962. His publications in Japanese include a major monograph on China's early industrialization.

Chūzō Ichiko, Professor of Oriental History at Ochanomizu University, Tokyo, was trained at Tokyo National University. His research has covered a range of topics in the social history of China since the late nineteenth century. He has been the leading figure in directing the attention of Japanese specialists on China to modern history through the development of The Seminar on Twentieth Century China at the Tōyō Bunko.

Mary Backus Rankin of Washington, D.C., received her Ph.D. from Harvard in 1966. She is continuing her work on the role of radical intellectuals in the Revolution of 1911 under a research grant from the Joint Committee on Contemporary China of the A.C.L.S. and the S.S.R.C. and has completed a book on the subject.

Harold Z. Schiffrin is Senior Lecturer in Chinese Studies at the Hebrew University, Jerusalem, from which he received his Ph.D. in 1961. He has done graduate work at the University of California at Berkeley and spent extensive research leaves in the Far East, London, and the United States. He is currently working on a major biography of Sun Yat-sen, volume 1 of which has been completed.

Mary Clabaugh Wright, Professor of History at Yale University, received her Ph.D. from Harvard in 1952. Before coming to Yale in 1959, she taught for 12 years at Stanford University. Her research interests, long focused on nineteenth-century Chinese history, had swung during the 1960s to the early years of the Chinese Revolution. She died in June 1970.

Ernest P. Young, Associate Professor of History at the University of Michigan, received his Ph.D. from Harvard in 1965. From 1965 to 1968 he was Assistant Professor of History at Dartmouth College.

Index